D1569338

Color Coded

Also by Walter Nugent

Progressivism: A Very Short Introduction

Habits of Empire: A History of American Expansion

Making Our Way: A Family History

Into the West: The Story of Its People

The American West: The Reader (*with Martin Ridge*)

Crossings: The Great Transatlantic Migrations, 1870–1914

Structures of American Social History

From Centennial to World War: American Society, 1876–1917

Modern America

Money and American Society, 1865–1880

The Money Question during Reconstruction

Creative History: An Introduction to Historical Study

The Tolerant Populists: Kansas Populism and Nativism

Color Coded

Party Politics in the American West
1950–2016

Walter Nugent

UNIVERSITY OF OKLAHOMA PRESS : NORMAN

This book has been selected to receive the Julian J. Rothbaum Prize for the highest standards of scholarship.

Publication is also made possible through the generosity of Edith Kinney Gaylord.

Library of Congress Cataloging-in-Publication Data

Names: Nugent, Walter T. K., author.
Title: Color coded : party politics in the American West, 1950–2016 / Walter Nugent.
Description: Norman : University of Oklahoma Press : Norman, [2018] | Includes bibliographical references and index.
Identifiers: LCCN 2018011171 | ISBN 978-0-8061-6169-3 (hardcover : alk. paper)
Subjects: LCSH: Party affiliation—West (U.S.)—History—20th century. | Party affiliation—West (U.S.)—History—20th century. | Political culture—West (U.S.) | Voting research—West (U.S.) | West (U.S.)—Politics and government.
Classification: LCC JK2271 .N84 2018 | DDC 324.2730978/09045—dc23
LC record available at https://lccn.loc.gov/2018011171

The paper in this book meets the guidelines for permanence and durability of the Committee on Production Guidelines for Book Longevity of the Council on Library Resources, Inc. ∞

1 2 3 4 5 6 7 8 9 10

To
The Other nÓg, again

Contents

Illustrations

Color Coded

Introduction
Party Shifts in the West

Politics has always been colorful. But since the tight Bush-Gore presidential campaign in 2000 the TV networks' constant portrayal of Republican votes and areas as red and Democratic ones as blue, politics has become color coded. Swing states, oscillating between red and blue, are now called purple. Other color schemes antedated this one, but repetition and familiarity have fastened it indelibly. This book looks at the politics of nineteen western states and how they shifted—or didn't—since 1950. Most of those states, the "stayers," were red or blue across the two-thirds of a century since then. The "shifters" were two states that turned from blue in 1950 to red more recently and two that went from red to blue. Five have been purple "swingers."[1]

Western politics has been understudied. Two striking changes in American politics since 1950 have been much remarked upon: the shift of the South from "solid Democratic" to "solid Republican," and the disappearance of moderate or liberal Republicans in the Northeast. Some who come to mind (to name a few senators) are Jacob Javits of New York, Leverett Saltonstall of Massachusetts, Clifford Case of New Jersey, and Margaret Chase Smith of Maine. In their place are Republicans who are from other parts of the country and definitely farther right, such as Ted Cruz of Texas, Thad Cochran of Mississippi, Mitch McConnell of Kentucky, and Jeff Sessions of Alabama before he became Trump's attorney general. Less dramatic and pervasive, hence less noticed than the section-wide changes in the South and Northeast, have been shifts in the West. But there have been some in that region, and they deserve a systematic look.

It is now two-thirds of a century since 1950, a period long enough to reveal secular trends. The following chapters start, then, with an occasional look back at the Progressive Era, the Great Depression and New Deal, and World War II. By 1950, most of the immediate fallout from the war was over. The Great Depression was a vivid and recent memory. But, despite the fears of economists and others that the Depression would return, it didn't. The 1950s, in many ways, saw the start of our recognizably modern country. Agricultural output greatly expanded, yet small farmers disappeared in favor of mechanized agribusiness. Cities and suburbs exploded all over the country, in the West from Houston to Albuquerque to Phoenix to Los Angeles, the Bay Area, Portland and Seattle up the coast, and Denver and Salt Lake City inland. The second Great Migration of black people brought them out of the rural South to northern *and western* cities. Immigration took off after 1965, especially from Latin America and Asia. Along with those demographic and geographic changes came the corporatizing and globalizing of manufacturing, finance, services, and other sectors; the gradual, painful, and partial start of true racial integration; and much else. Yet, amid these huge changes, the political framework of the Constitution and the two great political parties persisted without radical structural change— including the Electoral College, which twice, in 2000 and 2016, elected presidents who did not win pluralities of the people's votes.[2]

Why treat nineteen states here? The U.S. Census Bureau's West region includes thirteen, which are essential, but the six Great Plains states are also western.[3] The nineteen differ greatly in population and, therefore, in how many congressional districts they include. Two giants, California with fifty-three districts (as of the 2010s) and Texas with thirty-six, hold 58 percent of the West's House seats. Next are five middling-sized states, each with five to ten seats: Oklahoma five, Oregon six, Colorado seven, Arizona nine, and Washington ten. The remaining twelve are large in area but pygmies in population and House seats: Kansas, Nevada, and Utah have four, Nebraska and New Mexico three, Hawaii and Idaho two, and Alaska, Montana, North Dakota, South Dakota, and Wyoming only one; these twelve total, today, twenty-seven seats, fewer than either California or Texas.

In 1950 the lineup was very different. California had twenty-three seats and Texas twenty-one, the two largest in the West then as now. Yet together they had fewer than New York's forty-five. Only five states today have fewer House seats than they had in 1950:

Oklahoma had eight, now five; Kansas had six, now four; Nebraska had four, now three; Montana and North Dakota each had two, now one. All these are on the Great Plains, or mostly so. All of those whose populations and House seats have increased, except for Texas, are in the Mountain or Pacific West. From 1950 to the 2010s, Arizona went from two seats to nine, Colorado from four to seven, Nevada from one to four, New Mexico from two to three, Oregon from four to six, Utah from two to four, and Washington from six to ten.

Demographic gains or losses have varied across the nearly seven decades since 1950. In general, they reflect the depopulation of the rural and small-town Great Plains and the expansion of metropolitan areas. Such population patterns have varied from place to place, but these generalizations bear a rough truth. They are both cause and effect of economic and technological developments. Despite them, some locales resist political change, and cultural habits persist. Just to pick two examples, Colorado Springs stays dependably red and Honolulu dependably blue. Demography, conversely, can bring about political shifts even in stubbornly red or blue areas; Orange County, south of Los Angeles, at one time the epicenter of hard-right and Bircher conservatism, voted for Hillary Clinton in 2016, making her the first Democrat to carry that county since Franklin Roosevelt's 1936 landslide. Thus I discuss the effect on party allegiances and voting from demographic and economic change as necessary—and also religion where it played a role (or failed to).

What follows, then, is an examination of nineteen western states during the past two-thirds of a century, for the purpose of describing and explaining what has determined their partisan inclinations. Some states shifted radically, others slightly, some hardly at all. Taken together, they provide a grounded basis for considering partisan behavior in the West, whether red or blue or purple.

To do this, the first step was to gather voting data for each election beginning in 1950 and ending in 2016 for presidential electors, governors, U.S. senators, and members of the U.S. House of Representatives. In that period there have been over five thousand elections to these offices in the nineteen states.[4] With the vote counts in hand, patterns emerge. Kansas and Nebraska, which began Republican, have remained deep red. Idaho and Utah (and six others) have been almost as red. Hawaii and Washington have been consistently blue overall. Five have been purple, the true swing states: the southwestern cluster of New Mexico, Colorado, Nevada, and Arizona, plus Montana. Four states have shifted close to 180 degrees: Texas and Oklahoma, solidly Democratic in 1950, have become almost thoroughly red in recent years (and not solely because they resemble in some ways the Deep South just east of them). Contrariwise, California and Oregon, safely Republican in 1950, have become dependably Democratic. The chapters on Texas and California deserve and receive the most attention because of their size. Oklahoma and Oregon, the two smaller shifters, also merit individual chapters.

Though election returns are the bedrock sources for this book, most of the states have their own historiography. Fortunately, Texas and California have many relevant histories and biographies. Some of the other states have not been examined as they deserve. Historians and political scientists please note. There is plenty of good work yet to be done.

At first glance, one might think that *Color Coded* is a political history of the West since World War II. It resembles one, but its focus is more specific: party shifting (or its absence)—which states changed their party majority, when, why, and in which parts? Sometimes salient campaign issues or charismatic candidates came into play; at other times, more long-running demographic and economic changes were at work. This is a book of history, not political science. No theoretical proposition or thesis is being tested. The truth is in the narrative. Most of the changes, small or large, were incremental. Climactic turning points were less frequent than one might expect—Oklahoma's 1994 election, California's in 1958, and a few others. The process, even of radical change, was usually one of erosion and accretion. In short, it was more often glacial than seismic.

It also needs saying that this book is not about "political culture" or ideology. Others, including the now-large literature on conservatism, do that quite well. However, even very good treatments of "political culture" avoid treating elections, parties, personalities, events, issues, and organizations. *Color Coded*, instead, will do just that.[5]

To be sure, changes in party affiliations or labels do not necessarily represent changes in political culture or outlook. Party changes may instead underscore or clarify outlooks. The Oklahoma

Democrat of 1960 may not be all that different from the Oklahoma Republican of 1995. Nonetheless, it is a useful shorthand to fall back on the red-purple-blue color scheme that began in the networks' 2000 election night coverage, wherein blue meant Democratic, red meant Republican, and purple meant undecided or swinging. No state was or is thoroughly blue or red, if one surveys all elections and offices. Party labels also can and do mean different things depending on time and place. A Kansas or Oklahoma Democrat typically is more conservative than a Democrat from San Francisco, Portland, or Seattle. An evangelical Republican from Fort Worth might have arguments with a secular Republican from San Diego. But the labels do represent broad realities.

Some misimpressions commonly exist about the political West—for example, that it is more conservative than other sections. Some parts of it are, but the region as a whole is decidedly less conservative than the South. It is often believed by people farther east that, although the West is large in area, it is small(er) in population. The area part is true, but the West region has not been the smallest for some time and is home to more people than the Midwest. Is it a unit politically? Hardly, as this book shows. It lacks the political unity of New England or the South. At first glance, it seems that the western states that have saltwater coastlines are or have become blue. That is true of California, Oregon, Washington, and Hawaii—but not Alaska or Texas, though they are coastal states too. The Rocky Mountain states are reputedly rock-ribbed conservative. That is true of Idaho and Utah, at least recently, and of Wyoming and the parts of Oregon and Washington east of the Cascades. But it is not true of Montana, at least not all the time, or of New Mexico, Nevada, or Colorado. How and why they are not deserves comment, which comes in the following pages.

Seventeen presidential elections, scores of gubernatorial and senatorial elections, and literally thousands of elections to the House of Representatives combine to reveal a large and varied story. Economic changes such as the disappearance of small farms (and thus of farm and small-town people) in the Great Plains, the rise and later vicissitudes of aerospace and shipyards in California, the shrinking of Oregon's lumber industry and the explosion of high-tech in its "Silicon Forest," plus other economic and labor force developments underlay demographic movements, because people go where the jobs are and leave where they aren't. Demographic and economic changes like these inevitably result in political change.

Broad social trends do not, however, make history by themselves. This narrative is studded with individuals who made things happen. Henry Bellmon brought about the surge of the Republican Party in Oklahoma in the early 1960s. Rev. W. A. Criswell of Dallas's First Baptist Church enforced orthodoxy not only in religion but also in Texas's political Right. Monroe Sweetland resuscitated Oregon's moribund Democratic Party in the 1950s, and a decade later Tom McCall led that state's Republican Party along a centrist path. In 1958, Edmund G. "Pat" Brown won the first of his two terms as governor of California and made it a two-party state. Jesse Unruh, Alan Cranston, Phillip Burton, and Willie Brown pushed California ever farther into blue country. Women governors—Democrat Ann Richards of Texas in the early 1990s, and twenty years later Republicans Jan Brewer of Arizona, Susana Martinez of New Mexico, and Mary Fallin of Oklahoma—shattered the glass ceiling in their states. Dolores Huerta worked with Cesar Chavez and Phil Burton to mobilize Latino farmworkers in California's Central Valley. California sent two women, Dianne Feinstein and Barbara Boxer, to the Senate in 1992, where they stayed for over twenty-five years, and Washington also elected two female senators, Patty Murray and Maria Cantwell. Many other party builders, red and blue, made their marks on political change in the West from the 1950s onward.

The West produced six presidents in those years: Richard Nixon, Lyndon Johnson, Ronald Reagan, the George Bushes *père et fils*, and Barack Obama. Senate majority leaders Ernest McFarland came from Arizona, Mike Mansfield from Montana, and Harry Reid from Nevada; House speaker Nancy Pelosi has long represented San Francisco. Presidential candidates Barry Goldwater, George McGovern, Fred Harris, Jerry Brown, Bob Dole, and Mitt Romney were westerners. The interplay of large economic and demographic forces with individual actors has produced a complex and nuanced history.

The order of the following chapters is basically from red to blue. First come the two states that were deep blue in 1950 but became very red by 2000: Oklahoma (chapter 1) and Texas (chapter 2). Chapter 3 surveys the eight states that were red at the start of the period and have changed politically very little since then, even though each of them has elected a Democrat to high office occasionally and all (except Barry Goldwater's own Arizona) voted for Democrat Lyndon Johnson for president in 1964. No one of these states—Kansas, Nebraska, South Dakota, North Dakota, Wyoming, Utah, Idaho, and Alaska—has been hygienically, thoroughly, red or blue. Chapter 4 discusses the five purple states, the swingers, which are Arizona and Montana (reddish purple), Nevada, Colorado, and New Mexico (bluish purple). Then come the two states that were red in 1950 but later changed to blue: Oregon (chapter 5) and California (chapter 6). Finally, chapter 7 considers the two states that have been, on the whole, dependably blue: Hawaii and Washington. *Color Coded* concludes with some reflections on party building, term limits and incumbency, redistricting, religion in politics, and the surprise of 2016.

THE SWITCHERS, BLUE TO RED

1   Oklahoma: Starting Blue, Turning Deep Red

Is Oklahoma truly a western state? Visit the southeastern quarter of it, known as "Little Dixie," which includes Mississippi-reminiscent county names like Pushmataha and Atoka, and you would not think so. But visit the counties west of El Reno, and the Panhandle, where the early settlers were farmer-ranchers trying to make a living on wheat and cattle, and you would not doubt the state's western character. In truth, it is both southern and western, as is Texas. The best writers on American regionalism have agreed that Oklahoma cuts across, or better, combines, elements of both the South and the West.

Authorities differ. V. O. Key's magisterial *Southern Politics* (1949) has a chapter on Texas but not one on Oklahoma, nor is there even an index entry for Oklahoma. But Raymond Gastil's widely cited *Cultural Regions of the United States* (1975) places Texas and the southern two-thirds of Oklahoma in the "Western South," where "the white masses are religiously traditional, individualistic, against the use of alcohol. . . . They expect little of government, vote against bond issues, and for [George] Wallace or other populist candidates." The Western South is "thoroughly in the Southern Baptist world that I have taken as a principal marker of Southern Culture." Neal Peirce solved the problem by stressing geography and longitude rather than culture; he included the state in his fine *The Great Plains States of the United States* (1972).[1] It is unarguable that the state is part of the Great Plains tier. And it is also unarguable that in its politics and culture Oklahoma has been both southern and western. Consequently, Oklahoma's political culture has traditionally been conservative, in one sense or another, with greater or less intensity depending on candidates, issues, and the prevailing regional-national context.

In the spectrum of Goldwater-to-Reagan-to-Tea-Party conservatism, Oklahoma participated in its own ways. In Oklahoma, as elsewhere, Republican conservatism rested on several bases and perennial issues. Anti-union legislation appeared later than in most southern states, but a right-to-work law did pass in 2001. Modern conservatism's anti-regulatory, low-tax principles have been expressed for some time. The state was not hard-line opposed to civil rights for African Americans—it voted for George Wallace in 1968 far less than Deep South states did—and Governor Henry Bellmon, though certainly a GOP conservative (for his time, the 1960s), was no racist. Oklahomans have been strongly religious, as was most starkly demonstrated politically in the crucial 1994 election, which was a Republican victory resting in substantial part on a coalition of Baptists, other Protestants, Mormons like Congressman Ernest Istook, and conservative Catholics like soon-to-be-governor Frank Keating. In short, all of the elements of modern conservatism have been present, in an amalgam peculiar to itself and perhaps to Texas.

Oklahoma expressed its conservatism in its own way. But then, it had always had some of the ingredients—the tradition of self-made homesteading; the romantic (though not law-abiding) legend of the original Sooners, who literally jumped the gun in the land rushes of 1889 and later; and the idea, reinforced by oil booms, that anyone might strike it rich (and therefore had no use for "government handouts"). A key ingredient in Oklahoma's conservative mix was religion. It could act positively, providing help for the down and out, or negatively, fighting against abortion and lax sexual mores. Oklahoma had a submerged reservoir of conservative traditions and attitudes, and the efforts in 1994 by the Christian Coalition brought it to the surface. The state's conservatism, as was true elsewhere, comprised several unstable factions, but they have largely stayed together for more than two decades.[2]

Oklahomans, then, like their Great Plains neighbors to the south and the north, were receptive to modern conservatism, or various forms of it, as it developed across the South and parts of the West from the 1970s on. At times it built on remnants of the John Birch movement of the 1950s, though that was not especially strong in Oklahoma. At times it took a libertarian turn, resting in part on the radical individualism inherent in evangelicalism, as well as the Sooner frontier tradition. In the 1980s and 1990s emergent conservatism fed upon "social issues" such as "law and order," anti-abortion, and prayer in public schools—issues suggested as winning ones in Kevin Phillips's *Emerging Republican Majority* (1969)—and statements typical of Richard Nixon and other leading Republicans at that time. The Tea Party movement of 2010 did not engage all Oklahoma Republicans, but it was a reinforcement and yet another conservative mode.

Oklahoma thus participated, in its own way and its own time, in the wholesale shift of the South from solidly Democratic to solidly Republican in the 1960s and 1970s. It also participated in the deepening of political (and other) conservatism that was taking place in the Great Plains states, though most of them north of Oklahoma had traditionally voted Republican and did not shift party labels, as Oklahoma had to in order to reflect its increasingly palpable conservatism in the late twentieth century. I am well aware that there are different kinds of conservatives and liberals, and of Republicans and Democrats, but no one will gainsay the generalization that the Republican Party has, for at least a hundred years now, been the conservative party and the Democratic Party the more liberal. To use the color scheme first developed on television news, Oklahoma used to be blue, and now it is red.

It was not always thus. Oklahoma in 1950 was home to about two and a quarter million people, with an economy heavily invested in agriculture and oil. Many farmer-ranchers could still recall the land rushes of 1889–96 and the homesteading that followed. When Oklahoma became a state in 1907, it had more Socialists than New York[3] and a strong memory of the People's Party, which had flourished among farmers in the territorial period.[4] Political scientists were calling Oklahoma a "modified one-party state." Except for president, Sooners voted Democratic in the 1950s, as they traditionally had. The state had followed the national Republican flow briefly in 1920 and just after and decisively rejected Alfred E. Smith, Catholic and "wringing wet" on Prohibition, the Democratic presidential candidate in 1928. For the next twenty years, however, the Democratic presidential nominee carried Oklahoma solidly; Truman's percentage in Oklahoma in 1948 was his second-highest in the nation.

Oklahoma voted for Democrats Franklin D. Roosevelt (four times) and Truman but has voted Republican for president ever since, except for Lyndon Johnson in 1964, while staying (until recently) Democratic for other offices.[5] This pattern, which was also true in

Texas, has been called "presidential Republicanism." In the 1950s, Oklahomans elected Democrats for governor, for both U.S. Senate seats, and for five of the six congressmen. They enjoyed large majorities in registered voters and in both chambers of the state legislature. They elected down-ticket state and county officials through most of the rest of the century. Gradually, however, the GOP made inroads. Voters broke the Democrats' lock on the governorship in 1962 and on one Senate seat in 1968. The governorship has seesawed between the major parties, though since 2010 it has been safely Republican.[6]

Democrats won every election for seats in the Senate up to 1968, with only three exceptions, in 1920, 1924, and 1942. But aside from Democrat David Boren's three victories in 1978, 1984, and 1990, Republicans have won the Senate races every time since 1968. Democrats took four or five of the then-six House seats until 1994, but after that Republicans have won almost every seat, every election. The two chambers of the state legislature were the last to change, with Republican majorities finally in place in 2004 and 2006. The red shift in the state legislature occurred some years after Republicans began controlling U.S. Senate and House elections. A likely reason is that Democrats remained registered as such long after their real partisan preference changed because Republican primaries were often no-contests, and at least the Democratic primary was a way of making one's views felt. Except for a Republican majority elected to the lower house in 1920, both chambers had been historically Democratic and stayed that way until 2004.

Such was the timing of Oklahoma's "red shift." After Rick Santorum won Oklahoma's 2012 GOP presidential primary, a local political scientist remarked that "we are the reddest [state] in the Union."[7] How did a thoroughly Democratic state change so completely?

In 1950, when A. S. "Mike" Monroney was first elected senator and Johnston Murray governor, Democrats in statewide contests could rely on counties in the far western Panhandle and most of the southwestern, Red River, and eastern regions of the state. Republicans won in the northwestern and north-central counties next to Kansas, where much of their original settlement came from, and urban Tulsa. If one visualizes the state as two roughly equal northern and southern halves, in 1950 Murray and Monroney won the southern one, and the Republicans took much of the northern half as far east as (and including) Tulsa. The two big cities and their counties, Oklahoma and

Tulsa, have traditionally produced Republican majorities. After 1960 a Republican who did well in those two would win statewide. One who did poorly would be sunk by the more rural, more Democratic counties. Democratic hegemony held for another decade. The 1954 election put Democrat Raymond Gary in the governor's chair, cushioned by huge Democratic majorities of 109 to nineteen in the state house and thirty-nine to five in the state senate. Democrats Murray, Gary, and J. Howard Edmondson (1958) were all elected governor without serious Republican opposition. Oilman Robert Kerr, a lion of the Senate and mentor of Lyndon Johnson, held one Senate seat from 1949 until his sudden death in January 1963, and New Deal/ Fair Deal liberal Monroney held the other, winning three terms, in 1950, 1956, and 1962.

The results of the 1950 census reduced the state's congressional seats from eight to six, and they remained five to one or four to two Democratic through 1992. From 1952 through 1978, Democratic candidates won seventy-eight of the 105 contests for the House. Speaker Carl Albert in the southeastern 3rd District and Tom Steed in the mostly southwestern 4th District ran unopposed several times in these early years, like their famous neighbors across the Red River in Texas, Wright Patman and Sam Rayburn.

The dangers of such overwhelming control, of course, were factionalism and complacency. Legislators represented many local interests, and Raymond Gary worked with them all to build rural roads, modernize the state's extensive welfare system, and integrate the schools (with surprising smoothness) in line with the U.S. Supreme Court's *Brown v. Board* decision of 1954. Although Oklahoma has had anything but an untroubled racial history—recall the hideous 1921 race riot in Tulsa—the state did not resist school integration as the Deep South did. Gary cooperated with the rural old guard in the legislature and accomplished much.[8]

A serious factional division began after the 1958 election. The thirty-three-year-old J. Howard Edmondson defeated Oklahoma City developer W. P. Bill Atkinson in the Democratic gubernatorial primary and won the general election by about four to one, carrying every county. He managed to repeal Prohibition, institute central purchasing for state agencies, and start a merit system for state jobs, upsetting entrenched patronage arrangements. However, he neglected to discuss most of these changes with legislators, and within months

Edmondson had split with the state Democratic executive committee. In February 1960 local party conventions rejected Edmondson's
slates; his candidates lost the July primaries; and, in the fall, three
constitutional amendments that he proposed (including one to reapportion the legislature) were soundly defeated. Kennedy lost the state
to Nixon "above all else, for his religion," and some counties voted
Republican for the first time. By 1962, Oklahoma's Democratic Party
was "badly fractured."[9]

Into this breach, this opportunity, rode Henry Bellmon. Bellmon
was a burly farmer-rancher from north-central Oklahoma, a decorated tank commander on Iwo Jima and other Pacific battles, and a
very hard worker. After becoming state chairman of the vestigial
Republican Party in 1960, he traveled to every county seeking out the
scarce registered Republicans, and with them he built precinct and
county organizations. "I believed our support of Nixon [in 1960] was
the chief selling point," Bellmon later wrote.[10] Why Nixon appealed
to Sooners is not fully clear. His familiarity after eight years as Eisenhower's vice president probably helped, and Kennedy was rejected as
eastern, Boston, Harvard, Catholic, and liberal, thus uncongenial or
even anathema to Oklahoma's political culture on several grounds.

In the longer run, it was Bellmon's own assiduity that created a
new and lasting party and made him, as many have said, "the father of
Oklahoma's modern Republican Party." (It had never had an ancient
one.) Bellmon constructed a plan he called "GOP Countdown,"
and he hired a public relations firm to reassure "our major financial
contributors"—many of them oil-rich—that their money would be
used to maximum effect. He began a statewide county-by-county
fund-raising drive; promoted reregistration of voters to attract disgruntled Democrats; drew up a list of registered Republicans in every
county to discern precinct-level patterns; and replaced two-thirds of
the Republican state committee. The result was, in his own words,
"an active aggressive Republican organization in every county" for
the first time.[11] The average age of the three hundred state committee members "dropped overnight to the mid-thirties, roughly thirty
years below the previous average."[12]

In 1962, Bellmon was the consensus Republican candidate for
governor. He defeated the Democrat, Bill Atkinson, by a decisive
392,316 to 315,357. He "showed surprising statewide strength," even
in Little Dixie, and racked up large majorities in Tulsa and Oklahoma

Counties.[13] The Republican candidate for U.S. Senate on the same ticket, Hayden Crawford, failed to carry many of the counties that Bellmon won—Oklahoma County most notably but also its collar counties (Canadian, Cleveland, Pottawatomie) plus some west-central farming counties. It was Bellmon's personal appeal, on top of the reorganized party machinery that he had built in the preceding two years, that won the day for him. The Republican youth movement, the replacement of geriatric deadwood and sedentary oil and cattle grandees, was not fully in flight, but it was definitely off the ground. The Republican advance in 1962 was not the product of an ideological shift. It resulted from the combination of Democrats' disarray—the conflict between Howard Edmondson and the rural old guard—and Bellmon's sagacity in seizing this opportunity, plus his hard, shrewd work.

Proof of that lay in the Senate race. Two-term veteran Democrat Mike Monroney defeated Crawford, the Republican, by a solid 352,000 to 308,000. Half of Monroney's margin came from Oklahoma County. But Bellmon, running for governor, easily outpolled both senatorial candidates. Bellmon and the Republicans could look to a bright future.

No fewer than twelve candidates ran in the 1962 Democratic primary for governor, and when the top two vote getters met in the runoff developer Atkinson beat ex-governor Gary by 953 votes out of 462,781.[14] In the general election, when Gary would not endorse Atkinson, many Gary supporters then voted for Bellmon.[15] Upon Senator Kerr's sudden death in January 1963, Edmondson resigned the governorship with only a few days left in his term, and the new acting governor, George Nigh, appointed him to Kerr's seat. The voters did not like that. When Edmondson ran for the final two years of Kerr's term in late 1964, he lost to Fred Harris in the primary.

A few years later, the longtime political analyst of the *Daily Oklahoman*, Otis Sullivant, observed that more young people were "voting and thinking Republican than in former years when most of them were Democratic. It adds up to a changing political scene in Oklahoma, with more accent on youth and glamour."[16] Correct, but the youth movement had already begun by 1961.

As governor, Bellmon appointed a young black woman as the receptionist in his front office, shocking some first-time visitors unused to seeing a black face sitting behind a government desk in

Oklahoma City, according to his autobiography. No bigot, he later deplored the fact that "the waste of human resources which discrimination ha[d] caused in lives of women and minorities . . . [was] incalculable."[17] Bellmon also oversaw the redistricting mandated by the Supreme Court's one man, one vote rulings—thus one-third of the members of the legislature elected in 1964 suddenly came from Oklahoma and Tulsa Counties.[18] Extensive road building and repair along with a state employees' retirement system rounded out his successful and popular efforts.

Bellmon left office in 1966, the last Oklahoma governor constitutionally prohibited from succeeding himself. Dewey Bartlett, another Republican (and a Catholic, another break in tradition), succeeded him. From August 1967 to January 1968, Bellmon chaired Nixon's presidential campaign. Though he considered Nixon "no administrator," he admired him and agreed with him on many issues, foreign and domestic.[19]

Bellmon went to Washington after defeating three-term senator Monroney in 1968 and was reelected in 1974.[20] Though Republican to the core, he was never a hard-shell "movement" conservative. He supported welfare programs and the Panama Canal treaties, "was dubious of any position taken by the John Birch Society," and found Birchers "particularly repugnant."[21] In 1986 he rounded out his electoral career by winning another term as governor. It is worth noting that the Religious Right, which would play a large role in the 1990s, did not do so as Bellmon built the Oklahoma GOP. In 1960 and 1962, the "social issues"—actually, moral issues—had not yet become salient in American politics. They would at the end of the decade, when Nixon began talking them up and as the national press focused on campus disturbances, Woodstock, Stonewall, and other events upsetting to middle-class citizenry. But all that came after Bellmon's party-building years.

The Republican organization that Bellmon fathered became increasingly solid, "a more organized and centralized party [than] the state Democrats."[22] The latter before 1960 had become entrenched, complacent, and vulnerable, a collection of local satrapies. Rural districts were greatly overrepresented and remained so until redistricting began taking hold in 1965. Though that became fully effective only after several election cycles, it was another key factor producing the red shift.

Meanwhile, the state itself was changing demographically and economically. In the sixty years after the 1950 census, its population grew by 70 percent, of which nearly half was in Oklahoma and Tulsa Counties. Together with their collar counties, where suburbs were gobbling up farmland by annexation and home construction, they accounted for the bulk of the increase. Around Oklahoma County and City, Canadian and Cleveland Counties were major gainers; around Tulsa, Washington, Osage, Rogers, and Wagoner Counties shared or led the gains. Conversely, almost every county west of Canadian (county seat: El Reno) lost population, as was true up and down the Great Plains. The few exceptions included Texas County in the Panhandle, where new meatpacking plants attracted some thousands of immigrants; and Comanche County (Lawton), home of the army's Fort Sill, which more than doubled from all of the retail and service activity the post engendered. In smaller counties, very often the county seat gained people while the outlying areas lost. For example, Enid, the seat of Garfield County, increased 37 percent while the rest of the county lost 36 percent.[23]

Economic changes paralleled population shifts. As in other parts of the Great Plains, farms increased in average size but fell sharply in numbers. Around Clinton in west-central Oklahoma, for example, where scores of quarter-section homesteads once dotted the land, only a handful of farms remained by 2010, and they were better characterized as large agribusiness operations than as homesteads.[24] Two historians observed in the late 1970s that many survivors of the Great Depression had "changed from populist-style agitator to conservator of substantial assets." In the closing decades of the century, the Oklahoma farmer was "no longer Alfalfa Bill Murray's agrarian sage or the Socialists' desperate toiler. He [had become] a businessman."[25]

In 1940 the state held 180,000 farms averaging 194 acres; in 2009 it had 86,500, averaging 405 acres. Doubling in average size, the state's farms had halved in number.[26] Agriculture, once the state's largest economic sector, had become the smallest in 2009, far behind government (at all levels), services, and mining (including oil).[27] Young people did not stay on farms but went to Oklahoma City, Tulsa, and their spreading suburbs. They traded overalls for short-sleeved white shirts and thin ties and worked not on tractors but in corporate cubicles, absorbing the corporate ethos—including party identification and political issues. The young and suburban were replacing the old and rural. Fewer and fewer old-timers were still around to recall statehood or even the Dust Bowl and the Depression. With the cohort shift came stirrings of a political party shift.

For these many reasons, the Oklahoma Republican Party grew, quietly and not so quietly, during the 1960s and 1970s. It continued to elect its slate of presidential electors; it won the governorship in 1962 and 1966 and almost did so in 1970; it toppled three-term liberal senator Mike Monroney in 1968. Had it not been for David L. Boren's popularity, first as governor and then as three-term senator, it would have made a clean sweep of contests for U.S. senator from 1968 on, as it actually has since Boren resigned in 1994.

The one major exception to this conservative trend among the top offices was the emergence of Fred R. Harris in 1964. If the Republicans' comet in the 1960s was Bellmon, the Democrats' was Fred Harris. He came from a two-room house near Lawton, worked his way through the University of Oklahoma as a printer's devil, made Phi Beta Kappa as a history and political science major, and went on to become an outstanding student and head of his class in the law school. He was elected, at twenty-six, to the state senate in 1956 and was reelected in 1960.[28] He ran for governor in the May 1962 primary and, though he did not reach the runoff (Bill Atkinson and Raymond Gary outpolled him), he built valuable name recognition.

In 1964, Harris defeated incumbent J. Howard Edmondson in the primary for Kerr's old Senate seat. In the general election Harris faced former University of Oklahoma football coach Bud Wilkinson, a household name around the state. Harris campaigned with great vigor, shaking 150,000 hands (his own estimate), visiting hundreds of communities and every county, employing direct mail, billboards, a jingle, radio and TV ads, and a whistle-stop train. The Kerr family provided some financial help and three highly experienced staff persons. "Nobody had ever put together so personal a political organization in Oklahoma," Harris later wrote. Stressing his experience in government and Wilkinson's lack of it, he won by 22,000 votes, just over 51 percent. By his own analysis, he won for three reasons: "Wilkinson's decision to bring U.S. Senator Strom Thurmond [the South Carolina former Dixiecrat] to the state; President Johnson's national landslide win over . . . Goldwater; and a televised debate between Wilkinson and me." According to his biographer, historian

Richard Lowitt, Harris "put together a broad-based coalition that included organized labor, blacks, businessmen, traditional Democrats, teachers, and campus liberals."[29]

The 1964 election won Harris the final two years of Kerr's unfinished term, and in 1966 he gained a full six-year Senate term with about 54 percent to the Republican's 44 percent.[30] On the Washington scene, Harris and his vivacious half-Comanche wife, LaDonna, quickly gained attention and popularity. His liberal positions fit well with young colleagues like Birch Bayh of Indiana and Edward Kennedy of Massachusetts, and with the Great Society programs of President Johnson. He was tapped in 1968 to cochair (with Walter Mondale) Hubert Humphrey's presidential campaign. The following year, Humphrey appointed Harris chair of the Democratic National Committee.

In that role, Harris was in close contact with national Democratic liberals. But he was losing touch with his Oklahoma base. When he came out in opposition to the Vietnam War and in 1970 urged repeal of the Gulf of Tonkin Resolution, his Oklahoma support dwindled sharply. The Democratic Party of Oklahoma had long been factionalized around personalities—Raymond Gary Democrats, Howard Edmondson Democrats, Kerr Democrats—and now Harris Democrats. However, the personal coalition that had served him so well in 1964 and 1966 became unglued as he became more nationally prominent and visible as a liberal. It was easy to paint him as having "gone Washington." On the Republican side, Bellmon had no such problem; when he built the Oklahoma GOP there were not enough Republicans to factionalize, and Bellmon continued to run a tight ship through the 1980s. By 1971, Harris developed what he called "the new populism," his version of liberalism—a fairer "distribution of national income," "justice for minorities, women, and white workers, who paid an unfair share of social costs," reduction of military spending and more environmental regulation, and "above all [making] government 'responsive to the people's will.'" He also called for universal health insurance.[31] Harris's emphasis was almost entirely on economic issues, especially agrarian ones. Meanwhile, Republicans were increasingly stressing social issues—race, street riots, anti-war protests, campus unrest, "radical" feminism, "law and order."

By 1971, according to historian Jeff Bloodworth, Harris had become "profoundly unpopular back home." He declined to run for reelection in 1972 after he found himself far behind in polls.[32] Instead he resigned from the Democratic National Committee and began to campaign for the Democratic nomination for president. His fund-raising fell short, and so did his votes in several state primaries. In 1976 he tried again, but again he lost early primaries. Harris left politics for academic life at the University of New Mexico and has written almost twenty books on politics, plus works of fiction.

In 1968, Nixon soundly defeated Hubert Humphrey in Oklahoma, to no one's surprise. George Wallace took about 20 percent of the statewide vote, actually carrying two southeastern counties (Atoka and Pushmataha), outpolling Nixon in three Red River Democratic strongholds and outpolling Humphrey in three customarily Republican ones. For some, longtime party ties had loosened. The state's Populist/Socialist/New Deal/liberal tradition had withered. Harris was just about its last exemplar. Oklahomans, whether Democratic or Republican, were ever more manifestly conservative.[33]

By 1970 that underlying conservatism had strengthened. In the governor's race, Democrat David Hall defeated incumbent Republican Dewey Bartlett by only a tiny margin of 50.2 percent to 49.8 percent, each winning their traditional bases. However, Bartlett did better than usual in the suburbanizing counties around Oklahoma City and Tulsa.[34] Bartlett returned in 1972 and defeated Ed Edmondson, almost as narrowly, for the Senate seat being vacated by Fred Harris.

Bellmon's message was Oklahoma's wave of the future. Harris's was a reverberation of its agrarian past. Harris was the exception proving the rule that Oklahoma was moving to the right. Republicans did not win every election—far from it. But they won every presidential contest after 1964, their share of governorships, and (except for David L. Boren's three wins) every race for U.S. senator since 1968. In 1974, Boren was elected governor, and Bellmon, running for reelection to the Senate, narrowly defeated the hapless Ed Edmondson, J. Howard's brother. Bellmon carried the increasingly secure and suburban Cleveland and Canadian Counties south and west of Oklahoma City, and although he slipped somewhat in the northeast the election made him the first two-term Republican senator from Oklahoma. The deep inroads of conservatism were obvious when Raymond Gary, Democratic governor (1955–59) and from Little Dixie, endorsed Republican Bellmon for senator in 1974. Gary said that he did not "want either of our votes in the United States Senate to be influenced or controlled by the radical, left wing, liberal wrecking crew of the East or by the radical uncompromising labor union bosses of the nation."[35] Richard Nixon could not have said it better.

Elections for the U.S. House of Representatives proved more stubbornly resistant to Republican gains. Indeed, there was no sign of a Republican ascendancy in 1972, when Democrat James R. Jones won the 1st District Republican stronghold after veteran Republican Page Belcher (1953–73) retired.[36] A former aide to President Johnson, Jones was reelected until he, too, retired in 1987. For two years after the 1974 election, all six Oklahoma congressmen were Democrats.

That tide also began to turn in 1976. John Jarman, a moderate Democrat who had represented the Oklahoma City district since 1950, barely survived in 1974, defeating Republican Mickey Edwards by only 51.7 percent to 48.3 percent.[37] Early in 1975, Jarman declared himself a Republican, but evidently he decided that even that would not save him, and he did not run again in 1976. Edwards won the seat and was reelected through 1990, becoming "one of the leaders of the ideological right in Congress." He later chaired the American Conservative Union.[38] Edwards remained the lone Republican in the Oklahoma House delegation until Jones left the Tulsa seat and was succeeded by another conservative, James Inhofe, who held it until he was elected U.S. senator in 1994, which he continues to be.

From 1976 through 1992, Democrats won four seats and Republicans two—the 1st and 5th Districts. Of the six representatives, five were more conservative than their respective party caucuses in the House. The exception was Mike Synar from Muskogee, who won the 2nd District from 1978 through 1992 and voted on the liberal side much of the time. The 1994 *Almanac of American Politics* described him as "by far the most liberal of any white member from the South, more liberal than most Democrats from the North."[39] More typically Oklahoman were three other Democrats. Wes Watkins, successor in 1976 to House speaker Carl Albert in Little Dixie, "had one of the most conservative voting records of any young Democrat" in his first two terms. Watkins was reelected through 1988, ran for governor in 1994 and lost, then won back his seat in 1996 *as a Republican* and stayed for two more terms. Dave McCurdy, in the 4th District, was a Blue Dog member of the Democratic Leadership Council. Glenn English in the westernmost 6th District compiled "the most conservative voting record of Oklahoma Democrats."[40] Synar was the last true liberal, Democrat or Republican, elected to House or Senate from Oklahoma. By the early 1990s party labels still meant something, but that something, in the national context, was that an Oklahoma Democrat was right of center, and an Oklahoma Republican was usually far right of center.

The dam finally broke in 1994. From previously four Democrats to two Republicans, the Oklahoma delegation became five to one Republican. The last Democrat left standing was Bill Brewster in Little Dixie. Even he disappeared in 1996 when Watkins resurrected himself as a Republican, and the count became six to zero Republican. The only Oklahoma Democrats elected to the House after 1994 were Brad Carson in 1998 and 2000 and Dan Boren (son of the former senator) from 2004 through 2010, both in the 2nd District. Both were solid Blue Dogs. In 2016 all five members of the House delegation were conservative Republicans, and all were reelected handily. What had been a subtle but steady erosion of Democratic strength since 1960 became a conclusive shift to the Republicans, and as it turned out a lasting one. The secular trend became a rout in 1994, which in retrospect was a critical election in Oklahoma. Why, though, did the shift happen just then?

First, several elements coincided so that only two incumbents ran for reelection—Brewster (D-3rd) and Istook (R-5th). Thus most of the faces were fresh. In 1993, Glenn English resigned his 6th District seat and Republican Frank Lucas won a special election to succeed him. David Boren resigned his Senate seat in early 1994 to become president of the University of Oklahoma. Republican James Inhofe of the 1st District (Tulsa) and Democrat Dave McCurdy of the southwestern 4th squared off for Boren's Senate seat, opening up those two House seats. (Inhofe won the Senate race.) In the 2nd District, Mike Synar lost in the Democratic primary to a schoolteacher, some said because he voted for the Brady gun control bill and also because of failing health (he died in 1996, at forty-six).[41] Seats without incumbents running—"open seats"—often open the way for the other party, and that happened in Oklahoma's 2nd, 4th, and 6th Districts in 1994.[42] Dissatisfaction with President Bill Clinton and enthusiasm for Newt Gingrich's "Contract with America" helped make 1994 a Republican year, and the national vibes reverberated resoundingly in Oklahoma.

Second, and more crucial, a powerful new force appeared: the Religious Right. Almost every candidate with a fresh face had an identification with the Christian Coalition or were themselves evangelicals. Istook was a strong Mormon. Two Republican candidates, Steve Largent in the 1st District and J. C. Watts in the 4th, were former NFL players, familiar to fans of professional football. They were also well known as fundamentalists or Baptists. Inhofe, running for the Senate, had a sister who was "one of the most important Christian Right activists in the state." Christian Coalition "voter guides," of which tens of thousands were distributed, supported conservative social and economic issues and hence these candidates. Senator Don Nickles, though Catholic, had been known since his first election in 1980 "as a national Christian Right leader." The alliance on social issues between Protestant evangelicals and right-wing Catholics was beginning to become clear.[43] Baptists had an outright majority of Oklahoma churchgoers, with Methodists in second place. But denominational lines faded as evangelicals (as well as Catholics, most prominently Frank Keating, elected governor in 1994 and again in 1998) coalesced "against the perceived threat of secularism, with its attendant evils of women's liberation, gay rights, and political liberalism."[44]

Oklahoma Republicans have preserved and consolidated their 1994 tsunami in almost every election since. The state lost one of its House seats after the 2000 census; subsequent redistricting had some effects locally, but not nearly enough to arrest the deepening of the 1994 red shift. In 2002, Democrat Brad Henry won the governorship by a tiny six thousand votes in a three-way race, partly, it was said, because Little Dixie liked his support of cockfighting. Four years later he was reelected by a wider margin over Istook. But Henry was an exception. When David Boren resigned his Senate seat in 1994, Tulsa Republican congressman James Inhofe ran successfully against 4th District Democrat Dave McCurdy, and Inhofe has been elected ever since, most recently in 2014. When Don Nickles vacated the other Senate seat, 2nd District congressman Tom Coburn won it over Brad Carson; Coburn held it until 2014, when he declined to run again because of illness. James Lankford, a seminary graduate who had run youth camps for the Oklahoma Baptist Convention, and who had been the congressman representing Oklahoma City, ran successfully in 2014 for Coburn's two final years and won a full Senate term in

2016. All of these senators, from Nickles on, had fine conservative credentials and records and often had connections with conservative religious groups. Congress, the legislature, and voter registrations ratified Oklahoma's redness. After 2000 a Republican majority finally emerged in the state house, growing by 2012 to seventy-two Republicans versus twenty-nine Democrats. The state senate remained in Democratic hands until 2006 produced a tie at twenty-four, but 2012 brought thirty-six Republicans control over twelve Democrats. The red tide continued, and the result of the 2016 election was, for the house, twenty-six Democrats and seventy-five Republicans; for the senate, forty-two Republicans and six Democrats.

The transformation of the state from blue to red was a forty-year secular realignment capped by a decisive and only ostensibly sudden event in 1994, sprung by a concatenation of circumstances, seized on by the Christian Coalition. Over the decades, to summarize, several factors operated: the dry rot and factionalism of the Democrats; Henry Bellmon's energy, efficiency, and personal appeal; the rural to urban-suburban demographic shift; the one man, one vote redistricting; the aging of and disappearance of small farmers and their replacement by agribusiness or at least larger-capitalized family farms; the expansion of white-collar corporate jobs and lifestyles; and the increasing salience of social issues along with the collapse of Fred Harris's efforts to highlight economic ones. All of these factors were in place by 1994, and the activism of the Religious Right ignited the ready tinder.

2   Texas Roams from Blue to Red

It needs to be understood, to begin with, that the Texas Democratic Party as of 1950 was not a bastion of liberalism, any more than other southern states' Democratic parties were. Part of the New Deal coalition they may have been, especially on some national issues. But on state and local matters they were usually wedded to their region and to low-tax, lean-government conservatism, as subsequent history would show. Texas shared another characteristic with the South. It was frankly and proudly a one-party state. Within that party, however, lay factions and fiefdoms, coalescing into a liberal wing and a conservative wing. Although the Democratic spectrum was more a collection of shades than crudely bipolar, seeing the party as two factions explains much about it. Generally, the two sides recognized each other that way and fought in the Democratic primary as such.

The aim here is to explain the emergence of the Republican Party out of nowhere and ultimately into electoral dominance, as well as the concomitant erosion of the Democratic Party. In 1950, Texas had no Republican statewide elected officials, virtually no Republican primaries, and only a skeletal party apparatus. By 2015 almost the same could be said of the Democrats, and the Republicans ruled state politics. Why the sea change? To understand that requires some historical background. "Texas entered World War II a largely impoverished, rural, agricultural state, and emerged from the war decade thriving and far more urbanized and industrialized than ever before."[1] Texas was ripe for political change, which would inevitably, if slowly, follow the seismic economic and social changes of the 1940s.

THE BIG PICTURE

Imagine a state of 7.7 million people in 1950, of whom 40 percent lived on farms or country villages, and whose economy chiefly produced cattle, cotton, and oil.[2] In politics its determinative election was the Democratic Party primary. There was no Republican primary because there were no Republicans to speak of. It was a state where there was not a single Republican (or other non-Democrat) among the 191 members of the state house and senate, a state that had never elected a Republican governor or U.S. senator since Reconstruction after the Civil War. It sent no Republicans, only Democrats, to Congress. Democratic congressmen like Sam Rayburn and Wright Patman normally ran unopposed in the general election and often in their party's primary.

It was also a state in which poll taxes discouraged voting by poor folks, white or black, until 1966, and where the Democratic primary until 1944 or a little later was for whites only.[3] Even after the poll tax ended, Texas (with Oklahoma) was among the states with the lowest percentage of actual voters among the voting-age population.[4] That was the Texas political landscape in the 1950s, and it changed little before the 1960s, except for "presidential Republicanism"—voting for the Republican candidate for president (Dwight D. Eisenhower in 1952 and 1956) but sticking with Democrats in the Democratic primary, for state and local offices like sheriffs or judges, because only there did a voter have any choice about state or county government.

It was all a product of what can happen in a one-party state: politics divided not by party label but by factions—organized, in Texas, not so much around individual leaders as in some southern states (though certain leaders have been important, such as conservatives Allan Shivers and John Connally or liberal Ralph Yarborough), or around well-defined ideologies, but around "conservative" and "liberal" coalitions of economic and social interest groups. These could be somewhat fluid. They could cross party lines and could sometimes veer into a "moderate" category. But the common terms used by historians, political scientists, and journalists on Texas government and politics in the late twentieth century were "conservative" and "liberal." In Shivers's day (around 1950), "within the Democratic Party [there] was a division far more bitter than the one that exists today [2002] between the major parties—between liberal and conservative

Democrats over the rise of organized labor, support for New Deal programs, the continuation of racial segregation, the political clout of oil, and loyalty to the national Democratic party."[5]

The Rice University sociologist Chandler Davidson described the two great factions clearly in his 1990 *Race and Class in Texas Politics*. From the mid-1940s to the mid-1980s whites voted in primaries in a fairly consistent pattern according to socioeconomic class and income level. "Lower class Anglos" voted for liberal candidates (with the exception of the 1968 election when George Wallace ran). Liberal support waned as the class level rose from lower middle to upper middle and finally to "upper class."

It also eroded over time. When Franklin Roosevelt ran the third time, in 1940, over 50 percent of Dallas and Fort Worth voters supported him. In 1944, while the wealthiest donors to politics favored Republicans two to one, FDR pulled 71 percent of the state's vote. "In other words," writes Davidson, "this preference for the GOP [among the wealthiest] existed before the Dixiecrat party of 1948 and the Eisenhower campaigns of the 1950s. . . . Candidate ideology, rather than party label, then, is the predictor of upper-class preferences."[6] With few Republicans to vote for, conservatives became the Texas Regulars of 1944 and Dixiecrats of 1948—in Texas, the Shivercrats. Three decades later, upper-class Houston voters gave Jimmy Carter only 12 percent in 1976 and 11 percent to Walter Mondale in 1984. African American support for Democratic presidential candidates, and for Democrats on the liberal side running for governor or senator, remained persistently strong, often over 90 percent, from the 1940s through the 1980s and beyond. In 1984, 95 percent of black votes, but only 26 percent of white ones, went to Democrats Mondale and Ferraro. Class was still a factor, but race was more determining.[7] Mexican Americans did not vote for liberals quite as strongly but did so nonetheless by two-thirds or three-fourths. On issues, "the liberal-conservative conflict in Texas is quite similar to its national counterpart." Region has played a less telling role, with the Panhandle and the Hill Country—and, more recently, the suburbs of Dallas, Fort Worth, and Houston—voting more conservative, while central and south Texas, and Austin and Galveston, have been more liberal.[8]

Since Davidson wrote in the mid-1980s, however, the voting trend among Anglos, almost regardless of class, has been in the conservative, Republican direction. As of the mid-1980s, Davidson portrayed the Republicans of Texas as divided between an "establishment" wing represented by John Connally and a "right flank [which] consisted of militant religious fundamentalists, racial bigots, current or former members of the John Birch Society, homophobes, financial backers of mercenary anti-Sandinista troops, and advocates of conspiracy theories linking the Illuminati with the Trilateral Commission."[9] A recent history of Texas conservatism traces it much farther back.[10] Some of these players have changed in the thirty years since, but the intra-Republican factional split is worth noting, especially since the Texas Democratic Party, and with it liberalism, collapsed after 2000.

In the 1970s and 1980s, Texas Republican strength also battened on a in-migration of displaced and disgruntled Anglos from the Rust Belt. When they settled in Texas, a great many established themselves in suburbs in the Dallas–Fort Worth metroplex, Houston, Austin, and elsewhere, producing explosive growth of suburban counties, and of GOP votes. This migrant-to-suburb-to-Republican progression would become a bit less the norm after 2000 or 2005, but by then Texas had become a one-party state again—Republican rather than Democratic. In 1974, Republicans running for statewide offices won 29 percent of the votes; in 1996 they took 56 percent. Between 1970 and 2000 some suburban counties (e.g., Collin and Rockwall near Dallas and Fort Bend southwest of Houston) grew ten times over. Republican votes exploded there accordingly. The state, especially those suburbs, peopled with many midwestern newcomers, became Reagan country in the 1980s.

Texas in 1950 elected thirty-one senators and 150 representatives to its state legislature in Austin. Not one was a Republican. Every single one was a Democrat. In 2015 the legislature still included thirty-one senators and 150 representatives. But twenty senators, all but eleven, and ninety-nine representatives, all but fifty-two, were Republicans, creating near supermajorities that could override a governor's veto, if the governor happened to be a Democrat. In the persons of Rick Perry and Greg Abbott the governor decidedly was not a Democrat. In 1950, Texans also sent twenty-one congressmen (yes, all men) to Washington, all Democrats, many running unopposed in either the Democratic primary—the decisive contest then—or the general election. In 2014 the Texas delegation to the U.S. House had swelled to thirty-six, of whom twenty-five were Republicans and eleven were Democrats; the same division held in 2016. Both U.S.

senators were Democrats until Republican John Tower won Lyndon Johnson's former seat in 1961. In the 1992 election a Republican won the other seat, and so they have ever since. Democrats Kennedy (1960), Johnson (1964), Humphrey (1968), and Carter (1976) won Texas's electoral votes, but no later Democrat has managed it. Once part of the Democratic "Solid South," Texas has, over time, shifted its loyalty in one office after another, from president to legislature and even farther down the ballot, until it has become, in the twenty-first century, a deeply Republican state. The Democratic erosion, gradually accelerating in the 1980s and 1990s, became overwhelming except for African American and Hispanic voters after 2000. Why did this massive partisan shift happen?

LOYALISTS, REGULARS, SHIVERCRATS, AND OTHERS: THE 1940S AND 1950S

During the Depression-plagued 1930s, the Texas Democratic Party, as elsewhere, rallied around Franklin D. Roosevelt and his New Deal. By 1944, however, again as elsewhere, conservatives, calling themselves the "Texas Regulars," became "part of a South-wide movement among the upper classes to reassert [their] strength within the party." The plan was to thwart FDR's fourth-term effort "and throw the election into the House of Representatives." The plan failed, and Roosevelt carried Texas by 71 percent. The liberals won. But when their candidate for governor, Homer Rainey, was beaten in the 1946 primary by conservative Beauford Jester, control reverted to the conservatives.[11]

The 1948 election exhibited the bipolar shape of the Democrats. Texans strongly supported the party's presidential candidate, Harry S Truman, refusing to join the Strom Thurmond Dixiecrat defection that carried four Deep South states. Beauford Jester had won in 1946 (Texas then had a two-year term for governor) over liberal Homer Rainey, who had been fired in 1944 when as president of the University of Texas he defended some pro–New Deal faculty members and their political opinions. "Right-wing businessmen—predominantly Republicans—on the University of Texas board of regents . . . fired Rainey."[12] Jester won reelection more easily in 1948. He had been "acclaimed by the Texas Regulars," that is, the Texas Democrats who refused to support FDR's candidacy in 1944 for a fourth term (some still had not got over Roosevelt's dropping his vice president, Texan

John Nance Garner, from the 1940 third-term ticket and replacing him with Henry A. Wallace). Jester also had the backing of "Roosevelt Democrats who shied away . . . from Rainey." More broadly, conservative Democrats in Texas and elsewhere in the South opposed New Deal social and labor laws as well as perceived interference from federal agencies, and they favored states' rights and segregation. By 1948, to quote V. O. Key's classic *Southern Politics in State and Nation*, written at the time, the "battle of conservatives versus liberals . . . emerged in about as sharp a form as is possible under a one-party system. . . . All in all Texas has developed the most bitter intra-Democratic fight along New Deal and anti–New Deal lines in the South."[13]

The 1948 Senate race demonstrated the division fully. In the Democratic primary, former governor (1941–47) Coke Stevenson ran against six-term congressman Lyndon B. Johnson. Stevenson, a segregationist, led the 1944 Texas delegation's fight to deny FDR's nomination for a fourth term, backed the University of Texas regents' firing of Rainey that year, and was a champion of the anti–New Deal conservative Democrats.[14] Johnson was not perfectly liberal in state politics, nor would he be through the 1950s, but he was a firm Roosevelt-Truman supporter in national affairs, which brought much federal largesse to Texas. FDR "was like a daddy to me," he once said. The choices were clear.

The result of the Democratic senatorial primary was not. The result was Stevenson, 477,077; Johnson, 405,615; and eight others combined, about 320,000. Since no candidate won a clear majority, a runoff was required, and it gave Johnson 494,191 votes and Stevenson 494,104—making Johnson the winner by 87 votes. He went on to win the general election on November 2 by a two to one margin.[15] The initial results favored Stevenson by 362 votes, but several days later returns came in from Jim Wells County in south Texas, "a 'machine' county dominated by political boss George Parr," called "the Duke of Duval," which added 202 votes to the Johnson total, one vote to Stevenson's.[16] This put Johnson over the top statewide and earned him the sobriquet "Landslide Lyndon." But he was safely in the Senate.

Johnson's dubious victory scarcely meant that the Texas Democratic Party had gone liberal. Allan Shivers had been elected lieutenant governor in 1948 and succeeded to the top job when Beauford Jester suddenly died in July 1949. Shivers "was one of and at one

with Texas' business elite"; for him, "conservatism and segregationist views were inseparable."[17] For the next several years the liberal
and conservative wings fought bitterly for control of the party, and
therefore of the state government. Conservatives won the early
rounds. Incumbency helped Shivers, and he easily won reelection
in 1950 and again in 1952, though the liberals fielded an attractive
young candidate, Ralph W. Yarborough. But Shivers controlled the
party machinery, and the state convention in late May 1952 supported a slate of delegates to the national Democratic convention
uncommitted to President Truman or the to-be-chosen Democratic
nominee. The Texas liberal Democrats, led by Maury Maverick,
sent their own delegates to the convention, hoping to prevail as
party loyalists as they had against the conservative Texas Regulars
in 1944 and 1948.

Shivers's signature issue was tidelands oil. The question was
whether Texas would gain the revenue from oil drilling along its Gulf
coast, or whether the waters, the oil, and the money would remain
under federal control, which would divert significant royalties from
Texas. State control meant great profits for Texas oil interests and
possibly lower taxes for the people. Shivers and his fellow conservatives could also play on Texans' always-present state pride and their
history-based claim that "it had established ownership while an
independent republic from 1836 to 1845,"[18] and therefore that the
tidelands oil "rightfully" belonged to their state. For Shivers and his
supporters, tidelands "became almost as symbolic as the legendary
battle for the Alamo. To oppose or even suggest compromise became
unthinkable."[19] Shivers and attorney general (and future governor)
Price Daniel "attacked the national Democratic administration as
being corrupt and soft on communism, eroding the rights of the
states, and being outright thieves in attempting to steal the tidelands
oil from the schoolchildren of Texas. State control would direct much
of the oil income to the Permanent School Fund used for public education *and would mean a lower school tax burden for Texans.*"[20]

The 1952 national Democratic convention nominated Illinois
governor Adlai Stevenson for president. Stevenson would not commit
to leaving the tidelands in Texan hands, so Shivers and his faction, the
"Shivercrats," bolted and carried the party (and the state in November)
for the Republican presidential candidate, Dwight D. Eisenhower.
One can view this as the first break in Democratic hegemony. Others

would come, though they would take years, eventually turning the governorship, the two U.S. Senate seats, a majority of U.S. House seats, and finally the state legislature from Democrats to Republicans. Thus, writes one historian, Shivers "made presidential Republicanism acceptable"—voting for a Republican for president while continuing to vote Democratic for all other offices—not just in Texas but across the South.[21] The shift took decades to play out, and the Shivercrats remained the conservative wing of the state Democratic Party; they did not bolt to the state Republican Party, which was as yet nearly nonexistent anyway.

Shivers had successfully taken control of the state Democratic machinery not long after he became governor. After 1952, however, the liberal wing reinvigorated itself. It failed to prevent a second Eisenhower win in 1956, but it did rally around young liberal Ralph M. Yarborough.[22] Yarborough, from east Texas, earned a degree with high honors from the University of Texas law school. In the 1930s he became a protégé of Governor Jimmy Allred and, like him, was pro–New Deal. Yarborough became a successful litigator and then a judge in Austin. He saw combat duty in World War II, rising to lieutenant colonel. Neal Peirce described him as "a man of mercurial temperament, disdainful of the monied establishment . . . [and] the liberals' acknowledged leader and hero since 1952."[23] Yarborough ran against Shivers for governor in 1952 and 1954 and against Price Daniel in the 1956 primary after Shivers decided not to run again. Yarborough lost all three of those contests, but by narrower margins each time.[24] Although anti-communism and resistance to school integration resonated with many Texas voters, the liberal wing was gaining strength. Daniel resigned his Senate seat in January 1957 to become governor, and after an appointee served as senator for a few weeks Yarborough won a special election for the seat with support from organized labor.[25] The liberal wing of the Texas Democratic party—pro-labor, anti-segregation, minority-supported—had gained a major office.

But not much more. The 1950s, in fact, saw a Republican actually elected to a Texas House seat. Bruce Alger, first elected in 1954, was then a thirty-six-year-old former air force pilot who had become a real estate developer in Dallas. Alger inveighed and voted against "big government"—also called "creeping socialism"—whenever he could and once cast the lone vote in the House against free milk for schoolchildren. One historian wrote that Alger "was totally ineffective" as a congressman, "never passing or influencing any legislation."[26] He offered many bills, however. In 1962, for example, he proposed ending federal withholding tax from wages and salaries; pulling the United States out of the United Nations; creating an "alternative" internal revenue code; subjecting labor unions to anti-trust regulation; and adding a constitutional amendment "prohibiting government in business." These went nowhere, but he offered them almost perennially. His papers are replete with publications of most of the right-wing organizations and institutions of that day—the Manion Forum, the John Birch Society, Americans for Constitutional Action, *Human Events*, the "Dan Smoot Report," and others.[27] He "led the assault on urban redevelopment in Dallas," which he and his supporters deemed "socialistic."[28] In his philosophical outlook and personal intransigence, he greatly resembled the Tea Party faction of a half-century later. Liberals sat on their hands because the Democratic nominee in 1954 had worked for Eisenhower, thus letting Alger get in.[29] He kept his House seat for five terms and was finally swept out along with his hero, Barry Goldwater, in the Johnson landslide of 1964.

But Alger was the only Republican elected to Congress in these years except for one-termer Ed Foreman of Odessa, who in 1962 defeated an incumbent Democrat who had become involved in the Billy Sol Estes scandal. Foreman also lost reelection in 1964. Otherwise the Texas delegation, led by Rayburn and Johnson, remained pristinely Democratic through the 1950s. Through longevity and accumulating seniority, many of the Texans occupied major positions in Congress. Wright Patman of Texarkana, who represented District 1 in the northeast corner of the state from 1929 to 1975, chaired the House Banking, then Currency, Committee and was thus a national economic power. W. R. Poage of Waco represented District 11 from 1947 to 1977 and influenced agricultural policy. George Mahon of Lubbock represented District 19 for thirty-two years beginning in 1935; he chaired Appropriations. Paul Kilday of San Antonio, District 20, was in the House from 1939 to 1961; he led the Armed Services Committee. Jack Brooks of Beaumont (1953–93) chaired Government Operations, Olin "Tiger" Teague of College Station (1947–77) led Veterans' Affairs and then Science and Astronautics, and Jim Wright of Fort Worth (1955–89) reigned as House speaker through much of the 1980s.

Most prominent and powerful of all was the old lion, Sam Rayburn, first elected in 1912, who served as House speaker three different times before he was finally cut down by cancer in 1961. His was the 4th District, northeast of Dallas, along the Red River, just west of Patman's. In the 1950s, with Rayburn running the House and Lyndon Johnson as Senate majority leader, Texans led both houses of Congress. In a day when seniority was the key to power and control in the House of Representatives, Rayburn's decades of longevity explain much of his leadership. But seniority, though a necessary cause, was not sufficient.

Rayburn built a network of friends and associates, both in Washington and in his district. Like many a great leader, he knew his own mind and could explain his thinking in plain and clear terms. And his own mind was a liberal one, putting him in the political camp first of Wilsonian Progressivism, then the Roosevelt New Deal, then the Truman Fair Deal. His record over such a long period was thoroughly clean. Scandal never touched him, and after he died his net worth proved to be about $15,000, paltry for a man who held elective office for so many years. As his biographer wrote, both he and his 4th District were "a kind of political anachronism," a friends-and-neighbors community almost more typical of the nineteenth century than the mid- to late twentieth. His rock-solid base permitted him to take some positions that might have been unpopular in the district, but his vast personal network assured that voters would see him as "Mister Sam" rather than "that liberal."[30]

Most of these men ran unopposed in both the Democratic primaries and the general elections. Brooks, the first time he ran (1952), narrowly squeaked by in the Democratic primary but demolished a Republican opponent in the general, and for years to come he faced no one with the temerity to challenge him. The decisiveness of the Democratic primary, and the insignificance of the general election, is clear when we look at some of Patman's numbers, to take an example. Patman won his 1952 primary by about 41,000 to 20,000, but he needed only some 12,000 in 1950 to win the general. His neighbor Rayburn won his 1952 primary by about 30,000 to 15,000 but won the 1950 general, also unopposed, with only 12,400 votes.

It is difficult to grasp, yet true, that in the 1950s not one Republican was elected to either house of the Texas legislature. There were no Republican primaries. To all intents and purposes, there was no

Republican Party. Republicans were seldom even on the ballot, except for president and vice president. The result was "presidential Republicanism," since voters' only real choices other than for president were in the Democratic primary. And that is how matters remained for years to come.

The decisive Democratic primary was limited to white people until after the Supreme Court's ruling in *Smith v. Allwright* in 1944. Poll taxes, which effectively kept poor people, white or black, from voting, continued in Texas until 1966. How much the end of the white primary and the poll tax really expanded the electorate is uncertain. Texas's total vote in the 1952 presidential election was about 27 percent of its population as of the 1950 census, and the total presidential vote in 1972 was 31 percent of the 1970 population. The turnout in presidential elections continued to climb, but not by startling amounts. Conservative Democrats led by Governor John Connally changed the state constitution after 1966 to require annual voter registration—"the old poll tax system, but without the tax"—and to change the term of statewide elected officials, from the governor on down, from two years to four—with their elections to be held in off years when voter turnout was much lower than in presidential years. The results? Among other things, "primary participation plummeted."[31] Efforts to make it difficult for working-class and minority persons to vote have continued in the twenty-first century, when the conservatives in power became Republicans rather than Democrats as in the 1960s. Shivers's defection in 1952 had a lasting effect with regard to the eventual shift of the electorate from Democratic to Republican. If voting for Ike was not a sin, then maybe it was no longer sinful to vote for Republicans for other offices, should the opportunity arise. And the opportunity did arise, beginning with the race for U.S. senator in 1961.

Meanwhile, amid the seemingly stable political landscape, Texas was growing and changing. The United States and many other countries were experiencing a baby boom from the 1940s to the mid-1960s, raising the U.S. population from 132 million in 1940 to 203 million in 1970. Texas was growing at an even faster rate, from 6.4 million in 1940 to 11.2 million in 1970, an expansion of 75 percent. The sources were a high birth rate and low death rate (Texans were on average younger than people in older-settled states), along with migration from other states and countries. As elsewhere, large cities and suburbs outstripped smaller ones and rural areas. The four most populous counties—Bexar (San Antonio), Dallas, Harris (Houston), and Tarrant (Fort Worth)—collectively doubled between 1950 and 1970.

A STATEWIDE-ELECTED REPUBLICAN: JOHN TOWER

The 1960 election, with Lyndon Johnson running for vice president on the Democratic ticket, produced two major results. First, for the nation, the Kennedy-Johnson ticket carried Texas—by a thin 1,167,842 votes versus 1,121,602 for Nixon and Henry Cabot Lodge. By 46,000 votes, Kennedy and Johnson won Texas's electoral votes, and Illinois's by fewer than 10,000; without them the ticket would have lost. Second, for Texas, it laid the groundwork for a Republican to be elected U.S. senator the following year. In 1960, Texas law (pushed by Johnson himself) permitted Johnson to run on the general election ballot for vice president of the United States and also to run for reelection to the Senate. In his Senate race he faced a Republican political science professor at Midwestern University in Wichita Falls named John G. Tower. Tower lost, but he carried a more-than-respectable 41 percent of the votes.

When Johnson resigned his Senate seat, Governor Price Daniel appointed a conservative Democrat like himself, William Blakley of Dallas, a wealthy director of Braniff Airways, to fill the vacancy until a special nonpartisan election could take place to fill out the six-year term.[32] Seventy candidates including several prominent liberals entered the race, among them Maury Maverick Jr., Henry Gonzalez of San Antonio, and future House speaker Jim Wright of Fort Worth. All three had fine liberal credentials. Their candidacies had the self-defeating effect of splitting the liberal vote, and Blakley ran slightly ahead of all of them, while Tower led the pack. Tower had earned visibility and name recognition in 1960, and he was the obvious Republican candidate. To many people's astonishment, in the runoff Tower took 50.6 percent of the vote against 49.4 percent for Blakley.

Tower thus became the first Republican senator from Texas since the 1870s, and in fact the only Republican to win statewide office in that period. At five feet five inches, Tower was fond of introducing his speeches by announcing, "My name is Tower, but I don't."[33] Tower earned his master's degree at Southern Methodist University and then studied for a year at the London School of Economics. While there, he adopted his life-long costume of English-style bespoke suits and also deepened his fittingly conservative political views. He was the complete opposite of the stereotypical Texan cowboy image, which Shivers, for example, affected. Image aside, in 1961 and later Tower ran as a firm conservative, opposed to "alien socialist ideas" and "the radical New Frontier."

And Tower won with liberal help. Leaders of the liberal wing of the Texas Democratic Party, such as the editors of the very liberal *Texas Observer*, encouraged their readers and adherents to vote for Tower. Why? To begin creating a two-party political landscape in Texas; to break the hold of the conservatives over the Democratic Party organization; indeed to purify their party of the conservative stranglehold and thus put the liberals in charge. In the *Observer's* view, "the will of Texas liberal Democrats" is almost always thwarted, because "that party is controlled by provincial Dixiecrat conservatives in 'conservative' years, or by accommodating 'moderates,' well doused in oil, in moderate years. . . . Liberals want to free their party from the dead weight of the Dixiecrats, of whom Blakley is an unerring symbol; Republicans want to reorient Texas conservatism into a source of greater state prestige. At the intersection of these two basic objectives lies a vote for John Tower."[34]

The result, according to this thinking, would be a weakening of the conservatives' control of the Texas Democracy. People would then—it was assumed—elect liberal Democrats, while conservatives would either languish or move toward the weak and hapless Republican Party. The *Observer* argued that, "since politics is a game of risks . . . when the Republicans have finally accomplished their formidable task, liberals may well be defeated for governor and the state legislature. But they are defeated now anyway, by pseudo-Democrats who would be Republicans in any other state outside the South, and without the state sharing in the obvious advantages of a responsible two-party legislative system."[35]

As it turned out, the liberals got their wish in spades. Tower's election helped create a viable Republican Party where none had existed; it provided an alternative for conservative Democratic voters; it strengthened the liberals within the Democratic Party. But it became a classic case of "be careful what you wish for; you might get it." Neither the liberals nor anyone else imagined that a real second party would emerge and displace the Democracy as the dominant one by the turn of the century—electing governors, controlling the state legislature, and turning Texas into a deep-red Republican state. That took a while, but 1961 was a beginning, perhaps the beginning. As Gregory Curtis wrote years later, "That election began the rise of the Republicans in Texas. It also established the power of the liberals, who could keep the conservative Democrats from winning. And it exposed the liberals' fatal flaw; whenever victory was possible, they quarreled among themselves."[36] Tower, meanwhile, went on to serve twenty-four years in the Senate. He became a powerful Senate force on military and national security issues as chairman of the Senate Armed Services Committee.[37]

Some would insist that the Republicans' real turning point from fecklessness to viability came with Bill Clements's election as governor in 1978 (see below). Indeed, there was hardly any avalanche of down-ballot victories for Texas Republicans in the 1960s and into the 1970s. But, as with Shivers's supporting Eisenhower, bone-marrow Democratic loyalties were further diluted when Tower won (and stayed in office).[38] Tower's significance was to energize his party: "Keeping Tower in office remained the central focus of the Texas Republican Party, and the organization grew around him."[39] And thus one can reasonably claim that Tower's victory in 1961 is the birth date of the viable Texas Republican Party.[40] An irreverent view, but of some substance, is Richard Ben Cramer's:

> The GOP was growing in Houston [in 1962]—in fact it was on the rise all over Texas. (They'd even elected a Senator in '61, when LBJ had to give up his seat to assume the Vice Presidency. They got that runty professor, John Tower—a couple of Party leaders held him down on a table and shaved off his little Hitler mustache—and sent him out as a single-shot Republican against a field of about seventy Democrats . . . and he won!).[41]

CONNALLY RIGHT, YARBOROUGH LEFT

The Democrats' liberal wing hardly had its own way through the 1960s. Its conservative wing had been strong at least since the Texas Regulars of 1944, and the movement toward Republicanism actually began in Texas "before issues like abortion and gay rights replaced poverty and racial discrimination as the dominant moral issues of

American politics." Civil rights activism and legislation had never inspired conservatives. Senator Tower voted against the federal civil rights and voting rights acts of 1964 and 1965; George H. W. Bush opposed civil rights reform in his 1964 campaign against Yarborough; and the groundswell for Wallace in 1968 confirmed that racial conservatism was very much alive.[42] After the Tower surprise in 1961, conservative John Connally, still a Democrat, won the governorship in 1962. He gained national attention in the worst possible way, sitting next to John F. Kennedy in the car when the president was assassinated in Dallas on November 22, 1963. Connally survived, and by the end of the decade, with his ally Lyndon Johnson out of office, he asserted "iron rule of the State Democratic Executive Committee [and] further weakened the liberal forces within the state Democratic Party."[43]

During the 1960s, the liberal Ralph Yarborough served as Texas's other senator (and had since 1957). Through the decade, Yarborough led the liberal wing of the Democrats of Texas and was instrumental in the passage of much memorable legislation, especially in the areas of civil rights, education, and public health. Only two other Southern senators voted with him in favor of the Civil Rights Act of 1965. Governor Connally fought him bitterly, as Shivers had done in the 1950s, calling Yarborough an integrationist supported by communistic labor unions. Yarborough lost the governor's races of 1954 to Shivers and 1956 to Price Daniel, but he succeeded in the special election for senator in 1957 when Daniel resigned to become governor. Yarborough won the primary and the general election in 1958, and again in 1964 against future president George H. W. Bush, who had secret help from Governor Connally. But in 1970 Lloyd Bentsen upset Yarborough in the primary, stressing "social issues" such as urban and minority unrest, issues that would tar Oklahoma's Fred Harris at about the same time as being too liberal. Bentsen remained a Democrat (as Connally did not), going on to win four terms in the Senate, trying unsuccessfully for the presidential nomination in 1976, becoming the party's candidate for vice president in 1988 and later Bill Clinton's secretary of the treasury.

An indicator of conservative strength was the vote for George Wallace's third-party try in 1968. Of Texas's 254 counties, none gave Wallace an outright majority, but in sixteen he came in second, outrunning either Humphrey or Nixon. Four of those counties are in far western Texas, and the rest are along, or near, the Louisiana border in east Texas. (The statewide vote for president in 1968 gave Humphrey 41 percent, Nixon 40 percent, and Wallace 19 percent.)[44] Wallace tried again in 1972, was shot in May 1972 and became paralyzed, but continued to have a following, though diminished, in Texas and northward. By 1976, when Ronald Reagan tried to supplant Gerald Ford as the Republican presidential nominee, Texas was crucial for him. He was running behind in the spring. Some argue that "Texas represented Reagan's final Hail Mary pass of the '76 campaign." But on May 1, Reagan did win the Republican primary with 278,300 votes (66 percent) to Gerald Ford's 139,944 (33 percent), sweeping all twenty-four congressional districts.[45] Thus the Texas delegation to the national Republican convention was Reagan's, and with it he nearly unseated Ford, the incumbent president.

At that point, Wallace Democrats became Reagan Democrats, and they would remain so during the 1980s. The Reaganites in 1976 "*became* the Republican party [in Texas], and all wavering moderates had to get on Reagan's conservative bus or leave the party."[46] Wallace voters of 1968 and 1972 were "aggressively pursued" by the 1976 Reagan campaign, successfully and permanently. The vote total in the 1976 Republican primary was three times the Goldwater vote of 1964, the previous record.[47] Succinctly put, as Peter Adams wrote,

> Wallace's success in northern states [and in Texas] was due in large part to his law-and-order message, which resonated with working-class white voters who had been part of the Democratic Party coalition since the New Deal. He tapped into emotionally powerful issues among Northerners [and Texans] who resented federal programs that helped minorities; feared race riots and student protests against the [Vietnam] war; and viewed court-ordered busing as an intrusion by big government. After Wallace was suddenly eliminated from the political arena, these voters were adrift. The Republican Party easily turned the Wallace Democrats . . . into Reagan Democrats. In short, Ronald Reagan's victory in 1980 was aided in no small measure by the migration of the Wallace vote to the Republican Party. The same resentment of a government that is believed to favor minorities is at the heart of today's Tea Party.[48]

It helped the Republican cause that migration from the Midwest, "the Rustbelt," was heavy in the 1970s and 1980s, much of it settling in the suburbs of Houston and Dallas, which developed into Republican mainstays.[49]

With Yarborough gone and the conservative Democrat Preston Smith elected governor in 1970, the liberal wing was in eclipse in the early '70s. But a scandal arose over banker Frank Sharp's loans to legislators to buy stock in an insurance company he owned, in return for the legislators passing a couple of bills that benefited him. Smith vetoed the bills, clearing himself, but the lieutenant governor and the state house speaker and others were convicted of bribery.[50] Smith, though not charged with a crime, was sufficiently besmirched that he ran third in the 1972 primary behind liberal Frances "Sissy" Farenthold and rancher Dolph Briscoe. The conservative Briscoe defeated Farenthold in the runoff and then squeaked by Henry Grover, Texas's first modern Republican state senator, in the general.[51] Democratic Party unity was, however, as elusive as ever. Briscoe failed to control the party machinery. Democratic national committeewoman Billie Carr of Houston, a superb organizer who had supported Eugene McCarthy in 1968 and George McGovern in 1972, led the liberals to dominance by 1976.[52]

As conservatives departed to become Reagan Democrats, the liberals were left in charge. But of what? In 1971 only 20 percent of Texans thought of themselves as Republicans, compared to 52 percent who were self-styled Democrats.[53] And what kind of Democrat? Liberal, conservative, Wallace, or Reagan? In a situation reminiscent of 1961 when liberal Democrats urged each other to vote for Republican Tower rather than the conservative Democrat Blakley, in the hope of shooing the conservatives out of the Democratic Party, the liberal wing assumed in 1976 that when they took over the party machinery the conservative Democrats would simply become the defeated faction. Instead, as Paul Burka put it, the liberals' "belief that conservatives would continue their long-established habit of voting for Democrats proved to be a miscalculation."[54] The defeated faction instead became the disappearing faction. Two years later Texans elected a Republican governor.

BILL CLEMENTS, A REPUBLICAN GOVERNOR

In 1976 the liberal wing repeated its hubristic tactical error of 1961 by opposing and defeating Bentsen's presidential hopes in the Texas delegation to the Democratic nominating convention. They dreamed that, by nudging conservatives to become Republicans and leave the Democratic Party, it would thus become purely liberal. Alas for the liberal wing, too many did just that. The defeat of Bentsen within the party in 1976 pushed the conservatives out but, although it aimed to create a more purely liberal Democratic Party, all it did was siphon off conservatives into the Republican Party, which became more radically right rather than moderate like eastern Republicans. Thus, Billie Carr and the liberals, unwittingly and unintentionally, contributed to another tipping point in favor of the Republican Party. In the short term the Carr forces won, but in the long term they cut their own throats.

The result was not as planned—that the liberal Democrats would henceforth run state government. Instead, a Republican, Bill Clements, was elected governor in 1978, and he proceeded to appoint Republicans to "minor" offices around the state, among them a couple of hundred county judges. These "minor" officials became in many instances the nuclei of Republican county organizations.[55] First had come Shivers and "presidential Republicanism" (Jimmy Carter in 1976 was the last Democratic presidential candidate to carry Texas). Second came Tower, the first Republican senator. Third, Clements became the first Republican governor and patronage dispenser. Beneath these ticket leaders, Republicans began appearing in the Texas house and senate and the congressional delegation.

The Clements victory in 1978 was extremely narrow but nevertheless a major tipping point. Clements won the May 1978 Republican primary handily; he received just 115,000 votes, but that was enough. John Hill, a former chief justice of the state supreme court and former attorney general, won the Democratic primary, defeating incumbent Dolph Briscoe and former governor Preston Smith with a clear 52 percent. In the general election, Republican Clements squeaked by Hill, 49.96 percent to 49.24 percent, a difference of less than 17,000 votes out of the 2,370,000 cast.

Clements's win was shaky, but the man was not. He was an appealing candidate, compared to rather lackluster Democrats like Preston Smith and Briscoe. As one analyst put it, "Clements embodied the mythic, larger-than-life culture of Texas that many voters wanted to see in their governor."[56] Clements was an oilman who made his many millions in offshore drilling, beginning in the late 1940s when the tidelands issue became so important in Texas, especially to Texas conservatives. As deputy secretary of defense in the Nixon and Ford administrations, he could claim some government experience and, with his great wealth, he could tell Republicans that "we will not run out of money in the fourth quarter."[57] "He was perceived," wrote Senator Tower's biographer, "as a tough, self-made successful businessman who would provide leadership and management," rather than as an Austin politician, or at least that was the image his campaign wanted to portray. By late October, a UPI reporter estimated that Clements had spent a then-huge $6.4 million and had "closed the gap" with John Hill.[58] And he had, by almost the narrowest of margins—"almost" because Tower was reelected to his final term as senator by a margin of even fewer votes, just over 12,000.

How significant was Clements's victory, and how indicative of the future? Opinions have differed. Gilbert Garcia, in his book on Reagan's crushing of Gerald Ford in the 1976 Texas Republican primary, thinks that "in some ways Clements's [1978] win was a fortuitous one-off for the Texas GOP. Clements was a forerunner of the wealthy self-funding politician, and his outrageously deep pockets solved the Republican Party's perennial problem of running out of money in the crucial final weeks of gubernatorial campaigns. Also, the 1978 turnout was remarkably low, which benefited Clements, the candidate with the narrower base."[59] Another analysis says that "Hill was victimized by the polls that showed him way ahead, [by] low voter turnout—especially in minority precincts . . .—[and by] Clements's slick seven-million-dollar campaign, and specifically Clements's success in portraying himself as the conservative in the race against a big-spending liberal."[60] Probably Jimmy Carter's unpopularity at that moment reduced the Democratic vote, and the stagflating economy also contributed. Hill, though more accurately termed a moderate, seemed insufficiently conservative for Briscoe Democrats, and many of them—one source says 59 percent—voted for Clements.[61]

There is also disagreement on what the Clements-Tower wins did for the Texas GOP. One commentator has written that, because "Clements made no real effort to build his party's power base," he lost his 1982 reelection bid to Democrat Mark White, even though Democrats swept most statewide contests in that year. And a more fundamental change came in 1984 when Reagan again carried Texas and the very conservative Democrat-turned-Republican Phil Gramm beat liberal Lloyd Doggett for the Senate seat Tower was leaving.[62]

Perhaps. But others think Clements was, in fact, an avid party builder. In four years a governor can appoint about four thousand people to boards and commissions across the state, half of which require senate confirmation. Even after Clements lost the 1982 election, as a lame duck he appointed about a hundred—despite the screams of Mark White, who had just defeated him—and of course Clements continued to appoint conservatives.[63]

Another historian points out that Clements was especially successful in turning rural Texas, formerly a Democratic stronghold, to the GOP. Places once 80 percent Democratic had become 80 percent Republican by 2006. "How did Clements do it?" asked a former Clements insider. He recalled that Clements

> made a whole bunch of political appointments. There were places where there was no chance of winning, but if a Republican had a chance of winning, somebody was going to run as a Republican if they got the appointment. A few got beat, but by the time Clements left office three years later, we had appointed two to three hundred Republican judges, scattered all across Texas. Once you start breaking up the courthouse in rural Texas, you break up voting patterns and completely change the state.[64]

The Clements people hit any special election in "full campaign mode" while persuading officeholders and candidates to switch parties as congressman (and soon to be senator) Phil Gramm did in 1983.[65]

The 1978 results were far from a huge sweep for the Republicans. Undeniably, however, another corner had been turned away from the one-party past. Mark White, who defeated Clements in 1982, was the state attorney general and had first been appointed to statewide office by Dolph Briscoe in 1973. Thus White was, if not of the conservative wing, certainly not a liberal either. But he was clearly to the left of Clements. White proved lucky in several ways: the high inflation of the early 1980s followed by national recession; a disastrous oil blowout in the Gulf, in which one of Clements's drilling companies was involved (though it was not primarily culpable); Clements's Type-A CEO personality and consequent rough times with the legislature; the popular top of the Democratic ticket (Senator Lloyd Bentsen and

Lieutenant Governor Bill Hobby). Finally, the African American and Hispanic minorities, irked by Clements's economic measures, voted in substantial numbers for White.[66] The result was not predicted, least of all by the Clements people, but it produced over 53 percent for White and 46 percent for Clements.

White's four years as governor were famous for an educational reform commission led by Ross Perot, which was controversial and successfully court-tested. Known as House Bill 72, it lowered class sizes and reduced the funding gap between poor and wealthy districts. But it probably did not help White, nor did a severe drop in oil prices, which wrecked the state budget.[67] The fall 1986 election inverted the 1982 result: White lost to Bill Clements, with the numbers just about the reverse of White's victory in 1982. "The Texas economy was in free-fall . . . and a special session of the legislature imposed temporary tax increases."[68] The chronically taxophobic Texas electorate accordingly dismissed Mark White.

A ONE-AND-TWO-THIRDS-PARTY STATE?

Clements's second term, 1987–91, included some more abrasive episodes with the legislature, but also some successes. At its conclusion, Clements was seventy-two years old and "tired."[69] Neither of his terms, or White's sandwiched between them, had any great effect on party balance, other than the fact that his first election, in 1978, has to be seen as a tipping point if only because Clements broke the century-long tradition of Democratic governors. Thus it was significant, but not decisively so.

Texas was on its way to becoming a two-party state, but Republicans had not yet carried enough down-ballot statewide offices or escaped minority status in the legislature to have truly achieved that. Yet it could accurately be called a one-and-two-thirds-party state. Republicans had come a great distance from their nonentity status in the 1950s. The composition of the two major parties—the interest groups, the demographic profiles—as of the mid- to late 1980s shows how much had changed since the 1950s, the heyday of Rayburn and Johnson, and how much Texas politics was still in flux and subject to further change. Yet Republicans had the momentum. John Knaggs, Senator Tower's admiring political biographer, has pointed out that the "highly effective voter registration drive conducted by the Reagan-Bush Campaign [in 1984] resulted in more straight-ticket voting by Republicans in the high growth areas." The Nixon and Tower landslide of 1972 was not accompanied by Republican gains in congressional or legislative seats. In contrast, by 1984 the top of the Republican ticket was pulling along the rest.[70]

During the Reagan years, which were mostly the Bill Clements years in Texas, the GOP did well:

> Between 1984 and 1986, the number of candidates running in the Republican primary nearly doubled, from 584 to 1026. Meanwhile, the number of Republican primary voters jumped from 263,000 in 1982 to 543,000 in 1986 to more than a million in 1988. What's more, the Republican party probably has a more efficient system for recruiting and training candidates than the Democrats, and the GOP is better funded. . . . [In 1986] the state Republican party raised and spent $2.5 million . . . while the Democratic party spent less than $800,000.[71]

A 1986 statewide survey measured Texans' party preferences according to race, family income, hometown size, liberal/moderate/conservative philosophy, region, gender, length of time in Texas, and age. Some differences were not particularly significant, such as region or gender, but others were. Of "All Texans," party identification was 26 percent Republican, 32 percent "independent," and 35 percent Democratic. By race, however, differences were sharp. Anglos divided into 32 percent Republican, 36 percent independent, and 27 percent Democratic; African Americans split 11 percent Republican, 16 percent independent, 65 percent Democratic; and Hispanics were 14 percent Republican, 23 percent independent, 51 percent Democratic. Those with family incomes under $10,000 split 19 percent Republican, 24 percent independent, 46 percent Democratic; and those with incomes topping $30,000 divided 35 percent Republican, 32 percent independent, 28 percent Democratic. Democrats were least strong in "very large metros" but predominated in "towns/rural areas" as well as in length of time in Texas and age (over forty-five).[72]

These variables show consistently that as of the mid-1980s Democratic strength, except for minorities, was greatest among groups that were likely to shrink: small-town or rural residents, nonmigrants, and older folks. Republicans and independents, on the other hand, had an edge in big-city residence, recent migration into Texas, and youth.

The survey's authors summarized their analysis by saying, "The Texas Democratic party runs well among minority citizens, low-income voters of all races, people living outside large metropolitan areas, people who call themselves liberals or moderates, people who live in East or South Texas, older voters, women, members of labor unions, Jews, and some professionals."[73]

One variable to which these authors gave only passing attention is religion. They apparently sensed its growing relevance but they did not poll for it. They wrote, however: "Although traditional Republicans hold the upper hand in the state GOP [i.e., people like Connally or Clements], they face a stiff challenge from the religious conservatives . . . [who] are better organized and more strongly motivated than other Republican activists. As a result, they are a threat to the party's organizational structure."[74] The conclusion—from twenty-twenty hindsight—is that the state's becoming less rural and more metropolitan were not the only factors strengthening the Texas GOP. It was also helped as it attracted more migrants from the Midwest and elsewhere, as unions weakened, and as religious conservatives or fundamentalists became more vocal and visible. That would happen as the "social issues," local and national, commanded increasing attention. More on religion in a moment.

ANN RICHARDS: A DEMOCRATIC INTERLUDE?

The die of Republican supremacy and collapse of the Texas Democrats may already have been cast as of 1990. But elections do not ride entirely on the crest of demographic and economic trends. As Bill Clements's second term began ebbing away, it appeared likely that another Republican would succeed him, and that Democrats' hopes to elect another governor would be futile. Yet the 1990 election for governor came to be called the contest between "Claytie and the Lady," and the lady won.[75]

Ann Richards, born during the Great Depression, had fought her way through personal troubles and into leadership of the liberal wing of the state Democratic Party by the 1980s. Elected state treasurer in 1982, she gave the keynote address at the 1988 national Democratic convention, famously skewering the Republican candidate, fellow Texan and vice president George H. W. Bush. ("Poor George. He can't help it. He was born with a silver foot in his mouth.") In the 1990 Democratic primary for governor, she bested former governor

Mark White and attorney general Jim Mattox, winning 39.5 percent to Mattox's 36.8 percent, with White running far back of both. In the runoff, Richards soundly defeated Mattox—only to become a decided underdog behind Republican Clayton Williams in the general.

Williams was a strong conservative, an oilman and rancher from Fort Stockton in western Texas. With the help of able advisers, he sailed through the Republican primary. But those advisers "had no creative control in the general election." Williams portrayed himself as an old-time, typical Texan of myth and folklore, wearing cowboy garb, at one point riding his horse up the Capitol steps in Austin—but most of all becoming his own worst enemy, with a series of gaffes that especially repelled women. The most damaging and egregious was "his quip to reporters in March, during a rainy outing on his ranch, that 'the weather's like rape. If it's inevitable, you might as well lie back and enjoy it.'"[76] With that and other blunders, Williams frittered away an initially strong lead. He once claimed he was putting $20 million of his own money into the campaign, and perhaps he did. But Ann Richards's financial support came from small (under a hundred dollars) donors, of whom she attracted 33,000.[77] She won by just under 100,000 votes out of nearly four million. Twenty years after his defeat, Williams claimed that, despite losing, "I made it OK for Bubba to vote Republican."[78]

Other Democratic liberals lost, however. Jim Hightower, the agriculture commissioner and a strong liberal voice, lost to future governor Rick Perry, another Democrat-turned-Republican. Republican Kay Bailey Hutchison, the future senator, succeeded Richards as state treasurer. In seeking reelection in 1994, Richards faced George W. Bush and lost decisively.[79] Texas was not yet a clearly Republican majority state. Clayton Williams showed that a blundering super-macho Republican could lose, and Ann Richards showed that a liberal, outspokenly pro-choice Democrat could still win.[80] But not by much, and not against a better opponent, which Bush was. Bill Clinton's 1992 campaign did not seriously contest Texas, and Clinton lost the state. Texas Republicans could claim, with much justice, that the "national Democratic Party has no place for—and is no place for—Texas."[81] In 1994, according to exit polls, Richards took 85 percent of black voters and 71 percent of Hispanics, "but Bush received 62 percent of the white Anglo vote. . . . Richards received nearly two-thirds of the votes cast by people in the lowest income category, while Bush received almost two-thirds of the votes in the highest income category." By more than two to one, conservatives outnumbered liberals, giving Bush the clear advantage.[82] By then, more than a third of the state legislature and eleven of the thirty members of the Texas congressional delegation were Republicans. In the 1996 election, for the first time, more Texans voted for Republican congressional candidates (52.9 percent) than for Democrats (44.8 percent). Republicans have led in every election since.

THE RELIGIOUS FACTOR

The poet Christian Wiman spent many of his early years "in a twenty-five-foot trailer in a tiny, dying town in far West Texas," with his grandmother and great-aunt. "God was almost instinctive in them, so woven into the textures of their lives that even their daily chores, accompanied by hymns hummed under their breath, had an air of easy devotion."[83] Bred in the bone, one might say. More secular and more revealing of the social (as opposed to the individual) form of Texan religion was the heroine of Philipp Meyer's novel *The Sun:* "When her father died she had immediately stopped going to church. If prayer could not even keep your family alive, she did not see what good it was. But after she and Hank moved to Houston, she had started going again. You were marked if you didn't."[84]

Sincere belief, as well as social pressure, made religion a potent force in Texas politics. It had always played some role, but the amalgam of conservative, fundamentalist religion with right-wing politics was a late twentieth-century happening, and it did not form overnight. There was no abrupt tsunami as in Oklahoma in the 1994 election but a gradual strengthening of conservative forces allying religion with the state Republican Party. Evangelicals—not quite the same as fundamentalists though the overlap was substantial, especially in the largest denomination, the Southern Baptists—had difficulty with John F. Kennedy's Catholicism in 1960 and were attracted to Goldwater in 1964 and Nixon in 1968, becoming "presidential Republicans." Robert Wuthnow writes that "the 1964 election may have been mean and dirty, but it also showcased questions about morality that brought religion into the political sphere. Morality was the language in which citizens expressed concern that something they did not quite understand was terribly wrong. . . . Crime and violence, sex and gender, communism. And the Vietnam War became the focus of competing moral claims."[85]

From the 1960s on, "high-commitment evangelicals" became "the core of the Republican coalition" and about a third of state-wide Republican voters by the 1990s.[86] Mainline Protestants, which included the United Methodists, shifted Republican to an extent, but much less decisively than the high-commitment evangelicals. Southern Baptists' traditional support for Democrats became shaky by 1972, as was true of many people nationally, over a number of issues: the divide over the Vietnam War; "law and order" and apparent chaos in the cities; the civil rights movement—wasn't it moving "too fast"?[87] The four big issues were abortion, prayer in public schools, civic equality for gays and lesbians, and, "for some at least," teaching creationism through science textbooks.[88] As Wuthnow summarizes it, "Questions about feminism, the ordination of women as clergy, homosexuality, and abortion were beginning [in the 1970s] to mobilize religious leaders who felt that liberalization of long-held norms on these topics was fundamentally unbiblical."[89] Jerry Falwell began his Moral Majority in the late 1970s, and Pat Robertson founded the Christian Coalition in 1988. They and lesser televangelists reminded listeners unremittingly that public morality was in deep trouble. By the 1980s, Christian conservatives were targeting school boards, school superintendents' offices, and precinct and county conventions of the Republican Party. They made increasing inroads with wide cumulative impact over the next decade. At that time, a survey found that 54 percent of Texans regarded themselves as born-again, 72 percent believed the Bible to be inerrant and to be read literally, and 87 percent supported Christian prayers in the schools.[90]

Yet, prior to the early 1970s, the Texas Republican Party focused much more on economic issues than social or faith-based ones. Scholars of American religion disagree on how the Religious Right got started. Randall Balmer writes that the "real catalyst . . . was the attempt to defend against Internal Revenue Service attempts to rescind the tax exemption of racially segregated institutions, especially Bob Jones University and Jerry Falwell's segregated Liberty Christian Academy in the 1970s." Balmer cites such founders of the Religious Right as Paul Weyrich and Ed Dobson and the taxophobe Grover Norquist as "emphatically" denying that the abortion issue "played any role."[91]

In time, however, the Supreme Court's 1973 *Roe v. Wade* decision on abortion became the whipping boy of the Religious Right, in Texas and elsewhere. For the political scientist John M. Bruce it became the "central issue on the Christian Right agenda," with public education second—the absence of prayer in schools, the teaching of evolution rather than creationism, "encourag[ing] immoral behavior by providing information on contraception, homosexuality, AIDS, and basic human reproduction."[92] Opposition to gay rights and the Equal Rights Amendment were also conservative concerns.

Conservative Baptists, led by Rev. W. A. Criswell of the huge First Baptist Church of Dallas, and other clergy successfully captured the decisive denominational offices beginning in 1979 and continued to move the denomination in a fundamentalist direction through the 1980s. Baptists who were more moderate retained control of the Texas Baptist Convention, but the national organization, where Jerry Falwell played a critical role, attracted many Texans. In several ways 1979 is the "logical starting point for discussion of the Christian Right as a coherent political movement"—not only the takeover of the Southern Baptist Convention, but, as part of that, the creation of the Moral Majority by Falwell and others, aided by the conservative Catholic and Republican activist Richard Viguerie. In 1980, Baptists favored Reagan over their coreligionist Jimmy Carter by 56 percent to 42 percent. The Republican presidential advantage grew to 80 percent to 14 percent in 1996 (Dole over Clinton).[93] Many Baptists at first resisted joining Catholics in opposing abortion because they feared they might become tinctured with Catholic social action, which would have contravened the bedrock Baptist position on the separation of church and state.[94] They discovered they had little to fear. The Catholic hierarchy became much less outspoken on social justice issues than on abortion during the papacy of John Paul II, a stance that filtered down through Texas's bishops and clergy.

Through the 1980s, the Religious Right began to coalesce, and conservative religion began to merge with right-wing politics. The Religious Right existed in the 1970s, playing no "direct role in the party or electoral system," but it began to do so in the late 1980s and early 1990s because of "intense public reaction to the cultural wars and the simmering social issues, such as abortion." A key entity within the Religious Right was the Texas Christian Coalition, founded earlier but energized by new leader Dick Weinhold, who had been "the chief fund-raiser for Pat Robertson's campaign in 1988." By the 1994 election, the Religious Right/Texas Christian Coalition/high-commitment evangelicals were positioned to push Texas politics to the Republican Right decisively. "At least ten winning candidates for the U.S. Congress were aligned with or supported by the Christian Right in some way," and the slate for the Texas house and senate were similarly aligned. The result: "The formal structure of the Texas Republican Party [was] controlled by the Christian Right." In 1996 the Christian Right "held a virtual veto over the selection" of Texas's delegation to the national Republican convention.[95] A hopeful candidate who was not anti-abortion and outspoken about it had no chance.

How did the Religious Right do it? As James Lamare and his coauthors explain it, it succeeded "the old-fashioned way: it out-organized the opposition . . . [producing] a textbook example of how to obtain control over a party organization," beginning at the precinct committee and school board levels, then moving up to county and district positions, then the state organization, and ultimately the delegation to the national convention. It distributed three million voter guides. Its activists made countless phone calls. It had momentum and did not lose it. The result was the capture of the state party by 1994, and it did not let go after that. Weinhold left the leadership of the Texas Christian Coalition in 2001, and he was succeeded by Norm Mason, a friend and fellow resident of Sugar Land, the Houston suburb that was home to Congressman Tom DeLay.[96]

REDISTRICTING TWICE, 2001–2003

Ann Richards did not win reelection in 1994. It was a "Republican year" nationally as well as in Texas. President Bill Clinton's ratings were abysmal. The Religious Right was riding high. The Republican candidate for governor, George W. Bush, was much more palatable and gaffe-free than Clayton Williams had been in 1990. Kay Bailey Hutchison won the U.S. Senate seat that Lloyd Bentsen left to become Clinton's secretary of the treasury,[97] and the Republicans picked up two more Texas seats in the U.S. House. Bush, though a fairly traditional "economic" Republican rather than an evangelical, was quite acceptable to the Right. As Paul Burka wrote in *Texas Monthly*, Bush's "ideological stance is wholly compatible with the Christian Coalition's. Criticism of the sixties counterculture is a staple of his speeches."[98] Bush was reelected handily in 1998, as was Hutchison in 2000, and the Republicans kept picking up House seats and more and more of the Texas legislature.

The game was about over for the Texas Democratic Party. Before the 1998 campaign was under way, the attorney general, Dan Morales, held a press conference to announce he was not going to run for reelection. By doing so, he "made December 2, 1997, the day the Democratic party of Texas finally collapsed, not with a bang but a whimper." Morales, forty-one years old, had been elected three times to the Texas house and twice as attorney general. He had never been defeated, had a "69 percent approval rating, [was] honest and free of scandal, [and was] a Hispanic with a Harvard law degree."[99] Two decades earlier, or even one, Morales would have had a bright future in politics. But not by 1998. Republicans swept all statewide offices and kept their majorities in the legislature. Although they did not capture more U.S. House seats, that would change very soon, and decisively.

Republicans held steady in the 2000 election for state and federal offices. Then, the census of 2000 awarded Texas two more seats in the U.S. House because of population increase during the 1990s, giving Texas thirty-two seats. Republicans won fifteen of them. But that was not enough for congressman Tom DeLay (by then majority leader of the U.S. House), Texas house speaker Tom Craddick of Midland, and other Republicans. DeLay and Craddick were friends and allies and had sat virtually next to each other in the Texas house for years before DeLay went on to represent south-suburban Houston in Congress. David Dewhurst, another Houstonian, had been Texas land commissioner before being elected lieutenant governor in 2002, and he would be a major player in the final stages of the redistricting. Republicans had never controlled redistricting before, because they had never held majorities in the Texas house and senate before. For the next two years after the census's announcement, redistricting in Texas was a continuing arm-wrestle, which the Republicans ended up winning hands-down.

The story began almost peaceably. In the spring of 2001, state house speaker Pete Laney (Democrat) appointed and old friend, Representative Delwyn Jones (Democrat turned Republican) to chair the House Redistricting Committee, and Lieutenant Governor Bill Ratliff (Republican) appointed Senator Jeff Wentworth of San Antonio to chair the senate counterpart. Neither Jones nor Wentworth, though Republicans, were hyper-partisans with an overriding aim to increase the number of Republican House members and expunge Democrats. Wentworth, instead, aimed "to increase voter participation by creating as many competitive districts as possible." To Congressman Joe Barton (R-Ennis, between Dallas and Waco) the object was different. He wanted "to pick up at least seven seats"—the two new ones plus five then held by "WD-40s" (white Democrats over forty, i.e., who had been around a long time).[100] That was decidedly DeLay's aim as well. He would reach it, but it would take two years, along with the involvement of Governor Rick Perry, state and federal courts, the flight out-of-state of Democratic legislators who became known as the "Killer D's," and other excitement.

In May 2001 both the house and senate redistricting committees produced maps that would have allocated the two new seats resulting from the 2000 census between the parties. Neither proposal came to a vote. Democrats filed a suit before a Democratic judge in Travis County (Austin), and in October a federal court in Tyler would review his ruling. The Austin judge ruled on October 3 in such a way that the result would have been sixteen Republicans, thirteen Democrats, and three uncertain. But a week later the same judge produced a different plan that would have resulted in seventeen Democrats and fifteen Republicans. The state attorney general, at that time future senator John Cornyn, tried to have the state supreme court disallow that plan. It did so but then turned the matter back to the lower state court. The federal court then issued a plan that "protected all incumbents and created two new Republican districts, one in west Houston and one in north Dallas." These were the districts contested in the election of 2002. The result was seventeen Democrats and fifteen Republicans, the same as in 1996, 1998, and 2000, except for the addition of the two new Republican seats.[101]

This concluded the first redistricting in the wake of the 2000 census. The second followed right after the 2002 election and became a major political event of 2003, for both Texas and the nation. Its outcome governed the 2004 and subsequent elections until after the next census, in 2010. Steve Bickerstaff, the episode's historian, properly gives Tom DeLay a central role in the second redistricting, but he points out:

What happened in Texas in 2003 was not a result of the influence or planning of one person, or even a handful of persons. Instead, it was driven by a much more consequential partisan movement and was one facet of a ruthless and effective quest for power by persons and groups that share a common ideology and ambition. Activists within the Republican Party and major Republican donors played a critical role in convincing reluctant Texas Republican lawmakers to go along with an aggressive partisan redistricting plan despite their own reservations and substantial public opposition.[102]

The 2002 election had returned eighty-eight Republicans (out of 151) to the house, a first-time-ever Republican majority, putting the GOP in charge. In May, Speaker Craddick was prodded by his longtime colleague DeLay, now majority leader of the U.S. House, to come up with a new map, and the House Redistricting Committee did so on May 6, 2003. This map was intended to gerrymander out of office as many of the ten Anglo Democratic congressmen as possible while preserving the Latino and black Democrats and even adding one seat for each of those minorities.[103] To reopen a state's redistricting, after it had already been done in accord with the decennial census, was extremely unusual. Ohio had done it six times, but not since 1890. Other instances are rare or nonexistent.

With the house debate looming and Republican victory seemingly assured, fifty-one of the house Democrats slipped out of the state, depriving the chamber of its constitutionally required two-thirds quorum. They holed up in a motel in Ardmore, Oklahoma, thirty miles north of the state line and out of the reach of the Texas state police, who had been ordered to find them and bring them back. Such was the episode of the "Killer D's." DeLay pressured the U.S. departments of Homeland Security, Transportation, and Justice, as well as the Federal Aviation Authority, to track and possibly force the absentees to return, but to no avail. When the legislative session expired on May 15, they returned. The bill had not passed. But a month later, Governor Rick Perry convened a special session for the purpose of redistricting.[104]

This time the frustration of a quorum developed in the senate. Eleven Democratic senators took off for Albuquerque, stymieing action for a month. But one senator finally returned, and the bill passed in what was by then a third special session on October 12, 2003, with Lieutenant Governor David Dewhurst presiding over the senate. The U.S. Justice Department did not object to the redistricting map, and a federal court ruled that it was all right to redistrict twice between censuses. The 2004 election went ahead under the new district lines. Only three of the WD-40s—Chet Edwards, Lloyd Doggett, and Gene Green—survived. The Texas delegation went from seventeen to fifteen Democratic to twenty-one to eleven Republican. The Supreme Court approved the plan in 2005, except for requiring the borders of two seats to be revised, which did not change the outcome.[105]

Backlash followed. Craddick had used hardball tactics, which offended enough house members to lose him his speakership a couple of sessions later. DeLay lost his majority leadership, his House seat, and nearly his freedom after he was indicted in September 2005 for felony money laundering in connection with the redistricting, specifically by channeling corporate funds to help elect Republicans to the Texas house in 2002, who would thereupon support the second redistricting.[106] DeLay was convicted and sentenced to three years in prison. An appellate court set aside the conviction in 2013, and the Texas Court of Criminal Appeals upheld that judgment on October 1, 2014.[107] Bickerstaff's assessment is that

> the final redistricting plan was developed in secret by a small group of like-minded persons committed to maximizing Republican voting strength in 2004 and the future. Looming over the drawing up of the final map was the partisan aggressiveness of Congressman DeLay, the Republican congressional delegation, and other outside forces. . . . In 2003, neither the residents of the state nor the members of the Texas House or Senate had any significant impact on the final redistricting plan.[108]

It was done, too, with the consent and approval of the Bush White House.[109]

The 2010 census awarded Texas four more House seats. Certain Republican legislators urged a simple, quick solution: protect incumbents and split the four new seats to give Hispanic Democrats two and suburban Republicans two. But others, including Governor Perry and Attorney General Greg Abbott, devised a plan to leave the

Democrats one Hispanic-majority seat, taking the other three for the GOP. The Justice Department and federal courts weighed in. "After nearly a year and millions of dollars in court costs, the end result was nearly identical to what Republican incumbents had lobbied for in the first place," the two-two split.[110] It still gave Republicans the preponderance of Texas's House seats.

THE PERRY YEARS, AND CAN TEXAS REVERT TO BLUE, OR EVEN PURPLE?

The opening decade of the twenty-first century was a good time for Texas Republicans. Former governor George W. Bush was president. Rick Perry, pro-business but also at ease with the Religious Right, was governor through the entire decade and appointed every single state official and commissioner before he turned the job over to former attorney general Greg Abbott in January 2015. From 2004 on, the state's congressional delegation was strongly Republican, and the Texas house and senate held invincible Republican majorities, which continued to increase to just shy of two-thirds in both chambers in the 2014 election. Furthermore, "though Republicans had flipped only a few seats in the Legislature," wrote Erica Grieder in early 2015, "their caucuses had undoubtedly become more conservative. . . . there would be more than thirty Republican freshmen, most of them ideologically further to the right than their predecessors. . . . [Hence] Texas's 2014 general election and primaries produced a 2015 Legislature that is further to the right than the 2013 iteration."[111] Although Speaker Joe Straus was a relatively moderate Republican, and Lieutenant Governor Dan Patrick was more Religious Right than Tea Party, the "far-right element . . . fiscally inflexible and socially dogmatic—has become the mainstream." That did not bode well for any programs that new governor Greg Abbott might propose.[112]

Nor did it bode well for any comeback that Democrats might try to make. After the 2012 election—the reelection of Barack Obama with strong support from black and Hispanic minorities nationally and in Texas—opinion pieces (more hopes than predictions) appeared, proposing that by 2020 Texas would again have a Democratic majority, quite different from the old Shivers/Connally kind. Surmises of this sort rested largely on demography. Hispanics were becoming an ever-larger share of the state's population, from both in-migration and natural increase. In 2002 the state demographer, Steve Murdock

of Texas A&M, projected that by 2040 the state would have a Hispanic majority, whether in-migration continues or not.[113] Assuming
that Hispanics continue to vote roughly 70 percent Democratic, and
assuming that an increasing proportion of them will actually vote,
then a Democratic return to power is credible. Continued Hispanic
in-migration—and natural increase—might have turned Texas "to
at least comparatively purple by 2015."[114] In the words of political
scientist Cal Jillson, "For a half-century we have been waiting for the
moment that would galvanize Texas Latinos to seek citizenship, register to vote and storm the polls. Maybe this one [Trump's promise of
a border wall] will do it. I'm not betting on it."[115]

But it did not quite happen. And nothing certifies those two
assumptions about Hispanic voting. For one thing, if Hispanics vote
in greater numbers, there is no certainty that they will continue
to vote 65 or 70 percent Democratic. Republicans often say that
"Hispanics are really Republicans [i.e., social conservatives]; they
just haven't discovered that yet." As Paul Burka once wrote, "One
thing is certain. Demographic inevitability alone won't save the
Democrats." Their dream could become "a nightmare" if Hispanics
start splitting their votes.[116] A study done in 2006 indicated that
"Texas Hispanics were far more concerned about economic issues,
education, employment, and immigration policies than they were
about abortion or homosexuality."[117] That, of course, could cut two
ways. For the present, it meant that Hispanics, the majority of them
Catholic, would not be motivated by the anti-abortion monovision
of their bishops, who on that point walked hand-in-hand with evangelical Protestants.

Ethnicity has shaped partisan affiliation throughout American
history, but time dilutes it. Much else determines partisan strength.
Does the Texas Democratic Party have the elements necessary for
winning? It would require "the money, the down-ballot candidates,
the consulting talent, the PR muscle, the operatives, the issues
research team, the number crunchers, who constitute the worker
bees of a major political campaign . . . and . . . most important finding sympathetic voters and getting them to the polls."[118] The projec-
tions about Hispanic population growth—and, much less grounded,
Hispanic *voting* growth—afford Democrats some rays of hope (or
straws to grasp). So do a couple of other demographic turns. Unlike
the 1970s and 1980s, when Democratic voters clustered in small

towns and cities and were above the median age, Democrats in post-2000 or 2010 electorates have been more urban and younger than Republicans. Since 2000, Democrats have carried nearly all of the big cities, as distinct from the suburbs.[119] That is a solid base, and it is not all African American and Hispanic. "Upwardly mobile Asian and Latino families and younger whites" became increasingly important in 2006 and after, and courthouse races in Dallas and Houston became Democratic pickups. In the 2016 presidential, Trump got 52.2 percent, the lowest for the Republican standard bearer since the three-way races of 1992 and 1996, but still a majority. The congressional delegation remained twenty-five Republican, eleven Democratic, and the Texas house became ninety-four Republican, fifty-five Democratic.

Rural Texas has shifted from Democratic to Republican, but was it still critical to a win, as it used to be? Burka wrote after the 2008 election that the "Republicans are strongest where Texas isn't growing. The Democrats are strongest where it is growing"—that is, the reverse of the 1980s situation.[120] Are these some things the Republicans should worry about, or the Democrats should rest hopes on? Perhaps, but not for quite a while. When one considers that the utter replacement of the once-uncontested Democratic hegemony took decades, there is no compelling reason to think that a reversal of the present Republican hegemony would take any less time. Unless evangelical religion is diverted to some causes compatible with Democratic positions; unless Democrats produce candidates up and down the ticket who all have the charisma of the 1990 Ann Richards or the 2014 Wendy Davis; unless, unless, unless.

In the 1950s, a Republican Party was virtually nonexistent in Texas. In 2015 the same, or near it, was true of the Democratic Party. As Mimi Swartz of *Texas Monthly* wrote in 2016, "Texas Democrats' case of learned helplessness" has become "chronic. They hardly bother to run for dogcatcher. Wendy Davis's ignominious defeat in her 2014 run for governor proved it was time to start over, but strategic efforts have not taken off."[121]

First, Shivers and presidential Republicanism; then John Tower's election to the Senate, then Bill Clements becoming governor; and with accelerating speed through the 1990s and 2000s the capture of the Texas legislature and the congressional delegation—those were the outstanding turning points. Underlying them was a roster of elements: repulsion at disorder, crime in the streets, and related upheavals of the 1960s and '70s; dislike of candidates McGovern and Carter and attraction to Reagan; the spread of the Religious Right and its coalescence politically with the GOP; and much else—and finally sheer hard organizing work on top of the state's historic conservatism, whatever the party label. Texas's red shift should not revert to blue or even purple any time soon.

THE STAYERS, RELIABLY RED

3 The Red Belt:
Kansas, Nebraska, the Dakotas, Wyoming, Utah, Idaho, and Alaska

The Mountain states have a reputation of always voting Republican. That is partially true; Idaho, Wyoming, and Utah have seldom deviated from the GOP column. But others, such as Colorado and Montana, have oscillated and are historically purple, not red or blue. The Great Plains states, not only Texas and Oklahoma but the four to their north, are more deserving of the red reputation. There have been exceptions over the sixty-some years since 1950—a governor here, a senator there, and all of them voted for the Democrat Lyndon Johnson in 1964. But generally the four northern plains states, three in the Mountains, and Alaska have constituted an electoral red zone. Collectively, the reliably reds have thirty-three electoral votes, sixteen U.S. senators, and seventeen members of the U.S. House of Representatives.[1]

KANSAS

First, the northern Great Plains, beginning with Kansas and heading north. Kansas has been called "the essence of rural America,"[2] and until the one-time Confederacy switched from solid Democratic to solid Republican after 1965, Kansas was also the essence of Republican loyalty. A master's thesis done at Emporia State University some years ago described "the Kansan ethos." The author could as well have called it the "Kansas Republican ethos," because she considered it so deep-dyed as to smother any other political culture, not just the Democrats but including the People's Party of the 1890s.[3]

Many a commentator has observed how thoroughly and dependably Kansans have voted Republican. The *Almanac of American Politics* once described Kansas as "a state where Republicanism is the natural affiliation of the majority, and there the

Republican Party's base is broad. It includes not just rich people and country club members, but the mechanic at the garage and the clerk at the feed store; not just the banker and the lawyer, but the farmer and the minister."[4] Neal Peirce, in his *tour d'horizon* of the Great Plains states, remarked that "few states, in fact, are as consistently Republican as Kansas." Less flatteringly, Peirce also noted that William Allen White, the famous editor of the *Emporia Gazette*, wrote in the 1920s that Kansas was where things "happen first." But, Peirce went on to say, "today [the early 1970s] Kansas is scarcely the place where things happen 'first.' Indeed, nowhere on the American continent can the eclipse of a region or state as a vital force . . . be felt so strongly and poignantly as in Kansas." Kansas has undergone "a slide into obscurity." Not very kind, perhaps, but a reflection of how a one-time leader of the nation in both Populism and Progressivism, not to mention the pro- and anti-slavery extension fight of the 1850s, had become "fly-over country."[5]

The pattern of Kansas politics over the past two-thirds of a century is easily grasped. In every presidential election except 1964, the Republican candidate prevailed. In 1964, Lyndon Johnson bested Goldwater there, 54 percent to 45 percent. Otherwise, the Republican winners all captured majorities of the state vote, except for 1964 and 1992, when Ross Perot took 27 percent, suppressing George H. W. Bush's plurality to 39 percent, with Bill Clinton the runner-up at 34 percent. Other than Johnson, the last Democrat to win Kansas's electoral votes was FDR in 1932 and 1936.

Democrats have had better luck winning the governorship. Prior to 1974 the governor's term was still two years, and Republicans and Democrats each won six elections beginning in 1950. The Democrats' six were won by George Docking in 1956 and 1958 and by his son Robert four times from 1966 through 1972. The Dockings were bankers from Lawrence and Arkansas City. Peirce called George "a conservative Democrat" and Robert "his equally conservative son," who "won by holding onto traditional Democratic strongholds in the cities and within organized labor while being sufficiently conservative to sap off some of the normal Republican vote in the rural areas."[6] Beginning in 1974 when the term became four years (but limited to two terms at most), three Democrats were elected, including two women, Joan Finney in 1990 and Kathleen Sibelius in 2002 and again in 2006. Four Republicans won the office, at times relative moderates

like Bill Graves in 1994 and 1998, and at other times extreme conservatives (Sam Brownback in 2010 and 2014). In sum, the governorship
has been shared between the major parties more than any other major
office.

Not so the U.S. senatorships. Kansas has not elected a Democratic senator since 1932, a consistency unmatched by any other state.
Through the 1950s and into the 1960s, the two senators were Frank
Carlson, "a cautious, hard-working man of conservative-to-moderate
views," and Andrew Schoeppel, "a conservative oil and gas lawyer
from Wichita who opposed Eisenhower's foreign aid programs."
When Schoeppel died in office in 1962, he was succeeded by James B.
Pearson, another "moderate conservative in the Eisenhower-Carlson
tradition."[7] Carlson did not run for reelection in 1968. He was succeeded by a young congressman and war veteran from Russell, Robert
Dole, who represented Kansas with hitherto unparalleled visibility
as chair of the Republican National Committee in the early 1970s,
the party's vice presidential candidate (Gerald Ford's running mate)
in 1976, and its presidential candidate in 1996 (against Bill Clinton).
Pearson was a relative moderate, often working on legislation with
Democrats until he retired in 1978. Nancy Landon Kassebaum,
daughter of Alf Landon, the GOP's hapless presidential candidate in
1936, achieved considerable national prominence until she left the
Senate in 1997. When Dole resigned to run for president in 1996,
congressman Sam Brownback won election to that seat, and another
congressman, Pat Roberts, won the seat vacated by Kassebaum. In
2010, when Brownback was elected governor, congressman Jerry
Moran was elected to his Senate seat. Thus Kansas's senators have
ranged from the quietly obscure (Schoeppel) to highly visible nationally (Dole), have included one woman (Kassebaum), and ranged
from moderate (Pearson) to Tea Party conservative (Brownback). No
Democrats, however.

At one time, Kansas had eight House members. By 1950 the
delegation had shrunk to six, and then to five in 1962, and to four
in 1992 and since, reflecting the late twentieth-century population
losses on the rural Great Plains. Grain and livestock production continues to increase, but as agriculture and stockraising mechanized
after World War II they required fewer people to do those jobs. As in
Oklahoma, small farmers in Kansas either disappeared or stayed to
swallow up nearby neighboring homesteads and become agribusiness

operators themselves. After 1990 such rural population losses were offset by growth of metropolitan areas led by Johnson County (part of the Kansas City bistate complex), Sedgwick County (Wichita), and several smaller ones. The Kansas City stockyards, once second only in size to Chicago's, suffered greatly from a flood in 1951; Wyandotte County, where the yards were located, had been one of the few Democratic strongholds in the state, but thereafter it became less so. Meatpacking in recent years has flourished in the southwest, the Dustbowl of the 1930s, bringing population growth to towns like Liberal, Dodge City, and Garden City, the new "golden triangle of meatpacking"—all of which have multiplied since the 1980s, but without affecting political balances, since the newcomers were either noncitizens or did not vote. Other once-reliable Democratic counties such as Ellis, settled in the 1870s by German-Russian Catholics, either have lost population or their ethnic loyalties have become attenuated after four or five generations. Wyandotte County still leans Democratic, as does Douglas County (Lawrence), where the University of Kansas is located. But these have become islands in a Republican sea.

From 1950 through 2016, Kansans held 163 elections to the U.S. House. Democrats won thirty-two of those contests, Republicans 131. Multiple Democratic winners were Floyd Breeding (1956, 1958, 1960) in the then-southwestern District 5; Bill Roy (1970, 1972) in the northeast, then District 2; Martha Keys (1974, 1976), also in District 2; Dan Glickman (1976–92), nine-time winner in the Wichita district, then District 4; Jim Slattery (1982–92), who won six elections in District 2; and Dennis Moore (1998–2008), with six wins in District 3, the Kansas City–Lawrence district. Single-term wins took place in 1952 in District 1, then the northeast; in 1958 in the southeastern corner, then District 3; also in 1958 in the Wyandotte district, District 2; and Nancy Boyda won in 2006 in District 2, defeating five-term incumbent and former track champion Jim Ryun. In sum, Democrats, if they won at all, did so in the district that usually included Kansas City and Lawrence, occasionally Topeka also; and Wichita for Glickman's nine terms until a Christian Rightist, Todd Tiarht, defeated him in the Republican year of 1994. Except for a stray county here and there, notably Ellis, Kansans have voted for Republicans for Congress. Not many became nationally visible except for Bob Dole, who won his first of four terms in 1960, or Keith

Sibelius, who won the western Kansas district from 1968, when Dole went on to the Senate, through 1978.

Since Kansas has been so consistently Republican, its political history exhibits no turning points in the sense of the balance shifting from one party to the other. Within the Kansas Republican Party, however, a shift took place in the early 1990s as a major faction moved to the right. This shift can be traced to the local, precinct, and school board level in the late 1980s. But it became more visible from 1992, culminating in the takeover of the state party machinery in the 1990s and the capture, though briefly, of a majority on the state board of education in 1998.

The rightward shift, some say, first surfaced in the 1974 campaign for U.S. senator between two congressmen. The Democrat was Bill Roy, an obstetrician (and lawyer) from Topeka. Roy was first elected in 1970 from the northeastern district that then included Atchison, Topeka, Leavenworth, Manhattan, and part of Wyandotte County, and he was reelected in 1972. Bob Dole, his Republican opponent, represented the sparsely populated western Kansas district. Roy appeared to be well ahead. Then Dole started showing negative ads and billboards, accusing Roy of being "against" farmers, school lunches, and government economy. At a debate at the Kansas State Fair, Dole flung a question at Roy: "Why do you do abortions? And why do you favor abortion on demand?" Roy was blindsided. He had "performed abortions when the health of his patients required them," though personally he "had hated abortion since his residency . . . when he watched a teenage girl die in his emergency room because a back-alley abortionist had perforated her uterus."[8] But the accusation cost Roy many votes. On the weekend before the election, anti-abortionists "engineered an extensive literature 'drop' of an anti-Roy pamphlet, which included a picture of an aborted fetus. Caught off-guard, the Roy campaign failed to respond."[9] Dole squeaked by, 50.8 percent to Roy's 49.2 percent.[10] That was Dole's narrowest win among his House and Senate campaigns. Pro-life and pro-choice sides began to form; the abortion issue would continue, as in other states, to form the nucleus of the rightward shift among many Republicans.

Roe v. Wade "proved to be the trigger event that prompted an active Christian Right movement" in Kansas, according to its historians.[11] By the late 1980s, Pat Robertson's Christian Coalition threatened to take over the state Republican Party, which Senator Dole, as leader of the regular Republicans, found exceedingly irksome. In 1990 the social conservatives nearly threw out incumbent Republican governor Mike Hayden in the primary, and many defected in the general to the Democrat, state treasurer Joan Finney, who was pro-life.[12] The battle lines—all within the state Republican Party—tightened in the early 1990s. Senator Kassebaum "co-founded . . . the Republican Majority Coalition to combat the rise of the religious right,"[13] but the Religious Right fought on, capturing precinct committees and then county offices, led by state legislator David Miller, whom they managed to elect to chair the state party in 1990. By 1992 they were essentially in control of the party in Johnson and Sedgwick Counties (suburban Kansas City and Wichita).[14]

In 1994 came "the seminal event in establishing the legitimacy" of the right wing. Though moderate Republicans Bill Graves and Sheila Frahm won the governorship and lieutenant governorship, the Right won control of the Kansas house and kept a firm grip on the party organization. Because they favored less government on fiscal issues— taxes, expenditures—but more government on moral issues—especially abortion—they have been called "the polar faction," distinct from the more traditional "moderates."[15] Brakes, however, slowed the march of the Right. In 1998 moderate Graves crushed David Miller in the primary for governor, and in 2002 and 2006 Democrat Kathleen Sibelius trounced Republicans Tim Shallenberger and Jim Bennett. Both of those candidates, and thus the Right, were strong enough to win the Republican nominations, as were the post-Dole, post-Kassebaum senators, Sam Brownback and Pat Roberts.

The top offices eluded the Right in the 1990s, but they did elect Brownback to the House in 1994 and then to the Senate in 1996, and Vince Snowbarger and Tim Tiahrt to the House in 1996. Democrat Dennis Moore upset Snowbarger in 1996 and went on to several more terms. In one other area the Right won a victory in 1998, gaining a majority on the state board of education. Its agenda gained much unfavorable national publicity for Kansas. The majority promoted no sex education in the schools except abstinence, Christian messages in the schools, and "intelligent design" rather than Darwinian evolution.[16] The uproar was local as well as national, and in the 2000 primary, when five seats on the ten-member board were on the ballot, four Christian conservatives were defeated, and the board quickly voted to "approve revised science standards that emphasized evolution."[17]

The conservative agenda, as expressed in the legislature in the decade following 2005, included legislative control of the courts by contesting the reelection of moderate judges and supreme court justices and, in the Brownback administration, beginning in 2011, adoption of supply-side economics and the drastic reduction of state expenditure on education and other social areas. "What's the Matter with Kansas?," the question first asked by William Allen White in his 1896 editorial lampooning the Populists, was earning new answers. To the rightist faction that controlled the state party and most elections beginning in 2010, the answer was "nothing." Signs appeared, however, in 2016 that the Brownback/Far Right's grip was loosening. Supply-side economics—cutting taxes (and expenditure on schools and much else)—was not producing a promised economic takeoff in the state, but it was discomfiting voters. Several of the most conservative senators and House members, allies of Brownback, were thrown out in the Republican primary on August 2. Tim Huelskamp, the District 1 congressman and outspoken champion of the Tea Party/Freedom Caucus, lost the primary to a more moderate Roger Marshall, a physician. A columnist in the *Topeka Capital-Journal* even prophesied a "fall resurgence of Democrats, moderate GOP." That did not quite happen; as the highly respected electoral scholar at the University of Kansas, Burdett Loomis, put it, "This is a building process to get back to the moderate-conservative state I believe we are."[18]

NEBRASKA

Nebraska became a state in 1867, but it really exploded into life in the 1880s, when hundreds of thousands of optimistic settlers poured in and took up quarter-section plots of the U.S. public domain under the provisions of the Homestead Act of 1862 and subsequent federal land laws. The very first homestead claim was entered in southeastern Nebraska in January 1863, to a Union soldier. The great invasion awaited the welcoming rainfall of the 1880s, enticing several hundred thousand homesteaders across the Missouri River and along the Platte Valley. When the rainfall subsided in the late 1880s and through the 1890s, so did the influx. Nebraska adopted a seldom changing, conservative lifestyle and has kept it ever since.

Nebraska provided the nation with two exceptional statesmen early in its history. William Jennings Bryan was a compelling speaker who won the presidential nomination of his Democratic Party in 1896 as the champion of its agrarian wing, and he was also the nominee of the People's Party that year. He became the Democratic presidential candidate again in 1900 and 1908, and in 1913 he assumed the duties of secretary of state in Woodrow Wilson's cabinet. He resigned in 1915 when he believed that Wilson's threats toward Germany after the sinking of the *Lusitania* might pull the country into World War I. George W. Norris was a Progressive Republican who was elected to the House five times from 1902 through 1912, and then five times to the Senate, serving from 1913 to 1943. Norris is credited with the Norris-LaGuardia Act of 1932, which validated public employee unions, the law of 1933 creating the Tennessee Valley Authority, and the Rural Electrification Act of 1936, which brought electric power to farms and small towns in Nebraska and nationally that private utility companies had thought too expensive to serve. He and Bryan achieved much else as well.[19]

In 1942, Norris was defeated for reelection by Kenneth Wherry, who in the following eight years before his death in 1951 earned himself a reputation as an arch-conservative. Wherry was the first of several elected Nebraskans of that persuasion. Nebraska's political future was not to be marked with more Bryans or Norrises, but more by men like Wherry and his Nebraska colleague Hugh Butler, who served in the Senate until 1954. Nebraska elected senators who were conservative by the standards of 1950—Wherry and Butler. It did so again in 1970—Roman Hruska and Carl Curtis; again in 1985—Edward Zorinsky and J. James Exon; and again in 2010—Ben Nelson and Mike Johanns. Most were Republicans, a few were Democrats, but all were conservatives by the standards and contexts of their times. Bob Kerrey, a Democrat who was senator from 1989 to 2001, was a mild exception to the conservative pattern, the only one among the state's U.S. senators.

Nebraska, though steadfastly conservative politically, did change economically and demographically in the decades after 1950. As in the rest of the Great Plains states, its central and western regions saw people leave the one-time homesteads and small towns as stock and crop production mechanized, became more and more productive, but required ever fewer people. Meatpacking, for which Omaha, like Kansas City and Chicago, was once a mainstay, fled to much smaller and more remote cities near the ranches themselves, like Lexington, Grand Island, and Scottsbluff, on or near the 100th meridian. These towns expanded, but to a large extent with Hispanic packinghouse workers. Many did not or could not vote, so the migrant influx had little effect on politics. Nebraska had always had immigrants, but the earlier ones were German, Irish, Czech, or Scandinavian, who did play political roles. Not so the newest migrants. The state attracted some manufacturing, but military bases like the Strategic Air Command's Offutt near Omaha had probably a more significant impact, as did the service and financial sectors, led by the great investor and second wealthiest man in America, Warren Buffett of Omaha. Population shifts were reflected in legislative redistricting in 2011, and for the first time urban legislators were awarded "a slim legislative majority" over rural ones, who "watched their clear dominance wane on issues like education financing, water rights, economic development, agricultural property taxes and state spending."[20] Political change was incremental; it did not shift party balances; it was significant only locally.

The placid, noninnovative nature of Nebraska politics since 1950 is striking. There was no new Bryan, no new Norris. Kerrey was the nearest thing, but he was a party switcher, as were a number of other people elected to higher office. Some think that the nonpartisan character of the unicameral legislature weakened party loyalty and discipline. At any rate, the "branding iron" of party allegiance does not seem to have been as strong in Nebraska as in Kansas.

The story of the major offices since 1950 is uncomplicated. In every presidential election since 1940, Nebraskans have favored the Republican candidate, except for the Lyndon Johnson sweep of 1964. Back in 1896 and 1908, when Bryan was running, Nebraska voted for him, as it did twice for Democrat Wilson in 1912 and 1916 and for FDR in 1932 and 1936. But otherwise it has been consistently Republican.

The governorship has changed party hands more often, though it has been Republican since 1998: Mike Johanns was elected in 1998 and 2002, Dave Heineman in 2006 and 2010, and Pete Ricketts in 2014. Of the twenty-one gubernatorial elections beginning in 1950 through 2014, Republicans won twelve, Democrats nine. The term of office was two years until 1966, when (as in several states about that time) it was expanded to four. In the five elections from 1950 through 1958, four different men (three Republicans, one Democrat) won the job, but in 1960 Democrat Frank Morrison, a small-town lawyer, won the first of three terms. He supported the University of Nebraska and pioneered a state employees' retirement program, an income tax, and a public television network.[21] He was not, however, a raving liberal, but "a fiscal conservative described by some critics as 'a Copperhead Democrat of the Grover Cleveland stripe.'"[22] A Republican, Norbert Tiemann, won one term in 1966, followed by conservative Democrat James Exon in 1970 and 1974. Then came Lincoln attorney Republican Charles Thome in 1978, Democrat Bob Kerrey in 1982, Republican Kay Orr in 1986, and conservative Democrat Ben Nelson in 1990 and 1994, followed by the three recent Republicans mentioned above. So the office has seen some partisan shifts, though not really ideological ones.

The same applies to the state's seats in the U.S. Senate. Though not precisely paralleling the governor's races, the senatorial contests have followed a rough pattern of a conservative Democrat replacing, or being replaced by, an ultraconservative Republican. In 1950, Nebraska's senators were the very conservative Kenneth Wherry, who defeated George Norris in 1942, and Hugh Butler, equally conservative but not as outspoken. Butler was reelected in 1952 but died in office in 1954. Wherry, meanwhile, served as Senate Republican leader from 1949 to 1951 but also died in office, in November 1951. Fred Seaton, a relative moderate and later secretary of the interior in Eisenhower's cabinet, was appointed to Wherry's seat by the governor but did not run in 1952. In that year, Nebraskans reelected Butler and elected former governor Dwight Griswold to the Wherry seat.

In April 1954, Griswold also died in office, and 1954 became Nebraska's year of the seven senators (all Republicans). One seat was occupied by Butler until he died on July 1. Governor Robert Crosby appointed Sam Reynolds of Omaha two days later, to serve until the November election. In that election Roman Hruska of Omaha succeeded to the four remaining years of Butler's term. The other seat, which became open when Griswold died on April 12, was first filled by Eva Kelly Bowring, a ranch wife from Cherry County, whom Crosby appointed on April 16, with the understanding that her appointment would expire with the November election. A second woman, Hazel Hempel Abel of Lincoln, the vice chair of the state Republican Party, was elected—but only for the rest of the calendar year. She duly resigned on December 31. Finally, Congressman Carl Curtis of Minden won the November election for a full six-year term—Wherry's seat—defeating, among others, Governor Crosby in the August 10 primary. Curtis took office on January 1, 1955, to gain a few days' seniority before his elected term began later that month. Thus, Nebraska had a dizzying seven senators in one year—Butler, Griswold, Reynolds, Hruska, Bowring, Abel, and Curtis.

Bowring and Hempel are apparently the only cases in American electoral history of one woman succeeding another, and within the same year. Bowring was a senator for about six and a half months, Abel for about seven weeks. Bowring cast one hundred votes in the Senate, every one with her party's majority.[23] Abel was one of the sixty-seven senators who voted on December 2 to censure Joseph R. McCarthy of Wisconsin; Hruska was one of the twenty-two who voted against the censure resolution.[24] The two women "were leaders in their state parties, which probably accounted for their willingness to give up their short-tenured seats."[25] Perhaps. But Abel won her seat, short-term though it was, by defeating fifteen Republicans in the August 10 primary and a Democrat in the November special election, and she ran in the gubernatorial primary in 1960.[26]

Thus Nebraska began 1955 with the two new senators, Hruska and Curtis, and they would each be reelected three times, and each serve for more than twenty years, Hruska staying until 1977 and Curtis until 1979. Each compiled similar and almost impeccably conservative voting records. In the early 1970s, both scored virtually zero on measures supported by the Americans for Democratic Action and the League of Conservation Voters, but they earned almost perfect scores in the eyes of National Association of Businessmen, the American Security Council, and Americans for Constitutional Action.[27]

This long string of Republican senators allowed the *Almanac of American Politics* to announce, in its 1974 edition, that "Nebraska is the nation's most consistently Republican state."[28] But Hruska and Curtis were soon after replaced by Democrats: Ed Zorinsky and J. James Exon. Hruska resigned about a week before his term ended, and thus Zorinsky gained a little seniority. He was reelected in 1982 and died in office in March 1987. Exon, a former governor, won reelection in 1984 and 1990 and relinquished his seat to Republican Chuck Hagel in January 1997. Zorinsky was not as conservative as Hruska had been, but he was definitely right of center, particularly on cultural issues. He also voted for the Reagan tax cuts, for a balanced-budget amendment, and for the sale of AWACS to Saudi

Arabia. He scored well with the U.S. Chamber of Commerce and other conservative organizations, and only occasionally with centrists like conservationists and the League of Women Voters. Exon also voted for the Reagan tax cuts and a balanced-budget amendment, but overall he stood very close to the center on economic and foreign issues and leaned conservative on cultural ones.[29]

In 1988, in the next election after Zorinsky died, Democrat Bob Kerrey, a Medal of Honor winner in Vietnam and former governor (1983–87), defeated an interim appointee for the six-year term. He was reelected in 1994. Kerrey was by no means the most liberal Democrat in the Senate, but he clearly leaned farther left of center than any Nebraska senator since Norris. When Kerrey stepped down in 2000, former governor Ben Nelson, another Democrat, squeaked through; but he was handily reelected in 2006. He became known as the most conservative Democrat in the Senate but "resisted entreaties to switch parties."[30] When Nelson did not run in 2012, the Democrats' candidate became, again, former governor and senator Bob Kerrey.

Kerry lost, however, to Deb Fischer, a state senator whose family have a cattle ranch near Valentine, in Cherry County. In her 2012 Senate campaign, Fischer had support from conservatives including the Club for Growth, Sarah Palin, and Joe Ricketts of TD Ameri-Trade.[31] Kerrey returned to Nebraska from New York City, where he had spent several years as president of the New School. Kerrey took the Lincoln and Omaha counties, but Fischer carried rural Nebraska and won 58 percent to 42 percent. In the Senate she has taken firmly right-wing positions: pro-life, anti–tax increases, thorough reform of the Environmental Protection Agency, and opposition to "amnesty" for undocumented immigrants. On a liberal-conservative scale, Fischer's votes have been in the 70–80 percent conservative range.[32]

Exon's seat reverted to Republicans: Chuck Hagel in 1996 (and 2002), and then former governor Mike Johanns in 2008. Johanns's positions and votes did not vary greatly from Hagel's; mainly conservative, but with dashes of moderation or even working with Democrats on some measures, including the START treaty with Russia. Johanns voted for the nomination of Hagel to be Obama's secretary of defense, one of the few Republicans to do so (Fischer voted against).[33]

Johanns decided not to run for reelection in 2014. The winner of the Republican primary was Ben Sasse, a young Yale Ph.D. in history with several years of agency experience in Washington, D.C., and service as president of Midland University in Fremont, a small college with Lutheran roots. His Yale dissertation argued that the Religious Right's rise as a factor in American politics began not with *Roe v. Wade* in 1973 but with the Supreme Court decisions a decade earlier against Bible reading and compulsory prayer in public schools.[34] Sasse had support from the Club for Growth and was "a tea-party backed conservative," though he "has shied away from the tea party label."[35] In fact, one of his primary opponents in 2014 ran against Sasse from the right. Nonetheless, he has been, as he says he is, a "market-oriented conservative." He had only token Democratic opposition in his 2014 campaign and won with 64 percent of the vote.

In sum, Nebraska's senators since 1950 have always (since Norris) been conservative, whether Republican or Democrat. But, following the trend of the national Republican Party since the Reagan years, and the emergence of the Religious Right and, in 2009, the Tea Party, Nebraska's conservatism has intensified. The Nelsons and Kerreys have been replaced by the Fischers and Sasses. Nebraska has always been conservative, but lately more deeply so.

In the 1950s, Nebraska sent four representatives to the U.S. House. The 1960 census reduced the number to three, where it has stayed ever since. Republicans won all four seats, every time, from 1950 through 1956. But in the Democratic year of 1958 two of the seats, in the northeast and northwest, went to Democrats. Both were one-termers, ousted in 1960. In 1964 a Democrat won District 1, which included Lincoln. He was also a one-termer. In 1976 a Democrat won District 2, metropolitan Omaha; he won a second term in 1978 but then disappeared. In 1988, Democrat Peter Hoagland won that same district, was twice reelected, but in 1994 lost by less than a percentage point. In 2014 another Democrat, Brad Ashford, won that district, but he narrowly lost reelection in 2016. His political experience began as an intern for Hruska; he became a Democrat to back Bob Kerrey, switched back to the GOP in 1994 to help Omaha's Republican mayor (and former congressman), Hal Daub, and ran in 2014 as a Democrat for the Omaha seat.

All the other Nebraska congressfolk, beginning in 1950, were Republicans. Some were long-lived, most notably Doug Bereuter, who represented District 1, which has been eastern Nebraska from South Dakota to Kansas, including Lincoln but not the Omaha area. Bereuter was first elected in 1978 and was reelected through 2002.

He was succeeded by Jeff Fortenberry, reelected through 2016. The present representative for District 3, the western, larger half of the state, is the very conservative Adrian Smith, whose conservatism is rather similarly deep as his erstwhile neighbor's to the south in Kansas, Tim Huelskamp. It seems that, in the Great Plains states, the farther west one looks, the deeper red one sees.

SOUTH DAKOTA

The usual Great Plains population dynamics were taking effect in South Dakota in the postwar years through the 1970s: depopulating rural areas, the number of farms falling, the size of farms growing, people (especially the young, with high school and college educations) leaving for big cities such as Minneapolis and Chicago, or farther west from Los Angeles north to Seattle. Nothing surprising there. In about 1980 a change in state laws regarding interest rates changed South Dakota from a productive but shrinking grain-and-livestock state to a participant in a very up-to-date phenomenon: credit cards. Republican governor Bill Janklow saw to the repeal of century-old usury laws put in to protect small farmers from gouging mortgage rates. By 1980 small family farmers still existed, but they were no longer the backbone of the state's economy. Janklow invited large eastern banks, which were glad to come to a low-regulation, low-tax state. By the end of the 1990s, financial services had become the most vibrant and growing sector of the South Dakota economy. How it happened, the political change that preceded it, and the political fallout constitute the story here.

It needs to be said right away, however, that political change in South Dakota in the past several decades has been a matter of nuance, not dramatic change. It was a Republican state in 1950 and it is today. The presidential vote there since Eisenhower's day has gone Democratic only once, in 1964 for LBJ, as was true everywhere except Goldwater's own Arizona and five deep-Dixie states from Louisiana across to Georgia. The Republican presidential candidates secured solid majorities in every other contest except in 1992, when Ross Perot pulled 22 percent and limited George H. W. Bush to a 41 percent plurality, and 1996, when Perot took almost 10 percent, confining Robert Dole to 47 percent versus Bill Clinton's 43 percent. Even then, the Republican standard-bearer has not been in jeopardy.

The governorship has been nearly as monochrome Republican.

A Democrat, Ralph Herseth, won with 51 percent in 1958, when farmers were enraged about Ezra Taft Benson's agricultural policy; Democrat Dick Kneip won with 55 and 60 percent in 1970 and 1972, and again in 1974 with 54 percent, becoming the first to hold the office for four years, as South Dakota, like many other states at about that time, shifted away from two-year terms. Otherwise, Republicans won the right to serve in Pierre—notably the war hero Joe Foss in 1954 and 1956, marine fighter pilot at Guadalcanal and Medal of Honor winner, and later president of the National Rifle Association; Bill Janklow, the only person elected to four terms (1978, 1982, 1994, and 1998) and who brought the credit card industry to Sioux Falls; and Dennis Daugaard (2010, 2014), champion of restrictive anti-abortion laws in 2011 and 2013. Like the Republican Party nationally, South Dakota's governors, post-Kneip, have trended rightward.

Nineteen elections for U.S. senator have taken place in South Dakota starting in 1954. Of them, Republicans won ten, Democrats nine. For this office, as for the House of Representatives, South Dakotans have not voted Republican quite so consistently as they have for president or governor. The period began with two conservative Republicans, Karl Mundt and Francis Case, and has returned to conservatism with John Thune (2004, 2010, 2016) and former governor Mike Rounds (2014). Mundt served five terms in the House beginning in 1939, where he presided over the Un-American Activities Committee when it investigated Alger Hiss, followed by four successful elections to the Senate. There he presided over the Army-McCarthy hearings in the spring of 1954, voting later that year against censuring McCarthy. Mundt was described by the historian-philosopher Isaiah Berlin (then a British diplomat in Washington) in a confidential memo to the Foreign Office in 1943 as "an ignorant man, gifted with a somewhat slow intelligence, but sincere and constantly baffled by problems largely outside his mental scope."[36] In November 1969, Mundt was felled by a stroke and remained in office although he could never again participate actively. Francis Case was a member of the House for seven terms beginning with the 1936 election; he was elected senator in 1950, again in 1956, and served nearly two terms until he died in 1962. An aide to President Johnson described Case as "the little boy who throws his hand up before the child the teacher has called upon has had a chance to think of the answer. . . . Case was that little boy grown up, pale, square, and deadly dull."[37]

Case's successor in the Senate was George McGovern, elected in 1962 after two terms in the House and a losing campaign in 1960 against Mundt. During World War II, McGovern piloted B-24 Liberator bombers in thirty-five missions over Germany and nearby countries, earning a Distinguished Flying Cross for extremely hazardous exploits—experiences he chose not to mention when he later ran for president as an anti–Vietnam War candidate.[38] McGovern's father was a Methodist clergyman, and the family was hereditarily Republican. But McGovern was entranced by the speeches of Democratic presidential candidate Adlai E. Stevenson in 1952, as were others (see, e.g., California's "Adlai Clubs," chapter 6).[39] McGovern earned a Ph.D. in history at Northwestern University, writing on the Colorado coal strikes of 1913–14 that culminated in the Ludlow massacre of miners and their families, and he became a confirmed Democrat.[40]

In the summer of 1952, McGovern wrote seven articles (today they would be called op-eds) for his hometown newspaper, the Mitchell *Daily Republic*. These impressed the new state chair of the Democratic Party, who created a job, "state party executive secretary," and offered it to McGovern. McGovern accepted and traveled all over South Dakota from 1953 through 1955, shaking hands, making phone calls, visiting "receptions, courthouse meetings . . . private homes, farms, shops . . . [sending] tens of thousands of letters. . . . Looking for good county and precinct workers, recruiting candidates for office, raising money, discussing issues, and 'firing up the troops.'"[41] In this activity he paralleled party builders such as Henry Bellmon in Oklahoma and Monroe Sweetland in Oregon. Whether McGovern's efforts lasted as long as theirs is arguable; but, if not, one might blame his involvement in national affairs rather than in state governance, where Bellmon in particular had much staying power. With McGovern gone to Washington, Republicans continued to win the governorship and the House seats.

The Democrats' party building did not resume again until Bill Daugherty, state manager for the Robert Kennedy campaign in 1968, was elected lieutenant governor and worked to build "a coalition of farmers, college people, intellectual suburbanites, and labor and cutting down the Republican edge in the cities." These efforts resulted in Dick Kneip's election as governor in 1970 (and again in 1972 and 1974), capture of both House seats that year, and both chambers of the state legislature in 1972.[42] South Dakota had hardly become a Democratic state, but it was at least momentarily competitive. As two political scientists have written, "Almost single-handedly, McGovern turned the party around so that the citizens of the state continue to have a choice of political parties and candidates."[43] But in the mid-1970s the occupation of Wounded Knee by the American Indian Movement, and the backlash to that, in which Bill Janklow figured prominently as a prosecutor, propelled the electorate rightward again.[44] Democrats managed to capture a majority of seats in the state senate from 1971 to 1975 and the state house of representatives in the 1973–75 term, but otherwise they came up short. "Parity of strength between the two major parties during the mid-1970s—when each claimed about 46 percent of the electorate—was short-lived."[45]

McGovern ran in 1956 for the 1st District (eastern) congressional seat and won by 11,000 votes. He won a second term in 1958 but lost his challenge to Mundt's Senate seat in 1960. After Case died in office, McGovern defeated an appointed successor by 597 votes out of 254,000 cast. He was reelected in 1968 and 1974 by safer margins and was defeated resoundingly by Richard Nixon in the 1972 presidential election. He lost the Senate seat in 1980 to James Abdnor. But he had proved that a Democrat could break through the near-perfect Republican control of South Dakota politics. Another Democrat, James Abourezk, won the other Senate seat in 1972 after the stricken Mundt retired. Abourezk in turn lost in 1980 to the bumptious and voluble Larry Pressler, who won again in 1978 and 1984.

By then the Democrats had another winner, only slightly less prominent than McGovern: the young Tom Daschle, who won the first of four House terms beginning in 1978 and then took Abnor's Senate seat in 1986. Daschle went on to reelection in 1992 and 1998, becoming Senate majority leader for several years before falling in 2004 to John Thune by 4,508 votes of 391,000, or 50.6 percent for Thune, 49.4 percent for Daschle. Thune, a graduate of Biola University in Southern California (originally the Bible Institute of Los Angeles), enjoyed a solid base among the Religious Right.[46] That element had some political strength in South Dakota, but not as much as in the southern Plains. The legislature passed two abortion restriction measures in 2006 and 2008, but voters repealed both when they were put to ballot referenda.[47]

In 1986, Democrat Tim Johnson succeeded to Daschle's House seat, and he won reelection five times through 1994 before following

Daschle into the Senate in 1996. Republican Thune captured Johnson's House seat in 1996, was reelected in 1998 and 2000, very narrowly lost to Johnson in the 2002 Senate race, but upset Daschle in 2004. Johnson won again in 2008, but after suffering a stroke he declined to run in 2014. Republican former governor Mike Rounds won convincingly in that year, giving (with Thune) the state two Republican senators again.

In thirty-two elections to the U.S. House of Representatives from 1950 through 2016, Republicans won twenty-five, Democrats seventeen. South Dakota had two House districts from the 1950s until the 1982 election and has had one at-large representative from then on. The sole House seat has changed partisan hands about as often as the Senate seats, although beginning with Daschle's first election in 1978 either Daschle or Tim Johnson occupied it until Thune won it in 1996 when Johnson left to run for the Senate. Thune stayed for three terms until he, too, ran for the Senate in 2002 and lost by a hairsbreadth to Johnson. Thune then went on to his famous upending of majority leader Daschle in 2004.[48] The House seat, meanwhile, went to former governor Bill Janklow. He served less than a year when he ran a stop sign on a highway near Flandreau and killed a motorcyclist. Janklow immediately resigned his seat in Congress.[49] Democrat Stephanie Herseth, granddaughter of Governor Ralph Herseth (1959–61), won a special election to replace Janklow, to whom she had lost in 2002. She won the regular election in 2004 and again (by wide margins) in 2006 and 2008. But she lost in the Republican year of 2010 to conservative Republican Kristi Noem, 48 percent to 46 percent. Noem, having compiled a voting record that scored zero or near-zero from the Americans for Democratic Action, ACLU, and AFSCME and an 84 percent rating from the American Conservative Union, has retained the seat easily.[50]

Overall, then, South Dakota has earned long-term red state status by virtue of its almost unblemished Republican voting for president and governor and its election of Republicans 60–70 percent of the time for members of Congress.

NORTH DAKOTA

Of the six Great Plains states, North Dakota's redness is the least deep-dyed. One is tempted to call it pink, because it has frequently elected Democrats to three of the four major offices, though almost never for president. It would not, however, be accurate to call it "purple," which would mean it has been a swing state, which it has not; it has been generally consistent in its partisan leanings, giving incumbents multiple terms and seldom turning them out if they sought reelection. It has not been a state with a history of great shifts, rapid or even slow. If you cross its physical landscape, you don't see much change. And if you traverse its history, you won't see a lot of change there either. It has consistently been red, but with considerable dilution from time to time, and office to office.

Except for the presidency: like its southern neighbors, it has voted Republican for president since World War II except in 1964, when among many other states it departed from custom and voted for the Democrat, Lyndon Johnson. North Dakota voted for Eisenhower twice, Nixon three times, Ford, Reagan twice, both Bushes, McCain, Romney, and Trump from 1952 through 2016, by a majority of votes every time except in 1992, when Perot's 23 percent confined George H. W. Bush to only a comfortable plurality over Bill Clinton.

Such consistency has not been true of North Dakotans' votes for governor or members of Congress. In voting for governor, partisan choices have been rather different. Through the 1950s, Republicans Clarence Brunsdale and John E. Davis held the office, but in the 1960 election Democrat William L. "Bill" Guy won the first of four terms—two for two years each (1960 and 1962) and two for four years each (1964, 1968). Federal money came to North Dakota during Guy's governorship—missile bases, interstate highways, and more.[51] A farmer himself, Guy graduated from North Dakota Agricultural College (later, North Dakota State University) and taught agricultural economics there at one time. The state historical society credited him with creating a real two-party system in the state, though later events would cast doubt on that. He ran against Milton Young in 1974 for Young's U.S. Senate seat but lost by 177 votes out of about 230,000.[52] Guy was in fact succeeded by another Democrat, Arthur Link, who served two terms from 1973 to 1981. More of a moralist than Guy, Link opposed gambling, abortion, lowering the drinking age, and a state lottery, but he also, like Guy, ran a tight financial ship. The two gave North Dakotans twenty continuous years of Democratic leadership, conservative though it was. As historian David Danbom wrote in the early 1990s, "The Democrats' main strength [rests] in the fact that North Dakotans perceive them as the 'conservative' party; they are more likely than the Republicans to 'conserve' the redistributive federal programs on which North Dakotans have come to depend over the last half century [i.e., since the 1940s]."[53]

Only one other Democrat has been elected governor: George A. Sinner, who served two terms from 1985 to December 1992. Republicans have won the position ever since, usually for multiple terms: Ed Schafer (1992–2000), John Hoeven (2000–2010), Jack Dalrymple (2010–16), and Doug Burgum (2016–). Hoeven went on to the U.S. Senate, handily winning the 2010 election after Byron Dorgan retired.

North Dakota's senators have been Democrats even more often than its governors have been. From 1950 to 1974, Republicans won senatorial elections seven times, Democrats twice. But from 1974 through 2012, Republicans won twice and Democrats eleven times. The longevity, whether Republican or Democratic, has often been a product of incumbency. In making senatorial choices, North Dakotans for decades seem to have followed the adage, "If it ain't broke, don't fix it." As of 1950 the senior senator was William Langer, governor during much of the 1930s, elected to the Senate in 1940, and reelected in 1946, 1952, and 1958. The junior senator was Milton Young, elected in 1950 and four times thereafter, the last time being his 177-vote squeaker over Bill Guy in 1974. Both Langer and Young were Republicans. Langer, often called "Wild Bill," had been a prominent and flamboyant member of the Non-Partisan League in World War I days and was the archetype of the "midwestern isolationist" of the early and mid-twentieth century. He voted against American entry into the United Nations in 1945. The more sedate Young, "colorless and reticent" and "a thoroughly conventional and conservative midwestern Republican," was appointed to the Senate in 1945 on the death of his predecessor.[54] He went on to win five full terms and ultimately became the most senior Republican in the Senate.

After Langer died in office in 1959, an appointee served several months, and then Quentin Burdick, Democrat and Non-Partisan Leaguer, was elected to the seat. Burdick was reelected five times and ultimately died in office in 1988. Young, of the 1974 "landslide," decided not to run in 1980; he was succeeded by former Republican congressman Mark Andrews, who became that rare thing among North Dakota senators, a one-termer, when Democrat-NPL tax commissioner Kent Conrad defeated Andrews's reelection bid in 1984 by a very slim 2,100 votes. Conrad resumed the incumbent longevity tradition with reelections in 1994, 2000, and 2006. Conrad actually retired in 1992, and fellow former tax commissioner and Democrat-NPL candidate Byron Dorgan was elected to the seat. But then Quentin Burdick died, and in December 1992, in a special election, Conrad ran and won again. He had not quite left the Senate yet, so technically he held both of North Dakota's Senate seats for a few hours.[55] He would go on to win reelection in 1998 and 2004. Thus, for most of the 1990s and much of the 2000s, Conrad and Dorgan were the North Dakota senators, and both, because of their state-level experience, played significant roles in shaping the federal budget and finance. The senatorial scene changed when Dorgan left in 2010 and Conrad did so in 2012. Former three-term governor and Republican John Hoeven succeeded Dorgan. Hoeven "didn't have to campaign very hard. The Democrats barely put up a fight against a governor with an 80 percent approval rating."[56] In 2012 former attorney general and (yet again) tax commissioner Heidi Heitkamp, a Democrat who lost a bid for governor to Hoeven in 2000, won election to Conrad's seat. In her first year Heitkamp compiled a voting record that put her almost exactly in the center of the Senate, equidistant from both poles, liberal and conservative.[57] Hoeven leans conservative, but he "is no conservative absolutist" in the view of the *Almanac of American Politics*.[58]

Incumbency, longevity in office, and staying not far from the center—leaning left or right, but not very far—have characterized North Dakota's senators, with the arguable exception of William Langer. So it has been with the state's representatives in the U.S. House. There were two of them through 1970, but the slow growth of the state, until very recently, cut the delegation to one seat following the 1970 census. From 1950 through 1970, Republicans won twenty times, Democrats three times—future senator Quentin Burdick in 1958, Roland Redlin in 1964, and future governor Arthur Link in 1970. From 1972 through 2014, of twenty-two contests, Republicans won seven, Democrats fifteen. Both parties were helped by incumbency. Republican Mark Andrews won from 1964 through 1978—eight terms—until he ran for, and won, a Senate seat in 1970. His successor was Democrat Dorgan, who won six consecutive times until he made it to the Senate in 1992. Democrat Earl Pomeroy succeeded Dorgan in the House seat and won nine times before he was upended by Rick Berg in 2010. Berg then went for the Senate in 2012 but was beaten very narrowly by Heidi Heitkamp. The House seat went to

Republican Kevin Cramer in 2012, and he was reelected in 2014 and 2016. Cramer "defines himself as a climate change skeptic," and he came out early for Donald Trump in the spring of 2016, providing the candidate with policy advice on the subject.[59]

In sum, Democrats have won almost all of North Dakota's congressional contests from about 1974 on, except for Milton Young's last win in 1974, Andrews's House victories from 1970 through 1978 and his Senate win in 1980, and Cramer's two House wins. The governorship has almost always gone to a Republican since 1980, and presidential electors always except for 1964. So is North Dakota a Republican state? On balance yes, but not so committedly as the other Great Plains states. And if so, what kind of Republicans? The *Almanac of American Politics* has detected a shift toward redness, and more definitely conservative redness, since 2010—in other words, since the eruption of the Tea Party. Perhaps this has been so; Cramer's votes in 2013 and 2014 have been well to the right, and Governor Jack Dalrymple's anti-abortion law of 2013, "the nation's toughest," making the procedure illegal if a fetal heartbeat is detectable ("as early as six weeks into a pregnancy"),[60] would ratify the contention that the state's redness is deepening.

The most important event in recent North Dakota history has yet to have a clear, major impact on state politics. That has been the oil and gas boom in the state's northwest corner. The presence of oil in the Bakken Formation underneath northwest North Dakota and adjacent states and Canadian provinces had been known since 1951, but recovering it was technologically difficult until horizontal drilling and fracking began to be employed about 2007 and thereafter. The results have been a population boom unlike anything seen in North Dakota since the initial railroad-building and homesteading surge of 1890–1920. From statehood in 1889 up to 1920, hopeful farm families scrambled into the state, bringing its population to 649,000 in the latter year. But there it basically stayed, sliding to 618,000 in the 1970 census and recovering slightly to 642,000 in 2000.

Then, in the next decade, came the oil boom. The 2010 census counted 672,000, and the following five years brought a leap of 12.5 percent, bringing the official estimate on July 1, 2015, to 757,000 for the state.[61] The epicenter of the oil and gas mining was Williams County and its seat, Williston. Williams County had 22,398 people in the 2010 census and soared to 35,294, a rise of 57.6 percent, by

2015. Williston went from 14,716 in 2010 to 24,562 in 2015, a jump of 67 percent. In those five years, Williams was the second-fastest-growing county in the United States; the smaller McKenzie County, just to the south, was number one, rising 102 percent.[62] The unemployment rate for Williston and Williams County dropped below 2 percent. It is by no means certain, however, that the oil boom will continue, at least at that rate, because it became its own worst enemy, overproducing and thus contributing to the fall in world oil prices from 2014 on.

The political consequences of this demographic-economic boom are not yet clear. The office of secretary of state is sometimes used by political scientists to indicate respective Democratic and Republican strengths; in North Dakota the term is four years, elected in non-presidential years (e.g., 2006, 2010, 2014). While Williams County's population increased about 10 percent between 2006 and 2010 and 57.6 percent from 2010 to 2015, the total votes cast in the county for secretary of state also rose about 10 percent from 2006 to 2010, but only 9.3 percent from 2010 to 2014. Perhaps many of the newcomers were transient in some sense and did not vote; perhaps a minority did. The number of votes for the Republican candidate—the same person, a several-term incumbent—rose 31 percent (2006–10) and about 11 percent (2010–14).

Another elective office, the state's sole member of the House, is of course filled every two years. Democrat Pomeroy took about 46 percent of the Williams County vote in his last five elections (which he won, statewide); Republicans Rick Berg (2010) and Kevin Cramer (2012, 2014, 2016) won, on average, with 68 percent. The number of Republican votes in Williams County for Berg in 2010 was 6,278, and for Cramer in 2014 (the next off-year election) it was 6,922, a rise of 10.3 percent. This is not far from the number and percentage of Republican votes in the county for secretary of state. But it is well below the overall rise in population.

Future elections will provide more perspective and firmer conclusions about the political consequences, if any, of the Williston Basin oil boom. It has certainly not hurt the Republicans, but has it helped, and if so, by how much? An observer may sense that the movement in this normally Republican state has been to the right, to judge by the records of Cramer and Dalrymple and these population and voting statistics. But that sense is best left tentative. North Dakota, historically, has not been as red as Kansas or Nebraska, but it has not been purple or anywhere near blue. The question is only whether its redness is becoming deeper.

WYOMING

Change has come slowly to Wyoming over the past sixty-odd years. Its political coloration, red to begin with, has become, if anything, redder still. It has been the state with the smallest population, with fewer citizens and voters than an average congressional district anywhere else. Mining and minerals passed ranching and farming as the leading sector of the state's economy at least as early as the 1960s, and tourism became second. Before 1970 the one pocket of Democratic voters was along the line of the Union Pacific, close to what is now Interstate 80, running from Nebraska to Utah near the southern edge of the state. These voters were not so often railroad workers as miners of coal that kept the UP locomotives running. This activity waned as trains converted to diesel and the state's still prodigious output of coal became more mechanized. Meanwhile, the stock growers and ranchers in the central and northern parts of the state remained as deep-dyed Republican as they had traditionally been.[63] In recent years, Democratic voting has taken place, perhaps expectedly, around Laramie, site of the University of Wyoming, and, perhaps paradoxically, around resort-town Jackson, the wealthiest part of the state. Obama carried Teton County (Jackson) in both 2008 and 2012 and Albany County (Laramie) in 2008. Everywhere else, McCain and Romney prevailed. Obama's 33 percent in 2008 was lower than in any other state.[64] One assessment points out that "the two political parties in Wyoming have shared similar conservative assumptions on issues of economics and libertarian views on civil rights and individual freedoms."[65]

The presidential vote, in fact, has favored the Republican candidate throughout the state's post-1950 history except in 1964, when Lyndon Johnson's landslide extended even to Wyoming.[66] Since 1950 the voters have sent Democrats to the U.S. Senate only twice: Joseph C. O'Mahoney in 1954 and Gale McGee in 1958, 1964, and 1970. O'Mahoney was a New Deal Democrat who was appointed to fill a vacancy in 1933, was elected to a full term in 1934, and was reelected in 1940 and 1946. He lost in 1952 but ran and won again in 1954, then finally retired when his term expired early in 1961. O'Mahoney supported most New Deal and Fair Deal proposals and the Civil Rights Act of 1957. Gale McGee earned a Ph.D. in history at the University of Chicago and then joined the faculty of the University of Wyoming.[67] He maintained a lifelong interest in international affairs, spent a year as an aide to O'Mahoney, decided to run for the Senate in 1958 "on a program of youth and new ideas," helped put John F. Kennedy's nomination over the top at the 1960 Democratic convention, and—here his liberal credentials faltered, many would say—supported Johnson's policy on Vietnam. An editor in Denver wrote of him, "He was right in attacking the Birchers, but he's no flaming liberal."[68] After Malcolm Wallop defeated him in 1976, President Jimmy Carter appointed McGee to be U.S. ambassador to the Organization of American States, and he served four years in that capacity.[69]

While in the post-1950 years Democrats have won four senatorial elections—one by O'Mahoney and three by McGee—Republicans have won twenty-one. Names occasionally reoccur: Milward Simpson in 1962, his son Alan K. Simpson in 1978, 1984, and 1990. Except for the two Democrats, senators elected before the 1970s served one or two terms. Since then, three or even four terms have become normal. After Malcolm Wallop defeated McGee in 1976, he was reelected in 1982 and again in 1988. Alan Simpson, as just noted, won three terms. Craig Thomas won in 1994, 2000, and 2006 (and died of leukemia within a year of that). Mike Enzi first won in 1996 and has been reelected three times since, in 2002, 2008, and 2014. To date, John Barrasso has been elected in 2008 (to fill Thomas's vacancy) and 2012. Enzi, who has an M.B.A. in accounting, and Barrasso, who is an orthopedic surgeon, may be the most conservative pair of senators that any state is sending to Washington. The *National Journal* rated Enzi's votes in 2013 on economic bills as zero percent liberal, 95 percent conservative; on social issues, zero liberal and 92 percent conservative; on foreign matters, 5 percent liberal and 93 percent conservative; and his "composite" score, 4 percent liberal, 96 percent conservative. Barrasso's scores for 2013 were, on economic issues, 10 percent liberal, 87 percent conservative; social issues, zero and 92 percent; foreign, 5 and 93 percent; "composite," 7 and 93 percent. Barrasso, running in 2007, "noted that he had an 'A' rating from the National Rifle Association, voted for prayer in public schools, sponsored legislation 'to protect the sanctity of life,' and opposed gay marriage."[70] A conservative profile indeed.

Wyoming's sole seat in the House of Representatives has been held by Democrats slightly more often than its senatorships, but not by much. Beginning with William Henry Harrison in the early 1950s, a direct descendant of Old Tippecanoe, the ninth president, Republicans have held the position with only one exception. Democrat Teno Roncalio, son of Italian immigrants, native of Rock Springs on the Union Pacific, and winner of the Silver Star for his service in the Normandy invasion, edged out Harrison in 1964 by 2,200 votes out of 139,000. In 1966, Roncalio tried for the Senate but lost almost as narrowly to outgoing governor Clifford Hansen. Republican John Wold won the seat handily in 1968. He too ran for the Senate in 1970, losing to Gale McGee, thus opening up the House seat again to Roncalio. Roncalio won in 1970 even more narrowly than in 1964, defeating Harry Roberts by 608 votes out of 116,304. It was said that he "wears his liberal heart on his sleeve and has a dynamism that would probably mean longevity in office in most states; for Wyoming, he is simply too far to the left to win except in strongly Democratic years."[71] But he went on to win reelection in 1972, 1974, and 1976 by increasingly safer margins. He then decided to retire and did not run in 1978. His successor was Richard B. Cheney, who held the seat comfortably in the next five elections through 1988, leaving the House the next year to become secretary of defense in George H. W. Bush's administration, 1989–93. Cheney was elected vice president of the United States in 2000, the running mate of George W. Bush.

Wyoming's House seat has remained in Republican hands since Roncalio relinquished it in late 1978. After Cheney came Craig Thomas in 1990 and 1992, until he was elected to Wallop's Senate seat in 1994; then Barbara Cubin, elected in 1994 and six further elections through 2006. Her successor was Cynthia Lummis, elected in 2008 through 2014. Lummis was far from liberal—her composite *National Journal* score for 2013 was 32 percent liberal, 68 percent conservative, and she was a member of the Freedom Caucus—but she voted less impeccably conservatively than either Enzi or Barrasso. Lummis chose not to run in 2016. The Republican candidate and winner became Liz Cheney, daughter of the former vice president, thus creating a rare father-daughter succession to the same House seat, albeit with several other people in between.

The governorship is the one serious exception, among the top elective offices, to Republican dominance over the past nearly seventy years. Wyoming, like most states in the region, originally elected governors for two-year terms, but in 1955 (a little earlier than its neighbors) it went to four-year terms. Milward Simpson was the first beneficiary of this change, serving for only one term. In the Democratic year of 1958, John J. Hickey of Rawlins won the office, defeating Simpson. The deciding issue may have been local: the new interstate highways were soon to be built, and Simpson wanted I-90 and I-25 to intersect at Buffalo, south of Sheridan County. Voters around Sheridan were sore and sat out the election. "The balance was tipped toward Hickey, who proved to be more fiscally conservative than Simpson and equally defiant of federal government 'interference.'"[72]

But Hickey held the governorship only until January 1961, when he had himself appointed to the Senate seat vacated by the ailing O'Mahoney. Milward Simpson in turn defeated Hickey for the Senate seat in 1962. Hickey's term as governor was filled by another Democrat, secretary of state Jack Gage, who lost his bid for a full term in 1962 to Clifford Hansen.

As governor, Hansen oversaw passage of some moderately progressive laws, including one allowing state funds to match federal grants for education, "an enabling act for urban renewal, a minimum wage increase," and fair employment practices. In 1966, Hansen ran for the Senate and defeated Roncalio, 52 percent to 48 percent, and Hansen was reelected in 1972 by a much heftier margin. After that term ended in 1978, Hansen retired back to Wyoming. Stanley Hathaway, another Republican, followed for two terms as governor until January 1975, and he continued Hansen's moderate activism, streamlining state government, putting in a severance tax on coal and other minerals, and consolidating rural schools.[73]

Then followed twenty years, five terms, of Democrats as governor, from January 1975 to January 1995—three terms for Edgar Herschler and two for Mike Sullivan. A term-limit law passed in Wyoming in 1992 means that Herschler will always hold the longevity record for governors, unless the law is repealed or overturned. His first and third victories were by comfortable margins, though his second, in 1978, was close. Sullivan won against "name" opposition, first over Peter Simpson, son of Milward and older brother of Alan, and for his second term over Mary Hansen Mead, daughter of governor Clifford Hansen (and mother of future governor Matt Mead). After Herschler and Sullivan came the more usual two terms of Republican Jim

Geringer (1995–2003). But then another two-term Democrat, Dave Freudenthal, held office from 2003 to 2011, followed by Republican Matt Mead, elected in 2010 and again in 2014.

How to explain the seven wins of Democratic governors from 1975 through 2006, amid a plethora of Republicans elected not only for governor but for president, senator, and representative? The *Almanac of American Politics* suggests that the Democratic victories have resulted from "personal campaigning in such a tight-knit state." Perhaps, but that could apply to Republicans too. Surely, on average, both parties had equally effective glad-handers. Perhaps Neal Peirce was closer to an answer when he wrote, "While Wyoming usually votes Republican it votes first and foremost for the man, not the party. . . . Both parties have offered conservative candidates for office."[74] It may be that Wyoming conservatism, always present to some degree, hardened in the early twenty-first century (as evidenced by the voting records of Enzi, Barrasso, and Lummis), in step with the ideological hardening of the Right in other states. There was, however, no massive Tea Party surge in 2010 and after, no uncompromising abortion law as in South Dakota, no takeover of the state GOP by the Religious Right. "Organized religion," it has been said, "has not been a factor in the state's politics."[75] Perhaps Wyoming's people are simply too few and too scattered for such movements to take hold. An observation made over twenty years ago may sum it up best: "The state was closely contested from the New Deal days through the 1960s [viz., O'Mahoney and McGee], and by the 1980s this was one of the nation's most Republican states."[76] And except for a few governors, so it has remained.

UTAH

It is tempting to classify Utah as a switch state, moving from blue (or at least purple) to red in recent years. But, despite having elected a few Democrats not long after 1950, and almost none recently, the state has been rather consistently red, though lately more deeply so than before, say, 1980. It is the heart and soul of the "Mormon culture area," and the majority of its people have aligned themselves with the culturally conservative side of general American culture virtually since Utah was first settled by the Latter-day Saints in the late 1840s.[77] Historian friends of mine who taught at Utah State University and lived in Logan for over twenty years called the culture "an extreme case of normality." Its Republican officeholders have ranged from moderate to arch-conservative, and its few Democratic ones from moderately liberal (like Senator Frank "Ted" Moss) to centrist Blue Dog (like Congressman Jim Matheson, elected from 2002 through 2012 from Salt Lake City).

No state has completely excluded the nonmajority party; none has been purely Republican or Democratic. Even Kansas, Nebraska, and Wyoming have elected an occasional Democrat as governor or member of Congress. Utah voted for Franklin Roosevelt four times during the Great Depression and after, when the state's economy performed below the national average by almost every measure, and for Harry Truman in 1948.[78] In its first presidential election after statehood it voted 83 percent, highest in the nation, for the Democrat/Populist William Jennings Bryan, presumably for his championing of free coinage of silver, then a major Utahan product. In 1900, however, when Bryan ran a second time, Utah favored William McKinley and continued voting Republican, including in 1912 when it was joined only by Vermont in supporting William Howard Taft, the Republican in the three-way race won by Woodrow Wilson. Utah's electoral votes went to Wilson in 1916, when he "kept us out of war." But after the Roosevelt-Truman votes in 1932–48, Utah has never again voted for a Democrat except in 1964, when, like so many otherwise red states, it voted for Lyndon Johnson. Utah has generally not been intrigued with third-party candidates. George Wallace in 1968 polled only 6.4 percent in the state, less than half his national average, and John Anderson in 1980 won only 5.0 percent, below his national average of 6.6 percent. But in 1992, Ross Perot did better than Democrat Bill Clinton; Perot won 27.3 percent (nationally 18.9 percent) while Clinton won 24.7 percent, far behind Republican George H. W. Bush. In presidential elections, Utah now has six electoral votes, and they are a sure thing for the Republican candidate.

The governorship has been a different story, at least historically if not recently. Utah has always (since statehood) elected governors for four-year terms, unlike neighboring states, and in presidential rather than off years. It elected Democrats Henry Blood and Herbert Maw from 1932 through 1944, but in 1948 the voters chose the rightist Republican J. Bracken Lee, who would be reelected in 1952 and serve eight years. Lee represented, at least for a time, a conservative shift, corresponding to that of the national Republicans. He was an outspoken maverick throughout his career, first as mayor of his home town of Price (1935–48), then as governor for two terms (1949–57), and finally as mayor of Salt Lake City (1960–71). In those offices, according to his obituary in the *Deseret News*, "he was especially known for his fiscal conservatism and his strong stand against income tax, foreign aid, and the United Nations." He had dropped out of high school to join the U.S. Army in World War I, never graduated, and never went to college; his frugality as governor hit higher education especially hard, and educators at all levels opposed him. After he publicly criticized President Eisenhower, he "found church leaders, educators and politicians almost uniformly opposed to him," and he lost his bid for a third term in the 1956 Republican primary to George Dewey Clyde, who went on to win the 1956 general and reelection in 1960.[79] Lee ran for the U.S. Senate in 1958 and again in 1962 but had to settle for mayor of Salt Lake City.

After Clyde's two terms, Utah elected Democrats to the governorship in the next five elections. Calvin Rampton won the office in the same 1964 election that gave Utah's electoral votes to Lyndon Johnson, and Rampton was reelected in 1968 and 1972, the only person to win and serve three terms. In 1976 another Democrat, Scott M. Matheson, was elected, and he went on to win a second term in 1980. Thereafter, however, every governor has been a Republican. Rampton was a very popular governor, "with an unbeatable knack for conciliation and a pro-business/development stance." He reorganized state government for the first time since statehood and invested in public higher education, as Lee had not done.[80] Matheson was also a popular centrist, "not identified as either a liberal or a conservative," but he "had a penchant for the details and forms of governmental relations" and "advocated an alliance between government and the corporate community."[81]

The next five governors of Utah were Republicans—Norman H. Bangerter, Mike Leavitt, Olene Walker, Jon Huntsman Jr., and Gary Herbert. Bangerter, a home builder, also supported public education. Leavitt was elected in 1992, reelected in 1996, and reelected again in 2000, matching Rampton's three successes. But President George W. Bush appointed Leavitt administrator of the Environmental Protection Agency in August 2003 and as secretary of health and human services in January 2005, where he served to the conclusion of the Bush administration in January 2009. Olene Walker, Utah's only female governor, ascended to the office when Leavitt became EPA administrator. When the state legislature, dominated by her own party, passed a bill providing for vouchers for private schools, she vetoed it. She signed a bill ending Utah's then-unique use of firing squads to carry out death penalty sentences. In 2004 she belatedly decided to run for a full term, but other candidates had already gathered more support. Of eight candidates, she came in fourth, according to her *New York Times* obituary.[82]

The victor in 2004 was Jon Huntsman Jr., of a billionaire Mormon family. Huntsman worked in the Reagan White House and then in the George H. W. Bush administration, becoming ambassador to Singapore in 1992. After the Clinton hiatus, Huntsman served as a deputy U.S. trade representative. In March 2003 he resigned that position, and when Leavitt left for the EPA Huntsman ran for governor, won the 2004 Republican primary, and then the general 58 percent to 42 percent for Democrat Scott Matheson Jr. Huntsman was reelected in 2008 with 78 percent of the vote. He governed effectively, making tax and budget reforms, and was rewarded with high approval rates in polls. In early 2009, President Obama nominated him to be ambassador to China. He was confirmed unanimously and resigned the governorship in August. He returned in 2011 and began a campaign for the Republican nomination for president. But he was not far enough right for the party in that Tea Party heyday, and he dropped out in early 2012 and endorsed fellow Mormon and eventual nominee Mitt Romney. Gary Herbert, Huntsman's running mate in 2004 and 2008, succeeded to the governorship when Huntsman left, then won a special election in 2010 and full four-year terms in 2012 and 2016. Like Huntsman's, Herbert's policies nicely balanced conservative and moderate positions, and Utahans gave him a 74 percent approval rating in January 2015.[83]

Utah's senators have been even more consistently Republican than the governors. Of twenty-two Senate races in Utah from 1950 through 2012, Democrats won three, Republicans nineteen. Elbert D. Thomas, a staunch New Deal Democrat, internationalist, and Mormon, took away Reed Smoot's long-held Senate seat in the 1932 election and kept it until Thomas lost to Wallace Bennett in 1950. Beginning in 1950, Utah has elected only one Democrat to the Senate: Frank E. "Ted" Moss. Thanks in large part, ironically, to J. Bracken Lee, who would not sit still after losing the Republican primary in

1958 and ran as an independent, splitting the conservative vote, Moss squeaked through with 38.7 percent of the vote in that Democratic year, beating Watkins (34.8 percent) and Lee (26.4 percent). Some voters on the right were reputedly angry at Watkins for chairing the Senate committee that voted to censure the Wisconsin Republican demagogue senator Joseph R. McCarthy.[84] Moss's reelections in 1964 and 1970 were by safer, though not overwhelming margins—57 and 56 percent, respectively.

Moss was more liberal than his Wyoming neighbor, Gale McGee, and in the relatively liberal Democratic Senate of the 1960s and early 1970s he achieved much and rose to a lofty spot in the leadership.[85] Signature issues included nuclear disarmament, environmental purity, consumer protection, civil rights, women's rights, the space program, and keeping cigarette advertising from television. He did much to create the Canyonlands and Capitol Reef national parks, he fought for the Central Utah (water) Project, and more. In 1976, running for a fourth term, Moss was ousted by Orrin Hatch, who then kept winning elections, even surviving a Tea Party challenge in 2012.

Moss's colleague for most of his time in the Senate was Wallace Bennett, a former president of the National Association of Manufacturers, with a very different agenda and stance. He "seldom stray[ed] from the conservative fold."[86] Bennett, having won and served four terms, decided not to try again in 1974. The Republican nominee was Jake Garn, who would win and go on to win again in 1980 and 1986. Garn achieved an almost impeccable conservative voting record in the *National Journal* ratings, with strong interests and achievement in banking, housing, and defense issues. Garn stepped down before the 1992 election.

Garn's successor was Wallace Bennett's son, Robert, known widely as Bob. He narrowly won the Republican primary but defeated 2nd District Democratic congressman Wayne Owens 55 percent to 39 percent in the general. Bennett went on to compile a record nearly as conservative as his father's, but in 2010, up for reelection, he was blindsided by farther-right Mike Lee at the state Republican convention. Hatch, meanwhile, kept satisfying the Utah electorate with his generally conservative, but not extreme, positions, and kept getting elected, tacking to the right in 2012 to avoid being dumped at the state Republican convention, as happened to Bob Bennett. His seniority, as the most senior Senate Republican, is appreciated in the state. Mike Lee, who upended Bennett, fulfilled his far-right promise in his first and second years with a perfect rating from the American Conservative Union and other like-minded organizations.[87] His allies in the Senate have included Jim DeMint of South Carolina and Ted Cruz of Texas.

Utah's delegation to the U.S. House has been just over two to one Republican since 1950 but more heavily so since the 1980s. Of ten House contests in the 1970s, Democrats actually won six and Republicans four. But the score from 1982 (when Utah gained a third seat) through 1990 was Republicans eleven, Democrats four, of fifteen races; the same from 1992 through 2000, and about the same from 2002 to 2010. Only Salt Lake County, the heart of District 2, has gone Democratic with any consistency, and that was largely by victories from 2000 through 2012 by Jim Matheson, son of former governor Scott Matheson. And Jim was about as Blue Dog as any Democrat in the House. "Practic[ing] a careful centrism," known as the son of the popular governor, and "a shrewd campaigner," Jim Matheson survived for seven terms as the state grew increasingly conservative. He decided not to run again in 2014, giving the seat to the Brooklyn-born, Haitian-parented, and Mormon Mia Love, the first black Republican congresswoman ever. The most visible of the Utah delegation has been Jason Chaffetz, elected in 2008 and since from District 3, which includes Provo and has been "the most Republican district in Utah."[88] Chaffetz was one of the most outspoken young conservatives in Congress, but he resigned in May 2017 for unclear reasons. His successor is John Curtis, once mayor of Provo and, of course, a Republican. As with the "higher" offices, the trend in Utah's House elections has been, since 1980, the intensification of the redness.

In fact, a deepening of the red coloration has been measurable for every office. The eminent Brigham Young University historian Thomas G. Alexander dates the rise of a Republican majority from 1970 and the shift of the state's economy from colonial dependence on eastern capital to "a semiautochthonous state in which local people controlled an appreciable percentage of business enterprise."[89] One could quibble with the beginning date of the GOP ascendancy—it may have been a little earlier than 1970—and except for the New Deal political economy of the 1930s and 1940s Utah and the Mormon culture area have always had much that was conservative about them. And with the exits of governors Rampton and Matheson, and Senator Moss, the only question was whether dominance would be, as Ronald Reagan said of the two wings of his GOP, "the right, or the far right." By 2010, when Lee knocked off Bob Bennett and Huntsman was considered way too liberal to be a viable presidential candidate, the pendulum had swung, arguably, far right. Or was it an avalanche, with no reversal, instead of a pendulum?

IDAHO

In its early years, silver-producing Idaho voted several times for Democratic presidential candidates: William Jennings Bryan in 1896 and 1900, then Woodrow Wilson in 1912 and 1916. Hard hit by the Great Depression, the state voted four times for Franklin Delano Roosevelt, and in 1948 for Harry Truman. It also elected one of the Senate's leading Progressives, William E. Borah, who first went to Washington in 1907 and served until he died in office in 1940, by then dean of the Senate. The highest mountain in Idaho was named Borah Peak in 1934. But Borah was a Progressive *Republican*, and after the New Deal years very few Democrats have been elected governor or senator from Idaho. There have been a handful of exceptions, but for the most part the highest elective offices have been held by Republicans, and usually quite conservative ones.

Until about the 1960s, though the state overall was firmly Republican, the northern "Panhandle," the main silver-mining area where capital-labor conflicts erupted early in the twentieth century, was considered to be the one locus of Democratic strength, if there was one at all. The southeast, where most of the people lived a few miles on either side of the Snake River, was heavily Mormon, like adjacent northern Utah, and politically quite conservative. The one city of much size, Boise, was conservative. In the later years of the twentieth century, the Panhandle mines either closed or modernized and Democratic voting dwindled. Migrants arrived from California, and, as one wag put it, they came not for the natural beauty but because Orange County was not conservative enough for them. They solidified Idaho's conservatism. The area just north of Coeur d'Alene, around Hayden Lake, became home in the 1980s and 1990s to some of the most virulent racist and neo-Nazi elements in the United States.[90] John Birchers were in evidence in some communities. Hayden Lake remains a refuge for catastrophe thinkers who have built what they call "the American Redoubt" in preparation for the collapse of American civilization.[91] But after 2000—again, while the state as a whole was deep red—a few counties often voted Democratic. They were Blaine, which includes Sun Valley and Ketchum; Teton, adjacent to Wyoming's Teton County, which holds Jackson Hole; and Latah, home of the University of Idaho. Boise remains conservative, the home of several national market firms including building contractors Morrison-Knudson, Boise Cascade in energy, grocery retailing chain Albertson's, and potato king J. R. Simplot. It is not a branch-office town or a colony of eastern capital.

Like every other western state except Barry Goldwater's Arizona, Idaho voted for Lyndon Johnson for president in 1964, but very narrowly; Goldwater lost by about 2 percent here. Otherwise, like most of the red states discussed in this chapter, it supported the Republican candidate from 1952 through 2012. George Wallace took 12.5 percent in 1968, slightly below his national average, and Ross Perot won 27.0 percent in 1992, above his national average and only slightly below Bill Clinton's 28.4 percent. In most presidential elections in Idaho other than those two with significant third-party candidates, the Republican has defeated the Democrat by 60-some percent versus 30-some percent.

The governorship has not been quite as consistently Republican. Governors have served for four-year terms since before 1950 and are elected in the off year. In the seventeen contests for the office beginning in 1950 through 2014, Republicans won eleven and Democrats six. Of those six, Cecil Andrus won two (1970 and 1974), John V. Evans won two (1978 and 1982), and Andrus won two more (1986 and 1990). Thus two Democrats kept the Idaho governorship in Democratic hands for twenty-four consecutive years. Republican Len Jordan, later a senator, won the governorship in 1950 and was followed by Robert Smyllie for three terms beginning in 1954. Both Jordan and Smyllie were relative moderates, "attractive candidates" who benefited from Democrats' internal discord. Smyllie tried again in 1966 but lost in the GOP primary to Don Samuelson, "then a right-wing state senator known chiefly for his fight against a sales tax." But Samuelson "turned in a dismal performance both as an administrator and on the newly sensitive environmental issue," giving "hearty backing" to "mining interests that wanted to start mining molybdenum in the exquisite White Cloud area."[92] That would have meant a particularly destructive kind of surface mining, and Idahoans, proud and mindful of their vast wildernesses, could be (and were) persuaded to vote for a candidate who defended the mountains and open spaces.

In 1970, that candidate was Cecil Andrus, a "young Democrat and experienced state senator" who "made protection of the environment the central issue of his campaign."[93] Andrus defeated Samuelson in the general, 52 percent to 48 percent. He was reelected in 1974 by a much firmer 71 to 27 percent. As governor he compiled an admired record as an environmentalist and also pushed successfully for public kindergarten. In January 1977 he became secretary of the interior in President Jimmy Carter's administration, where he served four years. A signal achievement was his leadership in the creation in Alaska of the Arctic National Wildlife Refuge.[94]

The two years that remained in Andrus's second term were filled by Lieutenant Governor John V. Evans, also a Democrat; Evans was elected in his own right in 1978 and again in 1982 and thus was governor for ten years. Evans was also concerned with education and environment, particularly water rights, and he deployed both federal and state government to cushion the impact of the closing of the state's largest and oldest silver mine, in Shoshone County in the Panhandle, an event that cost 2,200 jobs.[95]

As Evans's tenth year as governor drew to a close, he ran for the U.S. Senate seat held by Steve Symms. Evans lost by about 12,000 votes and retired from politics. In that same election, 1986, Andrus made a comeback and won a third time, very narrowly, by 3,535 votes out of 383,000 cast. He successfully fought federal efforts to store nuclear waste in Idaho, and after he was reelected to his fourth term in 1990—with a very comfortable 68 percent of the vote—he pushed for the protection of endangered species of salmon on the Snake River. He had been governor for fourteen years, more than anyone else. To date, no Democrat has been elected governor since Andrus left office in early 1995.

The first in a string of Republicans who thereupon held the office was Phil Batt, an experienced state legislator who had also served as lieutenant governor under John Evans, though they were from different parties. Batt declined to run in 1998 for a second term. Dirk Kempthorne, a Republican party official who had been elected senator in 1992, ran for governor and won handily; he successfully ran for a second term in 2002. In May 2006, Kempthorne was nominated by

President George W. Bush to be secretary of the interior, and after confirmation he resigned as governor to stay at Interior for Bush's remaining three years. The lieutenant governor, Jim Risch, filled out the few months left of Kempthorne's term and then ran again for lieutenant governor, as Congressman C. L. "Butch" Otter became the Republicans' candidate for governor. Otter won in 2006, again in 2010, and a third time in 2014. Two years later, Risch ran for senator, won, and was reelected in 2014. Otter had carved out a conservative record as a congressman, and he continued to do so as governor. He opposed embryonic stem cell research, opposed federal abortion funding, and in 2003 achieved a zero percent rating from NARAL, the pro-choice organization, and from the AFL-CIO. He voted against same-sex marriage several times and supported immigration restriction and a fence along the Mexican border.[96]

The office of U.S. senator from Idaho has been in Republican hands even more than the governorship. Of twenty-four elections to the Senate from Idaho since 1950, twenty have gone to Republicans. The four Democratic wins were all by Frank Church. As the post-1950 period opened, the senators were Henry Dworshak, first elected in 1948 and a moderate conservative for the time, and Herman Welker, described by the veteran journalist Neal Peirce as "a vindictive right-winger who was a close ally of Wisconsin's Joseph McCarthy."[97] Dworshak was reelected in 1954 and 1960; Welker was a one-termer. Replacing him was Church, Idaho's sole Democratic senator since that time. Church was elected in 1956, defeating Welker's reelection bid, and Church was himself reelected in 1962, 1968, and 1974, finally falling to Steve Symms in 1980, Reagan's year, by 4,262 votes out of over 433,000 cast, or 49.7 percent to 48.8 percent.

Church was not only a Democrat but a liberal. His voting record in the Senate produced high marks from Americans for Democratic Action, the League of Women Voters, the National Farmers Union, and the Consumer Federation of America and very low ones from Americans for Constitutional Action on the right. He voted in the early 1970s for busing, consumer protection, the equal rights amendment, and a minimum tax on high incomes and against the Alaska pipeline and William Rehnquist's appointment to the Supreme Court.[98] Throughout his twenty-four years in the Senate, Church was most consistently interested in foreign policy and environmental matters. He opposed the Vietnam War and chaired watchdog committees overseeing intelligence gathering by federal agencies. He sponsored and led successful efforts to pass strong environmental and wilderness protection laws.[99] His positions were liberal but clearly acceptable to Idahoans. His uncompromising opposition to gun control no doubt helped him with many voters who were less than enthusiastic about some of his other positions. And his successful efforts to pass the Wilderness Act and the Wild and Scenic Rivers Act and to create several national recreation areas spoke to Idahoans' pride in their mountains and streams. He was thought of as heir of Idaho's earlier idol, Progressive Republican William E. Borah. As Peirce writes, "Church won in every region, among all income groups, in all types of farm precincts, and by the biggest percentage of all in lumbering and mining territory."[100] In his final campaign in 1980 his support for Carter's Panama Canal treaties provided his opponent, Steve Symms, with an issue that was an important factor in his narrow defeat, which was still by only one percentage point though it happened in the Reagan landslide year.[101]

Symms's voting record was virtually the polar opposite of Church's, and close at times to libertarian. But he seemed to sit well with the voters. They reelected him in 1986 over former governor John Evans. The other senator was James McClure, first elected in 1972 and reelected in 1978 and 1984. He was not quite as conservative in the Senate as Symms but a far cry from Church. He was described as being of the New Right, but "nonetheless a competent senator, of generally dependable views."[102] McClure was a leader of the "sagebrush rebellion," which fought to loosen restrictions on the uses of federal land and to further open up the public domain to private uses.[103] When McClure did not run again in 1990, he was succeeded by five-term 1st District congressman Larry Craig. Craig soon achieved "the most conservative voting record in the Senate in the 1992 *National Journal* ratings,"[104] and he was a leader in the nearly successful fight to pass a balanced-budget amendment. Craig was reelected in 1996 and 2002. His effectiveness ended abruptly when the news emerged in August 2007 that he had been arrested for lewd conduct in a men's room in the Minneapolis–St. Paul airport. He was convicted of disorderly conduct, resisted calls for resignation, and finished his Senate term, but there was no hope of his running again.

In 1992, Dirk Kempthorne, the mayor of Boise, succeeded Symms for a single term, then left the Senate in 1998 to run successfully for

governor. He was another fiscal conservative. Mike Crapo, "a faithful Mormon" from Idaho Falls, ran away with the election in 1998,
was reelected unopposed in 2004, and was reelected again in 2010
and 2016. He has not been quite as unremittingly conservative as,
say, Symms or even McClure. In 2008, as the self-besmirched Craig
departed the political scene, the other senatorship went to Jim Risch,
state senator for twenty-three years and lieutenant governor for five.
Crapo and Risch continue to represent Idaho in the Senate. Crapo has
compiled an almost perfect rating in the eyes of conservative groups,
and Risch was even more spotless, from the conservative viewpoint,
in the 2013 *National Journal* ratings.[105] As the congressional Republican party has moved to the right in recent years, Idaho has been part
of that movement.

Idaho, by virtue of its small population, has had two congressional districts since the early twentieth century. District 1 includes
the Panhandle and runs south through part of Boise to the Utah line.
District 2 includes the eastern and southeastern (heavily Mormon)
counties and the eastern side of Boise. From 1950 through 2016,
thirty-four cycles and sixty-eight contests have taken place. The total
result has been fifty-two Republican victories and sixteen Democratic.
The exceptions to Republican dominance have usually come from a
few Democrats who could get reelected, notably Cecil Andrus, Frank
Church, and Gracie Pfost, who won in the 1st District five times in
the 1950s. Richard Stallings, a history professor at Ricks College (now
Brigham Young University Idaho) in Rexburg, won the 2nd District
four times, 1984–90, but then ran against Kempthorne for senator
in 1992 and lost. Stallings's votes in the House were almost exactly
in the center.[106] A very different Democratic member from Idaho
was Walt Minnick, elected by a slim margin in 2008 to represent
District 1. Minnick was head of a wood products company and joined
the Blue Dog coalition when he arrived in the House; his votes were
well to the right of most Democrats. He was unseated in the 2010
(Tea Party) election by Raul Labrador, a Mormon from Puerto Rico.
Labrador has made common cause with the rightist Freedom Caucus
that forced out House speaker John Boehner.

In sum, Idaho was a conservative state in 1950 and has remained
so. Long-lived Democrats have been few: Cecil Andrus and John
Evans as governors, Senator Frank Church, four-term congressman
Richard Stallings. They have been thoroughly outnumbered by

Republicans starting with Robert Smyllie in the 1950s and since 2006 with Butch Otter as governors, Len Jordan and McClure as senators, and, among many others, the voluble Helen Chenoweth in the House (1995–2001).

ALASKA

When Alaska became the forty-ninth state in January 1959, the voters elected William A. Egan as governor, Edward L. "Bob" Bartlett and Ernest Gruening as the senators, and Ralph J. Rivers as the sole congressman. All were Democrats. The conventional wisdom then held that Alaska would be a Democratic state for the foreseeable future. But it did not come to pass. Even in 1960 there were rumblings against the Democratic hegemony that had characterized the territorial period. The local Democrats "were attacked for having failed to build roads, or to develop the tourist industry," or to support moving the state capital from small, distant Juneau to the largest population center, Anchorage. As noted at the time, "Practically all observers in Alaska are in agreement that the 1960 elections constituted a 'moral victory' for the Republicans," to the extent that "Alaska today is no longer a one-party state."[107] Before long, it would become one, but in the other direction.

Though the most important event in Alaska's late twentieth-century history was the discovery of huge oil deposits on the North Slope and the building of the pipeline to Valdez to create a way to bring the oil to markets, oil by itself did not swing Alaskan politics from blue to red; conditions and local issues were already in place at the time of statehood. True, the state's population soared from 226,000 in 1960 to 550,000 in 1990 to an estimated 740,000 in 2016, more than half of it in the Anchorage metropolitan area, but the oil boom was not the only incentive. The leading sources of migrants were the three West Coast states and Texas, and only some of those newcomers were oil patch roustabouts. Many came, as they did to Idaho, because California and Washington were not conservative enough for them, but more often because of the spreading word of job opportunities.[108] Republicans started to win elections in 1966, when Wally Hickel, a Republican, unseated Governor Egan in a close race, 50.0 percent to 48.4 percent, and Republican Howard Pollock defeated Rivers for the House seat by a slightly larger margin, 51.6 percent to 48.4 percent.

The Democratic senators were a bit more long-lived, but not by much. Bartlett, known to many as "the architect of Alaskan state-hood," was reelected with 75 percent of the vote in 1966, but he died in office in December 1968. Governor Hickel appointed Republican Ted Stevens to the seat, and Stevens was elected in his own right in 1970—and was reelected to full terms in 1972, 1978, 1984, 1990, 1996, and 2002. After being convicted of financial irregularities in 2008—the conviction was overturned the next year—Stevens lost his seventh bid for reelection. He died in a plane crash in 2010.

Gruening, whose sometime sobriquet was "father of Alaskan statehood," had been reelected in 1962, but in 1968 he lost in the Democratic primary to Mike Gravel. Gruening ran in the general as an independent but took only 17.4 percent of the vote. He was best known nationally as one of the two senators who voted in 1964 against the Gulf of Tonkin Resolution—the other nay vote came from Oregon's Wayne Morse—which President Johnson took as authoriza-tion for the massive expansion of the American military presence in Vietnam.

Gravel was elected in 1968 and reelected in 1974, thus keeping the "Gruening seat" in Democratic hands until after the 1980 elec-tion. Gravel, however, lost the Democratic primary that year to Clark Gruening, grandson of Ernest; but Clark was defeated in the general by Republican Frank Murkowski. Thus the apparently Democratic command of Alaska's high offices mostly evaporated in the late 1960s and disappeared completely by 1980.

A Democrat, Nick Begich, did win the sole House seat in 1970, upending Pollock, and Begich won again in 1972. But he disappeared on a flight from Anchorage to Juneau in October 1972, along with House majority leader Hale Boggs. A Republican, Don Young, won the House seat in the next election, and he has retained the seat through more than twenty elections. Stevens and Frank Murkowski held the two Senate seats through the 1980s and 1990s. Stevens, badly damaged by his criminal indictment, gave way to Mark Begich in 2008, son of Nick and the only Democrat to win an Alaskan Senate seat since Gravel in 1974. Frank Murkowski chose to run for governor in 2002 rather than try for the Senate again, and he won by a healthy margin. The Republican legislature arranged things so that Murkowski, rather than his Democratic predecessor, Tony Knowles, could fill the Senate seat. Murkowski appointed his daughter Lisa. She was elected to a full term in 2004. Up again in 2010, she lost the primary "to a tea-party-backed challenger [Joe Miller], only to come back to win the general election as a write-in candidate." Mark Begich ran for reelection in 2014 but lost to Dan Sullivan, who had support from the Club for Growth and the U.S. Chamber of Commerce.[109]

Given this history of races for governor, the Senate, and the House seat, it is no surprise to learn that Alaska since statehood voted only once for a Democrat for president, namely Lyndon Johnson in 1964, as did every other western state except Arizona. A state that started out looking blue quickly turned purple and then red within the next decade. The *Almanac of American Politics* has been justified in stating that Alaska is "a state which in national elections is one of the most Republican in the country"; "is solidly Republican, because national Democrats are seen as wanting to lock up Alaska's resources"; and "is heavily Republican, with a libertarian streak."[110] That was especially evident in 1992, when Ross Perot took 28 percent, his second-best showing (Maine was his best).[111]

The reasons for Alaska's redness are several but not very complicated. In contrast to, say, Oklahoma or Utah, religion has played no appreciable role; "Alaska had the lowest church attendance in the nation."[112] Its "libertarian streak," which the *Almanac* has several times alluded to, did not morph into a strong Tea Party movement in 2010; the state's politics were already right of center and were consistently focused on the state's natural resources. Oil had been a decisive factor ever since the North Slope's riches were discovered in the late 1950s along with the means of bringing the riches to markets—the pipeline to the ice-free port of Valdez. It began operating in 1977. The longevity of Senators Stevens and Murkowski and Congressman Young has depended on their unwavering defense and promotion of Alaskan resource interests.

But North Slope oil has proved to be finite. Production peaked in 1988 at two million barrels a day, and by 2014 it had fallen to under 500,000.[113] By 2016 not only was it dwindling, but world oil prices had fallen, the result in no small part of North Dakota's bonanza. The immediate consequence was a sharp tightening of the state budget, including severe cuts in higher education. Another result was further pressure to open the Arctic National Wildlife Reserve, in the northeastern corner of the state, to oil drilling. ANWR is suspected of having even greater oil deposits than the North Slope did before it was mined. Virtually all Alaskan politicians, regardless of party, have called for ANWR to be exploited, as has the national Republican Party. But lower-48 Democrats have resisted that on environmental grounds, which has not helped their party's popularity in Alaska.

Alaska's congressional delegation has often been more faithful to the state's peculiar interests than to the prevailing positions of the national parties. Stevens, for example, almost paralleled his Democratic colleague Gravel in the early 1970s. Both voted for the pipeline, for the equal rights amendment, and against gun control and the bombing of Cambodia. They differed on the nomination of William Rehnquist to the Supreme Court—Gravel against, Stevens for.[114] Ten years later Gravel was gone, replaced by Frank Murkowski. Both he and Stevens voted for Reagan's budget and 1981 tax cut, for aid to the rightist government of El Salvador, and for the sale of AWACS to Saudi Arabia. They differed on banning abortion—Murkowski for, Stevens against—which made Stevens "anathema to many right-wing colleagues."[115] By the early 1990s they both voted for the balanced-budget amendment and against Clinton's budgets, though they split on the North American Free Trade Agreement—Stevens against, Murkowski for. Stevens also took two un-Republican positions in the 1990s, to subsidize public television and to provide higher salaries and benefits to federal workers. Both of these were Alaska-centered issues, however, rooted in the desirability of more television access in isolated communities and support of the many federal employees in the state. Lisa Murkowski, while on balance conservative, proved to be somewhat less so as a senator than her father had been. Congressman Young, meanwhile, was earning *National Journal* ratings that showed him tilted strongly, but not exclusively, to the conservative side.[116]

Mark Begich, who in 2008 became the only Democrat elected to the Senate from Alaska since Mike Gravel in 1974, claimed that he was "an Alaska-*style* Democrat, which is to say, 'pro-gun rights, pro-oil and gas, pro-business, small business.'"[117] Yet his votes were more liberal than not; in 2011 and 2012 he was rated highly by AFSCME, the public-sector union, and the League of Conservation Voters but very low by the American Conservative Union and other organizations on the right.[118] He did not win reelection in 2014, losing to Republican Dan Sullivan. The only other Democrat who had any electoral success since the 1990s was Tony Knowles, one-time mayor of Anchorage. He was elected governor in 1994 by a plurality of 536 votes but was reelected in 1998 with a slightly less shaky 51.3 percent against an array of contenders. In 2004 he ran for the Senate but lost to Lisa Murkowski, and in 2006 he tried again for the governorship but lost to Sarah Palin.

Palin had beaten incumbent Frank Murkowski by a whopping 51 percent to 19 percent in the Republican primary. Palin claimed that Murkowski was planning to give the North Slope oil companies the rights to build the needed natural gas pipeline, and she saw it as a giveaway to the oil companies.[119] Palin was chosen by John McCain to run for vice president in 2008. They lost, and several months later, in July 2009, Palin resigned the governorship, turning it over to Lieutenant Governor Sean Parnell, who finished her term and won four years of his own in 2010. But he lost to independent Bill Walker, recently a Republican, in 2014. Parnell looked unbeatable until the Democratic candidate, Byron Mallott, called Walker and offered to run with him as lieutenant governor on a "unity ticket."[120] They won with 48 percent of the vote to Parnell's 46 percent. This left Mark Begich and Knowles as the only Democrats elected to any of the high offices since the 1980s. Bill Walker was elected governor in 2014 as an independent, but he was never a Democrat and had earlier run in a Republican primary. Walker, and Parnell before him, faced financial difficulties that Alaska had become unaccustomed to, as oil revenue continued to drop. Parnell was forced to cut taxes on Exxon Mobil, ConocoPhillips, and BP—taxes that Sarah Palin had imposed—in the hope of encouraging the oil companies to invest more in the North Slope.[121] That did not stop the bleeding. The Republican legislature made budget cuts in early 2016, but Walker used his line-item veto power to remove another $1.3 billion, which hit "public schools and the University of Alaska . . . [and] individual households [whose] oil investment dividend checks" would shrink, as would other state services.[122] As of mid-2016, however, there was no clear sign that such austerity would convert Alaska into a blue or even purple state politically.

It almost goes without saying that both houses of the Alaska legislature have had safe Republican majorities. The issues that Alaskans care about most strongly, especially the prudent mining of the great deposits of oil and gas it still sits upon, conform to the positions of the Republican Party nationally. If one wanted to predict, it would seem safe to foresee Alaska continuing to vote Republican for most offices, most of the time.

Henry Bellmon breathed life into the moribund Oklahoma Republican Party in 1960, became the first Republican to be elected governor of the Sooner State in 1962, and served later as U.S. senator and governor again. He has been called "the father of the modern Republican Party in Oklahoma." Cherokee Strip Museum Collection, Oklahoma Historical Society.

Four new Democratic senators, elected in the 1964 Johnson landslide: (*from left*) Walter Mondale (Minn.), Joe Tydings (Md.), Fred Harris (Okla.), and Robert Kennedy (Mass.). Courtesy of the *New Mexico Mercury.*

Democrat David Boren (*left*) defeated Republican James Inhofe (*right*) for Oklahoma's governorship in 1974. Then Boren ran successfully for the Senate in 1978, 1984, and 1990 and thereafter became president of the University of Oklahoma. Inhofe won election to the Senate in 1994, 1996, 2002, 2008, and 2014. Courtesy of the *Oklahoman*.

Congressman Bruce Alger, elected five times (1954–62) from Dallas, was the first Republican that Texas sent to the House in modern times. He was definitely not in the Rayburn-Johnson camp. His positions resembled those of the Tea Party several decades later. Courtesy of the Lyndon Baines Johnson Presidential Library, National Archives and Records Administration.

Texas Democratic stalwarts: (*from left*) Wright Patman of District 1 from 1929 to 1976 and chair of the House Banking Committee, Speaker Sam Rayburn from District 4, and Senator (1957–71) Ralph Yarborough. Courtesy of the Dolph Briscoe Center for American History, University of Texas at Austin.

Rev. W. A. Criswell was a theological and political conservative who served as pastor of the First Baptist Church of Dallas for decades. Many regarded him as the outstanding leader of the Religious Right in Texas. Courtesy of wacriswell.com.

William P. Clements Jr. with his wife Rita. In 1978, Clements became the first Republican elected governor in Texas since Reconstruction. He was defeated for reelection in 1982 but won another term in 1986. Along with John Tower's election to the Senate in 1961, Clements's victories were landmarks in Texas's Republican resurgence. Courtesy of Southern Methodist University.

In 1990, Democrat Ann Richards bested Republican Clayton Williams in the "Claytie and the Lady" campaign. Liberal and pro-choice, she lost reelection in 1994 to George W. Bush and to date has been the last Democrat to win the Texas governorship. Courtesy of the Richards family.

Three Texas Republican House members—(*from left*) Kenny Marchant, Bill Archer, and Bill Thomas—appeared with journalist Cokie Roberts at the 2015 House Ways and Means Committee dinner. Archer, a fiscal conservative, chaired the committee from 1995 to 2001. Courtesy of the United States Capitol Historical Society.

Two Democratic congressmen from Texas announce that they will not attend Donald Trump's presidential inauguration in 2017: Austin's Lloyd Doggett (*left*) and Houston's Joaquin Castro (*second from right*). Also pictured: Julián Castro, Joaquin's twin, mayor of San Antonio (2009–14) and secretary of housing and urban development (2014–17, *at Doggett's left*), and state representative Trey Martinez-Fischer (*center*). Photograph © Tom Reel/San Antonio Express-News/ZUMAPRESS.com.

A Republican wheelhorse, Hazel Abel was one of Nebraska's seven U.S. senators of 1954, and one of the first two female senators from the state. Elected for the remaining few weeks of Dwight Griswold's term, she resigned as promised on December 31. Courtesy U.S. House of Representatives

From a ranch in Nebraska's northwestern Cherry County, Eva Kelly Bowring became the other female Republican senator of 1954, serving from April to November, when Hazel Abel succeeded her. Courtesy of the Martin Luther King, Jr., Memorial Library, Washington, D.C.

Frank "Ted" Moss represented Utah in the Senate from 1959 to 1977 and joined Frank Church of Idaho, Mike Mansfield of Montana, and a few others as (mostly) liberal Democrats from the northern Rocky Mountain states. Moss was notably strong on environmental issues. Courtesy of the *Salt Lake Tribune*.

Clinton P. Anderson of New Mexico (*second from left*) held state offices in the 1930s, was elected to the House in 1940 and 1942, was secretary of agriculture under Truman, and was U.S. senator from 1949 to 1971. He was known as one of the most creative legislators ever to serve in Congress. Courtesy of the Forest History Society (FHS7159).

Atop the Senate in 1967: Mike Mansfield (D-Mont., *left*), majority leader, and Everett Dirksen (R-Ill., *right*), minority leader. Courtesy of the United States National Archives.

Morris "Mo" Udall followed his brother Stewart as the representative from Arizona's District 2, centering on Tucson, when Stewart became Kennedy's secretary of the interior. Morris held the seat until he retired in 1991. Courtesy of the U.S. National Archives and Records Administration, Carter White House Photographs Collection, NLC-WHSP-C-04018–9.

A trio of Arizona Udalls: (*from left*) interior secretary Stewart; uncle Jesse, chief justice of the Arizona supreme court; and congressman Mo. Courtesy of the University of Arizona.

Monroe Sweetland, who was chiefly responsible for rebuilding and liberalizing the Oregon Democratic Party in the 1940s and '50s. Courtesy of the Oregon Historical Society Research Library, bb005795.

Oregon's "maverick" senator Wayne Morse, a Republican who bolted that party in 1952, became an independent, and finally a Democrat. Courtesty of LBJ Presidential Library and Wikimedia Commons.

Another step toward the Beach Bill: Oregon's Republican governor Tom McCall (*right*) surveying the Pacific Coast beach at Rockaway in 1967, en route to preserving the state's coastline for public use. With state representative Sidney Barrett (*left*) and Oregon State University engineer Robert Schultz (*center*). Courtesy of the Oregon Historical Society and the *Oregonian*.

Earl Warren when governor of California. Courtesy of the Library of Congress Prints and Photographs Division, Washington, D.C. (LC-USZ62-41653).

California Republican senator William F. Knowland and his wife Helen, studying early returns in the 1958 governor's election, which he lost, along with the smiles. Courtesy of the *Oakland Tribune*.

California's Democratic governor Edmund G. "Pat" Brown meets with President Kennedy in 1961. Courtesy of the John F. Kennedy Presidential Library.

Phillip Burton represented districts in San Francisco in the California assembly from 1957 to 1964, and then the U.S. House from 1964 to 1983. More than any other person, he is credited (or damned) for the 1981 redistricting that tipped the political scales to the Democrats. He was a strong voice for social justice and environmental measures, and his biography (by John Jacobs) is aptly titled *A Rage for Justice*. Courtesy of the National Park Service.

John Burton was Phillip's younger brother and a liberal Democrat. He represented parts of San Francisco in the California assembly, then the U.S. House (1974–83), the assembly again, then the California senate, where he was president pro tem. He chaired the state's Democratic Party from 2009 to 2017. *Congressional Pictorial Directory* (Washington, DC: U.S. G.P.O., 1997), 16.

Democrat Willie Brown (*right*) served as a member of the California assembly from 1965 to 1995, the last fifteen years as its powerhouse speaker. Term-limited, he then ran for, and was elected, mayor of San Francisco and served from 1996 to 2004. Courtesy of the San Jose *Mercury News*.

Pete Wilson, Republican, elected governor of California in 1990 and 1994. His stands on immigration restriction helped him in 1994 but damaged his party in the longer run. Courtesy Wikimedia Commons and the Department of Defense.

Dianne Feinstein, Democratic senator from California since 1992. She was mayor of San Francisco from 1978 to 1988. Courtesy of Wikimedia Commons.

Republican governor Arnold Schwarzenegger in 2007, introducing President George W. Bush and Senator Dianne Feinstein. Courtesy of Jim Greenhill.

San Francisco congresswoman (since 1987) Nancy Pelosi was the first female speaker of the U.S. House of Representatives (2007–11). A protégée of the Burtons and a former chair of the California Democratic Party, she succeeded Phillip Burton's widow Sala, who like her husband died in office. Courtesy of Wikimedia Commons.

Senator Dan Inouye (D-Hawaii), chair of the Senate Select Committee on Intelligence, and Senator Barry Goldwater (R-Ariz.), vice-chair, in 1973. Courtesy of the Daniel K. Inouye Institute.

Washington's two Democratic senators in February 1969: Henry "Scoop" Jackson (*left*) and Warren Magnuson (*right*). Courtesy of the University of Washington Special Collections (Neg. UW19599).

THE SWINGERS, SHADES OF PURPLE

4   Arizona, Montana, Nevada, Colorado, and New Mexico

Five of the nineteen western states have not been consistently blue or red since 1950. Instead they have oscillated from one election to another, and in voting for one office or another. In the current color scheme, they have been varying shades of purple. Nor have they been consistent with one another. The sequence in this chapter's title places them from reddish purple to bluish, with Arizona very close to behaving like some of the always-red states and New Mexico and perhaps Colorado frequently blue, though not enough to qualify them as consistently so, which would put them in the Hawaii-Washington group.

These five states, as states, have not committed to one party or the other; but it is easy to identify parts of them that have been very consistent over time. The result is that small shifts of one part or another can move the entire state in a seemingly unpredictable or erratic direction. Then, in another election or two, it shifts the other way. Changes in demography and economics often play major roles. A fresh issue, an unusually appealing candidate, a scandal pinned on an incumbent, or other transient factors can cause a state's partisan leaning to shift. Perhaps it is more accurate to call these states not purple or inconsistent but finely balanced, easily tipped one way or another, with regard to elections to specific offices. Whatever we call them, they simply do not fit—*over time*—as simply red or blue. Purple will do, for want of a better term.

ARIZONA

A good case can be made for including Arizona among the persistently red states rather than among the swingers. It could perhaps go either way. Voting histories for president, senator, and the state legislature have been fairly consistently red, but votes for governor and the U.S. House have been more ambiguous. Compared to deep red states like Nebraska or North Dakota, Arizona has been a shade of purple.

From statehood in 1912 until the late 1940s, Arizona was a rather solidly Democratic state. Its presidential vote went to Woodrow Wilson twice, Franklin Roosevelt four times, and Harry Truman in 1948, and only three times to Republicans—Harding in 1920, Coolidge in 1924, and Hoover in 1928. It voted fourteen times for Democrats and only four times for Republicans for governor from 1912 through 1948. Only one Republican was elected to the U.S. Senate from 1912 through 1948, for a single term in the 1920s, while four Democrats were elected: Henry Ashurst served five terms, Carl Hayden seven, Ernest McFarland two, and Marcus Smith one. For nearly all of its first forty years as a state, Arizona was not unlike contemporaneous west Texas in its politics, a thinly populated and mostly rural state where "pinto Democrats" held most of the offices. Large in area but small in impact at the federal level, its representatives were happy to bring home some New Deal bacon and to work toward keeping whatever it could of Colorado River water.[1]

This changed in the late 1940s. Within a very few years, less than a decade, the state's political coloration changed to bright red. Beginning with Eisenhower in 1952, Arizona has voted for the Republican presidential candidate every time except 1996, when Bill Clinton edged out Bob Dole by about two percentage points. Of twenty-two elections for governor beginning in 1950, Republicans took fourteen, Democrats eight, all scattered unevenly across the six decades. Beginning in 1950, Carl Hayden won three of his seven Senate terms (in 1950, 1956, and 1962) and Dennis DeConcini won his three (in 1976, 1982, and 1988). They were the only Democratic senators from the state after 1950, whereas the voters elected Republicans sixteen times—Barry Goldwater to five terms, Paul Fannin twice, John McCain five terms, John Kyl three times, and Jeff Flake once. Thus Republicans have dominated that office in all elections after 1988. As for the House, Arizona's delegation has steadily increased, reflecting the state's remarkable population growth, from two seats through 1960 to nine after the 2010 census. There have been 171 contests for House seats from 1950 through 2016, of which Republicans have won 107 (62.6 percent) and Democrats sixty-four (37.4 percent). The party balance for House seats was fairly even in the 1950s and 1960s.

Thereafter Republicans usually prevailed, with Democratic victories largely limited to Morris Udall's in the 2nd District (mostly Tucson voters). The Republican redness lightened somewhat from 2002 through 2010, and the parties have run almost evenly since then. That is the main reason for classifying Arizona as a swing state, albeit reddish, along with the sprinkling of Democratic victories for other offices. The legislature has been quite stable with safe Republican majorities in both chambers since the 1970s.

Why did Arizona shift rather suddenly from "pinto Democratic" to Republican around 1950? For several reasons. One, underlying the others, was the development and spread of air conditioning in homes, offices, and factories and the electricity to operate it. Summer days of 100-plus degree heat were no longer unlivable. The state's population expansion led the nation for much of the post-1950 period. Maricopa County (which includes Phoenix) was home to about 332,000 people in 1950. It climbed to a million just after 1970, to over two million in 1990, and to 4.17 million in 2015.[2] Phoenix, the state capital as well as Maricopa County's seat, held 107,000 people in 1950, 600,000 by the early 1970s, and over 1.5 million by 2015. Tucson, the state's second city, had a population of 45,000 in 1950 and more than ten times that by 2010. Satellites and suburbs of Phoenix such as Chandler, Glendale, and Scottsdale had fewer than 10,000 in 1950 but were each close to a quarter-million by 2012.

Where did all these people come from? As in most U.S. migration streams, they came more from close-by places than distant ones: over time, from California, Texas, Oklahoma, and other Rocky Mountain states, followed by populous midwestern states such as Illinois. In the late 1940s and early 1950s, some arrivals were former servicemen who had been stationed in Arizona, or passed through it, and decided to come back to stay, often with newly formed families. Arizona was also a haven for retirees from places with harsher winters; they were a significant part of the state's in-migration, though not the only age group that arrived. Newcomers of every age came, except children and teenagers.[3] The reason for that was the nature of Arizona's postwar labor demand and job opportunities.

The prewar Arizona economy was extractive and agricultural, with the "three C's" dominating: cattle, copper, and cotton. World War II brought war-related industries as well as military bases, and, although the impact was not on the scale of California's, it was significant in the hitherto isolated and backwater Arizona. Importantly, the development and conscious, planned attraction of industries that were technologically advanced for their time required a trained, usually young, labor force. Looked at from the potential migrants' viewpoint, that meant attractive job opportunities. "In the most explosive growth period, between 1948 and 1963," wrote Neal Peirce, "Arizona led all the nation in seven important indexes of growth, from population to manufacturing employment to bank deposits." Copper, cotton, and cattle gave way to manufacturing, notably into what were then high-tech products for mass consumption. Jobs proliferated at Motorola, Sperry Rand, Hughes Aircraft, and General Electric, to cite only the leaders. By 1970 "the state's biggest employer [was] Motorola, which at one point had over 30,000 employees and still [in 1970 had] over 20,000. . . . The personal income of Arizonans rose in the 20-year span 1948–68 from $879 million to $5,034 million," or about sixfold.[4]

These changes in demography and economics had almost immediate political consequences. Migrants, Peirce wrote, were "heavily Midwestern, often Republican by heritage." Retirees "almost by definition" leaned Republican," and "even more important, the new industries in which younger settlers found employment were highly technical and not of the mass production type with strong industrial unions. Motorola, the biggest employer, is the finest example of this; it attracted technicians and engineers in large quantities and the unions never had a chance."[5]

They certainly never had a chance after Arizona passed a "right-to-work" law by constitutional amendment in 1946. The changes in demography and economics were real, but they were also led—specifically by the Phoenix chamber of commerce. Prominent in the organization was the head of the city's leading department store, Barry Goldwater, who had been writing anti-union, anti–New Deal editorials for the Phoenix *Gazette* for about ten years. When the very conservative owner of the *Indianapolis Star*, Eugene C. Pulliam (a winter visitor to Phoenix) bought the Phoenix papers, the *Republic* and the *Gazette*, in 1942, the local media monopoly neatly dovetailed with the business elite.[6] In March 1946,

> Herbert Williams, a building contractor recently returned to Phoenix after military service, was refused a construction contract because he employed nonunion building tradesmen. . . .

> Williams formed the Veterans Right-to-Work Committee
> [which] launched a petition drive to place a right-to-work
> amendment on the November ballot. Pulliam and Phoenix
> businessmen quickly lent their support. Barry Goldwater . . .
> agreed to head the committee's retailer's wing. . . . Editorials
> in the *Republic* and *Gazette* likened "domineering, self-serving
> labor bosses" to both Hitler and Communists.[7]

The measure passed easily.

Voters also approved an expanded city council that fall, putting Goldwater on it and placing Phoenix and Maricopa County in the business elite's control. There they would stay for over two decades, with the Republican Party, resurgent and revivified, in the saddle. It was business conservatism through and through; it was not a Religious Right or social-issues conservatism. "Dominating local politics between 1949 and 1975, Phoenix's Chamber of Commerce transformed local politics to lure industries and promote growth: reducing taxes on business and manufacturing, passing laws that hamstrung union organizing, and offering land grants and issuing industrial development bonds to support prospective businesses."[8]

In 1950 the state Republican convention "stampeded" the nomination of radio commentator Howard Pyle for governor. Goldwater managed a vigorous campaign for Pyle, who won a slender victory over longtime Democratic state auditor Ana Frohmiller.[9] Two years later Goldwater ran against U.S. Senator Ernest McFarland, then the Democratic majority leader, and won by three percentage points. John J. Rhodes, an attorney from Mesa, won the House seat in District 1, Maricopa County. Pyle was reelected in 1952 (governors had two-year terms before 1970). With the victories of Pyle, Goldwater, and Rhodes (who would win reelection through 1980, becoming a powerful national figure in the House), the Phoenix business-conservative Republicans had all but chased the rural Democrats from the principal offices, and so the political landscape would remain until the mid-1970s, with few exceptions.

The Republican ascendancy was never absolute, but over a few years it changed the state from rural blue to metropolitan red. The exceptions that preserved some Democrats included Carl Hayden's reelection in 1956 and again in 1962, after which the by-then nonagenarian finally succeeded in getting the Central Arizona Project passed, bringing water to Maricopa and other parts of the desert. In

1952, Democrat Harold Patten won District 2 (Tucson and most of the state except Maricopa County). Stewart Udall was elected to that district from 1954 through 1960, and when he became John F. Kennedy's secretary of the interior in 1961 his brother Morris succeeded to the district, winning it in every election from 1962 through 1990. When the state gained a third district, Democrat George Senner won it in 1962 and 1964. Ernest McFarland, after losing his Senate seat to Goldwater in 1952, won the governorship in 1954 and 1956 (but lost his Senate rematch with Goldwater in 1958). In many states 1958 was a Democratic year, so Goldwater's countercurrent win propelled him to national prominence, leading eventually to his presidential nomination in 1964.

Goldwater left the Senate when he ran for president in 1964, but he won back his seat in 1968 and was reelected in 1974 and (narrowly) in 1980. The brightest light for the Democrats was Dennis DeConcini winning the first of his three elections to the other Senate seat in 1976.

Otherwise, Republicans won the House seats through the 1950s, the 1960s, and the 1970s. The exception was Bob Stump in 1976–80, winning the district that included Flagstaff, west Phoenix, and Yuma. But he prudently switched parties for the 1982 and subsequent elections. The legislature, hitherto a Democratic monopoly, turned partially red in 1952, as Republican seats in the state house jumped from eleven to twenty-nine and four Republicans entered the state senate.[10] Republicans won more seats in 1954 and continued to nibble away at the Democrats' majorities. Yet it took the Supreme Court's one man, one vote decisions to reapportion the legislature in accord with population, reducing rural Democratic districts and increasing urban Republican ones, giving Republicans majorities in both chambers in the 1966 election.[11] Maricopa County had been electing two of twenty-eight senate seats; suddenly it had fifteen of thirty.[12]

In 1966 the state Republicans also won all the statewide offices and, in 1970, a majority on the state supreme court. They thereby controlled reapportionment after the 1970 census, when the state received yet another congressional seat. The Republican dominance took several election cycles, but it was solid by the end of the 1960s. Party registration, once overwhelmingly Democratic, also shifted Republican. Population continued to surge; corporations were recruited and provided jobs; the Phoenix business elite successfully kept control of an expanding state economy and kept the Far Right from taking over the party. Goldwater and friends took "a leading role in repulsing the right-wingers in primary elections and battles for common ground," according to Peirce, but in 1966 party stalwart Jack Williams was elected governor, and although not quite part of the hard right he had "some right-wing support" and "some rather reactionary views on education."[13] Williams was reelected in 1968 and, for the first four-year term for governors, in 1970. But he lost in 1974 to Raul Hector Castro, a Democratic lawyer and Pima County judge who had been born in the copper town of Cananea, Mexico. Lyndon Johnson had appointed him ambassador to El Salvador and then to Bolivia until 1969. The Democratic nominee for governor in 1970, he lost to Jack Williams. In a rerun in 1974, he defeated Williams narrowly. Castro resigned in 1977 to become Jimmy Carter's ambassador to Argentina. His successor, Wesley Bolin, abruptly died in office in early 1978, whereupon another Democrat, Arizona attorney general Bruce Babbitt, became governor. Babbitt was elected to full terms in 1978 and 1982. After completing nine years as governor in 1987, he capitalized on a press boomlet and ran for president in 1988, but he withdrew after lackluster showings in early primaries. He became president of the League of Conservation Voters, earning plaudits from environmentalists and criticism from Reaganites. Bill Clinton appointed him secretary of the interior in 1993, and he served through both Clinton terms until 2001.

The man whom Babbitt defeated for governor in 1978, car dealer Evan Mecham, won the office in 1986. The usually more fastidious *Almanac of American Politics* called him "a perennial political loser [he had run four times before] who won a three-way race in 1986 with 40 percent of the vote and immediately raised a national ruckus by rescinding the state's Martin Luther King holiday, prompting a boycott of the state by various conventioneers. . . . Recall petitions were circulated and he was impeached" and removed by the Republican legislature in April 1988. Arizona secretary of state Rose Mofford replaced him. Mecham continued to roil the state's political waters, running a sixth time for governor in 1990 and for senator in 1992, with no success.[14] Mofford, a Democrat, served as governor until early 1991, the first woman to hold the office. Three more would follow soon: Jane Dee Hill, Republican, 1997–2003 (finishing the term of Fife Symington, who became caught up in a real estate scandal and had to resign); Janet Napolitano, Democrat, elected in 2002 and serving until she became Obama's secretary of homeland security in 2009; and Jan Brewer, Republican, succeeding Napolitano and elected to a full term in 2012.[15] The governorship has thus swung between the major parties since the 1970s, going back to Castro and Babbitt.

The presidential vote of Arizonans did move Democratic in 1996, when Bill Clinton won, though not, so far, later than that. The state's congressional representatives have divided by party fairly evenly in recent years, since redistricting was moved from the legislature to the five-member Arizona Independent Redistricting Commission beginning in 2001. Two Republicans and two Democratic legislators appoint four members, and the fifth, to be neither a Democrat nor a Republican, is picked by the other four.[16] House seats, which split five to one Republican in 2000, loosened to six to two Republican in 2002 and 2004, then to four each in 2006, and actually five to three Democratic in 2008. The Tea Party year of 2010 brought a four to four split again, and 2012 brought a five to four Democratic edge. That reverted in 2014 and 2016 again to five to four Republican. It bears repeating that the state as a whole was unstable because two or three districts could easily shift, while most others were constant and predictable. The result is that "Arizona has become a competitive battleground for House seats. Its nine-member delegation includes four solid Republican districts, two solidly Democratic districts (with large Hispanic majorities), and three districts that could remain 'toss-up' for several more cycles. Those three districts—now [2015] represented by two Democrats and one Republican, all of them women—are based in the sprawling rural eastern part of the state, [plus] Tempe and Tucson [both university towns]."[17]

The bipartisan commission did not escape criticism. Its map in 2011 that included the new 9th District "infuriated Republicans." Governor Brewer threw out the map and accused the commission's chair of "gross misconduct." The senate removed the chair, but Arizona's top court rebuked Brewer and reinstated the chair, whereupon the commission voted to repass the map.[18]

The Peirce narrative, portraying a blue Arizona in the 1930s–1940s, then turning purple or even red in the 1950s–1960s under Goldwater and the Phoenix businesspeople, is correct, but there were always those exceptions; it was never a thorough reversal. Some parts of the state were always red: northern Phoenix and adjacent suburbs like Scottsdale, the eastern precincts of Tucson plus Prescott and the Mormon areas. But some were consistently blue: the Hispanic places such as west Tucson, south Phoenix, or Yuma and the major American Indian reservations (Navajo and Hopi). If these latter populations could be added to, Arizona would become nearly blue. Since 1950, Democrats have never won the presidential vote (except in 1996) or a senatorship (except for DeConcini's three wins). But they did take the governorship at times, most recently by Janet Napolitano in 2002 (very narrowly) and 2006 (comfortably), and certain House districts. By the 1990s, when Arizona had earned six districts, one was understood to be Hispanic—the one that Morris Udall had held until he had to retire for health reasons after 1990. It was then filled by Ed Pastor from the 1992 election through 2012 (renumbered a couple of times) and after that by Ruben Gallego. Another Hispanic district, now the 3rd, was carved out after the state gained two more House seats after the 2000 census, and it has been filled by the solidly left Raul Grijalva. The northern, or northeastern, part of the state, including Flagstaff and the major Indian reservations, has often (but not always) elected Democrats: Karan English in 1992, Harry Mitchell in 2006 and 2008, Ann Kirkpatrick in 2008, 2012, and 2014 until she ran (without success) for McCain's Senate seat in 2016. The district including much of Tucson was won in 2006 through 2010 by Democrat Gabrielle Giffords, who was shot in the head at a shopping mall rally. After redistricting, the general area sent Democrat Kyrsten Sinema to Washington in 2012, 2014, and 2016.

Almost regardless of party label, Arizona has elected to office people who ranged from moderately to deeply conservative. Except for the Udalls's environmentalism and the economic liberalism of the Hispanic members of Congress, few could be said to be on the left. Janet Napolitano (who was a centrist) was followed in the governorship by Jan Brewer, a rightist Republican, notably on immigration. Joe Arpaio, the harsh and vindictive sheriff of Maricopa County, was reelected several times, though he was defeated in 2016. Trent Gosar and J. D. Hayworth are or were voluble conservatives in Congress. Probably the most conservative of all was Trent Franks of the west Phoenix 8th District, but he resigned abruptly in late 2017 as a result of a sex scandal. Thus Arizona, all in all, has been a purple state, for at least the past forty years.

MONTANA

Montana is the fourth-largest state in area, and the forty-fourth in population as of 2015. It had two seats in the U.S. House before 1992 but lost one as a result of the 1990 census. Having recently just topped a million in population, it is unlikely to gain back that second House seat very soon. Once politically blue, when Anaconda Copper and Montana Power dominated the economy and the Mine, Mill, and Smelter Workers Union led many of the voters, it has become empurpled or even a bit reddish as those opposing entities have weakened or disappeared.

Montana's presidential vote has generally gone to the Republican candidate. Beginning with Eisenhower in 1952 through Trump in 2016, Republicans have taken fifteen of the seventeen contests, all but LBJ in 1964 and Bill Clinton in 1992 (very narrowly). Of the leading third-party candidates during the period, George Wallace did not do as well in Montana as he did nationally (13.5 percent nationally, but only 7.3 percent in Montana), but John Anderson in 1980 slightly exceeded his national average (6.6 percent nationally, 8.1 percent in Montana), and Ross Perot in 1992 went well beyond his national figure (18.9 percent nationally, 26.1 percent in Montana).

But the presidential vote, here as elsewhere, is not the whole story about party preference. The governorship in Montana is for a four-year term, elected in the same year as the presidency rather than an off year as is the case in many states. The two major parties have come out almost even since 1952, Democrats winning nine of the seventeen elections, Republicans eight. The recent trend has been Democratic—Brian Schweitzer in 2004 and 2008 and Steve Bullock in 2012 and 2016. The most recent Republican successes have been Marc Racicot in 1992 and 1996 and Judy Martz in 2000. Schweitzer and Bullock each won rather narrowly the first time but more solidly the second.

Senatorial elections have very often gone the Democrats' way. Of twenty-two elections beginning in 1952, Democrats took eighteen, Republicans four. Incumbency has generally helped. James E. Murray, nephew of the copper king and Irish immigrant James A. Murray, was elected in 1934 to the unexpired term of Thomas J. Walsh, who died in office. Murray won four more full terms, the final one in 1954; he died shortly after finishing it in early 1961. Aptly described as a liberal New Dealer, Murray played a major role in the 1938 Fair

Labor Standards Act, the Employment Act of 1946, and other labor legislation; he was joint author of the Wagner-Murray-Dingell bill to provide national health care. It was not enacted by the conservative congresses of the late 1940s, but it "laid the groundwork for adoption of the Medicare Amendment to the Social Security Act" in the mid-1960s, part of Johnson's Great Society.[19]

Murray's Montana colleague in the Senate after the 1952 election was Mike Mansfield, a native of New York City who came to Montana as a boy. When the United States entered World War I in 1917, Mansfield lied about his age (which was fourteen) to join the navy and served briefly until his youth was discovered, whereupon he joined the army, and then the marine corps, which sent him to the Philippines and China. For eight years in the 1920s he was a copper miner. Then he sought the education he had missed, earned a bachelor's and then a master's degree at the University of Montana, and taught East Asian history there from 1934 to 1942. His political career started when he ran for Congress in 1940. He lost but ran again in 1942 and won the first of five terms (1943–53). In 1952 he defeated Republican Zales Ecton, a McCarthy ally, for one of Montana's Senate seats. He was reelected in 1958, 1964, and 1970. When Lyndon Johnson resigned as majority leader in 1961 to become Kennedy's vice president, Mansfield took over the leadership and held it until he retired in 1977. He is still the longest-serving majority leader. He opposed the Vietnam War and excessive military spending, helped greatly in passing the Civil Rights Act of 1964 and the Voting Rights Act of 1965, and much else. He worked successfully "across the aisle" and helped bring about Nixon's famous trip to China, which led to U.S.-China diplomatic relations after decades of diplomatic silence. After he left the Senate, Mansfield was appointed ambassador to Japan by Jimmy Carter. Reappointed by Reagan, he stayed in Tokyo for ten years. He died in 2001, age ninety-eight. His *New York Times* obituary quotes Hugh D. Scott of Pennsylvania, the Republican minority leader when Mansfield left the Senate, as saying, "He's the most decent man I've ever met in public life."[20]

Murray's successor was another liberal Democrat, who won three terms in 1960, 1966, and 1972: Lee Metcalf. After serving in the Montana house and a term on the state supreme court, as well as in the army in World War II, Metcalf was elected in 1952 to Mansfield's U.S. House seat. Reelected to three more terms, he then won the

Senate seat that Murray was vacating. As a congressman and then as a senator, he focused on education and environment, especially the creation of wilderness areas in Montana.[21] John Melcher, another progressive who sponsored legislation to help Native Americans and distribute farm surpluses, won Mansfield's vacated seat in 1976 and was reelected once, in 1982. Republican Conrad Burns upended him in 1988, becoming the first Republican senator elected from Montana since Ecton in 1946. Burns also became Montana's first Republican senator to be reelected, which happened twice, in 1994 and 2000. As a one-time livestock auctioneer, he had a "common touch" with farmers and ranchers, but he was also "gaffe-prone," notably on racial matters.[22] Self-critical, Burns admitted in 2002 that "I can self-destruct in one sentence, sometimes in one word." In 2006, after Burns "was linked" to lobbyist Jack Abramoff, he lost his third reelection bid to John Tester.[23] Tester, with burr haircut and cowboy boots, looked the part of the rancher-farmer that he is. He defeated Burns in 2006 by about 3,500 votes out of nearly 400,000, but, reflecting Montana's centrist positions in his votes and statements, he was reelected in 2012 over six-term congressman Denny Rehberg by nearly 20,000. "He takes his party's side on key votes often enough to satisfy party leaders," wrote the *Almanac*, voting 51 to 58 percent liberal on economic, social, and foreign issues in 2012 and 2013.[24]

The Montana senators' longevity record was established by Max Baucus, who succeeded Metcalf in 1978 and then went on to win five more terms before retiring in 2014. He rose to become chair of the Senate Finance Committee and carved out a legislative record that was centrist rather than liberal. He "led the passage and enactment of Free Trade Agreements with 11 countries [and] was deeply involved in orchestrating congressional approval of permanent normal trade relations with China in 2000 and in facilitating China's entrance into the World Trade Organization in 2001."[25] His *National Journal* ratings moved from 70-plus percent liberal on economic issues in the early 1980s to 50-some percent in the early 1990s until the end of his Senate career. Yet he consistently earned high ratings from the American Civil Liberties Union and the League of Conservation Voters and generally low ratings from the American Conservative Union and other groups on the right.[26] He seemed to feel by 2013 that he might no longer be conservative enough for Montana, and he announced in April that he would not run again.[27] The following

December, President Obama nominated Baucus to be ambassador to China, and he was confirmed without dissent by the Senate in February 2014.

Governor Bullock thereupon appointed the lieutenant governor, John Walsh, who had strong military credentials and seemed a likely winner of a full Senate term in the fall. But it became clear during the summer that Walsh's master's thesis at the Army War College was partly plagiarized, and he had to withdraw.[28] The 2014 Senate election went to Steve Daines, a Republican who had won the state's house seat in 2012. He easily defeated a state senator, Amanda Curtis, who ran when the better-known former congressman, Pat Williams, declined to run for health reasons.[29] Daines, a former Procter & Gamble executive, proved to be a fiscal conservative (as he had been in the house) and a supporter of the Keystone pipeline, as was Tester (no surprise).

We spend some space on Montana's senators for several reasons. Some have been nationally prominent, most of all Mansfield but also Murray, Metcalf, and Baucus, and on the other side Conrad Burns. The three M's and Baucus gave Montana its greatest voice on the national stage—no mean feat for a state with four, then three, electoral votes and lacking even one city with a hundred thousand people. Additionally, since all but Burns and Daines were Democrats, they collectively provide a yardstick as to how Montana Democrats (and perhaps Mountain State ones generally) have gradually shifted to the right over the past several decades. Murray was a down-the-line New Dealer. Mansfield and Metcalf were Great Society liberals. Baucus was a centrist who voted with his party, urban though it had become, more often than not. Tester, perhaps a little less so, and his two victories were not by very comfortable margins. One sees, then, a rightward movement among these Democratic senators—not that they were ever clones of their Republican colleagues, or close to it, but rightward in comparison to their predecessors of the 1930s–1950s. If Montana is truly a swing state, which its electoral history says it is, it hasn't been swinging left lately. Pretty blue from the 1950s into the 1970s or even longer, it has developed a reddish tincture more recently.

As stated earlier, Montana had two members of the U.S. House through 1990 and only one from the election of 1992 onward. When there were two, the state was divided roughly along the Continental

Divide, District 1 being the western, more mountainous one, and District 2 being the roughly 60 percent of the state that is ranching and farming on the Great Plains. Stated succinctly, the political geography in the early 1980s was that "the eastern plains and Billings typically go Republican, and the western mountains and Butte, Great Falls, and Missoula usually go Democratic. . . . Billings, riding a local boom based on coal, is heavily Republican." District 1 included the miners of Butte and Anaconda, a shrinking cohort for many reasons: the collapse of the Anaconda Copper Company and its replacement by a nonunion corporation, and the dwindling of below-ground mining and the rise of surface strip mining, which meant a different kind of miner, wielding an earth mover rather than a pick. The district also included the state university at Missoula and often the one at Bozeman, and the Native American counties, also near the mountains.[30] More recently, with only one at-large district, "the Democratic tradition is strongest in the old mining towns like Butte and Anaconda, on Indian reservations (7 percent of Montanans are American Indians), in old railroad towns like Great Falls and Havre, in university towns like Missoula and Bozeman, and in the state capital, Helena. The Republican tradition is strongest in the population-losing eastern plains counties and in fast-growing Flathead and Ravalli Counties in the west."[31] And Billings.

In 1950–90, when there were two House seats, twenty-one contests took place in each district, a total of forty-two. In District 1, the western one, Democrats won nineteen, Republicans two. In District 2, the eastern plains one, Democrats won five times, Republicans sixteen. From 1992 on, the at-large district went Democratic twice and Republican eleven times. Incumbency was an advantage; House members seldom lost their seats unless they chose to run for an open Senate seat. Perennial incumbents in District 1, both Democrats, were Arnold Olsen, a lawyer from Butte, who was elected to five terms (1960–68), and Pat Williams, a Helena schoolteacher who first ran in 1978 when Baucus opened up the seat to run for the Senate and who was reelected through 1990 and twice more in 1992 and 1994 when Montana was reduced to the single at-large seat, for a total of nine terms. Perennials in District 2 were Republicans: Billings lawyer James F. Battin, who was elected to the House from 1960 through 1968, when he resigned to become federal district judge for Montana; and Ron Marlenee, a rancher-farmer from Scobey, a village on the northeast Montana plains. A common-touch Republican, he was elected eight times, from 1976 through 1990.

In the post-1992 single-district years, the hardiest perennial to date was Denny Rehberg, owner-manager of a large cattle-and-goat ranch near Billings. A Republican, he was an aide to Marlenee and Conrad Burns and then served in the state house until he was elected lieutenant governor. He ran against Baucus for the U.S. Senate in 1996 and lost. He ran and won the state's House seat in 2000 and five more times through 2010. In 2012 he ran against Tester for the Senate and lost, and then he became a Washington lobbyist. On social, economic, and foreign issues he compiled a strongly conservative voting record and supported the Iraq intervention.[32] Republican Steve Daines succeeded Rehberg in 2012 and went to the Senate in 2014; one-time navy Seal Ryan Zinke followed Daines in the House seat in 2014 and 2016 but was named in December 2016 by President-elect Trump to be secretary of the interior.

Those who left the House to run for the Senate included Mansfield in 1950, Metcalf in 1960, Melcher in 1976, Baucus in 1978, and Daines in 2014. All of these succeeded. Marlenee and Rehberg did not.

As we saw with Arizona, it is not that parts of a state swing; parts are relatively stable in their party affiliation. But small shifts in one or a few of those parts can swing the state. In Arizona, for example, voters in the Hispanic districts were mostly reliable Democrats, and voters in Scottsdale reliable Republicans. In Montana, Missoula goes Democratic, Billings Republican. But an economic spurt or failure, a home-town candidate, or (usually) a combination of small factors, including shoe leather or lack of it by precinct workers or an attractive or scurrilous TV ad, can shift the balance. Swing states have traditional and perennial party allegiances within them. But it takes fewer oddities to shift purple Montana than, say, deep-red Kansas.

NEVADA

It is tempting to classify Nevada as a shifter like Oklahoma or Texas rather than a swinger, but Nevada has never decisively shifted from one party to the other. It has gone back and forth. Nevada was deep blue in the 1930s and 1940s. "Democrats enjoyed unprecedented rule: no Republican won statewide office in Nevada during Roosevelt's presidency [1933–45]," writes Michael Green, "and most competitive races took place in Democratic primaries."[33] FDR carried

Nevada all four times, most decisively in 1936 with 72.8 percent of the votes cast. As elsewhere, his margins slipped in 1940 and 1944, and Truman squeaked by in 1948 with 50.4 percent over Dewey. In the 1950s the state drifted toward redness over time, definitely so in the 1980s, but slid back—for some offices but not all—into blue or at least purple territory after the late 1990s.

The Democratic solidity of the 1930s did not, however, signify that Nevadans were particularly liberal or New Dealish. Senator Pat McCarran was a Democrat from Reno who was first elected in 1932 and reelected in 1938, 1944, and 1950. He died in 1954 of a heart attack, age seventy-eight, after compiling a thoroughly anti–New Deal record. Indeed, as chair of the Senate Judiciary Committee and the Internal Security subcommittee, he investigated the Truman administration for possible Communist infiltrators. McCarran had some responsibility for the Civil Aeronautics Act of 1938 that authorized the Civil Aeronautics Authority, but he is better known for the Internal Security Act of 1950 and the nativist McCarran-Walter Immigration and Nationality Act of 1952, both of which were vetoed by Truman (and which Congress overrode both times). McCarran was "a friend" in some sense of the Spanish fascist dictator Francisco Franco and the Chinese Nationalist leader Chiang Kai-shek, as well as the red-baiting Senator Joseph McCarthy. A much later and very different Nevada Democratic senator, Harry Reid, said about him, "Pat McCarran was one of the most anti-Semitic . . . one of the most anti-black, one of the most prejudiced people who ever served in the Senate."[34] Through patronage appointments, from having put many young Nevadans through law school, and many other constituent services, McCarran became perhaps the closest thing to a political boss that Nevada had seen in the previous several decades. His contemporaries, such as at-large congressman Walter Baring and his Senate successor and protégé, Alan Bible, were scarcely New Deal/Fair Deal liberals either.

Nevada and its politics were already in rapid flux, however, before McCarran left the scene. The state had legalized gambling in 1931 when it was flat broke. "Gaming" (the Nevada term for gambling) bailed out the state finances but did not yet transform the economy. That began when Bugsy Siegel opened the Flamingo, the first large casino-hotel, in December 1946 and launched the Las Vegas strip.[35] Many casinos and luxury hotels followed. By 1989 "the importance of gambling to the state was almost absolute." Of the gainfully employed in the state, more than two out of three had jobs in that sector, and in Clark County (Las Vegas and nearby) 78 percent.[36] Several western states benefited in population and economically after World War II from new military installations and other federal infusions, and Nevada was one of them—notably (but not exclusively) Nellis Air Force Base and the nuclear test site. Yet gambling, tourism, and the explosion of Las Vegas and Clark County were more decisive. People came from California and other nearby states, which were themselves growing almost as rapidly. The ethnic composition of Nevada also changed. Hispanics, often of Mexican origin, were 5.6 percent of the state's population in 1970; in 2010 they were 26.5 percent. African Americans increased from 5.7 percent in 1970 to 8.1 percent in 2010. Asians—many of them Filipino—rose from 0.7 percent in 1970 to 7.2 percent in 2010.[37]

Gambling and associated industries brought in tourists, conventions, but also permanent residents. Nevada led the nation in population growth rate for much of the late twentieth century. In 1940 it contained just over 110,000 people, but by 1950 it had added 50,000, then 125,000 more by 1960, another 203,000 by 1970, and so on. By 2000 there were just under two million Nevadans, and by 2016 about 2.9 million.[38] The electorate reflected this explosiveness. Roosevelt won Nevada's three electoral votes in 1932 with 28,746 popular votes. Eisenhower won them with 50,498 in 1980, and Reagan did so with 155,017 in 1980. In 2008, Obama won the by-then five electoral votes with 533,736 popular votes, a nearly twenty-fold increase over Roosevelt's vote in 1932. As of 2015, about half of the population were registered voters: 571,144 Democrats, 475,326 Republicans, 280,809 "nonpartisans," 68,412 "Independent Americans," 11,918 Libertarians, and 13,307 "other."[39] Democrats had always outnumbered Republicans as registered voters, but, as in other states, that often did not guarantee Democratic election victories.

Prior to the 1982 election, Nevada had a single at-large seat in the U.S. House. Its population explosion earned it a second seat starting in 1982, then a third from 2002, and a fourth from 2012. In 1950 the state elected a "cow county" Republican, Charles H. Russell, from Elko and Ely, as governor—one of the few from neither Washoe County (the Reno area) or Clark County. Russell was elected to the at-large congressional seat in 1946, but in 1948 he was upended by a conservative Democrat, Walter S. Baring, "an open and unashamed segregationist"[40] who lost to Republican Cliff Young in 1952 and 1954 but bounced back to win the seat in 1956 and every election until 1972, when he lost in the Democratic primary to the more liberal James Bilbray. Neal Peirce wrote that Baring "has the distinction of voting the most conservative line of any Democratic Congressman outside the South."[41] The U.S. senators in 1950 were McCarran and Republican George Malone, another deep-dyed conservative first elected in the Republican "class of 1946." Often referred to as "Molly," Malone voted for the Taft-Hartley labor law and "became a reliable vote for conservative orthodoxy in the Senate of the 1950s." He was too far right for President Eisenhower, who said in 1956 that Malone along with McCarthy and Indiana's William Jenner were three Senate Republicans he could not count on. Malone won reelection in 1952 but lost to Democrat Howard Cannon in 1958.[42]

Thus, in the early and mid-1950s, Nevadans sent to Washington strong conservatives or at least right-of center senators and congressmen, whether Democrat or Republican. They also elected and reelected Russell as governor and, by comfortable margins, Eisenhower as president. In his history of Nevada, Michael Green quotes an NAACP official who called Nevada "the Mississippi of the West." Its representatives' voting records bore that out, as did the fact that African Americans were not welcome as customers, or to the better-paying jobs, on the Vegas Strip. They could appear as entertainers but were "barred from the premises when offstage."[43]

The conservative grip loosened in 1958, when Grant Sawyer soundly put to rest, 60 to 40 percent, Governor Russell's attempt to win a third term. In the same election, Howard Cannon sank Malone's reelection bid by almost as large a margin. Sawyer, just forty when elected, claimed that "ours was a more liberal social agenda than either Democratic or Republican politics had advocated in this state up to our time." He was right. In office, he worked at prison reform, tightened gambling regulation, cooperated with Pat Brown (then governor of California) to protect Lake Tahoe, secured color-blind hiring for state jobs, and worked to open casino nonmenial jobs to minorities. He was publicly critical of J. Edgar Hoover's unauthorized wiretapping of casinos, and Hoover retaliated with a letter to the Las Vegas *Sun* advising voters to elect Sawyer's opponent in 1966, Paul Laxalt. Laxalt won, 52 to 48 percent. Sawyer lived another thirty years, practicing law, and he is well and fondly remembered.[44]

While Sawyer was governor, a bulwark of Nevada conservatism disappeared. The population influx had toppled Reno and Washoe County from their traditional perch as the largest population center in the state. Las Vegas and Clark County went in front. But Washoe and Clark together quite outnumbered the other fourteen counties, although those "cow counties" were vastly larger in area—great expanses of uninhabited desert or, at best, grazing land. Beginning in 1915 the state legislature operated under what was known as the "little federal system," which apportioned the assembly (the lower house) by population but gave each county one member of the state senate. The Supreme Court ended that system with *Baker v. Carr* (1962) and *Reynolds v. Sims* (1964), the one man, one vote decisions: both chambers had to be apportioned by population. The legislature, prodded by federal judges, grudgingly reapportioned, and the power of the "cow counties" evaporated, to be assumed by Washoe and even more by Clark.[45] After the 2010 census, almost three-fourths of the assembly seats were elected in Clark County.

As Sawyer was more liberal than Russell, Howard Cannon was certainly more liberal than Malone (as was nearly anyone), and in 1964, running for reelection, despite facing serious opposition from Paul Laxalt, Cannon voted to end a southern filibuster holding up the Civil Rights Act. He defeated Laxalt by forty-eight votes statewide.[46] Cannon was reelected twice more, in 1970 and 1976, by much more comfortable margins, finally losing in 1982 to Chic Hecht, who proved to be a rather colorless one-termer, "probably the least prepossessing member of the Senate,"[47] who had been helped by the still-potent Reagan glow of that time.

Laxalt, Sawyer's successor as governor, was a fairly right-of-center Republican, a good friend of California's new governor, Ronald Reagan, but not a troglodyte like George Malone. Laxalt promoted the Nevada State Council on the Arts, continued Sawyer's prison reform efforts, and supported higher gambling and sales taxes,[48] *talking* conservatively rather than rigidly *acting* conservatively, rather like his neighbor Reagan. Laxalt did not run in 1970 for a second term, resulting in his replacement by a Democrat, Mike O'Callaghan, who defeated Lieutenant Governor Ed Fike in the general. O'Callaghan would win a second term in 1974.

In that year, however, Laxalt reappeared, running for the Senate seat being vacated by Alan Bible. Harry Reid, from the Clark County village of Searchlight, at that point O'Callaghan's lieutenant governor and a former assemblyman, was the Democratic candidate. Laxalt's strength in northern Nevada was enough to edge Reid by 624 votes out of nearly 170,000.[49] Laxalt was reelected easily in 1980 but did not run again in 1986, instead devoting much effort to the national Republican Party and to Reagan's success. As historian Green writes, "Reagan had long coattails."[50] As of the mid-1980s, Nevada had voted twice—by roughly two to one margins—for Reagan for president; it had two Republican U.S. senators; the assembly had a Republican majority; and the more northerly of the now two House seats was safely held by Republican Barbara Vucanovich, a one-time aide to Laxalt who in seven terms (1983–97) compiled "one of the most conservative voting records in Congress."[51] Only the governorship was in Democratic hands, after Richard Bryan defeated incumbent Robert List in 1982. The once conservative Democratic state of the 1940s had swung toward the GOP.

But the Democrats bounced back, and they were not the old McCarran-Baring Democrats at all. Two-term congressman Harry Reid won the Senate seat being vacated by Laxalt in 1986. Governor Bryan, reelected in 1986, squelched Chic Hecht's reelection bid in 1988 to give Nevada two Democratic senators. Democrat Jim Bilbray won the 1st District House seat (within Clark County) vacated by Reid, and Bilbray would win three more terms until Republican John Ensign nipped him by 1,433 votes (of 152,000) in the Republican year of 1994, continuing Nevada's recurring habit of close elections. Bryan's lieutenant governor, Bob Miller, succeeded him in Carson City and was elected to full terms in 1990 and 1994, thus serving as governor, ultimately, for just over ten years.

In 1992, Bill Clinton won Nevada's electoral votes with 37.3 percent of the popular vote versus George H. W. Bush's 34.7 percent and Ross Perot's 26.1 percent, well above Perot's national average of 18.9 percent. A Perot disciple, Charles Woods, seriously threatened Harry Reid in the Democratic senatorial primary. But Reid won the general election easily, for the first of his five terms. His closest race—another Nevada nail-biter—was against then-congressman John Ensign in 1998, when Reid slid through by 428 post-recount votes. A Libertarian, a candidate of the Natural Law Party, and "None of the above" (a uniquely Nevada ballot option) together took 19,023 votes, far more than Reid's margin over Ensign.[52] At the turn of the century the governor was Republican Kenny Guinn, the senators were Democrat Reid and Republican Ensign (who successfully ran in 2000), the southern 1st District congresswoman was Democrat Shelley Berkley, and the northern 2nd District congressman was Republican Jim Gibbons. The state senate had nine Democrats and twelve Republicans; the assembly, twenty-seven Democrats and fifteen Republicans. The usually perceptive *Almanac of American Politics* was perplexed by Nevada; in 2004 it remarked that the state had "a basic Republican proclivity," but in 2010 it said that its "historic preference" was Democratic.[53] In fact, neither party dominated. The state was purple.

Nevada's population continued to expand and diversify. Historian Green points out that the first major Latino influx happened in the 1970s, causing their percentage to triple "from 1970 to 1990 and again in the next two decades. . . . Hispanic numbers [also] grew in Washoe County." Some were Cubans, some Puerto Ricans, the majority Mexicans. In the 1990s, "while southern Nevada's populace grew 83.5 percent, the Asian and Hispanic populations each grew by 260 percent." As in other states, minority populations did not fully translate into minority votes, but when they did they tended to vote Democratic. In 2008 the state Democratic Party carried out a massive registration drive, "boosting [its] lead from 12,000 to 111,000" over the Republicans; that earned Obama 76 percent of the Hispanic vote, 94 percent of the black vote, and 67 percent of voters under thirty, carrying both Las Vegas and Reno.[54]

In 2008, Barack Obama won the state by 55 percent over John McCain's 43 percent, and Obama did almost as well in 2012, winning by 7 percent. In 2012, 2nd District Republican congressman Dean Heller edged out 1st District Democrat Shelley Berkley by one percentage point for the Senate seat being vacated by John Ensign, and the by-then four congressional seats divided two and two by party. Republicans picked up a third in 2014, but in 2016 they split evenly again, with a UNLV political scientist, 1st District Democrat Dina Titus, winning for the fourth time and Republican Mark Amodei, Carson City lawyer, winning the 3rd District for the third time. Harry Reid declined to run for a sixth term in 2016, after years as Senate majority or minority leader, the highest- and longest-ranking Nevada senator ever. Catherine Cortez Masto, Reid's pick as his Senate successor, had served as state attorney general for two terms. She won the seat over 3rd District congressman Joe Heck.

In 2014, Republican governor Brian Sandoval was reelected in a 71 to 24 percent "landslide," and Republicans "swept to majorities in the legislature and in statewide offices." But "Sandoval's moderation is . . . causing tension with the GOP's tea party wing," observed the *Almanac*.[55] The evidence from recent elections is that Nevada remains a swing state.

To summarize Nevada's voting behavior since 1950 for the four top offices: of seventeen elections for president, Republicans won ten, Democrats seven (Kennedy, Johnson, Bill Clinton twice, Obama twice, and Hillary Clinton). Starting in 2008, the Democrat has won the three most recent presidentials.

There have also been seventeen elections for governor, each for a four-year term, in the even-numbered off years. Republicans won nine, Democrats eight. Republican candidates have won all five times beginning in 1998 (Guinn twice, Gibbons once, and Sandoval twice).

Twenty-four senatorial elections have taken place, from McCarran in 1950 to Cortez Masto in 2016. Of those, Republicans won seven, Democrats seventeen (including Bible four, Cannon four, and Reid five). Incumbents usually won, but sometimes not: Hecht beat Cannon in 1982, but Bryan beat Hecht in 1988. And there were those squeakers: Cannon over Laxalt in 1964 by forty-eight votes, and Reid over Ensign in 1998 by 428 votes.[56]

Nevada had one at-large House seat through the 1980 election. From 1982 through 2000 it had two districts—the 1st District essentially much of Las Vegas, the 2nd District the rest of the state. From 2002 through 2010 it had three, the 3rd being a peculiar Y-shaped district that included most of Clark County outside of central Las Vegas. From 2012 through 2016, a fourth district was split from the 3rd District and consisted of northern Clark County and several sparsely populated counties north of it.

From 1950 through 2016 there have been a total of sixty-three contests for House seats. Democrats won thirty-three, Republicans thirty. From 1950 through 1990, Democrats won eighteen, Republicans eight, but from 1992 through 2016, Democrats won fifteen and Republicans twenty-two. In the one-seat at-large era from 1950 through 1980, Democrats won thirteen, Republicans three (but the frequently winning Democrat, Baring, was very conservative, as stated above). From 1982 through 2016, of eighteen races in Las Vegas, Democrats won sixteen (Reid in 1982 and 1984; James H. Bilbray in

1986, 1988, 1990, and 1992; Shelley Berkley seven times from 1998 through 2010; Dina Titus in 2012, 2014, and 2016); Republicans only twice (John Ensign in 1994 and 1996).

Outside of central Las Vegas the results have usually been Republican or mixed. In District 2, all of the state except Las Vegas from 1982 through the 2000 election, Republicans won ten contests, Democrats none at all: Vucanovich won from 1982 through 1994, Jim Gibbons in 1996, 1998, and 2000. From 2002 through 2010, when the district no longer included any of Clark County and was most of the state north of it, Republicans again prevailed with five wins (Jim Gibbons 2002, 2004; Dean Heller 2006, 2008, 2010), Democrats none. From 2012 through 2016, when the district was still largely northern (anchored in Reno), Mark Amodei won in 2012, 2014, and 2016. In sum, of eighteen House races in northern Nevada since 1982, Republicans won all of them, much like neighboring Utah, Idaho, and northeastern California.

In District 3 surrounding Las Vegas (Y-shaped from 2002 through 2010, smaller but still including parts of Clark County from 2012 through 2016) there were eight contests. Democrats won two (Titus in 2008, Jacky Rosen in 2016), Republicans six (Jon Porter 2002, 2004, 2006; Joe Heck 2010, 2012, 2014). District 4, created after the 2010 census, has been won twice by Democrats (Steven Horsford 2012, Ruben Kihuen in 2016) and once by a Republican (Cresent Hardy in 2014).

COLORADO

Colorado's credentials as a swing state are considerable. It is today more bluish than most of the purple states, but if one looks at it across the entire period since 1950 one sees ebbs and flows. Certain regions within the state have voted consistently for either Democrats or Republicans, but the state as a whole has exhibited what could be called uncertainty, or unpredictability, or inconsistency. As Courtney Daum and her colleagues write in their book *State of Change*, "The big picture is one of considerable party balance. . . . Whereas Colorado was a red state for most of the past thirty years [since the 1970s], it has now [ca. 2009] become a distinct shade of purple."[57]

The 1950s, politically, were a time of center to center-right conservatism for both parties. Eisenhower defeated Stevenson handily in Colorado in both 1952 and 1956. The governorship went Republican when Daniel I. J. Thornton, a cattle breeder from the Texas Pan-handle, ousted the Democratic incumbent, Walter Walford Johnson, in 1950. Thornton was reelected for another two-year term in 1952 and he continued to focus on agricultural matters. The senators were Eugene Milliken, first appointed in 1941 to fill a vacancy, elected in 1942 to complete a term, and reelected to full terms in 1944 and 1950. In all, Millikin was a senator for sixteen years, which included ten as chair of the Republican Senate Conference and two as chair of the Finance Committee. He was a Republican stalwart. The other Colorado senator in the early 1950s was Democrat Edwin C. Johnson, often called "Big Ed," born on the Kansas frontier in 1884. An "intra-party critic of the New Deal," he was elected governor twice (1932, 1934), senator three times (1936, 1942, 1948), and governor again in 1954. His successor as senator was the steadfastly conservative Republican Gordon Allott, who served three terms until Democrat Floyd Haskell defeated his fourth-term bid in 1972 by 9,588 votes out of over 900,000 cast. He is remembered for the Colorado River Basin Storage Act of 1968, a positive measure for preserving and providing water for the state.[58]

Cosponsoring that legislation in the House was Democrat Wayne Aspinall, whose twenty-four years as congressman from the Western Slope (he was elected from 1948 through 1970) earned him the chair of the House Interior Committee. In that role, from 1959 until he left in 1973, he had more impact on the western environment than any other single individual, except perhaps Stewart Udall.[59] "All mining, public land, reclamation, and Native American legislation had to pass through the House Interior Committee" and thus survive Aspinall's scrutiny. He led the efforts in 1956 to pass legislation authorizing several dams on the Colorado River, including Glen Canyon; he "allowed the Wilderness Act to pass his committee" but with "safeguards to protect the interests of traditional users of western lands."[60] His strategies often ran contrary to environmentalist opinion, as it strengthened in the 1960s and 1970s. David Brower of the Sierra Club has been quoted as lamenting that environmentalists found "dream after dream dashed on the stony continent of Wayne Aspinall."[61] Aspinall lost out in the Democratic primary in 1972, which he "blamed . . . primarily on redistricting, which removed half of the Western Slope from his congressional district that year while adding thousands of voters in Denver suburbs."[62]

Officeholders like Democrats Ed Johnson and Aspinall and Republicans Gordon Allott and J. Edgar Chenoweth (who was elected to eleven House terms from the southeastern 3rd District) bestowed on Colorado's politics of the 1950s and 1960s a conservative, albeit bipartisan, cast. That began to change after 1970. Conservatism still reigned in 1962, when the very rightist Republican Peter Dominick was first elected, defeating one-term Democrat John A. Carroll, and Dominick would win another term in 1968.

But Dominick was defeated for a third term in 1974 by Democrat Gary Hart. By then, liberal Democrats were surfacing and winning. Beginning in 1972, anti–Vietnam War sentiment, plus strengthening environmentalism—national liberal issues that were reaching the Denver and Boulder areas especially—elected several Democrats, very unlike previous ones such as Big Ed Johnson. The string of Democratic victories included Floyd Haskell's over Allott in a very tight contest. Pat Schroeder won her first election to District 1 (Denver) in 1972, and she was reelected until she retired in early 1997, a respected and popular liberal feminist voice. Mid-roader Frank Evans won District 3 for the first time in 1964 but kept increasing his margins and even carried Colorado Springs in 1970, such was the Democratic tide. Richard Lamm won the governorship in 1974 and was reelected in 1978 and 1982, creating a slow-growth, restrained-development environmentalist record for himself. Also in 1974, Gary Hart ousted Peter Dominick by a healthy margin. Tim Wirth, future senator, defeated the five-term Republican Donald Brotzman in the 2nd District. Colorado continued to vote for Republicans for president, except for LBJ in 1964 and Bill Clinton in 1992, and they consistently did so until 2008. But 1972–74 was a turning point, from old-style conservatism to more liberal candidates and issues, at least among the Democratic candidates. Republicans made a comeback when, in 1978, Bill Armstrong limited Floyd Haskell to only one Senate term, and Republicans kept winning the 4th and 5th Districts, which included the northern third of the state from Utah to Kansas and the more affluent Denver suburbs.

And of course Ronald Reagan won the presidential electors in 1980 and 1984. The fairly pronounced liberal Democratic shift of the early 1970s lost steam during the 1980s, and by the early 1990s Republicans were, if not exactly back in the saddle, certainly competitive. Colorado had swung again, this time to the middle, even to the right.

Coloradans were partaking of national trends on both sides: environmentalism and opposition to the Vietnam War on the left, Reaganism and Reaganomics on the right. They were also participating in population growth, not on the scale of Arizona or Nevada, but much more than the Plains states east of them. From 1950 to 1980, Colorado grew from 1.325 million to 2.89 million, or 117 percent, and from 1980 to 2010, from 2.89 to 5.03 million, or 74 percent, plus another half million (10.2 percent) by 2016. Hispanics were 5.8 percent of the state population in 1980 and rose to 20.7 percent of the much larger population by 2010. The other minorities according to the 2010 census were African Americans at 4.0 percent, Asians at 2.8 percent, and Native Americans at 1.1 percent.

Much of the growth was in Denver city and county, which has almost always voted Democratic. But growth was even faster in Denver's suburbs. Jefferson County to the west, Adams north and east, Arapahoe east, and Douglas south were all major gainers in the 1950s and 1960s and later. Neal Peirce, writing just after 1970, noted that in Jefferson "most of its people are middle income and vote Republican," and Arapahoe "is big country club territory, mostly upper income, and gold plate Republican." Adams was "the home of more low to middle income people—craftsmen, factory and foundry workers." In general, "the new Denver suburbanites, drawn by scientific-type jobs and the climate, tend to be an extremely well educated lot. But their education is in engineering and other technical fields, not education of a humanistic sort. . . . Many of these people grew up in conservative plains states like Iowa, Missouri, Kansas, and Nebraska." Pueblo still had its steel mills at that time, with strong AFL-CIO unions, and thus was a center of Democratic strength.[63] Boulder, home of the University of Colorado, was another blue county, like many counties with university towns elsewhere. The ski resort places such as Aspen, Vail, and Telluride, all postwar developments, have generally been politically liberal. Not so the Western Slope including Grand Junction, which has voted for conservatives, as has Colorado Springs, with its military bases and retirees, the Air Force Academy, and other federal presence. The Springs' county, El Paso, has almost always voted Republican, thus forming a conservative pole south of Denver just as Boulder has been a liberal pole north of it.

The growth noted by Peirce around 1970 did not stop. "Overall, the Denver area grew by 12 percent from 2000–2007, but by far the most explosive growth was in Denver's outer suburbs (Douglas, Elbert, Park, Gilpin, Clear Creek, and Broomfield Counties), which increased by nearly 42 percent." Hispanic growth in these suburbs was a "phenomenal" 61 percent. Democratic precinct workers and candidates carried out "aggressive voter identification and registration campaigns" in these areas starting in 2008 and gained steeply in registered voters.[64] In 2013 the Denver-Aurora-Boulder combined statistical area was home to 3,277,309 people, 60 percent of the state's population. At that time, a demographer concluded, "Colorado's Front Range continues to show steady growth . . . with the most urban counties showing the strongest population growth."[65] The state's economy, once dominated by mining and agriculture, more recently shifted in the sparsely populated eastern plains to ranching, while the also people-thin Western Slope engaged in energy extraction and, in a few fortunate towns, ski resorts and tourism. Along the urban Front Range was the mixture of services, state and federal government and the military, schools and universities, and technology firms both high and low—the urban mix typical of western (and other) metropolises.

As a whole, however, Colorado was a swing state before 1980 and after, despite these county-level and regional commitments one way or the other. In the early 1970s, according to the *Almanac of American Politics*, "newcomers . . . repudiated civic growth-boosters" by "reject[ing] the Winter Olympics and vot[ing] out hawkish and pro-development politicians for Vietnam war opponents and environmentalists. . . . Colorado in the 20 years since [by the 1990s] has become a laboratory, not only . . . of leftish reform but also . . . of rightish initiatives."[66]

The 1980s were a bit more reddish than the anti-war and anti-Olympics 1970s, but hardly decisively so. The poll results were mixed. Slow-growth governor Dick Lamm was reelected in 1978 and 1982, and he was followed in 1986 by another Democrat, Roy Romer, who stayed in office into 1999. In 1978, Republican Bill Armstrong defeated Floyd Haskell (who had ousted Allott in 1972) for one of the Senate seats, and Armstrong won again in 1984. But Democrat Gary Hart was reelected in 1980. After six terms, Tim Wirth left his Boulder-based 2nd District House seat in 1986 to run successfully for the Senate seat that Hart was vacating. Wirth was active on a number of issues, but he became best known as an advocate of slowing climate change and of the Kyoto Protocol. In 1982, when Colorado first voted for its sixth House seat, the two parties split with three wins each: Democrats won the Denver, Boulder, and Pueblo/Western Slope districts, and Republicans took the eastern plains, Colorado Springs, and a "U around Denver," its newer suburbs. A pattern much like this was to hold for some years. In 1984 a Republican won the 3rd District, but he lost the next time to Democrat (still) Ben Nighthorse Campbell, a Northern Cheyenne, who won the House seat two more times, then succeeded Wirth in the Senate as a Democrat. Switching parties, he was reelected as a Republican in 1998. Democrat Bill Clinton carried Colorado in 1992 by a plurality, as Ross Perot took 23.3 percent, above his national average.

Nighthorse Campbell's victory in 1998 was part of a momentary swing to the Republicans at that time, which included Bob Dole's win over Clinton in 1996, Wayne Allard's capture of the other Senate seat in that year, and the division of House seats, four to Republicans and two to Democrats, in 1992, 1994, 1996, 1998, and 2000. Republican Bill Owens won the governorship in 1998 by a half percentage point (but he was reelected in 2002 by almost two to one). So Colorado arrived at the twenty-first century still a swing state. Democrats had held the governorship for over twenty years by 1994, three terms for the environmentally minded Lamm and three for the more education-focused Romer. After Nighthorse Campbell changed parties, both senators were Republicans. Democrat David Skaggs held the 2nd District congressional seat from 1986 (when Wirth ran for the Senate) through 1996, when Mark Udall succeeded him. When Patricia Schroeder retired in early 1997, Diana DeGette followed in the 1st District and has been reelected to it through 2016. But when Colorado gained its seventh House seat after the 2000 census, the division in the 2002 election was Democrats two (Denver, Boulder), Republicans five. The legislature as of 1994 was Republican, in each chamber by three votes. It was slightly more Republican in 1996 and 2004. The GOP lost control of the state senate in 2000 but won it back in 2002. As elsewhere, redistricting was much disputed. By 2008, Democrats were in the majority in both chambers.

George W. Bush took Colorado's electoral votes in 2000 and again in 2004. Governor Owens won reelection in 2002. Then began a slow, sporadic, but definite shift that produced Democratic victories for the major offices more often than not. Also in 2004, when Campbell retired from the Senate, Representative Mark Udall of the 2nd District began a run, but he quickly withdrew for a more electable candidate, state attorney general Ken Salazar.[67] Salazar defeated the strongly conservative Pete Coors, of the Coors brewing family, who had survived a bruising primary fight with another conservative over gay rights. Obama appointed Salazar secretary of the interior in early 2009, and Governor Ritter appointed Michael Bennet in his place. Bennet ran in 2010 for the rest of Salazar's term, won, and was reelected in 2016. Meanwhile, Mark Udall won the other Senate seat when Allard retired in 2008. Thus the Democrats in 2008–10 had won the electoral votes, the governorship, both Senate seats, and both chambers of the state legislature. But the split of House seats, which became three Democratic and four Republican in 2004, remained that way in 2006. In that year the result was four Democrats, three Republicans, and in 2008, five to two. The count swung back in the Republican year of 2010 to three Democrats and four Republicans and remained that way in 2012, 2014, and 2016.

In the first several elections after 2000, some of the Republicans running for Congress became noted for their right-wing stances. Marilyn Musgrave of the 4th (Fort Collins and the plains) was a strong social conservative; she was elected in 2002, 2004, and 2006 but was beaten by businesswoman and public administrator Betsey Markey in 2008. Markey, in turn, lost in 2010 to Cory Gardner, a state legislator who opposed emergency contraception and tax increases (proposing instead a state "rainy day" fund) and urged tighter control of immigration. Gardner won again in 2012, and in 2014 he successfully ran against Mark Udall and won that Senate seat. Again, Colorado was swinging. Another widely noticed Republican House member of that era was Tom Tancredo of the 6th District, "a self-described religious right Republican" who served five terms after his first election success in 1998 and won much attention for his exceptionally strong anti-immigration stands.[68] He ran unsuccessfully for governor in 2010 against John Hickenlooper, a Democrat who was reelected in 2014. For their part, Democrats of note included John Salazar, brother of Ken, who won the 3rd District in 2004, 2006, and 2008 but lost in the Tea Party year of 2010; and Ed Perlmutter, first elected in 2006 from the 7th (part of the Denver area—Golden, Aurora, Arvada east to the Kansas line), who continued to win through 2016.

One narrative about recent Colorado politics portrays Republicans in the ascendant in the 1990s, controlling the legislature and the congressional delegation, passing term limits and no-tax-increases-without-referendum initiatives. Then the Democrats made a comeback, "led by liberal entrepreneurs such as Jared Polis. . . . One of the 'Gang of Four,' a group of high-powered political contributors who financed the resurgence of the party. . . . The group nurtured a web of liberal activist organizations, framed issues, chose their targets shrewdly, and helped reshape the political landscape."[69]

Perhaps. Yet the Colorado Democrats of the 2008 vintage did not conquer all, to the degree that Henry Bellmon did in 1960s Oklahoma or that Monroe Sweetland achieved in Oregon even earlier. They did make sure that Colorado remained a swing state, this time leaning a bit to the blue side. A team of political scientists believe that the "Gang of Four" story "overemphasizes the importance of wealthy donors, minimizes the role of the state's Democratic Party, and largely ignores the failures of the Republican Party." Admittedly, the "Gang" conducted an "aggressive effort to oust Republican Marilyn Musgrave in the Fourth District," but they did not play "a significant direct role in the other federal races."[70] Polis became the 2nd District congressman in 2008 and remains there, joining DeGette and Perlmutter, but the other four Representatives are Republicans. The governor, Hickenlooper, and one senator, Bennet, are Democrats, but the other, Cory Gardner, certainly is not. Democrats did very well in 2006 and 2008, with Obama winning 61 percent and Udall 63 percent of the Latino vote. But in 2010, the Tea Party year nationally, Republicans gained most statewide offices in Colorado, except for the governorship, which went to the Democratic mayor of Denver, John Hickenlooper. The Republican nomination went to Dan Maes, who was "a Tea Party favorite," whereupon the bomb thrower Tom Tancredo jumped into the race as an independent, splitting the Republican vote, and Hickenlooper sailed in. From 2000 on, the legislature has seesawed back and forth between the parties; the membership elected in 2014 was closely divided.[71] In 2016, Hillary Clinton won Colorado's electoral votes.

To summarize Colorado's electoral behavior since 1950 for the four principal offices: From 1952 through 2016, Coloradans (like everyone else) voted seventeen times for presidential electors. The Republican candidate prevailed twelve times, the Democrat five times—Johnson in 1964, Bill Clinton in 1992, Obama in 2008 and 2012, and Hillary Clinton in 2016. Of the most prominent third-party candidates, George Wallace in 1968 won 7.6 percent of the state vote, all in the Denver district (District 1), and below his national average of 13.5 percent. John Anderson in 1980 won 11.0 percent, almost twice his national average of 6.6 percent. Ross Perot in 1992 took a hefty 23.3 percent share in Colorado, above his national figure of 18.9 percent. Thus Coloradans, compared to the rest of the nation, under-voted for the segregationist Wallace but overvoted for the centrists Anderson and Perot.

There have been twenty gubernatorial elections beginning in 1950: for two-year terms through 1960 and for four-year terms from 1962 on, with the elections taking place in the even-numbered, non-presidential off years. Of the twenty, Republicans won seven, Democrats thirteen, including the three most recent ones (2006, 2010, and 2014).

U.S. senators have been elected twenty-three times in Colorado beginning in 1950. Republicans won thirteen of those, Democrats ten. The Republicans were Eugene Millikin in 1950; Gordon Allott in 1954, 1960, and 1966; Peter Dominick in 1962 and 1968; Bill Armstrong in 1978 (defeating Haskell) and 1984; Hank Brown in 1990; Wayne Allard in 1996 and 2002; Ben Nighthorse Campbell (as a Republican) in 1998; and Cory Gardner in 2014, upsetting Mark Udall. The Democrats were John Carroll in 1956; Floyd Haskell in 1972, defeating Allott; Gary Hart in 1974, defeating Dominick, and 1980; Tim Wirth in 1986; Ben Nighthorse Campbell (as a Demo-crat) in 1992; Ken Salazar in 2004; Mark Udall in 2008; and Michael Bennet in 2010 and 2016. Incumbents have usually won reelection for this and other offices, but here are two instances of Democrats unseating Republicans and two of Republicans unseating Democrats.

In the U.S. House of Representatives, Colorado had four seats through 1970. A fifth appeared in 1972, a sixth in 1982, and a sev-enth in 2002. Of 185 races, Democrats won 94 (50.8 percent) and Republicans won 91 (49.2 percent). Neither party has ever swept all the seats except in 1964, when Democrats took all four in the year of the Johnson landslide. The most volatile years were 2002 through 2008; Republicans won five of the seven in 2002, then four in 2004, then three in 2006, and finally only two of the seven in 2008. In the four elections since then, however, the split has been three Democrats (the Denver, Boulder, and suburban 7th District) and four Republicans (the Western Slope, the plains, Colorado Springs, and the south suburban 6th District). Denver and Boulder (presently the 1st and 2nd Districts) have almost always gone Democratic, and the Western Slope did so in the 1950s and 1960s when Aspinall held it, until he lost the 1972 primary. Republicans have consistently won it since, along with the plains, Colorado Springs, and the south suburbs and exurbs (once Tancredo's district).

In view of this history, Colorado continues to be classified as a purple, swing state. Republican for president more often than not (though not lately); Democratic for governor (including the past three times), but Republican (slightly) for senator, and a very even division of the House delegation, although there has been much consistency in specific districts. Some are locks for Democrats, others for Republicans.

What tips the balance? Why might Colorado shift parties? Answers are more suggestive than scientific. One, the amounts of money raised by a candidate, or in his or her behalf, for advertising, organizing, and getting out the vote. Second, an avoidance of gaffes (not to mention scandals, financial or sexual) during a campaign, yet at the same time putting forth a program or positions on issues and selling them to the voting public. Third, conveying an attractive personality, especially on media—now, after 2016, including social media. Fourth, party backing—campaigning, canvassing, and turning out the voters. In some places (Boulder and Colorado Springs are obvious examples within Colorado) loyalties are so entrenched that upsets are rare and difficult. In others, demographic and economic shifts may underlie, and support, political shifts. Those are also rare.

NEW MEXICO

Nate Silver, the pollster and pundit, remarked after Barack Obama's 57 percent win in 2008 in New Mexico that "over the course of the last ten presidential elections" the state "has grown somewhat more Democratic, going from what I call a 'maroon' state (somewhere between red and purple) to an 'indigo' state (somewhere between purple and blue.)"[72] It is true that the shades have shifted slightly and subtly over the years, but in the context of the other eighteen western states we are looking at, and in the context of the two-thirds of a century since 1950, they are all shades of purple. New Mexico, depending on the timing, the national mood, whether there is an incumbent running, and for which office, remains one of the swing states, although one is inclined to agree with Silver that since 2000 it has swung more often than not toward Democrats. Looking farther back, however, victories for the four major offices were pretty evenly distributed between the major parties in the 1970s, 1980s, and 1990s. Still farther back, to the 1950s and 1960s, Democrats usually prevailed in Senate and House elections, Republicans for presidential electors, and the governorship caromed back and forth for several cycles. Just as Montana has not been consistently red enough to be classified with its neighbors Idaho, Utah, Wyoming, and the Dakotas, New Mexico has not been blue enough, over time, to be linked to Hawaii and Washington. It is, and has been, a swinger, a purple state.

Dwight D. Eisenhower carried New Mexico in 1952 and again in 1956, as he did every one of the then-seventeen western states. The governor at the time was Republican Edwin Mechem, a lawyer from Alamogordo who was first elected in 1950 and to another two-year term in 1952.[73] He attempted in 1954, but failed, to dislodge Clinton P. Anderson from the latter's Senate seat. But Mechem tried in 1956 to regain the governorship, and he did so, defeating the incumbent Democrat, John F. Sims (whom he had beaten in 1952). Mechem lost his reelection bid in 1958 to John Burroughs by less than two thousand votes, but he defeated Burroughs in 1960, thus becoming the fifteenth, seventeenth, and nineteenth governor of the state. Democrat Jack M. Campbell beat Mechem's reelection effort in 1962 and would himself be reelected governor in 1964. About two weeks after Mechem lost in 1962, U.S. Senator Dennis Chavez died, and Mechem had himself appointed to replace Chavez. But his bid for a full term was thwarted by Joseph Montoya in the 1964 election. During his Senate year Mechem voted against the 1964 Civil Rights Act. In 1970, President Nixon appointed him a federal district judge, which became his final office.

Beginning with Mechem's reelection as governor in 1952, and for the next nine elections, the office switched people and parties seven times. Democrat Jack Campbell served two two-year terms (elected 1962 and 1964), as did Republican David Cargo (elected 1966 and 1968). From then on, governors were elected to four-year terms. Bruce King was the first, and the first of four successive Democrats who served through 1986. He won a nonconsecutive term in 1978 and another in 1990. From the 1950s through the 1980s, impermanence marked the state's governorship, and after that term limits assured it.

New Mexico's two seats in the Senate were marked much more by incumbency and stability. Through the 1950s, Democrats Dennis Chavez and Clinton P. Anderson were the state's senators, and they served it well. Whether voters always realized how important seniority was in that day's Senate, some no doubt did, and that made it possible for senators from a state like New Mexico, with comparatively meager industry and small population, to bring home a substantial amount of federal dollars, for defense, for the Sandia and Los Alamos laboratories, for the three Interstate highways (25, 40, and 10), and much else. Chavez was elected to the House three times beginning in 1930 and was a senator from 1935 to 1962. Anderson was elected to the House in 1940 and 1942, was Truman's secretary of agriculture from 1945 to 1948, and was elected to the Senate in 1948, 1954, 1960, and 1966, retiring in 1973 to much acclaim. Chavez was typical of New Mexico Hispanics. Not many were recent immigrants from Mexico. Some, Chavez's family included, had arrived two or three hundred years earlier, when Nuevo Mexico was a province of New Spain; they had been there far longer than any Anglos. For them, they did not move northward—the border moved southward. Chavez supported higher education, farmers, Native Americans, and labor.[74]

Anderson was a first-rate public administrator who held a number of state offices during the 1930s Depression and streamlined postwar food and agriculture production and distribution when he ran the Department of Agriculture in the late 1940s. As senator he chaired the Committee on Aeronautical and Space Sciences—the space program—during the years that culminated in putting men on the moon. He chaired several other Senate committees in his twenty-four years there, and in Peirce's words Anderson took up "where Chavez left off the fight for atomic, space, and military installations in New Mexico"; overall, Anderson was "one of the most creative legislators ever to serve in Congress."[75]

After Chavez died in November 1962, Governor Mechem had himself appointed to fill the vacancy, as noted, but he lost reelection in 1964 to three-term congressman Joseph Montoya, who won a full Senate term in that year and another in 1970. Montoya lost to Republican Harrison Schmitt in 1976, the first Republican senator elected in New Mexico since Bronson Cutting in 1934. Schmitt proved to be a one-termer when Jeff Bingaman defeated him in 1982. Bingaman went on to be reelected until he retired in 2013, when he was succeeded by Democrat Martin Heinrich. Anderson chose for health reasons not to run again in 1972, and Republican Pete Domenici won the seat; he would be reelected five times, serving until 2009. "Domenici's great work in the Senate is on the budget," wrote the 1996 *Almanac of American Politics*, and he chaired the Senate Budget Committee for much of the 1980s and 1990s hawkishly, though not as severely as the Gingrich Republicans in the House.[76] In late 2002 he left Budget to become chair of the Energy and Natural Resources Committee, and there, as always, he was attentive to New Mexican interests.[77] He won his reelections by healthy margins, but in late 2007 he made clear that he would not run again in 2008. Tom Udall, Democrat, a cousin of Colorado's Mark, won the seat in 2008 and was reelected in 2014. Except for Schmitt, New Mexico's senators enjoyed reelection and were all Democrats except for Schmitt and the long-lived Domenici.

As of 1950, New Mexico was entitled to two seats in the U.S. House, and in that year and through 1966 both were elected at-large. Democrats easily outpolled the Republican contenders every time. But in 1968, when the seats were given geographic boundaries, Republicans Manuel Lujan won the 1st (northern) District, and Ed Foreman won the southern one.[78] The two districts were divided by a roughly horizontal line—with Santa Fe and Albuquerque, heavily Hispanic Rio Arriba County, and many of the Native American pueblos in District 1. The southern district included "Little Texas," with its oil and ranching counties and such towns as Hobbs, Roswell, and Gallup. Over time, the northern district would trend Democratic, although it elected Manuel Lujan from 1968 through 1986, and the southern one became dependably Republican.

As a result of the 1980 census, New Mexico became entitled to a third district. From 581,000 in 1950 the state reached a million in population in 1970 and jumped another 28 percent to 1.3 million in 1980; it kept growing, passing two million in 2010, of which over 900,000 lived in the Albuquerque Metropolitan Statistical Area. Roughly 42 percent of the state population in 2010 was non-Hispanic white, and about 47 percent was Hispanic, according to the census. When New Mexico got its third district, the state divided into three parts: District 1 was basically Albuquerque, Bernalillo County around it, and some adjacent desert areas; District 2 was roughly the southern half with "Little Texas"; and District 3 included Santa Fe and the Hispanic counties north and west of it.

Bill Richardson, future governor and presidential candidate and despite his Anglo name a Hispanic, was the first representative from District 3, elected in 1982 and each time through 1996, when he left to become U.S. ambassador to the United Nations and then secretary of energy in the Clinton administration. Tom Udall won that seat in 1998 and held it through 2006, giving it up to run successfully for the Senate in 2008. Democrat Ben Ray Lujan won it from then through 2016. After Manuel Lujan retired in 1988, another Republican, Steven Schiff, won District 1, the Albuquerque district, and held it through 1996, and another Republican, Joe Skeen, won District 2. From 1982 through 2006, every election returned two Republicans and one Democrat to the House. Democrats won all three in 2006, and since then District 2 has reverted to a Republican and Albuquerque and the north (over 50 percent Hispanic and Indian) have voted for Democrats—lately, Ben Ray Lujan in District 3 and Michelle Lujan Grisham (a cousin of Ben Ray and a niece of Manuel) in District 1. Pete Domenici is reputed to have observed once that New Mexico politics has three parties: Republicans, Democrats, and Lujans.

In the two-thirds of a century since 1950, New Mexicans voted nine times for the Republican presidential candidate, eight times for the Democrat. They have almost always voted for the national winner; exceptions were Ford rather than Carter in 1976, and Gore in 2000 (by 366 votes, when over 21,000 were cast for the Green Party candidate) rather than George W. Bush. They were not drawn to George Wallace in 1968 (who took only 7.9 percent in New Mexico but 13.5 percent nationally) yet were close to the national average for John Anderson in 1980 (6.5 percent in New Mexico, 6.6 percent nationally) and for Ross Perot in 1992 (16.1 percent versus 18.9 percent nationally).

The governorship, which was for a two-year term through 1968 and for four years from 1970 on, went to Republicans eleven times and to Democrats eleven times, in the twenty-two elections for the office beginning in 1950.[79] There were also twenty-two elections for U.S. senator. Of them, Republicans won seven (Schmitt once, Domenici six times) and Democrats fifteen—Chavez in 1952 and

1958; Anderson in 1954, 1960, and 1966; Montoya in 1964 and 1970; Jeff Bingaman in 1982, 1988, 1994, 2000, and 2006; Tom Udall in 2008 and 2014; and Martin Heinrich in 2012.

From 1950 through 2016 there have been eighty-six contests for House seats. When the two seats were run at-large (1950–68), Democrats won all sixteen times. When the two seats became geographic in 1970, a Republican (Manuel Lujan) won all six times in District 1 and a conservative Democrat, Harold Runnels, took District 2, the southern one, through 1978. Since then, District 2 has unfailingly gone to a Republican—sheep rancher Joe Skeen from 1980 through 2000 and businessman Steve Pearce from 2000 through 2016. When the state received its third seat, effective in 1982, the Albuquerque district (District 1) continued to go to a Republican through 2006 (Steven Schiff from 1988 through 1996, then Rhodes Scholar Heather Wilson from 1998 through 2006). The northern, Santa Fe–anchored District 3 has always been Democratic (Bill Richardson 1982 through 1996, Tom Udall from 1998 through 2006, and Ben Ray Lujan from 2008). Of the eighty-six House races beginning in 1950, Republicans have won thirty-nine, Democrats forty-seven. District 2, including "Little Texas," has gone to a Republican every time except 2008; District 3 has always been Democratic. Bernalillo and District 1 always voted Republican through 2006, but it has been Democratic from 2008 through 2016.

With this voting record, it is tempting to include New Mexico among the blue states. But Susana Martinez's two victories for governor recently and Skeen's and Pearce's firm grip on District 2 continue to qualify it as purple, although it has been the most bluish of the group of five. Definitely blue, however, are the two states that were once red but have become decidedly blue: Oregon and California. We go there next.

THE SWITCHERS, RED TO BLUE

5   Oregon Becomes (Usually) Blue

In the early 1950s, Oregon had been voting Republican at every level for some time. Political scientists called it a "modified one-party state," a term they also applied to Oklahoma. But Oklahoma was then Democratic, and Oregon was then Republican. It had "been the most strongly Republican state on the Pacific Coast since 1932."[1] Then Oregon changed. By 1957 both U.S. senators were Democrats, as were three of the four U.S. representatives. The 1960s brought something of a Thermidor as Republicans won back both Senate seats and two of the four House seats. But a gradual shift toward the Democrats continued. Democrats have won every election for governor since 1986, every presidential election since 1988, and four of the five House seats in every election since 1990 except 1994. Only one Republican, Gordon Smith in 1996 and 2002, won a senatorial contest since five-termer Robert Packwood resigned in 1995. Democrats have had majorities in both houses of the state legislature more often than not and have kept a healthy lead in voter registration. Like Oklahoma, Oregon has shifted its party allegiance, but in the opposite direction.

From the early twentieth century until the 1950s, Oregon's pervasive Republicanism had a peculiarly progressive character, and, to be sure, the state had not invariably voted Republican. Democrat Woodrow Wilson won a plurality for president in 1912, and Democrats won the governorship in 1902, 1906, 1910, 1922, 1926, and 1934—roughly half the time. Activist William S. U'Ren led a coalition of workers, small-business people, and agrarians to create the "Oregon System," a set of Progressive measures including initiatives and referenda, popular election of U.S. senators, woman suffrage (Oregon was the seventh state where women could vote), and primary elections—in short, "direct democracy."[2] The reform spirit took a harsh turn in the 1920s as the Ku Klux Klan became powerful for a time, but the main pillars of the Oregon System remained in place.[3] With an economy resting on extractive industry—lumbering and diversified farming—the state grew at a moderate pace from 414,000 in 1900 to 1,090,000 in 1940 and (reflecting a boom during World War II) 1,521,000 in 1950, faster than the national rate but considerably slower than the West as a region.[4] Observers remarked on the state's ethnic, economic, and cultural homogeneity and the weakness of its party organizations compared to states to the east.

Party labels sometimes defied stereotypes. Charles L. McNary served in the Senate for Oregon from 1918 to 1944, the last eleven years (the New Deal and World War II years) as Republican minority leader. In 1919 he supported the Versailles Treaty and the League of Nations, unlike most Republicans; in the 1920s he coauthored the McNary-Haugen farm relief bill; and in the 1930s he was a principal force behind the federally built big dams on the Columbia River. A liberal Republican he certainly was. Contrariwise, and far to the right of McNary, was Charles H. Martin, elected to Congress from the Portland district in the early 1930s and then to a term as governor in 1934. He was a reactionary, racist, anti–New Deal southern (in word and deed though not location) Democrat, defying that party label as McNary, in many ways, defied his.

Nonetheless, the state's Republican tincture in the early and mid-twentieth century was strong. In presidential elections the GOP candidate generally won every time before 1988, except for Wilson in 1912, FDR all four times, and Lyndon Johnson in 1964. After 1950, Oregonians favored Eisenhower twice; Nixon in 1960, 1968, and 1972; then Ford; and Reagan twice. But starting with Dukakis in 1988, the Democratic candidate prevailed, usually by a solid margin.[5] Democratic strength lay in the northwestern counties with the largest cities, particularly Eugene (Lane County) and the Portland metropolitan area (Multnomah and Washington Counties). In 2012, Obama carried only ten of the state's thirty-six counties, all of them in the northwest, but they had the densest and largest urban and suburban populations.

Beginning in 1950, Oregonians have voted for governor eighteen times, including the 2016 special election. Republicans took all but two through 1982, but Democrats have won every time from 1986. Democrat Robert Holmes won a special election in 1956 to succeed

Republican Paul Patterson, who died in office, but two years later the moderate Republican Mark Hatfield defeated Holmes, and he repeated in 1962. An even more moderate Republican, Tom McCall, won two terms over Democrat Robert Straub in 1966 and 1970. Straub's third run, in 1974, succeeded over Republican Victor Atiyeh. Atiyeh unseated Straub four years later and was reelected in 1982. Since then, the governorship has gone to a string of Democrats: Neil Goldschmidt in 1986, Barbara Roberts in 1990, John Kitzhaber in 1994 and 1998, Ted Kulongoski in 2002 and 2006, Kitzhaber again in 2010 and 2014. Kitzhaber resigned in February 2015 in a conflict-of-interest scandal, and Kate Brown, the secretary of state, succeeded him. She won a special election in 2016 to complete the four-year term.

Oregon's U.S. senators (even when Republican) have also been fairly moderate within the national context. Guy Cordon, whom Richard Neuberger defeated in 1954, was the last Oregon senator who was a hard-nosed conservative. Of the twenty-three elections for senator from 1950 through 2016, Democrats won ten and Republicans thirteen. Five of the Republican victories were by Mark Hatfield and five more by Robert Packwood. Gordon Smith in 1996 and 2002 had two, and Wayne Morse won in 1950 while still a Republican. Hatfield and Packwood were mid-road Republicans, and Smith, though a little farther right, was not a hard-liner. Toward the end of his first term, Smith was regarded as "one of the more moderate" Senate Republicans, with about a 55 percent conservative voting record; after he lost to Jeff Merkley in 2008 he was still called "moderate and pragmatic."[6] None of the three was as liberal as Wayne Morse, who after winning in 1950 became an independent, then won in 1956 and 1962 as a Democrat, or Richard (1954) and Maurine (1960) Neuberger, or Ron Wyden in 1998, 2004, 2010, and 2016, or Merkley in 2008 and 2014. Ever since Packwood resigned in 1995 and Hatfield retired in 1996, mainstream-to-liberal Democrats have generally won.

House races have followed a similar if sharper trajectory. In the early 1950s, Oregon had four seats and Republicans held all of them, or (in the 1954 election) three of the four. But never again did the GOP win more than two of four, or (after 1980) two of five. Since 1990, with the sole exception of the Gingrich "Contract with America" year of 1994, Republicans have won only one of the five: the huge desert-like 2nd District east of the Cascades. Meanwhile, the Portland area (District 3) and the two major university towns, Eugene and Corvallis, have trended increasingly Democratic.

It was not always thus. From the mid-1950s into the 1970s, observers often noted a persistent rural-urban divide in Oregon but downplayed its political significance.[7] Across the state, party registrations were fairly balanced through the 1960s, becoming more Democratic everywhere through most of the 1970s. But, since then, and especially after 1990, the breach has grown wider, with the south and southwest becoming more Republican (and more economically stagnant) while the Portland area, much of the Willamette Valley, and the north coast have become more strongly Democratic. By 2010, indeed as early as the 1990s, there existed "a dramatic political divide between different regions of the state."[8] A survey of the congressional districts reflects this.

In the northwest (District 1), Republicans A. W. Norblad Jr. (through 1962) and Wendell Wyatt (1964–72) won every two years from the late 1940s through 1972. Both were liberal in the Republican context; Norblad had union support. In 1974, the Watergate year, Wyatt retired and Democrat Les AuCoin won the first of nine terms. He ran in the 1992 Senate race but lost to Packwood. From then on, Democrats have prevailed in the 1st District: Elizabeth Furse (1992–96, though by only 301 votes of 242,000 in 1994), David Wu (1998–2010), and Suzanne Bonamici in a special election in early 2012 after Wu resigned, and for full terms that fall and since. Thus a district once solidly Republican edged Democratic over time, with some help from redistricting (which added some Portland-area precincts to it).

District 2 could hardly be more different. It is the only one in the state to have pulled to the right over time. It elected Republicans in 1950–54, but then Al Ullman, a Democrat, won narrowly in 1956 and kept winning, usually by large margins, through 1978. He even ran unopposed in 1972. As a member and ultimately chair of the House Ways and Means Committee and as author of a number of major tax and other fiscal laws, Ullman became nationally more important than perhaps any Oregon House member ever. He nonetheless lost in 1980, the anti-incumbent Reagan year, by less than four thousand votes of 291,000. Republicans have won the 2nd District ever since—fortified by redistricting in 1982, the disappearance of sawmilling around 1990 and the working-class votes that went with it, and later by an influx of conservative Californians into the newly developing resort area of Bend and Deschutes County. Economically, the 2nd has become more connected to Boise than to Portland, as the Boise trade area now "dominates eastern Oregon."[9]

The opposite trend marked District 3, basically the Portland area. From 1954 on, which saw the first victory of the redoubtable Edith Green, the district has unfailingly been represented by Democrats— Green through 1972, Robert Duncan (1974–78), Ron Wyden (1980–94), and Earl Blumenauer (1996 onward). Portland thus strengthened as a Democratic stronghold. As of 1974 the *Almanac* regarded it as "only a mildly Democratic city,"[10] but by the 1980s it "voted solidly Democratic in national and state elections"[11] and has done so since. The 3rd District is ethnically complex: as of about 2008, Multnomah and Washington Counties were home to 40 percent of the state's fast-growing Hispanic population, and Portland held nearly 40,000 African Americans.[12]

Through 1980, District 4 basically consisted of the south-central and southwest parts of the state. The addition of the 5th District in 1982 split the old 4th but retained a centrist complexion in both. The redistricting did, however, intensify the conservative shift of the 2nd District by putting Salem and some other moderate areas in the new 5th. From 1950 through 1980, the old 4th District switched parties five times, ending with Democrat James Weaver (1974–84). Peter DeFazio, Democrat, has won ever since, through 2016, usually by wide margins.

District 5, from its creation in 1982, has included much of the Willamette Valley south of Portland and a couple of coastal counties. The Valley had strong Republican traditions but was "prime marginal territory" by the 1980s.[13] Republican Denny Smith, formerly of the 2nd District, won in 1982 through 1988, but by only 707 votes out of over 222,000 in 1988 over Democrat Mike Kopetski. In 1990, Kopetski defeated Smith by ten percentage points and won again in 1992. A Republican won narrowly in 1994. Democrat Darlene Hooley defeated him in 1996, held the seat through 2006, and another Democrat, veterinarian Kurt Schrader, has won since 2008.

In sum, Oregon's House elections have seen a distinct rightward shift east of the Cascades (District 2), a distinct liberal shift in the much more populous Portland area (District 3 and parts of Districts 1 and 5), and a moderately leftward drift elsewhere, paralleling the state's electoral patterns for president, governor, and U.S. senator.

Oregon's economy and demography changed strikingly between 1950 and 2010. The economy of 1950 was extractive, from several sources: ranching in the east, farming in the Willamette Valley, fishing on the coast, and above all, logging and lumbering in the Cascades and Coast Ranges. These sectors, as always, were subject to outside market forces. The huge spike in nationwide mortgage interest rates in the late 1970s and early 1980s smothered home building everywhere, and the Oregon wood products industry suffered greatly. By the late 1980s, the once-bustling harbor at Coos Bay had fallen nearly silent.[14] Environmental restrictions on fishing and farmers' use of Klamath River water, and on cutting old-growth forests to protect the spotted owl, also took their tolls. Some of Oregon's extractive sectors shrank, though agriculture remained relatively strong.

The state's growth economy increasingly trended toward light manufacturing, led by the Nike Corporation's campus at Beaverton outside Portland and advanced technology in the "Silicon Forest" centered in Washington County, just west of Portland. Tektronix became the state's "largest public employer" from the 1950s through the 1970s, by which time other high-tech firms sprouted in the area. Intel, the leading manufacturer of computer chips, though headquartered in California's Silicon Valley, opened in Washington County in 1976. It kept expanding its operations and payroll, becoming in turn the "largest public employer" by 2000. By then the Silicon Forest was home to several hundred high-tech firms.[15]

These economic changes paralleled the red-to-blue shift in the state's politics. The governor elected in 1934, Charles H. Martin, was a nominal Democrat but an extreme conservative. Martin had a long army career and retired as a major general. At the close of World War I he was given command of an all-black unit with the assignment "to break the spirit of the troops and disabuse them of any notions of equality."[16] After the army, though a registered Republican, Martin entered the Democratic primary in 1930 and won a write-in campaign and then the general, and thus he was elected to Congress for the Portland district (District 3) in 1930 and 1932. In 1934 he won the governorship. He successfully sought federal money for the Bonneville Dam but then tried to turn it over to private power companies. In every respect (except seeking the dam money) he opposed the New Deal. Secretary of Labor Frances Perkins was, in his mind, the foremost "red" (i.e., communist) in the Roosevelt administration. Martin was rabidly anti-union and used the Oregon state police to spy on unions, public power advocates, and even state legislators. The Oregon Commonwealth Federation, formed in 1936 to promote public power, labor unions, and other liberal causes, was to the governor simply a "gang . . . of young Jew[s] . . . communists, CIO's . . . and crackpots."[17]

Martin was not typical of the Oregon Democrats of that day. He was ousted in the 1938 primary, the victim (he claimed) of "a vicious communist conspiracy."[18] The Democrat who beat him thereupon lost to the Republican, and Republicans generally ruled the roost through the 1940s. In 1952 they "slightly strengthened their control of the state legislature." Oregon, wrote one observer, "is practically a one-party state" in which the Democratic organization was "feeble," split between a group of New Deal/Fair Dealers and "a motley group of opportunists."[19]

Martin was sufficiently odious that he inspired a new generation to revivify the Democratic Party, starting in the late 1940s. The leader of the young newcomers was Monroe Sweetland, the executive director of the Oregon Commonwealth Federation from its founding in November 1936 until it was dissolved in 1942. Martin spied on the OCF and his agents red-baited it. But the OCF aimed at getting rid of Martin in the spring 1938 primary, and they succeeded, as state senator Henry Hess prevailed by seven thousand votes.[20]

During World War II, Sweetland served with the American Red Cross in the Pacific. On his return he and fellow Democrat Howard Morgan succeeded by 1950 in gaining a Democratic majority of Oregon's registered voters for the first time in the twentieth century. They did it by building on the influx of war workers and others who migrated into Oregon in the 1940s. It was a slow, uphill struggle. In 1946, Republicans swept all four congressional seats, the governorship, and other offices. Sweetland's strategy, as historian William Robbins describes it, was "to begin 'at the bottom and build up strong and appealing legislative tickets.' Only then was it prudent to move toward higher offices." Democrats slowly started winning elections; they increased their seats in the state senate in 1948 from four to ten and in the house from two to eleven.[21] They lost all four congressional seats again in 1950, winning statewide only the attorney generalship. But they captured a U.S. Senate seat in 1954 and, in 1956, the other

Senate seat, the governorship, three of the four House seats, and the state legislature.[22]

Sweetland won election to the Oregon house in 1952 and to the senate in 1954 and 1958. He lost races for secretary of state in 1956 (very narrowly to Mark Hatfield) and 1960. But he continued to play a major role in Democratic affairs, including time as Democratic national committeeman. He has been called "the father of the modern Democratic party of Oregon"[23]—playing a parallel role, in many respects, to Henry Bellmon's in Oklahoma during those same years. Otherwise, they were distinctly unalike.

The victories in 1954 of Democrats Edith Green in the Portland district and Richard Neuberger for the U.S. Senate reflected not only population change but also the salience of public versus private power as an issue. The incumbent senator, Guy Cordon, was a conservative Republican of that era. He voted for the Taft-Hartley law in 1947, against the 1949 NATO treaty, and for the Bricker amendment of 1954, which would have limited presidential treaty-making power. He was "a typical Taft-wing, pro-business, small-government isolationist," voting against the Senate's censure of Joseph R. McCarthy and opposing the push for a Columbia Valley Authority along the lines of the TVA.[24] Neuberger, in contrast, "was undoubtedly the most attractive and best-known personality the [Democratic] party had in its ranks in 1954." Already a nationally known writer on politics in the Pacific Northwest and other topics, he was an outspoken proponent of public power and supporter of Franklin D. Roosevelt.[25] Neuberger did not win by much—50.2 percent to Cordon's 49.8. His ten-point margin in Portland put him over. With Green's victory in a district that twenty years earlier had elected "Iron Pants" Martin, the rural-to-urban shift in population was underpinning a return to a more liberal state politics.

Two years later, the Democrats did even better. Wayne Morse, the former dean of the University of Oregon Law School, won his first election as U.S. senator in 1944 and was reelected in 1950—as a Republican. But he was very different from Cordon. In 1952, after Eisenhower chose Richard Nixon as his running mate, Morse resigned from the Republican Party and became an independent. For the next three years Sweetland and Morgan (state party chairman from 1952 to 1956) worked to pull Morse into the Democratic Party, and Morse edged ever closer.[26] In 1954 he supported Neuberger rather than Cordon, and in 1955 he formally became a Democrat. In 1956 he was reelected, handily defeating former Oregon governor and Eisenhower's secretary of the interior, Douglas McKay.

Though not the only issue in the 1956 election, the argument over public versus private power had become a "most acrimonious dispute," particularly concerning what kind of dam, or dams, ought to be built, and by whom, on the Snake River: the Hells Canyon controversy. McKay represented the Eisenhower and Republican position that there should be three dams, built and operated by the private Idaho Power Company. Morse and Democrats promoted a single publicly built and operated "high dam." Voters in the normally conservative easternmost counties supported Morse and public (cheaper) power.[27] The Snake River/Hells Canyon fight was the first of several in Oregon environmental politics. Later would come the cleanup of the Willamette River and state control of the Pacific beaches, both popular measures. Less popular and more difficult for Democratic regulators were statewide land-use controls, which won close majorities, and in the 1990s the spotted owl and Klamath suckerfish controversies.

The 1956 election was a Democratic sweep, with wins by Morse, Robert Holmes for governor, and three of the four House seats—Al Ullman in District 2, Edith Green in District 3, and Charles Porter in District 4. Democrats won a thirty-seven to twenty-three majority in the state house and tied Republicans in the state senate at fifteen each.[28] The state's "traditional Republican hegemony" was over.[29] Perhaps the best summing-up of the mid-1950s shift is by historian Robert Burton:

> Democrats [Sweetland especially] altered the Oregon political scene by advantageous use of local and regional issues, selection of attractive candidates, and detailed party organization; but their success in 1956 was also the result, in part, of a retreat of the Republican Party to conservatism. This move polarized the position of the two parties, and led to widespread realignment of individual allegiances. The combination of these positive and negative forces brought the political fortunes of the Oregon Democratic Party to flood tide in 1956.[30]

In four years the Oregon Democracy had gone from weak minority status to victory across the board. Much of the credit goes to Sweetland's organizational work, aided by Morgan. Neuberger and

Morse, much more attractive candidates than Cordon and McKay, helped greatly. An influx of new voters, the expansion of logging, and other demographic-economic factors also contributed crucially. Locals opposed the Eisenhower administration's private-power plans for Hells Canyon. Morse campaigned aggressively, taking liberal positions on power, farm parity prices, "foreign aid, enlarged defense appropriations, the United Nations, desegregation, repeal of the Taft-Hartley Act, federal aid for health and education," and more. McKay, in contrast, hunkered down behind a barricade of conservative positions supported by an ossified party organization.[31] In 1958, a Democratic year nationally, the Democratic congressional candidates won by even larger margins. Oregon "has become a true two-party state," wrote political scientist John Swarthout, a huge change from the past as recent as 1952—with one large exception: Republican Mark Hatfield won the governorship.[32]

Floods can happen suddenly, but they can also recede suddenly. Republicans in the 1960s made "a strong comeback," wrote observer Neal Peirce. They did it "not so much through organization . . . as through the [more] appealing personalit[ies] of their major candidates, all of whom represented a moderate and sometimes downright liberal Republicanism that was close to the winning Oregon mainstream."[33] A roaring feud between Morse and Neuberger roiled the Democratic Party, one that went back to when Morse was the law school dean and Neuberger was an undergraduate.[34] It did not end until Neuberger's premature death from cancer in early 1960. Hatfield's victory in 1958 was the first of two as governor, to be followed by five for U.S. senator. In 1960 a Republican defeated Porter in the 4th District, as Nixon carried the electoral vote over Kennedy.[35] The 1960s would bring less success to the Democrats than they enjoyed in the 1950s. Morse won his final six years in 1962. He was one of only two senators to vote against the 1964 Gulf of Tonkin Resolution, which President Johnson sought to justify sending American forces to Vietnam. Morse continued loud opposition to the Vietnam War, and in 1966 he supported fellow Vietnam critic Republican Hatfield's election. The Democratic nominee, 4th District congressman Robert Duncan, supported the war. The Vietnam issue thus divided both Democrats and Republicans in Oregon. Morse lost his own reelection in 1968 to Packwood and died while opposing him in 1974.

In 1966, as Hatfield segued from the governorship to the U.S. Senate, the ineffable Tom McCall became governor. Thomas Lawson McCall, a unique political figure, was the grandson of two turn-of-the-century arch-Republicans: Massachusetts congressman and governor Sam McCall (d. 1923) and the financial buccaneer Tom Lawson (d. 1925). In 1954, his first run for public office (for 3rd District congressman) failed when he was backed by, and promoted, private power, whereas winner Edith Green advocated public power development.[36] McCall, by then a political analyst with a following, subsequently did the same on his daily television show in Portland. In 1961–62 he produced a documentary, "Pollution in Paradise," on the degradation of the Willamette River, and it established his credentials as an environmentalist. He also was clearly a "liberal Republican," speaking out against the Oregon GOP's support of Barry Goldwater. In 1964 he ran successfully for secretary of state, and in that office he investigated the finances of the Oregon John Birch Society.[37] In 1966, as Governor Hatfield was elected to the Senate, McCall defeated Democrat Robert Straub for governor.

McCall's first legislative victory was the July 1967 "Beach Bill." Originally Straub's idea, it ensured state ownership of Pacific beaches from the tideline inland to sixteen feet elevation. He then turned to statewide land-use planning, "the single most important crusade of his life."[38] McCall engineered passage in 1969 of S.B. 10, requiring local governments to devise zoning plans by 1971. In 1973 he strengthened it with S.B. 100, his—and the nation's—most comprehensive statewide land-use law. That created the Land Conservation and Development Commission (known as LCDC). Perennial conservative attempts to weaken or repeal it failed, often narrowly. In 1971, McCall also secured the "Bottle Bill," the first state law to provide cash deposits on returned soft-drink and other bottles.[39] He was reelected in 1970 over the same Democrat (Straub) whom he had defeated in 1966. To be sure, McCall did not achieve these things all by himself. Hatfield, when governor, made a good start on controlling runaway developers, and two state senators, Democrat Ted Hallock and Republican Hector Macpherson, helped move the land-use law through the legislature. But without McCall's energy and showmanship these measures would almost certainly not have happened.[40]

Straub was the only statewide Democratic winner in 1968 (reelected state treasurer), as Republicans "continue[d] their resurgence begun in the early 1960s."[41] His and McCall's positions on environmental and other issues were very close, enough so that their joint campaign appearances were often called "the Tom and Bob show." McCall shunned the Republican label and distanced himself from Nixon and the conservatives running the state party organization. Straub, on the other hand, consistently made sure that Oregonians knew he was a Democrat.

Neither McCall nor Straub was an anti-development preservationist. Rather, they promoted industrial development (even nuclear in McCall's case) and more accurately deserve to be seen as progressive conservationists. Straub, as state treasurer and candidate for governor in 1966, proposed the Willamette Greenway Project to "turn the land along the river into a 220-mile-long park stretching from Eugene to Portland." Rather than oppose the idea, McCall adopted it.[42] According to Robbins, McCall's two terms as governor were "serendipitous, paralleling significant improvements in water quality in Oregon's major river and the completion of the last of the Willamette Valley Project dams." A print, radio, and TV journalist himself, the Fourth Estate liked him. "Articulate, good at creating the facile metaphor, and with an oversized ego," McCall spoke to the issues persuasively and loudly.[43]

Straub was the Democrats' choice for governor four times (1966, 1970, 1974, 1978) but won only once, in the Democratic year of 1974, defeating Victor Atiyeh. In that year Packwood won reelection, but otherwise, as an *Oregonian* headline read, "Oregon sweep [for the Democrats] is most lopsided since that of 1878." They carried the state house thirty-eight to twenty-two and the state senate twenty-two to seven. In District 4, just beginning to suffer long-term recession in lumbering, Jim Weaver beat four-term Republican John Dellenback. McCall suggested that the Republicans should change their name, for it had grown toxic.[44]

But Straub soon ran into problems. Lacking McCall's charisma, he was beset by the mid-1970s energy crisis, a drought in 1975, and a troubled economy. In 1978 he lost to Victor Atiyeh, a relative conservative in the Oregon context who had beaten McCall in the GOP primary. But Atiyeh was better funded and better organized.[45] Atiyeh won another four years in 1982, despite severe recession, and became floor leader for Reagan at the Republican National Convention in 1984. Yet he was no hard-core reactionary; he promoted new industries, tourism, a statewide food bank, and other measures. As the moderates Hatfield and Packwood kept winning reelection and Republicans held two of the five House seats, the Democratic high tide of 1954–60 was long past. The Vietnam War and then Watergate had divided the two parties and on balance benefited the Democrats in Oregon. However, the energy crisis, the strengthening of the Reagan Right, and perhaps the 1979 Iran hostage episode did not.

By 1980, Oregon had moved from one-party Republican to a definitely two-party state, no sure thing for either. Reagan won only 48 percent of Oregon's presidential vote in 1980 (Carter had 39 percent, and the independent John Anderson 9.5 percent), though Reagan would carry 56 percent of the 1984 vote. Another change in the state's politics was the beginning of east-west (and to a lesser extent north-south) polarization. A bellwether of this was the end in 1980 of Al Ullman's electoral run in District 2. No doubt Ullman had been helped in the 1950s and 1960s by his public-power position on Hells Canyon; his district bordered on the Snake River. He had staved off a "red shift" in eastern Oregon for years. After twelve terms, Ullman lost reelection in 1980. The public versus private power issue had faded; the lumber industry was entering bleak times as high mortgage rates inhibited home building; an independent may have siphoned off votes he would otherwise have won; Reagan conservatism was attracting rural voters; and Ullman's preoccupations in Washington appeared to have caused him to lose touch with his district, one of the hardest to reach from D.C. In hindsight, however, Oregon's 2nd District had started to behave more like Idaho just east of it than like the Portland area and the Willamette Valley to its west.

Oregon received a fifth congressional seat after the 1980 census, and revised district lines took effect in the 1982 election. The new district, which included state capital Salem and other counties in the mid–Willamette Valley, voted Republican until 1990 but (except for 1994) has been Democratic ever since. Meanwhile the 2nd District, which has included only counties east of the Cascades since 1982, became solidly Republican. The national liberal-conservative polarization that began as the Reagan Revolution took hold, reinforced in 1994 with Newt Gingrich's "Contract with America." Until 1986, Republican candidates often did well: Atiyeh in 1982 (his second term), Reagan in 1984, Hatfield in 1984, Packwood in 1986, and the 2nd and 5th District House candidates from 1982 through 1988.

In 1986, however, Neil Goldschmidt, a Democrat, former Portland mayor, Jimmy Carter cabinet secretary, and Nike executive, won the governorship over liberal Republican Norma Paulus. The office has stayed in Democratic hands ever since.[46] The 5th District went Democratic in 1990, and the Republicans have won only the 2nd since then. Goldschmidt oversaw "the Oregon comeback," the state's recovery from several years of recession as well as reforms of workmen's compensation laws and the prison system. He surprised many when he declined to run again in 1990, though he was considered a probable shoo-in for reelection.[47] The Democrats united behind the secretary of state, Barbara Roberts, though she was not expected to defeat David Frohnmeyer, the attorney general and Republican candidate.

But she did. Al Mobley, an independent candidate, took 13 percent of the vote, much of which would probably have gone to Frohnmeyer. And here the story turns to the rise of the Christian Right in Oregon. Social issues—anti-abortion and anti–gay rights—surfaced in the late 1980s, the first organized far-right movement in the state since the John Birch Society twenty years earlier. The movement emerged in 1986 to challenge Senator Packwood in the Republican primary because he opposed recriminalizing abortion. Its candidate, a Baptist minister named Joe Lutz, did not win but took 42 percent of the vote. Encouraged by that, Lutz and his lead staffer, Lon Mabon, created the Oregon Citizens' Alliance.[48] Lutz soon disappeared and Mabon became the face and sparkplug of the OCA. In 1988 the Alliance promoted Ballot Measure 8, to reverse Governor Goldschmidt's ban on executive-branch discrimination against gays, and it passed, 53 percent to 47. (The Oregon Supreme Court overturned it in 1993.)

The OCA's high-water mark came in 1990 when Mobley took enough votes from Frohnmeyer to allow Barbara Roberts to defeat him. It tried again in 1992 to pass another anti-gay measure, but it failed, 56 percent to 44. The vote revealed a definite urban-rural split; the measure carried twenty-one of the state's thirty-six counties, all but one of them in eastern and southern Oregon. Support was weakest among Catholics and Jews (though neither group was large) and voters with college or graduate education and strongest among "self-identified fundamentalist Christians" and voters with high school or less education.[49] The OCA did succeed in passing a number of measures at the county or local level, but the state legislature subsequently annulled them. It tried statewide ballots again in 1994 and 2000 and into the following decade but failed. As of 1993 the OCA claimed a membership of 3,500, plus 12,000 volunteers and a mailing list of 250,000.[50] But the Alliance faded away after 2000, following anti-discriminatory court decisions and an apparent lack of traction for abortion and anti-gay issues. Its efforts had proved that in the right circumstances Mabon and the OCA could pass, or come close to passing, a ballot measure, but they could not conceivably elect a statewide official or even win a Republican primary. At the same time that the Christian Right was cementing Republican dominance in Oklahoma, its strength in Oregon was limited to some control of the state house of representatives in the 1990s.[51]

Barbara Roberts, a diligent but not very popular governor, decided in early 1994 not to run again, facing a probable primary challenge from John Kitzhaber.[52] That did not reflect any weakening of Democratic ascendancy. Quite the contrary. Democrat Mike Kopetski won the District 5 congressional seat in 1990 and 1992, and (except for 1994) Democrats Darlene Hooley and then Kurt Schrader followed him there. Elizabeth Furse, a liberal Democrat, won the 1st District in 1992, 1994, and 1996 and was also succeeded by Democrats.[53] Packwood was reelected in 1992 (though opposed by OCA) over longtime 1st District congressman Les AuCoin but resigned in September 1995 after the Senate Ethics Committee exposed his perennial sexual harassments.[54] Oregon also lost its other five-term senator, Mark Hatfield, who declined to run in 1996. The national GOP had turned well to his right, and he was aging.[55] Gordon Smith, the Republican president of the state senate, ran in early 1996 for Packwood's seat (with OCA backing) but lost to Representative Ron Wyden. Smith ran again in the fall for Hatfield's seat and won, one of the rare people to run twice in one year for the U.S. Senate. In the primary, Smith beat Lon Mabon 78 percent to 8,[56] and he won a second term in 2002. Mabon ran then as the "Constitution" candidate and got 1.7 percent of the vote. Smith proved the exception, along with 2nd District congressmen, to Democratic dominance after the Packwood-Hatfield departures.

The state continued to change in a polarized but liberal majority direction. Counties dependent on extractive industries moved to the right. Coos County, for example, a once-leading lumbering area before the recessions and market shifts of the late 1970s on, was voting solidly Democratic in 1954 and was the only county in the Pacific Northwest to vote for George McGovern in 1972. Coos voters registered over two to one Democratic in the 1980s. But by the mid-1990s Republicans won almost every election there for president or governor. In the Portland area, on the other hand, a youth movement further liberalized voters and candidates. The historian Carl Abbott saw a "turnover of generations" in the half decade 1969–73, when "the average age on Portland city council dropped by fifteen years," with similar changes elsewhere in the metro area and the legislature. Neil Goldschmidt, mayor of Portland from 1973 to 1979, became "the chief architect and beneficiary of the political transition."[57] Another historian of Oregon, Robert D. Johnston, observed in like vein that "during the 1980s, conservatives took back the Oregon Republican party. Unlike in [Guy] Cordon's era, however, this move to the right led only to Republican marginalization."[58]

Underlying these political shifts were demographic changes. As Multnomah County grew from 471,500 in 1950 to 735,300 in 2010, Washington County just to its west—soon to become the home of Oregon's high-tech Silicon Forest—exploded from 61,300 in 1950 to 245,800 in 1980 to 529,700 in 2010. Clackamas County, to Portland's south, expanded almost as much. Lane County, home of Eugene and the University of Oregon, nearly tripled from 125,800 in 1950 to 351,700 in 2010; similarly, Marion and its county seat, Salem, the state capitol. Elsewhere, the only county with anything close to those growth rates was Deschutes on the eastern slope of the Cascades, whose ascent from 21,800 in 1950 to 157,700 in 2010 was built on tourism and retirees. Most counties in southern and eastern Oregon stagnated or declined in population between 1950 and 2010.

Environmental questions have played important roles in Oregon's politics. The Hells Canyon issue, on which Neuberger and other Democrats favored a single federally built high dam rather than three privately built dams, benefited their party. Conversely, the Fish and Wildlife Service's declaration in 1990 that the spotted owl was endangered and that their old-growth forest habitat on public lands could not be cut, as well as the shutdown of Klamath River irrigation in 2001 to protect suckerfish, strengthened the anti-federal leanings of southern Oregon conservatives. But neither of the latter issues deflected the state's liberal trajectory. The urban-rural split was real both demographically and politically.

A final key to understanding political changes in Oregon, and where they have differed diametrically from Oklahoma, is religion. Oregon, along with Washington and Alaska, has a higher percentage of people unaffiliated with any religious denomination than other states and regions. Two national surveys in 2001 reported that Catholics were the largest denomination in the Pacific Northwest, with over a million adherents—but they were only 11.3 percent of the region's population. Far behind in second place at 4.7 percent were Holiness-Wesleyan-Pentecostals. Altogether, the affiliateds were 37.2 percent of the population, and the "nones" (unaffiliateds) were 62.8 percent. Political independency—not being either a declared Republican or Democrat—is more frequent than in other regions; yet voter turnout has been high as a rule, no doubt aided by Oregon's pioneering of voting by mail only. Whether the relation is causal and not just coincidental remains to be shown, but it is worth considering.[59]

The Democratic candidate for governor in 1994, John Kitzhaber, was (and is) a physician whose *chef d'oeuvre* as a legislator was the Oregon Health Plan. It listed, in rank order of deservedness of aid, dozens of diseases and other medical problems. Against former District 5 congressman Denny Smith, Kitzhaber won by 51 percent to 42. He defended the Health Plan and was reelected in 1998. Ron Wyden, the District 3 congressman first elected in 1980, succeeded to Packwood's Senate seat in early 1996, defeating Gordon Smith, who then won Hatfield's seat in the fall. Wyden continued his liberal ways, whereas Smith proved to be a moderate conservative. Yet the two cooperated on a number of issues important to Oregon. Wyden won a full term in 1998 and was reelected in 2004, 2010, and 2016. Smith ran for a third term in 2008 but was beaten by Oregon house speaker Jeff Merkley, a liberal internationalist from a blue-collar family.

Kitzhaber won a second term in 1998. Another Democrat, Ted Kulongoski, followed him in 2002. His was a bootstrap story, starting with a childhood in a Missouri orphanage. He joined the Marine Corps at nineteen and after four years left for college and law school, then won several terms in the Oregon house and senate, two terms as attorney general, and spent five years on the state supreme court. His Republican opponent in 2002, Kevin Mannix, was outspokenly anti-abortion and anti–new taxes. Kulongoski won by a relatively narrow 49 percent to 46. He was reelected in 2006 by a firmer margin,

51 percent to 43, despite Oregon suffering through a tough recession following the bursting of the dot-com bubble.

Oregon's unemployment rate in 2010 was an above-average 11 percent. It proved to be a Republican, indeed Tea Party, year. Kitzhaber, the two-term former governor, won the Democratic nomination. No one had ever won a third term. Only Tom McCall in 1978 had even attempted such a comeback, and he lost in the primary. The Republican nominee, Chris Dudley, had never held elective office but was well known as a former center for the Portland Trail Blazers of the NBA. Kitzhaber eked out a narrow win, 49.3 percent to 47.8. Reflecting the relative moderation of Oregon Republicans compared to right-shifting Republicans elsewhere, Dudley was "not a Tea Party candidate" and was more like Atiyeh, "a cautious conservative rather than a right-wing flamethrower." Thus "he mirror[ed] Kitzhaber, 'liberal on social and environmental issues but pragmatic and cautious in terms of finance and governance.'"[60] At the same time, Ron Wyden was reelected senator by 57 percent to 39. Earl Blumenauer in the 3rd District and Peter DeFazio in the 4th won perennially by large margins; other Democrats were less durable but still solid winners in the 1st and 5th Districts.

By 2010, was Oregon thoroughly blue? Kitzhaber's victory that year was very narrow. In the state legislature, Republicans took both houses in 1994 and at least one house in 1996 through 2002, and the lower house was tied in 2010. A ballot measure to legalize marijuana was defeated in 2012, but another (Measure 91), permitting limited amounts to be grown and kept for personal use, passed in 2014. The rift between eastern Oregon and the rest of the state grew wider in the 1980s and 1990s, and "since 2000, it has been a chasm." Oregon, said the Almanac of American Politics, "has been a Democratic state over the past two decades, but not always by wide margins," and the electoral record bears that out.[61] Obama trounced McCain 57 percent to 40 in 2008 and did nearly as well over Romney in 2012 (54 percent to 42). Hillary Clinton outpolled Trump by 50 percent to 39 in 2016. Demographic shifts favor the Democrats in the future—the state is now over 12 percent Hispanic—as appears true nationally.

The shift in Oregon's politics over the past six decades has been palpable, but not quite thorough. The GOP still exists in the state, even though the OCA failed to capture it around 1990 and the Tea Party movement made only minimal inroads around 2010. In 2014,

Merkley won another term in the Senate with 56 percent to the Republican's 37 percent, and Kitzhaber was reelected governor but by only 49.8 percent to 44.7 percent for Richardson, the Republican. In 2016, Kate Brown was elected governor over Republican Bud Pierce, 51 percent to 44 percent. Incumbent Democrats won the usual four U.S. House seats and Republican Greg Walden won east-of-Cascades District 2 by his usual 72 percent. The 2015 legislature was solidly Democratic, by an eighteen to twelve majority in the senate and thirty-five to twenty-five in the house. Oregon had not become quite as deep a blue as Oklahoma had become red.

But, if not complete, Oregon's blue shift was real. The long-term explanations include, early on, the large influx of war workers and their families, many of them African Americans previously rare in Oregon, concentrated in the Portland area. Sweetland and Morgan built on that demographic change. Against their organizational efforts, the ossified, elitist Republican leadership in Portland and the equally out-of-touch Iron Pants Martin wing of the Democratic Party had little defense. From the 1940s seed-time came the 1950s Democratic swing. Morse's switch and Neuberger's 1954 victory over Cordon provided fresh faces with focus. The state's long-term economic changes also aided the Democrats: from a broad base in agriculture and forest products, the thrust turned to technology and light manufacturing, epitomized by Silicon Forest and elsewhere in the Portland metro area, while the old economy languished and low-paying service jobs eroded the one-time blue-collar base.[62] After 2000, once-dominant agriculture, mining, and logging had dropped to only one or two percent of overall state product. Organizational effort, better candidates, and secular demographic and economic changes underlay the shift in Oregon's politics. Oregon also enjoyed clean government, thanks to its "robust transparency laws"; it had the lowest rate of convictions for corruption by public employees of any state (1.28 per 100,000).[63]

6 California

Ever since California became a state in 1850, it has grown faster than any other, been more ethnically diverse, and remained the nation's dreamland from Gold Rush days through the end of the twentieth century. Nobody talked or wrote about a Texas dream or a Colorado dream, but many did about "the California dream." After Alaska and Texas it is the third-largest state in area, and in 1962 it passed New York as the largest in population. It even grew during the Great Depression: during the 1930s the entire national population increased by a historically low 7 percent, but California rose by 22 percent. That was less than half its growth rate during the 1920s preceding, and the 1940s following, but still more than any other state, a million and a quarter people.[1]

Population increase meant political expansion. California elected twenty-three people to the U.S. House of Representatives in 1950. The census of that year awarded the state seven more, to thirty. Every ten years brought additions, to thirty-eight after the 1960 census, forty-three after the 1970, forty-five after the 1980, fifty-two after the 1990, and finally (so far) to fifty-three after the 2000. The 2010 census was the first ever that did not add to California's congressional delegation. But neither did it reduce it. New York once led the nation with forty-five representatives. After the 2010 census it had (and has) twenty-seven, about half as many as California. The shift in political weight from northeast to southwest is largely the result of California's enormous postwar population growth.

The state's postwar political change was not only in the size of its congressional delegation but also in direction—a bumpy and incomplete, but gradual secular shift from Republican to Democratic. Beginning in the 1930s, more voters registered as Democrats than Republicans by a hefty margin, but that rarely translated into Democratic victories at the polls. A principal reason was a peculiar California electoral practice, begun in the Progressive Era, called cross-filing. Candidates could file for an office under more than one party label. Earl Warren, a Republican, cross-filed as well in Democratic primaries, with much success. Cross-filing ended in the 1950s, but until then it gave Republicans an advantage. Democratic registered voters outnumbered Republican ones, but as long as a candidate could run in both parties' primaries that candidate could run as a Democrat even though he (or rarely, she) was really a Republican. In the 1950s, candidates were required to state on the ballot the name of the party they really belonged to. Democratic votes then began to catch up with Democratic registrations, as Republicans feared.

THE BIG PICTURE AGAIN

California was widely and accurately known as a Republican state in the early and mid-twentieth century. Governor (later Senator) Hiram Johnson, who masterminded California's political progressivism, was a Republican, and no Democrat was elected governor from 1894 to 1958, with the sole exception of Culbert Olson in 1938. Republicans dominated state offices, the assembly (the state's lower chamber) and senate, and local government from the 1910s through the 1940s. In the 1920s, Democrats won only twenty-five of 555 elections, none to a statewide office.[2] From 1930 until 1958, California strongly trended Republican.[3] When Upton Sinclair ran as a Democrat in 1934 on his EPIC (End Poverty in California) platform and lost, he "propelled California's Democrats down a road that was well to the left of the New Deal, costing them in the process their chance to control the state."[4] The New Deal never had the transforming effect in California that it had in many other states, because Sinclair tarred it with the brush of socialism, whereas a little later the moderate Republican governor Earl Warren co-opted some of its more palatable features.

Permanent voter registration by party arrived in 1932, and from then through the decade Democratic registrants overtook Republican ones (in 1934) and outnumbered them by 60 percent to 36 percent in 1942. The Democrats' share slipped slightly through the 1940s and 1950s but never fell below 55 percent.[5] Despite this imbalance, Republicans continued to win elections. Weak and factionalized Democratic organizations were one reason. But, arguably, cross-filing was chiefly responsible. It did not end until the 1950s. Until then, California was a solidly Republican state in all of its politics and was known as such.

The political scene started to shift in the 1950s. To summarize what happened over the next sixty-five years, we start with the votes for president. Contrary to their party preferences for other offices, Californians voted four times for FDR and for Truman in 1948. Then, from 1952 through 1988 (except for the Johnson landslide of 1964), their electoral votes went to the Republican candidates. The most recent shift came in 1992, when Clinton won a plurality (Ross Perot won 20 percent, keeping both major party candidates from an outright majority). Since then, Californians have given majorities to the Democratic candidates, most recently to Obama by more than 60 percent in 2008 and 2012. Hillary Clinton easily won the state in 2016, outpolling Republican Trump by 4.3 million votes, 61.5 percent to 31.5 percent.

Fourteen elections for U.S. senator took place from 1950 through 1988. Republicans won eight of those and Democrats won six (four by Democrat Alan Cranston). Since then through 2016, beginning in 1992, Dianne Feinstein and Barbara Boxer won all nine of their elections, and when Boxer retired Democratic attorney general Kamala Harris won the seat easily in 2016. Feinstein's first victory, in 1992, was to fill out the two remaining years of Republican Pete Wilson's term, which he left early to become governor. She won a full six-year term in 1994. The Feinstein and Boxer wins in 1992 and 1994 were fairly close, but thereafter their margins were comfortable. Thus one sees a shift toward the Democrats in 1992–94, but not a complete one; Republican Pete Wilson was reelected governor in 1994.

The governorship has changed partisan hands several times since the 1950s, though the secular trend favored the Democrats, as it did in presidential and senatorial voting. In 1950, Earl Warren won his third term with a nearly two to one victory over James Roosevelt. After President Eisenhower appointed Warren chief justice of the Supreme Court in 1953, he was succeeded in Sacramento by Republican Goodwin Knight. But in 1958 the combination of an attractive Democratic candidate and a disastrous Republican campaign (explanation to follow) gave a resounding victory, 60 percent to 40 percent, to Edmund G. "Pat" Brown over William Knowland. Brown was reelected in 1962 over former vice president Richard Nixon ("You won't have Nixon to kick around any more"), and in the context of congressional and legislative success Pat Brown's two wins, especially the first, were a turning point. California was moving from consistently Republican to—if not consistently Democratic—clearly a two-party state in gubernatorial elections. Pat Brown's win in 1958 was hailed as seismic, but his defeat for a third term by Reagan in 1966 cast doubt on that.

Of the seventeen contests for governor from 1950 through 2014, Republicans won nine and Democrats eight. With the exception of Republican Arnold Schwarzenegger in 2003's special election and then in the regular 2006 election, Democrats have won all of them since 1998. Earlier, of the twelve from Warren in 1950 through Wilson in 1994, Republicans won eight (Warren, Knight, Reagan twice, Deukmejian twice, and Wilson twice) and Democrats four (Pat Brown twice and Jerry Brown twice).

California's delegation to the U.S. House of Representatives grew ever larger with each census except 2010, as noted earlier. Republicans held a majority through 1956. But beginning in 1958—and that year could firmly be called a turning point with regard to House elections—Democrats have predominated, a few times by only two seats, but by 2014 and 2016 by twenty-five seats (thirty-nine Democrats, fourteen Republicans). On several occasions, control of redistricting, as federal censuses kept awarding more seats to the state, contributed to the Democrats' growing majorities. But even aside from that, the state's coloration became more and more blue.

Half of the California senate's forty members are elected in presidential years, and half in even-numbered off years. Republicans held clear majorities in the elections of 1950 through 1954. But after the 1956 election the senate split evenly, twenty Democrats and twenty Republicans. The 1958 result, when Pat Brown swept in, gave the Democrats their first clear majority, twenty-seven to thirteen. That became thirty to ten, the largest Democratic majority ever, as a result of the 1960 election. Republicans came back to within two seats in 1966, when Reagan was elected governor the first time, and actually won a two-seat majority in 1968. But that was their last. Since 1974, the (im)balance has been steady at twenty-five Democrats, fifteen Republicans, give or take a seat.

The eighty members of the assembly likewise contained Republican majorities from 1950 through 1956. Democrats have won control ever since, except for 1968 and 1994, when Republicans outnumbered them by one or two seats. Usually, however, since 1972 Democrats have held clear majorities of at least six seats and several times by as many as twenty or twenty-five. If there was a clear turning point, it was 1958, with less dramatic jumps in the 1970s and from 1998 onward.

Thus, the overall trend in California's elections for president, senator, governor, the U.S. House, and the two chambers of the state legislature, over the past sixty-five years, has been a shift from dependably Republican to dependably and deeply Democratic. Exceptions, as noted, have occurred, and thoroughly red Republican areas continue to exist.[6] The red-to-blue shift was not sudden or even complete.

Nor has the shift in partisan voting necessarily meant a shift from conservative to liberal. California has been famous for hippies, religious cults, celebrity divorces and multiple marriages, and other non-mainstream behavior. On the Right, it has been home to the John Birch Society and to less extreme but still very conservative enclaves in Orange and San Diego Counties, the mountain north, and lately the Central Valley. But the flamboyant few have garnered more than their share of media attention, and Californians are more accurately regarded as the moderate many. Earl Warren was a (moderate) Republican; Pat Brown was a (moderate) Democrat. Neither was extreme.

That said, we should note another form of voting behavior besides elections to public office. Voters also make choices on ballot initiatives, or propositions.[7] Often they have not contributed to California's liberal image and Democratic leanings. A prominent example was Proposition 14 in 1964, which reversed the Rumford fair-housing act passed the previous year by the legislature and signed by Governor Pat Brown. As Congress was passing the Civil Rights Act of 1964, a majority of Californians voted in the opposite direction. Proposition 13 of 1978 is the most famous and far-reaching initiative, drastically cutting property taxes and in effect defunding many state and local government services and programs. Prop 18 and others in 1994 were aimed at immigrants. There have been others less startling but, all told, ballot initiatives have often supported the observation that although California was becoming dependably Democratic it was not dependably liberal. A more accurate word to describe the state's politics is centrist, and so it has been since Earl Warren.

THE WARREN YEARS, CROSS-FILING, AND PAT BROWN

Earl Warren, the future chief justice, graduated from college and law school at the University of California at Berkeley. After U.S. Army service during World War I and five years as deputy city attorney of Oakland, he served as district attorney of Alameda County (which includes Oakland and Berkeley) from 1925 to 1939. In 1938 he cross-filed on both major party tickets for attorney general of California and won. In 1942 he was elected, again cross-filing, for the first of three times as governor of California. Warren grew up in, and imbibed, the spirit of California's Progressive Republicanism that had been put in place by Hiram Johnson (governor 1911–15 and senator from then until he died in 1945). The California Republican Party in the post-Johnson years included a very conservative wing. But with Warren as governor the watchword was "moderate activism rather than extremism."[8] Anti-communism was a very strong issue around 1950; Los Angeles Democratic senator Jack Tenney succeeded in outing "left-wingers" in 1950, but his influence was waning by 1952.[9] Richard Nixon played the red card successfully in his senatorial campaign of 1950 against Helen Gahagan Douglas, whom he called "the pink lady." Hollywood screenwriters and actors were investigated by the U.S. House Un-American Activities Committee, and many were then blacklisted. Warren mainly stayed above all this.

Warren was certainly "a loyal and effective Republican,"[10] and he was instrumental in creating the California Republican Assembly (CRA) in 1934 as a device to promote progressive candidates, since the formal party organizations were then forbidden by law to support specific candidates in their primaries. As a parallel organization but independent of the party itself, the CRA could—and was created in order to—promote primary candidates of the moderate Warren stamp, and thus to thwart the Far Right of that day. The CRA produced a broad supporting cast for Warren, and while he was governor from 1943 to 1953, the years of war and recovery, "a massive industrial war economy came into existence, regulated by a vastly enlarged governmental apparatus," including public works and "a vast investment in state-funded higher education."[11] Conservative interests such as the state medical association and chamber of commerce were not toothless, however, and after the war they shot down Warren's attempt to create state-supported medical insurance.

Warren portrayed himself as above the partisan fray, and he largely succeeded. Cross-filing was one of the reasons.

Cross-filing, enacted in 1913, was one of Hiram Johnson's major ways of weakening political party machinery. In its 1913 session, the legislature considered two bills concerning primary elections. One went to Governor Johnson's office. His staff added a cross-filing provision. As passed and signed by Johnson, it stated, "Nothing in this act contained shall be construed to limit the right of any person to become the candidate of more than one political party for the same office." The next legislature, in 1915, carried nonpartisanship further by omitting party labels from the names of candidates on ballots for state offices. Cross-filing favored Republicans and Progressives for the next twenty years, since they outnumbered Democrats until migrants from the South, black and white, began arriving in large numbers in the 1930s. Even when Democratic voters outnumbered Republicans by significant margins, familiarity with Republican incumbents kept many of them in office through cross-filing. Earl Warren cross-filed and won; it is said that many voters thought he was a Democrat. But Pat Brown cross-filed too, when he ran for state attorney general in 1950 and became the only Democrat elected to statewide office that year.[12]

By then, opposition to cross-filing had gathered force. In 1952, Democrats with labor support managed to qualify a ballot initiative repealing cross-filing. Republicans "recognized how dangerous" the initiative would be to them and proposed a measure keeping cross-filing but providing that candidates would show their party affiliations. Repeal failed, but the party label measure succeeded, and party labels started appearing on ballots in the 1954 election. From then on, Republicans' almost automatic electoral success started to ebb.[13] By 1959, Democrats had won majorities in the state assembly and senate, and they then repealed cross-filing altogether. As of the late 1940s, cross-filing had had "a devastating effect on the Democrats," even though Democrats outnumbered Republicans in voter registrations 2.9 million to 1.9 million. By the late 1950s, its weakening, then abolition, had a similar effect on the Republicans.[14]

Another, more grassroots movement breathed life into the California Democracy. When Adlai Stevenson of Illinois ran for president on the Democratic ticket in 1952, he lost to Eisenhower. But his liberal message and soaring, cerebral oratory inspired Democratic activists around the country and throughout California. Up to then, the Democrats' "base" was largely the membership of the labor unions in the state's aircraft and other defense-related industries. Immediately after the November 1952 election, young liberals outraged by Stevenson's defeat began forming "Adlai Clubs." By the time of the next election two years later, "425 local Democratic clubs with some 30,000 members" served as foot soldiers and provided financial support.[15] The 1954 election was also the first to have candidates identified by party label because of the partial rollback of cross-filing. In addition, liberal Democrats, led by Alan Cranston and others, had met in January 1953 at the Asilomar conference center at Pacific Grove on the Monterey Peninsula and laid the groundwork for a Democratic organization paralleling Earl Warren's California Republican Assembly. The new body, called the California Democratic Council (CDC), was formalized in November 1953.[16] It functioned for nearly twenty years as a liberal force—at times too liberal for some Democrats—nominating and backing candidates for state, local, and congressional offices in primaries and general elections, which the regular Democratic organization was statutorily prevented from doing. The CDC resembled in some ways the "Super PACs" that developed after 2010, but it could play a much more open and direct role in electioneering as well as fund-raising. The clubs, the party labeling, and the CDC became a triple threat to the state's longtime Republican hegemony.

Organized labor also became a key part of the Democratic base. Southern California, especially, had been a bulwark of anti-unionism through much of the early twentieth century, led by the *Los Angeles Times*. But the new defense industries were unionized. The rabid anti-unionism of the *Times* and the LA corporate leaders who supported it weakened as defense industries organized and the New Deal's Wagner Act took hold. The result was the revival of "the long dormant Democratic Party."[17]

These elements were aided by a disastrous Republican campaign in 1958, which produced a smashing Democratic victory. William F. Knowland, conservative Republican, was minority leader of the U.S. Senate. In early 1957 he let slip that he did not plan to run for reelection in 1958. His only stated reason at that time was his, and his wife Helen's, desire to leave Washington and go home to California. Many suspected Knowland of presidential ambitions, and it soon became clear that he planned to run for governor, presumably a better stepping stone than senator to the presidential nomination. The problem was that another Republican, Goodwin Knight, was the incumbent governor. Knowland, scion of the family that owned the *Oakland Tribune*, warned Knight that if he tried to be reelected his financial and party support would dry up. Vice President Nixon also supported Knowland and "wanted peace in his home state's party."[18] The upshot was "the Big Switch." Knowland would run for governor, and Knight would seek his vacated Senate seat.

Meanwhile, the Democrats produced a formidable candidate, Edmund G. "Pat" Brown, the state attorney general and the only Democrat to win any statewide office in many years. The primaries resulted in Brown versus Knowland for governor and Knight versus Democrat Clair Engle for senator. Also on the ballot that year was a right-to-work initiative, and Knowland threw his weight behind it. Helen Knowland, his wife, circulated a pamphlet by far-right Joseph Kemp calling labor leader Walter Reuther, the UAW president, "the man who plans to rule America." Kemp's pamphlet, and Helen Knowland's involvement, were seen as a "virulent" attack on Reuther.[19] The unions were energized by the right-to-work threat, and Brown, who condemned the pamphlet, used his prerogative as attorney general to retitle the proposition "Employer and Employee Relations" rather than the tendentious "Right to Work."[20] The CDC mobilized, and Brown defeated Knowland in the general election by 60 percent to 40. Engle beat Knight, 57 percent to 43. The anti-union Proposition 18 also lost by a 60 to 40 percent margin.[21]

If 1958 was not a historic turning point, it certainly changed fortunes for the Democrats, who, with the Brown and Engle victories, also won majorities in the assembly, senate, and congressional delegation. Once inaugurated, Brown believed he had a reform mandate and acted on it. The legislature passed thirty-five of Brown's forty significant proposals, a remarkable achievement that surpassed even Warren's or Hiram Johnson's.[22] Cross-filing completely ended. Racial discrimination in the job market ended, with a state Division of Fair Employment Practices created to enforce the principle. The famous California Master Plan for Higher Education, devised by Brown's classmate and by then president of the University of California, Clark Kerr, created the three-tier system of the University of California, the California state colleges, and two-year community colleges around the state. Brown devised a massive public works project, the California

Water Plan, to build a system of aqueducts and dams to bring water from the north, where it was plentiful, to the parched Central Valley. The cost of all these measures, and they were only the most visible of many new or expanded programs, was met by new taxes, resting on the state's exploding population and prosperity.

Brown's many proposals sailed through the legislature not only because he was a popular leader but also from the efforts of the chair of the Assembly Ways and Means Committee (and, from 1961, speaker), Jesse Unruh, a massive man and a primal force. The people approved of all this government action, and the 1960 election produced an unprecedented thirty to ten Democratic majority in the state senate and a repeat of 1958's forty-seven to thirty-three Democratic margin in the assembly. Favorite son Nixon, however, squeaked by Kennedy, 50.3 percent to 49.7 percent, in the presidential race.

THE SIXTIES

Toward the end of Brown's first term, perceptive observers were noticing a few stress fractures among the California Democrats. Party regulars were not at ease with CDC people; the unions were not always eye to eye with club movement activists. Through the 1964 election these were not serious or crippling. One historian writes that "the years between 1959 and 1963 were to see a radical transformation of the political landscape in California, with landmark legislation in fields ranging from civil rights to higher education to natural resources and to the rights of welfare recipients. The Brown administration and its allies in the legislature enacted an impressive legislative program that dramatically expanded the reach of the state."[23]

At that point, the Democrats were further strengthened by decennial reapportionment. California, the new census of 1960 found, deserved an additional eight seats in the U.S. House. Republicans had controlled the 1951 redistricting and thoroughly gerrymandered it to their own benefit. Now the Democrats had complete control of the legislature and the governorship, and it was time for payback.

The person in 1961 who would decide where those seats would be was assemblyman Bob Crown of Alameda County, with the help of "political technicians specializing in knowledge of census tracts." Jesse Unruh hired them. Unruh, assemblyman from Los Angeles and chair of the Assembly Ways and Means Committee, was itching and inching to become speaker. The state's population had increased by

50 percent since the 1950 census, much of it in Southern California. Crown and Unruh engineered what one observer called "one of the most significant gerrymanders ever conceived," resulting in the speakership for Unruh and the Democrats' capture of the eight new congressional seats mandated by the 1960 census.[24] California's congressional delegation shifted from sixteen Democrats and fourteen Republicans to twenty-five Democrats and thirteen Republicans. The GOP never again held a majority.[25] Unruh, with his almost overwhelming personality, was becoming (if he wasn't already) the most powerful member of the assembly, and in 1961 he did become assembly speaker and "turned it into the second-most powerful office in the state" until he left in 1969.[26] Willie Brown, the assembly powerhouse of the 1980s and early 1990s, entered the assembly when Unruh was speaker, and "over the years, Speaker Unruh and I also became friends. . . . Unruh taught me quite a lot. . . . He really was imaginative about using the gears and levers of power. He believed in re-machining things, not in just operating the levers. . . . Most [politicians] just want to do deals. I learned from Unruh that you could shape the game itself."[27]

The Crown-Unruh gerrymander of 1961 was an irreversible turning point. Combined with Pat Brown's landslide and the Democrats' comfortable capture of the assembly and senate in 1958, California was clearly no longer the Republican majority state of old. At the very least, it had become a two-party state. But how solid and permanent were the Democrats' gains? By no means had it become a one-party blue state. The 1961 gerrymander made a difference in the congressional delegation, but the Democrats' commanding lead in the legislature began in 1960, before the gerrymander. It could be overcome in the right circumstances.

Running for a second term in 1962, Pat Brown campaigned on his record of moderate Democratic liberalism, championing organized labor, welfare measures, and education. Former vice president Richard Nixon, his Republican opponent, resurrected the anti-communist, "subversive" issue that had served him well in his 1950 Senate race against Helen Gahagan Douglas. But that no longer resonated except among pockets of far-right strength, notably (but not exclusively) Orange County, headquarters of the John Birch Society. Brown won a clear victory over Nixon, 52 percent to 47 percent, ratifying his win of 1958. As historian Jonathan Bell writes, this was a time of "consolidating the political program of the California Democratic Party and . . . establishing a clear delineation between the parties on ideological grounds and preparing the ground for a major assault on inequities in access to economic resources" as well as aligning the Democratic Party with interest groups and convictions about individual rights, especially regarding "race, gender, and sexuality."[28] This would develop in a few years into championing of minority, women's, and gay rights.

The Democrats' espousal of minority rights did not wait long. Building on the federal Fair Employment Practice Commission Act of 1959, in 1963 the California legislature passed the Rumford Act, named after the African American assemblyman from Berkeley, Byron Rumford. Formally titled the "Fair Housing Act of 1963," it outlawed discrimination by race or ethnicity in home sales and purchases, and thus segregation and ghettoes. The act passed by large majorities in both chambers. In short order, the California Real Estate Association denounced it, claiming that such state interference in the free housing market was statist, socialistic, and un-American. The realtors were able to place a repeal proposition—Proposition 14—as a constitutional amendment on the 1964 ballot, and the voters approved it, 65 percent to 35 percent. The realtors' arguments were ingenious: support of the measure was support of freedom, not discrimination.

The fallout did not gratify the liberal Democrats, or African Americans, nor did the aftermath. In 1965 the Watts district of Los Angeles erupted in riot. Prop 14, "in the minds of many . . . played no small role in the black alienation that culminated in the Watts riots."[29] The California supreme court in 1966 and the U.S. Supreme Court in 1967 did not accept the realtors' argument and declared the amendment unconstitutional. The Rumford Act stood, but so did the memory of Watts. Also disquieting for the Democrats was the considerable support that unionized workers gave Prop 14. The liberal coalition had cracks. They would appear again in the 1966 gubernatorial election.

Factionalism and feuds bedeviled the Democrats during Brown's second term. The Rumford Act and Prop 14 divided segments of the Democrats' nascent base. External events, especially unrest at UC Berkeley in late 1964, just in time for the fall election, worked against Brown when he tried to cope by using the California Highway Patrol to disperse student protestors. The contest for U.S. senator was divisive when the terminally ill incumbent, Clair Engle, died on July 30. Who would be the party's candidate? Brown appointed Pierre Salinger, former press secretary to President Kennedy and newcomer to California politics. The CDC's favorite was Alan Cranston, the state controller. Salinger prevailed, but the split between the regular party (Brown, Unruh) and the CDC, whose leader, Si Casady of San Diego, was "an implacable foe of the Vietnam War" and therefore of President Johnson and Pat Brown, was widening.[30] The regular party and the CDC "had always coexisted uneasily, but now the break threatened to fracture the Democrats' hold on power."[31] Salinger lost in November to George Murphy, a Hollywood song-and-dance man, by a slim but clear margin.

In 1965 came Watts, a polarizing disaster for the Democrats and further support for the Right's "law and order" issue. Speaker Unruh, up to then Brown's good right hand in the assembly, had understood Brown to say in 1962 that he would support Unruh for governor in 1966. When Brown denied this and looked to run for a third term Unruh was profoundly offended. He continued to work with the governor, but in 1965 and 1966 his support cooled.[32]

Besides the disruption of Watts and the simmering Unruh-Brown disunion, on top of tension between the CDC and the regular Democratic organization, the Supreme Court's rulings on one man, one vote revised electoral politics. The first and more famous ruling—*Baker v. Carr* in March 1962—had little effect in California because the assembly "seemed to meet the population standard." But in December 1964 came *Reynolds v. Sims*, which mandated that both chambers "had to be apportioned on a one-man, one-vote basis."[33] The effect was to radically change the state senate.

Historically, the California senate's forty seats had been distributed by geography, with none of the fifty-eight counties getting more than one senator and a few counties combining to become one senatorial district. The absurd result was that Los Angeles County had one senator, and three counties in the High Sierras—Inyo, Mono, and Alpine—had one senator representing their 15,000 people. LA County's sole senator represented 6,500,000 people, thus producing a ratio of about 440 to 1.[34] After the California senate effectuated the Supreme Court ruling in 1965, the 1966 election redistributed its seats radically, throwing the balance of power to the eight counties of Southern California and away from northern and rural counties.[35]

The Democrats did not immediately or obviously benefit from the shift—in fact they lost seven seats in 1966. But that was in the context of the 1966 election, and the redistricting would help them down the road.

Brown's try for a third term was weakened in three ways before he even faced the Republican challenger. First, conservative Democratic mayor Sam Yorty of Los Angeles picked a primary fight against Brown. In a "personal and vindictive" campaign, with Yorty "strongly inferring that Brown was supported by Communists" and Brown calling Yorty "a right-wing 'fright peddler,'" Yorty won Orange County, almost won Los Angeles County, did well in the Central Valley and even in the Bay Area. Brown won statewide, but only by 1,355,262 votes to Yorty's 981,088, a poor showing for an incumbent, revealing that "anti-Brown sentiment was both statewide and preponderantly conservative." Second, Unruh's dudgeon continued, weakening Brown's support down to the precinct level. And third, disagreement over the Vietnam War, and the Johnson administration's conduct of it, split the CDC so badly that its "once Messiah-like fervor . . . had long been dissipated."[36]

The Democrats' fractures along with the external events of Berkeley, Watts, and elsewhere positioned the Republicans well in 1966. With much justice, it has been written that the passage of the Rumford Act in 1963, and other measures of Pat Brown's governorship, were the high-water mark of postwar Democratic liberalism—and that the capture of the California Republican Assembly by the hard Right marked the start of a Republican comeback. Not only did Reagan become governor, but Republicans won five of the six statewide offices and picked up five senate and seven assembly seats—though not enough to regain majorities—and three more congressional seats. With such a victory in 1966, it was clear in retrospect that Brown's and the Democrats' landslide in 1958 was not a complete turning point after all. But neither would 1966 prove to be a complete reversal of the Democrats' gains of 1958 to 1964. The nearly two to one victory of Prop 14, in the context of ongoing Democratic majorities in the legislature and the House delegation, revealed that California voters continued to be, at root, fairly moderate—or confused, or racist, or simply manipulated by signature seekers with clever rhetoric.

Ronald Reagan, fifty-five years old in 1966, had never held elective office and had been a registered Democrat until 1962. He had been

president of a labor union—his union, the Screen Actors' Guild—
and had led it effectively against some of the biggest Hollywood film
moguls. He had also emcee'd a weekly TV show, *The General Electric
Hour*, for several years beginning in 1954. GE also sent him around the
country to speak to its thousands of workers—on behalf of the company and its pro-business, anti-union stance, as developed by com-
munications vice president Lemuel Boulware. Reagan thus became
a spokesman for, and a believer in, "Boulwarism."[37] He had been a
strong anti-communist since the 1940s, when he detected communist
influence in Hollywood. Consistent with that, he became a prominent
conservative by the mid-1960s, though he was careful not to be identified with the hardest Right, the John Birch Society. Conservative leaders within the California Republican Party correctly identified him as
the ideal candidate to defeat Brown in 1966.

In the 1966 Republican primary, Reagan demolished a more
moderate candidate, San Francisco mayor George Christopher, 68
percent to 32 percent, demonstrating "his appeal to a much broader
spectrum of Republicans" than Goldwater had won two years earlier. The political public relations firm that guided Reagan's campaign had him stress three issues: "morality" (versus the New Left,
filthy speech, unwashed hippies in Berkeley); "taxes, spending"; and
"incumbency" (that Brown was a spendthrift and had been in office
too long).[38] The election was, as Matthew Dallek has written, "the
right moment" for Reagan. Unruh came out for Brown late in the
campaign—too late—and Reagan won by a margin close to Brown's
of 1958. As Dallek writes, "Reagan could not possibly have beaten
Brown prior to 1966; only civil rights [Rumford], Berkeley, Watts,
and Vietnam made it possible. It was Reagan's promise to arrest moral
decline that won him a million-vote victory."[39] A California Poll just
before the election showed a sharp drop in Brown support compared
to 1958 and 1962 among labor union members and their families and
among voters with less than high school education. Reagan owned the
law-and-order issue, as did the Republican Right in later years when
Reagan was gone. In 1966 he certainly captured the moment and
carried in with him nearly every Republican candidate for statewide
office. He reduced the Democrats' margins in the legislature (by six
assembly seats and seven senators) to "razor-thin majorities."[40]

Some regard 1966 as another turning point, reversing 1958.
California was not reverting to the pre-1958 Republican dominance,

however, and the election did not undo all the things that Brown did. As one observer concluded, "The Reagan administration would prove to be less of a 'decisive turning point' than its political spin doctors wanted Californians to believe. [It] did, however, represent the coming of age of a new party system in California in which each of the two main parties would become associated more categorically with a particular political worldview."[41] As governor, Reagan did not achieve a thoroughly conservative enactment of that worldview. He did cut some expenditures; he did fire Clark Kerr as university president, "whom conservatives had long seen as sympathetic to campus demonstrators" (though the demonstrators hardly thought so).[42] But more state dollars eventually went to the universities, and Reagan "acceded . . . to a substantial income tax increase." A state budget officer later termed Reagan "an evangelist, not a doer"—he said the right conservative things but did not pull back everything Brown had done.[43] Ideology was deliberately designed to replace pragmatism in the administration of public affairs, and so it appeared, as he cut the state's mental health program. But many costs were fixed or nearly so, and by the end of his first year, and in following years, Reagan had to move toward the center to "seemingly become a pragmatic politician."[44] Yet the conservative rhetoric continued. E. J. Dionne summed up Reagan's governorship as well as his presidency succinctly: "Reagan was an ideologue in his speeches, particularly before he became president, and he really believed the conservative gospel. But he was also intent on being both successful and popular. He would test limits, but not push beyond them if the political traffic would not bear what he had originally hoped for. This was obvious when he was governor of California."[45]

In 1968, Nixon won California by about three percentage points over Hubert Humphrey, with George Wallace winning 6.7 percent of the vote, about half his national level. Republican conservatives made some striking gains, winning majorities (albeit by only two or three seats) in the assembly and senate. Republican U.S. senator Thomas Kuchel, a moderate who had managed to remain aloof from his party's conservative wing and win election in 1956 and 1962, lost in the primary to outspokenly conservative Max Rafferty, the superintendent of public instruction. But Rafferty lost in the general to Alan Cranston, who would go on to win in 1974, 1980, and 1986. The conservative swing had limits, and Democrats maintained their twenty-one to seventeen edge in the congressional delegation.

THE SEVENTIES

In 1970 the Democrats lost one congressional seat but regained the assembly and senate majorities they had lost, very thinly, in 1968. George Murphy, the Hollywood friend of Reagan who was elected to the U.S. Senate in 1964 over Pierre Salinger, lost his reelection bid by ten percentage points to John V. Tunney, another Southern Californian, son of one-time heavyweight boxing champion Gene Tunney and law school roommate of Senator Edward M. Kennedy. Murphy strongly supported Nixon, Kissinger, and the Vietnam War; Tunney advocated withdrawal. For that and other reasons, Tunney won handily. He would, in turn, lose reelection in 1976 to S. I. Hayakawa, essentially on the law-and-order issue, as Hayakawa was best (and almost solely) known for facing down demonstrators when he was president of San Francisco State College.

Another conservative lost reelection when Rafferty, who had lost to Cranston in the senatorial race in 1968, lost reelection as superintendent of public instruction to his deputy, Wilson Riles, an African American. Rafferty had been a standard bearer of the Right; did his loss mean the voters were liberal after all? And in a contest with significance for the future, Pat Brown's son Jerry became secretary of state.

The main event in 1970, however, was Reagan's reelection campaign. Reagan faced no primary challenge. Among Democrats, Jesse Unruh sought the nomination for governor that Pat Brown had kept from him in 1966. Unruh's only serious rival was Sam Yorty, who ended up capturing less than half the number of votes he won against Brown in 1966. Unruh's major problem was his own recent record. He had dominated the assembly as speaker but had made some disastrous moves, including once locking in the assembly to force a vote. His last-minute support of Brown in 1966, his perennial distance from the CDC, and a capacity for making enemies as well as friends shook away Democratic elements (and moneybags) whose support he might have expected and surely needed. The result was an easy win for Reagan, though it was by about half the margin he enjoyed in 1966. Unruh never came close.[46] But Reagan proved to have no coattails this time, as shown by Murphy's loss and the failure to capture the assembly and senate, and thus the hope of controlling redistricting following the 1970 census. Liberalism in the style of Pat Brown or of the CDC no longer flourished, but conservatism à la Reagan, or

Nixon, not to say the John Birch Society, was not the people's choice either.[47]

Unruh, after his defeat in the 1970 governor's race, retreated from the legislature. In 1974 he ran and was elected state treasurer, a hitherto "bookkeeping office" that he, typically, made into a nexus of financial power through its oversight of state investments and pension funds. He held the job until he died of prostate cancer in summer 1987. He was such an outsized figure, both in personality and physique, that his withdrawal created something of a power vacuum, to be filled by a new cast of characters who led the California Democrats for the next fifteen to twenty years. First among them was Phillip Burton, who had been a major force in the assembly and then as leader of California's congressional delegation. In both roles he dominated redistricting in 1971 and 1981, making himself a founder of what became widely known as "the incumbent protection plan."

Burton, like Unruh, was a force of nature, with immense and not always smiling energy and possessing, as the title of John Jacobs's biography of him aptly states, "a rage for justice." Both men were Democrats, but there the resemblance stopped. Burton and Unruh had been rivals, and leaders of different factions, since they were undergraduates at the University of Southern California in the late 1940s. Unruh ran for the assembly from Hawthorne, a working-class suburb of Los Angeles, and was elected on his third try in 1954. Phillip Burton was elected to the assembly in 1956 on his second try from a San Francisco district that included North Beach, downtown, South of Market, and Chinatown. His campaigns "exemplified how a direct appeal to local constituencies and organizations of citizens could overturn the dominance of a small party elite."[48] For example, with the help of a Chinese American law school classmate, Burton "created a constituency in Chinatown that had never before existed," broadcasting campaign literature in Mandarin, identifying and stressing the issues that spoke to the people there—civil rights, immigration, "firecrackers—religious issue," a childcare center, and pensions for noncitizens.[49]

Burton stayed in the assembly until he was elected to the U.S. House in 1964, where he had a remarkable career, leading the creation of the Golden Gate National Recreation Area and always promoting support for the less fortunate. By 1976 he was chair of the Democratic caucus and ran for majority leader. He lost to Fort Worth's Jim Wright by one vote.[50] He remained in the House, where he was instrumental again in redistricting after the 1980 census. He died suddenly of a ruptured abdominal artery in the spring of 1983. His younger brother John was a trusted aide as an assemblyman from 1965 to 1974 and then as congressman from an adjacent San Francisco district from 1974 until 1983. John Burton returned to the assembly from 1988 to 1996 and then was a senator until he was term-limited out in 2004. By then his protégée Nancy Pelosi was distinguishing herself in Congress.

Another major Democratic figure was the aforementioned Willie Brown, an African American from San Francisco. First elected to the assembly in 1964, Brown rose to become speaker in 1980, which he remained through the ensuing decade until he was term-limited out in 1995. Thereupon he was elected mayor of San Francisco for two four-year terms. A "college buddy" of John Burton, Willie Brown "remembered idolizing Phillip Burton" yet regarded Jesse Unruh as his "friend and mentor."[51] Willie Brown could walk a tightrope and make it seem like an interstate highway.

But we are getting ahead of the story. Reagan's second term, 1971–75, found him at odds with the legislature. He did what he could to limit government by executive action. But, according to the pollster Mervyn Field, "he ha[d] polarized Democrats, the education and welfare people, state employees, and even some Republicans. What he offered was style—the citizen on detached duty—but there was an implied promise that he would solve problems. When he didn't, it created trouble."[52] The *Almanac of American Politics* concurred several years later. Reagan

> wanted to make California like Disneyland's Main Street, but it ended up in some respects looking more like Haight-Ashbury. He came to office in 1967 preaching against the drug culture and student rioting. He left the governorship in 1974 with marijuana, abortion, and pornography essentially legalized and the values of the student generation being propagated by the media and spreading to all groups. He came to office as an opponent of civil rights legislation. Yet when he left office there was a black mayor of Los Angeles, elected over conservative opposition.[53]

In the assembly, John Burton and Willie Brown thwarted Reagan's draconian cuts to old-age assistance and aid to dependent children.[54]

During Reagan's second term, in the early 1970s, redistricting and the 1974 election cemented the Democrats' strength. Although the CDC and the club movement that began in the 1950s "collapsed and died,"[55] Phil Burton and his allies held control over the five new congressional seats that the 1970 census was awarding to California. In the general election Democrats won three of the five, and eight more assembly seats. The redistricting stayed in effect only for the 1972 election, because Governor Reagan vetoed the plan in early 1973, throwing the issue to the state supreme court. Yet what the court decided benefited the Democrats even more, and in 1974 they won five more congressional seats, giving them a decisive twenty-eight to eighteen edge, plus a twenty-five to fifteen advantage in the senate and a fifty-three to twenty-five majority in the assembly.[56] These results were not simply due to redistricting. Watergate and the backlash from it not only forced Nixon from the presidency but benefited Democrats nationwide. In California, Jerry Brown squeaked past Republican state controller Houston Flournoy by 50 percent to 47 for the governorship, and Alan Cranston won reelection to the U.S. Senate resoundingly. On the face of it, Democrats were back in the saddle, after the Reagan interlude. A better, long-range view, however, would see state politics for the next twenty years seesawing between the two major parties with regard to presidential, gubernatorial, and senatorial elections. Democrats did hold majorities in the House delegation and state legislature through the period, but neither party won the higher offices consistently.

Jerry Brown's first governorship—he would return to Sacramento in 2011, after a twenty-year hiatus—flaunted a Spartan style, which to a degree overshadowed real accomplishments. He disdained the plutocratic pomp of his predecessor Reagan by driving himself around, *sans chauffeur,* in a Plymouth instead of a Cadillac like Reagan. He lived in a spare, almost monastic apartment rather than the governor's mansion. But there was substance as well as style. Leo McCarthy, onetime speaker of the assembly, later mused that Jerry Brown signed most, if not all, of the bills sent up to him, and the record shows that much got done. "So frankly," said McCarthy, "the years '75, '76, '77, '78 were, aside from the failure on property taxes, really pretty productive years, from a Democrat's point of view."[57]

In Jerry's first year "public school employees got collective bargaining rights; farm workers gained unemployment insurance coverage;

the maximum weekly insurance benefits were raised by $14, and the taxable wage base rate was increased from $4,200 to $7,000; employees' tips were protected by law from being skimmed off by employers. The jewel in the crown was the extension of collective bargaining rights to farm workers," with the creation of the Agricultural Labor Relations Board.[58] Brown also appointed an unprecedented number of women and minorities to state boards and the bench, and he pushed assiduously for education, workers' health and safety, and the environment.[59] He stopped the state's oil depletion allowance (which had been a big tax break for oil companies), opened city parks, reduced punishment for marijuana use while cracking down on heroin use; and assisted housing for low-income people.[60] All in all, he achieved a liberal agenda as his father did, but without the huge costs. The voters apparently approved, at least somewhat. In 1976, although Gerald Ford rather than Jimmy Carter carried California by a hair, and Hayakawa displaced John Tunney as U.S. senator, the Democrats increased their congressional and state senate seats by one and their assembly margin by four.

Yet a financial matter clouded Brown's first term. The American economy was beset by what journalists and economists were calling "stagflation," slow growth yet rising prices for oil and other necessities, and rising interest rates. In California inflation sent housing prices—and real estate taxes—soaring. Brown and the legislature stepped in, but too late and not strongly enough. They put together a tax relief bill in fall 1977 but it failed to pass the senate, chiefly because of resistance to its provision that tied a tax rate to personal income as well as property value, a "circuit breaker" that was intended to protect low- and middle-income owners and renters. In January 1978, Brown called a special session to pass an emergency tax relief measure and avoid a more draconian measure, but it was not in time to prevent something much more drastic.

PROP 13

In December 1977 a vulgarian agitator named Howard Jarvis, aided by Paul Gann in Northern California and backed financially by organized real estate interests, secured a place on the June 1978 ballot for a proposition (13) to place a lid of one percent on property taxes, based on market values as of 1975/76. It also limited increases in property taxes to two percent a year under the same owner, with any full reassessment taking place only when the property changed hands. The legislature could raise taxes only by a two-thirds or greater vote, with local tax increases also requiring two-thirds assent of voters. Since Prop 13 was a constitutional amendment, only another one could change it. Jarvis and Gann collected over a million valid signatures to place it on the June ballot. Despite warnings from the state Parent-Teachers' Association that it would hurt schools, from others that libraries and museums would close, that a broad range of state and local government services would be cut severely—speaker Leo McCarthy said it would be a disaster—Prop 13 passed in June with 65 percent of the vote. The turnout was 69 percent, "the highest of any off-year election at least since 1916, and probably ever."[61] The voters were in a glowering anti-tax mood, which Jarvis mobilized brilliantly through two support organizations—the United Organizations of Taxpayers and the Los Angeles Apartment Owners Association.[62] Prop 13 became a model for conservative tax-cutting movements around the country. It dovetailed with the Kemp-Roth proposal in Congress and with Reagan's stance both as governor and soon after as president.

The warnings from Speaker McCarthy and many others proved correct: many government functions were sharply reduced or stopped entirely. Property taxes did stabilize at a time when property values and mortgage rates continued to soar. Future assembly speaker Willie Brown called it a "stupid-ass" measure,[63] and journalist Peter Schrag twenty years later said it had made the state ungovernable. But Field Polls of public opinion consistently revealed public support for it, better than two to one, and repeal has been out of the question ever since.[64]

At the same time that voters almost across the political and economic spectrum voted for Prop 13, they defeated the aggressively nonliberal Prop 6, which would have required the dismissal of "all teachers who were gay or who promoted homosexuality."[65] Californians stopped economic activism by government (by cutting taxes) but also stopped social control. Were the voters conservative economically (for Prop 13), liberal socially (against Prop 6), or in between? Governor Brown tried to thwart Prop 13, but in late May he gave up and supported it and even began cutting state programs in anticipation of it.[66] In the November election, Jerry Brown won an easy victory over Republican attorney general Evelle Younger, 56 percent to 37 percent. But 1978 was not a good year for the Democrats. Though they kept their comfortable majorities, they lost four congressional seats and seven assembly seats. In 1980 the chief bright spot for them was Alan Cranston's election to the third of his four terms, handily defeating Paul Gann, the coarchitect of the Prop 13 success two years earlier.

THE EIGHTIES: BURTONS (PHILLIP AND JOHN) AND BROWNS (JERRY I AND WILLIE)

Democrats would lose a few more elections in 1980. In the presidential, Ronald Reagan carried his adopted state with about 53 percent to Democrat Jimmy Carter's 36 percent. Independent John Anderson managed only 8.6 percent, slightly above his national average. After Reagan ascended into the White House, he no longer played a significant role in California politics, though his coattails may have pulled in some Republicans in the next several elections. More likely, the Democrats' sagging fortunes in those years were the consequence of Democratic factionalism, notably in the Sacramento legislature, as Howard Berman tried and failed to unseat Speaker McCarthy in 1980 but produced a "bitterly divided" Democratic majority that "quarreled rancorously." The speakership went to neither Berman nor McCarthy but to Willie Brown.[67]

Despite the disputes and the erosion of a few seats, Democrats in 1981 still held a majority of twenty-three to seventeen in the senate, forty-seven to thirty-three in the assembly, and twenty-two to twenty-one in the congressional delegation. Among the Democratic House representatives was Phillip Burton, and Burton kept an iron hand on the reapportionment resulting from the 1980 U.S. census. Speaker Brown turned over reapportionment to Burton and his aide, Howard Berman's brother Michael, a pair with a minute knowledge of the state's precincts and how to weld them into legislative and congressional districts that Democrats would hold. Legislators were delighted; state senators could move up to safe congressional districts, and assembly members could succeed them in the senate.[68] For one, Howard Berman went to the U.S. House from a safe west Los Angeles district, and he was not alone. It was a win-win-win situation—if you were a Democrat. Many came out of the reapportionment very happy at succeeding to safer and often higher office. Furthermore, "the memory of the 1980 leadership battle was so traumatic for Democrats that they remained loath for more than a decade to engage in another one."[69] One other element prevented another factional fight: besides the happy reapportionment, and the memory of the 1980 bloodiness, Willie Brown's brains—and luck—kept him in the speakership for the next fifteen years, until he was term-limited out.[70]

With the 1981 redistricting complete, and after Republicans tried to court-test it but lost in the California supreme court, Burton might have relaxed. But his brother, John, who was the congressman from an adjacent district (San Francisco north of Market and west of Van Ness plus some precincts across the bridge in Marin County), did not like Washington (and was in bad physical shape) and so resigned his seat. Phil controlled who would replace him, and his pick was Nancy Pelosi, then the chair of the state Democratic Party. But she chose to stay home and continue raising her five teenage children. A Marin County woman who had heard John Burton speak in 1973 and volunteered to help in his congressional campaign, Barbara Boxer, had become president of the Marin County board of supervisors, and when John left Congress, she ran and won in John's district.[71] Congress and California were shocked when Phillip suddenly died on April 10, 1983. He had been instrumental in passing several progressive measures, including aid for black lung victims, creating OSHA (the Occupational Safety and Health Administration in the Department of Labor) as well as ERISA (the federal retirement security law), and other measures. He had done much, not just redistricting. His widow, Sala, succeeded him, but she died in early 1987 of colon cancer. This time Pelosi agreed to run, and she won the nomination in a special election in April 1987. The Burtons had played crucial roles, especially in the 1981 redistricting. And their legacy of paving the way to Congress for Boxer and Pelosi reverberated for another thirty years.[72]

Governor Brown could scarcely avoid some tarnish from the 1980 speakership fight, and he was damaged further by the "med fly" problem in the late summer of 1981. The Mediterranean fruit fly began causing severe damage to California's vital agricultural industry. Spraying with insecticides could control it, but the most effective insecticide, malathion, became highly controversial: did it also endanger people and animals and poison wells? Brown thought so and resisted spraying. Then the infestation spread rapidly, and the governor reversed himself and gave the go-ahead to aerial spraying. The reversal, reminiscent of his reversal on Jarvis-Gann (Prop 13) three years earlier, nibbled away at his credibility.[73] Nevertheless, in the spring of 1982 he easily won the Democratic nomination for the Senate seat being vacated by Sam Hayakawa.

The 1982 election proved the efficacy of Phil Burton's redistricting. "Democrats swamp GOP for Congress," headlined the *Los Angeles Times*, taking twenty-eight of forty-five House seats and picking up two state senate seats for a twenty-five to fifteen majority and one assembly seat for forty-eight to thirty-two control. Democrats also swept all but one statewide office.[74] But the top of the ticket, where Burton's writ did not run, went to Republicans. George Deukmejian, a native New Yorker and son of Armenian immigrants, was a lawyer by training. He had moved to Long Beach in his twenties. He was elected to two terms in the assembly, then to twelve years in the senate, and four years statewide in 1978 as attorney general. In the 1982 gubernatorial primary he defeated the lieutenant governor, and then, in the general, he nipped Los Angeles mayor Tom Bradley, 49.3 percent to 48.1 percent. Pete Wilson, mayor of San Diego, more easily won the open U.S. Senate seat over Governor Jerry Brown, 51.5 percent to 44.8 percent. The Democrats could hardly claim that California was theirs. In most respects, they had receded from their high-water marks of the Pat Brown days. Proposition 15, for handgun registration, became the state's most important issue in 1982 and was said by the *Almanac* to be "the main reason the state moved to the right while the nation was moving to the left." Bradley's support of Prop 15 "badly hurt" him and helped Deukmejian, who favored it. The *Almanac* went on to say that the issue

> seems to have brought into the electorate the other side of the baby boom, the people who did not necessarily graduate from college, who do not share the values of people who grew up protesting the Vietnam war and seeking women's liberation. These new voters are more likely to be family people (although they undoubtedly include many divorcees); despite their lack of college degrees they tend to be affluent. . . . they tend to be . . . devotees of country and western music rather than progressive rock.[75]

Republicans won almost every contest for president, Senate, and governor from 1982 through 1990: for president, Reagan in 1984, George H. W. Bush in 1988; for governor, Deukmejian, again over Bradley, in 1986; and Pete Wilson for a second Senate term in 1988 and for governor in 1990. The only Democratic exception was Senator Alan Cranston's fourth-term victory in 1986. On the other hand, Democrats maintained virtually their same large majorities in the congressional delegation and the two chambers of the state legislature. The *Almanac* claimed in 1984 that Democratic control of the legislature had become "the norm." Moreover, thanks to Jesse Unruh's efforts to put in place a large and professional staff, "the legislature deserves its high reputation, and the state government is highly competent."[76]

As governor, Deukmejian lived up to his conservative reputation. He had to, because Jerry Brown had left him with a large operating deficit, much of it the result of Prop 13's reduction of the state's income. The result was a "pragmatic alliance," an "uneasy partnership," between the "very conservative governor and the very liberal" speaker, Willie Brown. At times that produced gridlock, at other times muddling through. The state's population continued to expand and, with it, demand for expenditures for education, welfare, and infrastructure. Another huge claim on revenue was the criminal justice and incarceration system. "There was really only one issue that interested Deukmejian—fighting crime," wrote Willie Brown's biographer, James Richardson. He "built more prisons in eight years than California had built in the previous one hundred years. He toughened sentencing laws and doubled the number of convicted felons behind bars." Despite this financial drain, he still managed (with Willie's help) to support education, both K-12 and the higher education system.[77] How much Deukmejian owed his slim victory in 1982, and much more decisive one in 1986, to the fact that his opponent both times, Tom Bradley, was African American, can never be known. The preelection polls did not indicate that Bradley's race would make much difference. But probably it did. Political analysts ever since have referred to "the Bradley effect"—people, when polled, deny that race matters but then vote like it does.

THE EARLY NINETIES: RECESSION AND RETRENCHMENT

The California of 1990 was different from the California of Pat Brown (1950) or Jesse Unruh (the 1960s). The young veterans, black and white, men and women, who arrived right after World War II had become parents, even grandparents. The Sacramento-born writer

Joan Didion spends many pages in her 2003 book describing how working-class communities were damaged by the economic downturn of the early 1990s. In her account, Lakewood, just north of Long Beach, was created in the late 1940s much like the Levittowns on the East Coast, peopled with young families of veterans, earning good money from jobs at McDonnell Douglas, Rockwell, and other aerospace plants. But it all grew old, the people and the place (and there were many Lakewoods—Van Nuys, Canoga Park, El Segundo, and more). "The sad, bad times had actually begun, most people later allowed, in 1989, when virtually every defense contractor in Southern California began laying off. . . . Before 1991 ended, California had lost sixty thousand aerospace jobs. . . . some 800,000 jobs were lost in California between 1988 and 1993," according to the state's Commission on Finance. Over half were in Los Angeles County. Jesse Unruh hailed from Hawthorne, just southwest of LA. There, "life had changed. . . . World War II had turned the area into an aircraft manufacturing center, and the Cold War expanded it even more. The impoverished southwesterners of the late 1930s were now [in the late 1960s] the skilled craftsmen on plant floors, and their children were the engineers and scientists in the laboratories and offices upstairs." Many of such people became Reagan Democrats. Unruh in his 1970 campaign brought back some of them to voting Democratic, but not enough of them, and not soon enough.[78]

Didion describes the social dislocation—high school athletes degenerating into gangs of rapists.[79] Her account, however dyspeptic, described hard realities, not only for middle-class (really working-class) people but for those more comfortable: "The bell would eventually toll in Bel Air, where the people lived who held the paper on the people who held the mortgages in Van Nuys."[80] But her take was not the entire story. From the early 1990s into the early 2000s, "a cultural shift" was said to have happened in California "as employees of small businesses and high-tech companies replaced aerospace workers on the voting rolls. These [new] voters are often libertarian in their attitudes, favoring abortion rights and tolerant of alternative lifestyles." The Far Right, which had typified Orange and San Diego County Republicanism since the John Birch days, was being eroded by a tide of social issues.[81]

The California recession of the early 1990s—1992 and 1993 were the worst years—triggered outmigration. Oregonians, aghast with fear of a tidal wave of Californians, had sported "Don't Californicate Oregon" bumper stickers since the 1960s, but now with even more urgency.

Yet people still kept coming to California, often but not always Hispanics and Asians. Summarizing the census data, the *Almanac of American Politics* reported that, "in the first half of the 1990s, about 2 million Californians, mostly white and affluent, left for other Western states or moved east, while immigrants kept arriving. . . . California's Hispanic population rose from 16 percent in 1980 to 32 percent in 2000 and 36 percent in 2007. The Asian percentage was 5 percent in 1980, 11 percent in 2000, and 12 percent in 2007."[82] The trend would continue: "Between 2000 and 2010, the Asian population rose 31 percent and Hispanics rose 28 percent, while non-Hispanic whites declined more than 5 percent and blacks declined 1 percent."[83] The people of the state, historically more diverse than any other, became even more so.

The result, after the 1990 census, was another seven seats in the House of Representatives. That meant another reapportionment. Even without Phil Burton the Democrats came out ahead, increasing their share by four (to thirty) while the Republicans increased by three (to twenty-two). Speaker Willie Brown and the new Republican governor, Pete Wilson, stalemated each other's redistricting maps. Finally, Wilson threw the problem into the California supreme court, which "appointed special masters who finally undid Burton's 1981 remap, creating competitive districts up and down the state."[84]

Nevertheless, the economic downturn and President Bush's "decision to write off California" in his 1992 reelection campaign worked in favor of the Democrats.[85] Certain now-familiar trends were becoming apparent: Hispanic and African American minorities leaned strongly Democratic; suburbanites, especially from Orange County south through San Diego, leaned right-wing Republican. Other than San Diego, the largest cities—Los Angeles, San Jose, San Francisco, and Sacramento—were mostly Democratic strongholds. Republicans could count on only the far northeast and the counties along the Sierras, the Central Valley, and much of Orange and San Diego Counties. The traditional polarization between Northern and Southern California was weakening, being replaced by a coastal-interior divergence as the Central Valley began trending more Republican. Over the next twenty-five years, and especially after 2000, Republican numbers in the congressional delegation would slip—slowly, but persistently.

Pete Wilson had comfortably defeated Jerry Brown in 1982 for the Senate seat that Hayakawa was vacating. Wilson was reelected in 1988 by about the same margin over Leo McCarthy. He decided in 1990 to return to California and run for governor, and in that race he beat the mayor of San Francisco, Dianne Feinstein, by about 49 percent to 46 percent. Two years later Feinstein ran to fill the remaining two years of Wilson's Senate term, easily steamrolling Republican John Seymour, 54 percent to 38 percent. In the same election, congresswoman Barbara Boxer defeated right-wing Republican Bruce Herschensohn, 48 percent to 43 percent. Thus began the quarter-century incumbencies of the two women senators from the Bay Area. The thirty to twenty-two Democrat-to-Republican distribution of congressional seats in the 1992 election reflects how the political geography of California stood. Compared to the 1988 election, more women, Hispanics, Catholics, independents, and higher-income people voted, although minorities still undervoted: 45 percent of the state's residents were minorities, but they cast only 21 percent of the vote, whereas the 55 percent who were white non-Hispanics cast 79 percent.[86]

The twenty-four-year string of Democratic victories in California's presidential races began as Bill Clinton defeated George H. W. Bush, 46 percent to 33 percent. Independent Ross Perot took almost 21 percent, quite likely drawing support from both major parties and bringing in voters who would have voted for neither Clinton nor Bush.[87]

By the time of the 1990 census, coinciding with the economic slump in aerospace and other industries, the great postwar population surge that had gifted California with an unprecedented number of House representatives was nearly over. California continued to grow in population, but no longer at a faster rate than the rest of the country. The 1990 census, reflecting the surge of the 1980s, gave the state seven more House members; but the 2000 census awarded it only one, and the 2010 census, none. For the first time since statehood in 1850, California had to settle for a stable House delegation.

MID-NINETIES NATIVISM: RIGHT TURN TODAY, GOP TROUBLE TOMORROW

A Republican year nationally, 1994 was the year of Newt Gingrich and his "Contract with America," the year Republicans captured a majority in the House of Representatives for the first time since 1955.

In California "it was one of the darkest of economic times in the state's history," and Republican gains were substantial.[88] But the result was by no means a clean GOP sweep. In the congressional delegation, the Democrats lost three seats and the Republicans gained three, but that still left the Democrats with a narrow lead, twenty-seven to twenty-five, a lead that had begun with the 1956 election. Democrats also retained their majority in the California senate. But they lost their control of the assembly by two seats, thirty-nine to forty-one, as their average percentage of assembly votes fell from 56 to 51.[89] It appeared to end Willie Brown's fifteen-year reign as speaker. The wily Brown, however, persuaded Republican assemblyman Paul Horcher, from east Los Angeles County, to vote for him in return for being appointed vice chair of the Ways and Means Committee. This deadlocked the vote at forty to forty. Then Brown maneuvered—which took about six weeks—to have another Republican assemblyman disqualified on the ground that because he had been elected to the senate he was no longer eligible to vote on the speakership. Thus, Brown remained speaker for yet another session.[90] He resigned in June 1995 to run (successfully) for mayor of San Francisco, having been term-limited out of the assembly. As it happened, 1994 was the last election that resulted in a Republican majority in the assembly.

Other results of the 1994 election were longer lasting. Democrat Feinstein was elected to a full six-year term in the Senate, defeating Congressman Michael Huffington, and she would be reelected in 2000, 2006, and 2012. Her large margins in the Democratic strongholds of the Bay Area and Los Angeles County gave her 46.7 percent of the statewide vote, overcoming Huffington's 44.8 percent. Republican Pete Wilson started the campaign well behind Kathleen Brown, daughter of Pat and sister of Jerry, but the sagging economy and Wilson's "tough on crime" position, support for the death penalty, and hostility to illegal immigration pulled him ahead, and he was reelected governor by a healthy margin, 55 percent to 41 percent.[91] Typically for off-year elections, less than half—about 47 percent—of the eligible voters actually voted, but that was a six percent increase from 41 percent in the previous gubernatorial election in 1990. Quite possibly the much-talked-about Proposition 187, aimed at "illegal" immigration, raised voter interest and turnout. Wilson's strengths were in Southern California outside of Los Angeles County (i.e., Orange, San Diego, and the Inland Empire of Riverside, and San

Bernardino Counties) as well as the north coast and Sierra counties. He also was successful with conservative voters, non-Hispanic white men, Protestants, and voters above average in age and income—all traditionally Republican groups. The Wilson vote also correlated with yes votes on Prop 187.[92]

But Wilson's victory proved to be pyrrhic. He supported not only the crime-and-punishment issues but also some ballot propositions which, in the short run, pulled in many voters. Over time, however, after Wilson was long gone, and although courts overturned Prop 187, Republicans could not shake identification with his positions, which alienated Hispanics, the fastest-growing group in California's population.

In 1994, Wilson "made Proposition 187 a cornerstone of his successful reelection campaign."[93] Taking direct aim at "illegal immigrants," the ballot measure excluded them from "public social services, public health care services (unless emergency services mandated by federal law), and public school education at the elementary, secondary, and postsecondary levels." It also required providers of these services to verify that recipients were documented and "to report persons who are *suspected* undocumented immigrants to the California Attorney General and the Immigration and Naturalization Service." Prop 187 also made it "a felony to manufacture, distribute, sell, or use false citizenship or residency documents."[94] The measure passed comfortably, 59 percent to 41 percent, favored everywhere except the Bay Area; its support was especially strong in the Inland Empire and other Republican-leaning areas. White non-Hispanic men voted yes by 38 points; Latinos voted no by 46 points.[95] Wilson's campaign, said one observer, "whipped up a dormant xenophobia that is never far from California's political culture." That was not the case with federal judge Mariana R. Pfaelzer, who late in 1995 declared most sections of Prop 187 unconstitutional, because its refusal of health and welfare services contravened federal law that provided those services. Further, an earlier Supreme Court ruling, *Plyler v. Doe* (1982), disallowed exclusion of children of undocumented immigrants from public schools.[96]

The new nativism was not dead, however. Republican candidates were buoyed by Wilson's success with the immigration issue in 1994 and raised it again in the next two elections. California's "moderation" since the days of Earl Warren had been tested by the Rumford repeal in 1963 and now by Prop 187 in 1994, and the voters, certainly the white male voters, again rejected liberal ecumenism. In 1996 they had another chance to do so.

Prop 209 on that year's ballot was a constitutional amendment prohibiting affirmative action: there would be no consideration of race, sex, or ethnicity by state agencies in employment, contracting, or education. The voters passed it in November by about 55 percent to 45 percent. It was court-tested immediately—and since—but the courts have sustained it. Leading the support were Governor Wilson; his friend from earlier work on the Assembly Housing Committee, the African American university regent Ward Connerly; and two Cal State professors, Glynn Custred and Thomas Wood, who said they "were tired of seeing ethnic preferences run rampant in the California State University system."[97] Affirmative action has always been a hard sell, and the state leadership of the Democratic Party in California decided not to oppose Prop 209. Organized opposition did develop, much of it among young people both minority and white, but it was confined chiefly to the Bay Area and Los Angeles. University students opposed it; so did administrators.

Echoing the fight over the Rumford Act thirty years earlier, a Field Poll sampled public opinion just before the election and found that those favoring Prop 209 were planning to vote for Dole or Perot for president, were white, and (strongest of all categories) identified as Republican or conservative. Planning to oppose it were Clinton voters, Democrats, liberals, and, by about two to one, African Americans and Hispanics. All told, "public opinion polls showed a fairly consistent majority in favor," and it attracted "the highest voter participation rate (94 percent) of all twenty-seven measures on the March and September ballots." However, "the 55–45 percent outcome was decisive but not overwhelming," though it correlated very highly with the result in 1994 on Prop 187, aimed at the undocumenteds. It survived court tests within the following year.[98]

Prop 209 was not directly aimed at Hispanics in 1996, but it certainly did them no favors. Following on Prop 187 and also strongly backed by Pete Wilson, it was another reason why Hispanics did not vote Republican in California. A third reason arose in 1998, and the effect was direct. Prop 227 in that year would discontinue bilingual education in the state's schools. As historian Daniel Martinez HoSang writes, "Bilingual education programs had been won in the late 1960s and early 1970s by parents, activists, and advocates who were championing the needs of immigrant Latino and Asian American students left behind by a system that historically mandated English-only instruction." It appeared on the June 1998 primary ballot and passed, 61 percent to 39 percent. Conservatives supported it more heavily (though Republican gubernatorial candidate Dan Lungren did not), Democratic candidates for governor opposed it, and about one in three Hispanics voted for it.[99]

The cumulative result of Props 187, 209, and 227 was to alienate Hispanics from the Republican brand. Statistical correlations by historian John Allswang prove "a striking positive relationship in voting for Propositions 187, 209, and 227; between voting to end affirmative action and voting to end bilingual education, the correlation was .940, about as close to a perfect relationship as one will ever see in the real world." Allswang found a further correlation with a right-to-work proposition in 1998, Prop 226, which did not pass, but which indicates a consistent liberal-conservative split among the voters in the early and mid-nineties, the years of Wilson's second term.[100]

This is why Wilson's championing of Prop 187 and Republican/conservative support of all three ballot measures produced a victory in 1994 that was pyrrhic. As political scientist Sylvia Manzano has concluded, "The policy threat and harsh racial tones employed in the 1990s mobilized Californians at the polls. Latino voter turnout and Democratic-candidate support increased, while Republicans lost ground with white voters." California was already leaning strongly Democratic by the mid-1990s, but the hegemony was hardly complete, as Pete Wilson's victories and the illiberal measures revealed. It was already clear that, if the Republicans were to become consistent winners again, they had to attract the Hispanic minority. The propositions made that extremely difficult. Thus, in their perverse way, they became a significant marker in making California a blue state. They were not the only motivator of Hispanic voters; education and economic conditions have, over time, been more important. But they gave the GOP a lasting tincture that repelled Hispanics.[101]

GRAY DAVIS AND THE AGE OF ARNOLD

Californians voted again for Bill Clinton in 1996, and, uncomplicated by the Ross Perot candidacy of 1992, Clinton beat Dole 51 percent to 38 percent. Two years later Barbara Boxer was reelected to her second Senate term; Democrats held about steady in the congressional delegation; and they won twenty-five of the forty senate seats and, for the first time, fifty of the eighty assembly seats. In the governor's race Lieutenant Governor Gray Davis—Joseph Graham Davis Jr.—won a three-way primary and went on to defeat Attorney General Dan Lungren. Davis, a native of the Bronx who had lived in the Los Angeles area most of his life, took about 58 percent of the vote to Lungren's 38 percent. A Field Poll described the results as Davis "winning in nearly every region of the state and piling up majorities among Democrats, independents, moderate and liberal voters, men and women, and across all income, age, educational, race and ethnic groups. While union members favored Davis by a nearly three to one margin, Davis was also preferred among non-union households. . . . Protestant/Christian voters favored Lungren by a small margin, but all other religious groups voted overwhelmingly for Davis." In short, Davis swept every group except "Republicans and those who are ideologically conservative."[102] The impact on Hispanics was immediate: whereas Wilson won almost 40 percent of the group in 1990, Davis swamped Lungren in 1998 among Hispanics by 78 percent to 16 percent.[103]

In 2000, Democrats continued to win. California's fifty-four electoral votes went to Al Gore, who won 54 percent of the popular vote to George W. Bush's 42 percent. Feinstein won another Senate term even more decisively. Democrats took four more congressional seats away from Republicans—in Santa Barbara, LA, and San Diego—and maintained their large majorities in both chambers of the state legislature. California seemed deep blue. "There are those who thought that the 1998 election was the Republican Party's worst calamity. That was premature—2000 proved far worse," wrote political observers Lou Cannon and A. G. Block.[104]

For his first two and a half years, Governor Davis maintained most of his popularity, aided greatly by the healthy fiscal condition of the state resulting from the Silicon Valley and stock market expansions. As he had promised, he supported education at all levels, supported domestic partnerships, signed several gun control bills, and, more conservatively, stood by the death penalty and strict sentencing. He also earned a reputation as an environmentalist.

But by mid-2001 his luck was running out. What has become known as the dot-com bubble—the gross inflation of stocks, especially technology stocks on the Nasdaq index, but others as well—burst, slashing revenue and upending the state's finances. Additionally, the state suffered an energy crisis, a shortage of electricity, as a consequence of deregulation of the state's utilities in 1996. That put California at the mercy of out-of-state sellers of electricity. Price gouging and "rolling blackouts" resulted in summer 2001. Gray's administration had to buy electricity from private companies at exorbitant rates, further deepening the financial hole. Later, news channels showed electricity technicians and executives on national TV joking about how they had frivolously switched the lights (and air conditioning) on and off across California. But Governor Davis got much of the blame.[105] In March 2003 the Federal Energy Regulatory Commission determined that "Enron and five other energy companies had manipulated energy markets" in California. But it also said that the state was liable for $3 billion in unpaid electricity bills.[106] Davis faced an intractable budget situation and a hostile legislature.

Before that crisis, however, and though his approval ratings were sinking, he was reelected in 2002. The very competitive and hard-fought Republican primary produced a financial sector heir, Bill Simon, rather than the expected Dick Riordan, the mayor of Los Angeles. Davis spent a reputed $10 million to keep Riordan from winning the primary, and it paid off. Gray lived up to his reputation for negative campaign advertising, of which Simon was not innocent either. Each pulled down the other's popularity, so that the editor of the *California Journal* summed up the campaign as a cockroach (Davis as portrayed by Simon) or a reptile (Simon as portrayed by Davis).[107] The roach won, 47 percent to 42 percent, with 10 percent going to third-party candidates. Simon was relatively unknown to the voters, and Davis outspent him significantly, electing the incumbent.[108] Democrats took every statewide race ("for the first time since 1882," one political scientist pointed out) and held virtually steady in the congressional and legislative contests. Democratic efforts to energize naturalized Hispanics in Los Angeles and Orange Counties brought out new voters.[109] A Republican former aide to Vice President Dick Cheney told the unpleasant truth: "We're the biggest state in the nation—and the Democrats are in total control."[110]

From then on, Davis's luck disappeared entirely. The seriousness of the budget crisis and the rolling electricity blackouts persuaded increasing numbers that Davis had to go. Darrell Issa, a very conservative Republican congressman from San Diego County who had hopes of succeeding Davis, funded the recall in its early stages out of his $400 million fortune acquired from making and selling car alarms. Only once before, in North Dakota in 1921, had a governor been recalled. But Davis became the second, less than a year after he was reelected. The vote came on October 7, 2003. The ballot asked two questions: should Davis be recalled, and who should succeed him? (Unlike a regular election, there was no primary to weed out competitors.) The answer to the first was yes by 55 percent, and to the second was Arnold Schwarzenegger. To Issa's dismay, the Austrian weightlifter-actor whose name every voter knew from the movies became the party's preference, and he won the crowded field with 49 percent. In a special election like this one, there was no runoff.

In office, Schwarzenegger persuaded voters to support a $15 billion bond issue, which would tide over the state government until its immediate cash-flow problems were addressed. In 2005 he announced several initiatives that would make it harder for schoolteachers to gain tenure; limit public-sector unions' political contributions; control state expenditures; and depoliticize redistricting. All four failed.[111] But in 2006 he was reelected governor by 56 percent to 39 percent for the Democrats' Phil Angelides, the state treasurer, even though Democrats continued to sweep the other state offices and maintain their preponderance in the congressional delegation and both houses of the legislature. The "incumbent protection" redistricting continued to operate. Meanwhile, a Field Poll identified "megatrends" in the 2006 election for governor: a decrease in white non-Hispanic voters from 79 percent in 1990 to 67 percent; an increase in Hispanic voters from 10 percent in 1990 to 19 percent; and a divide between coastal and inland California, with the coastal areas favoring Democrats and the inlanders (usually) voting Republican.[112] The long-range implication, especially regarding Hispanics, favored the Democrats.

The voters were exhibiting a kind of schizophrenia regarding Schwarzenegger's governorship. As he was being reelected handily, almost every one of his ballot propositions lost, and the Democratic legislature thwarted him as well. By fall 2008, midway through his second term, 38 percent of polled voters approved of his performance and 52 percent disapproved—better than Davis's rating just before he was recalled, but not good. Yet murmurings of recalling Schwarzenegger gained little traction.[113] He continued to be cheerful, even as spending on the prison system outstripped higher education: "The same fiscal year that the state spent $6 billion on prisons, it had invested just $4.7 billion on higher education."[114] He left office a happy warrior, despite a spreading sense—locally and in national media—that California, with its two-thirds requirement to pass a budget or raise taxes, with the ravages of Prop 13, and with the governor and the legislature at loggerheads, had become "ungovernable." He did manage to get the voters to support, by 61 percent to 39 percent, an initiative to turn redistricting over to a nonpartisan commission. It would begin operations after the 2010 census.[115]

Californians' vote in the presidential election of 2008 confirmed, rather than deviated from, the Democratic orientation that had been building since the 1990s. Polls during 2008 showed a consistent safe lead, almost always over 50 percent, for the Obama-Biden ticket over McCain-Palin.[116] The election result in November, after the market crash and the onset of the Great Recession, was Obama 61 percent, McCain 37 percent. (The result in 2012 was almost identical: Obama 60 percent, Romney 37.) Obama's margin was greater than Lyndon Johnson's in 1964 or Reagan's in 1984 and was the highest since FDR won 67 percent in 1936. African Americans voted 94 percent for Obama, Hispanics 74 percent, and Asians 64 percent, according to exit polls. Obama did well with people in the fifty to sixty-four age cohort (Baby Boomers), broke even among the over-sixty-fives, and did very well (76 percent) among under-thirties, especially first-time voters. Obama's victory in the general election happened despite his losing to Hillary Clinton in the California Democratic primary. The Democratic majorities in the congressional delegation and the state assembly and senate did not change at all from the 2006 result.

JERRY II

As Schwarzenegger left office in January 2011 without solving California's revenue needs, his popularity sank to Gray Davis's level.[117] The 2010 election returned none other than Jerry Brown to the governorship. In 1982 he had decided not to run for a third term as governor and tried for the Senate seat that Hayakawa was vacating, but he lost to Los Angeles mayor Tom Bradley in the primary. Bradley lost narrowly to Pete Wilson in the general. Jerry spent much of the 1980s out of politics, then made a run in 1992 for president and lost to Bill Clinton. In 1998 he ran for mayor of Oakland and won

easily, was reelected in 2002, and was generally credited with revital-
izing the city. In 2006 he ran successfully for state attorney general
and then carried out some high-profile prosecutions. In 2010, since
Schwarzenegger was not running again for governor, Brown defeated
eBay CEO Meg Whitman 54 percent to 41 percent, with strong
support from women, independents, Hispanics, and in LA County,
though he was strong elsewhere as well.[118] Thus began his third term,
a.k.a "Jerry II." He would be more successful than he was previously,
as Jerry I.

Brown, like his predecessors Schwarzenegger, Davis, and Wilson,
took advantage of California's ballot initiative procedure to act when
something stalled in the legislature. When the Republican minority prevented passage of a state budget because of the two-thirds requirement,
an initiative in 2010 lowered it to a simple majority. Another initiative
legalized the "top two" primary, whereby the two leading vote-getters
in a primary, *regardless of party*, would face each other in the general.
A third measure took redistricting out of the hands of the legislature
(or the Burtons) and assigned it to a fourteen-member commission of
citizens.[119] It first operated in 2011, and though indeed nonpartisan the
results did not make Democrats unhappy. They increased their lead in
the congressional delegation by four (thirty-eight to fifteen) and in the
senate and assembly to more than two-thirds. Prop 30 raised tax rates
at the wealthy end and also raised the sales tax by a quarter percent,
putting the state budget in balance. Brown also was able to provide
more funding for education, raise the minimum wage, and address climate change. The supermajorities in the legislature replaced stalemate
with action. Nevertheless, Brown was watchful about pressure from
the legislature to overspend. "If I took my foot off the brake," he said,
"we'd be back in the red within six months."[120]

Thus able to pass budgets and even raise taxes, California had
become "governable" again, under Democratic aegis. It could become
even more so, according to the historian Robert Cherny, if further
changes were made, including getting rid of the two-thirds requirement for tax increases, abolishing term limits, limiting campaign
contributions to registered voters in California, and others.[121] At any
rate, California governance was proceeding more smoothly under
Jerry II than it had for some years. In 2014, Brown was reelected by
a larger margin than in 2010—59 percent to the Republican banker
Neel Kashkari's 41 percent.

By the beginning of his fourth term, Jerry II enjoyed an approval rating of 56 percent with disapproval of only 32 percent. His voter approval, a Field Poll concluded, "spans most of the major demographic, regional and political subgroups of the state's electorate." Only "strong conservatives" disapproved.[122] After the 2014 and 2016 elections, Democrats outnumbered Republicans in the California congressional delegation thirty-nine to fourteen. The senate had twenty-six Democrats and fourteen Republicans, the assembly after 2016 fifty-five Democrats and twenty-five Republicans. Regarding immigrants, voters supported paths to citizenship for undocumenteds if they were employed, learned English, and paid back taxes, and they approved of in-state tuition for them at public universities.[123] In 2016 the voters passed initiatives to legalize marijuana, 56 percent to 44, and to require background checks for ammunition purchases and ban large-capacity ammunition magazines, 63 percent to 37. In the 1990s, Democratic voting did not always mean liberal opinions on ballot measures. Twenty years later, by 2016, the voters had become more liberal.

From a reliably Republican state through the mid-1950s—albeit moderately so under Earl Warren—California incrementally had become one of the deepest blue states in the union. George H. W. Bush did not contest it when he ran for reelection in 1992, considering it a lost cause. Al Gore spent no campaign money there in 2000 because he considered it a sure winner. And it was. Looking back across sixty-some years, the most startling turning point was the 1958 election, when Pat Brown sank William Knowland and began a period when Democrats were competitive. Very gradually, and despite reversals under Reagan, Deukmejian, and Pete Wilson, Democratic candidates began winning elections with votes becoming commensurate with their longtime advantage in registrations. By the early 1990s California had become a blue state, though not in all respects a liberal one.

Interestingly, and in contrast with Texas and Oklahoma, organized religion played at best a small role. Despite being the home of megachurches, and historically of utopian communities and a strong Religious Right in Orange County, much of the Central Valley, and a few other places, California (like Oregon and Washington) has been more secular than devout. It is also very diverse, with 40 percent of the country's Buddhists and "most Hindus and Muslims—70,000

Muslims in Los Angeles County alone," according to a 2015 study. "California is 28 percent Catholic, 20 percent Evangelical Protestant, and 10 percent mainline Protestant. This is in contrast to the United States as a whole, where 70 percent of Christians are Protestant."[124] In 1994, for example, the Christian Right existed in California, led by the state Christian Coalition and the Traditional Values Coalition out of Anaheim. White evangelicals indeed voted 60 percent Republican, but they were just 24 percent of the Republican vote in that year. "Nones"—people who did not claim a church affiliation—voted 24 percent Republican and 46 percent Democratic.[125]

Yet, even as it became a key faction in the Republican Party, the Christian Right in California, quite unlike its dominant positions in Oklahoma and elsewhere, refrained from stressing opposition to gay rights or abortion. In the 1992 Republican primary, the moderate John Seymour crushed William Dannemeyer, an anti-abortion and anti-gay congressional veteran, 51 percent to 27 percent. Running for governor and senator in 1994, Republicans Pete Wilson and Michael Huffington were both pro-choice and instead appealed to Christian Rightists on such issues as high taxes, crime, "illegal" immigration, and family values.[126] About two-thirds of California voters favored *Roe v. Wade*, according to a poll in 2010, and that had not changed "over the course of fifteen separate Field Poll measures taken on this issue since 1987."[127] No victory march for the Christian Right in California.

Not unrelated was the near-absence of a Tea Party movement in 2009–10, although Republicans deemed insufficiently conservative could be "primaried out."[128] In January 2010 a Field Poll reported that 28 percent of those polled "identify with it [Tea Party] either a lot (12 percent) or some (16 percent) and 11 percent believed that Obama was not born in the U.S. with 22 percent more saying they were not sure."[129] The contrast with Texas was much argued and remarked about.[130]

Why had California changed politically? Conservative columnist Fred Barnes had an answer: "It's pretty simple why Republicans collapsed in California. The state changed. They didn't. The Hispanic and Asian electorates grew without attracting heavy GOP attention. In 1990, Republicans were 39 percent of registered voters. Today they're 29 percent. In the past two decades, 4 million middle-class [white] families have left California. The guess is a majority were

Republicans. . . . The demographics are daunting for Republicans."[131]

Barnes elided the contributions that Pete Wilson and the 1990s ballot measures made to furthering Republican long-term decline. Demography was destiny, as it often is, and its reality could not be evaded or reversed. E. J. Dionne summed it up as follows: "California telescoped the demographic changes the nation is going through, so its transformation from Ronald Reagan's base to a Democratic bastion ought to be an alarming portent for conservatives. 'The one thing no one can stop,' said Representative Ted Lieu, a Los Angeles–area Democrat who was elected to Congress in 2014, 'is that every month, the rest of America looks more like California.'" Prop 187 in 1994, and Pete Wilson's strong support of it, "simultaneously turned off Hispanic voters from the GOP and mobilized many of them into the political process. The same thing is now [2016] happening nationally as the Republican party is pressured by its political base to repeat the California GOP's mistake on immigration."[132]

The 2010 census and subsequent population surveys have shown the rapid increase in minority populations, especially Hispanics and Asians. They as well as African Americans have trended more and more strongly Democratic, especially in California but also nationally. Xavier Becerra, until recently the congressman for downtown Los Angeles, including strongly Korean, Chinese, Japanese, and Filipino neighborhoods, has said that, "when he was first elected to Congress in 1992, a large share of Asian Americans leaned Republican. That's no longer true," and the perception that the Republican Party is unfriendly to immigrants and minorities, going back at least to Pete Wilson's 1994 campaign, continues to strengthen.[133] Nationally, and certainly in California, diversity characterizes America's demographic change.[134] Unless something radically changes the demography, the Democrats will benefit. But Ted Lieu is probably correct.

The results of the 2016 election confirmed and continued the preceding trends. Hillary Clinton won 8.8 million votes versus Donald Trump's 4.5 million, or 61.5 percent to 31.5 percent, with the Libertarian and Green candidates taking 5.4 percent. Clinton carried thirty-three counties, including all of the populous ones, even Orange, the longtime Republican Right's bastion, by more than 100,000 votes. No Democratic presidential candidate had carried Orange County since FDR in 1936.[135] Most of the Trump counties were in the Central Valley or along the Sierras; the largest was Kern (county seat, Bakersfield), where Trump won 130,000 votes to Clinton's 99,000. But Clinton took 2.5 million in Los Angeles County to Trump's 770,000. The contest for U.S. senator to fill the place of retiring Barbara Boxer pitted two Democrats, because they had been the top vote-getters in the interparty primary earlier: Congresswoman Loretta Sanchez and Attorney General Kamala Harris, who won 62.4 percent of the votes. Of the fifty-three House seats, Democrats won thirty-nine, Republicans fourteen. The state senate went twenty-seven Democratic to thirteen Republican; the assembly, fifty-five Democratic to twenty-five Republican.[136] California remained deep blue, and a more liberal blue than had been true in the 1990s or 2000s. Rumblings about the aging leadership at the top of the California Democrats—Boxer, Feinstein, Pelosi, and Jerry Brown all being over seventy-five—were offset by the emergence of young(er) leaders such as Harris, Becerra, Toni Atkins (speaker of the assembly), Kevin de León (senate leader), Lieutenant Governor Gavin Newsom, and others, all in the prime of life.[137]

California has certainly changed since 1950, demographically and economically, and hence politically. It continues to grow, if not as fast as in the postwar, Baby Boom years. And it seems sure to keep giving fifty-some electoral votes to whatever Democrat runs for president.

THE BLUE STAYERS

7   Basically Blue:
Hawaii and Washington

It is tempting to conclude that being washed by the waters of the Pacific immerses one in liberal politics, or at least in voting Democratic, because that's true of Washington, Oregon, California, and Hawaii and has been for some time. But then there is Alaska. Perhaps the generalization works only if the water is relatively warm, especially if it is perpetually warm and the weather in general is constant, pleasant, and predictable. So it is with Hawaii.

The fiftieth state and the forty-ninth, Alaska, are uniquely not contiguous with the other forty-eight. They also have in common that their political coloration during their territorial periods changed shortly after reaching statehood, and changed (so far) permanently. This surprised both sides. As Brett Melendy writes, "The prevailing Republican view [nationally] in the 1950s was that statehood for Hawaii would bring three of their party to the halls of Congress, offsetting the anticipated three Democrats from Alaska."[1] Alaska at the close of its territorial period and into the 1960s had its Gruening, Bartlett, and other Democrats, but for one reason or another they were soon replaced by Republicans. Hawaii, in its territorial period, seemed invincibly Republican. Southern Democrats opposed Hawaiian statehood not simply because it would add two senators who likely would vote for civil rights laws, but even more because it would violate white supremacy by giving equal status to the mixed-race, white-minority territory.[2] Hawaii's politics reflected the interests of the "Big Five" planters, processors, and exporters, along with other white elites with chamber of commerce mindsets. But by statehood in 1959, and into the early 1960s, the state turned Democratic and has remained so ever since. It quickly became more blue than any of the red states discussed in chapter 3 are red. Washington is also blue, but a lighter shade; its coastal region, west of the Cascades, accounts for most of the blueness, while the bulk of its land area, east of the mountains but more sparsely populated, is not very blue at all. Its neighbor Oregon splits in a similar way, as we see in chapter 5.

HAWAII

The Aloha State topped 1.4 million in population in 2015, almost three times what it was in 1950. It is very ethnically divided and has been throughout the twentieth century and into the twenty-first, though only in the 1950s and later have nonwhite minorities made themselves felt electorally. Hawaii was the first state with a nonwhite majority. As of 1970, the population was a third Japanese, a fifth Native Hawaiian or partly so, a fifth white, with sizeable Filipino, Chinese, Portuguese, and other groups. This distribution has not changed much in subsequent decades except that whites have become about a quarter of the people. Other than the Native Hawaiians and the whites who began arriving in the nineteenth century, the other groups came in the early twentieth, mainly as workers in the then-dominant pineapple and sugar plantations. By the late territorial period (the 1950s), these European and Asian groups had reached their third and fourth generations and had become as Hawaiian as the whites and the Native Hawaiians.[3]

Well before the U.S. engorgement of the islands in 1898, a group called "the Big Five"—"three island-based corporations, one mainland firm, and one British company"—controlled sugar and pineapple production, processing, and marketing. As "the islands' leading conservative force," they also controlled politics when territorial government came into being, and through "numerous interlocking directorates [they could] keep a stranglehold on the islands' economy."[4]

Three postwar developments changed Hawaii's politics. One was the "rapid unionization of the state's great sugar and pineapple plantations right after the war . . . which forced plantation workers to collaborate across race lines." Nonsegregated public schools and intermarriage sped the sense of unity around class instead of race and ethnicity. The ILWU—the International Longshoremen's and Warehousemen's Union—was critical in forging worker unity. As Melendy wrote, "Following a series of struggles sometimes resembling sieges, island laborers gained a voice in their working conditions, made the Democratic party a viable political force, gained control of the territorial legislature, and dominated elected and appointed state offices from 1962" onward.[5]

The second change was the McCarran-Walter immigration act of 1952, which was illiberal in many ways but did finally permit Asians to become citizens. "With the coming of age of their citizen children, the Nikkei [ethnic Japanese who have immigrated, and their descendants] formed a formidable voting bloc that revitalized the Democratic Party and dislodged the Republican plantation oligarchy."[6]

A third factor was the return of the Nisei (literally, second-generation immigrants) from World War II. The exploits of the 442nd Regimental Combat Team and the 100th Infantry Battalion in Italy, all-Nisei outfits and the most decorated units in the army, fighting for the United States despite the incarceration of the West Coast Japanese Americans (some of whom joined those units), gave their members and families no inclination to sense any racial inferiority; the returning veterans "were in no mood to return to a second-class role in the Island structure." Many took advantage of the GI bill to get college and professional educations, including soon-to-be-recognized names such as Inouye, Matsunaga, and Ariyoshi.[7] The elements were in place for the eclipse of the Big Five–dominated conservative territorial government with a much different one.

The first elections under statehood came in 1959. The pioneer U.S. senators were Oren Long, an educator-social worker and Democrat who had been appointed territorial governor in the early 1950s by Truman; and a Republican businessman, Hiram Fong, who enjoyed the support of the ILWU. Fong, the first Chinese American member of Congress, was reelected twice, leaving the Senate in January 1977. Long did not run again when his term expired in 1962, and he was succeeded then by Daniel Inouye, a combat veteran who had lost his right arm with the 442nd in Italy. Inouye served as a senator for just over fifty years. Of serious mien, he played prominent roles in the Watergate hearings of 1974 and again in the Iran-Contra hearings of 1987 and was Hawaii's best-known political figure for decades.

On November 8, 1960, 184,705 Hawaiians cast their first votes for president of the United States. John F. Kennedy won the three electoral votes by 115 popular votes; an inevitable recount upheld Kennedy's victory. In the election for congressman-at-large, 182,639 people voted, and Dan Inouye won by 89,015, or 74.4 percent. Democrats were in the saddle and would remain so; the only shift ever in

Hawaii's party balance had taken place. Since statehood, from 1960 through 2016, Hawaii has voted Republican for president only twice (Nixon in 1972 and Reagan in 1984) and for Democrats the other thirteen times.

In the 1964 presidential election, Hawaii voted like every other western state except Arizona, but more so. It supported Lyndon Johnson by 78.8 percent to Goldwater's 21.2 percent. It gave Hubert Humphrey about 60 percent in 1968 and Richard Nixon about 39 percent. The third-party, pro-segregation American Independent ticket of George Wallace received 1.44 percent, the lowest proportion of any state.[8] The most racially diverse state was Wallace's weakest. In 1972, however, it gave the incumbent Nixon 62.5 percent to McGovern's 37.5 percent. The next two elections went to Democrat Jimmy Carter narrowly, by about two percentage points, in both 1976 and 1980. In the latter year, independent John Anderson picked up 10.6 percent, well above his national average of 6.6 percent. Hawaii's second Republican vote for president came in 1984, when it gave 55 percent to incumbent Reagan. Since then the Democrat has always won, although in 1992 Ross Perot took 13.8 percent and prevented Bill Clinton from winning a clear majority. Clinton's reelection in 1996 and the votes for Gore in 2000 and Kerry in 2004 were all with 54 or 55 percent. Obama, Hawaii-born, won about 71 percent of Hawaii's votes both times, and in 2016 Hillary Clinton captured 62.2 percent to Donald Trump's 30.0 percent, with the Libertarian, Green, and other candidates totaling 7.8 percent.

Hawaii's governors were appointed by the president in the territorial period. The last one, William F. Quinn, an Irish Catholic lawyer, was appointed by Eisenhower in 1957. Statehood meant that governors would be elected for four-year terms in off years. Quinn ran and won what was more accurately a three-and-a-half-year term, defeating another Irish Catholic, a Honolulu police officer and Democrat named John A. Burns. When Eisenhower appointed Quinn, he reportedly said, "I hope you can do something about the communist influence out there." He had likely been told that Harry Bridges, head of the ILWU, had been a member of the Communist Party USA in the 1930s. But, as a newspaperman observed, Bridges worked for the benefit of working-class Hawaiians, not the international communist movement.[9]

Quinn was also part of the Eisenhower administration's hope of building strong GOP organizations in the Pacific territories. He came into office with a "patronage bonanza" and "got to make some 550 appointments. . . . Beside his cabinet, he nominated all judges and hundreds of members of boards and commissions." But after the 1959 special election he was undercut by his lieutenant governor, Jimmy Kealoha, who insisted on making half the appointments, and a few members of the still-Republican majority in the state senate joined with Democrats to thwart the governor on some appointments and policies. Bottom line: "The disarray caused by power grabs and Quinn's inability to master them led to his defeat for re-election in 1962." Kealoha ran against Quinn in the 1962 primary, splitting the Republican vote.[10] Meanwhile, the ILWU and the Nisei veterans had been solidifying and building a Democratic organization, carrying John Burns to the governorship. He was reelected in 1966 and 1970. By late 1973, Burns was very ill with cancer, and although he kept the office its duties were taken over by his lieutenant governor, George Ariyoshi, who won in his own right in 1974. By then, the once-Republican legislature had passed permanently to the Democrats. The balance in 1974 was seventeen Democrats and eight Republicans in the state senate, and thirty-five Democrats and sixteen Republicans in the lower chamber. Later elections favored the Democrats more and more.

Ariyoshi was reelected in 1978 and 1982 despite primary opposition from Frank Fasi, the vigorous mayor of Honolulu. He might have been reelected again, but Hawaii had already succumbed to the national craze for term limits, and he had become ineligible to serve another term. His lieutenant governor, John Waihee, racially a Native Hawaiian (though also partly Chinese and white), defeated congressman Cecil Heftel in the 1986 primary and a Republican in the general, although by a narrow 52 to 48 percent. His 1990 victory was easier.[11] The 1994 election nearly saw the Democratic succession interrupted; Waihee's lieutenant governor, Filipino-descended Ben Cayetano, won with 35.8 percent of the vote as Fasi, running on his self-created "Best Party" ticket, picked up 30.0 percent. Republican congresswoman Pat Saiki took 28.6 percent, and a Green Party candidate won 3.4 percent.

Cayetano won another term in 1998, with a thin victory (49.5 to 48.2 percent) over Republican Linda Lingle. Lingle was a St. Louis native who went to college in Southern California and moved to Hawaii—Molokai, then Maui—in her twenties. Beginning in 1980 she was elected to five terms on the Maui County Council, and in 1990 she ran successfully for mayor of Maui, a four-year term. She was reelected in 1994. She built a record of careful budgeting yet encouraging tourism (Maui's potential was still to be realized) and job growth. By 1998 her political reputation had made her a plausible challenger to Cayetano. Even though she lost, she had the credibility to become state Republican chairperson, and as such she oversaw the election of more Republicans to the legislature.

In 2002 she won her party's nomination for governor. In that year the Democrats nominated Cayetano's lieutenant governor, Mazie Hirono. This time, Lingle won by a comfortable five percentage points, in a rare contest between two women, one Japanese-born, the other a Jew. Lingle thus became the first Republican, male or female, of any ethnicity, to be elected governor of Hawaii since William Quinn in 1959. She had substantial funding support from the Republican Jewish Coalition and AIPAC (American-Israel Public Affairs Committee, or "Israel lobby"), the leading Jewish organizations on the right, and as governor she followed a right-leaning agenda as far as the still-Democratic legislature would let her. She took centrist positions on abortion and the death penalty but promoted deregulation of businesses and decentralization of the state's unitary educational district (which she did not get done).[12] She was reelected in 2008 by a 62 to 35 percent margin when the Democrats were unable to persuade their presumably frontline candidates to run, and she outspent the Democrat, state senator Randy Iwase, about twenty to one.

In her second term, Lingle followed a more rightward path, in line with the directional shift of the GOP nationally. She closed a program of medical care for legal immigrants, reducing Medicaid coverage, and vetoed a measure passed by the legislature to legalize same-sex civil unions. She also quarreled with Hawaii's public-sector unions, which had become a mainstay of state Democratic power. "As agriculture and the docks became less important, the ILWU's power has waned; it has been replaced by the public employee unions," including the teachers.[13] As her gubernatorial term was coming to a close, and with Senator Dan Akaka retiring, she made a run for the Senate seat and won the Republican primary in August 2012. The Democrats nominated Mazie Hirono, who by then had been elected several times to one of Hawaii's two U.S. House seats. This time

Hirono won, 62 to 37 percent, about the same margin Lingle had achieved in her 2006 reelection as governor.[14]

The 2010 election brought Honolulu Democratic congressman Neil Abercrombie to the governorship. He had compiled a House record admired by many in his party, but as governor he proved abrasive and antagonistic to important party elements, and despite a much larger war chest he lost the 2014 primary to David Ige, a state senator.[15] Ige went on to defeat the Republican comfortably. Thus, in fifteen gubernatorial elections beginning with William Quinn at the time of statehood, Democrats won all of them except Quinn himself and Lingle in 2002 and 2006.

Hawaii's votes for U.S. senator have, if anything, been even more blue than its elections for governor. Hawaii has had seven senators since 1959. Only one has been a Republican, Hiram Fong, one of Hawaii's first two senators, twice reelected (1964, 1970). As a territorial legislator in 1945, Fong supported the "Little Wagner Act," allowing agriculture workers to join unions. In turn, labor supported him as an exception to its blanket backing of Democrats.[16]

The other senator-from-statehood, Democrat Oren E. Long, had been territorial governor in the early 1950s. His term lasted only until 1962 (Fong's to 1964), and Long decided not to run again. Stepping into the Senate race was Hawaii's first member of the House—there was only one, at-large, until after the 1960 census—Daniel K. Inouye. Medal of Honor winner for his exploits in France and Italy in World War II, he went on to win eight more elections to the Senate, rising to president pro tempore in 2010. For decades he was, far and away, Hawaii's most respected political figure.

Fong's successor was Spark Matsunaga, who ran for the House seat that Inouye vacated when he went to the Senate in 1962. Matsunaga ultimately served fourteen years in the House and another fourteen in the Senate until he died in office in 1990. Like Inouye, he was a decorated combat veteran, serving chiefly in the Nisei 100th Infantry Battalion. He fought successfully for the $20,000-per-prisoner reparation to the Japanese Americans still living who had been incarcerated in concentration camps during the war.[17]

The contest in 1990 to fill Matsunaga's seat was between Republican Pat Saiki, who had won the 1st District (central Honolulu) House seat in 1986 and 1988, and Daniel Akaka, who had filled the 2nd District seat (outer Honolulu and the rest of the islands) since

1976. Akaka, a Native Hawaiian, took Matsunaga's seat in 1990 by appointment of Governor Waihee. His Senate votes classify him as a solid Democratic liberal, with special efforts on civil rights bills. Congressman Ed Case, who had long been at odds with the state organization, challenged him in the 2006 primary, but Akaka had the support of Inouye, Abercrombie, and labor. Akaka won, in both Honolulu and the outer islands.[18]

With Inouye's death and Akaka's retirement, both in 2012, the long era of the two Dans ended. To fill Inouye's seat, Governor Abercrombie appointed his lieutenant governor, Brian Schatz. The other seat went to Mazie Hirono, who pushed back Ed Case in the Democratic primary, 58 to 41 percent, and then defeated ex-governor Lingle in the general. Schatz downed a Republican businessman, 69.8 to 27.7 percent, in 2014 to finish the final two years of Inouye's term. He was already compiling a voting record to tie him with Chris Murphy of Connecticut and Chuck Schumer of New York as the most liberal senator.[19]

The people whom Hawaii has sent to the U.S. House of Representatives have also been mainstream liberal Democrats, with few exceptions. Since statehood, Hawaii has held fifty-eight regular House elections and two special elections. Republican Pat Saiki won in 1986 and 1988; in 1990 she ran for the Senate but lost to Akaka. Republican Charles Djou won a special election in May 2010 when Ed Case and Colleen Hanabusa split the Democratic vote, but Djou lost in November to Hanabusa after Case dropped out. Of the fifty-eight regular House elections, Democrats have won fifty-six, and the parties split the two special elections. Incumbents have won remarkably often, with seats opening up usually because the holder decided to run for governor or senator; rarely has an incumbent been rejected, Governor Abercrombie being a rare and recent example.

That staying power began with the first congressman, Dan Inouye, who ran successfully for the Senate in 1962. Patsy Mink won six successive House terms from 1964 through 1974, then lost to Matsunaga in the 1976 senatorial primary. Mink won back the House seat in 1990, won another seven times, the last one posthumously in 2002 after she died of pneumonia on September 28 with her name still on the ballot in November. Matsunaga's successor in the 1st District was Cecil Heftel, who won five terms before he ran for governor in 1986 and lost to John Waihee in the primary. Mink's successor was Akaka,

who won seven House terms before he went to the Senate. When
the 1st District seat became open after Saiki tried for senator, it was
filled in 1990 by Neil Abercrombie, who went on to win ten terms
before he won the governorship in 2010. The only "nonestablishment"
Democratic congressman was Ed Case, who won Mink's seat in late
2002 and was reelected in 2004 but then lost a challenge in 2006 to
Akaka. Case voted to the right of Hawaii's Democratic mainstream,
and party regulars (Inouye, Akaka et al.) considered him a maverick.

All told, fourteen people have represented Hawaii in the U.S.
House since statehood. One, Djou, served only a few months;
another, Mark Takai, was elected in 2014 but died of pancreatic cancer before completing his term.[20] Despite the fact that the elements
that created the Democratic predominance in Hawaii in the 1950s—
the return of the Nisei (like Inouye), full citizenship for Asians, and
the strength of the ILWU—had aged and weakened some time ago,
the party and its fairly liberal wing have continued to win office.
Hawaii remains multiethnic, but whites like Schatz have begun to
play larger roles. The Public Employees Union has replaced the ILWU
as the labor union mainstay of the Democrats. The *Washington Post*
summed it up early in 2014: "In Hanabusa's candidacy, what remains
of Inouye's mostly Japanese-American political machine is fighting
for supremacy against a younger and whiter progressive wing. . . .
After Inouye's passing, [Randy] Perreira and his workers have lined
up behind Schatz." Perreira is president of the Government Employees Association, the state's largest union.[21] Meanwhile, the legislature
has been deeper than ever in Democratic hands; in 2013 and 2015
they outnumbered Republicans in the senate twenty-four to one, and
in the House forty-four to seven.[22] That preponderance held in 2016:
in 2017 the senate was unanimously Democratic and the house had
forty-five Democrats, five Republicans, and an independent.[23]

WASHINGTON

The other arguably blue state in the West has been Washington. It
is not now, and never has been, as blue as Hawaii, but it is generally
regarded as a Democratic state, with good reason, and has trended
more decidedly that way since the 1990s. Washington had a sporadi-
cally liberal tincture in the early twentieth century, when it elected
Miles Poindexter to the Senate. But Poindexter was a Progressive
Republican, not a Democrat. The Seattle general strike, which lasted

five days in February 1919, attested to the strength of organized labor in shipbuilding and other industries; but after it was over it was seized upon by conservatives as a bogeyman of bolshevism, despite its utter lack of violence. In the 1930s and 1940s, Washingtonians gave their presidential electoral votes to FDR all four times and to Truman in 1948; but so did the majority of Americans. The Washington of the first half of the twentieth century grew from a half million in 1900 to well over two million in 1950, most rapidly from 1900 to 1910 and in the 1940s, with its economy based on lumbering, agriculture, and marine-related activity. Boeing was founded in Seattle in 1916, expanded greatly in World War II, and kept on producing both military and civilian aircraft in the following decades. Its downside was its volatility because of dependence on Pentagon contracts. Its payroll in Washington State in 1969 included 101,000 workers, but that plummeted to 30,000 two years later. It rebounded, but it was a huge rollercoaster. Microsoft, Amazon, Starbucks, and the like would arrive later in the century; their more stable markets ameliorated some of Boeing's ups and downs.[24] By 2017, Amazon's "footprint of 8.1 million square feet" of office space equaled the combined next forty employers in the city.[25]

In 1950, Washington's political coloration was very light blue. It had given 52.6 percent of its presidential votes to Harry Truman two years before, a couple of points above the national average. Most of the counties in the state, whether west or east of the Cascades, favored Truman, although a few of the farming counties did not. The governor, Republican Arthur B. Langlie, had been mayor of Seattle in the late 1930s and was elected governor in 1940. He failed reelection in 1944 but won another term in 1948 and a third in 1952. Overall a conservative, frugal, moralistic reformer, Langlie was by no means a progressive in the tradition of Poindexter. In 1956 he ran against incumbent Democrat Warren Magnuson for the U.S. Senate and lost with 39 percent to Magnuson's 61 percent.

Magnuson had won four terms in the U.S. House from the 1st District (north Seattle) beginning in 1936. After a stint as a naval officer in the South Pacific early in World War II, he ran successfully for an open Senate seat in 1944. He would be reelected five times by safe margins, until Republican attorney general Slade Gorton unseated him, 54 percent to 46 percent, in the Reagan year of 1980. By then his seniority had elevated him to president pro tem of the Senate.

By all accounts he was respected and well regarded. The voters liked his record in support of environmental measures, such as keeping oil supertankers out of Puget Sound and protecting marine mammals—orcas, sea otters, and others—and the fishing industry. He saw to it that Washington received (more than) its fair share of federal money for highways, dams, and other public works when he was chair of the Senate Commerce and Appropriations committees, and he obtained money for the 1962 Seattle and 1974 Spokane world's fairs, for cancer research, and for agencies that morphed into the National Institutes of Health and the National Oceanographic and Atmospheric Administration. He could work both sides of the aisle, and he was friendly with Teamster president Dave Beck, with Seattle business leaders, and with his former colleague Lyndon Johnson, who was best man when Magnuson married in 1964. He accomplished much for his state, and the voters appreciated it.[26]

Magnuson's colleague in the Senate for over thirty years was another Democrat, Henry M. "Scoop" Jackson, who defeated conservative Republican and McCarthy ally Harry P. Cain in 1952. Jackson also would be reelected five times, serving until he died in office on September 1, 1983. Thus "Maggie" and "Scoop" were Washington's senators through most of the 1950s as well as the 1960s and 1970s. Jackson was somewhat better known nationally than Magnuson and was reelected with even larger margins, the greatest being with 82.4 percent in 1970. That indicates something of the character of the Washington electorate, because at that point opposition to the Vietnam War was very strong in many parts of the country and in the Democratic Party, and Jackson was clearly and vociferously on record as a supporter of it.

He was sometimes called "the senator from Boeing" and a "Cold War liberal." His strong views on national defense, including support for the anti-ballistic missile, made him a progenitor of the "neoconservatives" who were prominent in the George W. Bush administration. Indeed, two of them, Richard Perle and Paul Wolfowitz, were members of the "Jackson circle." But defense issues were not his only concerns and contributions. As chair of the Senate Interior Committee, he led in passage of the National Historic Preservation Act of 1966, creating the National Register of Historic Places, and three years later he brought about his "most far-reaching contribution to environmental protection," the National Environmental Policy Act, which President Nixon signed. If many Washingtonians disagreed with Jackson on Vietnam, they could applaud what he did for the environment, and even more, perhaps, in getting federal money for projects that meant jobs.

In the long view—one might say an Olympian view because this is Washington's story—the years from 1980 to 1992 were a time of relative upheaval in elections to the Senate compared to the long tenures of Magnuson and Jackson that preceded them and the Murray-Cantwell period that came some years later. Slade Gorton, Republican, defeated Magnuson in 1980, but Gorton lost his reelection bid in 1986 to Democrat Brock Adams. Undeterred, Gorton ran for Jackson's old seat in 1988. Governor John Spellman had appointed former governor Dan Evans to it, and Evans won a special election to certify his occupancy of the remaining five years of the term after Jackson died. But Evans did not like the Senate and declined to run for reelection. Gorton thus became the Republican candidate, and he defeated Democrat Mike Lowry by a slim 51 to 49 percent edge. This time Gorton was longer-lived, and he won reelection in the Republican year of 1994. By then, Patty Murray had won (in 1992) the former Magnuson-Adams seat, taking the Democratic primary and then the general over five-term District 8 congressman Rod Chandler.

Murray, from Seattle's northern suburb of Bothell, got into politics by going to Olympia in 1980 and arguing to preserve a community college class she was teaching on parent education, and which was threatened with defunding. According to legend, "a state legislator told her gruffly, 'You're just a mom in tennis shoes. You can't make a difference.'"[27] Whether she saved her class is unrecorded, but she saved the quotation and used it effectively in her later campaigns—for the school board, then for the state senate, and then in 1992 for the U.S. Senate. There she has been effective on educational, environmental, and foreign policy issues and has been part of the Democratic leadership while working across the aisle, most famously to forge with Congressman Paul Ryan the Bipartisan Budget Act of 2013. Resuming Washington's predilection for incumbents, she won again in 1998, defeating 3rd District congresswoman Linda Smith; in 2004 over 5th District congressman George Nethercutt; in 2010 over perennial hopeful Dino Rossi, who had previously lost two campaigns for the governorship; and in 2016 over former legislator and Republican state chair Chris Vance, 59 percent to 41 percent. In her five Senate campaigns Murray has won not overwhelmingly yet securely, with 54, 58, 55, 52, and 59 percent of the vote.

Since 2000, Murray's colleague has been Maria Cantwell, who came to the Seattle area from her native Indiana in 1983 to work for California senator Alan Cranston. In 1986 she ran successfully for the Washington house and was reelected in 1988 and 1990. In 1992 she contested the 1st District congressional seat, which had not elected a Democrat since 1950, but Cantwell broke the jinx—for one term. Upset in 1994, she left politics to become a marketing executive with an internet firm, RealNetworks, and made tens of millions—which financed her run in 2000 for Slade Gorton's Senate seat. The vote was extremely close, and after a recount Cantwell had won by just over two thousand votes of two and a half million cast. A libertarian won almost 65,000 votes, a small portion of which would have reelected Gorton. But Cantwell did win, and she thus became the second female Democratic senator from Washington. She was reelected much more comfortably in 2006 and again in 2012. Murray's and Cantwell's voting records have by no means been identical, but they both average out to roughly 75 percent on the liberal end of the spectrum, and higher than that on social issues.[28]

During the long careers of Senators Magnuson and Jackson, Washingtonians of course participated in many other elections. When Arthur Langlie left the governorship to run—unsuccessfully—for Magnuson's Senate seat in 1956, a Democrat succeeded him: Albert Rosellini, born in Tacoma of Italian immigrants. He gained a second term in the 1960 election but lost in 1964 to Republican Dan Evans. Rosellini cleaned up "atrocious conditions" in the state's prisons and mental hospitals, promoted the University of Washington Medical Center, and built (under budget) the famous floating bridge that carries State Route 520 across Lake Washington, thereby uniting Seattle with its high-tech eastern suburbs.[29] His Italian name and Catholic faith raised some suspicions that he might have connections with mob elements, but he was never indicted, much less convicted, of anything, despite J. Edgar Hoover era FBI surveillance.[30]

Beginning with Evans's defeat of Rosellini in 1964, the governorship changed hands, and parties, three times in the next twenty years. Evans gave the keynote at the 1968 Republican convention but did not endorse the nominee, Nixon, instead sticking with Nelson Rockefeller. As governor, Evans championed higher education, helping create the state's community college system and the experimental Evergreen State College. He was a supporter, morally and fiscally, of the University of Washington. In his second term he created the state Department of Ecology and promoted environmental issues in a number of ways. In 1972 he was elected to a third consecutive term, defeating Rosellini once more. Early on, in 1965, "Evans openly condemned the John Birch Society and its attempt to infiltrate the Republican party." In the 1970s analysis of Neal Peirce, "Evans and his friends represent a modern, pragmatic form of Republicanism so progressive in tone . . . that the Republican party today appears to be the more progressive party of the state."[31] Out of office, he was appointed by Governor John Spellman to the Senate in 1983 when Jackson died, and Evans then won the special election to fill the five remaining years of Jackson's term.[32]

Evans's successor in Olympia was Washington's only female governor up to that time, Democrat Dixy Lee Ray. She was a marine biologist of some distinction, a faculty member at the University of Washington. Nixon appointed her to the Atomic Energy Commission in 1972, and she chaired it from 1973 to 1975, after which Gerald Ford made her assistant secretary of state for oceans, international environment, and scientific affairs. She resigned after six months because Secretary of State Henry Kissinger never consulted her. In 1976, without previous political experience or party affiliation, she ran for governor in the Democratic primary, won by about a percentage point, and then won the general, 53 percent to 45 percent, over Republican John Spellman, a King County executive. As governor she was a resolute defender of nuclear power and thus at odds with many Democrats, and she feuded with Senator Magnuson when she tried to admit oil-laden supertankers into Puget Sound. In 1980 she lost the Democratic primary to future congressman Jim McDermott, 56 percent to 41 percent.[33]

McDermott, in turn, lost the general to John Spellman. A moderate-to-progressive Republican, Spellman had the good luck to run in the Reagan year of 1980 but the bad luck to be in office during the severe recession that hit the state in the early 1980s. An environmentalist, he stopped oil companies from building a pipeline under Puget Sound and took other positions that were as unloved among Republican partisans as Dixy Lee Ray's pro-nuclear advocacy was among her Democrats. Spellman lost his bid for reelection in 1984 to

Democrat and Weyerhaeuser heir Booth Gardner, 53 percent to 47 percent. Spellman was the last Republican governor, to date, elected in Washington State.[34] Gardner won a second term in 1988, and he was followed by a string of Democrats—Mike Lowry, "a strong liberal," in 1992, Gary Locke in 1996 and 2000, Christine Gregoire in 2004 and 2008, and Jay Inslee in 2012 and 2016.[35] All were elected by margins of four to eighteen percentage points except Gregoire in 2004, who required several recounts and suits before she prevailed over Republican Dino Rossi by 129 votes out of 2.7 million cast. To sum up, the governorship alternated between parties several times since the 1950s, but it has been in Democratic hands since 1984.

Elections to the state legislature take place in even-numbered years. The term is two years for the house and four years for the senate, but staggered so that half the senators are elected in one year, the other half two years later, providing overlap. Of the thirty-four biennial elections to the senate from 1950 through 2016, Democrats won majorities twenty-seven times, Republicans seven, although twice, in 1980 and 1986, a Democrat switched to the Republicans, shifting the majority to the GOP, and in 2016 the result was twenty-four Republicans, twenty-four Democrats, and one "independent Democrat," meaning a virtual tie. Elections to the house gave Democrats twenty-five majorities, Republicans seven, with two ties in 1978 and 1998. Few real exceptions to Democratic control took place. Both houses went Republican from Democratic in the Eisenhower year of 1952, although by small margins. In the Reagan year of 1980 the senate shifted to Republican when one Democrat changed parties, and the house went Republican by fourteen votes. But both chambers reverted to Democratic control in 1982. The third period of Republican success was 1994 and 1996, when they eked out slim majorities in the senate and more substantial ones in the house. Again, Democrats soon regained majorities.[36]

Washington's congressional races have exhibited fairly clear patterns since 1950. With six seats in 1950, the state gained a seventh seat in 1952 as a result of its population surge in the 1940s. It added an eighth in 1982, a ninth in 1992, and a tenth in 2012. Except when new districts were carved out of the existing ones, the boundaries of districts have not changed radically: District 1 has been the north side and suburbs of Seattle, including Redmond, extending sometimes across the Sound as well; District 2, Everett, Bellingham, and north to the Canadian border; District 3, the southwest corner of the state; District 4, immediately east of the Cascades; District 5, Spokane and the Pelouse; District 6, much of Tacoma plus Bremerton; District 7, the rest of Seattle; District 8, eastern suburbs of Seattle, usually including Mercer Island and Bellevue; District 9, part of Tacoma and nearby suburbs; District 10, Olympia and just east of it. From 1950 through 2016 inclusive, there have been 272 elections in Washington to the U.S. House. Democrats won 156 (57.4 percent), Republicans 116 (42.6 percent). Recently, from 1996 through 2016 inclusive, there have been 102 elections, with Democrats improving their preponder- ance slightly, winning sixty-one (59.8 percent) to the Republicans' forty-one (40.2 percent). Overall, therefore, the blue has become a little deeper in the past thirty years.

The shifts have not been evenly distributed geographically. The 1st District has elected Democrats twelve times and Republicans twenty-two times (1950–2016), but there has been a blue shift over time: Republicans won consistently through the 1950s, 1970s, and 1980s, but except for 1994 and 1996 Democrats have won every time since, including present governor Jay Inslee (1998–2010) and Suzan DelBene (2012, 2014, and 2016). Microsoft's headquarters, Nintendo of America's, and part of Google make much of the district a land of techies, to Democrats' benefit. District 2 elected Democrats twenty-five times and Republicans nine times, six of which were in 1952–62 and the other three in 1994–98.

District 3 is the closest to a swing district. With twenty-three Democratic victories and eleven Republican, it appears similar to District 2, including six wins by psychologist and outdoorsman Brian Baird (1998–2008). But although five of the Republican wins were in the 1950s, four have been very recent (2010–16), and with the removal in 2011 of Olympia to create the new District 10 it may remain Republican or at least closely contested for a while. In Baird's era, District 3 was "one of only nine districts in the country with a Cook Partisan Voting Index of 'Even,' meaning its political perfor- mance closely approximates the national average," but as of 2015 "it now leans Republican by [two] percentage points."[37]

District 4 is a safe Republican district. Since 1950, Democrats have won only six times, five of them from 1970 through 1978. Republican "Doc" Hastings held it from 1994 through 2012. The easternmost District 5 appears about even on the historical record, with nineteen Republican wins and fifteen Democratic, but all of the latter were by House speaker Tom Foley from 1964 through 1992. Since then Republicans have carried the 5th, including (since 2004) Cathy McMorris Rodgers, chair of the House Republican conference.

West of the Cascades, except for District 3, Democrats have mostly prevailed. In District 6 no Republican has won since 1962. In District 7 a Republican was elected only in 1962; Democrats won the other thirty-three, notably Jim McDermott from 1988 through 2014. The 8th District was created in 1982 to include Republican voters, and it has done so all eighteen times since. District 9 elected a Republican in 1994, but otherwise District 9 and the new District 10 have voted Democratic. As a rough generalization, the two districts east of the Cascades, plus the Seattle-suburban 8th, have become firmly Republican, with the 3rd leaning that way, while the other seven have voted more consistently Democratic.

The state's votes for president have roughly followed the trends described for governor, members of Congress, and the legislature: fairly evenly balanced in the 1950s and very gradually shifting more Democratic over time, except for the 1980s, when the blue trend stalled for Reagan, and then gave way to Democratic preponderance in the 2000s and 2010s. After voting for FDR and Truman, Washington chose Eisenhower in both 1952 and 1956, both times by percentages slightly below his national figure (the state 54 percent each time, the nation 55 and 57 percent). In 1960 it went for Nixon over Kennedy by about 30,000 votes out of 1.24 million cast. Again, in 1964 its percentage for Lyndon Johnson was about one point above his overall mark.

In 1968, Washington gave its electoral votes to Democrat Hubert Humphrey (47 percent) rather than Richard Nixon (45 percent). George Wallace's segregationist American Independent ticket won 7.4 percent of Washingtonians' votes, well below his national figure of 13.5 percent. In 1972, however, Nixon trounced George McGovern in Washington as he did in most states, though not as soundly as across the country. The state stuck with the Republican candidate in 1976, as Gerald Ford took 50 percent to Jimmy Carter's 46 percent, the rest going to a scattering of minor candidates.

Ronald Reagan helped make Washington red in 1980 and 1984. Neither Reagan nor Carter did as well in the state as they did nationally, in part because independent John Anderson won 10.6 percent of Washington's votes as against his 6.6 percent nationally. In 1984, without the Anderson distraction, Reagan won again in the state, but as in his previous election not with as decisive a margin as he did nationally.

Reagan was the last Republican presidential candidate, to date, to win Washington State. Dukakis beat the senior Bush in 1988, and Clinton did so in 1992. Clinton won 43.4 percent, George H. W. Bush 32.0 percent, and Ross Perot 23.7 percent, well beyond Perot's 18.9 percent nationally. Clinton captured Washington again in 1996 with just under 50 percent to Dole's 37 percent, with Perot taking about 9 percent and the Green and other candidates winning the rest. The blue coloration of the state manifested itself in 2000 as Gore beat the younger Bush, 50.2 percent to 44.0 percent, with Ralph Nader, the Green candidate, winning 4.1 percent; it did so again in 2004 as Kerry beat Bush there by about 53 to 46 percent.

Obama won decisively in 2008 (58 to 41 percent for John McCain) and in 2012 (56 to 41 percent for Mitt Romney).[38] Hillary Clinton outpolled Trump by a half million votes in 2016, taking 54.3 percent. Thus, of seventeen presidential contests held in Washington from 1952 through 2016, Republicans won seven and Democrats ten. But there was a shift over time: Republicans won consistently from 1952 through 1984, except for 1964 and 1968, whereas Democrats have won in 1988 and each time since. That, and the other evidence presented in the preceding pages, qualifies Washington as a Democratic state—not as deep blue as Hawaii, but it qualifies.

Reflections

The several thousand elections recapitulated in these chapters are interesting in themselves and in what they reveal about the partisan trends in the nineteen states of the West. Several other aspects of political behavior, however, have not been confronted, though they reappear in several, if not all, of the nineteen. We reflect upon them here. We begin with party building: do efforts to re-create— or simply to create a party organization where none functionally existed—have common elements amid these histories? We have also encountered the rise of, and pushback against, term limits. Incumbency also deserves a look; how common and advantageous has it been? Redistricting after each census, and at unusual times (as in Texas in 2003–5), majorities' temptation to gerrymander, and the emergence of nonpartisan electoral commissions deserve some remarks. We conclude with a brief consideration of the surprising election of 2016.

SO YOU WANT TO BUILD A PARTY?

As the preceding chapters show, there are many ways to build, or resuscitate, or just hang on to a political party's majority in a state. But they all have in common the smart use of the tools at hand—whatever media and money are available—and hard work. That can be generated by many motives, none unfamiliar: greed for "pelf," eagerness for "privilege," for power, for atavistic identification with a party's history (often mythology), or simply conviction or idealism. But right, left, or center, party building requires serious, intelligent effort. Of course, it also requires leadership—forceful, genial, or just clever. It takes money, "the mother's milk of politics," as Jesse Unruh said in 1962. Yet, by itself, money is not determinative; the bigger war chest doesn't always win the election. So now, some retrospective looks at party building in the nineteen-state West.

In this survey of those states across two-thirds of a century, several examples of successful party building stand out. In Oklahoma, Henry Bellmon took an almost nonexistent Republican Party by the scruff of the neck in the early 1960s and propelled it into existence and, ultimately, into overwhelming control of state government. In South Dakota in the 1950s, George McGovern turned from the threshold of a promising academic career to make his Democratic Party more than competitive; unfortunately for the party, his departure into national prominence removed his spark and the South Dakota Democracy reverted to minority status. In Oregon in the late 1940s and into the 1950s, Monroe Sweetland engineered the shift of the state from red to blue, and of the Democratic Party from reaction to liberalism; he even forced the state Republican Party to adopt at least centrist positions and candidates. In Arizona, Barry Goldwater and his colleagues in the Phoenix chamber of commerce recast the state's politics unswervingly to the right. The giant states of Texas and California changed their predominant parties radically over time—Texas from blue to red, California from red to blue, and each was (and is) too large to attribute those shifts to any one personality. In each, several agents of change and fresh coalitions brought about those alterations. John Tower, though not himself a builder, became a rallying point for Republicans in Texas; then Bill Clements led them into the governorship; Tom DeLay and friends brought about a (so far) permanent GOP dominance in the Texas congressional delegation. Jesse Unruh in Los Angeles and Phillip Burton in San Francisco extended Democratic supremacy in those cities, and Alan Cranston and others converted the "Adlai Clubs" of the early 1950s into an effective California Democratic Council. Dan Inouye, his fellow Nisei, and the longshoremen's union made Hawaii the bluest state in the West. Other examples dot the preceding pages.

What did these party builders have in common? Almost all of them were young in their most active party-building years, from their mid-twenties to early forties. They had the vigor and commitment of youth. They also had charisma: the dedication to a political party and what they understood its principles to be—whether social democracy or individualistic free enterprise or somewhere between—and the ability to attract followers and to persuade them to join their cause. Youth and charisma are no surprises. Besides them, as a practical matter, a leader needed time and money: "time" often meant a profession like the law or part-time duties like public office that permitted organizing and contacting; "money" could be one's own or funds provided by others, like Bellmon's oilman angel. These essentials limited the presence of women among the statewide or metropolitan-wide party builders. Thus, few women were major leaders before 2000, though Dolores Huerta of Hispanic California, Joan Finney of Kansas, and Texas's Barbara Jordan, Ann Richards, and Frances "Sissy" Farenthold were important leaders from the 1970s to the 1990s. As for being young, Bellmon, McGovern, Goldwater, Sweetland, Cranston, Phil Burton, and others were most effective when they were not long out of college or the military and in their thirties or forties. Older than that, they either faded or went on to elective office. Maintaining contact with the communities or states they were involved with was important. McGovern's statewide organizing of South Dakota's Democrats, as mentioned, slipped after he went to the Senate, whereas Bellmon's efforts continued after he became governor. The countercase in Oklahoma was Fred Harris, the bright star of liberalism until he went to the Senate and then held prestigious national offices. However, he lost touch with his home-state support.

In states like Oklahoma and South Dakota, the party builders drove many miles and talked with many locals in cafes and barber shops, on streets, and on farms. They also replaced county committee members if they were inattentive or ineffective, retired the geriatric, and recruited the young. They were attentive to the issues and positions that cemented coalitions, most obviously labor unions for the Democrats (which often meant thwarting so-called right-to-work legislation) and corporate and chamber of commerce people for Republicans. The Religious Right was often a Republican bloc as well, but in some states, especially in the Southwest and Great Plains, it could overwhelm and take over the local and state party organizations. Party building—and maintenance—were essential to winning office. Ingenious use of existing institutions such as ballot initiatives and electoral reforms (such as term limits) also marked western party building in recent decades.

TERM LIMITS, INCUMBENCY, AND REDISTRICTING

A flurry of extensions of gubernatorial terms took place between 1962 and 1974. Several western states had specified two-year terms for governor in their original constitutions, often with the thought that legislatures, the more "popular" branch of government, would be more in control. Of the nineteen western states examined, eleven have had four-year gubernatorial terms at least since 1950, and eight had two-year terms. Each of those eight expanded its governor's term to four years, beginning with Colorado in 1962 and concluding with Kansas, South Dakota, and Texas, effective in 1974.[1] As these states gradually became less rural, more efficient and professional executive agencies and government became achievable and desirable, and the four-year term at the top helped.

About twenty years after the movement to extend the terms of governors and other statewide elected officials to four years, a movement arose to limit not only governors but also legislators and, its proponents hoped, members of Congress to a restricted number of elected terms. The heyday of the term-limits movement ran from 1990 to 1994. It succeeded especially in states that had ballot initiatives, the device usually employed rather than new laws, since legislators were understandably unenthusiastic about voting themselves out of office, even down the road. Of the nineteen states, eight have legislative term limits.[2] Another five of the nineteen enacted limits; however, they were later repealed either by the legislature or the state supreme court, not for the content of the laws but on more technical grounds.[3] Attempts to limit the number of terms to which a member of Congress could be elected passed in several states. These laws were court-challenged. The leading organization promoting term limits defended them, but the Supreme Court struck them down on the ground that, since members of the U.S. House and Senate were federal officers, they could not be term-limited by a state,[4] only by an amendment to the U.S. Constitution. State chapters of the League of Women Voters in Arkansas and Maine sued successfully to overturn term-limit laws in their states, and the national League came out in opposition in 1991.[5]

U.S. Term Limits, Inc., has been the major advocacy organization for term limits. Its argument has been to promote and elect "citizen legislatures, not career politicians," and to stand up "against government malpractice." Opponents have argued that the means for limiting terms already exist, namely, elections. The term-limits movement has purported to be nonpartisan, but its proponents have been on the right, beginning with the 1994 "Contract with America,"

Newt Gingrich's program. The Heritage Foundation supported the idea at that time. In 2008, Senator Jim DeMint, Republican of South Carolina, proposed a constitutional amendment that would have allowed limits on members of Congress.[6] It has been remarked that the term-limits movement arose when it did because, going into the 1994 election campaign, the Democrats had controlled the House for forty years. The only apparent way to break that hold was to unseat incumbents. As it happened, the Republicans won the House anyway in 1994 without the help of term limits.

Incumbency was indeed common, indeed normal, in the late twentieth century. In the nineteen western states, 5,335 elections for the four major offices took place from 1950 through 2016 inclusive. There were 319 for presidential elections, 358 for governors, 441 for U.S. senators, and 4,217 for members of the House of Representatives.[7] Nationally, three incumbent presidents were defeated when they ran for another term: Gerald Ford in 1976, Jimmy Carter in 1980, and George H. W. Bush in 1992. In these cases and in those when the incumbent was reelected, the western states generally followed the national pattern. When governors ran for reelection, they seldom lost. In only nine cases did an incumbent governor run in, and lose, the next general election. They include Pat Brown's loss to Reagan in 1966 and Ann Richards's to the younger George Bush in 1994. In recent decades governors have often been term-limited, which at least prevents them from losing reelection.

Senators have not been immune in that way, have therefore often run successive times, and have lost reelection more often than governors—though still not often. In the nineteen western states, there have been twenty-nine senatorial defeats for reelection since 1950, with Oregon and South Dakota leading with four each. Six states, however, have never voted out an incumbent senator running for reelection. Of all the elections to the House from those states, only 118 incumbents running for reelection have been defeated. The term-limits proponents had a point. Once someone was elected to high office, they usually were able to keep it. The term-limiters' argument was that they would likely become complacent or corrupt. Opponents of term limits argued that reelected officials gain ever more experience, expertise, and contacts that benefit their state or district.[8]

Incumbency has always been aided by the friendly drawing of district lines, sometimes called "the incumbent protection plan." The

Burton brothers' redistrictings in California and the Tom DeLay redistricting in Texas in 2003 are cases in point, and there have been others less dramatic. Some western states have turned over redistricting to election commissions, nonpartisan or at least less partisan. Having the most consequential impact on districting were the Supreme Court's one man, one vote decisions of the early and mid-1960s, which in many states (including Texas and California, as described above) greatly reduced rural representation and expanded urban-metropolitan. As well, the Voting Rights Act of 1965 mandated district lines assuring representation of minorities, which resulted in sharp increases in African American voters as well as elected officials, notably in Texas.[9]

Of the thirteen states across the country that have commissions whose task is to decide or suggest what the borders of state legislative districts should be, eight are in the West: Alaska, Arizona, California, Colorado, Hawaii, Idaho, Montana, and Washington. Additionally, Oklahoma and Texas have "backup commissions" to decide on district lines "if the legislature is unable to agree." No two of these commissions are exactly alike in their makeup and how they are selected, but they all have overt bipartisanship in common. The California Citizens' Redistricting Commission, resulting from Proposition 11 of 2008, which took effect in 2011, is the most elaborate and the largest, with fourteen members. Washington's commission has five and is perhaps the simplest: "The majority and minority leaders in each legislative chamber each select one registered voter to serve as commissioner, and those four commissioners choose a nonvoting fifth commissioner to serve as chair."[10] Nonpartisan or bipartisan commissions largely developed in the 1990s and 2000s and have not stamped out contentiousness. As one scholar writes, "Clearly the use of independent commissions is no panacea," because in several instances their proposals were "thrown out in court." "Even in Idaho, a state dominated by one party, it took the [commission] three rounds to develop maps that would withstand judicial scrutiny" in 2001.[11]

Several other patterns emerge from the political history of the nineteen states, and each could fruitfully be explored in depth (and some have been). One example is the Religious Right. It was strong, even at times politically decisive, in Texas and Oklahoma, but not in California or the secular Pacific Northwest. Why? And why was there no significant "Religious Left"? A strong one existed early in the twentieth century, in many manifestations, which may be collectively called "the Social Gospel."

Another pattern is areas that remain persistently liberal or conservative. Red voters have tended lately to reside in rural areas, which can cross state lines. For example, Oregon's east-of-Cascades District 2 borders on Idaho's District 1, as does Washington's District 5, and all are red and have been for some time. New Mexico's District 2, mostly coterminous with "Little Texas," votes much like adjacent Texas districts in the Panhandle, the Permian Basin, and nearby. Eastern Colorado's politics resemble western Kansas's, next door, much more than Denver's. Metropolitan areas have generally been blue, more so in recent times than earlier. Portland was purple in the 1940s and 1950s and has become deep blue; Phoenix was dark red in Goldwater's day but has taken on a purplish tone more recently. Few places outside the West can match the deep blue of Denver and its inner suburbs, or Seattle, San Francisco, or Los Angeles. In the Mountain and Plains states, with small populations and few congressional districts, the largest metro areas are economically centered on agriculture and resource extraction. Those cities trend red; examples are Oklahoma City, Tulsa, Wichita, Billings, and Boise. (Omaha has often been an exception.) Towns with broad-based arts-and-sciences universities with professional schools in law, medicine, business, music, and others—Lawrence, Lincoln, Boulder, Missoula, Eugene, Tucson, for example—have usually been blue patches in red surroundings; A&M universities, however, have been less so.

Radicals of various stripes have surfaced in the West from time to time: the Sagebrush Rebellion in some of the Mountain states around 1980; the survivalists around Hayden Lake, in the Idaho Panhandle, since the 1990s; the secessionists in northeastern California and northeastern Colorado since 2010. They garner media attention but not votes because they exist for the most part outside the two dominant parties. All of these patterns collectively underscore the fact that it is tempting, although mistaken, to overgeneralize about the West. The region is more accurately understood politically as a collection of states or, even better, of parts of states.

THE 2016 SURPRISE

The result of the 2016 presidential election was a great surprise even to most pollsters and pundits and probably to Donald Trump himself.

It is possible that Hillary Clinton's momentum was stopped and suppressed when the director of the FBI, James Comey, reopened the issue of her e-mails ten days before the election, only to close the investigation on the eve of the election, or that Russian cybermeddling had a negative effect. These events cannot be measured definitively, only speculated upon.

Another culprit, from the Clinton point of view, may well have been the oft-remarked-upon social media like Facebook and Twitter and the use of them by Trump and the Right. President Obama, in a postelection interview with the *New Yorker*'s David Remnick, said that "an explanation of climate change from a Nobel prize–winning physicist looks exactly the same on your Facebook page as the denial of climate change by somebody on the Koch brothers' payroll." Truth and fact, settled science and reasoned policy, stumbled when attacked by conspiracy theories and negatives, in Obama's view.[12]

It is easier to state who voted for Clinton or Trump than to explain why. The demographer William H. Frey reported two days after the election that exit polls showed that "Trump bested Democrat Clinton by a net of 6,414,252 votes among voters *over* age 45 [whereas among] voters *under* age 45, Clinton received a net of 6,679,191 votes more than Trump." "Racial minorities . . . made up 37 percent of voters under age 30," whereas "whites constituted 78 percent of the voters over age 45 and 87 percent of those over age 65. And 65 percent of the older whites are not college graduates." In short, "non college whites comprised 37 percent of all voters and favored Trump over Clinton by more than 2 to 1." Frey identifies a "cultural generation gap, a disconnect between older, primarily working class, whites and the increasingly diverse and globalized nation we are becoming." The older whites, especially in the Rust Belt, perceive that "America's culture and way of life has changed for the worse" since the 1950s, whereas "millennials, minorities, and whites with college degrees . . . see it as a change for the better."[13]

Until late on election night, the Clinton forces touted their "firewall" in Rustbelt states that Democratic presidential candidates normally won, notably Pennsylvania, Ohio, Michigan, and Wisconsin. Trump won Ohio by more than 400,000 votes but barely squeaked by in the other three by a total of 77,744 votes.[14] That gave him 46 electoral votes. Without them, his total of 306 would have fallen to 260, and Clinton's 232 would have risen to 278, enough to cross the victory threshold of 270. In that sense, from the Democratic stand-point, the Rustbelt "misbehaved."[15]

The West, however, did not. The blue Pacific states remained deep blue. Pennsylvania, Michigan, and Wisconsin may have mis-behaved, that is, voted otherwise than observers expected them to. The Pacific states, though, stayed on their customary trajectory. The hitherto "swing states" Colorado, Nevada, and New Mexico voted more firmly than previously for the Democratic candidate. Arizona went closely for Trump, remaining a purplish swinger. The Pacific states have become the Democrats' firewall, if there is one, not the eastern Rustbelt. The Great Plains and the northern Rocky Mountain states went decisively for Trump, continuing their long-term pattern. Texas did not lurch, or even slip very much, toward Clinton; Trump carried the state 52.2 percent to Clinton's 43.2 percent. Romney did a little better in 2012 than Trump did in 2016. The most populous Texas counties continued to increase in Democratic percentage of presidential vote, from Obama's in 2012 to Hillary Clinton's in 2016: Dallas rose from 57.1 to 60.8 percent; Harris (Houston) from 49.4 to 54.0 percent; Bexar (San Antonio) from 51.6 to 54.2; Travis (Austin) from 60.1 to 65.8 percent; and El Paso from 65.5 to 69.1 percent. The only large county to maintain a Republican plurality was Tarrant (Fort Worth), though it slipped from 57.1 percent in 2012 to 51.7 percent in 2016.[16] Wistful Democrats hoping to sip of victory waters in Texas would be tantalized but could only hope for 2020 (or 2024, or whenever). Until a viable state and local party organization revives, Democrats will surely continue to lose elections in Texas. And just as Texas (and Oklahoma) remained deep red in 2016, California and the other Pacific states became bluer than ever. The large counties in California voting for Clinton included Los Angeles (71.8 percent), San Diego (56.3 percent), San Francisco (84.5 percent), and Sacra-mento (58.0 percent). As noted earlier, the one-time home of the Far Right, Orange County, voted for a Democrat for the first time since 1936—Clinton getting 59.9 percent to Trump's 42.3 percent.

At the close of 2013, columnist Dan Balz of the *Washington Post* surveyed the political scene, contrasting states controlled by Repub-licans—governor and both chambers of the legislature—and those controlled by Democrats. Assessing issues one by one—taxation, economic stimuli, same-sex marriage, and others—he concluded that the "red-state-blue-state divide" had deepened, forming two different approaches to government, "one . . . grounded in principles of lean and limited government and on traditional values; the other . . . built on a belief in the essential role of government and on tenets of cultural liberalism."[17] The two approaches, or philosophies, have become even more distinct in the intervening years. In a companion piece, Balz singled out Texas and California as the "behemoths in size, population, history, and influence" that "stand at opposite poles in the debate over red-state vs. blue-state governance." He concludes that these two "behemoths" preeminently "stand as proxies for the national debate about the size and shape of government and which direction a divided America should go in the future."[18]

More recently and even more pointed, Alan Howard, a cultural anthropologist from the University of Hawaii, contrasted "red America" with "blue America." "Red" emphasizes property rights, gun rights, and absence of regulation "without regard for the common good." "Blue" believes that "freedom implies the right to pursue personal goals without being encumbered by government regulation; the right to worship as we please, to choose as partners and marry whomever we please," and more.[19] These are two distinct cultures, in essence.

The West's two political and demographic giants, Texas and California, have gone their separate ways on opposite trajectories over the nearly seven decades since 1950. They exemplify two different versions of America. The blue pole and the red pole are the products of deep and long-developing trends. They did not quickly become such polar opposites, and they will no more quickly dissolve their respective redness and blueness. The color codes would seem here to stay.

Appendix
Election Results, 1950–2016

The results of the 5,335 elections that constitute the database for this book, and the percentages of the votes for the candidates, are arranged alphabetically by state, from Alaska through Wyoming. The initial table for each state contains the results of the elections for president, governor, and U.S. senator. After that come tables for the elections to the U.S. House of Representatives from that state. The percentages do not always add up to 100, but rather sometimes to 99 or 101, because of rounding error and, in some elections, because scattered minor candidates or write-ins have not always been included. In a few very closely contested elections, raw vote counts rather than percentages are provided.

As noted earlier, the source for elections of presidential electors, U.S. senators, and members of the U.S. House of Representatives is the website of the clerk of the U.S. House, which contains returns from 1920 through 2014. For 2016, not yet online, I used "Election Results 2016" on the *New York Times* website. All had 100 percent of precincts reported. For state governor results, in most cases I consulted the websites of the appropriate official in charge of elections for that state, usually the secretary of state, though at times it was an election commissioner or board. If that source did not go back far enough, I sometimes consulted state blue books or other sources. I was almost always able to find an official, credible source.

National or regional political party affiliations are given as abbreviated below. State-specific or otherwise local parties are explained via footnotes.

MAJOR POLITICAL PARTIES

Am Ind	American Independent Party (in some states, affiliates known as American Party or Independent American Party)
Con	Constitution Party
conserv	unspecified "conservative"
D	Democratic Party
Green	Green Party of the United States
ind	running independently of any party
IPP	Independent Progressive Party
La Raza	Partido Nacional de la Raza Unida
Lib	Libertarian Party
NLP	Natural Law Party
Peace Fr	Peace and Freedom Party
Populist	Populist (or People's) Party
Prog	Progressive Party
Proh	Prohibition Party
R	Republican Party
Reform	Reform Party USA
Soc	Socialist Party of America/Socialist Party USA
SLP	Socialist Labor Party
SWP	Socialist Workers Party

Alaska Election Results

Alaska has had one at-large House district since statehood.

	PRESIDENT	GOVERNOR	SENATE	HOUSE AT-LARGE
1960	Nixon 50.9 Kennedy 49.1		Bartlett D 63.4 McKinley R 36.6	Rivers D 56.8 Rettig R 43.2
1962		Egan D 52.3 Stepovich R 47.7	Gruening D 58.1 Stevens R 41.9	Rivers D 54.5 Thomas R 45.5
1964	Johnson 65.9 Goldwater 34.1			Rivers D 51.5 Thomas R 48.5
1966		Egan D 48.4 Hickel R 50.0 Grasse ind 1.6	Bartlett D 75.5 McKinley R	Rivers D 48.4 Pollock R 51.6
1968	Humphrey 42.6 Nixon 45.3 Wallace 12.1		Gravel D 45.1 Rasmuson R 37.4 Gruening D 17.4	Begich D 45.8 Pollock R 54.2
1970		Egan D 52.4 Miller R 46.1 Anderson Am Ind 1.5	Kay D 40.4 Stevens R 59.6	Begich D 55.1 Murkowski R 44.9
1972	McGovern 34.6 Nixon 58.1 Schmitz 7.2		Guess D 22.7 Stevens R 77.3	Begich D 56.2 Young R 43.8
1974		Hammond R 45,602 Egan D 45,381 Vogler Am Ind 4,740	Gravel D 58.3 Lewis R 41.7	Hensley D 46.2 Young R 53.8
1976	Carter 35.7 Ford 57.9 Macbride 5.5			Hopson D 28.9 Young R 70.8 write-in 0.2
1978		Croft D 20.2 Hammond R 39.1 Kelly ind 12.3 Wright ind 1.9 Hickel write-in 26.4	Hubbs D 24.1 Stevens R 75.6	Rodey D 44.6 Young R 55.4
1980	Carter 26.4 Reagan 54.3 Anderson 7.0 Clark 11.7		C Gruening D 45.9 F Murkowski R 53.7	Parnell D 25.9 Young R 73.8
1982		Sheffield D 46.2 Fink R 37.2 Randolph Lib 14.9 Vogler Am Ind 1.7		Carlson D 28.8 Young R 71.1
1984	Mondale 29.9 Reagan 66.7 Bergland 3.1		Havelock D 28.8 Stevens R 71.2	Begich D 41.7 Young R 55.0 Breck Lib 3.2
1986		Cowper D 47.3 Sturgelewski R 42.6 3 others 8.7	Olds D 44.0 F Murkowski R 54.0	Begich D 41.0 Young R 56.4 Breck Lib 2.3
1988	Dukakis 36.2 Bush 59.5			Gruenstein D 37.2 Young R 62.4
1990		Knowles D 30.9 Sturgelewski R 26.2 Hickel ind 38.9 Others 4.0	Beasley D 32.1 Stevens R 66.2 write-in 1.6	Devens D 47.8 Young R 51.6
1992	Clinton 30.2 Bush 39.4 Perot 28.4 6 others 1.4		Smith D 38.4 F Murkowski R 53.0 Jordan Green 8.3	Devens D 42.8 Young R 46.7 Milligan Green 3.9 States ind 6.2
1994		Knowles D 41.8 Campbell R 40.8 Coghill ind 13.0 Sykes Green 4.1		Smith D 32.7 Young R 56.9 Whitmore Green 10.2
1996	Clinton 33.3 Dole 50.8 Perot 10.9 Nader 3.1		Obermeyer D 10.3 Stevens R 76.7 Whittaker Green 12.5	Lincoln D 36.4 Young R 59.4 Grames Green 1.9 Nemec Am Ind 2.1
1998		Knowles D 51.3 Lindauer R 17.9 3 others 12.6 Taylor write-in 18.3	F Murkowski R 74.5 Sonneman D 19.7 Gottlieb Green 3.2 Kohlhaas Lib 2.3	Young R 62.6 Duncan D 34.6 Grames Green 2.7
2000	Gore 27.7 Bush 58.6 Nader 10.1 4 others 3.2			D Young R 69.6 Greene D 16.5 A Young Green 8.2 2 others 5.5
2002		F Murkowski R 55.9 Ulmer D 40.7 4 others 3.4	Stevens R 78.2 Vondersaar D 10.5 Sykes Green 7.2 2 others 3.9	Young R 74.5 Greene D 17.3 deForest Green 6.3 Clift Lib 1.7
2004	Kerry 35.5 Bush 61.1 4 others 3.2		Knowles D 45.5 L Murkowski R 48.6 5 others 5.9	Young R 71.1 Higgins D 22.4 Feller Green 3.8 Anders Lib 2.4
2006		Knowles D 41.0 Palin R 48.3 Halcro ind 9.5 3 others 1.1		Benson D 40.0 Young R 56.6 3 others 3.2
2008	Obama 37.9 McCain 59.4 3 others 2.2		Begich D 47.8 Stevens R 46.5 Bird Am Ind 4.2 Others 1.6	Berkowitz D 45.0 Young R 50.1 Wright Am Ind 4.5 write-in 0.4
2010		Berkowitz D 37.7 Parnell R 59.1 Others 3.3	L Murkowski ind 99.0	Crawford D 30.5 Young R 69.0 write-in 0.5
2012	Obama 40.8 Romney 54.8 Others 4.5			Cissna D 28.6 Don Young R 63.9 others 7.4
2014		Walker ind 48.1 Parnell R 46.4 Others 5.5	Sullivan R 48.8 Begich D 45.6 2 others 5.6	Young R 51.6 Dunbar D 40.8 McDermott Lib 7.6
2016	Trump 51.3 Clinton 36.6		L Murkowski R 44.3 Miller D 29.5 Others 26.2	Young R 50.5 Lindbeck D 36.5 McDermott Lib 10.1 Other 2.9

Arizona Election Results: President, Governor, Senator

Year	PRESIDENT	GOVERNOR	SENATE
1950		JH Pyle R 50.8 A Frohmiller D 49.2	C Hayden D 62.8 B Brockett R 37.2
1952	Eisenhower 58.4 Stevenson 41.6	J Pyle R 60.2 J Haldeman D 39.8	B Goldwater R 51.3 E McFarland D 48.1
1954		E McFarland D 52.5 J Pyle R 47.5	
1956	Eisenhower 61.0 Stevenson 38.9	E McFarland D 59.6 H Griffen R 50.5	C Hayden D 61.4 R Jones R 38.6
1958		P Fannin R 55.1 R Morrison D 44.9	B Goldwater R 56.1 E McFarland D 43.9
1960	Nixon 55.5 Kennedy 44.4	P Fannin R 59.3 L Ackerman D 40.7	
1962		P Fannin R 54.8 S Goddard D 45.2	C Hayden D 54.9 E Mecham R 45.1
1964	Goldwater 50.4 Johnson 49.5	S Goddard D 53.2 R Kleindienst R 46.8	P Fannin R 51.4 R Elson D 48.6
1966		J Williams R 53.8 S Goddard D 46.2	
1968	Nixon 54.8 Humphrey 35.0 Wallace 9.6	J Williams R 57.8 S Goddard D 42.2	B Goldwater R 57.2 R Elson D 42.8
1970		J Williams R 50.9 RH Castro D 49.1	P Fannin R 56.0 S Grossman D 44.0
1972	Nixon 61.6 McGovern 30.4		
1974		RH Castro D 50.4 R Williams R 49.6	B Goldwater R 58.3 J Marshall D 41.7
1976	Carter 39.8 Ford 56.4 McCarthy 2.6 2 others 1.25		D DeConcini D 54.0 S Steiger R 43.3 3 others 2.7
1978		B Babbitt D 52.5 E Mecham R 44.8 2 others 2.7	
1980	Reagan 60.6 Carter 28.2 Anderson 8.8 others 2.4		B Goldwater R 49.5 B Schulz D 48.4 others 2.1
1982		B Babbitt D 62.5 L Corbet R 32.5 S Steiger Lib 5.0	D DeConcini D 56.9 P Dunn R 40.3 R Clemons Lib 2.8
1984	Reagan 66.4 Mondale 32.5 Lib 1.1		
1986		E Mecham R 39.7 C Warner D 34.5 B Schulz ind 25.9	J McCain R 60.5 R Kimball D 39.5
1988	Bush 60.0 Dukakis 38.9 Paul 1.1		D DeConcini D 56.7 K DeGreen R 41.1 R Tompkins Lib 1.8
1990		F Symington R 49.7 T Goddard D 49.2 7 others 2.1	
1992	Bush 38.5 Clinton 36.5 Perot 23.8 others 0.2		J McCain R 55.8 C Sargent D 31.6 E Mecham ind 10.5 3 others 2.1
1994		F Symington R 52.5 E Basha D 44.3 J Buttrick Lib 3.1	J Kyl R 53.7 S Coppersmith D 39.5 S Grainger Lib 6.8
1996	Clinton 46.5 Dole 44.3 Perot 8.0 Browne 1.0		
1998		JD Hull R 60.9 P Johnson D 35.5 K Gallant Lib 2.7 4 others 0.9	J McCain R 68.7 E Ranger D 27.2 3 others 4.1
2000	Bush 51.0 Gore 44.7 Nader 3.0 3 others 0.5		J Kyl R 79.3 W Toel ind 7.8 V Hansen Green 7.8 B Hess Lib 5.1
2002		J Napolitano D 46.2 M Salmon R 45.2 R Mahoney ind 6.9 B Hess Lib 1.7	
2004	G Bush 54.9 Kerry 44.9 3 others 0.2		J McCain R 76.7 S Starky D 20.6 E Hancock Lib 2.6
2006		J Napolitano D 62.6 L Munsil R 35.4	J Kyl R 53.3 J Pederson D 43.5 R Mack Lib 3.2
2008	McCain 53.6 Obama 45.1 6 others 1.3		
2010		J Brewer R 54.3 T Goddard D 42.5 5 others 3.2	J McCain R 59.1 R Glassman D 34.8 D Nolan Lib 4.7 Green 1.5
2012	Romney 53.5 Obama 44.5		J Flake R 49.2 R Carmona D 46.2 M Victor Lib 4.6
2014		D Ducey R 53.5 F DuVal D 41.6 B Hess Lib 3.3 others 1.0	
2016	Trump 49.5 Clinton 45.4 Johnson 3.9 Stein 1.2		J McCain R 53.4 A Kirkpatrick D 41.1 G Swing Green 5.5

Arizona Elections to the U.S. House, Districts 1–5

Arizona had two congressional districts from 1950 through 1960: District 1 was Maricopa County, and District 2 the rest of the state. The 1960 census added a third district; Maricopa continued to be District 1, District 2 went to Pima and Yuma (Tucson and Yuma city), and District 3 the central and northern areas. District 4 was added for the 1972 election, with District 1 assigned to south Phoenix, Mesa, and Tempe; District 2 to Tucson and most of Pima County; District 3 to west Phoenix, part of Yuma County, and Flagstaff; and District 4 to east Maricopa County northeast to the Utah line. District 5 was in place for the 1982 election, covering east Tucson and Pima County, and the other four districts included parts of Maricopa County and radiated out to the state's borders.

	DISTRICT 1	DISTRICT 2	DISTRICT 3	DISTRICT 4	DISTRICT 5
1950	J Murdock D 60.5 C Divelbiss R 39.4	H Patten D 69.1 J Curnutte R 30.9			
1952	J Rhodes R 54.0 J Murdock D 46.0	H Patten D 56.8 W Frey R 43.1			
1954	J Rhodes R 53.1 D Adams D 46.9	S Udall D 62.1 H Zipf R 37.9			
1956	J Rhodes R 54.9 W Mahoney D 45.1	S Udall D 60.1 J Speiden R 39.9			
1958	J Rhodes R 59.2 J Haldiman D 40.7	S Udall D 60.9 J Speiden R 39.1			
1960	J Rhodes R 59.3 R Harless D 40.8	S Udall D 55.8 M Matheson R 44.3			
1962	J Rhodes R 58.7 H Peterson D 41.3	M Udall D 58.3 R Burke R 41.7	G Senner D 56.1 J Clark R 43.9		
1964	J Rhodes R 55.3 J Ahearn D 44.7	M Udall D 58.7 W Kimble R 41.3	G Senner D 51.5 S Steiger R 48.5		
1966	J Rhodes R 67.1 P Riggs D 32.9	M Udall D 59.6 A McGinnis R 40.4	S Steiger R 56.9 G Senner D 43.0		
1968	J Rhodes R 71.6 R Miller D 28.4	M Udall D 70.3 A McGinnis R 29.7	S Steiger R 63.4 R Watkins D 36.7		
1970	J Rhodes R 68.5 G Pollock D 31.5	M Udall D 69.1 M Herring R 29.9	S Steiger R 62.1 O Beatty D 37.9		
1972	J Rhodes R 57.3 G Pollock D 42.7	M Udall D 63.5 G Savoie R 36.5	S Steiger R 63.2 J Brown D 47.0	J Conlan R 53.0 T Wykoff D 37.0	
1974	J Rhodes R 51.1 P Fullinwider D 42.3 J Sanders LLJ 6.6[1]	M Udall 62.0 K Dolgaard R 38.0	S Steiger R 51.1 P Bosch D 48.9	J Conlan R 55.3 B Brown D 44.7	
1976	J Rhodes R 57.3 P Fullinwider D 40.7 S Dodge Lib 1.4 H Braun ind 0.6	M Udall D 59.3 L Gutterson R 39.4 M Emmerling Lib 2.4	B Stump D 47.5 F Koory R 42.3 B McCune ind 10.2	E Rudd R 48.6 T Mason D 48.2 P Harper Lib 3.1	
1978	J Rhodes R 71.0 K Graves D 29.0 J Bach Lib 1.1 B McDonald SWP 0.9	M Udall D 52.5 T Richey R 45.4	B Stump D 85.0 K Cooke Lib 15.0	E Rudd R 63.1 M McCormick D 33.8	
1980	J Rhodes R 73.3 S Jancek D 21.4 I Leitch Lib 4.2 R Roper SWP 1.1	M Udall D 58.1 R Huff R 40.4 B Stefanov Lib 1.5	B Stump D 64.3 B Croft R 30.0 S Hayse Lib 5.7	E Rudd R 62.6 L Miller D 37.4	
1982	J McCain R 65.9 B Hegarty D 30.5 R Dodge Lib 3.6	M Udall D 70.9 R Laos R 27.4 J Sampson YSA 1.7[2]	B Stump R 63.3 P Bosch D 36.7 D Stauffer Lib 3.9	E Rudd R 65.7 W Earley D 30.4	J McNulty D 49.7 J Kolbe R 48.3 R Auster Lib 2.0
1984	J McCain R 78.1 H Braun D 21.9	M Udall D 87.7 L Torrez PBP 12.3[3]	B Stump R 71.8 B Schuster D 26.5 L Valencia Lib 1.8	E Rudd R 100	J Kolbe R 50.9 J McNulty D 48.2 H Johnson Lib 0.9
1986	J Rhodes R 71.3 H Braun D 28.7	M Udall D 73.3 S Clark R 23.3 L Torrez PBP 3.5	B Stump R 100	J Kyl R 64.6 P Davis R 35.4	J Kolbe R 64.9 J Ireland D 35.1
1988	J Rhodes R 72.1 J Fillmore D 27.9	M Udall D 73.3 J Sweeney R 26.7	B Stump R 68.9 D Moss D 28.6 J Parsons LWL 2.6[4]	J Kyl R 87.1 G Sprunk Lib 12.9	J Kolbe R 67.8 J Belcher D 32.2
1990	J Rhodes R 99.5 2 write-ins 0.5	M Udall D 65.9 J. Sweeney R 34.1	B Stump R 56.6 R Hartstone D 43.4	J Kyl R 61.3 M Ivey D 38.7	J Kolbe R 64.8 C Phillips D 35.2
1992	S Coppersmith D 51.3 J Rhodes R 44.6 T Goldstein Peace Fr 4.1	E Pastor D 56.0 D Shooter R 30.0 D Detaranto Lib 4.0	B Stump R 61.5 R Hartstone D 34.4 P Volponi NLP 4.2	J Kyl R 59.2 W Wybeck D 26.7 D Collings ind 9.7 T McDermott Lib 4.4	J Kolbe R 66.5 J Toevs D 29.7 P Willis Lib 4.7
1994	M Salmon R 56.0 C Blanchard D 39.0 B Howarth Lib 4.9	E Pastor D 62.3 R McDonald R 32.7 J Bertrand Lib 5.0	B Stump R 70.1 H Sprague D 29.9	J Shadegg R 60.2 C Cure D 36.0 M Yannone Lib 3.8	J Kolbe R 67.7 G Auerbach D 28.7 P Murphy Lib 3.5
1996	M Salmon R 60.2 J Cox D 39.8	E Pastor D 65.0 J Buster R 30.8 A Bangle Lib 4.2	B Stump R 66.5 A Schneider D 33.5	J Shadegg R 66.8 M Milton D 33.2	J Kolbe R 68.7 M Nelson D 25.9 J Zajac Lib 2.8 E Finkelstein Reform 2.5
1998	M Salmon R 64.6 D Mendoza D 35.4	E Pastor D 67.8 E Barron R 28.0 R Duncan Lib 3.1 G Schultz Reform 1.1	B Stump R 67.3 S Starky D 32.7	J Shadegg R 64.7 E Ehst D 31.2 2 others	J Kolbe R 51.6 T Volgy D 45.2 P Murphy Lib 2.5 B Connery Reform 0.8
2000	J Flake R 53.6 D Mendoza D 42.4 J Burroughs Lib 4.0	E Pastor D 68.5 G Barenholz R 26.9 G Weber Lib 2.6 B Shelor NLP 2.0	B Stump R 65.7 G Scharer D 31.4 E Carlson Lib 3.0	J Shadegg R 64.0 B Jankowski D 32.7 E Hancock Lib 3.3	J Kolbe R 60.1 G Cunningham D 35.3 M Green Green 3.1 A Nost Lib 1.4
2002	R Renzi R 49.2 G Cordova D 45.6 E Porr Lib 5.1	T Franks R 59.9 R Camacho D 36.5 E Carlson Lib 3.5	J Shadegg R 67.3 C Hill D 30.3 M Yannone Lib 2.4	E Pastor D 67.4 J Barnert R 27.8 A Gibbons Lib 4.8	J Hayworth R 61.2 C Columbus D 36.3 W Severin Lib 2.6
2004	R Renzi R 58.5 P Babbitt D 36.2 J Crockett Lib 5.2	T Franks R 59.2 R Camacho D 38.5 P Gammill Lib 2.4	J Shadegg R 80.1 M Yannone Lib 19.9	E Pastor D 70.1 D Karg R 25.7 G Fallon Lib 4.2	J Hayworth R 59.5 E Rogers D 38.2 M Kielsky Lib 2.3
2006	R Renzi R 51.8 E Simon D 43.4 D Schlosser Lib 4.8	T Franks R 58.6 J Thrasher D 38.9 P Gammill Lib 2.5	J Shadegg R 59.3 H Paine D 38.2 M Yannone Lib 2.5	E Pastor D 72.5 D Karg R 23.9 R Harders Lib 3.6	H Mitchell D 50.4 J Hayworth R 46.4 W Severin Lib 3.1
2008	A Kirkpatrick D 55.9 S Hay R 39.4 B Maupin ind 3.4 T Eichenauer Lib 1.3	T Franks R 59.4 J Thrasher D 37.2 P Gammill Lib 2.3 W Crum Green 1.1	J Shadegg R 54.1 B Lord D 42.1 M Shoen Lib 3.9	E Pastor D 72.1 D Karg R 21.2 R DeWitt Green 3.6 J Cobb Lib 3.1	H Mitchell D 53.2 D Schweikert R 43.6 W Severin Lib 3.3
2010	P Gosar R 49.7 A Kirkpatrick D 43.7 N Patti Lib 6.6	T Franks R 64.9 J Thrasher D 31.1 P Gammill Lib 4.1	B Quayle R 52.2 J Hulburd D 41.1 M Shoen Lib 5.0 L Clark Green 1.6	E Pastor D 66.9 J Contreras R 27.5 J Cobb 3.0 R DeWitt Green 2.6	D Schweikert R 52.0 H Mitchell D 43.2 N Coons Lib 4.8
2012	A Kirkpatrick D 48.8 J Paton R 45.1 K Allen Lib 6.1	R Barber D 50.4 M McSally R 49.6	R Grijalva D 58.4 G Mercer R 37.1 B Guerra Lib 4.5	P Gosar R 66.8 J Robinson D 28.4 J Pamelia Lib 3.8 R Grayson AE 1.0[5]	M Salmon R 67.2 S Morgan D 32.8
2014	A Kirkpatrick D 52.6 A Tobin R 47.4	M McSally R 109,704 R Barber D 109,543	R Grijalva D 55.7 G Mercer R 44.2	P Gosar R 70.0 M Weisser D 25.8 C Rike Lib 4.2	M Salmon R 59.6 J Woods D 30.4
2016	T O'Halleran D 50.7 P Babeu R 43.3 R Parrish Green	M McSally R 57.0 M Heinz D 43.0	R Grijalva D 100 4 write-ins	P Gosar R 71.5 M Weisser D 28.5	A Biggs R 64.1 T Fuentes D 35.9

[1] Life Liberty Justice. [2] Young Socialist Alliance. [3] People Before Profit Alliance. [4] Land-Water-Legacy. [5] Americans Elect Party of Arizona.

Arizona Elections to the U.S. House, Districts 6–9

District 6 appeared in 1992, with District 5 becoming most of Tucson, plus Pima and Cochise Counties, District 6 running from the northern edge of Phoenix to Utah, District 2 west Phoenix and north and west to California and Utah, and the other four covering parts of Phoenix and Maricopa County. District 7 and District 8 appeared in 2002 and the numbers were reshuffled: District 1 was assigned to the northern half of the state, District 2 to Phoenix, Glendale, and Sun City, District 3 to north Phoenix and Paradise Valley, District 4 to southwest and downtown Phoenix (a heavily Hispanic area), District 5 to Tempe and Scottsdale, District 7 to Yuma and the southwest (also Hispanic), and District 8 to Tucson. The 9th District appeared in 2012: District 1 became the northeast including Flagstaff; District 2, Tucson and the southeast corner of the state; District 3, the southwest from Nogales to California; District 4, the western areas from part of Yuma north to Utah including Prescott; and Districts 5–9 covering parts of Maricopa County.

	DISTRICT 6	DISTRICT 7	DISTRICT 8	DISTRICT 9
1992	K English *D* 53.0 D Wead *R* 41.4 S Stannard *ind* 5.6			
1994	J Hayworth *R* 54.6 K English *D* 41.5 S Fuller *Lib* 3.9			
1996	J Hayworth *R* 47.6 S Owens *D* 46.6 R Anderson *Lib* 5.8			
1998	J Hayworth *R* 53.0 S Owens *D* 43.7 R Anderson *Lib* 3.3			
2000	J Hayworth *R* 61.4 L Nelson *D* 35.6 R Duncan *Lib* 3.0			
2002	J Flake *R* 65.9 D Thomas *D* 31.6 A Wagner *Lib* 2.5	R Grijalva *D* 59.0 R Hieb *R* 37.1 J Nemeth *Lib* 3.9	J Kolbe *R* 63.3 M Ryan *D* 33.6 J Duarte *Lib* 3.1	
2004	J Flake *R* 79.4 C Sritar *D* 20.6	R Grijalva *D* 62.1 J Sweeney *R* 33.7 D Kaplan *Lib* 4.3	J Kolbe *R* 60.4 E Bacal *D* 36.2 R Anderson *Lib* 3.4	
2006	J Flake *R* 74.8 J Blair *Lib* 25.2	R Grijalva *D* 61.1 R Drake *R* 35.4 J Cobb *Lib* 3.6	G Giffords *D* 54.3 R Graf *R* 42.1 2 others 3.6	
2008	J Flake *R* 62.4 R Schneider *D* 34.5 R Biondi *Lib* 3.0	R Grijalva *D* 63.3 J Sweeney *R* 32.8 R Petrulsky *Lib* 3.9	G Giffords *D* 54.7 T Bee *R* 42.8 P Davis *Lib* 2.5	
2010	J Flake *R* 66.4 R Schneider *D* 29.1 D Tapp *Lib* 3.1 R Grayson *Green* 1.4	R Grijalva *D* 50.2 R McClurg *R* 44.2 H Meyer *ind* 2.8 G Keane *Lib* 2.7	G Giffords *D* 48.8 J Kelly *R* 47.3 S Stoliz *Lib* 3.9	
2012	D Schweikert *R* 61.3 M Jette *D* 33.3 2 others 5.4	E Pastor *D* 81.7 J Cobb *Lib* 18.3	T Franks *R* 63.3 G Scharer *D* 35.1 S Dolgos *AE* 1.6[1]	K Sinema *D* 48.7 V Parker *R* 44.6 P Gammill *Lib* 6.6
2014	D Schweikert *R* 64.9 J Williamson *D* 35.1	R Gallego *D* 74.9 J Cobb *Lib* 14.8	T Franks *R* 75.8 S Dolgos *AE* 24.2	K Sinema *D* 54.7 W Rogers *R* 41.9 P Gammill *Lib* 3.5
2016	D Schweikert *R* 62.1 J Williamson *D* 37.9	R Gallego *D* 75.2 E Nunez *R* 24.7	T Franks *R* 68.5 M Salazar *Green* 31.4	K Sinema *D* 60.9 D Giles *R* 39.0

[1] Americans Elect Party of Arizona.

California Election Returns: President, Governor, Senator

In the California election results, *R-D* and *D-R* indicate use of the cross-filing procedure. For example, in 1952 William Knowland filed as the candidate of both the Republican and Democratic Parties. See discussion of cross-filing in chapter 6.

	PRESIDENT	GOVERNOR	SENATE
1950		E Warren R 64.9 J Roosevelt D 35.1	Nixon R 59.2 HG Douglas D 40.8
1952	Eisenhower 56.9 Stevenson 43.1		W Knowland R-D 87.7 R Borough IPP 11.9 others 0.4
1954		G Knight R 56.8 R Graves D 43.1	
1956	Eisenhower 55.6 Stevenson 44.4		T Kuchel R 54.0 R Richards D 45.6 others 0.4
1958		P Brown D 59.8 W Knowland R 40.2	C Engle D 57.0 G Knight R 42.9
1960	Nixon 50.3 Kennedy 49.7		
1962		P Brown D 51.9 R Nixon R 46.9 others 1.2	T Kuchel R 56.3 R Richards D 43.5 other 0.2
1964	Johnson 59.2 Goldwater 40.8		G Murphy R 51.5 P Salinger D 48.5
1966		R Reagan R 57.6 P Brown D 42.3	
1968	Nixon 47.8 Humphrey 44.7 Wallace 6.7		A Cranston D 51.8 M Rafferty R 40.9 P Jacobs Peace Fr 1.3
1970		R Reagan R 52.8 J Unruh D 45.1	JV Tunney D 53.9 G Murphy R 44.3 2 others 1.6
1972	Nixon 55.0 McGovern 41.5		
1974		J Brown D 50.1 H Flournoy R 47.3 2 others 2.5	A Cranston D 60.5 HL Richardson R 36.2 2 others 3.3
1976	Ford 49.3 Carter D 47.6		SI Hayakawa R 50.2 JV Tunney D 46.9 3 others 2.9
1978		J Brown D 56.1 E Younger R 36.5 E Clark ind 5.5 2 others 2.0	
1980	Reagan 52.7 Carter 35.9 Anderson 8.6		A Cranston D 56.5 P Gann R 37.1 D Bergland Lib 2.4 D Wald Peace Fr 2.4 J Griffin Am Ind 1.6
1982		G Deukmejian R 49.3 T Bradley D 48.1 3 others 2.6	P Wilson R 51.5 J Brown D 44.8 3 others 3.7
1984	Reagan 57.5 Mondale 41.3		
1986		G Deukmejian R 60.5 T Bradley D 37.4 3 others 2.1	A Cranston D 49.3 E Zschau R 47.9 3 others 2.8
1988	Bush 51.1 Dukakis 47.6		P Wilson R 52.8 L McCarthy D 44.0 3 others 3.2
1990		P Wilson R 49.3 D Feinstein D 45.8 3 others 5.0	
1992	Clinton 46.0 Bush 32.6 Perot 20.6		D Feinstein D 54.3 (2 yrs) J Seymour R 38.0 3 others 7.7 B Boxer D 47.9 B Herschensohn R 43.0 3 others 9.1
1994		P Wilson R 55.2 K Brown D 40.6 3 others 4.2	D Feinstein D 46.7 (full term) M Huffington R 44.8 4 others 8.4
1996	Clinton 51.1 Dole 38.2		
1998		G Davis D 58.0 D Lungren R 38.4 5 others 3.7	B Boxer D 53.0 M Fong R 43.0 5 others 4.0
2000	Gore 53.5 Bush 41.7		D Feinstein D 55.9 T Campbell R 36.6 5 others 7.5
2002		G Davis D 47.3 B Simon R 42.4	
2004	Kerry 54.4 Bush 44.4		B Boxer D 57.8 B Jones R 37.8 3 others 5.4
2006		A Schwarzenegger R 55.9 P Angelides D 39.0 4 others 5.2	D Feinstein D 59.5 D Mountjoy R 35.1 4 others 5.4
2008	Obama 61.1 McCain 37.0		
2010		J Brown D 53.8 M Whitman R 40.9 4 others 5.3	B Boxer D 52.2 C Fiorina R 42.2 4 others 5.6
2012	Obama 60.2 Romney 37.1		D Feinstein D 62.5 E Emken R 37.5
2014		J Brown D 59.2 N Kashkari R 40.8	
2016	Clinton 61.5 Trump 31.5		K Harris D 62.4 L Sanchez D 37.6

California Elections to the U.S. House, Districts 1–3

As a result of frequent renumbering, California's share of congressional districts rose from twenty-three in 1950 to fifty-three in 2002. The northern area bordering Oregon has consistently had the fewest districts, while San Diego and Imperial Counties, bordering Mexico, have gotten the most districts. In general, District 1 has included the Pacific coast north of Marin County; District 2, the northeast along the Sierras until 1982, when it was confined to inland areas; and District 3, mostly Sacramento until 1992, after which it included counties north of that city. The second column gives the statewide total percentage vote for Democrats and Republicans, the number of districts contested, and how many each major party won.

	STATE SPLIT	DISTRICT 1	DISTRICT 2	DISTRICT 3
1950	52.2R, 44.1D (23) 13R, 10D	H Scudder R 54.0 R Kent D 46.0	C Engle D-R 100	L Johnson R-D 100
1952	52.4R, 44.5D (30) 20R, 10D	H Scudder R-D 86.3 C Sullivan IPP 13.6	C Engle D-R 100	J Moss D 50.8 L Wood R 47.8 H Thomsen Ind 1.4
1954	49.2R, 49.1D 19R, 11D	H Scudder R 59.1 M Kortum D 40.9	C Engle D-R 100	J Moss D 65.3 J Phillips R 34.7
1956	47.7R, 52.3D 17R, 13D	H Scudder R 53.6 C Miller D 46.4	C Engle D-R 100	J Moss D 68.6 N Stevenson R 31.4
1958	40.0R, 60.0D 14R, 16D	C Miller D 54.9 F Dupuis R 45.1	H Johnson D 61.0 C Tarr R 39.0	J Moss D-R 100
1960	46.1R, 53.9D 14R, 16D	C Miller D 51.6 F Dupuis R 48.4	H Johnson D 62.7 F Nagel R 37.3	J Moss D 100
1962	48.1R, 51.9D (38) 13R, 25D	C Miller D 50.7 D Clausen R 49.2	H Johnson D 64.7 F Nagel R 35.4	J Moss D 74.8 G Smith R 25.2
1964	47.1R, 52.9D 13R, 25D	D Clausen R 59.1 G McCabe D 40.9	H Johnson D 64.6 C Merriam R 35.4	J Moss D 74.3 E Gjelsteen R 25.7
1966	53.2R, 46.8D 16R, 22D	D Clausen R 64.9 T Storer D 34.7 others 0.4	H Johnson D 70.9 W Romack R 29.1	J Moss D 67.5 T Feil R 32.5
1968	54.4R, 44.1D 17R, 21D	D Clausen R 75.1 D Duffy R 21.4 2 others 3.5	H Johnson D 60.8 O Dunaway R 37.5 Am Ind 1.7	J Moss D 56.0 E Duffy R 41.8 Am Ind 2.2
1970	49.0R, 49.4D 18R, 20D	D Clausen D 63.4[1] W Kortum R 36.6	H Johnson D 77.9 L Gilbert R 19.2 J Carigg Am Ind 2.9	J Moss D 61.6 E Duffy R 36.6 A Priest Am Ind 1.9
1972	46.5R, 52.0D (43) 20R, 23D	D Klausen R 62.2 W Nighswonger D 34.1 Peace Fr 3.7	H Johnson D 68.3 F Callahan R 28.6 D Paradis Am Ind 3.1	J Moss D 69.9 J Rakus R 30.1
1974	40.6R, 56.8D 15R, 28D	H Johnson D 85.9 D Paradis Am Ind 14.1	D Clausen R 53.0 O Klee D 42.7	J Moss D 72.3 I Lenei R 27.7
1976	43.2R, 55.8D 14R, 29D	H Johnson D 73.9 J Taylor R 26.1	D Clausen R 56.0 O Klee D 41.0 Peace Fr 3.0	J Moss D 72.9 G Marsh R 27.1
1978	47.6R, 51.1D 17R, 26D	H Johnson D 59.4 J Taylor R 40.6	D Clausen R 52.0 N Bork D 45.3 Peace Fr 2.8	R Matsui D 53.4 S Smoley R 46.6
1980	51.2R, 44.8D, 3.3 Lib 20R, 23D	E Chappie R 53.7 H Johnson D 39.9 J McLarin Lib 6.4	D Clausen R 54.2 N Bork D 42.0 D Mosier Lib 2.6 Peace Fr 1.3	R Matsui D 70.6 J Murphy R 26.5 B Daniel Lib 2.9
1982	47.5R, 50.3D (45) 17R, 28D	D Bosco D 49.8 D Clausen R 47.2 D Redick Lib 2.9	G Chappie R 57.9 J Newmyer D 40.5 Peace Fr 1.6	R Matsui D 89.6 B Daniel Lib 7.5 Peace Fr 2.9
1984	49.4R, 48.3D 18R, 27D	D Bosco D 62.3 D Redick R 37.7	G Chappie R 69.5 H Cozad D 30.5	R Matsui 100
1986	45.9R, 52.3D 18R, 27D	D Bosco D 67.5 F Sampson R 26.6 Peace Fr 5.9	W Herger R 58.3 S Swendiman D 39.6 H Pendery Lib 2.2	R Matsui D 75.9 L Landowski R 24.1
1988	44.5R, 52.7D 18R, 27D	D Bosco D 62.9 S Vanderbilt R 28.4 Peace Fr 8.7	W Herger R 58.8 W Meyer D 38.5 H Pendery Lib 2.6	R Matsui D 71.2 L Landowski R 28.8
1990	46.0R, 49.0D 19R, 26D	F Riggs R 43.3 D Bosco D 41.9 Peace Fr 14.8	W Herger R 63.7 E Rush D 31.2 R Crain Lib 5.1	R Matsui D 60.3 L Landowski R 34.8 D McCann Lib 4.9
1992	41.5R, 51.7D (52) 22R, 30D	D Hamburg D 47.6 F Riggs R 45.1 M Howard Lib 3.0 Peace Fr 4.3	W Herger R 65.2 E Freedman D 28.0 H Pendery Lib 6.8	V Fazio D 51.2 H Richardson R 40.3 R Crain Lib 8.6
1994	48.8R, 47.6D 25R, 27D (reg) 26R, 26D (spec)	F Riggs R 53.3 D Hamburg D 46.7	W Herger R 64.2 M Jacobs R 26.0 D Kidd Am Ind 7.3 H Pendery Lib 2.5	V Fazio D 49.7 T Lefever R 46.1 R Crain Lib 4.1
1996	45.3R, 49.6D 23R, 29D	F Riggs R 49.6 M Alioto D 43.5 E Rossi Lib 6.9	W Herger R 60.8 R Braden D 33.7 W Brunner Lib 2.4 P Thiessen NLP 3.0	V Fazio D 53.5 T Lefever R 41.1 T Erich Reform 3.5 E Donelle Lib 1.9
1998	43.9R, 51.4D 24R, 28D	M Thompson D 61.8 M Luce R 32.9 E Rossi Lib 2.7 Peace Fr 2.5	W Herger R 62.5 R Braden D 34.5 P Thiessen NLP 3.0	D Ose R 52.4 S Dunn D 45.0 R Crain Lib 2.6
2000	42.6R, 51.8D 20R, 32D	M Thompson D 65.0 R Chase R 28.0 E Rossi Lib 2.7 C Kreier NLP 3.0 P Elizondo Reform 1.3	W Herger R 65.7 S Morgan D 28.2 C Martin Lib 2.6 J McDermott NLP 3.5	D Ose R 56.2 B Kent D 40.4 D Tuma Lib 2.3 C Jones NLP 1.1
2002	45.1R, 51.3D (53) 20R, 33D	M Thompson D 64.1 L Wiesner R 32.4 K Bastian Lib 3.5	W Herger R 65.8 M Johnson D 29.3 C Martin Lib 2.2 P Thiessen NLP 2.7	D Ose R 62.5 H Beeman D 34.4 D Tuma Lib 3.1
2004	43.3R, 53.5D 20R, 33D	M Thompson D 66.9 L Wiesner R 28.3 P Elizondo Green 4.8	W Herger R 66.9 M Johnson D 33.1	D Lungren R 61.9 G Castillo D 34.8 D Tuma Lib 3.2
2006	37.4R, 53.1D 19R, 34D	M Thompson D 66.2 J Jones R 29.0 P Elizondo Green 3.2 Peace Fr 1.6	W Herger R 64.2 A Sekhon D 32.5 E Hinesley Lib 3.4	D Lungren R 59.5 B Durston D 37.8 D Tuma Lib 1.7 Peace Fr 1.0
2008	36.7R, 59.9D 19R, 34D	M Thompson D 68.1 Z Starkewolf R 23.4 C Wolman Green 8.5	W Herger R 57.9 J Morris D 42.1	D Lungren R 49.5 B Durston D 43.9 D Tuma Lib 2.3 Peace Fr 4.3
2010	44.9R, 55.1D 19R, 34D	M Thompson D 62.8 L Hanks R 31.0 M Rodrigues Lib 2.6 C Wolman Green 3.6	W Herger R 57.1 J Reed D 42.8	D Lungren R 50.1 A Bera D 43.2 D Tuma Lib 2.4 J Leidecker Am Ind 2.5 Peace Fr 1.8
2012	37.1R, 60.6D 15R, 38D	D LaMalfa R 57.4 J Reed D 42.6	J Huffman D 71.2 D Roberts R 26.8	J Garamendi D 54.2 K Vann R 45.8
2014	41.4R, 57.0 14R, 39D	D LaMalfa R 61.0 H Hall D 39.0	J Huffman D 75.0 D Mensing R 25.0	J Garamendi D 52.7 D Logue R 47.3
2016	34.9R, 64.3 16R, 37D	D LaMalfa R 59.1 J Reed D 40.9	J Huffman D 76.9 D Mensing R 23.1	J Garamendi D 59.4 N Cleek R 40.6

[1] The website of the clerk of the U.S. House has Kortum and Clausen reversed. Clausen's incumbency was uninterrupted and Kortum lost in 1970, according to obituaries in local newspapers.

California Elections to the U.S. House, Districts 4–7

In general, District 4 in the 1950s was the west side of San Francisco; the number went to seven counties northwest of Sacramento in 1962, then was restricted mostly to Yolo County in 1982; was given to seven counties along the Nevada border in 1992; and to Mother Lode areas in 2002. District 5 was the east side of San Francisco in the 1950s–1980s; that district number went to Sacramento in 1992. District 6 was Contra Costa County in the 1950s, parts of San Francisco in the 1960s–1980s, and mostly Marin County since. District 7 has been parts of the East Bay.

	DISTRICT 4	DISTRICT 5	DISTRICT 6	DISTRICT 7
1950	F Havenner D 67.2 R Smith R 32.8	J Shelley D-R 100	G Miller D-R 100	J Allen R 55.3 L Cook D 44.7
1952	W Mailliard R 55.0 F Havenner D 45.0	J Shelley D-R 100	R Condon D 50.6 J Baldwin R 49.4	J Allen R-D 84.2 J Johnson ind 15.6
1954	W Mailliard R 61.2 P O'Rourke D 36.7 G Andersen ind 2.1	J Shelley D-R100	J Baldwin R 50.9 R Condon D 49.1	J Allen R 53.0 S Crook D 47.0
1956	W Mailliard R 61.9 J Quigley D 38.1	J Shelley D-R 100	J Baldwin R 53.7 H Quinney D 42.3	J Allen R 52.8 L Cross D 47.2
1958	W Mailliard R 60.0 G Collins D 40.0	J Shelley D-R 100	J Baldwin R 51.0 H Jewel D 49.0	J Cohelan D 50.9 J Allen R 49.1
1960	W Mailliard R 65.3 P Davies D 34.7	J Shelley D 83.7 N Verreos R 16.3	J Baldwin R 58.7 D Page D 41.3	J Cohelan D 57.0 L Sherman R 42.9
1962	R Leggett D 56.5 L Honsinger R 43.5	J Shelley D 80.4 R Charles R 19.5	W Mailliard R 58.7 J O'Connell D 41.3	J Cohelan D 64.5 L Cantando R 35.5
1964	R Leggett D 71.9 I Norris R 28.1	P Burton D 100	W Mailliard R 63.6 T O'Toole D 36.3	J Cohelan D 66.1 L McNutt R 33.9
1966	R Leggett D 59.4 T McHatton R 40.5	P Burton D 71.3 T Macken R 28.7	W Mailliard R 76.6 L Grim D 23.4	J Cohelan D 63.9 M Champlin R 35.3
1968	R Leggett D 55.5 J Shumway R 41.6	P Burton D 72.0 W Velasquez R 24.2 Peace Fr 3.8	W Mailliard R 72.8 P Drath D 27.2	J Cohelan D 62.9 B Hilburn R 29.6 Peace Fr 7.5
1970	R Leggett D 68.0 A Gyorke R 32.0	P Burton D 70.8 J Parks R 29.2	W Mailliard R 53.4 R Miller D 46.6	R Dellums D 57.3 J Heady R 41.3 Peace Fr 1.4
1972	R Leggett D 67.4 B Chang R 32.6	P Burton D 81.8 E Powell R 18.2	W Mailliard R 52.0 R Boas D 48.0	R Dellums D 56.0 P Hannaford R 38.0 Am Ind 6.0
1974	R Leggett D 100	J Burton D 59.3 T Caylor R 38.0 Peace Fr 2.7	P Burton D 71.4 T Spinosa R 21.7 2 others 6.9	G Miller D 55.6 G Fernandez R 44.4
1976	R Leggett D 75,844 A Dehr R 75,193	J Burton D 61.8 B Fanning R 38.2	P Burton D 66.1 T Spinosa R 27.0 2 others 6.9	G Miller D 74.7 R Vickers R 23.3 Am Ind 2.0
1978	V Fazio D 55.4 R Hime R 44.6	J Burton D 66.8 D Skore R 44.3	P Burton D 68.3 T Spinosa R 28.0 Am Ind 3.7	G Miller D 63.4 P Gordon R 33.7 Am Ind 2.8
1980	V Fazio D 65.3 A Dehr R 29.7 R Burnside Lib 5.0	J Burton D 51.1 D McQuaid R 45.3 D Dougherty Lib 3.6	P Burton D 69.4 T Spinosa R 25.6 R Childs Lib 5.0	G Miller D 63.3 G StClair R 31.4 S Snow Lib 3.1 Am Ind 2.2
1982	V Fazio D 63.9 R Canfield R 36.1	P Burton D 57.9 M Marks R 40.4 J Raimondo Lib 1.6	B Boxer D 52.4 D McQuaid R 44.6 2 others 3.0	G Miller D 67.2 P Vallely R 30.2 2 others 2.6
1984	V Fazio D 61.4 R Canfield R 36.7 R Pope Lib 1.9	S Burton D 72.3 T Spinosa R 23.8 2 others 3.9	B Boxer D 68.0 D Binderup R 29.7 H Creighton Lib 2.3	G Miller D 66.7 R Thakar R 33.3
1986	V Fazio D 70.2 F Sampson R 29.8 Peace Fr 6.6	S Burton D 75.2 M Garza R 22.1 2 others 2.7	B Boxer D 73.9 F Ernst R 26.1	G Miller D 66.6 R Thakar R 33.4
1988	V Fazio D 99.3	N Pelosi D 76.4 B O'Neill R 19.3 2 others 4.3	B Boxer D 73.4 W Steinmetz R 26.6	G Miller D 68.4 J Last R 31.6
1990	V Fazio D 54.7 M Baughman R 39.3 B Bigwood Lib 6.0	N Pelosi D 77.2 A Nichols R 22.8	B Boxer D 68.1 B Boerum R 31.9	G Miller D 60.5 R Payton R 39.5
1992	J Doolittle R 49.8 P Malberg D 45.7 P McHargue Lib 4.5	R Matsui D 68.6 R Dinsmore R 25.5 3 others 5.9	L Woolsey D 65.2 B Filante R 33.6	G Miller D 70.3 D Scholl R 25.2 Peace Fr 4.5
1994	J Doolittle R 61.3 K Hirning D 34.0 D Falconi Lib 8.8	R Matsui D 68.5 R Dinsmore R 29.0 Am Ind 2.5	L Woolsey D 58.1 M Nugent R 37.6 2 others 4.3	G Miller D 69.7 C Hughes R 27.4 Peace Fr 2.9
1996	J Doolittle R 60.5 K Hirning D 36.1 P McHargue Lib 3.4	R Matsui D 70.4 R Dinsmore R 26.1 3 others 3.4	L Woolsey D 61.8 D Hughes R 34.0 2 others 4.2	G Miller D 71.8 N Reece R 22.3 2 others 5.9
1998	J Doolittle R 62.6 D Shapiro D 34.4 D Winterrowd Lib 3.0	R Matsui D 71.9 R Dinsmore R 26.0 D Tuma Lib 2.1	L Woolsey D 68.0 K McAuliffe R 29.7 A Barreca NLP 2.2	G Miller D 76.7 N Reece R 23.3
2000	J Doolittle R 63.4 M Norberg D 31.5 W Frey Lib 3.0 R Ray NLP 2.1	R Matsui D 68.7 K Payne R 26.1 3 others 5.2	L Woolsey D 64.3 K McAuliffe R 28.3 J Moscoso Green 4.7 2 others 2.7	G Miller D 76.5 C Hoffman R 21.1 M Sproul NLP 2.4
2002	J Doolittle R 64.8 M Norberg D 31.9 2 others 3.3	R Matsui D 70.5 R Frankhuizen R 26.4 T Roloff Lib 3.1	L Woolsey D 66.7 P Erickson R 29.6 2 others 3.7	G Miller D 70.7 C Hargrave R 26.4 S Wilson Lib 2.8
2004	J Doolittle R 65.4 D Winters D 34.6	R Matsui D 71.4 M Dugas R 23.3 2 others 5.3	L Woolsey D 72.6 P Erickson R 27.4	G Miller D 76.1 C Hargrave R 23.9
2006	J Doolittle R 49.1 C Brown D 45.9 D Warren Lib 5.1	D Matsui D 70.8 C Yan R 23.5 2 others 5.7	L Woolsey D 70.2 T Hooper R 26.1 R Friesen Lib 3.7	G Miller D 84.0 C McConnell Lib 16.0
2008	T McClintock R 50.2 C Brown D 49.8	D Matsui D 74.3 P Smith R 20.8 Peace Fr 4.9	L Woolsey D 71.7 M Halliwell R 24.1 J Smolen Lib 4.3	G Miller D 72.8 R Petersen R 21.8 2 others 5.4
2010	T McClintock R 61.3 C Curtis D 31.4 B Emery Green 7.3	D Matsui D 72.0 P Smith R 25.3 Peace Fr 2.7	L Woolsey D 65.9 J Judd R 29.6 2 others 4.4	G Miller D 68.3 R Tubbs R 31.7
2012	T McClintock R 61.1 J Uppal D 36.9	M Thompson D 74.5 R Loftin R 25.5	D Matsui D 75.1 J McCray R 24.9	A Bera D 51.7 D Lungren R 48.3
2014	T McClintock R 60.0 A Moore R 40.0	M Thompson D 75.7 J Hinton ind 24.3	D Matsui D 72.7 J McCray R 27.3	A Bera D 50.4 D Ose R 49.6
2016	T McClintock R 62.7 R Derlet D 37.3	M Thompson D 76.9 C Santamaria R 23.1	D Matsui D 75.4 R Evans R 24.6	A Bera D 51.2 S Jones R 48.8

California Elections to the U.S. House, Districts 8–11

In general, District 8 included Oakland and some nearby East Bay communities until 1992; thereafter it has included north and east San Francisco. District 9 included coastal San Mateo County, southern Alameda County, and parts of Santa Clara County in the 1950s–1960s, thereafter mostly southern Alameda; in the 1990s, Berkeley and Oakland too, and from 2002, not Alameda County. District 10 included San Jose and Santa Clara County in the 1950s–1960s, but the number shifted to south Alameda and part of San Jose in 1972; southern Alameda County in the 1980s and other inland East Bay areas thereafter. District 11 included Stockton in the 1950s; San Jose and some of Santa Clara County in the 1960s; northern San Mateo County in the 1970s–1980s; and Stockton and most of San Joaquin County from 1992 on.

	DISTRICT 8	DISTRICT 9	DISTRICT 10	DISTRICT 11
1950	J Anderson R-D 83.1 J Peterson ind 16.9	A Hunter R 52.0 C White D 48.0	T Werdel R 53.6 A Walker D 46.4	E Bramblett R 52.1 M Walker D 47.9
1952	G Miller D-R 100	J Younger R 53.1 H Taggart D 45.3 IPP 1.6	C Gubser R 59.2 A Johnson D 39.1 IPP 1.1	L Johnson R 87.1 IPP 12.9
1954	G Miller D 65.4 J Ritchie R 34.6	J Younger R 54.5 H Taggart R 45.5	C Gubser R 61.2 P Birmingham D 38.8	L Johnson R 52.6 C Sugar D 47.4
1956	G Miller D 65.6 R Watkins R 34.4	J Younger R 60.3 McKay D 39.7	C Gubser R 60.7 W Vatcher D 39.3	J McFall D 53.1 L Johnson R 46.9
1958	G Miller D-R 100	J Younger R 58.8 E Oddstad D 41.2	C Gubser R 54.6 R Bryan D 45.4	J McFall D 69.3 F Van Dyke R 30.7
1960	G Miller D 62.0 R Hannon R 38.0	J Younger R 59.2 J Kaster D 40.8	C Gubser R 58.9 R Bryan D 41.1	J McFall D 65.4 C Bull R 34.6
1962	G Miller D 72.5 H Petersen R 27.5	D Edwards D 65.9 J Donovan R 34.0	C Gubser R 60.7 J Thurber D 39.3	J Younger R 62.3 W Keller D 37.7
1964	G Miller D 70.2 D McKay R 29.7	D Edwards D 69.8 W Hyde R 30.2	C Gubser R 63.1 E Carman D 36.9	J Younger R 54.8 M Sullivan D 45.2
1966	G Miller D 65.4 R Britton R 34.6	D Edwards D 63.1 W Durkee R 36.8	C Gubser R 69.1 G Leppert D 30.9	J Younger R 59.4 M Sullivan D 40.6
1968	G Miller D 64.0 R Britton R 36.0	D Edwards D 56.5 L Fargher R 43.5	C Gubser R 67.3 G Takeda D 30.9 Peace Fr 1.8	P McCloskey R 79.3 U Whitaker D 19.6 Peace Fr 1.0
1970	G Miller D 69.0 M Crane R 31.0	D Edwards D 69.1 M Guerra R 28.5 Am Ind 2.3	C Gubser R 62.0 S McLean D 36.8 Am Ind 1.2	P McCloskey R 77.5 R Gomperts D 21.0 others 1.5
1972	P Stark D 52.9 L Warden R 47.1	D Edwards D 72.3 H Smith R 25.2 E Kaiser Am Ind 2.6	C Gubser R 64.6 F Gillette D 35.4	L Ryan D 60.4 C Chase R 37.0 N Kudrovzeff Am Ind 2.6
1974	R Dellums D 56.5 J Redden R 39.7 J Holland Am Ind 3.8	P Stark D 70.6 E Adams R 29.4	D Edwards D 77.0 J Enright R 23.0	L Ryan D 75.7 B Merdinger R 21.3 N Kudrovzeff Am Ind 3.1
1976	R Dellums D 62.1 P Breck R 34.7 Peace Fr 3.2	P Stark D 70.8 J Mills R 27.1 Peace Fr 2.1	D Edwards D 72.0 H Smith R 24.5 Am Ind 3.5	L Ryan D 61.1 B Jones R 35.4 N Kudrovzeff Am 3.5
1978	R Dellums D 57.4 C Hughes R 42.6	P Stark D 65.4 R Allen R 30.5 Peace Fr 4.1	D Edwards D 67.1 R Hansen R 32.9	L Ryan D 60.5 D Welch R 35.6 N Kudrovzeff Am Ind 3.9
1980	R Dellums D 55.5 C Hughes R 39.2 T Mikuriya Lib 5.4	P Stark D 55.3 B Kennedy R 41.1 S Clanin Lib 3.6	D Edwards D 62.1 J Lutton R 27.9 2 others 9.9	T Lantos D 46.4 B Royer R 43.3 3 others 10.3
1982	R Dellums D 55.9 C Hutchison R 44.1	P Stark D 60.7 B Kennedy R 39.3	D Edwards D 62.7 B Herriott R 33.7 2 others 3.7	T Lantos D 57.1 B Royer R 39.7 3 others 3.2
1984	R Dellums D 60.3 C Connor R 39.7	P Stark D 69.9 J Beaver R 26.3 M Fuhrig Lib 3.8	D Edwards D 62.4 R Herriott R 34.3 2 others 3.3	T Lantos D 69.9 J Hickey R 28.2 N Kudrovzeff 1.8
1986	R Dellums D 60.0 S Eigenberg R 37.9 Peace Fr 2.1	P Stark D 69.7 D Williams R 30.3	D Edwards D 70.5 M LaCrone R 26.6 2 others 2.9	T Lantos D 74.1 B Quraishi R 25.9
1988	R Dellums D 66.6 J Cuddihy R 31.2 Peace Fr 2.2	P Stark D 73.0 H Hertz R 27.0	D Edwards D 86.2 K Watson Lib 13.8	T Lantos D 71.0 B Quraishi R 24.4 3 others 4.6
1990	R Dellums D 61.3 B Galewski R 38.7	P Stark D 58.4 V Romero R 41.6	D Edwards D 62.7 M Patrosso R 37.3	T Lantos D 65.9 B Quraishi R 28.8 J Genis Lib 5.3
1992	N Pelosi D 82.5 M Wolin R 11.0 2 others 6.5	R Dellums D 71.9 B Hunter R 23.5 Peace Fr 4.6	B Baker R 52.0 W Williams D 48.0	R Pombo R 47.6 P Garamendi D 45.6 C Roberts Lib 6.8
1994	N Pelosi D 81.8 E Cheung R 18.2	R Dellums D 72.2 D Wright R 22.6 Peace Fr 5.1	B Baker R 59.3 E Schwartz D 38.6 Peace Fr 2.1	R Pombo R 62.1 R Perry D 34.9 J Miller Lib 3.0
1996	N Pelosi D 84.3 J Raimondo R 12.4 D Smithstein NLP 3.3	R Dellums D 77.0 D Wright R 18.5 2 others 4.5	E Tauscher D 54.1 B Baker R 47.2 3 others 4.2	R Pombo R 59.3 J Silva D 36.2 2 others 4.5
1998	N Pelosi D 85.8 D Martz R 12.0 D Smithstein NLP 2.1	B Lee D 82.8 C Sanders R 13.2 2 others 4.0	E Tauscher D 53.5 C Ball R 43.4 2 others 3.1	R Pombo R 61.4 R Figueroa D 36.2 J Baird Lib 2.3
2000	N Pelosi D 84.4 A Sparks R 11.7 2 others 3.8	B Lee D 84.9 A Washington R 9.8 2 others 5.2	E Tauscher D 52.6 C Hutchison R 44.2 V Janlois NLP 3.1	R Pombo R 57.8 T Santos D 38.1 2 others 4.0
2002	N Pelosi D 79.6 M German R 12.5 J Pond Green 6.3 I Spivack Lib 1.7	B Lee D 81.4 J Uduinsky R 15.2 J Eyer Lib 3.4	E Tauscher D 75.6 S Harden Lib 24.4	R Pombo R 60.3 E Shaw D 39.7
2004	N Pelosi D 82.9 J DePalma R 11.5 Others 5.5	B Lee D 84.5 C Bermudez R 12.3 J Eyer Lib 3.2	E Tauscher D 65.7 J Ketelson R 34.3	R Pombo R 61.2 J McNerney D 38.8
2006	N Pelosi D 80.4 M Denunzio R 10.7 P Berg Lib 1.5 K Keefer Green 7.4	B Lee D 86.3 J Dendulk R 10.7 J Eyer Lib 2.9	E Tauscher D 66.4 D Linn R 33.5	J McNerney D 53.3 R Pombo R 46.7
2008	N Pelosi D 71.9 D Walsh R 9.7 C Sheehan Ind 16.2 P Berg Lib 2.3	B Lee D 86.1 C Hargrave R 9.7 J Eyer Lib 4.2	E Tauscher D 65.1 N Gerber R 31.1 Peace Fr 3.7	J McNerney D 55.3 D Andal R 44.7
2010	N Pelosi D 80.1 J Dennis R 15.1 2 others 4.8	B Lee D 84.3 G Hashimoto R 10.8 3 others 5.0	J Garamendi D 58.8 G Clift R 37.9 J Cloward Green 3.3	J McNerney D 48.0 D Harmer R 46.9 Christenson Ind 5.2
2012	P Cook R 57.4 G Imus R 42.6	J McNerney D 55.6 R Gill R 44.4	J Denham R 52.7 J Hernandez D 47.3	G Miller D 69.7
2014	P Cook R 67.6 B Conaway D 32.4	J McNerney D 52.4 A Amador R 47.6	J Denham R 56.1 M Eggman D 43.9	M DeSaulnier D 67.3 T Phan R 32.7
2016	P Cook R 62.3 R Ramirez D 37.7	J McNerney D 57.4 A Amador R 42.6	J Denham R 51.7 M Eggman D 48.3	M DeSaulnier D 72.1 R Petersen R 27.9

California Elections to the U.S. House, Districts 12–15

In the 1950s these districts included much of the Central Valley, but in successive redistrictings after that they progressively moved more tightly toward the south end of the Bay Area. After 2000, District 12 included Daly City and the San Mateo peninsula, District 13 included southern Alameda County, District 14 included Palo Alto, Mountain View, and Silicon Valley; and District 15 covered Santa Clara County and the northern two-thirds of San Jose.

	DISTRICT 12	DISTRICT 13	DISTRICT 14	DISTRICT 15
1950	P Hillings R 60.0 S Zetterberg D 39.9	N Poulson R-D 84.8 E Davidson ind 15.1	S Yorty D 49.3 J Hardy R 36.8 C Bass ind 13.8	McDonough R-D 87.1 J Cole ind 12.8
1952	O Hunter R-D 100	E Bramblett R 51.0 W Hays D 49.0	H Hagen D 51.0 T Werdel R 49.0	McDonough R-D 100
1954	B Sisk D 53.8 O Hunter R 46.2	C Teague R 52.5 T O'Reilly D 47.5	H Hagen D 65.1 A Blain R 34.9	G McDonough R 56.9 F O'Sullivan D 43.1
1956	B Sisk D 73.0 R Moore R 27.0	C Teague R 59.6 W Stewart D 40.4	H Hagen D 63.0 M Tisdel R 37.0	G McDonough R 57.9 E Petty D 42.1
1958	B Sisk D 81.1 D Halpin R 18.9	C Teague R 57.0 W Stewart D 43.0	H Hagen D 100	G McDonough R 52.0 E Petty D 47.9
1960	B Sisk D 100	C Teague R 65.0 B Finch D 35.0	H Hagen D 56.5 R Arnett R 43.5	G McDonough R 51.3 N Martell D 48.6
1962	B Talcott R 61.3 W Seward D 38.7	C Teague R 64.9 G Holgate D 35.1	J Baldwin R 62.9 C Weidner D 37.1	J McFall D 70.0 A Young R 30.0
1964	B Talcott R 61.9 S Bolz D 38.1	C Teague R 57.4 G Taylor D 42.6	J Baldwin R 64.9 R Koch D 35.1	J McFall D 70.9 K Gibson R 29.1
1966	B Talcott R 77.2 G Barron D 22.7	C Teague R 67.5 C Storke D 32.5	J Waldie D 56.4 F Newman R 43.5	J McFall D 57.0 S VanDyken R 43.0
1968	B Talcott R 94.9 A Holliday Am Ind 5.1	C Teague R 65.9 S Sheinbaum D 34.1	J Waldie D 71.6 D Schuh R 26.6 L Hamilton Am Ind 1.9	J McFall D 53.8 S VanDyken R 46.2
1970	B Talcott R 63.6 O Riordan D 33.9 Peace Fr 2.5	C Teague R 58.2 G Hart D 40.8 M Jordet Am Ind 1.1	J Waldie D 74.5 B Athan R 25.5	J McFall D 63.1 S VanDyken R 35.6 G Gillings Am Ind 1.3
1972	B Talcott R 54.0 J Camacho D 43.1 S Montieth Am Ind 2.9	C Teague R 73.9 L Cleveland D 26.1	J Waldie D 77.6 F Sims R 22.4	J McFall D 100
1974	P McCloskey R 69.1 G Gilmor D 30.9	N Mineta D 52.6 G Milias R 42.4 2 others 5.1	J McFall D 70.8 C Gibson R 24.1 R Blain Am Ind 5.1	B Sisk D 71.9 C Harner R 28.1
1976	P McCloskey R 66.2 D Harris D 31.3 J Cooney Am Ind 2.5	N Mineta D 66.8 E Konnyu R 31.2 W Herrell Am Ind 2.1	J McFall D 72.5 R Blain R 27.5	B Sisk D 72.2 C Harner R 27.8
1978	P McCloskey R 73.1 K Olsen D 21.5 2 others 5.4	N Mineta D 57.5 D O'Keefe R 39.5 Peace Fr 3.0	N Shumway R 53.4 J McFall D 42.6	T Coelho D 60.1 C Patterakis R 39.9
1980	P McCloskey R 72.2 K Olsen D 18.6 2 others 9.2	N Mineta D 58.9 T Gagne R 35.5 2 others 5.6	N Shumway R 60.7 A Cerney D 36.2 D Housley Lib 3.0	T Coelho D 71.8 R Schwartz R 25.2 M Pullen Lib 3.0
1982	E Zschau R 63.0 E Lynch D 33.5 B White Lib 3.5	N Mineta D 65.9 T Kelly R 31.4 A Hinkle Lib 2.7	N Shumway R 63.4 B Reed D 36.6	T Coelho D 63.7 E Bates R 34.0 S Gerringer Lib 2.3
1984	E Zschau R 61.7 M Carnoy D 36.0 Kudrovzeff Am Ind 2.3	N Mineta D 65.2 J Williams R 33.0 J Redding Lib 1.8	N Shumway R 73.3 P Carlson D 23.9 F Colburn Lib 2.8	T Coelho D 65.5 C Harner R 32.7 R Harris Lib 1.8
1986	E Konnyu R 59.5 L Weil D 37.2 B White Lib 3.3	N Mineta D 69.7 B Nash R 30.3	N Shumway R 71.6 B Steele D 26.1 B Daniel Lib 2.3	T Coelho D 71.0 C Harner R 27.2 R Harris Lib 1.8
1988	T Campbell R 51.7 A Eshoo D 46.0 T Grey Lib 2.3	N Mineta D 67.1 L Sommer R 29.8 J Webster Lib 3.1	N Shumway R 62.6 P Malberg D 37.4	T Coelho D 69.8 C Harner R 28.2 R Harris Lib 2.1
1990	T Campbell R 60.9 R Palmer D 33.7 C Olson Lib 5.5	N Mineta D 58.0 D Smith R 35.7 J Webster Lib 6.3	J Doolittle R 51.5 P Malberg D 48.5	G Condit D 66.2 C Burris R 33.8
1992	T Lantos D 68.8 J Tomlin R 23.3 2 others 7.8	P Stark D 60.2 V Teyler R 31.6 Peace Fr 8.2	A Eshoo D 56.7 T Huening R 39.0 2 others 4.3	N Mineta D 63.5 R Wick R 31.2 D Dieterly Lib 5.0 write-in 2.2
1994	T Lantos D 66.3 D Wilder R 37.6	P Stark D 64.6 L Molton R 30.2 B Gough Lib 5.1	A Eshoo D 60.6 B Brink R 39.4	N Mineta D 59.9 R Wick R 40.1
1996	T Lantos D 71.7 S Jenkins R 23.7 2 others 4.6	P Stark D 65.2 J Fay R 30.4 T Savage Lib 4.4	A Eshoo D 64.8 B Brink R 31.2 3 others 4.0	T Campbell R 58.5 D Lane D 34.8 3 others 6.6
1998	T Lantos D 74.0 R Evans R 21.1 M Maloney Lib 4.9	P Stark D 71.2 J Goetz R 26.6 K Beylikjian NLP 2.1	A Eshoo D 68.6 C Haugen R 28.4 2 others 2.9	T Campbell R 60.5 D Lane D 37.9 F Strutner NLP 1.5
2000	T Lantos D 74.5 M Garza R 20.8 2 others 4.7	P Stark D 70.4 J Goetz R 24.3 3 others 5.3	A Eshoo D 70.2 B Quraishi R 25.8 2 others 4.0	M Honda D 54.3 J Cunneen R 42.2 2 others 3.6
2002	T Lantos D 68.1 M Maloney R 24.8 M Abu-Ghazalah Lib 7.1	P Stark D 71.1 S Mahmood R 22.1 3 others 6.9	A Eshoo D 68.2 J Nixon R 28.2 A Carver Lib 3.7	M Honda D 65.8 L Hermann R 31.0 J Landauer Lib 3.2
2004	T Lantos D 68.0 M Garza R 20.8 2 others 11.1	P Stark D 71.6 G Bruno R 24.0 M Stroberg Lib 4.4	A Eshoo D 69.8 C Haugen R 26.6 B Holtz Lib 3.7	M Honda D 72.0 R Chukwu R 28.0
2006	T Lantos D 76.1 M Maloney R 24.0	P Stark D 74.9 G Bruno R 25.1	A Eshoo D 71.1 R Smith R 24.2 2 others 4.7	M Honda D 72.3 R Chukwu R 27.7
2008	J Speier D 75.1 G Conlon R 18.5 3 others 6.4	P Stark D 76.4 R Chui R 23.6	A Eshoo D 69.8 R Santana R 22.2 2 others 8.0	M Honda D 71.7 J Cordi R 23.3 P Myers Green 5.1
2010	J Speier D 75.6 M Moloney R 22.1 M Williams Lib 2.4	P Stark D 72.0 F Baker R 27.7 write-in 0.3	A Eshoo D 69.1 D Chapman R 27.8 P Lazaga Lib 3.1	M Honda D 67.6 S Kirkland R 32.4
2012	N Pelosi D 85.1 J Dennis R 14.9	B Lee D 86.8 M Singleton ind 13.2	J Speier D 78.9 D Bacigalupi R 21.1	E Swalwell D 52.1 P Stark D 47.9
2014	N Pelosi D 83.3 J Dennis R 16.7	B Lee D 88.5 D Sundeen R 11.5	J Speier D 76.7 R Chew R 23.3	E Swalwell D 69.8 H Bussell R 30.2
2016	N Pelosi D 80.9 P Picus ind 19.1	B Lee D 90.8 S Caro R 9.2	J Speier D 80.9 A Cardenas R 19.1	E Swalwell D 73.8 D Turner R 26.2

California Elections to the U.S. House, Districts 16–19

In the 1950s, these district numbers were assigned to parts of the Los Angeles area. In the 1960s, Districts 17 and 19 remained in south LA County and Districts 16 and 18 covered the central and southern parts of the San Joaquin Valley. That remained true in the 1970s and 1980s, except that District 19 represented Santa Barbara County and some coastal areas north of it. Since 1992 these became the districts for much of San Jose as well as Monterey, Stanislaus and San Benito Counties, and southern San Joaquin including much of Fresno (District 19).

	DISTRICT 16	DISTRICT 17	DISTRICT 18	DISTRICT 19
1950	D Jackson R 59.2 E Murray D 40.7	C King D-R 100	C Doyle D 50.5 C Hosmer R 49.5	C Holifield D-R 90.8 M Weiss ind 9.1
1952	D Jackson R 59.7 J Harter D 40.2	C King D 54.6 R Finch R 44.1 1 other 1.3	C Hosmer R 55.5 J Kennick D 44.5	C Holifield D-R 87.0 2 others 12.8
1954	D Jackson R 60.8 M. Hogue D 39.2	C King D 60.1 R Finch R 39.9	C Hosmer R 55.0 J Kennick D 45.0	C Holifield D 74.8 R Pritchard R 25.2
1956	D Jackson R 60.8 B Fleming D 39.2	C King D 64.9 C Franklin R 35.1	C Hosmer R 59.2 R Simpson D 40.7	C Holifield D 73.8 R Reynolds R 26.2
1958	D Jackson R 57.8 M Lennard D 42.2	C King D 75.3 L DiMiceli R 24.7	C Hosmer R 60.0 H May D 40.0	C Holifield D 83.4 H Leppek R 16.6
1960	A Bell R 55.4 J Pacht D 44.6	C King R 67.7 T Coffee R 32.3	C Hosmer R 69.9 P Ahern D 30.0	C Holifield D 78.2 G McWilliams R 21.8
1962	B Sisk D 71.9 A Selland R 28.1	C King R 67.2 T Bruinsma R 32.8	H Hagen D 58.9 R Arnett R 41.1	C Holifield D 61.6 R Ramsay R 38.4
1964	B Sisk D 66.8 D Harris R 33.2	C King R 67.7 R Muncaster R 32.3	H Hagen D 66.7 J Williams R 33.3	C Holifield D 65.4 E Hunt R 34.6
1966	B Sisk D 71.3 C White R 28.6	C King R 60.8 D Cortum R 39.2	B Mathias R 55.9 H Hagen D 44.1	C Holifield D 62.2 W Sutton R 37.7
1968	B Sisk D 62.5 D Harris R 35.4 J Carroll Am Ind 2.2	G Anderson D 50.7 J Blatchford R 48.1 Peace Fr 1.1	B Mathias R 65.2 H Hagen D 33.4 E Williams Am Ind 1.4	C Holifield D 63.2 B Jones R 34.1 W Cook Am Ind 2.6
1970	B Sisk D 66.4 P Sanchez R 30.5 J Scott Am Ind 3.0	G Anderson D 62.2 M Donaldson R 35.5 Peace Fr 1.0 R Copeland Am Ind 1.3	B Mathias R 63.2 M Miller D 35.5 N Hensley Am Ind 1.3	C Holifield D 70.4 B Jones R 29.6
1972	B Sisk D 79.1 C Harner R 20.9	P McCloskey R 60.2 J Stewart D 39.8	B Mathias R 66.5 V Lavery D 33.5	C Holifield D 67.2 K Fisher R 27.9 Peace Fr 4.9
1974	B Talcott R 49.2 J Camacho D 47.9	J Krebs D 51.9 B Mathias R 48.1	W Ketchum R 52.6 G Seielstad D 47.4	R Lagomarsino R 56.5 J Loebl R 43.5 D Mauro Am Ind 2.9
1976	L Panetta D 53.4 B Talcott R 46.6	J Krebs D 65.7 H Andreas R 34.3	W Ketchum R 64.2 D Close D 35.8	R Lagomarsino R 64.4 D Sisson D 35.6
1978	L Panetta D 61.4 E Seastrand R 38.6	C Pashayan R 54.5 J Krebs D 45.5	W Thomas R 59.3 B Sogge D 40.7	R Lagomarsino R 71.7 J Zamos D 24.3 Peace Fr 4.0
1980	L Panetta D 71.0 J Roth R 24.5 2 others 4.5	C Pashayan R 70.6 B Johnson D 29.4	W Thomas R 71.0 C Lodise D 29.0	R Lagomarsino R 77.7 M Miller D 17.6 J Trotter Lib 4.7
1982	L Panetta D 85.4 R Arnold R 14.6	C Pashayan R 54.0 G Tackett D 46.0	R Lehman D 59.5 A Fondse R 38.3 M Fritz Lib 2.2	R Lagomarsino R 61.1 F Frost D 35.8 2 others 3.1
1984	L Panetta D 70.8 P Ramsey R 27.7 B Anderson Lib 1.5	C Pashayan R 72.5 S Lakritz D 27.5	R Lehman D 67.3 D Ewen R 32.7	R Lagomarsino R 67.3 J Carey D 30.9 Peace Fr 1.8
1986	L Panetta D 78.4 L Darrigo R 19.2 2 others 2.4	C Pashayan R 60.2 J Hartnett D 39.8	R Lehman D 71.3 D Crevelt R 28.7	R Lagomarsino R 71.9 W Norris D 26.8 G Hasara Lib 1.4
1988	L Panetta D 78.6 S Monteith R 21.4	C Pashayan R 71.5 V Lavery D 28.5	R Lehman D 69.9 D Linn R 30.1	R Lagomarsino R 50.2 G Hart D 48.5 R Donaldson Lib 1.2
1990	L Panetta D 74.2 J Reiss R 22.0 B Tucker Lib 3.8	C Dooley D 54.5 C Pashayan R 45.5	R Lehman D 100	R Lagomarsino R 54.6 A Ferguson D 44.4 M Lorentz ind 1.0
1992	D Edwards D 62.0 T Bundesen R 32.0 Peace Fr 6.0	L Panetta D 72.0 B Campbell R 23.7 2 others 4.2	G Condit D 84.7 K Ahlstrom Lib 15.3	R Lehman D 46.9 T Cloud R 46.4 Peace Fr 6.2 write-in 0.5
1994	Z Lofgren D 65.0 L Smith R 35.0	S Farr D 52.2 B McCampbell R 44.5 C Coffin Green 3.3	G Condit D 65.5 T Carter R 31.7 J Morzella Lib 2.8	G Radanovich R 56.8 R Lehman D 39.6 D Comstock Lib 3.6
1996	Z Lofgren D 65.7 C Wojslaw R 30.2 2 others 4.2	S Farr D 58.9 J Brown R 37.8 J Black NLP 3.4	G Condit D 65.7 B Conrad R 31.8 2 others 2.5	G Radanovich R 66.6 P Barile D 28.3 2 others 5.1
1998	Z Lofgren D 72.8 H Thayn R 23.4 J Black NLP 3.8	S Farr D 64.5 B McCampbell R 32.7 2 others 2.8	G Condit D 86.8 L Degroat Lib 13.2	G Radanovich R 79.4 J Richter Lib 20.6
2000	Z Lofgren D 72.1 H Thayn R 23.3 2 others 4.6	S Farr D 68.6 C Engler R 24.7 4 others 6.7	G Condit D 67.1 S Wilson R 31.3 P Riskin NLP 1.6	G Radanovich R 64.9 D Rosenberg D 31.7 3 others 3.4
2002	Z Lofgren D 67.0 D McNea R 29.8 D Umphress Lib 3.2	S Farr D 68.1 C Engler R 27.0 2 others 4.9	D Cardoza D 51.3 D Monteith R 43.4 2 others 5.3	G Radanovich R 67.3 J Veen D 30.0 P McHargue Lib 2.7
2004	Z Lofgren D 70.9 D McNea R 26.3 M Welch Lib 2.8	S Farr D 66.7 M Risley R 29.2 3 others 4.1	D Cardoza D 67.5 C Pringle R 32.5	G Radanovich R 66.0 J Bufford D 27.2 L Mullen Green 6.7
2006	Zoe Lofgren D 72.7 C Winston R 27.3	S Farr D 75.8 A DeMaio R 22.6 write-in 1.6	D Cardoza D 65.5 J Kanno R 34.5	G Radanovich R 60.6 T Cox D 39.4
2008	Z Lofgren D 71.3 C Winston R 24.1 S Wells Lib 4.6	S Farr D 73.9 J Taylor R 25.8 write-in 0.3	D Cardoza D 100	G Radanovich R 98.4 2 write-ins 1.6
2010	Z Lofgren D 67.8 D Sahagun R 24.3 E Gonzalez Lib 7.9	S Farr D 66.7 J Taylor R 29.9 2 others 3.4	D Cardoza D 58.5 M Berryhill R 41.5	J Denham R 69.6 L Goodwin D 35.1 write-in 0.3
2012	J Costa D 57.4 B Whelan R 42.8	M Honda D 73.5 E Li R 26.5	A Eshoo D 70.5 D Chapman R 29.5	Z Lofgren D 75.2 R Murray R 26.8
2014	J Costa D 50.7 J Tacherra R 49.3	M Honda D 51.8 R Khanna D 48.2	A Eshoo D 67.8 R Fox R 32.2	Z Lofgren D 67.2 R Murray R 32.8
2016	J Costa D 58.0 J Tacherra R 42.0	R Khanna D 61.0 M Honda D 39.0	A Eshoo D 71.1 R Fox R 28.9	Z Lofgren D 73.9 B Lancaster R 26.1

California Elections to the U.S. House, Districts 20–23

These district numbers pertained to parts of Los Angeles County in the 1950s through the 1980s, except for parts of Ventura in the 1970s (District 20) and San Luis Obispo in the 1980s (also District 20). From 1992 the numbers were attached to areas north of LA: the southern San Joaquin Valley and nearby coastal counties (parts or all of Kings, Kern, San Luis Obispo, Santa Barbara, and Ventura).

	DISTRICT 20	DISTRICT 21	DISTRICT 22	DISTRICT 23
1950	C Hinshaw R-D 85.1 W Esterman ind 10.7 other 4.2	H Sheppard D 57.4 R Reynolds R 42.6	J Phillips R-D 100	C McKinnon D 51.0 L Gehres R 49.0
1952	C Hinshaw R-D 100	E Hiestand R 53.6 E Burkhalter D 46.4	J Holt R 60.4 D McHenry D 39.5	C Doyle D-R 87.3 2 others 12.7
1954	C Hinshaw R 71.2 E Radding D 28.8	E Hiestand R 58.7 B Roskam D 41.3	J Holt R 58.2 B Costley D 41.8	C Doyle D 70.9 F Bussing R 27.3 O Thompson ind 1.8
1956	H Smith R 70.8 E Radding D 29.2	E Hiestand R 62.6 B Stethem D 37.4	J Holt R 59.8 I Glasband D 40.2	C Doyle D-Proh 70.9 C Calvin R 29.1
1958	H Smith R 65.9 R Farrell D 34.0	E Hiestand R 51.9 R Brown D 48.1	J Holt R 55.4 I Glasband D 44.6	C Doyle D 100
1960	H Smith R 70.1 G Sadler D 29.9	E Hiestand R 58.4 R Brown D 41.6	J Corman D 51.1 L Blanchard R 48.9	C Doyle D 74.2 E Schwartz R 25.8
1962	H Smith R 70.6 L Mayer D 29.4	G Hawkins D 84.5 H Smith R 15.4	J Corman D 53.6 C Foote R 46.4	C Doyle D 64.2 D Clawson R 35.8
1964	H Smith R 67.9 B Kaufman D 32.1	G Hawkins D 90.3 R Lundy R 9.7	J Corman D 50.5 R Cline R 49.5	D Clawson R 55.4 H van Petten D 44.5
1966	H Smith R 73.4 R Freschi D 26.6	G Hawkins D 84.8 N Hodges R 15.2	J Corman D 53.4 R Cline R 46.5	D Clawson R 67.4 E O'Connor D 32.6
1968	H Smith R 69.3 D White D 29.2 Peace Fr 1.5	G Hawkins D 93.7 R Lundy R 8.4	J Corman D 56.9 J Holt R 41.4 Peace Fr 1.7	D Clawson R 64.9 J Sperrazzo D 35.1
1970	H Smith R 69.1 M Stolberg D 29.7 E Harper Am Ind 1.2	G Hawkins D 94.5 S Johnson R 5.5	J Corman D 59.4 T Hayden R 39.5 C Johnson Am Ind 1.2	D Clawson R 63.3 J Chapman D 36.7
1972	C Moorhead R 57.4 J Binkley D 42.6	G Hawkins D 82.9 R Lundy R 17.1	J Corman D 67.6 B White R 29.3 Peace Fr 3.1	D Clawson R 61.4 C Tuohey D 38.6
1974	B Goldwater R 61.2 A Mathews D 38.8	J Corman D 73.5 M Nadell R 26.5	C Moorhead R 55.7 R Hallin D 44.3	T Rees D 71.5 J Roberts R 28.5
1976	B Goldwater R 67.2 P Corman D 32.8	J Corman D 66.5 E Hogan R 28.8 Peace Fr 4.7	C Moorhead R 62.6 R Salley D 37.4	A Beilenson D 60.2 T Bartman R 39.8
1978	B Goldwater R 66.4 P Lear D 33.6	J Corman D 59.5 R Walsh R 35.9 Peace Fr 4.6	C Moorhead R 64.6 R Henry D 35.4	A Beilenson D 65.6 J Barbara R 34.4
1980	B Goldwater R 78.8 M Miller D 17.0 C Darwin Lib 4.2	B Fiedler R 74,674 J Corman D 73,898 2 others (3.1%)	C Moorhead R 63.9 P O'Donnell D 31.9 W Susel Lib 4.3	A Beilenson D 63.2 B Winckler R 31.5 J Lieb Lib 5.3
1982	W Thomas R 68.1 R Bethea D 31.9	B Fiedler R 71.8 G Margolis D 24.1 D Wiener Lib 4.1	C Moorhead R 73.6 H Goldhammer D 23.5 R Gerringer Lib 3.0	A Beilenson D 59.6 D Armor R 40.5
1984	W Thomas R 70.9 M LeSage D 29.1	B Fiedler R 72.3 C Davis D 25.9 R Leet Lib 1.8	C Moorhead R 85.2 M Yauch Lib 14.8	A Beilenson D 61.6 C Parrish R 36.9 L Leathers Lib 1.6
1986	W Thomas R 72.6 J Moquin D 27.4	E Gallegly R 68.4 G Saldana D 28.2 D Wiener Lib 3.4	C Moorhead R 73.8 J Simmons D 23.0 2 others 3.2	A Beilenson D 65.7 G Woolverton R 31.8 2 others 2.5
1988	W Thomas R 71.1 L Reid D 27.1 D Bersohn Lib 1.8	E Gallegly R 69.1 D Stevens D 28.8 R Jay Lib 2.1	C Moorhead R 57.4 J Simmons D 26.0 2 others 4.5	A Beilenson D 63.5 J Salomon R 33.1 2 others 3.4
1990	W Thomas R 59.8 M Thomas D 34.5 W Dilbeck Lib 5.6	E Gallegly R 58.4 R Freiman D 34.0 P Christensen Lib 7.6	C Moorhead R 60.0 D Bayer D 34.1 2 others 5.9	A Beilenson D 61.7 J Salomon R 34.2 Peace R 4.1
1992	C Dooley D 64.9 E Hunt R 35.1	W Thomas R 65.2 D Vollmer D 34.7	M Huffington R 52.5 G Ochoa D 34.9 M Lorenz Green 9.5 H Dilbeck Lib 3.0	E Gallegly R 54.3 E Ferguson D 41.5 J Wood Lib 4.3
1994	C Dooley D 56.7 P Young R 43.3	W Thomas R 68.1 J Evans D 27.7 M Hodges Lib 4.0	A Seastrand R 49.3 W Capps D 48.5 D Bersohn Lib 2.2	E Gallegly R 66.2 K Ready D 27.5 2 others 6.3
1996	C Dooley D 56.5 T Harvey R 39.1 J Richter Lib 4.4	W Thomas R 65.9 D Vollmer D 26.5 3 others 7.6	W Capps D 48.4 A Seastrand R 44.2 4 others 7.3	E Gallegly R 59.6 R Unruhe D 35.1 2 others 5.3
1998	C Dooley D 60.7 C Unruh R 39.3	W Thomas R 78.9 J Evans, Reform 21.1	L Capps D 55.0 T Bordonaro R 43.1 2 others 1.9	E Gallegly R 60.1 D Gonzalez D 39.9
2000	C Dooley D 52.3 R Rodriguez R 45.5 2 others 2.2	W Thomas R 71.6 P Martinez D 24.8 J Manlon Lib 3.6	L Capps D 53.1 M Stoker R 44.3 3 others 2.5	E Gallegly R 54.1 M Case D 40.7 3 others 5.3
2002	C Dooley D 63.7 A Minuth R 34.3 V Swearingen Lib 2.0	D Nunes R 70.5 D LaPere D 26.2 J Richter Lib 3.3	W Thomas R 73.3 J Corvera D 23.7 D Coates Lib 2.9	L Capps D 59.0 B Rogers R 38.6 J Hill Lib 2.4
2004	J Costa D 53.4 R Ashburn R 46.6	D Nunes R 73.2 F Davis D 26.8	W Thomas R 100	L Capps D 63.0 D Regan R 34.4 M Favorite Lib 2.6
2006	J Costa D 100	D Nunes R 66.7 S Haze D 29.9 J Miller Green 3.3	K McCarthy R 70.7 S Beery D 29.3	L Capps D 65.2 V Tognazzini R 34.8
2008	J Costa D 74.3 J Lopez R 25.7	D Nunes R 68.4 L Johnson D 31.6	K McCarthy R 100	L Capps D 68.1 M Kokkonen R 31.9
2010	J Costa D 51.7 A Vidak R 48.3	D Nunes R 100	K McCarthy R 100	L Capps D 57.8 T Watson R 37.6 2 others 4.6
2012	S Farr D 74.1 J Taylor R 25.9	D Valadao R 57.8 J Hernandez D 42.2	D Nunes R 61.9 O Lee D 38.1	K McCarthy R 73.2 T Phillips ind 26.8
2014	S Farr D 75.2 R Kabat ind 24.8	D Valadao R 57.8 A Renteria D 42.2	D Nunes R 72.0 S Aguilera-M D 28.0	K McCarthy R 74.8 R Garcia D 25.2
2016	J Panetta D 70.8 C Lucius R 29.2	D Valadao R 56.7 E Huerta R 43.3	D Nunes R 67.6 L Campos D 32.4	K McCarthy R 69.2 W Reed D 30.8

California Elections to the U.S. House, Districts 24–27

These districts, newly created in 1952, covered parts of Los Angeles County and city from then until 2002, except for District 27 in the 1950s, which was assigned to San Bernardino County. From 2002, Districts 24 and 25 covered Santa Barbara as well as Ventura, Inyo, Mono, and San Bernardino (Gallegly, McKeon, Capps) Counties. District 26 included northeast suburbs (Dreier), and District 27 included much of the San Fernando Valley (Sherman).

	DISTRICT 24	DISTRICT 25	DISTRICT 26	DISTRICT 27
1952	N Poulson R-D 87.2 / B Sharp IPP 12.6	P Billings R 64.3 / W Sayre D 35.7	S Yorty D-R 87.9 / H Alexander IPP 11.9	H Sheppard D 55.0 / C Hilliard R 45.0
1954	G Lipscomb R 56.9 / G Arnold D 43.1	P Hillings R 65.2 / J Sobieski D 34.8	J Roosevelt D 60.1 / T Owings R 39.9	H Sheppard D 64.8 / M Barrett R 35.2
1956	G Lipscomb R 61.9 / F Porter D 38.1	P Hillings R 63.8 / J Sobieski D 36.2	J Roosevelt D 68.9 / E Gibbons R 31.2	H Sheppard D-R 100
1958	G Lipscomb R 56.3 / W Ware D 43.6	G Kasem D 135,009 / P Lieberg R 134,406	J Roosevelt D 72.2 / C Wright R 27.8	H Sheppard D 72.3 / R Castle R 27.7
1960	G Lipscomb R 59.7 / N Hass D 40.3	J Rousselot R 53.6 / G Kasem D 46.4	J Roosevelt D 73.4 / W McIntyre R 26.6	H Sheppard D 66.8 / R Castle R 33.2
1962	G Lipscomb R 70.3 / K Mellon D 29.7	R Cameron D 53.1 / J Rousselot R 45.9	J Roosevelt D 68.3 / D Beltz R 31.7	E Burkhalter D 52.1 / E Hiestand R 47.9
1964	G Lipscomb R 67.9 / B Stevens R 32.1	R Cameron D 55.4 / F Walton R 44.6	J Roosevelt D 70.4 / G Seton R 29.6	E Reinecke R 51.7 / T Bane D 48.3
1966	G Lipscomb R 76.2 / E McNall D 23.7	C Wiggins R 52.5 / R Cameron D 47.4	T Rees D 62.3 / I Teichner R 37.7	E Reinecke R 65.3 / J Howard D 34.6
1968	G Lipscomb R 72.8 / F Neal R 27.2	C Wiggins R 68.6 / K Shirey D 31.4	T Rees D 65.5 / I Teichner R 31.3 / Peace Fr 3.2	E Reinecke R 72.2 / J Butchko D 27.8
1970	J Rousselot R 65.1 / M Evers D 32.4 / 2 others 2.6	C Wiggins R 63.3 / L Craven D 35.1 / K Scanlon Am Ind 1.6	T Rees D 71.3 / N Friedman R 25.8 / 2 others 2.9	B Goldwater R 66.7 / T Kimmel D 30.5 / 2 others 2.8
1972	J Rousselot R 70.1 / L Mandell D 29.9	C Wiggins R 64.9 / L Craven D 31.9 / A Romirez Am Ind 3.1	T Rees D 68.6 / P Rutta R 27.9 / Peace Fr 3.5	B Goldwater R 57.4 / M Novak D 42.6
1974	H Waxman D 64.2 / E Graham R 32.8 / D Davis Am Ind 3.0	E Roybal D 100	J Rousselot R 58.8 / P Conforti D 41.2	A Bell R 63.8 / J Dalessio D 32.6 / Peace Fr 3.6
1976	H Waxman D 67.8 / D Simmons R 32.2	E Roybal D 71.9 / J Madrid R 22.0 / Peace Fr 6.1	J Rousselot R 65.6 / B Latta D 34.4	R Dornan R 54.7 / G Familian D 45.3
1978	H Waxman D 62.7 / H Schaefer R 32.6 / Peace Fr 4.8	E Roybal D 67.4 / R Watson R 32.6	J Rousselot R 100	R Dornan R 51.0 / C Peek D 49.0
1980	H Waxman D 63.8 / R Cayard R 27.1 / 3 others 9.1	E Roybal D 66.0 / R Ferraro R 28.4 / W Mitchell Lib 5.6	J Rousselot R 70.9 / J Lisoni D 24.4 / W Wagener Lib 4.7	R Dornan R 51.0 / C Peck D 46.5 / J Sievers Lib 2.5
1982	H Waxman D 65.1 / J Zerg R 31.0 / J Mandel Lib 4.0	E Roybal D 85.5 / D Gorham Lib 14.5	H Berman D 59.6 / H Phillips R 40.4	M Levine D 59.5 / B Christensen R 37.0 / Z Richardson Lib 3.5
1984	H Waxman D 63.4 / J Zerg R 33.2 / 2 others 3.4	E Roybal D 71.7 / B Bloxom R 24.1 / A Bajada Lib 4.2	H Berman D 62.8 / M Ojeda R 37.2	M Levine D 55.0 / R Scribner R 41.8 / 2 others 3.3
1986	H Waxman D 87.9 / 2 others 12.1	E Roybal D 76.1 / G Hardy R 21.3 / T Brown Lib 2.6	H Berman D 65.1 / R Kerns R 34.9	M Levine D 63.7 / R Scribner R 34.3 / 2 others 2.0
1988	H Waxman D 72.2 / J Cowles R 23.8 / 2 others 4.0	E Roybal D 85.5 / 2 others 14.5	H Berman D 70.3 / B Broderson R 29.7	M Levine D 67.5 / D Galbraith R 29.6 / W Fulco Lib 2.8
1990	H Waxman D 68.9 / J Cowles R 25.6 / Peace Fr 5.5	E Roybal D 70.0 / S Renshaw R 24.8 / R Scott Lib 5.2	H Berman D 61.1 / R Dahlson R 34.8 / B Zimring Lib 4.1	M Levine D 58.2 / D Cohen R 37.2 / Peace Fr 4.5
1992	A Beilenson D 55.5 / T McClintock R 39.1 / Peace Fr 5.4	B McKeon R 51.9 / G Gilmartin D 33.0 / 4 others 15.0	H Berman D 61.0 / G Forsch R 30.1 / 2 others 8.8	C Moorhead R 49.7 / D Kahn D 39.4 / 3 others 10.9
1994	A Beilenson D 49.4 / R Sybert R 47.5 / J Koehler Lib 3.1	B McKeon R 64.9 / J Gilmartin D 31.4 / D Cutler Lib 3.7	H Berman D 63.7 / G Forsch R 32.2 / E Miller Lib 5.2	C Moorhead R 53.0 / D Kahn D 42.1 / 2 others 4.9
1996	B Sherman D 49.4 / R Sybert R 43.6 / 3 others 7.0	B McKeon R 62.4 / D Trautman D 33.2 / 2 others 4.4	H Berman D 65.9 / B Glass R 28.6 / 2 others 5.5	J Rogan R 50.2 / D Kahn D 43.2 / 3 others 6.6
1998	B Sherman D 57.3 / R Hoffman R 38.5 / 3 others 4.2	B McKeon R 74.7 / B Acker Lib 25.3	H Berman D 82.5 / 3 others 17.5	J Rogan R 50.7 / B Gordon D 46.4 / B New Lib 2.8
2000	B Sherman D 66.0 / J Doyle R 29.8 / 2 others 4.2	B McKeon R 62.2 / S Gold D 33.2 / 2 others 4.6	H Berman D 84.1 / 2 others 15.9	A Schiff D 52.7 / J Rogan R 43.8 / 2 others 3.5
2002	E Gallegly R 65.2 / F Rudin D 31.8 / G Harber Lib 3.1	B McKeon R 65.0 / B Conaway D 31.1 / F Consolo Lib 3.9	D Dreier R 63.7 / M Mikels D 33.5 / R Weissbuch Lib 2.7	B Sherman D 62.0 / R Levy R 38.0
2004	E Gallegly R 62.8 / B Wagner D 33.9 / S Bechman Green 3.3	B McKeon R 64.4 / T Willoughby D 35.6	D Dreier R 53.6 / C Matthews D 42.8 / R Weissbuch Lib 3.6	B Sherman D 62.3 / R Levy R 33.3 / E Carter Green 4.5
2006	E Gallegly R 62.0 / J Martinez D 38.0	B McKeon R 60.0 / R Rodriguez D 35.7 / D Erickson Lib 4.4	D Dreier R 57.0 / C Matthews D 37.9 / 2 others 5.2	B Sherman D 65.8 / P Hankwitz R 31.2
2008	E Gallegly R 58.2 / M Jorgenson D 41.8	B McKeon R 57.7 / J Conaway D 42.3	D Dreier R 52.6 / R Warner D 40.4 / T Brown Lib 6.9	B Sherman D 66.1 / N Singh R 26.2 / T Denton Lib 6.7
2010	E Gallegly R 59.9 / T Allison D 40.1	B McKeon R 61.8 / J Conaway D 38.2	D Dreier R 54.1 / R Warner D 36.5 / 2 others 9.3	B Sherman D 65.2 / M Reed R 34.8
2012	L Capps D 58.1 / A Maldonado R 44.9	B McKeon R 54.8 / L Rogers D 45.2	J Brownley D 52.7 / T Strickland R 47.3	J Chu D 64.0 / J Orswell R 36.0
2014	L Capps D 51.9 / C Mitchum R 48.1	S Knight R 53.3 / T Strickland R 46.7	J Brownley D 51.3 / J Gorell R 48.7	J Chu D 59.4 / J Orswell R 40.6
2016	S Carbajal D 53.4 / J Fareed R 46.6	S Knight R 53.1 / B Caforio D 46.9	J Brownley D 60.4 / R Dagnesses R 39.6	J Chu D 67.4 / J Orswell R 32.6

California Elections to the U.S. House, Districts 28–31

Districts 28–30, created in 1952, included the south coast (Orange County), inland (Riverside and Imperial Counties), and most of San Diego County in the 1950s. They (and District 31, created in 1962) thereafter covered central and south Los Angeles. The 1992 redistricting gave them more northerly areas, but still within LA County, from Santa Monica eastward into the San Gabriel Valley.

	DISTRICT 28	DISTRICT 29	DISTRICT 30	DISTRICT 31
1952	J Utt R 63.0 L Van Deerlin D 37.0	J Phillips R-D 100	B Wilson R 59.6 D Austin D 40.4	
1954	J Utt R 66.2 H Enderle D 33.8	J Phillips R 57.9 B Shangle D 42.0	B Wilson R 60.4 R McIntire D 39.6	
1956	J Utt R 64.5 G Shepard D 35.5	J Saund D 51.5 J Odlum R 48.4	B Wilson R 66.7 G Cheney D 33.3	
1958	J Utt R 58.2 T Boyett D 41.8	J Saund D 62.4 J Babbage R 37.6	B Wilson R 55.3 L Van Deerlin D 44.7	
1960	J Utt R 60.9 M Woods D 39.1	J Saund D 57.1 C Jameson R 42.9	B Wilson R 59.3 W Wencke D 40.7	
1962	A Bell R 64.0 R Felixson D 36.0	G Brown D 55.6 H Richardson R 44.3	E Roybal D 56.5 G McDonough R 43.5	C Wilson D 52.2 G Hahn R 47.8
1964	A Bell R 65.6 G Gottlieb D 34.4	G Brown D 58.6 C Farrington R 41.4	E Roybal D 66.3 A Feder R 33.7	C Wilson D 64.0 N Shanahan R 36.0
1966	A Bell R 72.3 L Sherman D 27.7	G Brown D 51.1 B Orozco R 48.9	E Roybal D 67.3 H O'Bryant R 33.6	C Wilson D 63.4 T Smith R 36.6
1968	A Bell R 71.2 J Pratt D 26.9 *Peace Fr* 1.9	G Brown D 52.3 B Orozco R 47.7	E Roybal D 67.5 S Cavnar R 32.5	C Wilson D 58.9 J Dunn R 39.1 *Am Ind* 2.0
1970	A Bell R 69.3 D McLaughlin D 25.9 2 others 4.8	G Danielson D 62.6 T McMann R 37.4	E Roybal D 68.3 S Cavnar R 29.9 *Am Ind* 1.8	C Wilson D 73.2 F Casmir R 26.8
1972	A Bell R 60.7 M Shapiro D 37.5 *Peace Fr* 1.8	G Danielson D 62.8 R Ferraro R 33.5 *Peace Fr* 3.7	E Roybal D 68.4 B Brophy R 28.6 *Peace Fr* 3.0	C Wilson D 52.3 B Valentine R 42.5 *Peace Fr* 5.2
1974	Y Burke D 80.3 T Neddy R 19.7	G Hawkins D 100	G Danielson D 74.2 J Perez R 25.8	C Wilson D 70.5 N Bridges R 26.8 *Peace Fr* 2.7
1976	Y Burke D 80.2 E Skinner R 19.8	G Hawkins D 85.4 M Germonprez R 11.2 S Leburg *ind* 3.3	G Danielson D 74.4 H Couch R 25.6	C Wilson D 100
1978	J Dixon D 100	G Hawkins D 85.0 U Fields R 15.0	G Danielson D 71.4 H Ares R 28.6	C Wilson D 67.8 D Grimshaw R 32.2
1980	J Dixon D 79.2 R Reid R 16.9 E Ghermann *Lib* 3.9	G Hawkins D 86.1 M Hirt R 11.1 E Smith *Lib* 2.8	G Danielson D 72.1 A Platten R 23.5 B Hobbs *Lib* 4.4	M Dymally D 64.4 D Grimshaw R 35.6
1982	J Dixon D 78.9 D Goerz R 18.7 D Meleney *Lib* 2.4	G Hawkins D 79.8 M Mackaig R 20.2	M Martinez D 53.9 J Rousselot R 46.1	M Dymally D 72.4 H Minturn R 27.6
1984	J Dixon D 75.6 B Jett R 22.4 D Frederick *Lib* 2.0	G Hawkins D 86.6 E Goto R 13.4	M Martinez D 51.8 R Gomez R 43.4 *Am Ind* 4.9	M Dymally D 70.7 H Minturn R 29.3
1986	J Dixon D 76.4 G Adams R 21.3 H Johnson *Lib* 2.3	G Hawkins D 84.5 J Van de Brooke R 14.5 W Boctor *Lib* 0.9	M Martinez D 62.5 J Almquist R 35.5 K Goldsworthy *Lib* 2.0	M Dymally D 70.3 J McMurray R 27.6 *Peace Fr* 2.1
1988	J Dixon D 76.1 G Adams R 19.8 2 others 4.1	G Hawkins D 82.8 R Franco R 13.7 G Gilmore *Lib* 3.5	M Martinez D 59.9 R Ramirez R 36.3 2 others 3.8	M Dymally D 71.6 A May R 25.5 *Peace Fr* 2.9
1990	J Dixon D 72.7 G Adams R 22.2 2 others 5.1	M Waters D 79.4 B DeWitt R 18.6 W Boctor *Lib* 2.0	M Martinez D 58.2 R Franco R 37.0 G Feger *Lib* 4.8	M Dymally D 67.1 E Sato R 32.9
1992	D Dreier R 58.4 A Wachtel D 37.5 2 others 5.0	H Waxman D 61.3 M Robbins R 25.7 3 others 13.0	X Becerra D 58.4 M Waksberg R 24.0 3 others 17.6	M Martinez D 62.6 R Franco R 37.4
1994	D Dreier R 67.1 T Randle D 30.4 J Baker *Lib* 2.5	H Waxman D 68.0 P Stepanek R 28.3 M Binkley *Lib* 3.8	X Becerra D 66.2 D Ramirez R 28.2 R Weilburg *Lib* 5.6	M Martinez D 59.1 J Flores R 40.9
1996	D Dreier R 60.7 D Levering D 36.9 K Saurenman *Lib* 2.4	H Waxman D 67.6 P Stepanek R 24.6 3 others 7.8	X Becerra D 72.3 P Parker R 18.7 3 others 9.0	M Martinez D 67.5 J Flores R 28.0 M Everling *Lib* 4.6
1998	D Dreier R 57.6 J Nelson D 39.3 3 others 3.1	H Waxman D 73.9 M Gottlieb R 22.6 2 others 3.5	X Becerra D 81.2 P Parker R 18.8	M Martinez D 70.0 F Moreno R 22.6 3 others 7.3
2000	D Dreier R 56.8 J Nelson D 39.9 3 others 3.3	H Waxman D 75.7 J Scileppi R 19.2 2 others 5.1	X Becerra D 83.3 T Goss R 11.8 2 others 4.9	H Solis D 79.4 K Lieberg-Wong *Green* 9.1 2 others 11.5
2002	H Berman D 71.4 D Hernandez R 23.2 K Ross *Lib* 5.4	A Schiff D 62.6 J Scileppi R 33.4 T Brown *Lib* 4.0	H Waxman D 70.4 T Goss R 29.6	X Becerra D 81.2 L Vega R 18.8
2004	H Berman D 71.0 D Hernandez R 23.3 K Ross *Lib* 5.7	A Schiff D 64.7 H Scolinos R 30.4 2 others 4.9	H Waxman D 71.2 V Elizalde R 28.8	X Becerra D 80.2 L Vega R 19.8
2006	H Berman D 73.9 S Kesselman R 19.1 2 others 7.0	A Schiff D 63.5 W Bodell R 27.4 3 others 9.1	H Waxman D 71.5 D Jones R 26.4 *Peace Fr* 2.1	X Becerra D 100
2008	H Berman D 99.9 write-in	A Schiff D 68.9 C Hahn R 26.7 A Pyeatt *Lib* 4.3	H Waxman D 100	X Becerra D 100
2010	H Berman D 69.5 M Froyd R 22.4 C Rodriguez *Lib* 8.0	A Schiff D 64.8 J Colbert R 32.0 W Cushing *Lib* 3.2	H Waxman D 64.6 C Wilkerson R 31.9 2 others 3.4	X Becerra D 83.8 S Smith R 16.2
2012	A Schiff D 76.5 P Jennerjahn R 23.5	T Cardenas D 74.1 D Hernandez *ind* 25.9	B Sherman D 60.3 H Berman D 39.7	G Miller R 55.2 B Dutton R 44.8
2014	A Schiff D 76.5 S Stokes *ind* 23.5	T Cardenas D 74.6 W Leader R 25.4	B Sherman D 65.6 M Reed R 34.4	P Aguilar D 51.7 P Chabot R 48.3
2016	A Schiff D 78.0 L Solis R 22.0	T Cardenas D 74.7 R Alarcon D 25.3	B Sherman D 72.6 M Reed R 27.4	P Aguilar D 56.1 P Chabot R 43.9

California Elections to the U.S. House, Districts 32–35

Created in 1962, these four districts originally included parts of southern Los Angeles County (Compton, Long Beach), San Bernardino County, and Orange County. After 2002 they covered much of the eastern and southern city of Los Angeles and some adjacent suburbs (Monterey Park, Rosemead).

	DISTRICT 32	DISTRICT 33	DISTRICT 34	DISTRICT 35
1962	C Hosmer R 70.7 J Johovich D 29.2	H Sheppard D 59.0 W Thomas R 41.0	R Hanna D 55.9 R Geier R 44.1	J Utt R 68.5 B Shamsky D 31.5
1964	C Hosmer R 68.9 M Cullen D 31.1	K Dyal D 51.7 J Pettis R 48.3	R Hanna D 58.2 R Geier R 41.7	J Utt R 65.0 P Carpenter D 35.0
1966	C Hosmer R 80.1 T Odell D 19.9	J Pettis R 53.5 K Dyal D 46.5	R Hanna D 55.8 F LaMagna R 44.3	J Utt R 73.1 T Lenhart D 26.9
1968	C Hosmer R 73.8 A Gottlieb D 24.1 Am Ind 2.1	J Pettis R 66.3 A Bellard D 32.0 Am Ind 1.7	R Hanna D 50.9 B Teague R 49.1	J Utt R 72.5 T Lenhardt D 25.1 Am Ind 2.4
1970	C Hosmer R 71.5 W Mallonee D 26.5 Peace Fr 1.9	J Pettis R 72.2 C Wright D 27.8	R Hanna D 54.5 B Teague R 44.0 Am Ind 1.5	J Schmitz R 67.0 T Lenhart D 30.3 Peace Fr 2.7
1972	C Hosmer R 65.9 D Murray D 32.0 Peace Fr 2.2	J Pettis R 75.1 K Thompson D 24.9	R Hanna D 67.2 J Ratterree R 28.9 Amican 3.9	G Anderson D 74.8 V Brown R 25.2
1974	G Anderson D 87.7 Am Ind 9.3 Peace Fr 3.1	D Clawson R 53.4 B White D 43.1 Am Ind 3.5	M Hannaford D 49.7 B Bond R 46.3 2 others 3.9	J Lloyd D 60,709 V Veysey R 60,102
1976	G Anderson D 72.2 C Young R 27.8	D Clawson R 55.1 T Snyder D 44.9	M Hannaford D 50.7 D Lungren R 49.3	J Lloyd D 53.3 L Brutocao D 46.7
1978	G Anderson D 71.4 S Mathison R 22.4 Am Ind 6.1	W Grisham R 56.0 D Kazarian D 44.0	D Lungren R 53.7 M Hannaford D 43.7 Am Ind 2.6	J Lloyd D 54.0 D Dreier R 46.0
1980	G Anderson D 65.9 J Adler R 30.8 T Cosgrove Lib 3.3	W Grisham R 70.9 F Anderson D 29.1	D Lungren R 71.8 Simone D 24.1 Peace Fr 4.1	D Dreier R 51.8 J Lloyd D 45.4 Peace Fr 2.8
1982	G Anderson D 58.0 B Lungren R 39.6 Peace Fr 2.4	D Dreier R 65.2 P Servelle D 32.2 2 others 2.6	E Torres D 57.2 P Jackson R 42.8	J Lewis R 68.3 R Erwin D 31.7
1984	G Anderson D 60.7 R Fiola R 36.6 2 others 2.7	D Dreier R 70.6 C McDonald D 26.0 2 others 3.4	E Torres D 59.8 P Jackson R 40.2	J Lewis R 85.5 Peace Fr 14.5
1986	G Anderson D 68.5 J Robertson R 29.4 Peace Fr 2.1	D Dreier R 71.7 M Hempel D 26.8 Peace Fr 1.5	E Torres D 60.3 C House R 39.7	J Lewis R 76.9 R Hall D 23.1
1988	G Anderson D 66.9 S Kahn R 29.6 2 others 3.5	D Dreier R 69.2 N Gentry D 26.2 2 others 4.6	E Torres D 63.2 C House R 35.0 C Swinney Lib 1.8	J Lewis R 70.4 P Sweeney D 27.7 J Shuman Lib 1.9
1990	G Anderson D 61.5 S Kahn R 38.5	D Dreier R 63.7 G Webb D 31.4 G Lightfoot Lib 4.9	E Torres D 60.7 J Eastman R 39.3	J Lewis R 60.6 B Norton D 32.9 J Johnson Lib 6.5
1992	J Dixon D 87.2 2 others 12.8	L Roybal-Allard D 63.0 R Guzman R 30.4 2 others 6.6	E Torres D 61.3 J Hernandez R 34.0 C Swinney Lib 4.7	M Waters D 82.5 N Truman R 14.0 2 others 3.5
1994	J Dixon D 77.6 E Farhat R 17.6 Peace Fr 4.8	L Roybal-Allard D 81.5 K Booker Peace Fr 18.5	E Torres D 61.7 A Nunez R 34.1 C Swinney Lib 4.2	M Waters D 78.1 N Truman R 21.9
1996	J Dixon D 82.4 L Ardito R 12.4 2 others 5.2	L Roybal-Allard D 82.1 J Leonard R 14.1 H Johnson Lib 3.8	E Torres D 68.4 D Nunez R 26.6 2 others 5.0	M Waters D 85.5 E Carlson R 12.1 Am Ind 2.4
1998	J Dixon D 86.7 L Ardito R 11.3 V Melosevich Lib 2.0	L Roybal-Allard D 87.2 W Miller R 12.8	G Napolitano D 67.6 E Perez R 28.6 2 others 3.8	M Waters D 89.3 G Mego Am Ind 10.7
2000	J Dixon D 83.5 K Williamson R 12.1 2 others 4.3	L Roybal-Allard D 84.5 W Miller R 11.5 2 others 3.9	G Napolitano D 71.3 R Canales R 22.5 J Simon NLP 6.2	M Waters D 86.5 C McGill R 10.8 2 others 2.6
2002	H Solis D 68.8 E Fischbeck R 27.5 M McGuire Lib 3.7	D Watson D 82.5 A Kim R 14.1 C Tate Lib 3.4	L Roybal-Allard D 74.0 W Miller R 26.0	M Waters D 77.5 R Moen R 20.4 G Mego Am Ind 3.1
2004	H Solis D 85.0 L Faegre Lib 15.0	D Watson D 88.6 R Weber Lib 11.4	L Roybal-Allard D 74.5 W Miller R 25.5	M Waters D 80.5 R Moen R 15.1 2 others 4.4
2006	H Solis D 83.0 L Faegre Lib 17.0	D Watson D 100	L Roybal-Allard D 76.8 W Miller R 23.2	M Waters D 83.7 2 others 16.3
2008	H Solis D 100	D Watson D 87.6 D Crowley R 12.4	L Roybal-Allard D 77.1 C Balding R 22.9	M Waters D 82.6 T Hayes R 13.2 H Peters Lib 4.2
2010	J Chu D 71.0 E Schmerling R 29.0	K Bass D 86.1 J Andion R 13.9	L Roybal-Allard D 77.2 W Miller R 22.8	M Waters D 79.3 B Brown R 20.7
2012	G Napolitano D 65.7 D Miller R 34.3	H Waxman D 54.0 B Bloomfield ind 46	X Becerra D 86.6 S Smith R 14.4	G McLeod D 56.9 J Baca D 44.1
2014	G Napolitano D 59.7 A Alas R 40.3	T Lieu D 59.2 E Carr R 40.8	X Becerra D 72.5 A Edwards D 27.5	N Torres D 63.5 C Gagnier D 36.5
2016	G Napolitano D 61.6 R Hernandez D 38.4	T Lieu D 66.4 K Wright R 33.6	X Becerra D 77.2 A Edwards D 22.8	N Torres D 72.4 T Fischella R 27.6

California Elections to the U.S. House, Districts 36–39

Districts 36–38 were created after the 1960 census, and originally were assigned to San Diego (36 and 37) and Riverside and Imperial (38) Counties. District 39 was new after the 1970 census. In the 1970s and 1980s, they covered the eastern San Gabriel Valley, most of San Bernardino County, and much of Orange. Since the 1990s they have been assigned to southern parts of LA County from Venice through Watts and Long Beach to Fullerton.

	DISTRICT 36	DISTRICT 37	DISTRICT 38	DISTRICT 39
1962	B Wilson R 61.8 W Godfrey D 38.2	L van Deerlin D 51.3 D Wilson R 48.6	M Martin R 55.9 J Saund D 44.1	
1964	B Wilson R 59.1 Q Whelan D 40.9	L van Deerlin D 58.2 D Wilson R 41.7	J Tunney D 52.8 P Martin R 47.2	
1966	B Wilson R 72.7 W Godfrey D 27.1	L van Deerlin D 61.1 S Vener R 38.8	J Tunney D 54.5 R Barry R 45.5	
1968	B Wilson R 71.6 D Lindgren D 28.4	L van Deerlin D 64.7 M Schaefer R 35.3	J Tunney D 62.8 R Hunter R 35.4 2 others 1.9	
1970	B Wilson R 71.5 D Hostetter D 24.2 2 others 4.2	L van Deerlin D 72.1 J Kuhn R 24.5 2 others 3.3	V Veysey R 49.8 D Tunno D 48.8 Am Ind 1.4	
1972	W Ketchum R 52.7 T Lemucchi D 43.5 B Armour Am Ind 3.8	Y Burke D 73.2 G Tria R 24.7 Peace Fr 2.1	G Brown D 56.3 H Snider R 43.7	A Hinshaw R 65.7 J Black D 34.3
1974	G Brown D 62.6 J Osgood R 32.3 W Pasley Am Ind 5.1	J Pettis R 63.0 B Vincent D 33.1 J Ortman Am Ind 3.9	J Patterson D 54.0 D Rehmann R 41.3 2 others 4.7	C Wiggins R 55.2 B Farris D 40.4 P Scalera Am Ind 4.4
1976	G Brown D 61.6 G Carner R 33.5 Am Ind 5.0	S Pettis R 71.1 D Nilson D 26.1 Am Ind 2.8	J Patterson D 63.6 J Combs R 36.4	C Wiggins R 58.6 B Farris D 41.4
1978	G Brown D 62.9 D Carmody R 37.1	J Lewis R 61.4 D Corcoran D 34.8 Am Ind 3.8	J Patterson D 58.6 D Goedeke R 41.4	W Dannemeyer R 63.7 B Farris D 36.3
1980	G Brown D 52.5 J Stark R 43.4 H Histen Lib 4.0	J Lewis R 71.6 D Rusk D 25.1 L Morris Lib 3.3	J Patterson D 55.5 A Jacobson R 40.0 C Heiser Lib 4.4	W Dannemeyer R 76.3 L Lahtinen D 23.7
1982	G Brown D 54.3 J Stark R 45.7	A McCandless R 59.1 S Cross D 38.5 M Wruble Lib 2.4	J Patterson D 52.4 B Dohr R 43.4 A Barr Lib 4.2	W Dannemeyer R 72.2 F Verges D 26.0 Peace Fr 1.8
1984	G Brown D 56.6 J Stark R 43.4	A McCandless R 63.6 D Skinner D 36.4	B Dornan R 53.2 J Patterson D 45.0 Peace Fr 1.9	B Dannemeyer R 76.2 R Ward D 23.8
1986	G Brown R 57.1 B Henley R 42.9	A McCandless R 63.7 D Skinner D 36.3	B Dornan R 55.3 R Robinson D 42.4 L Connelly Lib 2.3	B Dannemeyer R 74.5 D Vest D 24.0 Peace Fr 1.6
1988	G Brown D 54.0 J Stark R 42.5 2 others 3.5	A McCandless R 64.3 J Pearson D 33.1 B Flickinger Lib 2.6	B Dornan R 59.5 J Yudelson D 35.6 2 others 4.9	B Dannemeyer R 73.8 D Marquis D 22.7 L Connelly Lib 3.3
1990	G Brown D 52.7 B Hammock R 47.3	A McCandless R 48.0 R Waite D 43.5 2 others 5.5	B Dornan R 58.1 B Jackson D 41.9	B Dannemeyer R 65.3 F Hoffman D 30.8 Peace Fr 3.9
1992	J Harman D 48.4 J Flores R 42.2 3 others 9.4	W Tucker D 85.7 Peace Fr 14.3	S Horn R 48.6 E Braude D 43.4 2 others 8.0	E Royce R 57.3 M McClanahan D 38.2 J Dean Lib 4.4
1994	J Harman D 93,939 S Brooks D 93,127 J Tyler Lib (2.5%) Am Ind (1.9%)	W Tucker D 77.4 G Wilson Lib 22.3	S Horn R 58.5 P Mathews D 36.8 2 others 4.7	E Royce R 66.4 B Davis D 29.0 J Dean Lib 4.6
1996	J Harman D 52.5 S Brooks R 43.9 2 others 3.6	J Millender-M D 85.0 M Voetee R 15.0	S Horn R 52.6 R Zbur D 42.7 2 others 4.7	E Royce R 62.8 B Davis D 31.9 J Dean Lib 5.3
1998	S Kuykendall R 48.9 J Hahn D 46.6 3 others 4.5	J Millender-M D 85.1 S Lankster R 14.9	S Horn R 52.9 P Mathews D 44.3 D Bowers Lib 2.7	E Royce R 62.6 C Groom D 34.0 2 others 3.4
2000	J Harman D 48.4 S Kuykendall R 46.6 3 others 5.0	J Millender-M D 82.3 V Van R 11.3 2 others 6.4	S Horn R 48.4 G Schipske D 47.5 2 others 4.1	E Royce R 62.9 G Kanel D 31.3 2 others 5.8
2002	J Harman D 61.4 S Johnson R 35.0 M McSpadden Lib 3.6	J Millender-M D 71.1 O Velasco R 26.3 H Peters Lib 2.6	G Napolitano D 54.8 A Burrola R 40.8 A Cuperus Lib 4.4	Linda Sanchez D 54.8 T Escobar R 40.8 R Newhouse Lib 4.4
2004	J Harman D 62.0 P Whitehead R 33.5 2 others 4.6	J Millender-M D 75.1 V Van R 20.2 H Peters Lib 4.8	G Napolitano D 100	Linda Sanchez D 60.7 T Escobar R 39.3
2006	J Harman D 63.4 B Gibson R 31.9 2 others 4.7	J Millender-M D 82.4 H Peters Lib 17.6	G Napolitano D 75.3 S Street R 24.7	Linda Sanchez D 65.9 J Andion R 34.1
2008	J Harman D 68.6 B Gibson R 31.4	L Richardson D 74.9 N Dibs ind 24.4 write-in 0.6	G Napolitano D 81.7 C Agrella Lib 18.3	Linda Sanchez D 69.7 D Lenning R 30.3
2010	J Harman D 59.6 M Fein R 34.7 H Peters Lib 5.6	L Richardson D 68.4 S Parker R 23.2 N Dibs ind 8.4	G Napolitano D 73.5 R Vaughn R 26.5	Linda Sanchez D 63.3 L Andre R 32.6 Am Ind 4.1
2012	R Ruiz D 52.9 M Mack R 47.1	K Bass D 86.4 M Osborne R 13.6	Linda Sanchez D 67.5 B Campos R 32.5	E Royce R 57.8 J Chen D 42.2
2014	R Ruiz D 54.2 B Nestande R 45.8	K Bass D 84.3 A King R 15.7	Linda Sanchez D 59.1 B Campos R 40.9	E Royce R 68.5 P Anderson D 31.5
2016	R Ruiz D 62.1 J Stone R 37.9	K Bass D 81.1 C Wiggins D 18.9	Linda Sanchez D 70.5 R Downing R 29.5	E Royce R 57.2 B Murdock D 42.8

California Elections to the U.S. House, Districts 40–43

These four districts were created as a result of the 1970 census and were first contested in 1972. In the 1970s and 1980s they basically covered the south coast from Costa Mesa and Newport Beach through San Diego, as well as Imperial County to the Arizona border (District 43). In 1992 they were reassigned to include more inland areas—San Bernardino, Inyo, and Riverside Counties and part of Orange County.

	DISTRICT 40	DISTRICT 41	DISTRICT 42	DISTRICT 43
1972	B Wilson *R* 67.8 F Caprio *D* 30.3 Peace *Fr* 1.9	L van Deerlin *D* 74.1 D Kau *R* 25.9	C Burgener *R* 67.4 B Lowe *D* 29.2 A Moths *Am Ind* 3.4	V Veysey *R* 52.7 E Robles *D* 37.3
1974	A Hinshaw *R* 63.3 R Wilson *D* 31.0 *Am Ind* 5.7	B Wilson *R* 54.4 C O'Connor *D* 43.1 *Am Ind* 2.5	L van Deerlin *D* 69.9 W Marden *R* 30.1	C Burgener *R* 60.4 B Bandes *D* 39.6
1976	R Badham *R* 59.3 V Hall *D* 40.7	B Wilson *R* 57.7 K Golden *D* 42.3	L van Deerlin *D* 76.0 W Marden *R* 24.0	C Burgener *R* 65.0 P Kelly *D* 35.0
1978	R Badham *R* 65.9 J McGuy *D* 34.1	B Wilson *R* 58.1 K Golden *D* 41.9	L van Deerlin *D* 73.7 L Mattera *R* 26.3	C Burgener *R* 68.7 R Brooks *D* 31.3
1980	R Badham *R* 70.2 M Dow *D* 21.8 D Mahaffey *Lib* 8.0	B Lowery *R* 52.7 B Wilson *D* 43.2 J Alldredge *Lib* 4.1	D Hunter *R* 53.3 L van Deerlin *D* 46.7	C Burgener *R* 86.6 T Metzger *D* 13.4
1982	R Badham *R* 69.5 P Haseman *D* 26.1 Peace *Fr* 2.4	B Lowery *R* 68.9 T Brandenburg *D* 28.8 E Hale *Lib* 2.3	D Lungren *R* 69.0 J Spellman *D* 28.3 Peace *Fr* 2.7	R Packard *R* (write-in) 36.8[1] P Archer *D* 32.1 J Crean *R* 31.1
1984	R Badham *R* 64.4 C Bradford *D* 34.0 Peace *Fr* 1.6	B Lowery *R* 63.5 B Simmons *D* 33.7 S Baase *Lib* 2.9	D Lungren *R* 73.0 M Brophy *D* 24.6 Peace *Fr* 2.4	R Packard *R* 74.1 L Humphreys *D* 22.8 P Avery *Lib* 8.1
1986	R Badham *R* 59.8 B Sumner *D* 37.7 Peace *Fr* 2.5	B Lowery *R* 67.8 D Kripke *D* 30.4 D Rider *Lib* 1.8	D Lungren *R* 72.8 M Blackburn *D* 24.7 Peace *Fr* 2.5	R Packard *R* 73.1 J Chirra *D* 24.0 P Avery *Lib* 2.9
1988	C Cox *R* 67.0 L Lenney *D* 29.9 2 others 3.0	B Lowery *R* 65.6 D Kripke *D* 30.9 2 others 3.6	D Rohrbacher *R* 64.2 G Kimbrough *D* 33.0 Peace *Fr* 2.8	R Packard *R* 71.7 H Greenebaum *D* 25.7 D Muhe *Lib* 2.7
1990	C Cox *R* 67.6 E Gratz *D* 32.4	B Lowery *R* 49.2 D Kripke *D* 43.6 Peace *Fr* 7.2	D Rohrbacher *R* 59.3 G Kimbrough *D* 36.5 R Martin *Lib* 4.2	R Packard *R* 68.1 R Arnold *Lib* 13.8 Peace *Fr* 18.1
1992	J Lewis *R* 63.1 D Rusk *D* 31.1 Peace *Fr* 5.8	J Kim *R* 59.6 B Baker *D* 34.4 Peace *Fr* 5.9	G Brown *D* 50.7 D Rutan *R* 44.0 F Ward *Lib* 5.4	K Calvert *R* 88,987 M Takano *D* 88,468 others 13,184
1994	J Lewis *R* 70.7 D Rusk *D* 29.3	J Kim *R* 62.1 E Tessier *D* 37.9	G Brown *D* 51.1 R Guzman *R* 48.8	K Calvert *R* 55.1 M Takano *D* 38.7 G Berkman *Lib* 6.3
1996	J Lewis *R* 75.9 B Conaway *D* 29.0 2 others 6.1	J Kim *R* 58.5 R Waldron *D* 33.0 2 others 8.5	G Brown *D* 50.5 L Wilde *R* 49.5	K Calvert *R* 54.7 G Kimbrough *D* 38.0 3 others 7.3
1998	J Lewis *R* 64.9 B Conaway *D* 31.9 M Maybena *Lib* 3.2	G Miller *R* 53.2 E Ansari *D* 40.7 3 others 6.1	G Brown *D* 55.3 E Pirozzi *R* 40.3 2 others 4.4	K Calvert *R* 55.7 M Rayburn *D* 38.7 2 others 6.5
2000	J Lewis *R* 79.9 M Lindberg *Lib* 10.0 F Schmidt *NLP* 10.1	G Miller *R* 58.9 R Favila *D* 37.4 D Kramer *NLP* 3.7	J Baca *D* 59.8 E Pirozzi *R* 35.1 J Ballard *Lib* 2.7 G Hartley *NLP* 2.4	K Calvert *R* 73.7 B Reed *Lib* 15.6 N Adam *NLP* 10.7
2002	E Royce *R* 67.6 C Avalos *D* 29.5 C McGlawn *Lib* 2.9	J Lewis *R* 67.4 K Johnson *D* 29.6 K Craig *Lib* 3.0	G Miller *R* 67.8 R Waldron *D* 29.0 D Yee *Lib* 3.2	J Baca *D* 66.4 W Neighbor *R* 30.5 E Mohler *Lib* 3.1
2004	E Royce *R* 67.9 J Williams *D* 32.1	J Lewis *R* 82.9 P Mottahedek *Lib* 17.1	G Miller *R* 68.1 L Myers *D* 31.9	J Baca *D* 66.4 E Laning *R* 33.6
2006	E Royce *R* 66.8 F Hoffman *D* 30.7 P Inman *Lib* 2.6	J Lewis *R* 66.9 L Contreras *D* 33.1	G Miller *R* 100	J Baca *D* 64.5 S Folkens *R* 35.5
2008	E Royce *R* 62.5 C Avalos *D* 37.5	J Lewis *R* 61.6 T Prince *D* 38.4	G Miller *R* 60.2 E Chau *D* 39.8	J Baca *D* 69.1 J Roberts *R* 30.9
2010	E Royce *R* 66.8 C Avalos *D* 33.2	J Lewis *R* 63.2 P Meagher *D* 36.8	G Miller *R* 62.2 M Williamson *D* 31.9 M Lambert *Lib* 5.9	J Baca *D* 65.5 S Folkens *R* 34.5
2012	L Roybal-Allard *D* 58.9 D Sanchez *D* 41.1	M Takano *D* 59.0 J Tavaglione *R* 41.0	K Calvert *R* 60.6 M Williamson *D* 39.4	M Waters *D* 71.2 B Flores *D* 28.6
2014	L Roybal-Allard *D* 61.2 D Sanchez *D* 38.8	M Takano *D* 56.6 S Adams *R* 43.4	K Calvert *R* 65.7 T Sheridan *D* 34.3	M Waters *D* 71.0 J Wood *R* 29.0
2016	L Roybal-Allard *D* 71.4 R Gonzalez *ind* 28.6	M Takano *D* 65.0 D Shepherd *R* 35.0	K Calvert *R* 58.8 T Sheridan *D* 41.2	M Waters *D* 76.1 O Navarro *R* 23.9

[1] Crean defeated Packard in the GOP primary by a small margin. Packard then ran a write-in campaign and won.

California Elections to the U.S. House, Districts 44–47

Districts 44 and 45 were created after the 1980 census and were first contested in the 1982 election. In the 1980s they covered southern portions of San Diego County, but from 1992 they were assigned to Riverside County, including Palm Springs. After 2002 they covered San Bernardino city, some of Riverside County, and Orange County (San Clemente). Districts 46 and 47 were created after the 1990 census and were first contested in 1992. They have represented parts of Orange County.

	DISTRICT 44	DISTRICT 45	DISTRICT 46	DISTRICT 47
1982	J Bates D 64.9 S Gissendanner R 31.8 J Conole Lib 3.2	D Hunter R 68.6 R Hill D 29.2 J Sanders Lib 2.2		
1984	J Bates D 69.7 N Campbell R 28.0 J Conole Lib 2.2	D Hunter R 75.1 D Guthrie D 22.9 P Wright Lib 2.0		
1986	J Bates D 64.2 B Mitchell R 33.1 2 others 2.7	D Hunter R 76.9 H Ryan D 21.2 L Schwartz Lib 1.9		
1988	J Bates D 59.7 B Butterfield R 36.5 D Thompson Lib 3.8	D Hunter R 74.0 P Lepiscopo D 24.0 P Willis Lib 2.0		
1990	R Cunningham R 46.3 J Bates D 44.8 2 others 8.9	D Hunter R 72.8 J Shea Lib 27.2		
1992	A McCandless R 54.2 G Smith D 40.1 P Turner Lib 5.7	D Rohrbacher R 54.5 P McCabe D 39.0 G Copeland Lib 6.5	R Dornan R 50.2 R Banuelos D 41.0 R Newhouse Lib 8.8	C Cox R 64.9 J Anwiler D 30.3 Peace Fr 4.8
1994	S Bono R 56.2 S Clute D 38.6 Am Ind 6.3	D Rohrbacher R 69.1 B Williamson D 30.9	R Dornan R 57.1 M Farber D 37.2 R Newhouse Lib 5.7	C Cox R 71.7 G Kingsbury D 25.0 V Wagner Lib 3.4
1996	S Bono R 57.8 A Rufus D 38.6 2 others 3.7	D Rohrbacher R 61.0 S Alexander D 33.2 2 others 5.8	Loretta Sanchez D 46.7[1] R Dornan R 45.7 3 others 7.6	C Cox R 65.7 T Laine D 28.9 2 others 5.5
1998	M Bono R 60.1 R Waite D 35.7 J Meuer NLP 4.2	D Rohrbacher R 58.7 P Neal D 37.3 2 others 4.0	Loretta Sanchez D 56.4 R Dornan R 39.3 2 others 4.3	C Cox R 67.6 C Avalos D 29.5 3 others 2.9
2000	M Bono R 59.2 R Oden D 37.9 2 others 2.9	D Rohrbacher R 62.1 T Crisell D 32.4 2 others 5.5	Loretta Sanchez D 60.2 G Tuchman R 35.0 2 others 4.8	C Cox R 65.6 J Graham D 30.0 2 others 4.3
2002	K Calvert R 63.7 L Vandenberg D 31.6 P Courtney Green 4.8	M Bono R 65.2 E Kurpiewski D 32.7 R Miller-B Lib 2.1	D Rohrbacher R 61.7 G Schipske D 34.5 K Gann Lib 3.7	Loretta Sanchez D 60.6 J Chavez R 34.7 Lib + write-ins 4.7
2004	K Calvert R 61.6 L Vandenberg D 35.0 Peace Fr 3.4	M Bono R 66.6 R Meyer D 33.4	D Rohrbacher R 61.9 J Brandt D 32.6 2 others 5.5	Loretta Sanchez D 60.4 A Coronado R 39.6
2006	K Calvert R 60.0 L Vandenberg D 37.0 Peace Fr 3.0	M Bono R 60.7 D Roth D 39.3	D Rohrbacher R 59.6 J Brandt D 36.7 D Chang Lib 3.7	Loretta Sanchez D 62.3 T Nguyen R 37.7
2008	K Calvert R 51.2 B Hedrick D 48.8	M Bono Mack R 58.3 J Bornstein D 41.7	D Rohrbacher R 52.5 D Cook D 43.1 2 others 4.4	Loretta Sanchez D 70.1 R Avila R 25.6 Am Ind 5.1
2010	K Calvert R 55.6 B Hedrick D 44.4	M Bono Mack R 51.5 S Pougnet D 42.1 Am Ind 6.4	D Rohrbacher R 62.2 K Arnold D 38.8	Loretta Sanchez D 53.0 V Tran R 39.3 C Iglesias ind 7.8
2012	J Hahn D 60.2 L Richardson D 39.8	J Campbell R 58.5 S King D 41.5	Loretta Sanchez D 63.9 J Hayden R 36.1	A Lowenthal D 56.6 G DeLong R 43.4
2014	J Hahn D 86.7 Peace Fr 13.3	M Walters R 65.1 D Leavens D 34.9	Loretta Sanchez D 59.7 A Nick R 40.3	A Lowenthal D 56.0 A Whallon R 4.40
2016	N Barragan D 52.2 I Hall R 47.8	M Walters R 58.6 R Varasteh D 41.4	L Correa D 70.0 B Nguyen D 30.0	A Lowenthal D 63.7 A Whallon R 36.3

[1] Loretta Sanchez. Her sister, Linda Sanchez, represented the 39th District from 2002.

California Elections to the U.S. House, Districts 48–51

These districts resulted from the 1990 census and were first contested in 1992. They have covered the coast from Laguna Niguel (District 48, 1990s) or Newport Beach (District 48, 2000s) to much of San Diego and Imperial Counties.

	DISTRICT 48	DISTRICT 49	DISTRICT 50	DISTRICT 51
1992	R Packard R 61.1 M Farber D 29.2 T Lowe Lib 3.8 D White Peace Fr 5.8	L Schenk D 51.1 J Jarvis R 42.7 J Wallner Lib 4.3 M Zaslow Peace Fr 1.9	B Filner D 56.6 T Valencia R 28.9 B Hutchinson Lib 11.3 R Batchelder Peace Fr 3.1	R Cunningham R 56.1 B Herbert D 33.7 B Holmes Lib 4.1 M Clark Peace Fr 4.1 R Roe Green 2.1
1994	R Packard R 73.4 A Leschick D 23.3 D White Peace Fr 4.4	B Bilbray R 48.5 L Schenk D 46.0 2 others 5.5	B Filner D 56.7 M Acevedo R 35.4 3 others 7.9	R Cunningham R 66.9 R Tamerius D 27.7 2 others 5.3
1996	R Packard R 65.9 D Farrell D 26.9 2 others 7.2	B Bilbray R 52.6 P Navarro D 41.9 3 others 5.5	B Filner D 61.9 J Baize R 32.4 3 others 5.7	R Cunningham R 65.1 R Tamerius D 28.9 3 others 6.0
1998	R Packard R 76.9 D Muhe Lib 10.2 S Miles NLP 12.9	B Bilbray R 48.8 C Kehoe D 46.6 3 others 4.6	B Filner D 100	R Cunningham R 62.0 D Kripke D 34.7 2 others 4.3
2000	D Issa R 61.4 P Kouvelis D 28.3 3 others 10.2	S Davis D 49.6 B Bilbray R 46.2 2 others 4.2	B Filner D 68.3 B Divine R 27.6 2 others 4.1	R Cunningham R 64.3 G Barraza D 30.4 2 others 5.3
2002	C Cox R 68.4 J Graham D 28.4 J Cobb Lib 3.1	D Issa R 77.2 K Dietrich Lib 22.0 write-in 0.8	R Cunningham R 64.3 D Stewart D 32.3 M Fontanesi Lib 3.3	B Filner D 57.9 M Garcia R 39.3 J Keup Lib 2.7
2004	C Cox R 65.0 J Graham D 32.2 B Cohen Lib 2.9	D Issa R 62.6 M Byron D 34.9 L Grossmith Lib 2.5	R Cunningham R 58.4 F Busby D 36.5 3 others 5.1	B Filner D 61.6 M Giorgino R 35.1 M Metti Lib 3.3
2006	J Campbell R 59.9 S Young D 37.2 B Cohen Lib 2.9	D Issa R 63.3 J Criscenzo D 33.4 L Grossmith Lib 3.2	B Bilbray R 53.1 F Busby D 43.5 2 others 3.4	B Filner D 67.4 B Miles R 30.2 D Litwin Lib 2.4
2008	J Campbell R 55.6 S Young D 40.7 D Patterson Lib 3.7	D Issa R 58.3 R Hamilton D 37.5 L Grossmith Lib 4.3	B Bilbray R 50.2 N Leibham D 45.2 W Dunlap Lib 4.6	B Filner D 72.7 D Joy R 24.2 D Litwin Lib 3.0
2010	J Campbell R 59.9 B Krom D 36.5 M Binkley Lib 3.6	D Issa R 62.8 H Katz D 31.5 2 others 5.7	B Bilbray R 56.7 F Busby D 39.0 2 others 4.4	B Filner D 60.1 N Popaditch R 39.9
2012	D Rohrabacher R 61.0 R Varasteh D 39.0	D Issa R 58.2 J Tetalman D 41.8	D Hunter R 67.7 D Secor D 32.3	J Vargas D 71.5 M Crimmins R 28.5
2014	D Rohrabacher R 64.1 S Savary D 35.9	D Issa R 60.2 D Peiser D 39.8	D Hunter R 71.2 J Kimber D 28.8	J Vargas D 68.8 S Meade R 31.2
2016	D Rohrabacher R 58.3 S Savary D 41.7	D Issa R 50.3 D Applegate D 49.7	D Hunter R 63.5 P Malloy D 36.5	J Vargas D 72.8 J Hidalgo R 27.2

California Elections to the U.S. House, Districts 52–53

District 52, first contested in 1992, included the eastern suburbs of San Diego County plus Imperial County in the 1990s, and since then about two-thirds of San Diego County. District 53, first contested in 2002, has included much of the city of San Diego plus Coronado.

	DISTRICT 52	DISTRICT 53
1992	D Hunter *R* 52.9 J Gastil *D* 41.2 2 others 5.9	
1994	D Hunter *R* 64.0 J Gastil *D* 31.1 2 others 5.0	
1996	D Hunter *R* 65.5 D Wesley *D* 29.8 3 others 4.8	
1998	D Hunter *R* 75.7 L Badler *Lib* 14.3 A Pelton *NLP* 10.0	
2000	D Hunter *R* 64.7 C Barkacs *D* 31.3 2 others 4.0	
2002	D Hunter *R* 70.2 P Moore-K *D* 25.8 M Benoit *Lib* 4.1	S Davis *D* 62.2 B VanDeWeghe *R* 37.8
2004	D Hunter *R* 68.2 B Keliher *D* 27.6 M Benoit *Lib* 3.2	S Davis *D* 66.1 D Hunzeker *R* 28.9 2 others 5.0
2006	D Hunter *R* 64.6 J Rinaldi *D* 32.0 M Benoit *Lib* 3.40	S Davis *D* 67.6 J Woodrum *R* 30.0 E Lippe *Lib* 2.4
2008	D Hunter *R* 56.4 M Lumpkin *D* 38.9 M Benoit *Lib* 4.7	S Davis *D* 68.5 M Crimmins *R* 27.5 E Teyssier *Lib* 4.1
2010	D Hunter *R* 63.1 R Lutz *D* 32.1 M Benoit *Lib* 4.9	S Davis *D* 62.3 M Crimmins *R* 34.0 P Dekker *Lib* 3.7
2012	S Peters *D* 51.2 B Bilbray *R* 48.8	S Davis *D* 61.4 N Popaditch *R* 38.6
2014	S Peters *D* 51.6 C DeMaio *R* 48.4	S Davis *D* 58.8 L Wilske *R* 41.2
2016	S Peters *D* 56.5 D Gitsham *R* 43.5	S Davis *D* 67.0 J Veltmeyer *R* 33.0

Colorado Election Results: President, Governor, Senator

	PRESIDENT	GOVERNOR	SENATOR
1950		D Thornton R 52.4 W Johnson D 47.2 SLP 0.3	E. Millikin R 53.3 M Carroll D 46.8
1952	Eisenhower 60.3 Stevenson 39.0 others 0.8	D Thornton R 57.1 J Metzger D 42.4	
1954		E Johnson D 53.6 D Brotzman R 46.4	G Allott R 51.3 J Carroll D 48.7
1956	Eisenhower 59.6 Stevenson 39.9 SLP 3.3 other 1.3	S McNichols D 51.3 D Brotzman R 48.7	J Carroll D 50.2 D Thornton R 49.8
1958		S McNichols D 60.7 P Burch R 39.3	
1960	Nixon 54.6 Kennedy 44.9 others 0.5		G Allott R 53.7 R Knous D 45.8
1962		J Love R 56.7 S McNichols D 42.6 others 0.7	P Dominick R 53.6 J Carroll D 45.6 3 others 0.8
1964	Johnson 61.4 Goldwater 38.3		
1966		J Love R 54.0 R Knous D 43.5 other 2.5	G Allott R 58.0 R Romer D 42.0
1968	Nixon 50.9 Humphrey 41.2 Am Ind 7.6		P Dominick R 58.6 S McNichols D 41.4
1970		J Love R 52.5 M Hogan D 45.2 others 2.3	
1972	Nixon 62.9 McGovern 34.8 Am Ind 1.8		F Haskell D 49.4 G Allott R 48.4 2 others 2.2
1974		R Lamm D 53.2 J Vanderhoof R 45.7	G Hart D 59.2 P Dominick R 40.8
1976	Ford 54.6 Carter 43.0 ind 2.4		
1978		R Lamm D 58.8 T Strickland R 38.5 others 2.7	W Armstrong R 59.3 F Haskell D 40.7
1980	Reagan 56.7 Carter 32.0 Anderson 11.1		G Hart D 50.8 M Buchanan R 49.2
1982		R Lamm D 65.7 J Fuhr R 31.7 3 others	
1984	Reagan 53.4 Mondale 35.1 5 others		W Armstrong R 64.2 N Dick D 34.6 3 others
1986		R Romer D 58.2 T Strickland R 41.0 others 0.8	T Wirth D 49.9 K Kramer R 48.4 others 1.7
1988	Bush 53.1 Dukakis 45.3		
1990		R Romer D 61.9 J Andrews R 35.4 2 others 2.7	H Brown R 55.7 J Heath D 41.7 2 others 2.7
1992	Clinton 40.1 Bush 35.9 Perot 23.3		B Campbell D 51.8 T Considine R 42.7 3 others 5.5
1994		R Romer D 55.5 B Benson R 38.7 4 others 5.8	
1996	Dole 45.8 W Clinton 44.4 Perot 6.6		W Allard R 51.4 Tom Strickland D 45.7
1998		B Owens R 49.1 G Schoettler D 48.4 2 others 2.5	B Campbell R 62.5 D Lamm D 35.0 4 others 2.5
2000	Bush 50.7 Gore 42.4 Green 5.2 7 others		
2002		B Owens R 62.6 R Heath D 33.7 2 others 3.7	W Allard R 50.7 Tom Strickland D 45.8 4 others 3.5
2004	Bush 51.7 Kerry 47.0 9 others		K Salazar D 51.3 P Coors R 47.4 5 others 1.3
2006		B Ritter D 57.0 B Beauprez R 40.2 3 others 2.8	
2008	Obama 53.7 McCain 44.7 16 others		M Udall D 52.8 B Schaffer R 42.5 2 others
2010		J Hickenlooper D 51.0 Tancredo ACN 36.4[1] D Maes R 11.1	M Bennet D 48.1 K Buck R 46.4 5 others 5.5
2012	Obama 51.5 Romney 46.1		
2014		J Hickenlooper D 49.3 B Beauprez R 46.0 4 others 4.8	C Gardner R 48.5 M Udall D 46.0 2 others 4.0
2016	Clinton 47.3 Trump 44.4 Johnson 5.0 Stein 1.3		M Bennet 49.2 D Glenn 45.3 L Williams Lib 3.5

[1] American Constitution Party.

Colorado Elections to the U.S. House, Districts 1–4

From 1950 through the 1970 election, Colorado's four districts assigned District 1 to Denver, District 2 to the northeast quarter of the state, District 3 to the southeast quarter, and District 4 (Aspinall's) basically west of the Continental Divide. The 1972 redistricting added a fifth district. Denver kept District 1 (Schroeder); District 2 included the area just west of Denver plus Boulder; District 3 covered the southern third of the state from Utah to Kansas; District 4, the northern third from Utah to Kansas; and District 5, several Denver suburbs plus Colorado Springs. In the 1982 redistricting, the basically east-west orientation of the 1970s gave way to a north-south orientation: Denver stayed District 1; District 2 included some northern Denver suburbs plus Longmont and Boulder; District 3 became the western half including Pueblo; District 4 covered the Plains counties plus Greeley and Fort Collins; District 5 became Colorado Springs and some Denver suburbs; and the new District 6 formed a "U" around Denver including Aurora. The 1992 redistricting kept this configuration with minor changes. With the addition of District 7 in 2002, the arrangement became Denver, still District 1; Boulder into the mountains, District 2; the southwest and west from Pueblo to Utah, District 3; the plains including Fort Collins, District 4; Colorado Springs and some mountains, District 5; southern suburbs of Denver, District 6; and a strip from Golden, Arvada, and Aurora to Kansas, District 7.

	DISTRICT 1	DISTRICT 2	DISTRICT 3	DISTRICT 4
1950	B Rogers D 50.3 R Luxford R 48.3 2 others 1.3	W Hill R 57.5 G Bickel D 38.9 1 other 0.5	J Chenoweth R 51.6 J Marsalis D 48.4	W Aspinall D 57.3 J Evans R 42.7
1952	B Rogers D 50.8 M Knuckles R 48.6 1 other 0.6	W Hill R 63.1 R Williams D 36.9	J Chenoweth R 57.7 J Marsalis D 42.2	W Aspinall D 39,676 H Shults R 39,647
1954	B Rogers D 55.6 E Harris R 44.1 1 other 0.3	W Hill R 55.3 L Wilkinson D 44.7	J Chenoweth R 53.0 A Adams D 47.0	W Aspinall D 53.5 C Wilson R 46.5
1956	B Rogers D 57.8 R McCollum R 42.2	W Hill R 53.4 B Johnson D 46.6	J Chenoweth R 50.2 A Adams D 49.8	W Aspinall D 61.8 H Caldwell R 38.2
1958	B Rogers D 66.7 J Harpel R 33.3	B Johnson D 54.2 J Mackie R 45.8	J Chenoweth R 63,655 F Betz D 63,112	W Aspinall D 63.7 J Wells R 36.3
1960	B Rogers D 60.0 R Rolander R 40.0	P Dominick R 57.6 B Johnson D 42.4	J Chenoweth R 52.0 F Stewart D 48.0	W Aspinall D 68.5 C Casteel R 31.5
1962	B Rogers D 56.0 W Chenoweth R 44.0	D Brotzman R 61.9 C McBride D 38.1	J Chenoweth R 54.6 A Tomsic D 45.4	W Aspinall D 58.7 L Sommerville R 41.3
1964	B Rogers D 67.5 G Jones R 31.9 1 other 0.6	R McVicker D 50.6 D Brotzman R 49.4	F Evans D 51.2 J Chenoweth R 48.9	W Aspinall D 63.0 E Lamm R 37.0
1966	B Rogers D 56.0 G Pearson R 44.0	D Brotzman R 51.7 R McVicker D 47.1 1 other 1.2	F Evans D 51.7 D Enoch R 48.3	W Aspinall D 58.6 J Johnson R 41.4
1968	B Rogers D 45.7 F Kemp R 41.5 G Barnwell Am Ind 12.8	D Brotzman R 62.9 R McVicker D 37.1	F Evans D 52.2 P Bradley R 47.9	W Aspinall D 54.7 F Anderson R 45.3
1970	J McKevitt R 51.5 C Barnes D 45.3 S Carpio La Raza 3.2	D Brotzman R 63.4 R Gebhardt D 36.6	F Evans D 63.6 J Mitchell R 33.4 M Serna La Raza 1.3 2 others 1.6	W Aspinall D 55.1 B Gossard R 44.9
1972	P Schroeder D 52.1 J McKevitt R 47.9 M Serna La Raza 0.8 1 other 0.2	D Brotzman R 66.3 F Brush D 33.4	F Evans D 66.3 C Brady R 33.7	J Johnson R 51.0 A Merson D 49.0
1974	P Schroeder D 58.9 F Southworth R 41.2	T Wirth D 51.9 D Brotzman R 48.1	F Evans D 67.9 E Records R 32.1	J Johnson R 52.0 J Carroll D 48.0
1976	P Schroeder D 53.5 D Friedman R 46.5 2 others 0.6	T Wirth D 50.5 E Scott R 49.5	F Evans D 52.0 M Takaki R 48.0	J Johnson R 54.0 D Ogden D 34.8 D Davis ind 9.2 H Thiel ind 1.9
1978	P Schroeder D 61.5 G Hutcheson R 37.0 Adley SWP 1.5	T Wirth D 52.9 E Scott R 47.1	R Kogovsek D 69,669 H McCormick R 69,303 H Olshaw ind 2,470	J Johnson R 61.2 M Smith D 38.8
1980	P Schroeder D 60.0 N Bradford R 37.9 J Mason Lib 2.2	T Wirth D 52.9 J McElderry R 41.4 P Grant Lib 1.7	R Kogovsek D 54.9 H McCormick R 43.7 J Glennie Lib 1.4	H Brown R 68.4 P Barragan D 29.5 C Molson-S. Lib 2.1
1982	P Schroeder D 60.3 A Decker R 37.4 R White Lib 2.3	T Wirth D 61.8 J Buechner R 36.4 C Jackson Lib 1.7	R Kogovsek D 53.4 T Wiens R 44.9 2 others 1.8	H Brown R 69.7 C Bishopp D 30.3
1984	P Schroeder D 62.0 M Downs R 36.3 2 others 1.7	T Wirth D 53.2 M Norton R 45.5 J van Sickle Lib 1.3	M Strang R 57.1 W Mitchell D 41.9	H Brown R 71.1 M Bates D 27.4 R Fitzgerald Lib 1.5
1986	P Schroeder D 68.4 J Wood R 31.6	D Skaggs D 51.4 M Norton R 48.5	B Campbell D 51.9 M Strang R 48.1	H Brown R 69.8 D Sprague D 30.2
1988	P Schroeder D 69.9 J Wood R 30.1	D Skaggs D 62.7 D Bath R 37.3	B Campbell D 78.1 J Zartman R 21.9	H Brown R 73.1 C Vigil D 26.9
1990	P Schroeder D 63.7 G Roemer R 36.3	D Skaggs D 60.6 J Lewis R 39.3	B Campbell D 70.2 B Ellis R 28.2 H Fields CP 1.6[1]	W Allard R 54.1 R Bond D 45.9
1992	P Schroeder D 68.8 R Aragon R 31.2	D Skaggs D 60.7 B Day R 32.6 V Tharp AGRA[2] 6.7	S McInnis R 54.7 M Callihan D 43.7 K Nelson Populist 1.6	W Allard R 57.9 T Reder D 42.2
1994	P Schroeder D 60.0 W Eggert R 40.0	D Skaggs D 56.7 P Miller R 43.2	S McInnis R 69.6 L Powers D 30.4	W Allard R 72.3 C Kipp D 27.7
1996	D DeGette D 56.9 J Rogers R 40.2 R Combs Lib 2.9	D Skaggs D 57.0 P Miller R 38.2 2 others 4.7	S McInnis R 68.9 A Gurule D 31.1	B Schaffer R 56.1 G Kelley D 38.0
1998	D DeGette D 66.9 N McClanahan R 30.1	M Udall D 49.9 B Greenlee R 47.4 P West NLP 2.7	S McInnis R 66.1 R Kelley D 31.5 B Maggert Lib 2.4	B Schaffer R 59.3 S Kirkpatrick D 40.7
2000	D DeGette D 68.7 J Thomas R 27.3	M Udall D 55.0 C Cox R 38.6 R Forthofer Green 4.4 D Baker Lib 2.0	S McInnis R 65.9 C Imrie D 29.1	B Schaffer R 79.5 3 others 20.5
2002	D DeGette D 66.3 K Chlouber R 29.6 3 others 4.1	M Udall D 60.1 H Hume R 36.8 3 others 3.1	S McInnis R 65.8 D Berckefeldt D 31.3 2 others 2.9	M Musgrave R 55.0 S Matsunaka D 41.7 J Shroyer Lib 3.4
2004	D DeGette D 73.5 R Chicas R 24.4	M Udall D 67.2 S Hackman R 30.4 N Olsen Lib 2.4	J Salazar D 50.6 G Walcher R 46.6 J Krug ind 2.9	M Musgrave R 51.1 S Matsunaka D 44.8
2006	D DeGette D 79.7 T Kelly Green 20.3	M Udall D 68.3 R Mancuso R 28.3 2 others 3.4	J Salazar D 61.6 S Tipton R 36.5 2 others 1.9	M Musgrave R 45.6 A Paccione D 43.1 Eidsness Reform 11.3
2008	D DeGette D 72.0 G Lilly R 23.8 M Buchanan Lib 4.2	J Polis D 62.6 S Starin R 33.9 J Calhoun Green 2.9 1 other 0.6	J Salazar D 61.6 W Wolf R 38.4	B Markey D 56.2 M Musgrave R 43.8
2010	D DeGette D 67.4 M Fallon R 28.8 3 others 3.8	J Polis D 57.4 S Bailey R 37.9 2 others 4.7	S Tipton R 50.1 J Salazar D 45.8	C Gardner R 52.5 B Markey D 41.4
2012	D DeGette D 68.1 D Stroud R 27.0 F Atwood Lib 3.5 G Swing Green 1.3	J Polis D 55.9 K Lundberg R 38.5 R Luallin Lib 3.1 S Hall Green 2.3	S Tipton R 53.4 S Pace D 41.1 T Casida La Raza 3.1 G Gilman Lib 2.3	C Gardner R 58.5 B Shaffer D 36.7 B Gilliland Lib 3.0 1 other 1.6
2014	D DeGette D 65.7 M Walsh R 29.2 2 others 5.2	J Polis D 56.5 G Leing R 43.5	S Tipton R 58.1 A Tapia D 35.7 2 others 6.2	K Buck R 64.8 V Meyers D 29.2 2 others 6.1
2016	D DeGette D 67.7 C Stockham R 27.8 D Dinges Lib 4.4	J Polis D 56.6 N Morse R 37.4 P Longstreth Lib 5.8	S Tipton R 54.5 G Schwartz D 40.6 G Kent Lib 4.8	K Buck R 63.7 B Seay D 31.4 B Griffith Lib 4.7

---

[1] Colorado Populist Party.   [2] American Grass Roots Alternative.

Colorado Elections to the U.S. House, Districts 5–7

	DISTRICT 5	DISTRICT 6	DISTRICT 7
1972	W Armstrong *R* 62.3 B Johnson *D* 36.4 P Boyls *Lib* 1.2		
1974	W Armstrong *R* 57.7 B Galloway *D* 38.5 S Johnson *ind* 3.8		
1976	W Armstrong *R* 66.4 D Hores *D* 33.6		
1978	K Kramer *R* 59.8 G Frank *D* 34.4 L Bridges *ind* 5.8		
1980	K Kramer *R* 72.4 E Schreiber *D* 25.3 J Lanning *Lib* 2.3		
1982	K Kramer *R* 59.5 T Cronin *D* 40.5	J Swigert *R* 62.2 S Hogan *D* 35.6 J Green *Lib* 2.3	
1984	K Kramer *R* 78.6 W Geffen *D* 21.4	D Schafer *R* 89.4 J Heckman *CP* 10.6[1]	
1986	J Hefley *R* 69.8 B Story *D* 30.2	D Schaefer *R* 65.0 C Norris *D* 33.5 J Heckman *CP* 1.5	
1988	J Hefley *R* 75.1 J Mitchell *D* 24.9	D Schaefer *R* 63.0 M Ezzard *D* 35.6 J Heckman *CP* 1.3	
1990	J Hefley *R* 66.4 C Johnston *D* 30.0 K Hamburger *CL* 3.5[2]	D Schaefer *R* 64.5 D Jarrett *D* 35.5	
1992	J Hefley *R* 71.1 C Oriez *D* 25.7 K Hamburger *Lib* 3.2	D Schaefer *R* 60.9 T Kolbe *D* 39.1	
1994	J Hefley *R* 100	D Schaefer *R* 69.8 J Hallen *D* 28.0 J Heckman *CP* 1.4 S Dawson *NLP* 0.8	
1996	J Hefley *R* 72.0 M Robinson *D* 28.1	D Schaefer *R* 56.1 J Fitz-Gerald *D* 37.8	
1998	J Hefley *R* 72.7 K Alford *D* 25.9	T Tancredo *R* 55.9 H Strauss *D* 41.5 G Newman *NLP* 2.6	
2000	J Hefley *R* 82.7 K Kantor *Lib* 12.3 R MacKenzie *NLP* 5.0	T Tancredo *R* 53.9 K Toltz *D* 42.1 2 others	
2002	J Hefley *R* 69.4 C Imrie *D* 24.7 B Baker *Lib* 6.0	T Tancredo *R* 66.9 L Wright *D* 30.0 A Katz *Lib* 3.1	B Beauprez *R* 81,789 M Feeley *D* 81,668 3 others 3.8
2004	J Hefley *R* 70.5 F Hardee *D* 27.0 A Roberts *Lib* 2.5	T Tancredo *R* 59.5 J Conti *D* 39.1 2 others 1.4	B Beauprez *R* 54.7 D Thomas *D* 42.8 C Harkins *ACN* 2.5[3]
2006	D Lamborn *R* 59.6 J Fawcett *D* 40.3	T Tancredo *R* 58.6 B Winter *D* 39.9 J Woehr *Lib* 1.5	E Perlmutter *D* 54.9 R O'Donnell *R* 42.1 2 others 3.0
2008	D Lamborn *R* 60.0 H Bidlack *D* 37.0 B Scott *ACN* 2.9	M Coffman *R* 60.7 H Eng *D* 39.3	E Perlmutter *D* 63.5 J Lerew *R* 36.5
2010	D Lamborn *R* 65.8 K Bradley *D* 29.3 2 others 4.9	M Coffman *R* 65.7 J Flerlage *D* 31.5 R McNealy *Lib* 2.9	E Perlmutter *D* 53.4 R Frazier *R* 41.8 B Bailey *Lib* 4.8
2012	D Lamborn *R* 65.2 D Anderson *ind* 17.3 J Pirtle *Lib* 7.2 M Luzov *Green* 5.8 K Harvell *ACN* 4.2	M Coffman *R* 48.6 J Miklosi *D* 45.0 K Polhemus *ind* 3.8 P Provost *Lib* 2.4	E Perlmutter *D* 53.2 J Coors *R* 41.1 D Campbell *ACN* 2.9 B Bailey *Lib* 2.6
2014	D Lamborn *R* 59.8 I Halter *D* 40.2	M Coffman *R* 52.0 A Romanoff *D* 42.9 2 others 5.1	E Perlmutter *D* 54.9 D Ytterberg *R* 45.1
2016	D Lamborn *R* 62.3 M Plowright *D* 30.7 M McRedmond *Lib* 6.8	M Coffman *R* 50.9 M Carroll *D* 42.6 N Olsen *Lib* 4.9 R Worthey *Green* 1.4	E Perlmutter *D* 55.1 G Athanasopoulos *R* 39.7 M Buchanan *Lib* 5.0

[1] Concerns of People.   [2] Colorado Libertarian.   [3] American Constitution Party.

Hawaii Election Results

Hawaii had one House seat in its first two elections (1958 and 1960) and two ever since. They were elected at-large from 1962 through 1968. Then, in 1970, Honolulu (or most of it) became District 1 and the rest of the islands became District 2. Only minor changes have taken place since then.

	PRESIDENT	GOVERNOR	SENATE	HOUSE	AT-LARGE
1959		W Quinn R 51.1 J Burns D 48.7	O Long D H Fong R		
1960	Kennedy 92,410 Nixon 92,295			D Inouye D 74.4 F Titcomb R 25.6	
1962		J Burns D 58.3 W Quinn R 41.7	D Inouye D 69.4 B Dillingham R 30.6	T Gill D 123,649 S Matsunaga D 123,599 A Evenson R 70,880 R Sutton R 46,292	
1964	Johnson 78.8 Goldwater 21.2		H Fong R 53.0 T Gill D 46.4 D Domine ind 0.4	S Matsunaga D 35.7 P Mink D 27.2 J Milligan R 22.8 R Sutton R 14.3	
1966		J Burns D 51.1 R Crossley R 48.9		S Matsunaga D 34.1 P Mink D 34.3 J Carroll R 16.4 J Kealoha R 15.2	
1968	Humphrey 59.8 Nixon 38.7 Wallace 1.5		D Inouye D 83.4 W Thiessen R 15.0 O Lee Peace Fr 1.6	S Matsunaga D 37.4 P Mink D 34.4 N Blaisdell R 18.2 G Dubois R 9.0 P Lombardi Peace Fr 0.5 I Olsen Peace Fr 0.6	

				DISTRICT 1	DISTRICT 2
1970		J Burns D 57.7 S King R 42.4	H Fong R 51.6 C Heftel D 48.4	S Matsunaga D 72.9 R Cockey R 27.1	P Mink D 100.0
1972	Nixon 62.5 McGovern 37.5			S Matsunaga D 54.7 F Rohlfing R 45.3	P Mink D 57.1 D Hansen R 42.9
1974		G Ariyoshi D 54.6 R Crossley R 45.5	D Inouye D 82.9 J Kimmel Proh 17.1	S Matsunaga D 59.3 Paul R 40.7	P Mink D 62.6 Coray R 37.4
1976	Carter 50.6 Ford 48.1 Lib 1.3		S Matsunaga D 53.7 W Quinn R 40.6 RH Johnson Lib 0.5 A Hodges Proh 4.7 J Kimmel ind 0.5	C Heftel D 43.6 F Rohlfing R 39.1 K Hoshijo IGG 17.3[1]	D Akaka D 79.5 H Inouye R 15.3 3 others 5.2
1978		G Ariyoshi D 54.5 J Leopold R 44.3		C Heftel D 73.3 W Spillane R 21.2 2 others 5.5	D Akaka D 85.7 C Isaak R 11.4 A Fritts Lib 2.9
1980	Carter 44.8 Reagan 42.9 Anderson 10.6 others 1.7		D Inouye D 77.9 C Brown R 18.4 B Shasteen Lib 3.6	C Heftel D 79.8 A Noble R 16.1 R Johnson Lib 4.1	D Akaka D 89.9 D Smith Lib 10.1
1982		G Ariyoshi D 45.2 F Fasi ind 28.6 D Anderson R 26.1	S Matsunaga D 80.1 C Brown R 17.0 F Bernier-Nachwey ind 2.9	C Heftel D 89.9 R Johnson Lib 10.1	D Akaka D 89.2 A Fritts Lib 4.6 G Mills ind 6.1
1984	Reagan 55.1 Mondale 43.8 3 minor			C Heftel D 82.7 W Beard R 14.8 C Winter Lib 2.4	D Akaka D 82.2 A Shipley R 14.6 A Fritts Lib 3.2
1986		J Waihee D 52.0 D Anderson R 48.0	D Inouye D 73.6 F Hutchinson R 26.4	P Saiki R 59.2 M Hannemann D 37.5 B Harris Lib 3.3	D Akaka D 76.1 M Hustace R 21.7 K Schoolland Lib 2.2
1988	Dukakis 54.3 Bush 44.8 3 others 2.9		S Matsunaga D 76.6 M Hustace R 20.7 K Schoolland Lib 2.8	P Saiki R 54.7 M Bitterman D 43.2 B Harris Lib 2.1	D Akaka D 88.9 L Mallan Lib 11.1
1990		J Waihee D 59.8 F Hemmings R 38.6 2 others 1.6	D Akaka D 54.0 P Saiki R 44.6 K Schoolland Lib 1.4	N Abercrombie D 60.0 M Liu R 38.7 R Taylor Lib 1.3	P Mink D 66.3 A Poepoe R 30.6 L Mallan Lib 3.1
1992[2]	Clinton 46.8 Bush 35.7 Perot 13.8 4 minor 1.0		D Inouye D 54.4 R Reed R 25.6 L Martin Green 13.0 R Rowland Lib 2.0	N Abercrombie D 68.4 W Sutton R 22.0 R Johnson Lib 3.5	P Mink D 67.8 K Price R 20.7 L Mallan Lib 4.9
1994		B Cayetano D 35.8 F Fasi Best 30.0 P Saiki R 28.6 K Dudley Green 3.4	D Akaka D 68.0 M Hustace R 22.9 R Rowland Lib 3.8	N Abercrombie D 51.4 O Swindle R 41.5 2 others 2.9	P Mink D 64.6 R Garner R 22.3 L Bartley Lib 5.2
1996	Clinton 55.4 Dole 30.8 Perot 7.4 Nader 2.8 3 others 1.0			N Abercrombie D 48.5 O Swindle R 44.7 2 others 3.0	P Mink D 57.1 T Pico R 29.1 3 others 8.4
1998		B Cayetano D 49.5 L Lingle R 48.2 G Peabody Lib 1.1	D Inouye D 76.4 C Young R 17.2 Mallan Lib 2.9	N Abercrombie D 59.8 G Ward R 35.3 NLP 2.0	P Mink D 66.3 C Douglass R 23.2 N Chun Lib 6.1
2000	Gore 55.3 Bush 37.1 Nader 5.8 4 others 0.9		D Akaka D 67.7 J Carroll R 22.8 3 others 2.5	N Abercrombie D 62.3 P Meyers R 25.8 J Murphy Lib 2.1	P Mink D 57.3 R Francis R 33.4 L Duquesne Lib 2.3
2002		L Lingle R 51.1 M Hirono D 46.6 4 others 1.5		N Abercrombie D 68.6 M Terry R 23.4 J Bracken Lib 2.1	P Mink D 52.0 B McDermott R 37.1 2 others 3.5
2003[3]					E Case D 43.2 M Matsunaga D 30.2 C Hanabusa D 7.9 B Marumoto R 5.9 B McDermott R 5.6 39 others
2004	Kerry 53.7 Bush 46.0 2 others 0.7		D Inouye D 72.7 C Cavasso R 20.2 2 others 3.3	N Abercrombie D 60.5 D Tanonaka R 32.0 E Young D 2.9	E Case D 60.9 M Gabbard D 36.1
2006		L Lingle R 61.7 R Iwase D 34.9 2 others 2.1	D Akaka D 60.3 C Thielen R 36.1 L Mallan Lib 1.8	N Abercrombie D 66.4 R Hough R 29.3	M Hirono D 59.8 B Hogue R 38.2
2008	Obama 71.5 McCain 26.4 4 others 1.5			N Abercrombie D 70.6 S Tataii R 17.4 L Zhao Lib 3.5	M Hirono D 69.8 R Evans R 18.7 2 other 3.3
2010[4]				C Djou R 39.4 C Hanabusa D 30.8 E Case D 27.6 11 others 1.5	
2010		N Abercrombie D 57.8 D Aiona R 40.8 2 others 1.3	D Inouye D 71.9 C Cavasso R 20.7 3 others 3.5	C Hanabusa D 53.2 C Djou R 46.8	M Hirono D 72.2 J Willoughby R 25.3 2 others 2.5
2012	Obama 70.1 Romney 27.7 2 others 1.6		M Hirono D 61.6 L Lingle R 36.8	C Hanabusa D 53.5 C Djou R 44.4	T Gabbard D 76.8 K Crowley R 18.6
2014		D Ige D 49.5 D Aiona R 37.1 M Hannemann ind 11.7 J Davis Lib 1.7	B Schatz D 69.8 C Cavasso R 27.7	M Takai D 51.9 C Djou R 48.1	T Gabbard D 78.7 K Crowley R 18.6 J Kent Lib 2.6
2016	Clinton 62.2 Trump 30.0 Johnson 3.7 Stein 3.0 others 1.1		B Schatz D 73.6 J Carroll R 22.2 others 4.2	C Hanabusa D 68.1 S Ostrov R 21.5	T Gabbard D 76.2 A Kaaihue R 17.7

[1] Independent for Godly Government.   [2] Beginning in 1992, official returns in Hawaii counted blank votes. Consequently, many subsequent races appear not to total 100 percent. Actual vote percentages are given here.   [3] Special election to replace Mink.   [4] May special election.

Idaho Election Results

Since the 1912 election, Idaho has had two House seats. District 1, historically, has included the western third of the state from Canada to Nevada and Utah. District 2 has included the southeastern area between Montana and Utah. The boundary has shifted to run west of, through, or east of Boise. Recently it has been moving incrementally westward to reflect greater population growth.

	PRESIDENT	GOVERNOR	SENATE	HOUSE DISTRICT 1	HOUSE DISTRICT 2
1950		L Jordan R 52.6 C Wright D 47.4	H Dworshak R 51.9 C Burtenshaw D 48.1 H Welker R 61.7 DW Clark D 38.3	J Wood R 41,823 G Pfost D 41,040	H Budge R 57.1 J Hawley D 42.9
1952	Eisenhower 65.5 Stevenson 34.5			G Pfost D 54,725 J Wood R 54,134	H Budge R 66.2 P Jensen D 33.8
1954		R Smylie R 54.2 C Hamilton D 45.8	H Dworshak R 62.9 G Taylor D 37.1	G Pfost D 54.9 E Schwiebert R 45.1	H Budge R 60.8 W Whitaker D 39.2
1956	Eisenhower 61.2 Stevenson 38.8		F Church D 56.2 H Welker R 38.7 G Taylor D 5.1	G Pfost D 55.1 L Shadduck R 44.9	H Budge R 59.9 J Reynolds D 40.1
1958		R Smylie R 51.0 AM Derr D 49.0		G Pfost D 62.4 A Curtis R 37.6	H Budge R 55.0 T Brennan D 45.0
1960	Nixon 53.8 Kennedy 46.2		H Dworshak R 52.3 B McLaughlin D 47.7	G Pfost D 60.4 T Leupp R 39.6	R Harding D 51.2 H Budge R 48.8
1962		R Smylie R 54.6 V Smith D 45.4	F Church D 54.8 J Hawley R 45.2 L Jordan R 51.0 G Pfost D 49.0	C White D 53.0 E Schwiebert R 47.0	R Harding D 52.9 O Hansen R 47.1
1964	Johnson 50.9 Goldwater 49.1			C White D 51.7 D Mattmiller R 48.3	G Hansen R 52.2 Harding D 47.8
1966		D Samuelson R 41.4 C Andrus D 37.1 Swisher ind 12.1 Jungert ind 9.2	L Jordan R 55.4 R Harding D 44.6	J McClure R 51.8 C White D 48.2	G Hansen R 70.3 B Brunt D 29.7
1968	Nixon 56.8 Humphrey 30.7 Wallace 2.5		F Church D 60.3 G Hansen R 39.7	J McClure R 59.4 C White D 40.5	O Hansen R 52.5 D Manning D 43.9 Am Ind 3.6
1970		C Andrus D 52.2 D Samuelson R 47.8		J McClure R 58.2 W Brauner R 41.8	O Hansen R 65.8 J Wells D 31.6 J Anderson Am Ind 2.6
1972	Nixon 70.9 McGovern 28.7 Am Ind 10.3		J McClure R 52.3 B Davis D 45.5 J Stoddard Am Ind 2.2	S Symms R 55.6 E Williams D 44.4	O Hansen R 69.2 W Ludlow D 27.1 J Thiebert Am Ind 3.8
1974		C Andrus D 70.9 J Murphy R 26.5 N Victor Am Ind 2.6	F Church D 56.1 B Smith R 42.2 J Stoddard Am Ind 1.8	S Symms R 58.3 JR Cox D 41.7	G Hansen R 55.7 M Hanson D 44.3
1976	Ford 60.0 Carter 37.2 McCarthy 1.7 Lib 1.1			S Symms R 54.6 K Pursley D 45.4	G Hansen R 50.6 S Kress D 49.4
1978		J Evans D 58.8 A Larsen R 39.6 W Loveless Am Ind 1.7	J McClure R 68.4 D Jensen D 31.6	S Symms R 59.9 R Truby D 40.1	G Hansen R 57.3 S Kress D 42.7
1980	Reagan 66.4 Carter 25.2 Anderson 6.2 Lib 1.9 Am Ind 0.3		S Symms R 49.7 F Church D 48.8 L Fullmer Lib 1.5	L Craig R 53.7 G Nichols D 46.3	G Hansen R 58.8 D Bilyeu D 41.2
1982		J Evans D 52.9 P Batt R 47.1		L Craig R 53.7 L La Rocco D 46.3	G Hansen R 52.3 Stallings D 47.7
1984	Reagan 72.4 Mondale 26.4 Lib 0.7 Populist 0.6		J McClure R 72.2 P Busch D 26.0 D Billings Lib 1.8	L Craig R 68.6 B Heller D 31.4	R Stallings D 101,266 G Hansen R 101,133
1986		C Andrus D 49.9 D Leroy R 49.0 Miller ind 1.1	S Symms R 51.6 J Evans D 48.4	L Craig R 65.2 B Currie D 32.3 D Shepherd ind 2.6	R Stallings D 54.4 M Richardson R 45.6
1988	Bush 62.1 Dukakis 36.0 2 others 1.9			L Craig R 65.8 J Givens D 34.2	R Stallings D 63.4 D Watkins R 33.8 D Bramwell Lib 2.8
1990		C Andrus D 68.1 R Fairchild R 31.9	L Craig R 61.3 R Twilegar D 38.7	L La Rocco D 53.0 S Smyser R 47.0	R Stallings D 63.6 S McDevitt R 36.4
1992	Bush 42.0 Clinton 28.4 Perot 27.0 ind 2.3 Lib 0.2		D Kempthorne R 56.5 R Stallings D 43.5	L LaRocco D 58.0 R Gilbert R 37.5 J Abel ind 2.6 S Kinsey ind 1.9	M Crapo R 60.8 JD Williams D 35.4 S Kauer ind 2.1 D Mansfield ind 1.7
1994		P Batt R 51.1 L Echohawk D 45.2 R Rankin ind 3.7		H Chenoweth R 55.4 L LaRocco D 44.6	M Crapo R 75.0 P Fletcher D 25.0
1996	Dole 53.0 Clinton 34.1 Reform 12.9 3 others		L Craig R 57.0 W Minnick D 39.9 M Charbonneau ind 2.0 S Vegors NLP 1.0	H Chenoweth R 50.0 D Williams D 47.6 M Ellis NLP 2.5	M Crapo R 68.8 J Seidl D 29.5 J Butler NLP 1.7
1998		D Kempthorne R 67.7 R Huntley D 29.1 P Rickards ind 3.2	M Crapo R 69.5 B Mauk D 28.4 G Mansfield NLP 2.1	H Chenoweth R 55.2 D Williams D 44.8	M Simpson R 52.5 R Stallings D 44.7 Ratner NLP 2.8
2000	Bush 69.1 Gore 28.4 Nader 2.5 4 others			CL Otter R 67.4 L Pall D 32.6 2 others	M Simpson R 70.7 C Williams D 25.9 D Bramwell Lib 3.3
2002		D Kempthorne R 56.3 J Brady D 41.7 D Adams Lib 2.0	L Craig R 65.1 A Blinken D 32.6 D Bramwell Lib 2.3	CL Otter R 58.6 B Richardson D 39.0 S Gothard Lib 4.6	M Simpson R 68.2 E Kinghorn D 29.1 J Lewis Lib 2.8
2004	Bush 69.3 Kerry 30.7 3 others		M Crapo R 99.2	CL Otter R 69.6 N Preston D 30.4	M Simpson R 70.7 L Whitworth D 29.3
2006		CL Otter R 52.7 J Brady D 44.1 2 others		B Sali R 52.7 L Grant D 47.3 3 others	M Simpson R 64.3 J Hansen D 35.7 2 others
2008	McCain 63.0 Obama 37.0 3 others		J Risch R 62.5 L LaRocco D 37.0 R Rammell ind 5.8 2 others 2.9	W Minnick D 50.6 B Sali R 49.4	M Simpson R 71.0 D Holmes D 28.9
2010		CL Otter R 59.1 K Allred D 32.9 J Kemp ind 5.9 Dunlap Lib 1.3 Pro-Life 0.9	M Crapo R 71.2 PT Sullivan D 24.9 R Bergquist Con 3.9	R Labrador R 51.0 W Minnick D 41.3 D Olson ind 5.8 Washburn Lib 1.9	M Simpson R 68.8 M Crawford D 24.4 B Schad ind 6.8
2012	Romney 64.5 Obama 32.6 3 others			R Labrador R 63.0 J Farris D 30.8 R Oates Lib 3.9 Pro-Life 2.4	M Simpson R 65.2 N LaFavour D 34.8
2014		CL Otter R 53.5 AJ Balukoff D 38.6 J Bujak Lib 4.1 Others 3.9	J. Risch R 65.3 N. Mitchell D 34.7	R Labrador R 65.0 S Ringo D 35.0	Simpson R 61.4 R Stallings D 38.6
2016	Trump 59.2 Clinton 27.5 McMullin 6.7 G Johnson 4.1 others 2.4		M Crapo R 66.1 J Sturgill D 27.8 R Writz Con 6.2	R Labrador R 68.2 J Piotrowski D 31.8	M Simpson R 62.9 J Martinez D 29.4 A Tomkins Con 7.7

Kansas Election Results: President, Governor, Senator

	PRESIDENT	GOVERNOR[1]	SENATE
1950		E Arn R 53.8 K Anderson D 44.5	F Carlson R 54.2 Aiken D 43.8
1952	Eisenhower 68.8 Stevenson 30.5 Proh 0.7	E Arn R 56.3 C Rooney D 41.7	
1954		F Hall R 53.0 G Docking D 46.0	A Schoeppel R 56.3 G McGill D 41.8 D White Proh 1.8
1956	Eisenhower 65.4 Stevenson 34.2 Proh 0.3	G Docking D 55.5 W Shaw R 42.1 H Lytle Proh 2.4	F Carlson R 57.9 G Hart D 40.5 Hester Proh 1.6
1958		G Docking D 56.5 C Reed R 42.5	
1960	Nixon 60.5 Kennedy 39.1 Proh 0.4	J Anderson R 55.5 G Docking D 43.6 Proh 1.0	A Schoeppel R 54.6 F Theis D 43.8 C Cowen Proh 1.6
1962		J Anderson R 53.4 D Saffels D 45.6	F Carlson R 62.4 (full term) K Smith D 35.9 G Kline Proh 1.6 J Pearson R 56.2 (unexp. term) P Aylward D 42.5 C Cowen Proh 1.3
1964	Johnson 54.1 Goldwater 45.1 Proh 0.6 SLP 0.2	W Avery R 50.9 H Wiles D 47.1	
1966		R Docking D 54.8 W Avery R 43.9	J Pearson R 52.1 F Breeding D 45.2 E Dodge Proh 1.4 G Snell conserv 1.2
1968	Nixon 54.8 Humphrey 34.7 conserv 10.2 Proh 0.3	R Docking D 51.9 R Harman R 47.6	R Dole R 60.1 W Robinson D 38.7 J Hyskell Proh 1.3
1970		R Docking D 54.3 K Frizzell R 44.7	
1972	Nixon 67.7 McGovern 29.5 Proh 0.5 conserv 2.4	R Docking D 62.0 M Kay R 37.1	J Pearson R 71.4 A Tetzlaff D 23.0 H Hadin Proh 1.5 G Miller conserv 4.1
1974		R Bennett R 49.5 V Miller D 49.0 Proh 1.5	R Dole R 50.8 Roy D 49.2
1976	Ford 52.5 Carter 44.9 5 others 2.6		
1978		J Carlin D 49.4 R Bennett R 47.3 others 3.3	N Kassebaum R 53.9 B Roy D 42.4 J Maher conserv 3.0 R Mikels Proh 0.7
1980	Reagan 57.8 Carter 33.3 Anderson 7.0 Lib 1.5 others 0.3		R Dole R 63.8 J Simpson D 36.2
1982		J Carlin D 53.2 S Hardage R 44.5 others 2.4	
1984	Reagan 66.3 Mondale 32.6 4 others 1.1		N Kassebaum R 76.0 J Maher D 21.1 4 others 2.8
1986		M Hayden R 51.9 T Docking D 48.1	R Dole R 70.0 G MacDonald D 30.0
1988	Bush 55.8 Dukakis 42.6 ind 1.7		
1990		J Finney D 48.6 M Hayden R 42.6 ind 8.8	N Kassebaum R 73.6 D Williams D 26.4
1992	Bush 38.9 Clinton 33.7 Perot 27.0 Lib 0.4		R Dole R 62.7 G O'Dell D 31.0 C Campbell-Cline ind 4.0 M Kirk Lib 2.2
1994		W Graves R 64.1 J Slattery D 35.9	
1996	Dole 54.3 Clinton 36.1 Reform 8.6 others 1.0		S Brownback R 53.9 (unexp. term) J Docking D 43.3 D Klassen Reform 2.8 P Roberts R 62.0 (full term) S Thompson D 34.4 M Marney Reform 2.3 S Rosile Lib 1.2
1998		W Graves R 73.4 T Sawyer D 22.7 2 others	S Brownback R 65.3 P Feleciano D 31.6 T Oyler Lib 1.6 A Bauman Reform 1.6
2000	Bush 58.0 Gore 37.2 Green 3.4 4 others 1.4		
2002		K Sibelius D 52.9 T Shallenburger R 45.1 2 others	P Roberts R 82.5 S Rosile Lib 9.1 G Cook Reform 8.4
2004	Bush 62.0 Kerry 36.6 3 others 1.4		S Brownback R 69.2 L Jones D 27.5 S Rosile Lib 1.9 G Cook Reform 1.4
2006		K Sibelius D 57.9 J Barnett R 40.4 2 others 1.6	
2008	McCain 56.6 Obama 41.7 3 others		P Roberts R 60.1 J Slattery D 36.5 R Hodgkinson Lib 2.1 J Martin Reform 1.4
2010		S Brownback R 63.2 T Holland D 32.3 2 others 4.4	J Moran R 70.0 L Johnston D 26.3 2 others 3.4
2012	Obama 37.9 Romney 59.7 Johnson 1.7		
2014		S Brownback R 49.5 P Davis D 46.1 Lib 4.0	P Roberts R 53.1 G Orman ind 42.5 Lib 4.3
2016	Trump 56.6 Clinton 36.0 Johnson 4.6 Stein 1.9		J Moran R 62.1 P Wiesner D 32.2 R Garrard Lib 5.5

[1] The best source for Kansas governors, from statehood through the 1980s, is Homer E. Socolofsky, *Kansas Governors* (Lawrence: University Press of Kansas, 1990).

Kansas Elections to the U.S. House, Districts 1–6

Kansas had six House districts in the 1950 through 1960 elections. District 1 covered the northeast; District 2, Kansas City and Johnson County south to near Pittsburg; District 3, the southeast corner; District 4, the Flint Hills and Wichita; District 5 the large southwest; District 6 the large northwest. After the 1960 census, District 6 disappeared, and the numbers were reassigned, with District 1 becoming the western half, District 2 the northeast corner, District 3 Kansas City and Lawrence, District 4 the western Flint Hills and Wichita, and District 5 the southeast. From 1972 through 1980, District 2 included northern Wyandotte County plus Topeka, Manhattan, and Atchison, with District 3 including southern Wyandotte and Johnson Counties and Lawrence. District 4 included

(continued on opposite page)

	DISTRICT 1	DISTRICT 2	DISTRICT 3
1950	A Cole *R* 66.5	E Scrivner *R* 52.2	M George *R* 54.7
	E Stewart *D* 33.5	M Sullivant *D* 47.8	B Griffith *D* 45.3
1952	H Miller *D* 51.5	E Scrivner *R* 57.3	M George *R* 59.5
	A Cole *R* 48.5	C Rice *D* 42.7	F Hedges *D* 40.5
1954	W Avery *R* 54.3	E Scrivner *R* 54.7	M George *R* 55.4
	H Miller *D* 45.7	N George *D* 45.3	W Monypeny *D* 44.6
1956	W Avery *R* 53.1	E Scrivner *R* 54.9	M George *R* 55.0
	H Miller *D* 45.9	N George *D* 45.1	D Hargis *D* 45.0
	H Hadin *Proh* 1.1		
1958	W Avery *R* 51.2	N George *D* 50.8	D Hargis *D* 51.7
	R Domme *D* 47.4	E Scrivner *R* 49.2	M George *R* 48.3
	M Hadin *Proh* 1.4		
1960	W Avery *R* 63.1	R Ellsworth *R* 52.3	W McVey *R* 51.2
	M Gardiner *D* 36.9	N George *D* 47.7	D Hargis *D* 48.8
1962	R Dole *R* 55.8	W Avery *R* 65.2	R Ellsworth *R* 63.4
	F Breeding *D* 44.2	H Kehoe *D* 34.8	B Sparks *D* 36.6
1964	R Dole *R* 51.2	C Mize *R* 51.1	R Ellsworth *R* 62.2
	B Bork *D* 48.8	J Montgomery *D* 48.9	A Dial *D* 37.8
1966	R Dole *R* 68.6	C Mize *R* 62.9	L Winn *R* 53.0
	B Henkle *D* 31.4	H Wiles *D* 37.1	M Rainey *D* 45.0
			H Shomber *conserv* 2.0
1968	K Sibelius *R* 51.4	C Mize *R* 67.6	L Winn *R* 62.8
	G Meeker *D* 48.6	R Swan *D* 32.4	N George *D* 37.2
1970	K Sibelius *R* 56.8	W Roy *D* 52.4	L Winn *R* 53.0
	B Jellison *D* 43.2	C Mize *R* 44.9	J DeCoursey *D* 45.7
		F Kilian *conserv* 2.7	W Redding *conserv* 1.3
1972	K Sibelius *R* 77.2	W Roy *D* 60.9	L Winn *R* 71.0
	M Coover *D* 21.6	C McAtee *R* 37.3	C Barsotti *D* 25.4
	D Scoggin *Proh* 1.2	B Failey *conserv* 1.8	W Redding *conserv* 3.7
1974	K Sibelius *R* 58.4	M Keys *D* 55.0	L Winn *R* 62.9
	D Smith *D* 32.9	J Peterson *R* 43.9	S Wells *D* 35.0
	T Morgan *Am Ind* 7.5	D Scoggin *Proh* 1.1	T Oakes *Am Ind* 2.1
	L Miller *Proh* 1.2		
1976	K Sibelius *R* 73.0	M Keys *D* 50.7	L Winn *R* 68.7
	R Yowell *D* 27.0	R Freeman *R* 47.5	P Rhoads *D* 29.0
		D Scoggin *Proh* 0.7	W Hyatt *Am Ind* 2.3
		C Ijams *Am Ind* 1.1	
1978	K Sibelius *R* 100	J Jeffries *R* 52.0	L Winn *R* 100
		M Keys *D* 48.0	
1980	P Roberts *R* 62.3	J Jeffries *R* 53.9	L Winn *R* 55.5
	P Martin *D* 37.7	S Keys *D* 46.1	D Watkins *D* 41.8
			J Stewart *conserv* 2.7
1982	P Roberts *R* 68.4	J Slattery *D* 57.5	L Winn *R* 59.2
	K Roth *D* 30.3	M Kay *R* 42.5	W Kostar *D* 38.3
	K Earnest *Lib* 1.4		G Blair *Lib* 2.5
1984	P Roberts *R* 75.9	J Slattery *D* 60.1	J Meyers *R* 54.8
	D Ringer *D* 23.3	J Van Slyke *R* 39.0	J Reordon *D* 39.9
	C Scoggin *Proh* 0.9	K Peterson *Proh* 0.9	J Ralph *ind* 5.3
1986	P Roberts *R* 76.5	J Slattery *D* 70.6	J Meyers *R* 100
	D Lyon *D* 23.5	P Kline *R* 29.4	
1988	P Roberts *R* 100	J Slattery *D* 73.3	J Meyers *R* 73.6
		P Meinhardt *R* 26.7	L Kunst *D* 26.4
1990	P Roberts *R* 62.7	J Slattery *D* 62.8	J Meyers *R* 60.1
	D West *D* 37.3	S Morgan *R* 37.2	L Jones *D* 39.9
1992	P Roberts *R* 68.3	J Slattery *D* 56.2	J Meyers *R* 58.0
	D West *D* 29.3	J Van Slyke *R* 40.8	T Love *D* 37.6
	S Rosile *Lib* 2.4	J Clack *Lib* 3.0	F Kaul *Lib* 4.4
1994	P Roberts *R* 77.4	S Brownback *R* 65.7	J Meyers *R* 56.6
	T Nichols *D* 22.6	J Carlin *D* 34.3	J Hancock *D* 43.4
1996	J Moran *R* 73.5	J Ryun *R* 52.2	V Snowbarger *R* 49.8
	J Divine *D* 24.5	J Frieden *D* 45.5	J Hancock *D* 45.4
	B Earnest *Lib* 2.0	A Clack *Lib* 2.3	R Gardner *Reform* 3.4
			C Clack *Lib* 1.4
1998	J Moran *R* 80.7	J Ryun *R* 61.0	D Moore *D* 52.4
	J Phillips *D* 19.3	J Clark *D* 39.0	V Snowbarger *R* 47.6
2000	J Moran *R* 89.3	J Ryun *R* 67.4	D Moore *D* 50.0
	J Warner *Lib* 10.7	S Wiles *D* 29.3	P Kline *R* 46.9
		D Hawver *Lib* 3.3	C Mina *Lib* 3.1
2002	J Moran *R* 91.1	J Ryun *R* 60.4	D Moore *D* 50.2
	J Warner *Lib* 8.9	D Lykins *D* 37.5	A Taff *R* 46.0
		A Clack *Lib* 2.0	D Martin *Lib* 0.6
			D Bly *Reform* 2.3
2004	J Moran *R* 90.7	J Ryun *R* 56.1	D Moore *D* 54.8
	J Warner *Lib* 9.3	N Boyda *D* 41.3	K Kobach *R* 43.3
		D Hawvere *Lib* 2.6	J Bellis *Lib* 1.0
			R Wells *Reform* 0.9
2006	J Moran *R* 78.6	N Boyda *D* 50.6	D Moore *D* 64.6
	J Doll *D* 20.0	J Ryun *R* 47.1	C Abner *R* 33.7
	S Cain *Reform* 1.5	R Tucker *Reform* 2.3	R Conroy *Reform* 1.7
2008	J Moran *R* 81.9	L Jenkins *R* 50.6	D Moore *D* 56.4
	J Bordonaro *D* 13.3	N Boyda *D* 46.2	N Jordan *R* 39.7
	J Warner *Lib* 2.1	R Garrard *Lib* 1.5	J Bellis *Lib* 2.8
	K Burton *Reform* 2.7	L Martin *Reform* 1.7	R Tucker *Reform* 1.1
2010	T Huelskamp *R* 73.7	L Jenkins *R* 63.1	K Yoder *R* 58.4
	A Julka *D* 22.8	C Hudspeth *D* 32.3	S Moore *D* 38.6
	others 3.5	R Garrard *Lib* 4.5	J Talbert *Lib* 2.9
2012	T Huelskamp *R* 100	L Jenkins *R* 57.0	K Yoder *R* 68.4
		T Schlingensiepen *D* 38.7	J Balam *D* 31.5
		D Hawver *Lib* 4.2	
2014	T Huelskamp *R* 67.9	L Jenkins *R* 57.0	K Yoder *R* 60.0
	J Sherow *D* 32.0	M Wakefield *D* 38.6	K Kultala *D* 39.9
		C Clemmons *Lib* 4.3	
2016	R Marshall *R* 65.8	L Jenkins *R* 60.9	K Yoder *R* 51.3
	A LaPolice *ind* 26.2	B Potter *D* 32.5	J Sidie *D* 40.5
	K Burt *Lib* 7.5	J Bates *Lib* 6.5	S Hohe *Lib* 8.0
	T Huelskamp *ind* 0.3		

Kansas Elections to the U.S. House, Districts 1–6 *(continued)*

Wichita and Hutchinson. District 5 included Emporia and east-central counties. District 1 extended eastward to include Salina. Redistricting through the 1980s put Lawrence in District 2 and all of Wyandotte in District 3. After the 1990 census, Kansas lost its fifth seat, which was split between District 3 (Wyandotte, Johnson, and Douglas Counties) and District 4 (centered on Wichita). After 2010, District 1 included the western two-thirds of the state, extending one county east of Manhattan to the Shawnee County line. District 3 held only the populous Wyandotte and Johnson Counties and the northern part of Miami County, with Douglas (Lawrence) now in District 2, which runs from the Nebraska line to Oklahoma, bordering Missouri to the east. District 4 continued to center on Wichita.

	DISTRICT 4	DISTRICT 5	DISTRICT 6
1950	E Rees *R* 58.9 L Donnell *D* 41.1	C Hope *R* 61.8 R Bock *D* 38.2	W Smith *R* 59.5 F Wasinger *D* 40.5
1952	E Rees *R* 59.4 B Porter *D* 40.6	C Hope *R* 70.9 A McAnarney *D* 29.1	W Smith *R* 62.5 H Santry *D* 37.5
1954	E Rees *R* 56.2 R Green *D* 43.8	C Hope *R* 64.8 R Bock *D* 35.2	W Smith *R* 53.3 E Mahoney *D* 46.7
1956	E Rees *R* 53.8 J Montgomery *D* 46.2	F Breeding *D* 50.5 J Crutcher *R* 49.5	W Smith *R* 51.1 E Mahoney *D* 48.9
1958	E Rees *R* 50.7 W Moore *D* 49.3	F Breeding *D* 53.1 C Hope Jr *R* 46.9	W Smith *R* 43,782 E Mahoney *D* 43,549 J Jones *Proh* 1,624
1960	G Shriver *R* 55.2 W Robinson *D* 44.8	F Breeding *D* 55.5 J Hunter *R* 44.5	R Dole *R* 59.2 W Davis *D* 40.8
1962	G Shriver *R* 66.8 L Wetzel *D* 33.2	J Skubitz *R* 53.3 W Myers *D* 46.7	
1964	G Shriver *R* 59.3 J Glaves *D* 40.7	J Skubitz *R* 56.4 R Russell *D* 43.6	
1966	G Shriver *R* 68.7 P Gerling *D* 31.3	J Skubitz *R* 60.9 D Bass *D* 39.1	
1968	G Shriver *R* 64.7 P Kelly *D* 35.3	J Skubitz *R* 64.5 A Bramble *D* 35.5	
1970	G Shriver *R* 63.2 J Juhnke *D* 34.9 G Snell *conserv* 1.9	J Skubitz *R* 66.1 T Saar *D* 33.9	
1972	G Shriver *R* 73.2 J Stevens *D* 24.9 W Nobbs *Proh* 2.0	J Skubitz *R* 72.3 L Kitch *D* 27.7	
1974	G Shriver *R* 48.9 B Cheney *D* 42.5 J Stevens *Am Ind* 8.7	J Skubitz *R* 55.2 F Gaines *D* 44.8	
1976	D Glickman *D* 50.3 G Shriver *R* 48.4 R Cowdrey *Am Ind* 1.3	J Skubitz *R* 60.7 V Olson *D* 36.2 G Rutherford *Am Ind* 3.2	
1978	D Glickman *D* 69.5 J Litsey *R* 30.5	B Whittaker *R* 57.0 D Allegrucci *D* 41.4 J Blackwell *Proh* 1.6	
1980	D Glickman *D* 68.9 C Hunter *R* 31.1	B Whittaker *R* 74.2 D Miller *D* 24.1 J Blackwell *Statesman* 1.7	
1982	D Glickman *D* 73.9 G Caywood *R* 24.4 K Peterjohn *Lib* 1.7	B Whittaker *R* 67.6 L Rowe *D* 31.1 J Conger *Lib* 1.2	
1984	D Glickman *D* 74.4 W Krause *R* 25.6	B Whittaker *R* 73.6 J Barnes *D* 25.2 V Bacon *Proh* 1.2	
1986	D Glickman *D* 64.5 B Knight *R* 35.5	B Whittaker *R* 71.1 K Myers *D* 28.9	
1988	D Glickman *D* 64.0 L Thompson *R* 36.0	B Whittaker *R* 70.2 J Barnes *D* 29.8	
1990	D Glickman *D* 70.8 R Grund *R* 29.2	D Nichols *R* 59.3 G Wingert *D* 40.7	
1992	D Glickman *D* 51.7 E Yost *R* 42.1 S Warren *Lib* 6.2		
1994	T Tiahrt *R* 52.9 D Glickman *D* 47.1		
1996	T Tiahrt *R* 50.1 R Rathbun *D* 46.6 S Warren *Lib* 3.3		
1998	T Tiahrt *R* 58.3 J Lawing *D* 38.5 C Newland *Taxpayers* 3.2		
2000	T Tiahrt *R* 54.4 C Nolla *D* 42.0 S Rosile *Lib* 3.6		
2002	T Tiahrt *R* 60.6 C Nolla *D* 37.0 M Warren *Lib* 2.4		
2004	T Tiahrt *R* 66.1 M Kinard *D* 31.1 D Loomis *Lib* 2.8		
2006	T Tiahrt *R* 63.5 G McGinn *D* 33.9 J Holt *Reform* 2.6		
2008	T Tiahrt *R* 63.4 D Betts *D* 32.4 S Rosile *Lib* 1.9 S Ducey *R* 1.1		
2010	M Pompeo *R* 58.7 R Goyle *D* 36.4 others 4.9		
2012	M Pompeo *R* 62.2 R Tillman *D* 31.5 T Jefferson *Lib* 6.2		
2014	M Pompeo *R* 66.6 P Schuckman *D* 33.3		
2016	M Pompeo *R* 60.6 D Giroux *D* 29.6 G Bakken *Lib* 2.8 M Allen *ind* 6.9		

Montana Election Results

Montana had two House seats from 1950 through 1990, splitting the state at roughly the Continental Divide. From 1992 onward, Montana has had one at-large seat.

	PRESIDENT	GOVERNOR	SENATE	HOUSE DISTRICT 1	HOUSE DISTRICT 2
1950				M Mansfield D 60.9 R McGinnis R 39.1	W D'Ewart R 54.0 J Holmes D 44.8 C Kinsey Prog 1.2
1952	Eisenhower R 59.7 Stevenson D 40.3	JH Aronson R 51.0 JW Bonner D 49.0	M Mansfield D 50.7 Z Ecton R 48.6 L Price Prog 0.7	L Metcalf D 50.3 W Rankin R 48.9 L Hamilton Soc 0.8	W D'Ewart R 62.0 W Fraser D 38.0
1954			J Murray D 50.4 W D'Ewart R 49.6	L Metcalf D 56.0 W Page R 44.0	O Fjare R 50.6 L Anderson D 49.4
1956	Eisenhower R 57.1 Stevenson D 42.9	JH Aronson R 51.4 AH Olsen D 48.6		L Metcalf D 62.0 B McDonald R 38.0	L Anderson D 50.9 O Fjare R 49.1
1958			M Mansfield D 76.2 L Welch R 23.8	L Metcalf D 69.5 J Walterskirchen R 30.5	L Anderson D 61.0 A Jones R 39.0
1960	Nixon 51.2 Kennedy 48.7	D Nutter R 55.1 P Cannon D 44.9	L Metcalf D 50.7 O Fjare R 49.3	A Olsen D 53.3 G Sarsfield R 46.7	J Battin R 50.9 L Graybill D 49.1
1962				A Olsen D 52.8 W Montgomery R 47.2	J Battin R 55.4 L Graybill D 44.6
1964	Johnson 59.0 Goldwater 40.6 3 others 0.5	T Babcock R 51.3 R Renne D 48.7	M Mansfield D 64.5 A Blewett R 35.5	A Olsen D 53.9 W Montgomery R 46.1	J Battin R 54.1 J Toole D 45.9
1966			L Metcalf D 53.2 T Babcock R 46.8	A Olsen D 50.8 D Smiley R 49.2	J Battin R 60.2 J Melcher D 39.8
1968	Nixon 50.6 Humphrey 41.6 Wallace 7.3 3 others 0.5	F Anderson D 54.1 T Babcock R 41.9 W Montgomery NR[1] 4.0		A Olsen D 53.6 D Smiley R 46.4	J Battin R 67.8 R Kelleher D 32.2
1970			M Mansfield D 60.5 B Wallace R 39.5	D Shoup R 64,388 A Olson D 63,175	J Melcher D 64.1 J Rehberg R 35.9
1972	Nixon 57.9 McGovern 37.8 Wallace 4.2	T Judge D 54.1 E Smith R 45.9	L Metcalf D 52.0 H Hibbard R 48.0	D Shoup R 53.7 A Olson D 46.3	J Melcher D 76.0 D Forester R 24.0
1974				M Baucus D 54.8 D Shoup R 45.2	J Melcher D 63.0 J McDonald R 37.0
1976	Ford 52.8 Carter 45.4 Am Ind 1.8	T Judge D 61.7 B Woodahl R 36.6 C Mahoney ind 1.7	J Melcher D 64.2 S Burger R 35.8	M Baucus D 66.4 B Diehl R 33.6	R Marlenee R 54.9 T Towe D 45.1
1978			M Baucus D 55.7 L Williams R 44.3	P Williams D 57.3 J Waltermire R 42.7	R Marlenee R 56.9 T Monahan D 43.1
1980	Reagan 56.8 Carter 32.4 Anderson 8.1 Lib 2.7	T Schwinden D 55.4 J Ramirez R 44.6		P Williams D 61.4 J McDonald R 38.6	R Marlenee R 59.0 T Monahan D 41.0
1982			J Melcher D 54.5 L Williams R 41.7 L Dodge Lib 3.9	P Williams D 59.7 B Davies R 37.2 D Doig Lib 3.0	R Marlenee R 53.7 H Lyman D 44.2 W Deitchler Lib 2.1
1984	Reagan 60.5 Mondale 38.2 Lib 1.4	T Schwinden D 70.3 P Goodover R 26.4 L Dodge Lib 3.2	M Baucus D 56.9 C Cozzens R 40.7 N Halprin Lib 2.4	P Williams D 65.6 G Carlson R 31.9 R Warren Lib 2.4	R Marlenee R 65.9 C Blaylock D 34.1
1986				P Williams D 61.7 D Allen R 38.3	R Marlenee R 53.4 B O'Brien D 46.6
1988	Bush 52.1 Dukakis 46.2 2 others 1.7	S Stephens R 51.9 T Judge D 46.1 W Morris Lib 1.9	C Burns R 51.9 J Melcher D 48.1	P Williams D 60.8 J Fenlason R 39.2	R Marlenee R 55.5 B O'Brien D 44.5
1990			M Baucus D 68.1 A Kolstad R 29.4 W Deitchler Lib 2.5	P Williams D 61.1 B Johnson R 38.9	R Marlenee R 63.0 D Burris R 37.0
1992	Clinton 37.6 Bush 35.1 Perot 26.1 Gritz 0.9 Lib 0.2	M Racicot R 51.3 D Bradley D 48.7		P Williams D 50.4 R Marlenee R 47.0 J Wilverding Lib 2.6	
1994			C Burns R 62.4 J Mudd D 37.6	P Williams D 48.7 C Jamison R 42.2 S Kelly ind 9.1	
1996	Dole 44.2 Clinton 41.3 Perot 13.6 2 others 1.1	M Racicot R 79.2 J Jacobson D 20.8	M Baucus D 49.5 D Rehberg R 44.7 B Shaw Reform 4.7 S Heaton NLP 1.0	R Hill R 52.4 B Yellowtail D 43.2 J Brooks NLP 4.4	
1998				R Hill R 53.0 D Deschamps D 44.4 M Fellows Lib 1.7 W Sullivan Reform 0.9	
2000	Bush 58.4 Gore 33.4 Nader 5.9 4 others 2.3	J Martz R 51.0 M O'Keefe D 47.1 S Jones Lib 1.9	C Burns R 50.6 B Schweitzer D 47.2 G Lee Reform 2.2	D Rehberg R 51.5 N Keenan D 46.3 J Tikalsky Lib 2.2	
2002			M Baucus D 62.7 M Taylor R 31.7 2 others 5.5	D Rehberg R 64.6 S Kelly D 32.7 M Fellows Lib 2.7	
2004	Bush 59.1 Kerry 38.6 4 others	B Schweitzer D 50.4 B Brown R 46.0 B Kelleher Green 1.9 S Jones Lib 1.7		D Rehberg R 64.4 T Velasquez D 32.8 M Fellows Lib 2.8	
2006			J Tester D 49.2 C Burns R 48.3 S Jones Lib 2.6	D Rehberg R 58.9 M Lindeen D 39.1 M Fellows Lib 2.0	
2008	McCain 49.5 Obama 47.3 Paul 2.2 2 others 1.0	B Schweitzer D 65.5 R Brown R 32.5 S Jones Lib 2.0	M Baucus D 72.9 B Kelleher R 27.1	D Rehberg R 64.2 J Driscoll D 32.4	
2010				D Rehberg R 60.4 D McDonald D 33.9 M Fellows Lib 5.7	
2012	Romney 55.4 Obama 41.7	S Bullock D 48.9 R Hill R 47.3 R Vandevender Lib 3.8	J Tester D 48.6 D Rehberg R 44.9 D Cox Lib 6.6	S Daines R 53.3 K Gillan D 42.7 D Kaiser Lib 4.0	
2014			S Daines R 57.8 A Curtis D 40.1 R Roots Lib 2.1	R Zinke R 55.4 J Lewis D 40.4 M Fellows Lib 4.2	
2016	Trump 56.5 Clinton 36.0 Johnson 5.6 Stein 1.6	S Bullock D 50.2 G Gianforte R 46.4 T Dunlap Lib 3.4		R Zinke R 56.2 D Juneau D 40.5 R Breckenridge Lib 3.3	

1 New Reform Party.

Nebraska Voting Results: President, Governor, Senator

	PRESIDENT	GOVERNOR	SENATE
1950		V Peterson R 53.8 W Raecke D 44.1	
1952	Eisenhower 69.1 Stevenson 30.9	R Crosby R 61.4 W Raecke D 38.6	H Butler R 69.1 S Long D 27.8 D Dell (petition) 3.1 D Griswold R 63.6 W Ritchie D 36.4
1954		V Anderson R 60.3 W Ritchie D 39.7	C Curtis R 61.1 K Neville D 38.9 R Hruska R 60.9 J Green D 39.1
1956	Eisenhower 65.5 Stevenson 34.5	V Anderson R 54.3 F Sorrell D 40.2 G Morris ind 5.6	
1958		R Brooks D 50.2 V Anderson R 49.8	R Hruska R 55.6 F Morrison D 44.4
1960	Nixon 62.1 Kennedy 37.9	F Morrison D 52.0 J Cooper R 48.0	C Curtis R 58.9 R Conrad D 41.1
1962		F Morrison D 52.2 F Seaton R 47.8	
1964	Johnson 52.6 Goldwater 47.4	F Morrison D 60.0 D Burney R 40.0	R Hruska R 61.4 R Arndt D 38.6
1966		N Tiemann R 61.5 P Sorenson D 38.4	C Curtis R 61.2 F Morrison D 38.8
1968	Nixon 59.8 Humphrey 31.8 Wallace 8.4		
1970		JJ Exon 53.8 N Tiemann R 43.8 A Walsh Am Ind 2.4	R Hruska R 52.5 F Morrison D 47.5
1972	Nixon 70.5 McGovern 29.5		C Curtis R 53.2 T Carpenter D 46.8
1974		JJ Exon D 59.2 R Marvel R 35.4 E Chambers ind 5.4	
1976	Ford 59.2 Carter 38.4 3 others		E Zorinsky D 52.9 J McCollister R 47.1
1978		C Thone R 55.9 G Whelan D 44.0	J Exon D 67.7 D Shasteen R 32.3
1980	Reagan 65.6 Carter 26.0 Anderson 7.0 Lib 1.4		
1982		B Kerrey D 50.6 C Thone R 49.3	E Zorinsky D 66.6 J Keck R 28.6 B Walsh (petition) 4.8
1984	Reagan 70.6 Mondale 28.8 3 others 0.6		JJ Exon D 52.0 N Hoch R 48.0
1986		K Orr R 52.9 H Boosalis D 47.0	
1988	Bush 60.2 Dukakis 39.2 2 others 0.6		B Kerrey D 56.7 D Karnes R 41.7 E Chambers ind 1.6
1990		B Nelson D 49.9 K Orr R 49.2	J Exon D 59.0 H Daub R 41.0
1992	Bush 46.6 Clinton 29.4 Perot 23.6 2 others 0.4		
1994		B Nelson D 73.0 G Spence R 25.6 others 1.4	B Kerrey D 54.9 J Stoney R 45.1
1996	Dole 53.8 Clinton 35.0 Reform 10.6 3 others 0.6		C Hagel R 57.4 B Nelson D 42.6
1998		M Johanns R 53.9 B Hoppner D 46.0	
2000	Bush 62.3 Gore 33.3 Nader 3.5 3 others 0.9		B Nelson D 51.1 D Stenberg R 48.9
2002		M Johanns R 68.7 S Dean D 27.5 P Rosberg ind 3.8	C Hagel R 82.8 C Matulka D 14.6 ind + Lib 2.6
2004	Bush 59.1 Kerry 38.6 4 others		
2006		D Heinemann R 73.6 D Hahn D 24.5 2 others	B Nelson D 63.9 P Ricketts R 36.1
2008	McCain 56.5 Obama 41.6 5 others		M Johanns R 57.5 S Kleeb D 40.1 2 others 2.4
2010		D Heinemann R 72.9 M Meister D 26.1	
2012	Obama 38.0 Romney 59.8		D Fischer R 57.8 B Kerrey D 42.2
2014		P Ricketts R 57.2 C Hassebrook D 39.2 M Ellsworth Lib 3.5	B Sasse R 64.3 D Domina D 31.5 2 others 4.2
2016	Trump 59.9 Clinton 34.4 Lib + Green 5.8		

Nebraska Elections to the U.S. House, Districts 1–4

Nebraska had four House seats before 1962, and three since then. In the 1950s, District 1 was a strip along the southern border from Colorado to Missouri; District 2 was the Omaha area; District 3 was the northeast; District 4, the largest (slightly more than half the state's area), was in the northwest. From 1962, generally, the Omaha area has been District 2; District 1 has been west of it from South Dakota to Kansas and including Lincoln; and District 3 has been the western two-thirds or more.

	DISTRICT 1	DISTRICT 2	DISTRICT 3	DISTRICT 4
1950	C Curtis *R* 54.5 C Miles *D* 45.5	H Buffett *R* 63.5 E O'Sullivan *D* 36.5	K Stefan *R* 67.0 D Peterson *D* 33.0	A Miller *R* 65.8 H Holtorf *D* 34.2
1952	C Curtis *R* 72.1 S Freeman *D* 27.9	R Hruska *R* 56.1 J Hart *D* 43.9	R Harrison *R* 71.9 A Dusatko *D* 28.1	A Miller *R* 73.4 F Lee *D* 26.6
1954	R Weaver *R* 58.6 F Morrison *D* 41.4	J Chase *R* 53.0 J Hart *D* 47.0	R Harrison *R* 65.2 E Luther *D* 34.8	A Miller *R* 70.4 C Laird *D* 29.6
1956	P Weaver *R* 66.9 S Freeman *D* 33.1	G Cunningham *R* 53.4 J Benesch *D* 44.9 A Misegadis (petition) 1.7	R Harrison *R* 62,645 L Brock *D* 62,399	A Miller *R* 65.7 C Laird *D* 34.3
1958	P Weaver *R* 53.4 C Callan *D* 46.6	G Cunningham *R* 64.8 F Casey *D* 35.2	L Brock *D* 55.1 R Harrison *R* 44.9	D McGinley *D* 52.3 A Miller *R* 47.7
1960	P Weaver *R* 55.5 G Whelan *D* 44.5	G Cunningham *R* 66.6 J Benesch *D* 33.4	R Beermann *R* 51.3 L Brock *D* 48.7	D Martin *R* 51.1 D McGinley *D* 48.9
1962	R Beermann *R* 50.3 C Callan *D* 44.4 G Menkens *ind* 5.3	G Cunningham *R* 69.4 T Bonner *D* 30.6	D Martin *R* 65.6 J Hoffman *D* 34.4	
1964	C Callan *D* 51.3 R Beermann *R* 48.7	G Cunningham *R* 53.2 R Swenson *D* 46.8	D Martin *R* 52.8 W Colwell *D* 47.2	
1966	R Denney *R* 51.1 C Callan *D* 48.9	G Cunningham *R* 64.3 R Fellman *D* 35.7	D Martin *R* 73.0 J Homan *D* 27.0	
1968	R Denney *R* 54.1 C Callan *D* 43.4 H Hamilton *ind* 2.5	G Cunningham *R* 55.2 Mrs F Morrison *D* 44.9	D Martin *R* 67.8 J Dean *D* 32.2	
1970	C Thone *R* 50.6 C Callan *ind* 26.2 G Burroughs *D* 23.2	M Collister *R* 51.9 J Hlavacek *D* 48.1	D Martin *R* 59.5 D Searcy *D* 40.5	
1972	C Thone *R* 64.2 D Berg *D* 35.8	J McCollister *R* 63.9 P Cooney *D* 36.1	D Martin *R* 69.6 W Fitzgerald *D* 30.4	
1974	C Thone *R* 53.3 H Dyas *D* 46.7	J McCollister *R* 55.2 J Lynch *D* 44.8	V Smith *R* 80,992 W Ziebarth *D* 80,255	
1976	C Thone *R* 73.2 P Anderson *D* 26.8	J Cavanaugh *D* 54.6 L Terry *R* 45.4	V Smith *R* 72.9 J Hansen *D* 24.7 W Steen *Am Ind* 2.4	
1978	D Bereuter *R* 58.1 H Dyas *D* 41.9	J Cavanaugh *D* 52.3 H Daub *R* 47.7	V Smith *R* 80.0 M Fowler *D* 20.0	
1980	D Bereuter *R* 78.7 R Story *D* 21.3	H Daub *R* 53.1 R Fellman *D* 43.8 S Putney *Lib* 3.1	V Smith *R* 83.9 S Ditus *D* 16.1	
1982	D Bereuter *R* 75.1 C Donaldson *D* 24.9	H Daub *R* 56.8 R Fellman *D* 43.2	V Smith *R* 100.0	
1984	D Bereuter *R* 74.1 M Bauer *D* 25.9	H Daub *R* 65.0 T Cavanaugh *D* 35.0	V Smith *R* 83.3 T Vickers *D* 16.7	
1986	D Bereuter *R* 64.5 S Burns *D* 35.5	H Daub *R* 58.6 C Calinger *D* 41.4	V Smith *R* 69.8 S Sidwell *D* 30.2	
1988	D Bereuter *R* 66.9 C Jones *D* 33.1	P Hoagland *D* 50.7 J Schenken *R* 49.3	V Smith *R* 79.0 J Racek *D* 21.0	
1990	D Bereuter *R* 64.8 L Hall *D* 35.2	P Hoagland *D* 58.1 A Milder *R* 41.9	B Barrett *R* 51.1 S Scofield *D* 48.9	
1992	D Bereuter *R* 59.7 G Finnegan *D* 40.3	P Hoagland *D* 51.2 R Staskiewicz *R* 48.8	B Barrett *R* 71.7 L Fisher *D* 28.3	
1994	D Bereuter *R* 62.6 P Combs *D* 37.4	J Christensen *R* 49.9 P Hoagland *D* 49.0	B Barrett *R* 78.7 G Chapin *D* 21.3	
1996	D Bereuter *R* 70.0 P Combs *D* 30.0	J Christensen *R* 56.9 J Davis *D* 40.2 2 others 2.9	B Barrett *R* 77.5 J Webster *D* 22.5	
1998	D Bereuter *R* 73.6 D Eret *D* 26.4	L Terry *R* 65.7 M Scott *D* 34.3	B Barrett *R* 84.6 J Hickman *Lib* 15.4	
2000	D Bereuter *R* 66.3 A Jacobsen *D* 31.1 D Oenbring *Lib* 2.6	L Terry *R* 65.9 S Kiel *D* 31.1 J Graziano *Lib* 3.1	T Osborne *R* 82.1 R Reynolds *D* 15.7 J Hickman *Lib* 2.2	
2002	D Bereuter *R* 85.4 R Eckerson *Lib* 14.6	L Terry *R* 63.4 J Simon *D* 33.0 2 others	T Osborne *R* 93.2 J Hickman *Lib* 6.8	
2004	J Fortenberry *R* 54.2 M Connealy *D* 43.0 S Larrick *Green* 2.8	L Terry *R* 61.1 M Thompson *D* 36.1 2 others 2.8	T Osborne *R* 87.5 D Anderson *D* 10.6 2 others 2.0	
2006	J Fortenberry *R* 58.3 M Moul *D* 41.7	L Terry *R* 54.7 J Esch *D* 45.3	A. Smith *R* 55.0 S Kleeb *D* 45.0	
2008	J Fortenberry *R* 70.4 M Yashirin *D* 29.6	L Terry *R* 51.9 J Esch *D* 48.1	A Smith *R* 76.9 J Stoddard *D* 23.1	
2010	J Fortenberry *R* 71.3 I Harper *D* 28.7	L Terry *R* 60.8 T White *D* 39.2	A Smith *R* 70.2 R Davis *D* 17.9 D Hill (petition) 12.0	
2012	J Fortenberry *R* 68.3 K Reiman *D* 31.7	L Terry *R* 50.8 J Ewing *D* 49.2	A Smith *R* 74.2 M Sullivan *D* 25.8	
2014	J Fortenberry *R* 69.0 D Crawford *D* 31.0	B Ashford *D* 48.6 L Terry *R* 46.0 S Laird *Lib* 5.3	A Smith *R* 75.5 M Sullivan *D* 24.5	
2016	J Fortenberry *R* 69.5 D Wik *D* 36.6	D Bacon *R* 48.9 B Ashford *D* 47.7 S Laird *Lib* 3.3	A Smith *R* 100	

Nevada Voting Results: President, Governor, Senator

	PRESIDENT	GOVERNOR	SENATE
1950		C Russell R 57.6 V Pittman D 42.4	P McCarran D 58.0 G Marshall R 42.0
1952	Eisenhower 61.4 Stevenson 38.6		G Malone R 51.7 T Mechling D 48.3
1954		C Russell R 53.1 V Pittman D 46.9	A Bible D 58.1 E Brown R 41.9
1956	Eisenhower 58.0 Stevenson 42.0		A Bible D 52.6 C Young R 47.4
1958		G Sawyer D 59.9 C Russell R 40.1	H Cannon D 57.6 G Malone R 42.4
1960	Kennedy 51.2 Nixon 48.8		
1962		G Sawyer D 66.8 O Gragson R 33.2	A Bible D 65.3 W Wright R 34.7
1964	Johnson 58.6 Goldwater 41.4		H Cannon D 67,336 P Laxalt R 67,288
1966		P Laxalt R 52.2 G Sawyer D 47.8	
1968	Nixon 47.5 Humphrey 39.3 Wallace 19.7		A Bible D 54.7 E Fike R 45.3
1970		M O'Callaghan D 48.1 E Fike R 43.8 C Springer ind 4.4 D Hansen Am Ind 3.7	H Cannon D 57.7 W Raggio R 41.2 H DeSellem Am Ind 1.2
1972	Nixon 63.7 McGovern 36.3		
1974		M O'Callaghan D 67.4 S Crumpler R 17.1 J Housaton Ind Am 15.5	P Laxalt R 47.0 H Reid D 46.6 J Doyle Ind Am 6.4
1976	Ford 50.2 Carter 45.8 3 others 4.0		H Cannon D 63.0 D Towell R 31.5 others 5.5
1978		R List R 56.2 R Rose D 39.7 T Jefferson Ind Am 1.7 John Grayson Lib 0.8 None of above 1.7	
1980	Reagan 63.6 Carter 27.4 Anderson ind 7.2 Lib 1.8		P Laxalt R 59.3 M Gojack D 37.9 A Hacker Lib 2.8
1982		Richard Bryan D 53.4 R List R 41.8 D Becan Lib 1.9	C Hecht R 51.2 H Cannon D 48.8
1984	Reagan 66.8 Mondale 32.4 Lib 0.8		
1986		R Bryan D 71.9 P Cafferata R 25.0 None of above + others 3.1	H Reid D 50.0 J Santini R 44.5 K Cromwell Lib 1.9 Other 3.6
1988	Bush 60.0 Dukakis 38.7 others 1.3		R Bryan D 51.3 C Hecht R 47.1 J Frye Lib 1.6
1990		B Miller D 64.8 J Gallaway R 29.9 None of above 2.8 J Frye Lib 2.5	
1992	Clinton 37.3 Bush 34.7 Perot 26.1 6 others 1.9		H Reid D 51.1 D Dahl R 40.2 5 others 8.7
1994		B Miller D 52.7 J Gibbons R 41.3 D Hansen Ind Am 2.6 None of above + Lib 3.4	R Bryan D 50.9 H Furman R 41.0 4 others 8.1
1996	Clinton 43.9 Dole 42.9 Perot 9.5 5 others 3.7		
1998		K Guinn R 51.6 J Laverty Jones D 42.0 2 others 3.4 None of above 2.9	H Reid D 208,621 J Ensign R 208,220 M Cloud Lib 8,129 M Williams NLP 2,781 None of above 8,113
2000	Bush 49.5 Gore 45.9 8 others 4.6		J Ensign R 55.1 E Bernstein D 39.7 None of above + others 5.2
2002		K Guinn R 68.2 J Neal D 22.0	
2004	Bush 50.5 Kerry 47.9 5 others 1.6		H Reid D 61.1 R Ziser R 35.1 4 others 4.8
2006		J Gibbons R 47.9 D Titus D 43.9 C. Hansen Ind Am 3.4	J Ensign R 55.4 J Carter D 41.0 3 others 3.7
2008	Obama 55.1 McCain 42.7 5 others 2.2		
2010		B Sandoval R 53.4 R Reid D 41.6 6 others	H Reid D 50.3 S Angle R 44.6 others 5.2
2012	Obama 52.4 Romney 45.7		S Berkley D 44.7 D Heller R 45.9
2014		B Sandoval R 70.6 R Goodman D 23.9 None of above + others 5.6	
2016	H Clinton 47.9 Trump 45.5 Other 6.6		C Cortez Masto D 47.1 J Heck R 44.7 4 others + "none" 8.2

Nevada Elections to the U.S. House, Districts 1–4

Nevada had one at-large House seat from 1950 through 1980. It gained a second in 1982, a third in 2002, and a fourth in 2012. From 1982 through 2000, District 1 included much of Clark County, and District 2 covered the rest of the state. From 2002 through 2010, District 1 remained Las Vegas; the new District 3, a "Y"-shaped ring around it; and District 2 the other counties, of which Washoe (Reno) was the most populous. From 2012, the districts became District 1, much of Las Vegas; District 2, roughly the northern half of the state including Reno and Carson City; District 3, southern Clark County including Henderson and Boulder City; and District 4, northern Las Vegas.

	DISTRICT 1	DISTRICT 2	DISTRICT 3	DISTRICT 4
1950	W Baring D 52.7 B MacKenzie R 47.3			
1952	C Young R 50.5 W Baring D 49.5			
1954	C Young R 54.5 W Baring D 45.5			
1956	W Baring D 54.2 R Horton R 45.8			
1958	W Baring D 66.9 R Horton R 33.1			
1960	W Baring D 57.5 G Malone R 42.5			
1962	W Baring D 71.6 C Adair R 28.4			
1964	W Baring D 63.3 G von Tobel R 36.7			
1966	W Baring D 67.6 R Kraemer R 32.4			
1968	W Baring D 72.1 J Slattery R 27.9			
1970	W Baring D 82.5 R Charles R 17.5			
1972	D Towell R 52.2 J Bilbray D 47.8			
1974	J Santini D 55.8 D Towell R 36.4 J Hansen Ind Am 7.8			
1976	J Santini D 77.0 W Earhart R 12.1 others 10.9			
1978	J Santini D 72.4 B O'Mara R 24.3 L West Lib 3.3			
1980	J Santini D 70.0 V Saunders R 26.8 H Mangrum Lib 3.3			
1982	H Reid D 57.5 P Cavnar R 42.5	B Vucanovich R 55.5 M Gojack D 41.3 T Vuceta Lib 3.2		
1984	H Reid D 56.1 P Cavnar R 42.5 J Morris Lib 1.5	B Vucanovich R 71.2 A Barbano D 25.8 D Becan Lib 3.0		
1986	J Bilbray D 54.1 B Ryan R 44.0 G Morris Lib 1.8	B Vucanovich R 58.4 P Sferrazza D 41.6		
1988	J Bilbray D 64.0 L Lusk R 33.7 P O'Neill Lib 2.3	B Vucanovich R 57.3 J Spoo D 40.6 K Cromwell Lib 2.2		
1990	J Bilbray D 61.4 B Dickinson R 34.4 B Moore Lib 4.2	B Vucanovich R 59.1 J Wisdom D 34.0 D Becan Lib 6.9		
1992	J Bilbray D 57.9 J Pettyjohn R 38.0 S Kjar Lib 4.1	B Vucanovich R 47.9 P Sferrazza D 43.3 D Hansen Ind Am 4.9 D Becan Lib 2.8 D Golden Populist 1.1		
1994	J Ensign R 73,769 J Bilbray D 72,333 G Wood Lib 6,065	B Vucanovich R 63.5 J Greeson D 29.2 T Jefferson Ind Am 4.3 L Avery NLP 3.0		
1996	J Ensign R 50.1 B Coffin D 43.5 3 others 6.4	J Gibbons R 58.5 S Wilson D 35.2 3 others 6.2		
1998	S Berkley D 49.2 D Chairez R 45.6 2 others 5.1	J Gibbons R 81.0 C Horne Ind Am 8.3 L Tomburello Lib 7.5 R Winquist NLP 3.1		
2000	S Berkley D 51.7 J Porter R 44.2 3 others	J Gibbons R 64.3 T Cahill D 29.8 7 others		
2002	S Berkley D 52.9 L Boggs-McDonald R 42.1 4 others	J Gibbons R 74.3 T Souza D 20.0 J Hansen Ind Am 3.6 3 others	J Porter R 56.1 D Herrera D 37.3 3 others	
2004	S Berkley D 66.0 R Mickelson R 31.1 J Duensing Lib 2.9	J Gibbons R 67.2 A Cochran D 27.5 2 others 5.4	J Porter R 54.4 T Gallagher D 40.4 2 others 5.1	
2006	S Berkley D 64.8 K Wegner R 31.2 2 others 4.0	D Heller R 50.3 J Derby D 44.9 2 others 4.7	J Porter R 48.5 T Hafen D 46.6 2 others 5.0	
2008	S Berkley D 67.7 K Wegner R 28.3 2 others 4.0	D Heller R 51.8 J Derby D 41.4 3 others 6.7	D Titus D 47.4 J Porter R 42.3 4 others 10.3	
2010	S Berkley D 61.8 K Wegner R 35.3 2 others 3.0	D Heller R 63.3 N Price D 32.7 other 4.0	J Heck R 48.1 D Titus D 47.5 3 others 4.4	
2012	D Titus D 63.6 C Edwards R 31.5 2 others 4.9	M Amodei R 57.6 S Koepnick D 36.3 2 others 6.1	J Heck R 50.4 J Oceguera D 42.9 2 others 6.8	S Horsford D 50.1 D Tarkanian R 42.1 2 others 7.8
2014	D Titus D 56.8 A Teijeiro R 37.9 2 others 5.3	M Amodei R 65.7 K Spees R 27.9 J Hansen ind 6.3	J Heck R 60.8 E Bilbray D 36.1 3 others 3.1	C Hardy R 48.5 S Horsford D 45.8 2 others 5.7
2016	D Titus D 61.9 M Perry R 28.8 2 others 9.4	M Amodei R 58.3 C Evans D 36.9 2 others 4.8	J Rosen D 47.2 D Tarkanian R 46.0 2 others 6.8	R Kihuen D 48.5 C Hardy R 44.5 2 others 7.0

New Mexico Results: President, Governor, Senator

	PRESIDENT	GOVERNOR	SENATE
1950		E Mechem R 53.7 J Miles D 46.3	
1952	Eisenhower 55.4 Stevenson 44.3 4 others 0.3	E Mechem R 53.8 E Grantham D 46.2	D Chavez D 51.1 P Hurley R 48.9
1954		J Simms D 57.0 A Stockton R 43.0	C Anderson D 57.3 E Mechem R 42.7
1956	Eisenhower 57.8 Stevenson 41.8 3 others 0.4	E Mechem R 52.2 J Simms D 47.8	
1958		J Burroughs D 50.5 E Mechem R 49.5	D Chavez D 62.7 F Atchley R 37.3
1960	Kennedy 50.1 Nixon 49.4 2 others 0.5	E Mechem R 50.3 J Burroughs D 49.7	C Anderson D 63.4 W Colwes R 36.6
1962		J Campbell D 53.0 E Mechem R 47.0	
1964	Johnson 59.2 Goldwater 40.2 2 others 0.6		J Montoya D 54.7 E Mechem R 45.3
1966		D Cargo R 51.7 G Lusk D 48.3	C Anderson D 53.1 A Carter R 46.9
1968	Nixon 51.8 Humphrey 39.7 Wallace 7.9 2 others 5.5		
1970		B King D 51.3 P Domenici R 46.4 J Salazar ind 1.6 other 0.8	J Montoya D 52.9 A Carter R 47.1
1972	Nixon 1.1 McGovern 36.6 Am Ind 2.3		P Domenici R 54.0 J Daniels D 46.0
1974		J Apodaca D 49.9 J Skeen R 48.8 Am Ind 1.3	
1976	Ford 50.7 Carter 48.3 4 others 1.0		H Schmitt R 57.1 J Montoya D 42.9
1978		B King D 50.5 J Skeen R 49.4	P Domenici R 53.4 T Anaya D 46.6
1980	Reagan 55.0 Carter 36.8 Anderson 6.5 4 others 1.7		
1982		T Anaya D 53.0 J Irick R 47.0	J Bingaman D 53.8 H Schmitt R 46.2
1984	Reagan 59.7 Mondale 39.2 5 others 1.1		P Domenici R 71.9 J Pratt D 28.1
1986		G Carruthers R 53.0 R Powell 47.0	
1988	Bush 51.9 Dukakis 46.9 5 others 1.2		J Bingaman D 63.3 B Valentine R 36.7
1990		B King D 54.7 F Bond R 45.3	P Domenici R 72.9 T Benavides D 27.0
1992	Clinton 45.9 Bush 37.3 Perot 16.1 7 others 0.7		
1994		G Johnson R 55.5 B King D 44.5	J Bingaman D 54.0 C McMillan R 46.0
1996	Clinton 49.2 Dole 41.9 Reform 5.8 Green 2.4 2 others 0.7		P Domenici R 64.7 A Trujillo D 29.8 A Gutmann Green 4.4 Lib 1.1
1998		G Johnson R 54.5 M Chavez D 45.5	
2000	Gore 286,783 Bush 286,417 Nader 21,251 4 others		J Bingaman D 61.7 B Redmond R 38.3
2002		B Richardson D 55.5 J Sanchez R 39.1 D Bacon Green 5.5	P Domenici R 65.0 G Tristani D 35.0
2004	Bush 49.8 Kerry 49.0 ind 0.5		
2006		B Richardson D 68.8 J Dendahl R 31.2	J Bingaman D 70.6 A McCulloch R 29.3
2008	Obama 56.9 McCain 41.8 4 others 1.3		T Udall D 61.3 S Pearce R 38.7
2010		S Martinez R 53.4 D Denish D 46.6	
2012	Obama 55.3 Romney 44.7		M Heinrich D 53.0 H Wilson R 47.0
2014		S Martinez R 57.2 G King D 42.8	T Udall D 55.6 A Weh R 44.4
2016	Clinton 48.3 Trump 40.0 Johnson 9.3 Stein 1.2 others 1.1		

New Mexico Elections to the U.S. House, Districts 1–3 and At-Large

New Mexico had two at-large House seats at the 1950 through 1960 elections. The two were districted from 1962 through 1980, with District 1 assigned to the northeast part of the state, including Santa Fe and Albuquerque; District 2 included the rest. A third seat was added in 1982. Albuquerque (Bernalillo County and some counties east of it) became District 1, the southern part of the state including Little Texas became District 2, and the northwestern third to half became District 3, including Santa Fe, Los Alamos, and Farmington in the 1980s, and some other northern counties thereafter. District lines have not changed much since: Bernalillo, District 1; the south, District 2; the north, District 3.

	AT-LARGE	AT-LARGE	
1950	A Fernandez *D* 97,691 S Mason *R* 75,447	J Dempsey *D* 97,187 J Armijo *R* 68,752	
1952	J Dempsey *D* 121,477 H Berkshire *R* 112,297	A Fernandez *D* 119,925 E Guthmann *R* 109,595	
1954	J Dempsey *D* 111,711 T Childers *R* 77,151	A Fernandez *D* 109,816 W Cobean *R* 76,528	
1956	J Dempsey *D* 129,625 D Cornell *R* 114,719	A Fernandez *D* 128,330 F Atchley *R* 112,531	
1958	J Montoya *D* 124,924 G McKim *R* 70,925	T Morris *D* 115,928 W Thompson *R* 72,922	
1960	J Montoya *D* 176,514 J Robb *R* 124,101 2 others 1,659	T Morris *D* 172,577 E Balcomb *R* 123,683	

	DISTRICT 1	DISTRICT 2	DISTRICT 3
1962	J Montoya *D* 52.5 J Redman *R* 47.5	T Morris *D* 64.4 J Lopez *R* 35.6	
1964	T Morris *D* 61.8 M Sims *R* 38.2	J Walker *D* 51.6 J Redman *R* 48.4	
1966	T Morris *D* 55.9 S Cook *R* 44.1	J Walker *D* 50.5 R Davidson *R* 49.5	
1968	M Lujan *R* 52.8 T Morris *D* 466.6 W Higgs *ind* 0.5	E Foreman *R* 50.5 J Walker *D* 49.1 W Sedillo *ind* 0.4	
1970	M Lujan *R* 58.5 F Chavez *D* 41.5	H Runnels *D* 51.4 E Foreman *R* 48.6	
1972	M Lujan *R* 55.7 E Gallegos *D* 44.3	H Runnels *D* 72.2 E Presson *R* 27.8	
1974	M Lujan *R* 58.6 R Mondragon *D* 39.7 *Am Ind* 1.7	H Runnels *D* 66.7 D Trubey *R* 31.9 *Am Ind* 1.4	
1976	M Lujan *R* 72.1 R Garcia *D* 27.4 *La Raza* 0.5	H Runnels *D* 70.3 D Trubey *R* 29.7	
1978	M Lujan *R* 62.6 R Hawk *D* 37.5	H Runnels *D* 100.0	
1980	M Lujan *R* 51.0 B Richardson *D* 49.0	J Skeen *R* 38.0 D King *D* 34.0 D Runnels *ind* 28.0	
1982	M Lujan *R* 52.5 J Hartke *R* 47.5	J Skeen *R* 58.4 C Chandler *D* 41.6	B Richardson *D* 64.5 M Chambers *R* 35.4
1984	M Lujan *R* 64.9 C Asbury *D* 34.0 *Lib* 1.1	J Skeen *R* 74.3 P York *D* 25.7	B Richardson *D* 60.8 L Gallegos *R* 37.8 S Jones *Lib* 1.5
1986	M Lujan *R* 70.9 M Garcia *D* 29.1	J Skeen *R* 62.9 M Runnels *D* 37.1	B Richardson *D* 71.3 D Cargo *R* 28.7
1988	S Schiff *R* 50.6 T Udall *D* 47.2 *Lib* 2.1	J Skeen *R* 100.0	B Richardson *D* 73.1 C Salazar *R* 26.9
1990	S Schiff *R* 70.2 R Vigil-Giron *D* 29.8	J Skeen *R* 100.0	B Richardson *D* 74.4 P Archuletta *R* 25.6
1992	S Schiff *R* 62.6 R Aragon *D* 37.4	J Skeen *R* 56.4 D Sosa *D* 43.6	B Richardson *D* 67.4 FG Bemis *R* 30.0 E Nagel *Lib* 2.6
1994	S Schiff *R* 73.9 P Zollinger *D* 26.1	J Skeen *R* 63.3 B Chavez *D* 31.9 R Johnson *Green* 4.9	B Richardson *D* 63.6 FG Bemis *R* 34.1 E Nagel *Lib* 2.4
1996	S Schiff *R* 56.6 J Wertheim *D* 37.1 2 others 6.3	J Skeen *R* 55.9 ES Baca *D* 44.1	B Richardson *D* 67.2 B Redmond *R* 30.5 E Nagel *Lib* 2.2
1998	H Wilson *R* 48.4 P Maloof *D* 41.9 R Anderson *Green* 9.7	J Skeen *R* 57.9 ES Baca *D* 42.1	T Udall *D* 53.1 B Redmond *R* 43.3 C Miller *Green* 3.6
2000	H Wilson *R* 50.4 J Kelly *D* 43.3 D Kerlinsky *Green* 6.4	J Skeen *R* 58.1 M Montoya *D* 41.9	T Udall *D* 67.2 L Lutz *R* 32.8
2002	H Wilson *R* 55.3 R Romero *D* 44.7	S Pearce *R* 56.2 J Smith *D* 43.7	T Udall *D* 100.0
2004	H Wilson *R* 54.5 R Romero *D* 45.5	S Pearce *R* 60.2 G King *D* 39.8	T Udall *D* 68.7 G Tucker *R* 31.3
2006	H Wilson *R* 50.2 P Madrid *D* 49.8	S Pearce *R* 59.4 A Kissling *D* 40.5	T Udall *D* 74.7 R Dolin *R* 25.3
2008	M Heinrich *R* 55.7 D White *R* 44.3	H Teague *D* 56.0 E Tinsley *R* 44.0	B Lujan *D* 56.7 D East *R* 30.5
2010	Heinrich *D* 51.9 J Barela *R* 48.1	S Pearce *R* 55.4 H Teague *D* 44.6	B Lujan *D* 57.0 T Mullins *R* 43.0
2012	M Grisham *D* 59.2 J Arnold-Jones *R* 40.8	S Pearce *R* 59.1 E Erhard *D* 40.9	B Lujan *D* 63.1 J Byrd *R* 36.9
2014	M Grisham *D* 58.6 M Frese *R* 41.4	S Pearce *R* 64.4 R Lara *D* 35.5	B Lujan *D* 61.5 J Byrd *R* 38.5
2016	M Grisham *D* 65.1 R Priem *R* 34.9	S Pearce *R* 62.7 ML Soules *D* 37.3	B Lujan *D* 62.4 M Romero *R* 37.6

North Dakota Voting Results

In the 1950s the state had two seats, contested at large. In the 1960s the eastern 40 percent became District 1 and the western 60 percent District 2. From 1972 onward, North Dakota has had one at-large House seat.

	PRESIDENT	GOVERNOR	SENATE	HOUSE AT-LARGE	HOUSE AT-LARGE
1950		N Brunsdale R 66.3 C Byerly D	M Young R 67.6 H O'Brien D 32.4	F Aandahl R 119,047 E Schumacher D 62,322	U Burdick R 110,534 E Johansson D 32,946
1952	Eisenhower 71.0 Stevenson 28.4	N Brunsdale R 78.7 O Johnson D 21.3	W Langer R 66.3 H Morrison D 23.2 F Aandahl (write-in) 10.4	U Burdick R 181,218 E Nesemeier D 49,829	O Krueger R 156,829
1954		N Brunsdale R 64.2 C Bymers D 35.8		U Burdick R 124,845 P Lanier D 64,089	O Krueger R 106,341 R Vendsel D 49,183
1956	Eisenhower 61.7 Stevenson 38.1	J Davis R 58.5 W Warner D 41.5	Young R 63.6 Q Burdick D 36.0 Townley ind 0.4	U Burdick R 143,514 A Geelan D 85,743	O Krueger R 136,003 S Hocking D 83,284
1958		J Davis R 53.1 J Lord D 46.9	W Langer R 57.2 R Vendsel D 41.5 2 others 1.3	Q Burdick D 99,562 S Hocking D 78,889	D Short R 97,862 O Nordhougen R 92,124
1960	Nixon 55.4 Kennedy 44.5	W Guy D 52.6 C Dahl R 47.4		D Short R 135,579 R Vendsel D 120,773	H Nygaard R 127,118 A Anderson D 109,207
				DISTRICT 1	**DISTRICT 2**
1962		W Guy D 50.4 M. Andrews R 49.6	M Young R 60.7 Lanier D 39.3	H Nygaard R 54.6 S Anderson D 45.3	D Short R 54.0 R Vogel R 46.0
1964	Johnson 58.0 Goldwater 41.9	W Guy D 55.7 D Halcrow R 44.3	Q Burdick D 57.7 T Kleppe R 42.4	M Andrews R 52.2 G Sinner D 47.4 2 others 0.5	R Redlin D 52.6 D Short R 47.5
1966				M Andrews R 66.2 B Hoffner D 33.8	T Kleppe R 51.9 R Redlin D 48.1
1968	Nixon 55.9 Humphrey 38.2 Wallace 5.7	W Guy D 54.8 R McCarney R 43.7 L Landsberger ind 1.5	Young R 64.8 Lashkowitz D 33.8 ind 1.4	M Andrews R 71.9 B Hagen D 26.2 ind 1.9	T Kleppe R 49.96 R Redlin D 48.80 R Kleppe ind 1.3
1970			Q Burdick D 61.2 T Kleppe R 37.8 R Kleppe ind 0.9	M Andrews R 65.7 J Brooks D 34.3	A Link D 50.2 R McCarney R 49.8
				AT-LARGE	
1972	Nixon 62.1 McGovern 35.8 Wallace 2.0	A Link D 51.0 R Larsen R 49.0		M Andrews R 72.7 R Ista D 27.1	
1974			M Young R 114,852 W Guy D 114,675 K Gardner ind (0.1%) J Jungroth ind (2.8%)	M Andrews R 55.7 B Dorgan D 44.3	
1976	Ford 51.7 Carter 45.8 9 others	A Link D 51.6 R Elkin R 46.5 other 1.9	Q Burdick D 62.1 R Stroup R 36.6 C Haggard Am Ind 1.3	M Andrews R 62.4 L Omdahl D 36.0 R Kleppe Am Ind 1.6	
1978				M Andrews R 67.0 B Hagen D 30.9 2 others 2.1	
1980	Reagan 64.3 Carter 26.3 Anderson 7.8 7 others	A Olson R 53.6 A Link R 46.4	M Andrews R 70.3 K Johanneson D 29.0 2 others 0.8	B Dorgan D 56.8 J Smykowski R 42.5 2 others 0.7	
1982			Q Burdick D 62.8 G Knorr R 34.0 other 3.2	B Dorgan D 71.6 K Jones R 27.7 Proh 0.7	
1984	Reagan 64.8 Mondale 33.8 8 others	G Sinner D 55.3 A Olson R 44.7		B Dorgan D 78.7 L Altenburg R 21.3	
1986			K Conrad D 49.8 M Andrews R 49.1 A Bourgois ind 1.1	B Dorgan D 75.5 S Vinje R 23.4 G Kopp ind 1.1	
1988	Bush 56.0 Dukakis 43.0 4 others	G Sinner D 59.9 L Mallberg R 40.1	Q Burdick D 59.4 E Strinden R 39.0 K Gardner Lib 1.5	B Dorgan D 70.9 S Sydness R 28.2 K Brekke Lib 1.0	
1990				B Dorgan D 65.2 E Schafer R 34.8	
1992	Bush 4.2 Clinton 32.2 Perot 23.1	E Schafer R 56.8 N Spaeth D 39.4 2 others 3.8	B Dorgan D 59.0 S Sydness R 38.9 T Asbridge ind 2.1	E Pomeroy D 56.8 J Korsmo R 39.4 other 3.8	
1994			K Conrad D 58.0 B Clayburgh R 42.0	E Pomeroy D 52.3 G Porter R 45.0 J Germalic ind 2.7	
1996	Dole 47.0 Clinton D 40.1 Perot 12.2 3 others	E Schafer R 66.2 L Kalldor D 33.8		E Pomeroy D 55.1 K Cramer R 43.2 K Loughhead ind 1.7	
1998			B Dorgan D 63.1 D Nalewaja R 35.1 H McLain Reform 1.7	E Pomeroy D 56.2 K Cramer R 41.1 K Loughhead ind 2.7	
2000	Bush 60.7 Gore 33.1 Nader 2.5 others 3.8	J Hoeven R 55.0 H Heitkamp 45.0	K Conrad D 61.4 D Sand R 38.6	E Pomeroy D 52.9 J Dorso R 44.6 2 others 2.5	
2002				E Pomeroy D 52.4 R Clayburgh R 47.6	
2004	Bush 62.9 Kerry 35.5 3 others	J Hoeven R 71.3 J Satrom D 27.4 ind 1.4	B Dorgan D 68.3 M Liffrig R 31.7	E Pomeroy D 59.6 D Sand R 40.4	
2006			K Conrad D 68.8 D Grotberg R 29.5 2 others 1.6	E Pomeroy D 65.7 M Mechtel R 34.3	
2008	McCain 53.3 Obama 44.6	J Hoeven R 74.4 T Mathern D 23.5		E Pomeroy D 62.0 D Sand R 38.0	
2010			J Hoeven R 76.2 T Potter D 22.2 K Hanson Lib 1.6	R Berg R 54.9 E Pomeroy D 45.1	
2012	Romney 58 Obama 39	J Dalrymple R 63.1 R Taylor D 34.3 2 others 2.6	H Heitkamp D 50.5 R Berg R 49.5	K Cramer R 54.9 P Gulleson D 41.7 others 3.4	
2014				K Cramer R 55.6 G Sinner Jr D 38.5 J Seaman Lib 5.9	
2016	Trump 63.0 Clinton D 27.2 Johnson Lib 6.2	D Burgum R 76.7 M Nelson D 19.4 Lib 3.9	J Hoeven R 78.5 E Glassheim D 17.0 others 4.6	K Cramer R 69.2 C IronEyes D 23.8 J Seaman Lib 7.0	

Oklahoma Election Results: President, Governor, Senator

	PRESIDENT	GOVERNOR	SENATE
1950		J Murray D 51.1 J Ferguson R 48.6	M Monroney D 54.8 B Alexander R 45.2
1952	Eisenhower 54.6 Stevenson 45.4		
1954		R Gary D 58.6 R Sparks R 41.3	R Kerr D 55.8 F Mock R 43.7 2 ind 0.5
1956	Eisenhower 55.1 Stevenson 44.9		M Monroney D 55.3 D McKeever R 44.7
1958		JH Edmondson D 74.1 P Ferguson R 19.9 others 5.9	
1960	Nixon 59.0 Kennedy 41.0		R Kerr D 54.8 H Crawford R 44.6 B Brown ind 0.5
1962		H Bellmon R 55.3 WP Atkinson D 44.4 R Zavitz ind 0.3	M Monroney D 53.2 H Crawford R 46.3 P Beck ind 0.4
1964	Johnson 55.7 Goldwater 44.3		F Harris D 51.2 B Wilkinson R 48.8
1966		Dewey Bartlett R 55.6 Prescott Moore D 43.7 H Ingram ind 0.5	F Harris D 53.7 P Patterson R 46.3
1968	Nixon 47.7 Humphrey 32.0 Wallace 20.3		H Bellmon R 51.7 M Monroney D 46.2 Am Ind 2.1
1970		D Hall D 48.4 D Bartlett D 48.1 R Little Am Ind 3.4	
1972	Nixon 73.7 McGovern 38.1 Am Ind 4.5 other 0.2		D Bartlett R 51.4 E Edmondson D 47.6 3 others 1.0
1974		D Boren D 63.9 J Inhofe R 36.0	H Bellmon R 49.4 E Edmondson D 48.9 P Trent ind 1.7
1976	Ford 49.96 Carter 48.74 ind 1.29		
1978		G Nigh D 51.7 R Shotts R 47.2 3 others 1.0	D Boren D 65.5 B Kamm R 32.9 4 others
1980	Reagan 60.5 Carter 35.0 Anderson 3.3 Lib 1.2		D Nickles R 53.5 A Coats D 43.5 3 others
1982		G Nigh D 62.0 T Daxon R 37.6 ind 0.3	
1984	Reagan 68.6 Mondale 30.7 Lib 0.7		D Boren D 75.6 B Crozier R 23.4 Lib 0.9
1986		H Bellmon R 47.4 D Walters D 44.5 J Brown ind 6.6 N Little ind 1.4	D Nickles R 55.2 JR Jones D 44.8
1988	Bush 57.9 Dukakis 41.3 2 others 0.8		
1990		D Walters D 57.4 B Price R 32.7 T Ledgerwood ind 9.9	D Boren D 83.2 S Jones R 16.8
1992	Bush 42.6 Clinton 34.0 Perot 23.0 Lib 0.3		D Nickles R 58.6 S Lewis D 38.2 2 others 3.3
1994		F Keating R 46.9 J Mildren D 29.6 W Watkins ind 23.5	J Inhofe R 55.2 McCurdy D 40.0 D Corn ind 4.8
1996	Dole 48.3 Clinton 40.4 Perot 10.8 Lib 0.5		J Inhofe R 56.7 J Boren D 40.1 3 others 3.2
1998		F Keating R 57.9 L Boyd D 40.9 H Heidberg Reform 1.2	D Nickles R 66.4 D Carroll D 31.3 2 others 2.3
2000	Bush 60.3 Gore 38.4 2 others		
2002		B Henry D 43.3 S Largent R 42.6 G Richardson ind 14.1	J Inhofe R 57.3 D Walters D 36.3 J Germalic ind 6.4
2004	Bush 65.6 Kerry 34.4		T Coburn R 52.8 B Carson D 41.2 S Bilyeu ind 6.0
2006		B Henry D 66.5 E Istook R 33.5	
2008	McCain 65.6 Obama 34.4		J Inhofe R 56.7 A Rice D 39.2 S Wallace ind 4.1
2010		M Fallin R 60.5 J Askins D 39.6	T Coburn R 70.6 J Rogers D 26.1 2 others 3.2
2012	Romney 66.8 Obama 33.2		
2014		M Fallin R 55.8 J Dorman D 41.0 2 others 3.2	J Inhofe R 68.0 M Silverstein 28.5 3 others 3.4 J Lankford R 67.9 (unexp. term) C Johnson D 29.0 other 3.2
2016	Trump 65.3 Clinton 28.9 Johnson Lib 5.7		J Lankford R 67.7 M Workman D 24.6 others 7.7

Oklahoma Elections to the U.S. House, Districts 1–4

Oklahoma had eight House seats in 1950 and promptly lost two. It kept six from 1952 through 2000 but lost another at that point and has elected five from 2002 on. The six-seat configuration that began in 1952 basically held through 1968: Tulsa and some of north-central were District 1, the northeastern Indian area was District 2, Little Dixie (the southeast) was District 3, the counties east of Oklahoma City were District 4, Oklahoma City and Norman were District 5, and the southwest and panhandle were District 6. That changed somewhat (notably Norman shifting to District 4). From 1972 through 1982 some marginal changes occurred. From 1984 through the 1990s, Tulsa and Osage Counties remained District 1, District 2 was the northeast and Tulsa environs, District 3 still Little Dixie, District 4 became the southwest including Norman and part of Oklahoma City, District 5 covered the bulk of Oklahoma City, and District 6 included the western plains and some minority precincts in Oklahoma City. With the loss of the sixth seat from 2002, the geography was District 1, Tulsa north to Kansas; District 2, much of the former District 2 and eastern counties of former District 3; District 3, the old 6th District (western plains) and some north-central counties; District 4, mostly the southwestern counties; and District 5, basically Oklahoma City. No significant redistricting has taken place since 2010.

	DISTRICT 1	DISTRICT 2	DISTRICT 3	DISTRICT 4
1950	Schwabe R 52.9 Gilmer D 47.1	Stigler D 66.2 Crain R 33.8	Albert D 82.9 Powell R 17.1	Steed D 68.1 Young R 31.9
1952	Belcher R 58.6 Dickey D 41.3	E Edmondson D 59.2 Easton R 38.8 3 ind 2.0	Albert D 78.0 McSherry R 22.0	Steed D 58.7 Goode R 40.6 Akin ind 0.6
1954	Belcher R 58.9 Crowley D 41.2	E Edmondson D 64.7 P Butler R 35.3	Albert D 83.3 J Butler R 16.7	Steed D 100
1956	Belcher R 57.2 Moreland D 42.8	E Edmondson D 60.3 P Butler R 39.7	Albert D 76.5 Wallace R 23.0 ind 0.5	Steed D 61.1 Potter R 38.8
1958	Belcher R 50.8 Wright D 48.3 Brasier ind 0.8	E Edmondson D 79.1 Ritter R 20.9	Albert D 90.9 Wallace R 9.1	Steed D 74.0 Calkin R 26.0
1960	Belcher R 63.8 Land D 36.2	E Edmondson D 56.9 Sharp R 43.1	Albert D 74.9 Sherritt R 25.1	Steed D 60.8 Crall R 39.2
1962	Belcher R 68.6 Wright D 31.4	E Edmondson D 56.7 Sharp R 43.4	Albert D 100	Steed D 100
1964	Belcher R 63.5 Martin D 36.5	E Edmondson D 61.4 Lange R 38.6	Albert D 79.0 McSherry R 21.0	Steed D 100
1966	Belcher R 69.7 Cadenhead D 30.4	E Edmondson D 53.6 Garrison R 46.4	Albert D 77.2 Pate R 22.8	Steed D 36,719 Branscum R 36,355
1968	Belcher R 59.3 Jarboe D 40.7	E Edmondson R 54.9 RG Smith R 45.1	Albert D 68.4 Beasley R 31.6	Steed D 53.7 JV Smith R 46.4
1970	Belcher R 55.7 JR Jones D 44.3	E Edmondson D 70.8 Humphries R 29.2	Albert D 100	Steed D 63.7 J Wilkinson 3 34.9 2 ind 1.4
1972	JR Jones D 55.5 Hewgley R 44.5	McSpadden D 71.2 Toliver R 28.8	Albert D 93.3 Marshall ind 6.6	Steed D 71.3 Crozier R 28.7
1974	JR Jones D 67.9 Mizer R 32.1	Risenhoover D 59.0 Keen R 40.9	Albert D 100	Steed D 100
1976	JR Jones D 54.0 Inhofe R 45.1	Risenhoover D 54.0 Stewart R 46.0	Watkins D 82.0 Beasley R 17.2 ind 0.8	Steed D 74.9 Stanley R 22.0 Trent ind 3.1
1978	JR Jones D 59.9 Unruh R 40.1	Synar D 54.8 Richardson R 45.2	Watkins D 100	Steed D 60.3 Robb R 39.7
1980	JR Jones D 58.4 Freeman R 41.6	Synar D 54.0 Richardson R 46.0	Watkins D 100	McCurdy D 51.0 Rutledge R 49.0
1982	JR Jones D 54.1 Freeman R 45.9	Synar D 72.6 Striegel R 27.4	Watkins D 82.2 Miller R 17.8	McCurdy D 65.0 Rutledge R 34.3 2 others 0.7
1984	JR Jones D 52.2 F Keating R 47.3 Neal Lib 0.5	Synar D 74.1 Rice R 26.0	Watkins D 77.8 Miller R 22.3	McCurdy D 63.6 J Smith R 35.3 Mobley Lib 1.0
1986	Inhofe R 54.8 Allison D 42.8 McCullough ind 2.4	Synar D 73.3 Rice R 26.7	Watkins D 78.1 Miller R 21.9	McCurdy D 76.2 Humphreys R 23.8
1988	Inhofe R 52.6 Glassco D 47.4	Synar D 64.9 Phillips R 35.1	Watkins D 100	McCurdy D 100
1990	Inhofe R 56.0 Glassco D 44.0	Synar D 61.3 Gorham R 38.7	Brewster D 80.4 Miller R 19.6	McCurdy D 73.6 Bell R 26.4
1992	Inhofe R 52.8 Selph D 47.2	Synar D 55.5 Hill R 41.1 Vardeman ind 3.4	Brewster D 75.1 Stokes R 24.9	McCurdy D 70.7 Bell R 29.2
1994	Largent R 62.7 Price D 37.3	T Coburn R 52.1 Cooper D 47.9	Brewster D 73.7 Tallant R 26.2	JC Watts R 51.7 Perryman D 43.2 Tiffee ind 5.1
1996	Largent R 68.2 Amen D 27.6 several 4.3	Coburn R 55.5 G Johnson D 44.5	Watkins R 51.4 Roberts D 45.2 Demaree ind 3.3	Watts R 57.7 Crocker D 40.0 Murphy Lib 2.4
1998	Largent R 61.8 Plowman D 38.2	Coburn R 57.7 Pharaoh D 39.8 Jones ind 2.4	Watkins R 61.9 Roberts D 38.1	Watts R 61.5 Odom D 38.5
2000	Largent R 69.3 Lowe D 29.3 Lib 1.5	Carson D 54.9 Ewing R 41.8 Mavis Lib 3.3	Watkins R 86.6 Yandell ind 9.2 Lib 4.2	Watts R 64.9 Weatherford D 31.1 2 others 3.9
2002	Sullivan R 55.6 Dodd D 42.1 ind 2.2	Carson D 74.1 Pharaoh R 25.9	Lucas R 75.6 Murphy ind 24.4	Cole R 53.8 Roberts D 46.2
2004	Sullivan R 60.2 Dodd D 37.5 Krymski ind 2.3	Boren D 65.9 Smalley R 34.1	Lucas R 82.2 Wilson ind 17.8	Cole R 77.8 Bradshaw ind 22.2
2006	Sullivan R 63.6 Gentges D 30.9 Wortman ind 5.5	Boren D 72.7 Miller R 27.3	Lucas R 67.4 Barton D 32.5	Cole R 64.6 Spake D 35.4
2008	Sullivan R 66.2 Oliver D 33.8	Boren D 70.5 Wickson R 29.5	Lucas R 69.7 Robbins D 23.6 Michael ind 6.7	Cole R 66.0 Cummings D 29.2 Joyce ind 4.8
2010	Sullivan R 76.8 O'Dell ind 23.2	Boren D 56.5 Thompson R 43.5	Lucas R 78.0 Robbins D 22.0	Cole 100
2012	Bridenstine R 63.5 Olson D 32.0 Allen ind 4.5	Mullin R 57.3 Wallace D 38.3 Fulks ind 4.3	Lucas 75.3 Murray D 20.0 Sanders ind 4.8	Cole R 67.9 Bebo R 27.6 Harris ind 4.5
2014	Bridenstine R 100	Mullin R 70.0 Everett D 24.6 ind 5.4	Lucas R 78.6 Robbins D 21.4	Cole R 70.8 Smith D 24.7 ind 4.5
2016	Bridenstine R 100	Mullin R 70.6 Harris-Till 23.2 ind 6.2	Lucas R 78.3 Robbins 21.7	Cole R 69.6 Owen 26.1

Oklahoma Elections to the U.S. House, Districts 5–8

	DISTRICT 5	DISTRICT 6	DISTRICT 7	DISTRICT 8
1950	Jarman D 58.8 Barnes R 41.1	Morris D 67.1 Campbell R 32.9	Wickersham D 67.1 Cornell R 32.9	Belcher R 53.4 Wilson D 46.6
1952	Jarman D 62.4 Burch R 37.6	Wickersham D 63.3 Cornell R 36.7		
1954	Jarman D 66.1 Young R 33.9	Wickersham D 69.3 Russell R 30.7		
1956	Jarman D 63.7 Hobbs R 36.3	Morris D 68.9 Coogan R 31.1		
1958	Jarman D 82.3 Hobbs R 17.6	Morris D 66.7 Coogan R 33.3		
1960	Jarman D 66.5 Hobbs R 33.5	Wickersham D 68,192 Wheeler R 68,116		
1962	Jarman D 68.9 Pointon R 31.1	Wickersham D 53.5 Gibson R 46.5		
1964	Jarman D 70.8 Cowan R 29.2	J Johnson D 56.7 Auchinclosss R 43.3		
1966	Jarman D 69.6 Gregg R 30.4	JV Smith R 51.4 J Johnson D 48.7		
1968	Jarman D 73.6 Leeper R 26.3	Camp R 55.3 Goodwin D 44.7		
1970	Jarman D 73.1 Campbell R 26.9	Camp R 64.2 Cassity D 35.8		
1972	Jarman D 60.4 Keller R 39.6	Camp R 72.7 Schmitt D 27.3		
1974	Jarman D 51.7 Edwards R 48.3	English D 53.2 Camp R 44.4 Basore ind 2.4		
1976	Edwards R 49.9 Dunlap D 47.4 4 others 2.8	English D 71.1 McCurley R 28.9		
1978	Edwards R 80.0 Knipp D 20.0	English D 74.2 Hunter R 25.8		
1980	Edwards R 68.5 Hood D 28.0 Rushing Lib 3.6	English D 64.7 McCurley R 35.3		
1982	Edwards R 67.3 Lane D 28.9 Trent ind 3.9	English D 75.4 Moore R 24.6		
1984	Edwards R 75.7 Greeson D 21.9 Robinson Lib 2.5	English D 58.9 Dodd R 41.1		
1986	Edwards R 70.6 Compton D 29.4	English D 100		
1988	Edwards R 72.2 Montgomery D 27.8	English D 73.1 Brown R 26.9		
1990	Edwards R 69.6 Baggett D 30.4	English D 80.0 Burns R 20.0		
1992	Istook R 53.4 Williams D 46.6	English D 67.8 Anthony R 32.2		
1994	Istook R 78.2 Keith ind 21.9	Lucas R 70.2 Tollett D 29.8		
1996	Istook R 69.7 Forsythe D 27.1 Kennedy ind 3.2	Lucas R 63.9 Barby D 36.1		
1998	Istook R 68.2 Smothermon D 31.8	Lucas R 65.0 Barby D 33.2 ind 1.9		
2000	Istook R 68.5 McWatters D 27.2 2 others 4.4	Lucas R 59.3 Beutler D 39.1 Lib 1.5		
2002	Istook R 62.2 Barlow D 32.4 Davis ind 5.4			
2004	Istook R 66.1 B Smith D 33.9			
2006	Fallin R 60.4 Hunter D 37.3 ind 2.3			
2008	Fallin R 65.9 Perry D 34.1			
2010	Lankford R 62.5 Coyle D 34.6 2 others			
2012	Lankford R 58.8 Guild D 37.3			
2014	Russell R 60.1 McAffrey D 36.3 3 ind 3.6			
2016	Russell R 57.1 McAffrey D 36.8			

Oregon Election Results: President, Governor, Senator

	PRESIDENT	GOVERNOR	SENATE
1950		D McKay R 66.1 A Flegel D 34.0	W Morse R 74.8 H Latourette D 23.2
1952	Eisenhower 60.6 Stevenson 38.9		
1954		P Patterson R 56.9 J Carson D 43.1	R Neuberger D 50.2 G Cordon R 49.8
1956	Eisenhower 55.3 Stevenson 44.8	R Holmes D 50.5 E Smith R 49.5	W Morse D 54.2 D McKay R 45.8
1958		M Hatfield R 55.4 R Holmes D 44.7	
1960	Nixon 52.6 Kennedy 47.3		M Neuberger D 54.6 E Smith R 45.4
1962		M Hatfield R 50.6 R Thornton D 45.5	W Morse D 54.2 Sig Unander R 45.8
1964	Johnson 63.7 Goldwater 36.0		
1966		T McCall R 55.3 R R Straub D 44.7 D	M Hatfield R 51.8 R Duncan D 48.2
1968	Nixon 49.8 Humphrey 43.8 Wallace 6.1		R Packwood R 50.2 W Morse D 49.8
1970		T McCall R 55.6 R Straub D 44.2 write-in 0.2	
1972	Nixon 52.4 McGovern 42.3		M Hatfield R 53.7 W Morse D 46.2
1974		R Straub D 57.7 V Atiyeh R 42.1 write-in 0.1	R Packwood R 55.4 B Roberts D 44.6
1976	Ford 47.8 Carter 47.6		
1978		V Atiyeh R 54.9 R Straub D 45.1	M Hatfield R 61.7 V Cook D 38.3
1980	Reagan 48.3 Carter 38.7 Anderson 9.5		R Packwood R 52.1 T Kulongoski D 44.0 T Nathan Lib 3.8
1982		V Atiyeh R 61.4 T Kulongoski D 35.9 Lib + write-ins 2.9	
1984	Reagan 55.9 Mondale 43.7		M Hatfield R 66.6 M Hendriksen D 33.4
1986		N Goldschmidt D 51.9 N Paulus R 47.9 write-in 0.3	R Packwood R 63.6 R Bauman D 36.4
1988	Dukakis 51.3 Bush 46.6		
1990		B Roberts D 45.7 D Frohnmeyer R 40.0 A Mobley ind 13.0 Lib 1.3	M Hatfield R 53.8 H Lonsdale D 46.2
1992	Clinton 42.5 Bush 32.5 Perot 24.2		R Packwood R 52.4 L AuCoin D 46.7
1994		J Kitzhaber D 51.0 D Smith R 42.4 E Hickam Am Ind 4.8 Lib + write-ins 1.9	
1996	Clinton 47.1 Dole 39.1 Perot 8.8		G Smith R 49.8 T Bruggere D 45.9 6 others 4.3
1998		J Kitzhaber D 64.4 B Sizemore R 30.0 6 others 5.5	R Wyden D 61.1 J Lim R 33.8
2000	Gore 47.0 Bush 46.5 Nader 5.0		
2002		T Kulongoski D 49.0 K Mannix R 46.2 T Cox Lib 4.6 write-in 0.2	G Smith R 57.4 B Bradbury D 40.5 L Mabon Con 1.7 Lib 2.4
2004	Kerry 51.4 Bush 47.2		R Wyden D 63.4 A King R 31.7
2006		T Kulongoski D 50.8 R Saxton R 42.7 3 others + write-in 6.5	
2008	Obama 56.7 McCain 40.4		J Merkley D 48.9 G Smith R 45.6 D Brownlow Con 5.2 others 0.3
2010		J Kitzhaber D-IPO 49.3[1] Chris Dudley R 47.8	R Wyden D 57.2 J Huffman R 39.2 4 others 3.5
2012	Obama 54.2 Romney 42.2		
2014		J Kitzhaber D 49.9 D Richardson R 44.1 4 others 6.0	J Merkley D 55.8 M Wehby R 37.3
2016	Clinton 50.1 Trump 39.1 Johnson 4.7 Stein 2.5 others 3.6	K Brown D 50.7 B Pierce R 43.5 3 others 5.8	R Wyden D 56.6 M Callahan R 33.3 5 others 10.1

[1] Kitzhaber was nominated by the Democratic Party and also by the Independent Party of Oregon.

Oregon Elections to the U.S. House

From the 1950 election through 1980, Oregon had four House districts. District 1 covered the northwest from the Columbia River down the coast; District 2 was the two-thirds of the state east of the Cascades; District 3 was Multnomah County (Portland) and some suburbs; and District 4 was the southwest. Except for shifts of a few counties here and there, these numbers and assignments changed very little for those thirty years. The only serious change since then came when District 5 was created for the 1982 election. It was carved out of parts of Districts 1 and 4 and included a couple of coastal counties but was chiefly "the heart of the Willamette Valley," as the *Almanac of American Politics* once put it, including Oregon City, Corvallis, and Salem.

	DISTRICT 1	DISTRICT 2	DISTRICT 3	DISTRICT 4	DISTRICT 5
1950	W Norblad R 66.5 R Hewitt D 33.5	L Stockman R 55.5 V Bull D 44.5	H Angell R 50.7 C Donaugh D 43.6 2 others 5.6	H Ellsworth R 59.5 D Shaw D 40.5	
1952	W Norblad R 68.0 R Jones D 32.0	S Coon R 58.5 J Jones D 41.5	H Angell R 54.0 A Corbett D 46.0	H Ellsworth R 66.3 W Swanson D 33.7	
1954	W Norblad R 63.0 D Mitchell D 37.0	S Coon R 52.5 A Ullman D 47.5	E Green D 52.4 T McCall R 47.6	H Ellsworth R 55.9 C Porter D 44.1	
1956	W Norblad R 54.7 J Lee D 45.3	A Ullman D 50.6 S Coon R 49.4	E Green D 61.6 P Roth R 38.4	C Porter D 51.3 H Ellsworth R 48.7	
1958	W Norblad R 54.9 R Thornton D 45.1	A Ullman D 61.7 M Weatherford R 38.3	E Green D 65.8 J Johnston R 34.2	C Porter D 56.4	
1960	W Norblad R 65.1 M Owens D 34.9	A Ullman D 59.6 R Phair R 40.4	E Green D 63.9 W Lee R 36.1	E Durno R 51.1 C Porter D 48.9	
1962	W Norblad R 61.9 R Whipple D 38.1	A Ullman D 64.0 R Chandler R 36.0	E Green D 66.0 S Hartman R 34.0	R Duncan D 54.0 C Fisher R 46.0	
1964	W Wyatt R 53.0 R Whipple D 47.0	A Ullman D 68.1 E Thoren R 31.9	E Green D 65.6 L Dean R 34.4	R Duncan D 64.8 P Jaffarian R 35.2	
1966	W Wyatt R 74.4 M Cross D 25.6	A Ullman D 63.2 E Thoren R 36.8	E Green D 67.0 L Dean R 33.0	Dellenback R 62.7 C Porter D 37.3	
1968	W Wyatt R 80.6 T Baggs D 19.4	A Ullman D 63.9 M Root R 36.1	E Green D 69.8 D Warren R 30.2	Dellenback R 59.0 E Fadeley D 41.0	
1970	W Wyatt R 71.8 V Cook D 28.2	A Ullman D 71.2 E Thoren R 28.8	E Green D 73.7 R Dugdale R 26.3	Dellenback R 58.4 J Weaver D 41.6	
1972	W Wyatt R 68.6 R Bunch D 31.4	A Ullman D 100	E Green D 62.4 M Walsh R 37.6	J Dellenback R 62.6 C Porter D 37.4	
1974	L AuCoin D 56.0 D O'Scannlain R 44.0	A Ullman D 78.2 K Brown R 21.8	R Duncan D 70.4	J Weaver D 52.9 J Dellenback R 47.1	
1976	L AuCoin D 58.6 P Bladine R 41.4	A Ullman D 72.0 T Mercer R 28.0	R Duncan D 83.9 M Simon ind 16.1	J Weaver D 50.0 J Lausmann R 35.1 2 ind 14.9	
1978	L AuCoin D 62.9 N Bunick R 37.1	A Ullman D 69.1 T Hicks R 30.9	R Duncan D 84.6 M Simon Labor 15.4	J Weaver D 56.2 J Laumann R 33.8	
1980	L AuCoin D 65.9 L Engdahl R 34.1	D Smith R 48.8 A Ullman D 47.5 L Marbet ind 3.7	R Wyden D 78.2 D Conger R 21.8	J Weaver D 54.8 M Fitzgerald R 45.2	
1982	L AuCoin D 53.8 B Moshofsky R 46.2	RF Smith R 55.6 L Willis D 44.4	R Wyden D 78.2 T Phelan R 21.8	J Weaver D 59.0 R Anthony R 41.0	D Smith R 51.2 R McFarland D 48.8
1984	L AuCoin D 53.1 B Moshofsky R 46.9	RF Smith R 57.0 L Willis D 43.0	R Wyden D 72.3 D Davis R 27.7	J Weaver D 58.2 B Long R 41.8	D Smith R 54.5 R McFarland D 45.5
1986	L AuCoin D 61.7 T Meeker R 38.3	RF Smith R 60.2 L Tuttle D 338.8	R Wyden D 85.9 T Phelan R 14.1	P DeFazio D 72.0 B Long R 28.0	D Smith R 60.5 B Ross D 39.5
1988	L AuCoin D 69.6 E Molander R 30.4	RF Smith R 62.7 L Tuttle D 37.3	R Wyden D 99.4 other 0.6	P DeFazio D 72.0 J Howard R 28.0	D Smith R 50.2 M Kopetski D 49.8
1990	L AuCoin D 63.1 E Molander R 30.4 R Livingston ind 6.5	RF Smith R 68.0 J Smiley D 32.0	R Wyden D 80.7 P Mooney R 19.3	P DeFazio D 85.8 T Nathan Lib 14.2	M Kopetski D 55.0 D Smith R 45.0
1992	E Furse D 52.0 T Meeker R 48.0	RF Smith R 67.1 D Ferguson D 32.9	R Wyden D 77.1 A Ritter R 18.6 B Bobbier Lib 4.2	P DeFazio D 71.4 R Schulz R 28.6	M Kopetski D 63.9 J Seagraves R 36.1
1994	E Furse D 47.7 B Witt R 47.6 D Wilson Lib 2.0 B Gillett Am Ind 2.6	W Cooley R 57.3 S Kupilas D 38.7 G Sublett Lib 3.9	R Wyden D 72.5 E Hall R 19.4 M Brunelle ind 6.1 G Nanni Lib 1.9	P DeFazio D 66.8 J Newkirk R 33.2	J Bunn R 49.9 C Webber D 46.9 J Zimmer Lib 3.3
1996	E Furse D 51.9 B Witt R 45.3 R Johnson Lib 2.3 others 0.6	RF Smith R 61.7 M Dugan D 36.5 F Wise Lib 1.7	E Blumenauer D 66.9 S Bruun R 26.3 J Keating Pac Green 3.7[1] others 3.0	P DeFazio D 65.7 J Newkirk R 28.4 others 5.9	D Hooley D 51.2 J Bunn R 46.0 others 2.8
1998	D Wu D 50.1 M Bordonaro R 47.2 others 2.8	G Walden R 61.5 K Campbell D 34.8 others 3.7	E Blumenauer D 84.9 B Knight Lib 9.3 R Webb Soc 1.51 others 1.3	P DeFazio 70.1 S Webb R 28.6 K Sorg Soc 1.2	D Hooley D 54.9 M Shannon R 40.5 4 others 4.6
2000	D Wu D 58.3 C Starr R 38.0 others 3.7	G Walden R 73.6 W Ponsford D 26.4	E Blumenauer D 66.8 J Pollock R 23.6 others 9.6	P DeFazio D 68.0 J Lindsey R 30.6 Soc + other 1.4	D Hooley D 56.8 B Boquist R 43.2
2002	D Wu D 62.7 J Greenfield R 34.0 B King Lib 3.2	G Walden R 71.9 P Buckley D 25.8 M Wood Lib 2.3	E Blumenauer D 66.8 S Seale R 26.7 others 6.5	P DeFazio D 63.8 L VanLeeuwen R 34.4 others 1.8	D Hooley D 54.8 B Boquist R 45.2
2004	D Wu D 57.5 G Ameri R 38.1 other 4.3	G Walden R 71.6 J McColgan D 25.6 other 2.7	E Blumenauer D 70.9 T Mars R 23.7 others 5.5	P DeFazio D 61.0 J Feldcamp R 37.6 others 1.4	D Hooley D 52.9 J Zupancic R 44.3 2 others 2.8
2006	D Wu D 62.8 D Kitts R 33.7 others 3.5	G Walden R 66.8 C Voisin D 30.4 others 2.8	E Blumenauer D 74.5 B Broussard R 23.5	P DeFazio D 62.2 J Feldcamp R 37.8 others 2.1	D Hooley D 54.0 M Erickson R 42.8 2 others 3.2
2008	D Wu D 71.5 J Haugen ind 14.9 4 others 11.0	G Walden R 69.5 N Lemas D 25.8 3 others 4.8	E Blumenauer D 74.5 D Lopez R 20.8 2 others 7.0	P DeFazio D 82.3 J Germond Con 12.9 M Beilstein Pac Green 3.9 others 0.9	K Schrader D 54.3 M Erickson R 38.3 4 others 7.4
2010	D Wu D 54.8 R Cornilles R 41.9 3 others 3.2	G Walden R 73.9 J Segers D 26.1	E Blumenauer D 70.0 D Lopez R 24.6 2 others 5.3	P DeFazio D 59.1 A Robinson R 43.6 Pac Green 1.7	K Schrader D 51.2 S Bruun R 46.0 Pac Green 1.7
2012	S Bonamici D 59.7 D Morgan R 33.1 2 others 7.2	G Walden R 68.6 J Segers D 29.1 J Tabor Lib 2.1	E Blumenauer D 74.5 R Green R 19.8 2 others 5.6	P DeFazio D 59.1 A Robinson R 38.8 C Huntting Lib 1.7 others 0.2	K Schrader D 54.0 F Thompson R 42.4 2 others 3.5
2014	S Bonamici D 57.3 J Yates R 34.5 J Foster Lib 4.0 S Reynolds Pac Green 4.0	G Walden R 70.6 A Christofferson D 25.6 S Durbin Lib 3.6 other 0.3	E Blumenauer D 72.3 J Buchal R 19.6 4 others 8.1	P DeFazio D 58.6 A Robinson R 37.5 others 3.9	K Schrader D 53.7 T Smith R 39.3 3 others 7.0
2016	S Bonamici D 59.6 B Heinrich R 37.0 K Sheahan Lib 3.2	G Walden R 71.7 J Crary D 28.3	E Blumenauer D 71.8 D Walker ind 20.4 D Delk Prog 7.3 others 0.4	P DeFazio D 55.5 A Robinson R 39.7 others 4.8	K Schrader D 53.5 C Willis R 43.0 M Sandnes Pac Green 3.4 others 0.2

---

[1] Pacific Green, Oregon affiliate of the Green Party of the United States.

South Dakota Election Results

South Dakota had two House districts from the 1950 through the 1980 elections. In 1950 the dividing line was the Missouri River, with District 1 east of it and District 2 west of it. Because population grew faster in the eastern district, the boundary shifted eastward in 1966 and 1972. Since the 1982 election, South Dakota has had one representative, elected at-large.

	PRESIDENT	GOVERNOR	SENATE	HOUSE DISTRICT 1	HOUSE DISTRICT 2
1950		S Anderson R 60.9 J Robbie D 39.1	Case R 63.9 Engel D 36.1	Lovre R 60.8 Tice D 39.2	Berry R 60.3 Bober D 39.7
1952	Eisenhower 69.3 Stevenson 30.7	S Anderson R 70.2 S Iverson D 29.8		Lovre R 68.4 Wells D 31.6	Berry R 69.0 Bangs D 31.1
1954		J Foss R 56.7 EC Martin D 43.3	Mundt R 57.3 Holum D 42.7	Lovre R 58.0 Dunn D 42.0	Berry R 62.8 Satterlee D 37.2
1956	Eisenhower 58.4 Stevenson 41.6	J Foss R 54.4 R Herseth D 45.6	Case R 50.8 Holum D 49.2	McGovern D 52.4 Lovre R 47.6	Berry R 55.9 Eastman D 44.1
1958		R Herseth D 51.4 P Saunders R 48.6		McGovern D 53.4 Foss R 46.6	Berry R 55.6 McCullen D 44.4
1960	Nixon 58.2 Kennedy 41.8	A Gubbrud R 50.7 R Herseth D 49.3	Mundt R 52.5 McGovern D 47.6	Reifel R 54.8 Fitzgerald D 45.2	Berry R 59.8 Raff D 40.3
1962		A Gubbrud R 56.1 R Herseth D 43.9	McGovern D 127,458 Bottum R 126,861	Reifel R 59.3 Nauman D 40.7	Berry R 61.5 Clarkson D 38.5
1964	Johnson 55.6 Goldwater 44.4	N Boe R 51.7 J Lindley D 48.3		Reifel R 57.6 May D 42.5	Berry R 56.0 Brown D 44.0
1966		N Boe R 57.7 R Chamberlin D 42.3	Mundt R 66.3 Wright D 33.7	Reifel R 66.7 Richter D 33.3	Berry R 60.6 Allmon D 39.5
1968	Nixon 53.3 Humphrey 41.9 Am Ind 4.8	F Farrar R 57.7 R Chamberlin D 42.3	McGovern D 56.8 Gubbrud R 43.2	Reifel R 58.0 Denholm D 42.0	Berry R 59.3 Garner D 40.7
1970		R Kneip D 54.8 F Farrar R 45.2		Denholm D 55.9 Gunderson R 44.0	Abourezk D 52.2 Brady R 47.8
1972	Nixon 54.2 McGovern D 45.5	R Kneip D 60.1 C Thompson R 39.9	Abourezk D 56.0 Hirsch R 42.0	Denholm D 60.5 Vickerman R 39.5	Abdnor R 54.8 McKeever D 45.1
1974		R Kneip D 53.6 J Olson R 46.4	McGovern D 53.0 Thorsness R 47.0	Pressler R 55.3 Denholm D 44.7	Abdnor R 67.8 Weiland D 32.2
1976	Ford 50.4 Carter 48.9 Lib 0.5			Pressler R 79.8 Guffey D 19.4 Stevens ind 0.9	Abdnor R 69.8 Mickelson D 30.2
1978		W Janklow R 57.0 R McKillips D 43.0	Pressler R 66.8 Barnett D 33.2	Daschle D 64,683 Thorsness R 64,544	Abdnor R 56.1 Samuelson D 43.9
1980	Reagan 60.5 Carter 31.7 ind 6.5 Lib 1.2		Abdnor R 58.2 McGovern D 39.4 Peterson ind 2.4	Daschle D 65.8 Kull R 34.2	Roberts R 58.4 Stofferahn D 41.6
				AT-LARGE	
1982		W Janklow R 70.9 M O'Connor D 29.1		Daschle D 51.5 Roberts R 48.4	
1984	Reagan R 63.0 Mondale D 36.5 other 0.4		Pressler R 74.5 Cunningham D 25.5	Daschle D 57.4 Bell R 42.6	
1986		G Mickelson R 51.8 R Herseth D 48.2	Daschle D 51.6 Abdnor R 48.4	Johnson D 59.2 Bell R 40.8	
1988	Bush 52.8 Dukakis 46.5 ind 0.2			Johnson D 71.8 Volk R 28.3	
1990		G Mickelson R 58.9 B Samuelson D 41.1	Pressler R 52.4 Muenster D 45.1 Sinclair ind 2.5	Johnson D 67.5 Frankenfeld R 32.5	
1992	Bush 40.6 Clinton 37.1 Perot 21.8 2 others		Daschle D 64.9 Haar R 32.5 2 others 2.6	Johnson D 69.1 Timmer R 26.9 3 others 4.0	
1994		W Janklow R 65.4 J Beddow D 40.5 Lib 4.1		Johnson D 59.8 Berkhout R 36.6 Wieczorek ind 3.5	
1996	Dole 46.5 Clinton 43.0 Perot 10.0 Lib 0.5		Johnson D 51.3 Pressler R 48.7	Thune R 57.7 Weiland D 36.9 Nelson ind 3.2 Evans ind 2.1	
1998		W Janklow R 64.0 B Huhoff D 32.9	Daschle D 62.2 Schmidt R 36.4 Dale Lib 1.4	Thune R 75.1 Moser D 24.9	
2000	Bush 60.3 Gore 37.6 3 others			Thune R 73.4 Hohn D 24.9 Lerohl Lib 1.7	
2002		M Rounds R 56.8 J Abbott D 41.9 2 others 1.3	Johnson D 49.6 Thune R 49.5 Evans Lib 0.9	Janklow R 53.5 Herseth D 45.6 Begay Lib 0.9	
2004	Bush 59.9 Kerry 38.4 3 others		Thune R 50.6 Daschle D 49.4	Herseth D 53.4 Diedrich R 46.0 Begay Lib 0.7	
2006		M Rounds R 61.7 J Billion D 36.1 2 others 2.2		Herseth D 69.1 Whalen R 29.3 Rudebusch Lib 1.6	
2008	McCain 53.2 Obama 44.7 3 others		Johnson D 62.5 Dykstra R 37.5	Herseth D 67.0 Lien R 32.2	
2010		D Daugaard R 61.5 S Heidepriem D 38.5	Thune R 100	Noem R 48.1 Herseth D 45.9 Marking ind 6.0	
2012	Romney 58 Obama 40			Noem R 57.4 Varilek D 42.6	
2014		D Daugaard R 70.5 S Wismer D 25.4 ind 4.1	Rounds R 50.4 Weiland D 29.5 2 others 20.1	Noem R 66.5 C Robinson D 33.5	
2016	Trump 61.5 Clinton 31.7		Thune R 71.8 Williams 28.2	Noem R 64.1 Hawks D 35.9	

Texas Election Results: President, Governor, Senator

	PRESIDENT	GOVERNOR[1]	SENATE
1950		A Shivers *D* 89.9 R Currie *R* 10.1	
1952	Eisenhower 53.1 Stevenson 46.7 4 others	AShivers *D* 74.6 A Shivers *R* 25.4	P Daniel *D* 100
1954		A Shivers *D* 89.5 T Adams *R* 10.4	LB Johnson *D* 84.6 C Watson *R* 14.9 other 0.4
1956	Eisenhower 55.3 Stevenson 44.0 Con 0.7	P Daniel *D* 78.4 WR Bryant *R* 15.2 P O'Daniel *ind* 6.4	
1958		P Daniel *D* 88.1 E Mayer *R* 11.9	R Yarborough *D* 74.6 R Whittenburg *R* 23.6 other 1.8
1960	Kennedy 50.5 Nixon 48.5 Con 0.8 2 others	P Daniel *D* 72.7 W Steger *R* 27.3	LB Johnson *D* 58.0 J Tower *R* 41.1 B Logan *Con* 0.9 J Tower *R* 50.6[2] W Blakley *D* 49.4
1962		J Connally *D* 54.4 J Cox *R* 45.6	
1964	Johnson 63.3 Goldwater 36.5 Con 0.2	J Connally *D* 73.8 J Crichton *R* 26.0 other 0.2	R Yarborough *D* 56.2 GHW Bush *R* 43.6 Con 0.2
1966		J Connally *D* 72.8 TE Kennerly *R* 25.8 2 others 1.4	J Tower *R* 56.4 W Carr *D* 43.2 other 0.5
1968	Humphrey 41.1 Nixon 39.9 Wallace 19.0	P Smith *D* 57.0 PW Eggers *R* 43.0	
1970		P Smith *D* 53.4 Eggers *R* 46.6	L Bentsen *D* 53.3 GHW Bush *R* 46.6
1972	Nixon 66.2 McGovern 33.3 3 others	D Briscoe *D* 47.9 H Grover *R* 45.0 R Muniz *La Raza* 6.3 others 0.8	J Tower *R* 53.4 B Sanders *D* 44.3 F Amaya *La Raza* 1.9 other 0.5
1974		D Briscoe (4 yr) 61.4 Jim Granberry *R* 31.1 R Muniz *La Raza* 5.6 others 1.9	
1976	Carter 51.1 Ford 48.0 3 others		L Bentsen *D* 56.8 A Steelman *R* 42.2 2 others
1978		B Clements *R* 49.96 J Hill *D* 49.24	J Tower *R* 49.8 R Krueger *D* 49.3 L Diaz de Leon *La Raza* 0.8 M Pendas *SWP* 0.2
1980	Reagan 55.3 Carter 41.4 *ind* 2.5 *Lib* 0.8		
1982		M White *D* 53.2 Clements *R* 45.9	L Bentsen *D* 58.6 J Collins *R* 40.5 2 others 0.9
1984	Reagan 61.9 Mondale 36.1 *ind* 0.3		P Gramm *R* 58.5 L Doggett *D* 41.4
1986		B Clements *R* 52.7 M White *D* 46.1 *Lib* + other 1.3	
1988	Bush 56.0 Dukakis 43.3 2 others		L Bentsen *D* 59.2 B Boulter *R* 40.0 J Daiell *Lib* 0.8
1990		A Richards *D* 49.5 C Williams *R* 46.9 J Daiell *Lib* 3.3 write-in 0.3	P Gramm *R* 60.2 H Parmer *D* 37.4 G Johnson *Lib* 2.3
1992	Bush 40.6 Clinton 37.1 Perot 22.0 other		
1994		GW Bush *R* 53.5 A Richards *D* 45.9 *Lib* 0.6	KB Hutchinson *R* 60.8 R Fisher *D* 38.3 *Lib* 0.8
1996	Dole 48.8 Clinton 43.8 Reform 6.7 3 others		P Gramm *R* 54.8 V Morales *D* 43.9 2 others 1.3
1998		GW Bush *R* 68.2 G Mauro *D* 31.2 others 0.6	
2000	Bush 59.3 Gore 38.0 Nader 2.2 2 others		KB Hutchinson *R* 65.1 G Kelly *D* 32.3 2 others 2.6
2002		R Perry *R* 57.8 T Sanchez *D* 40.0 others 2.2	J Cornyn *R* 55.3 R Kirk *D* 43.3 3 others 1.4
2004	Bush 61.1 Kerry 38.2 other		
2006		R Perry *R* 39.0 C Bell *D* 29.8 C Strayhorn *ind* 18.1 K Friedman *ind* 12.4 others 0.6	KB Hutchinson *R* 61.7 B Radnofsky *D* 36.0 S Jameson *Lib* 2.3
2008	McCain 55.5 Obama 43.7 2 others		J Cornyn *R* 54.8 R Noriega *D* 42.8 Y Schick *Lib* 2.3
2010		R Perry *R* 55.0 B White *D* 42.3 others 2.7	
2012	Romney 58.0 Obama 42.0		T Cruz *R* 56.9 P Sadler *D* 41.0 *Lib* 2.1
2014		G Abbott *R* 59.2 W Davis *D* 38.8	J Cornyn *R* 61.6 D Alameel *D* 34.4
2016	Trump 52.2 Clinton 43.2 3 others 4.6		

[1] Standard sources augmented by the Texas State Historical Society online *Texas Almanac*.   [2] 1961 special election.

Texas Election Results for the U.S. House of Representatives, Districts 1–4

In 1950, Texas had twenty-one seats in the U.S. House of Representatives. Because its population has increased at a faster rate than the whole country, it has added seats after every census since then. From 1952 through 1960 it had twenty-two; 1962–70, twenty-three; 1972–80, twenty-four; 1982–90, twenty-seven; 1992–2000, thirty; 2002–10, thirty-two; and 2012–20, thirty-six. Inevitably this has meant that district numbers have shifted. The lowest numbers have always been in the northeast of the state and along its eastern border. Districts with numbers in the teens have usually been assigned to the Panhandle, El Paso, and other western areas. Numbers in the 20s and 30s have usually been attached to Houston, Dallas, and other metropolitan areas, where population has grown fastest.

Through the 1950s and 1960s, Districts 1 through 4 were those along the Red River and the entire eastern border south to the Gulf of Mexico. Redistricting in 1967, which remained in place through the 1970s, removed the Gulf coast from District 2 but assigned District 3 to part of Dallas. In the 1980s, Districts 1 and 2 remained along the Arkansas and Louisiana border, District 3 remained around Dallas, but District 4 no longer touched the Red River but included several counties east of Dallas and west of District 1. In the 1990s and 2000s, District 4 abutted the Red River again and the first three were not much changed. Changes in 2012 moved District 1 south of the river but still along the eastern border, District 2 now became part of the Gulf coast including Port Arthur, District 3 remained much the same; and District 4 included the northeast corner of the state.

The second column gives the statewide total percentage vote for Democrats and Republicans, the number of districts contested, and how many each major party won. For example, the 1950 election produced 90.5 percent of votes for Democratic candidates and 9.5 for Republicans. Of the twenty-one districts contested, Democrats won twenty-one, Republicans none.

	STATE SPLIT	DISTRICT 1	DISTRICT 2	DISTRICT 3	DISTRICT 4
1950	90.5D, 9.5R (21) 21D	Patman D 100	Combs D 100	Beckworth D 91.5 Kennedy R 8.5	Rayburn D 100
1952	98.7D, 1.3R (22) 22D	Patman D 100	Brooks D 79.0 Reed R 21.0	Gentry D 100	Rayburn D 100
1954	87.0D, 12.9R 21D, 1R	Patman D 100	Brooks D 100	Gentry D 100	Rayburn D 100
1956	85.8D, 14.0R 21D, 1R	Patman D 100	Brooks D 100	Beckworth D 83.5 Kennedy R 16.5	Rayburn D 100
1958	87.6D, 11.9R 21D, 1R	Patman D 100	Brooks D 100	Beckworth D 100	Rayburn D 100
1960	82.4D, 14.6R 20D, 2R	Patman D 100	Brooks D 69.7 Naumann R 29.9 other 0.4	Beckworth D 100	Rayburn D 100
1962	67.4D, 32.6R (23) 21D, 2R	Patman D 67.4 Timberlake R 32.6	Brooks D 68.7 James R 31.3	Beckworth D 52.0 Steger R 48.0	Roberts D 72.0 Harrington R 28.0
1964	68.7D, 31.3R 23D	Patman D 74.5 Jones R 25.5	Brooks D 52.7 Greco R 37.3	Beckworth D 59.3 Warren R 40.7	Roberts D 81.4 Benfield R 18.6
1966	82.4D, 16.4R 21D, 2R	Patman D 100	Dowdy D 100	Pool D 53.4 Collins R 46.6	Roberts D 100
1968	71.8D, 28.2R 20D, 3R	Patman D 100	Dowdy D 100	Collins R 59.4 Hughes D 40.6	Roberts D 100
1970	73.0D, 26.0R 20D, 3R	Patman D 78.5 Hogan R 21.5	Dowdy D 100	Collins D 60.6 Mead D 39.4	Roberts D 100
1972	70.4D, 28.9R (24) 20D, 4R	Patman D 100	Wilson D 73.8 Brightwell R 26.2	Collins R 73.3 Hughes D 26.7	Roberts D 70.3 Russell R 29.7
1974	72.2D, 27.3R 21D, 3R	Patman D 68.6 Farris R 31.4	Wilson D 100	Collins R 64.7 Collum D 35.3	Roberts D 74.9 LeTourneau R 25.1
1976	64.7D, 34.9R 22D, 2R	S Hall D 83.7 Hogan R 16.3	Wilson D 95.0 other 5.0	Collins R 74.0 Shackelford D 26.0	Roberts D 72.7 Glenn R 37.3
1978	58.9D, 40.8R 20D, 4R	S Hall D 78.1 Hudson R 21.9	Wilson D 70.1 Dillion R 30.0	Collins R 100	Roberts D 61.4 Glenn R 38.6
1980	59.1D, 39.5R 19D, 5R	S Hall D 100	Wilson D 69.3 Pannill R 29.5 Lib 1.2	Collins R 79.3 Porter D 18.0 Lib 2.7	R Hall D 52.3 Wright R 47.7
1982	64.8D, 32.8R (27) 22D, 5R	S Hall D 97.5 Lib 2.5	Wilson D 94.3 Lib 5.7	Bartlett R 77.1 McNees D 21.8	R Hall D 73.8 Collomb R 25.3
1984	57.6D, 42.3R 17D, 10R	Hall D 100	Wilson D 59.2 Dugas R 40.7	Bartlett R 83.0 Westbrook D 17.0	R Hall D 57.9 Blow R 42.1
1986	57.0D, 42.0R 17D, 10R	Chapman D 100	Wilson D 56.7 Gordon R 40.5	Bartlett R 94.1 2 others 5.9	R Hall D 71.6 Blow R 28.5
1988	58.6D, 39.3R 19D, 8R	Chapman D 62.3 McQueen R 37.8	Wilson D 87.7 Lib 12.3	Bartlett R 81.8 Cowden D 18.2	R Hall D 66.4 Sutton R 32.1 Lib 1.5
1990	53.8, 45.7R 19D, 8R	Chapman D 61.0 Hodges R 39.0	Wilson D 55.6 Peterson R 44.5	Bartlett R 100	R Hall D 100
1992	49.9D, 47.8R (30) 21D, 9R	Chapman D 100	Wilson D 56.1 Peterson R 43.6	Johnson R 86.1 Donahue Lib 9.0	R Hall D 58.1 Bridges R 39.8
1994	55.7D, 42.1R 19D, 11R	Chapman D 55.3 Blankenship R 40.9	Wilson D 57.0 Peterson R 43.0	Johnson R 91.0 Donahue Lib 9.0	R Hall D 58.8 Bridges R 39.8
1996	44.8D, 52.9R 17D, 13R	Sandlin D 51.6 Merritt R 46.7 Palms NLP 1.7	Turner D 52.2 Babin R 45.6 3 others 2.1	Johnson R 73.0 Cole D 24.5 2 others 2.6	R Hall D 63.8 J Hall R 34.3
1998	44.2D, 51.6R 17D, 13R	Sandlin D 59.4 Boerner R 40.6	Turner D 58.5 Babin R 40.8 Lib 0.8	Johnson R 91.2 Lib 8.8	R Hall D 57.6 Lohmeyer R 40.9 Lib 1.5
2000	46.8D, 49.0R 17D, 13R	Sandlin D 55.8 Willingham R 43.4 Lib 0.8	Turner D 91.1 Lib 8.9	Johnson R 71.6 Zachary D 25.7 Lib 2.7	R Hall D 60.3 Newton R 37.9 Lib 1.8
2002	39.0D, 57.7R (32) 17D, 15R	Sandlin D 56.5 Lawrence R 43.6	Turner D 60.8 Brookshire R 38.2 Lib 1.0	Johnson R 74.0 Molera D 24.3 Lib 1.7	R Hall D 57.8 Graves R 40.3
2004	39.0D, 57.7R 11D, 21R	Gohmert R 61.5 Sandlin D 37.7	Poe R 55.5 Lampson D 42.9	Johnson R 85.6 ind 8.1	R Hall R 68.2 Nickerson D 30.4
2006	44.5D, 50.9R 13D, 19R	Gohmert R 68.0 Owen D 30.2 Lib 1.7	Poe R 65.6 Binderim D 32.7 Lib 1.7	Johnson R 62.5 Dodd D 34.9 Lib 2.6	R Hall R 64.4 Melancon D 33.5
2008	39.6D, 55.8R 13D, 19R	Gohmert R 87.6 Owen ind 12.4	Poe R 88.9 Wolfe Lib 11.1	Johnson R 59.7 Daley D 38.0 Lib 2.2	R Hall R 68.8 Melancon D 29.3 Lib 1.9
2010	30.6D, 64.4R 9D, 23R	Gohmert R 89.7 Lib 10.3	Poe R 88.6 Lib 11.4	Johnson R 66.3 Lingenfelder D 31.3 others 2.4	R Hall R 73.2 Hathcox D 22.0 2 others 4.8
2012	38.5D, 57.8R (36) 12D, 24R	Gohmert R 71.4 McKellar D 26.9 Lib 1.6	Poe R 64.8 Dougherty D 32.7 2 others 2.5	Johnson R 100	R Hall R 73.0 Hathcox D 24.1 2 others 3.0
2014	33.1D, 60.3R 11D, 25R	Gohmert R 77.5 McKellar D 22.5	Poe R 67.9 Letsos D 29.6 2 others 2.4	Johnson R 82.0 Blair Green 18.0	Ratcliffe R 100
2016	37.1D, 57.2R 11D, 25R	Gohmert R 73.9 McKellar D 24.1 other 2.0	Poe R 60.6 Bryan R 36.0 2 others 3.3	Johnson R 61.2 Bell D 34.6 2 others 4.2	Ratcliffe R 88.0 Wommack D 12.0

Texas Elections to the U.S. House, Districts 5–8

From 1950 through 1970, District 5 included Dallas County, which elected Republican Bruce Alger from 1954 through 1962. District 6 ran south of Dallas County to Bryan in Brazos County. District 7 included Lufkin and Nacogdoches, east of District 6 and west of Districts 2 and 3; in 1965 the number was reassigned to the west side of Houston and suburbs, electing George H. W. Bush and then Bill Archer. District 8 was the north half of Harris County and the city of Houston. From 1972 through 1990, District 5 included only the south part of Dallas County; District 6 lost two counties but now included Waxahatchie, College Station, and some Fort Worth suburbs; Districts 7 and 8 now included the west and northeast sides of Houston. Some shrinkage affected these four districts during 1992–2000. From 2002 onward, District 5 has included east and southeast Dallas County and ten counties to the southeast; District 6 has included most of Arlington and the southern edge of Fort Worth; and Districts 7 and 8 continue to cover the west and northeast sides of Houston.

	DISTRICT 5	DISTRICT 6	DISTRICT 7	DISTRICT 8
1950	JF Wilson D 100	Teague D 98.1 Blumrosen R 1.9	Pickett D 100	A Thomas D 77.8 Hanna R 22.2
1952	Wilson D 100	Teague D 100	Dowdy D 100	Thomas D 100
1954	B Alger R 52.9 Savage D 47.1	Teague D 100	Dowdy D 100	Thomas D 62.1 Buttler R 37.4 other 0.5
1956	Alger R 55.6 Wade D 44.4	Teague D 100	Dowdy D 100	Thomas D 60.4 Friloux R 38.0 Miller Con 1.6
1958	Alger R 52.6 Sanders D 47.4	Teague D 100	Dowdy D 99+	Thomas D 88.1 Nesmith R 11.9
1960	Alger R 57.3 Pool D 42.7	Teague D 100	Dowdy D 100	Thomas D 68.6 Farris R 21.9 Nesmith Con 9.6
1962	Alger R 56.3 B Jones D 43.7	Teague D 100	Dowdy D 88.3 Ramage R 11.7	Thomas D 71.4 Farris R 28.6
1964	E Cabell D 57.5 Alger R 42.5	Teague D 82.2 VanWinkle R 17.8	Dowdy D 83.7 Orr R 16.3	Thomas D 76.8 Gilbert R 23.3
1966	Cabell D 61.0 Burgess R 39.0	Teague D 100	GHW Bush R 57.1 Briscoe D 42.4 Con 0.5	Eckhardt D 92.3 Con 7.7
1968	Cabell D 61.4 Wagoner R 38.6	Teague D 100	Bush R 100	Eckhardt D 70.6 Stevens R 29.4
1970	Cabell D 59.8 Crowley R 40.3	Teague D 100	W Archer R 64.8 Greenwood D 35.2	Eckhardt D 100
1972	Steelman R 55.7 Cabell D 44.3	Teague D 72.6 Nigliazzo R 27.4	Archer R 82.3 Brady D 17.7	Eckhardt D 64.6 Emerich R 34.7 Other 0.7
1974	Steelman R 52.0 McKool D 48.0	Teague D 82.9 Nigliazzo R 17.0	Archer R 79.2 Brady D 20.8	Eckhardt D 72.2 Whitefield R 27.8
1976	Mattox D 54.0 Judy R 44.6 Am Ind 1.5	Teague D 65.9 Mowery R 33.4 other 0.7	Archer R 100	Eckhardt D 60.6 Gearhart R 39.2 other 0.1
1978	Mattox D 50.3 Pauken R 49.2 other 0.6	Gramm D 65.1 Mowery R 34.9	Archer R 85.1 Hutchings D 14.9	Eckhardt D 61.5 Gearhart R 38.5
1980	Mattox D 51.0 Pauken R 48.8 other 0.2	Gramm D 70.9 Haskins R 29.1	Archer R 82.1 Hutchings D 16.4 Lib 1.4	Fields R 51.8 Eckhardt D 48.2
1982	Bryant D 64.8 Devany R 33.7 2 others 1.5	Gramm D 94.5 Lib 5.5	Archer R 85.0 Scoggins D 14.0	Fields R 56.7 Allee D 42.6 Lib 0.6
1984	Bryant D 100	Barton R 56.6 Kubiak D 43.4	Archer R 86.7 Willibey D 13.3	Fields R 64.5 Buford D 35.5
1986	Bryant D 58.5 Carter R 40.7 Lib 0.8	Barton R 55.8 Geren D 44.2	Archer R 87.4 Kniffen D 11.9 Lib 0.7	Fields R 68.4 Mann D 31.6
1988	Bryant D 60.8 Williams R 38.2	Barton R 67.6 Kendrick D 32.4	Archer R 79.1 Richards D 20.9	Fields R 100
1990	Bryant D 59.5 Rucker R 37.7 Lib 2.7	Barton R 66.5 Welch D 33.1 write-in 0.4	Archer R 100	Fields R 100
1992	Bryant D 58.9 Stokley R 37.3 Lib 3.8	Barton R 71.9 Dietrich D 28.1	Archer R 100	Fields R 77.0 Robinson D 23.0
1994	Bryant D 50.0 P Sessions R 47.3 others 2.6	Barton R 75.6 Jesmore D 22.0 Lib 2.3	Archer R 100	Fields R 92.1 ind 7.9
1996	Sessions R 53.1 Pouland D 46.9	Barton R 77.1 Richardson ind 12.8 Anderson Lib 7.0	Archer R 81.4 Siegmund D 15.1 2 ind 3.5	Brady R 41.5 Fontenot R 38.9 Newman D 13.6 Musemeche D 6.0
1998	Sessions R 55.7 Morales D 43.5 Lib 1.8	Barton R 73.0 Boothe D 25.9 Lib 1.2	Archer R 93.4 Lib 6.6	Brady R 92.9 Lib 7.2
2000	Sessions R 54.0 Coggins D 44.4 Lib 1.5	Barton R 88.1 Lib 11.9	Culberson R 73.9 Sell D 24.4 Lib 1.7	Brady R 91.6 Lib 8.4
2002	Hensarling R 58.2 Chapman D 40.2 others 1.5	Barton R 70.4 Alvarado D 27.7 2 others 2.0	Culberson R 89.2 Lib + other 10.8	Brady R 93.2 Lib 6.9
2004	Hensarling R 64.5 Bernstein D 32.9 Lib 2.7	Barton R 66.0 Meyer D 32.7 Lib 1.3	Culberson R 64.1 Martinez D 33.3 Lib + ind 2.6	Brady R 68.9 Wright D 29.7 Lib 1.4
2006	Hensarling R 61.8 Thompson D 35.6 Lib 2.6	Barton R 60.5 Harris D 37.1 Lib 2.5	Culberson R 59.2 Henley D 38.4 Lib 2.4	Brady R 67.3 Wright D 32.7
2008	Hensarling R 83.6 Lib 16.4	Barton R 62.0 Otto D 35.6 Lib 2.4	Culberson R 55.9 Skelly D 42.4 Lib 1.7	Brady R 72.5 Hargett D 24.8 Lib 2.7
2010	Hensarling R 70.5 Berry D 27.5 Lib 2.0	Barton R 65.9 Cozad D 31.2 Lib 2.9	Culberson R 81.5 Lib + write-ins 18.6	Brady R 80.3 Hargett D 17.3 Lib 2.5
2012	Hensarling R 64.4 Mrosko D 33.2 Lib 2.4	Barton R 58.0 Sanders D 39.2 Lib + Green 2.7	Culberson R 60.8 Cargas D 36.4 Lib + Green 2.8	Brady R 77.3 Burns D 20.3 Lib 2.4
2014	Hensarling R 85.4 Ashby Lib 14.6	Barton R 61.1 Cozad D 36.4 Lib 2.4	Culberson R 63.3 Cargas D 34.5 Lib 2.2	Brady R 89.3 Perry Lib 10.7
2016	Hensarling R 80.6 Ashby Lib 19.4	Barton R 58.3 Woolridge D 39.0 Green 2.6	Culberson R 56.2 Cargas D 44 43.8	Brady R 100

Texas Elections to the U.S. House, Districts 9–12

From 1950 through 1970, District 9 covered the Gulf coast from Galveston to Victoria and inland; District 10 included Austin, the Hill Country, and some counties eastward; District 11 ran between District 6 and Austin and included Waco and Temple; and District 12 was Tarrant County (Fort Worth). From 1972 through 2004, District 9 ran northeast of Houston and included the eastern Gulf coast (Galveston, Port Arthur, Texas City, Beaumont); the other three districts had some small changes. The DeLay redistricting, effective 2006, resulted in District 9 becoming southwest Houston, District 10 taking in only the north suburban part of Travis County (Austin) and running eastward to northwest Harris (Houston), District 11 moving westward to include Odessa, Midland, and much of the Hill Country, and District 12 becoming the western part of Fort Worth and two suburban counties.

	DISTRICT 9	DISTRICT 10	DISTRICT 11	DISTRICT 12
1950	Thompson D 100	Thornberry D 100	Poage D 100	Lucas D 80.6 Neely R 19.4
1952	Thompson D 100	Thornberry D 100	Poage D 100	Lucas D 100
1954	Thompson D 100	Thornberry D 100	Poage D 100	Wright D 100
1956	Thompson D 100	Thornberry D 100	Poage D 100	Wright D 100
1958	Thompson D 100	Thornberry D 100	Poage D 100	Wright D 100
1960	Thompson D 94.1 Rogers Con 6.0	Thornberry D 98.2 Brown Con 1.9	Poage D 100	Wright D 100
1962	Thompson D 66.3 Oaks R 33.7	Thornberry D 63.3 Dobbs R 36.7	Poage D 100	Wright D 60.6 Barron R 39.4
1964	Thompson D 75.3 Oakes R 24.8	Pickle D 75.8 Pratt R 24.2	Poage D 81.5 Isenhower R 18.5	Wright D 68.5 Dielman R 31.5
1966	J Brooks D 100	Pickle D 74.3 Sumner R 24.5 Con 1.1	Poage D 94.9 Dunn conserv 5.1	Wright D 100
1968	Brooks D 60.5 Pressler R 39.4	Pickle D 62.0 Gabler R 37.9	Poage D 96.5 Dunn R 3.5	Wright D 100
1970	Brooks D 64.5 Pressler R 35.5	Pickle D 100	Poage D 100	Wright D 100
1972	Brooks D 66.2 Reed R 33.8	Pickle D 91.2 SWP 8.8	Poage D 100	Wright D 100
1974	Brooks D 62.0 Ferguson R 38.0	Pickle D 80.4 Weiss R 19.6	Poage D 81.6 Clements R 17.2 ind 1.1	Wright D 78.7 Garvey R 21.3
1976	Brooks D 100	Pickle D 76.8 McClure R 23.2	Poage D 57.4 Burgess R 42.6	Wright D 75.8 Durham R 23.8 Am Ind 0.4
1978	Brooks D 63.3 Evans R 36.7	Pickle D 76.3 Hudspeth R 23.6	Leath D 51.7 Burgess R 48.4	Wright D 68.5 Brown R 31.5
1980	Brooks D 100	Pickle D 59.1 Biggar R 38.8 Lib 2.1	Leath D 100	Wright D 59.9 Bradshaw R 39.3 Lib 0.7
1982	Brooks D 67.6 Lewis R 30.3 Lib 2.1	Pickle D 90.1 2 others 9.9	Leath D 96.3 others 3.7	Wright D 68.9 Ryan R 30.5 Lib 0.6
1984	Brooks D 58.9 Mahan R 41.1	Pickle D 100	Leath D 100	Wright D 100
1986	Brooks D 61.5 Duperier R 38.5	Pickle D 72.3 Rylander R 27.7	Leath D 100	Wright D 68.7 McNeil R 31.3
1988	Brooks D 100	Pickle D 93.4 Lib 6.6	Leath D 95.4 Lib 4.6	Wright D 100
1990	Brooks D 57.7 Meyers R 42.3	Pickle D 64.9 Beilharz R 31.3 Lib 3.8	Edwards D 53.4 Shine R 46.6	Geren D 71.3 McGinn R 28.7
1992	Brooks D 53.6 Stockman R 43.5 Lib 2.9	Pickle D 67.7 Spiro R 26.2 2 others + write-ins 6.1	Edwards D 67.4 Broyles R 32.6	Geren D 62.8 Hobbs R 37.2
1994	Stockman R 51.9 Brooks D 45.7 others 2.4	L Doggett D 56.3 Baylor R 39.8 3 others 3.9	Edwards D 59.2 Broyles R 40.8	Geren D 68.7 Anderson R 31.4
1996	Lampson D 52.8 Stockman R 47.2	L Doggett D 56.2 T Doggett R 41.4 ind + Lib 2.4	Edwards D 56.8 Mathis R 42.4 NLP 0.8	Granger R 57.8 Parmer D 41.1
1998	Lampson D 63.7 Cottar R 36.3	L Doggett D 85.2 Lib 14.8	Edwards D 82.4 Lib 17.6	Granger R 61.9 Hall D 36.3
2000	Lampson D 59.2 Williams R 39.7 Lib 1.1	L Doggett D 84.6 Lib 15.4	Edwards D 54.8 Farley R 44.3 Lib 0.8	Granger R 100
2002	Lampson D 58.6 Williams R 40.3 Lib 1.1	L Doggett D 84.4 Lib 15.6	Edwards D 51.6 Farley R 47.1 Lib 1.3	Granger R 91.9 Lib 8.1
2004	A Green D 72.2 Molina R 26.6 Lib 1.2	McCaul R 78.6 Fritsche Lib 15.4 write-in 6.0	Conway R 76.8 Raasch R 21.8 Lib 1.4	Granger R 72.3 Alvarado D 27.7
2006	A Green D 100	McCaul R 55.3 Ankrum D 40.4 Lib 4.3	Conaway R 100	Granger R 67.0 Morris D 31.1 Lib 2.0
2008	A Green D 93.7 Lib 6.4	McCaul R 53.9 Doherty D 43.1 Lib 3.0	Conaway R 100	Granger R 67.6 Smith D 30.6 Lib 1.8
2010	A Green D 75.7 Mueller R 22.9 Lib 1.4	McCaul R 64.7 Ankrum D 33.1 Lib 2.3	Conaway R 80.8 Quillian D 15.4 Lib + Green 3.7	Granger R 71.9 Smith D 25.1 Lib 3.0
2012	A Green D 78.5 Mueller R 19.7 Lib + Green 1.8	McCaul R 60.5 Cadien D 36.3 Lib 3.2	Conaway R 78.6 Riley D 18.6 Lib 2.8	Granger R 70.9 Robinson D 26.7 Lib 2.4
2014	A Green D 90.8 Lib 9.2	McCaul R 62.2 Walter-Cadien D 34.1 Lib 3.7	Conaway R 90.3 Lange Lib 9.7	Granger R 71.3 Greene D 26.3 Lib 2.4
2016	A Green D 80.6 Martin R 19.4	McCaul R 57.3 Cadien D 38.4 Lib 4.2	Conaway R 89.5 Landholt Lib 10.5	Granger R 69.4 Bradshaw D 26.9 Lib 3.7

Texas Elections to the U.S. House, Districts 13–16

During the 1950s and 1960s, District 13 included Red River counties west of District 4 and Wichita Falls. District 14 was Corpus Christi and inland counties to the north and south. District 15 included border counties from Maverick through Webb (Laredo) and Cameron (Brownsville). District 16 covered the southwest, Odessa to El Paso. Through the 1970s and 1980s, District 13 ran from Wichita Falls through Amarillo and included much of the Panhandle; District 14 remained at Corpus Christi, included Victoria, but lost some inland counties; District 15 lost Laredo and other territory but kept Zapata through Cameron (Brownsville, Harlingen) and McAllen; District 16 was the westernmost district, keeping El Paso but losing Odessa and Midland. Changes thereafter were relatively minor, except for District 14, which lost Corpus Christi and centered on Brazoria and Galveston, south of Houston.

	DISTRICT 13	DISTRICT 14	DISTRICT 15	DISTRICT 16
1950	Gossett D 100	Lyle D 100	Bentsen D 100	Regan D 100
1952	Ikard D 100	Lyle D 100	Bentsen D 100	Regan D 100
1954	Ikard D 100	Bell D 93.8 DeWitt R 6.2	J Kilgore D 100	Rutherford D 100
1956	Ikard D 100	Young D 87.3 Stichter R 12.7	Kilgore D 100	Rutherford D 64.6 Gibson R 35.4
1958	Ikard D 100	Young D 100	Kilgore D 100	Rutherford D 100
1960	Ikard D 100	Young D 100	Kilgore D 100	Rutherford D 58.9 Chapman R 18.0 Con 23.1
1962	Purcell D 67.1 Meissner R 32.9	Young D 70.4 Hoover R 29.6	Kilgore D 100	Foreman R 53.8 Rutherford D 46.2
1964	Purcell D 75.1 Corse R 24.8	Young D 77.6 Patton R 22.4	de la Garza D 69.4 Coulter R 30.7	White D 55.7
1966	Purcell D 57.0 Norwood R 43.0	Young D 100	de la Garza D 100	Foreman R 44.4 White D 100
1968	Purcell D 55.8 Crowley R 44.2	Young D 100	de la Garza D 100	White D 73.5 Slaughter R 26.5
1970	Purcell D 64.9 Staley R 35.1	Young D 100	de la Garza D 76.2 Martinez R 23.8	White D 82.7 Provencio R 17.3
1972	Price D 54.8 Purcell D 45.2	Young D 100	de la Garza D 100	White D 100
1974	Hightower D 57.6 Price R 42.4	Young D 100	de la Garza D 100	White D 100
1976	Hightower D 59.3 Price R 40.4 Am Ind 0.3	Young D 61.4 Holford R 38.6	de la Garza D 74.3 McDonald R 25.6	White D 57.8 Shackelford R 42.2
1978	Hightower D 74.9 Jones R 25.2	Wyatt D 72.5 Yates R 27.5	de la Garza D 66.3 McDonald R 33.9	White D 70.1 Giere R 29.9
1980	Hightower D 55.0 Slover R 45.0	Patman D 56.8 Conclin R 43.2	de la Garza D 70.0 McDonald R 30.0	White D 84.6 Lib 15.4
1982	Hightower D 63.6 Slover R 35.3	Patman D 60.7 Wyatt R 38.6 Lib 0.7	de la Garza D 95.7 Lib 4.3	Coleman D 53.9 Haggerty R 44.2
1984	Boulter R 53.0 Hightower D 47.0	Sweeney R 51.3 Patman D 48.7	de la Garza D 100	Coleman D 57.4 Hammond R 42.6
1986	Boulter R 64.9 Seal D 35.1	Sweeney R 52.4 Laughlin D 47.7	de la Garza D 100	Coleman D 65.7 Gillis R 34.3
1988	Sarpalius D 52.4 Milner R 47.5	Laughlin D 53.3 Sweeney R 45.9 Lib 0.9	de la Garza D 94.0 Lib 6.1	Coleman D 100
1990	Sarpalius D 56.5 Waterfield R 43.5	Laughlin D 54.4 Dial R 45.7	de la Garza D 100	Coleman D 95.7 write-in 4.4
1992	Sarpalius D 60.3 Boulter R 39.7	Laughlin D 68.1 Garza R 27.2 Vreeland ind 4.7	de la Garza D 60.5 Haughey R 39.5	Coleman D 51.9 Taberski R 48.1
1994	Thornberry R 55.4 Sarpalius D 44.6	Laughlin D 55.6 Deats R 44.4	de la Garza D 58.9 Haughey R 39.4 ind 1.6	Coleman D 57.1 Ortiz R 42.9
1996	Thornberry R 66.9 Silverman D 32.3 NLP 0.8	Paul R 51.1 Morris D 47.6 NLP 1.3	Hinojosa D 62.3 Haughey R 36.7 NLP 1.0	Reyes D 70.7 Ledesma R 27.6 NLP 1.8
1998	Thornberry R 67.9 Harmon D 31.0 Lib 1.1	Paul R 55.3 Sneary D 44.5 write-in 0.3	Hinojosa D 58.4 Haughey R 41.6	Reyes D 87.9 2 others 12.1
2000	Thornberry R 67.6 Clinesmith D 31.1 Lib 1.2	Paul R 59.7 Sneary D 40.3	Hinojosa D 88.5 Lib + write-ins 11.5	Reyes D 68.3 Power R 30.2 Lib 1.5
2002	Thornberry R 79.3 Reese D 20.7	Paul R 68.1 Windham D 31.9	Hinojosa D 100	Reyes D 100
2004	Thornberry R 92.3 Lib 7.7	Paul R 100	Hinojosa D 57.8 Thamm R 40.8 Lib 1.4	Reyes D 67.5 Brigham R 31.1 Lib 1.4
2006	Thornberry R 74.3 Waun D 23.0 Lib 2.6	Paul R 60.2 Sklar D 39.8	Hinojosa D 61.7 Haring R 23.7 Zamora R 14.6	Reyes D 78.6 Strickland R 21.4
2008	Thornberry R 77.7 Waun D 22.3	Paul R 100	Hinojosa D 65.7 Zamora R 31.9 Lib 2.3	Reyes D 82.2 ind + Lib 17.9
2010	Thornberry R 87.1 ind+ Lib 13.0	Paul R 76.0 Pruett D 24.0	Hinojosa D 55.7 Zamora R 41.6 Lib 2.7	Reyes D 58.1 Besco R 36.6 Lib + write-ins 5.3
2012	Thornberry R 91.0 Deek Lib 6.2 Houston Green 2.9	Weber R 53.5 Lampson D 44.6 Lib + Green 1.9	Hinojosa D 60.9 Brueggemann R 36.9 Lib 2.3	O'Rourke D 65.4 Carrasco R 32.9 Lib 1.7
2014	Thornberry R 84.3 Minter D 12.8 Lib + Green 2.9	Weber R 61.9 Brown D 36.1 Lib 2.1	Hinojosa D 54.0 Zamora R 43.3 Lib 2.7	O'Rourke D 67.5 Roen R 29.2 Lib 3.3
2016	Thornberry R 90.0 Lib + Green 10.0	Weber R 61.9 Cole D 38.1	Gonzalez D 57.3 Westley R 37.7 Lib + Green 5.0	O'Rourke D 85.7 Lib + Green 14.3

Texas Elections to the U.S. House, Districts 17–20

From 1950 through 1970, District 17 covered seven counties from just west of Tarrant County (Fort Worth) to the edge of the Panhandle; it included Abilene. District 18 was Amarillo and the northern Panhandle; District 19 was the Staked Plains including Lubbock. District 20 was Bexar County (San Antonio). From 1972 through 1990, most changes in these districts were minor except that the number 18 was reassigned from Amarillo to central Houston, and District 20 was narrowed to central San Antonio, losing the northern part of Bexar County. This configuration largely held through the 1990s. From 2006 the number 17 was given to parts of former District 11, District 18 circled Houston, District 19 remained the Lubbock district but expanded to include Big Spring and Abilene, and District 20 remained central and west-side San Antonio.

	DISTRICT 17	DISTRICT 18	DISTRICT 19	DISTRICT 20
1950	Burleson D 100	Rogers D 52.5 Guill R 47.5	Mahon D 93.9 Temple R 6.1	Kilday D 100
1952	Burleson D 100	Rogers D 100	Mahon D 100	Kilday D 100
1954	Burleson D 100	Rogers D 64.8 LaMaster R 35.2	Mahon D 100	Kilday D 100
1956	Burleson D 100	Rogers D 100	Mahon D 100	Kilday D 100
1958	Burleson D 100	Rogers D 100	Mahon D 100	Kilday D 100
1960	Burleson D 77.8 Mossholder R 22.2	Rogers D 100	Mahon D 85.6 Anderson Con 14.4	Kilday D 100
1962	Burleson D 100	Rogers D 58.8 Seale R 41.2	Mahon D 67.1 Taylor R 32.9	H Gonzalez D 100
1964	Burleson D 76.5 Bridges R 23.5	Rogers D 55.0 Price R 45.0	Mahon D 77.7 Phillips R 22.3	H Gonzalez D 64.6 O'Connell R 35.4
1966	Burleson D 100	Price R 59.5 Miller D 40.5	Mahon D 100	Gonzalez D 87.1 2 others 12.9
1968	Burleson D 100	Price R 65.2 Brown D 34.8	Mahon D 100	H Gonzalez D 81.4 Schneider R 18.6
1970	Burleson D 100	Price R 100	Mahon D 100	H Gonzalez D 100
1972	Burleson D 100	Jordan D 80.6 Merritt R 18.3 SWP 1.2	Mahon D 100	H Gonzalez D 96.9 SWP 3.1
1974	Burleson D 100	Jordan D 84.7 Mitchell R 14.1 SWP 1.2	Mahon D 100	H Gonzalez D 100
1976	Burleson D 100	Jordan D 85.5 Wright R 14.0 SWP 0.5	Mahon D 54.6 Reese R 45.4	H Gonzalez D 100
1978	Stenholm D 68.1 Fisher R 31.8	Leland D 96.8 SWP 3.2	Hance D 53.2 GHW Bush R 46.8	H Gonzalez D 100
1980	Stenholm D 100	Leland D 79.9 Kennedy R 17.9 Lib 2.2	Hance D 93.5 Lib 6.5	H Gonzalez D 81.9 Nash R 17.2 Lib 0.8
1982	Stenholm D 97.1 Lib 2.9	Leland D 82.6 Pickett R 14.7 Lib 2.7	Hance D 81.5 Hicks R 17.4 Lib 1.1	H Gonzalez D 91.5 2 others 8.5
1984	Stenholm D 100	Leland D 78.8 Beaman R 19.0 ind 2.2	Combest R 58.1 Richards D 41.9	H Gonzalez D 100
1986	Stenholm D 100	Leland D 90.2 ind 9.8	Combest R 62.0 McCathern D 38.0	H Gonzales D 100
1988	Stenholm D 100	Leland D 92.9 Lib 7.1	Combest R 67.7 McCathern D 32.3	H Gonzalez D 70.7 Travino R 27.5 Lib 1.8
1990	Stenholm D 100	Washington D 100	Combest R 100	H Gonzalez D 100
1992	Stenholm D 66.1 Sadowski R 33.9	Washington D 64.7 Blum R 32.6 Lib 2.7	Combest R 77.4 Moser D 22.6	H Gonzalez D 100
1994	Stenholm D 53.7 Boone R 46.3	Jackson-Lee D 73.5 Burley R 24.4 2 others 2.1	Combest R 100	H Gonzalez D 62.5 Colyer R 37.5
1996	Stenholm D 51.7 Izzard R 47.4	Jackson-Lee D 77.1 4 others 22.9	Combest R 80.4 Sawyer D 19.6	H Gonzalez D 63.2 Walker R 34.6 Lib 1.3
1998	Stenholm D 53.6 Izzard R 45.3	Jackson-Lee D 89.9 Lib 10.1	Combest R 83.7 Blankenship D 16.4	C Gonzalez D 63.2 Walker R 35.5 Lib 1.3
2000	Stenholm D 59.0 D Clements R 35.5 Lib 5.5	Jackson-Lee D 76.5 Levy R 22.2 Lib 1.4	Combest R 91.6 Lib 8.4	C Gonzalez D 87.7 Lib 12.3
2002	Stenholm D 51.3 Beckham R 47.4 Lib 1.2	Jackson-Lee D 77.0 Abbott R 21.7 Lib 1.4	Combest R 91.6 Johnson Lib 8.4	C Gonzalez D 100
2004	Edwards D 51.2 Wohlgemuth R 47.4 Lib 1.4	Jackson-Lee D 88.9 ind + Lib 11.1	Neugebauer R 58.5 Stenholm D 40.0 Lib 1.5	C Gonzalez D 65.5 Scott R 32.0 Lib + ind 2.5
2006	Edwards D 58.1 Taylor R 40.3 Lib 1.6	Jackson-Lee D 76.6 Hassan R 19.1 Lib 4.3	Neugebauer R 67.7 Ricketts D 29.8 Lib + write-ins 2.5	C Gonzalez D 87.3 Idrogo Lib 12.7
2008	Edwards D 53.0 Curnock R 45.5 Lib 1.5	Jackson-Lee D 77.3 Mendoza R 20.3 Lib 2.3	Neugebauer R 72.4 Fullingim D 24.9 Lib 2.6	C Gonzalez D 71.9 Litoff R 25.2 Lib 2.9
2010	Flores R 61.8 Edwards D 36.6 Lib 1.6	Jackson-Lee D 70.2 Faulk R 27.3 Lib 2.6	Neugebauer R 77.8 Wilson D 19.1	C Gonzalez D 63.6 Trotter R 34.5 Lib 1.9
2012	Flores R 79.9 Easton Lib 20.1	Jackson-Lee D 75.0 Seibert R 22.6 Lib 2.4	Neugebauer R 85.0 Peterson Lib 15.0	Castro D 63.9 Rosa R 33.5 Lib + Green 2.6
2014	Flores R 64.6 Haynes D 32.4 Lib 3.0	Jackson-Lee D 71.8 Seibert R 24.8 ind + Green 3.5	Neugebauer R 77.2 Marchbanks D 18.4 Lib + write-ins 4.5	Castro D 75.7 Blunt Lib 24.3
2016	Flores R 60.8 Matta D 35.2 Lib 4.0	Jackson-Lee D 73.5 Bartley R 23.6 Green 2.9	Arrington R 86.7 Lib + Green 13.3	Castro D 79.7 Lib + Green 20.3

Texas Elections to the U.S. House, Districts 21–24

Ever since 1950, District 21 has been the Hill Country district, varying only marginally in each redistricting. District 22 was first contested in 1958 and has always covered the southern (or nearby) parts of Houston; it was held by Democrat Bob Casey from 1958 through 1974 and by Republicans Ron Paul in 1978, 1980, and 1982 and Tom DeLay from 1984 through 2004. District 23, from its first contest in 1966, has run along the Rio Grande, including Laredo before 2006 and counties to the northwest, nearly to El Paso, since then; it is the largest district in Texas. District 24 began its existence in 1972 to include central and southwest Dallas and westward to part of Fort Worth; from 1978 through 2002 it was won by Democrat Martin Frost, who became a victim of the DeLay redistricting. It has since included parts of Dallas, Tarrant, and Denton Counties.

	DISTRICT 21	DISTRICT 22	DISTRICT 23	DISTRICT 24
1950	Fisher D 100			
1952	Fisher D 100			
1954	Fisher D 100	(at large) Dies D 88.0 Nolan R 12.0		
1956	Fisher D 100	(at large) Dies D 99.1		
1958	Fisher D 100	Casey D 61.7 Kennerly R 32.9 write-in 5.4		
1960	Fisher D 100	Casey D 58.3 Noonan R 39.2 Con 2.5		
1962	Fisher D 76.2 Mayer R 23.8	Casey D 53.5 Baker R 46.5	(at large) Pool D 56.1 Barry R 43.9	
1964	Fisher D 78.1 Claypool R 21.9	Casey D 58.1 Barry R 41.9	(at large) Pool D 66.9 Hayes R 32.7 Con 0.4	
1966	Fisher D 100	Casey D 100	Kazen D 96.4 Con 3.6	
1968	Fisher D 60.8 Alexander R 39.2	Casey D 62.3 Blaney R 37.7	Kazen D 100	
1970	Fisher D 61.3 Gill R 38.7	Casey D 55.6 Busch R 44.4	Kazen D 100	
1972	Fisher D 56.8 Harlan R 43.2	Casey D 70.2 Griffin R 29.0 Am Ind 0.8	Kazen D 100	Milford D 65.1 C Roberts R 34.9
1974	Krueger D 52.6 Harlan R 45.2 others 2.2	Casey D 69.6 Paul R 28.4	Kazen D 100	Milford D 76.1 Beaman R 20.4 Am Ind 3.5
1976	Krueger D 71.0 Locke R 26.7 others 2.2	Gammage D 96,535 Paul R 96,267	Kazen D 100	Milford D 63.4 Berman R 36.1 Am Ind 0.5
1978	Loeffler R 57.0 Wolff D 43.0	Paul R 50.5 Gammage D 49.4	Kazen D 89.7 Mata La Raza 10.3	Frost D 54.1 Berman R 45.9
1980	Loeffler R 76.5 Sullivan D 22.8 Lib 0.7	Paul R 51.0 Andrews D 48.3 ind 0.6	Kazen D 69.8 Locke R 30.1	Frost D 61.3 Smothers R 38.7
1982	Loeffler R 74.5 Stough D 24.6	Paul R 100	Kazen D 55.3 Wentworth R 44.3 Lib 0.5	Frost D 72.9 Patterson R 26.0
1984	Loeffler R 80.6 Sullivan D 19.4	DeLay R 65.3 Williams D 34.7	Bustamante D 100	Frost D 59.5 Burk R 40.5
1986	L Smith R 60.6 Snelson D 38.5 Lib 0.9	DeLay R 71.8 Director D 28.3	Bustamante D 90.7 Lib 9.3	Frost D 67.2 Burk R 32.8
1988	L Smith R 93.2 Lib 6.8	DeLay R 67.4 Walker D 31.4 Lib 1.2	Bustamante D 64.5 Gonzales R 33.6 Lib 1.8	Frost D 92.6 Lib 7.4
1990	L Smith R 74.8 K Roberts D 25.2	DeLay R 71.2 Director D 28.8	Bustamante D 63.5 J Gonzales R 36.6	Frost D 100
1992	L Smith R 72.2 Gaddy D 23.7 Lib 4.1	DeLay R 68.9 Konrad D 31.1	Bonilla R 59.1 Bustamante D 38.4 Lib 2.6	Frost D 59.8 Masterson R 40.2
1994	L Smith R 90.0 ind 10.0	DeLay R 73.8 Cunningham D 23.8 ind 2.5	Bonilla R 62.6 Rios D 37.4	Frost D 52.8 Harrison R 47.2
1996	L Smith R 76.4 Wharton D 22.4 NLP 2.2	DeLay R 68.1 Cunningham D 31.9	Bonilla R 61.8 CP Jones D 36.4 NLP 1.8	Frost D 55.7 Harrison R 39.1 2 others 5.2
1998	L Smith R 91.4 Lib 8.6	DeLay R 65.2 Kemp D 33.7	Bonilla R 63.8 C Jones D 35.1	Frost D 57.4 Terry R 40.9 2 others 1.6
2000	L Smith R 75.9 Green D 22.2 Lib 2.0	DeLay R 60.4 Matranga D 36.1 2 others 3.5	Bonilla R 59.3 Garza D 38.8 Lib 1.9	Frost D 61.8 Wright R 36.7 write-in 1.5
2002	L Smith R 72.9 Courage D 25.3 Lib 1.8	DeLay R 63.2 Riley D 35.0 2 others 1.8	Bonilla R 51.5 Cuellar D 47.2 2 others 1.3	Frost D 64.7 Ortega R 33.9 Lib 1.4
2004	L Smith R 61.5 R Smith D 35.5	DeLay R 55.2 Morrison D 41.1 2 others 3.7	Bonilla R 69.2 Sullivan D 29.4 Lib 1.3	Marchant R 64.0 Page D 34.2 Lib 1.8
2006	L Smith R 60.1 Courage D 24.5 5 others 15.4	Lampson D 51.8 Gibbs write-in 41.8 3 others 5.4	Rodriguez D 54.3 Bonilla R 45.7	Marchant R 59.8 Page D 37.2 Lib 3.0
2008	L Smith R 80.0 Stohm Lib 20.0	Olson R 52.4 Lampson D 45.4 Lib 2.2	Rodriguez D 55.8 Larson R 41.9 Lib 2.3	Marchant R 56.0 Love D 41.1
2010	L Smith R 68.9 Melnick D 27.9 Lib 3.3	Olson R 67.5 Rogers D 29.8 Lib 2.7	Canseco R 49.4 Rodriguez D 44.4 3 others 6.2	Marchant R 81.6 Lib 18.4
2012	L Smith R 60.5 Duval D 35.4 Lib 4.1	Olson R 64.0 Rogers D 32.0 2 others 4.0	Gallego D 50.3 Canseco R 45.6 2 others 4.1	Marchant R 61.0 Rusk D 36.0 Lib 3.0
2014	L Smith R 71.8 Shields Lib 13.5 Diaz Green 14.7	Olson R 66.5 Briscoe D 31.6 Lib 1.9	Hurd R 49.8 Gallego D 47.7 Lib 2.5	Marchant R 65.0 McGehearty D 32.3 Lib 2.6
2016	L Smith R 57.0 Wakely D 36.4 2 others 6.5	Olson R 59.5 Gibson D 40.5	Hurd R 48.3 Gallego D 47.0 Lib 4.7	Marchant R 56.2 McDowell D 39.3 2 others 4.5

Texas Elections to the U.S. House, Districts 25–28

New in 1982, District 25 covered Pasadena, the Ship Channel, and southern Harris County, but after the 2003–6 redistricting the number shifted to parts of Austin plus Hayes, Bastrop, and five other counties southward. District 26 also began with the 1982 election and has included most of Denton County and some adjacent areas. District 27 was the southern Gulf coast from just north of Corpus Christi to the border from 1982 until 2012, when it was changed to run northward along the coast, rather than southward. District 28 was first contested in 1992 and has run from Laredo on the border northward to Bexar County.

	DISTRICT 25	DISTRICT 26	DISTRICT 27	DISTRICT 28
1982	Andrews D 60.4 Faubion R 37.9 2 others 1.7	Vandergriff D 69,782 Bradshaw R 69,438	Ortiz D 64.0 Luby R 33.8 Lib 2.1	
1984	Andrews D 64.0 Patterson R 36.0	Armey R 51.2 Vandergriff D 48.8	Ortiz D 63.6 Moore R 36.3	
1986	Andrews D 100	Armey R 68.1 Richardson D 31.9	Ortiz D 100	
1988	Andrews D 71.4 Loeffler R 27.7 Lib 1.0	Armey R 69.3 Reyes D 30.7	Ortiz D 100	
1990	Andrews D 100	Armey R 70.4 Caton D 29.6	Ortiz D 100	
1992	Andrews D 56.0 McKenna R 41.4 Lib 2.7	Armey R 73.1 Caton D 26.9	Ortiz D 55.5 Kimbrough R 42.7 Lib 1.9	Tejeda D 87.1 Lib 12.9
1994	K Bentsen D 52.3 Fontenot R 45.0 2 others 2.7	Armey R 76.4 Bryant D 22.5 Lib 1.1	Ortiz D 59.4 Stone R 40.6	Tejeda D 70.9 Slatter R 27.6 Lib 1.5
1996	K Bentsen D 57.3 McKenna R 42.7	Armey R 73.6 Frankel D 26.4	Ortiz D 64.7 Gardner R 33.9 NLP 1.5	Tejeda D 75.4 Cude R 23.4 NLP 1.2
1998	K Bentsen D 57.8 Sanchez R 41.3 Lib 0.8	Armey R 88.1 Lib 11.9	Ortiz D 63.2 Stone R 35.2 Lib 1.5	Rodriguez D 90.4 Lib 9.5
2000	K Bentsen D 60.1 Sudan R 38.5 Lib 1.4	Armey R 72.5 Love D 25.6 Lib 1.9	Ortiz D 63.4 Ahumada R 34.0 Lib 2.7	Rodriguez D 89.0 Lib 11.0
2002	Bell D 54.8 Reiser R 43.1 2 others 2.1	Burgess R 74.8 LeBon D 22.8 2 others 2.4	Ortiz D 61.1 Ahumada R 36.5 Lib 2.4	Rodriguez D 71.1 Perales R 26.9 Lib 2.0
2004	Doggett D 67.6 Klein R 30.8 Lib 1.7	Burgess R 65.8 Reyes D 32.7	Ortiz D 63.2 Vaden R 34.9 Lib 2.0	Cuellar D 59.0 Hopson R 38.6 Lib 2.4
2006	Doggett D 67.3 Rostig R 26.3 2 others 6.4	Burgess R 60.2 Barnwell D 37.3 Lib 2.6	Ortiz D 56.8 Vaden R 38.9 Lib 4.3	Cuellar D 67.6 Enriquez D 20.3 Avery conserv 12.11[1]
2008	Doggett D 65.8 Morovich R 30.4 Lib 3.7	Burgess R 60.2 Leach D 36.4 Lib 3.4	Ortiz D 58.0 Vaden R 29.0	Cuellar D 68.7 Fish R 29.2 Lib 2.1
2010	Doggett D 52.9 Campbell R 44.8 Lib 2.3	Burgess R 67.1 Durrance D 30.7 Lib 2.3	Farenthold R 50,976 Ortiz D 50,179	Cuellar D 56.4 Underwood R 41.9 Lib 1.7
2012	Williams R 58.4 Henderson D 37.4 Lib 4.1	Burgess R 68.3 Sanchez D 28.7 Lib 3.0	Farenthold R 56.8 Harrison D 39.2 2 others 4.0	Cuellar D 67.9 Hayward R 29.8 2 others 2.3
2014	Williams R 60.2 Montoya D 36.2 Lib 3.5	Burgess R 82.7 Boler Lib 17.3	Farenthold R 63.6 Reed D 33.7 Lib 2.7	Cuellar D 82.1 Aikens Lib 13.3 Cary Green 4.6
2016	Williams R 58.3 Thomas D 37.7 Lib 3.9	Burgess R 66.4 Mauck D 29.6 Lib 4.0	Farenthold R 61.7 Barrera D 38.3	Cuellar D 66.2 Hardin R 31.3 Green 2.5

[1]Results of the special election held Nov. 7, 2006.

Texas Elections to the U.S. House, Districts 29–32

District 29, around Houston and including some of Pasadena, was intended to be Hispanic and continues to be. District 30 has been called Dallas's majority-black district, but it has also developed a considerable Hispanic population. The 31st District, first contested in 2002, originally lay east and north of Austin and extended eastward to northwest Houston, but in the 2003 redistricting it was given a much more north-south orientation, including Williamson County northward toward Fort Worth. From 2012 it became coterminous with Williamson and Bell Counties, east and north of Austin. District 32, also new in 2002, covered north Dallas suburbs. The same four members have represented these districts since they were created.

	DISTRICT 29	DISTRICT 30	DISTRICT 31	DISTRICT 32
1992	G Green D 64.9 Ervin R 35.1	Johnson D 71.5 Cain R 25.1 Lib 3.4		
1994	G Green D 73.4 Eide R 26.6	Johnson D 72.7 Cain R 25.6 Lib 1.7		
1996	G Green D 67.5 Rodriguez R 31.0 other 1.5	Johnson D 54.6 Hendry R 18.3 6 others 27.1		
1998	G Green D 92.9 2 others 7.2	Johnson D 72.2 Kelleher R 26.7 Lib 1.0		
2000	G Green D 73.3 Vu R 25.6	Johnson D 91.8 Lib 8.2		
2002	G Green D 95.2 Lib 4.8	Johnson D 74.3 R Bush R 24.2 Lib 1.5	Carter R 69.1 Bagley D 27.4 3 others 3.6	Sessions R 67.7 Dixon D 30.4 2 others 1.9
2004	G Green D 94.2 Lib 5.9	Johnson D 93.0 Lib 7.0	Carter R 64.8 Porter D 32.5 Lib 2.8	Sessions R 54.3 Frost D 44.0 Lib 1.7
2006	G Green D 73.5 Story R 24.4 Lib 2.0	Johnson D 80.2 Aurbach R 17.7 Lib 2.2	Carter R 58.5 Harrell D 38.8 Lib 2.7	Sessions R 56.4 Pryor D 41.3 Lib 2.3
2008	G Green D 74.6 Story R 23.9 Lib 1.5	Johnson D 82.5 Wood R 15.9 Lib 1.7	Carter R 60.3 Ruiz D 36.6 Lib 3.2	Sessions R 57.3 Roberson D 40.6 Lib 2.2
2010	G Green D 64.7 Morales R 34.1 Lib 1.3	Johnson D 75.7 Broden R 21.7 Lib 2.6	Carter R 82.6 Lib 17.5	Sessions R 62.6 Raggio D 34.9 Lib 2.5
2012	G Green D 90.0 2 others 10.0	Johnson D 78.8 Washington R 19.0 Lib 2.2	Carter R 61.3 Wyman D 35.0 Lib 3.7	Sessions R 58.3 McGovern D 39.5 Lib 2.3
2014	G Green D 89.5 Stanczak Lib 10.5	Johnson D 87.9 2 others 12.1	Carter R 64.0 Minor D 32.0 Lib 4.0	Sessions R 61.8 Perez D 35.4 Lib 2.7
2016	G Green D 72.5 Garza R 24.0 2 others 3.6	Johnson D 77.9 Lingerfelt R 19.0 2 others 3.1	Carter R 58.4 Clark D 36.5 Lib 5.2	Sessions R 71.1 Rankin Lib 19.0 Stuard Green 10.0

Texas Elections to the U.S. House, Districts 33–36

Created as a result of the 2010 census and first contested in 2012, these four districts reflect recent population growth scattered around the state. The 33rd District is between Dallas and Fort Worth and includes Arlington, Irving, and Grand Prairie. The 34th District covers the southernmost Gulf coast including Brownsville. District 35 is a narrow strip anchored in Austin at the north end and San Antonio at the south (and people-heavier) end. District 36 includes eastern suburbs of Houston and also several nonurban counties to the east.

	DISTRICT 33	DISTRICT 34	DISTRICT 35	DISTRICT 36
2012	Veasey D 72.5 Bradley R 25.8 Green 1.7	Vela D 61.9 Bradshaw R 36.2 Lib 1.9	Doggett D 63.9 Narvaiz R 32.0 others + write-ins 4.0	Stockman R 70.7 Martin D 26.6 Lib 2.7
2014	Veasey D 86.5 Reaves Lib 13.5	Vela D 59.5 Smith R 38.6 Lib 2.0	Doggett D 62.5 Narvaiz R 33.3 2 others 4.2	Babin R 76.0 Cole D 22.1 2 others 2.0
2016	Veasey D 73.7 Mitchell R 26.3	Vela D 62.7 Gonzalez R 37.3	Doggett D 63.1 Narvaiz R 31.6 2 others 5.4	Babin R 88.6 Ridley Green 11.4

Utah Election Results: President, Governor, Senator

	PRESIDENT	GOVERNOR[1]	SENATOR
1950			W Bennett R 53.9 E Thomas D 45.8
1952	Eisenhower 58.9 Stevenson 41.1	J Bracken Lee R def E Glade D	A Watkins R 54.3 WK Granger D 45.7
1956	Eisenhower 64.6 Stevenson 35.4	GD Clyde R def LC Romney D and JB Lee ind	W Bennett R 54.0 A Hopkin D 46.0
1958			F Moss D 38.7 A Watkins R 34.8 JB Lee ind 26.4
1960	Nixon 54.8 Kennedy 45.2	GD Clyde R 52.7 B Bardecker D 47.3	
1962			W Bennett R 52.4 D King D 47.6
1964	Johnson 54.9 Goldwater 45.1	C Rampton D 57.0 M Melich R 43.0	F Moss D 57.3 E Wilkinson R 42.7
1968	Nixon 56.5 Humphrey 37.1 Wallace 6.4	C Rampton D 68.7 C Buehner R 31.3	W Bennett R 53.7 M Weilenmann D 45.8 1 other
1970			F Moss D 56.2 L Burton R 42.5 Amer Ind 1.3
1972	Nixon 67.6 McGovern 26.4 Am Ind 6.0	C Rampton D 70.1 N Strike R 29.9	
1974			J Garn R 50.0 W Owens D 44.1 Am Ind 5.9
1976	Ford 62.4 Carter D 33.6 Am Ind 2.5 5 others	S Matheson D 52.0 V Romney R 46.0 2 others 2.0	O Hatch R 55.6 F Moss D 42.9 2 others
1980	Reagan 72.8 Carter 20.6 ind 5.0 6 others	S Matheson D 55.2 B Wright R 44.2 other 0.4	J Garn R 73.6 D Berman D 25.5 2 others 0.9
1982			O Hatch R 58.3 T Wilson D 41.4 2 others 0.3
1984	Reagan 74.5 Mondale 24.7 6 others	N Bangerter R 55.9 W Owens D 43.8 Am Ind 0.3	
1986			J Garn R 72.3 C Oliver D 26.5 2 others 1.2
1988	Bush 66.2 Dukakis 32.0 7 others	N Bangerter R 40.1 T Wilson D 38.4 M Cook ind 21.1 2 others 0.4	O Hatch R 67.1 BH Moss D 31.7 2 others
1992	Bush 43.4 Clinton 24.7 Perot 27.3 Populist 3.8 9 others	M Leavitt R 42.2 M Cook ind 33.6 S Hanson D 23.3	R Bennett R 55.4 W Owens D 39. 3 others
1994			O Hatch R 68.8 P Shea D 28.3 4 others 2.9
1996	Dole 54.5 Clinton 33.3 Perot 10.0 10 others	M Leavitt R 75.0 J Bradley D 23.3 3 others 1.7	
1998			R Bennett R 64.0 S Leckman D 33.0 ind 3.0
2000	Bush 66.8 Gore 26.3 Nader 4.7 6 others	M Leavitt R 55.8 B Orton D 42.7 ind 1.5	O Hatch R 65.6 S Howell D 31.5 2 others 2.9
2004	Bush 71.5 Kerry 26.0 5 others	J Huntsman R 57.7 S Matheson D 41.4 other 0.9	R Bennett R 68.7 RP Van Dam D 28.4 2 others 2.9
2006			O Hatch R 62.4 P Ashdown D 31.1 4 others 6.5
2008	McCain 62.6 Obama 34.4 5 others	J Huntsman 79.6 B Springmeyer D 19.7 Lib 2.6	
2010		G Herbert R 64.1 (special elec.) P Corroon D 31.9 ind, Lib 4.0	M Lee R 61.6 S Granato D 32.8 Lib 5.7
2012	Romney 74.6 Obama 25.4	G Herbert R 69.6 P Cooke D 28.1 Lib 2.3	O Hatch R 66.3 S Howell D 30.4 other 3.2
2016	Trump 45.1 Clinton D 27.2 McMullin 21.3 Johnson 3.5 others 3.0	G Herbert R 66.6 M Weinholtz D 28.9 B Kamerath Lib 310 other 1.4	M Lee R 68.1 M Snow D 27.1 others 4.8

[1] No quantitative data found for 1952 and 1956 governor elections.

Utah Elections to the U.S. House, Districts 1–4

Utah had two House districts in 1950, added a third for the 1982 election, and a fourth for 2012. From 1950 through 1964, District 2 included Tooele, Utah, Salt Lake, and Davis Counties—the urban center—and District 1 the rest of the state. A few counties shifted in 1966 and 1972. When District 3 was created for 1982, all were renumbered. District 1 was now the north, including Logan and the western tier from Idaho south to Arizona. The new district became District 2 and included Salt Lake County. The former District 1 became District 3, including Utah County (Provo, Orem), part of Salt Lake County, and east to Colorado and south to Arizona. Redistricting in 1992 and 2002 moved around parts of Salt Lake County into the more Republican adjacent districts. The new District 4, effective in 2012, in the 2014 *Almanac*'s words "would consist of heavily Republican suburbs south of Salt Lake City and the northern reaches of prohibitively Republican northern Utah County."

	DISTRICT 1	DISTRICT 2	DISTRICT 3	DISTRICT 4
1950	Granger D 51.1 Jones R 49.0	Bosone D 53.4 Priest R 46.6		
1952	Stringfellow R 60.5 ER McKay D 39.5	Dawson R 52.5 Bosone D 47.5		
1954	Dixon R 53.3 Granger D 46.6	Dawson R 57.2 Bosone D 42.8		
1956	Dixon R 60.9 Gronning D 39.1	Dawson R 57.6 McConkie D 42.4		
1958	Dixon R 53.8 Peterson D 46.1	King D 51.1 Dawson R 48.9		
1960	Peterson D 65.939 Stevenson R 65,871	King D 50.8 Lloyd R 49.2		
1962	Burton R 50.9 Peterson D 49.1	Lloyd R 53.9 Jenkins D 46.1		
1964	Burton R 56.0 Bruhn D 44.0	King D 57.5 Judd R 42.5		
1966	Burton R 66.5 Melville D 33.5	Lloyd R 61.2 King D 38.8		
1968	Burton R 68.1 Maughab D 31.9	Lloyd R 61.6 Ross D 38.3		
1970	KG McKay D 51.3 Richards R 47.9 Am Ind 2.7	Lloyd R 52.3 Nance D 46.6 Am Ind 1.1		
1972	KG McKay D 55.4 Wolthuis R 42.0 Am Ind 2.6	Owens D 48.9 Lloyd R 39.5 Bangerter Am Ind 11.7		
1974	KG McKay D 62.6 Inkley R 31.5 Am Ind 5.9	Howe D 49.5 Harmsen R 46.9 Am Ind 3.0 Lib 0.6		
1976	KG McKay D 58.2 Ferguson R 39.8 Am Ind 2.0	Marriott R 52.4 Howe D 40.1 McCarty write-in 7.4		
1978	KG McKay D 51.1 Richardson R 46.2 Am Ind 2.3	Marriott R 62.2 Firmage D 35.3 2 others		
1980	Hansen R 52.1 KG McKay D 47.9	Marriott R 67.0 Monson D 30.3 3 others		
1982	Hansen R 62.8 Dirks D 37.2	Marriott R 53.8 Farley D 46.2	Nielson R 76.9 Huish ind 23.9	
1984	Hansen R 71.3 Abrams D 28.2 Lib	Monson D 105,549 Farley D 105,044 3 others	Nielson R 74.4 Baird D 25.0 Lib	
1986	Hansen R 51.6 G McKay D 48.5	Owens D 55.2 Shimizu R 43.8 2 others	Nielson R 66.6 Gardiner D 32.7	
1988	Hansen R 59.8r G McKay D 40.2	Owens D 57.4 Snelgrove R 41.1 Lib	Nielson R 66.8 Stringham D 30.8 2 others	
1990	Hansen R 52.1 Brunsdale D 43.8 Am Ind 4.0	Owens D 57.6 Atwood R 39.8 2 others	Orton D 58.4 Snow R 36.5 2 others	
1992	Hansen R 65.3 Holt D 28.0 ind 6.7	Shepherd D 50.5 Greene R 46.8 2 others	Orton D 58.9 Harrington R 36.7 4 others	
1994	Hansen R 64.6 Coray D 35.5	Waldholtz R 45.8 Shepherd D 35.9 Cook ind 18.3	Orton D 59.0 Thompson R 39.8 SWP 1.2	
1996	Hansen R 68.3 Sanders D 30.0 NLP 1.7	Cook R 55.0 Anderson D 42.4 2 others	Cannon R 51.1 Orton D 47.3 3 others	
1998	Hansen R 67.7 Beierlein D 30.4 Lib	Cook R 52.8 Eskelsen D 43.5 4 others	Cannon R 76.9 ind + Lib	
2000	Hansen R 69.0 Collinwood D 27.2 3 others	Matheson D 55.9 Smith R 41.3 3 others	Cannon R 58.5 Dunn D 37.3 3 others	
2002	Bishop R 60.9 Thomas D 36.8 4 others	Matheson D 49.4 Swallow R 48.7 Lib 0.7 Green 1.2	Cannon R 67.4 Woodside D 29.0 Lib 3.6	
2004	Bishop R 67.9 Thompson D 29.1 2 others	Matheson D 54.8 Swallow R 43.2 3 others	Cannon R 63.4 Babka D 32.5 3 others	
2006	Bishop R 63.0 Olsen D 32.4 2 others	Matheson D 59.0 Christensen R 37.3 3 others	Cannon R 57.7 Burridge D 32.2 2 others	
2008	Bishop R 64.9 Bowen D 30.5 2 others	Matheson D 63.4 Dew R 34.5 2 others	Chaffetz R 65.6 Spencer D 28.3 Con 6.1	
2010	Bishop R 69.2 Bowen D 23.9 2 others	Matheson D 50.5 Philpot R 46.1 3 others	Chaffetz R 72.3 Hyer D 22.9 3 others	
2012	Bishop R 71.5 D McAleer D 24.7 other 3.8	Stewart R 63.7 Seegmiller D 34.3 other 2.1	Chaffetz R 76.6 Simonsen D 23.4	Matheson D 48.8 Love R 48.5 Lib 2.7
2014	Bishop R 64.2 D McAleer D 28.9 2 others 6.8	Stewart R 61.1 Luz Robles D 33.6 2 others 5.3	Chaffetz R 74.4 Wonnacott D 23.3 other 2.3	Love R 51.7 Owens D 48.3
2016	Bishop R 65.9 Clemens D 26.4 2 others 7.6	Stewart R 61.6 Albarran D 33.9 Con 4.5	Chaffetz R 73.5 Tryon D 27 26.5	Love R 53.8 Owens D 41.3 Con 4.9

Washington Election Results: President, Governor, Senator

	PRESIDENT	GOVERNOR	SENATOR
1950			W Magnuson D 53.4 W Williams R 46.0 2 others 0.6
1952	Eisenhower 54.3 Stevenson 44.6 5 others	A Langlie R 52.7 H Mitchell D 47.4	H Jackson D 56.2 H Cain R 43.5 2 others 0.3
1954			
1956	Eisenhower 53.9 Stevenson 45.4	A Rosellini D 54.6 E Anderson R 45.0 SLP 0.4	W Magnuson D 61.1 A Langlie R 38.9
1958			H Jackson D 67.3 W Bantz R 31.4 3 others 1.3
1960	Nixon 50.7 Kennedy 48.3 SLP 0.9 2 others	A Rosellini D 50.3 L Andrews R 48.9 2 others 0.8	
1962			W Magnuson D 52.1 R Christensen R 47.3 2 others 0.6
1964	Johnson 62.0 Goldwater 37.4 2 others	D Evans R 55.8 A Rosellini D 43.9 SLP 0 0.3	H Jackson D 73.2 L Andrews R 28.2
1966			
1968	Humphrey 47.2 Nixon 45.1 Wallace 7.4 4 others	D Evans R 53.3 J O'Connell D 46.7 2 others 1.0	W Magnuson D 64.4 J Metcalf R 35.3 2 others 0.3
1970			H Jackson D 82.4 C Elicker R 16.0 2 others 1.6
1972	Nixon 56.9 McGovern 38.6 Wallace 4.0 5 others	D Evans R 50.8 A Rosellini D 42.8 3 others 6.4	
1974			W Magnuson D 60.7 J Metcalf R 36.1 3 others 3.2
1976	Ford 50.0 Carter 46.1 ind 2.4 8 others	DL Ray D 53.1 J Spellman R 44.4	H Jackson D 71.8 G Brown R 24.2 4 others 4.0
1980	Reagan 49.7 Carter 37.3 ind 10.6 6 others	J Spellman R 56.7 J McDermott D 43.3	S Gorton R 54.2 W Magnuson D 45.8
1982			H Jackson D 69.0 D Jewett R 24.3 2 others 6.7
1984	Reagan 56.1 Mondale 42.6 8 others	B Gardner D 53.3 J Spellman R 46.7	
1986			B Adams D 50.7 S Gorton R 48.7
1988	Dukakis 50.0 Bush 48.5 5 others	B Gardner D 62.2 B Williams R 37.8	S Gorton R 51.1 M Lowry D 48.9
1992	Clinton 43.4 Bush 32.0 Perot 23.7 7 others	M Lowry D 52.2 K Eikenberry R 47.8	P Murray D 54.0 R Chandler R 46.0
1994			S Gorton R 55.7 R Sims D 44.3
1996	Clinton 49.8 Dole 37.3 ind + Green 2.8 Perot 8.9 5 others	G Locke D 58.0 E Craswell R 42.0	
1998			P Murray D 58.4 L Smith R 41.6
2000	Gore 50.2 Bush 44.6 Green 4.1 7 others	G Locke D 58.4 J Carlson 39.7	M Cantwell D 48.7 S Gorton R 48.6 Lib 2.6
2002			
2004	Kerry 52.8 Bush 45.6 7 others	C Gregoire D 1,373,361 D Rossi 1,363,228 Lib 2,259	P Murray D 55.0 G Nethercutt R 42.7 2 others 2.3
2006			M Cantwell 56.9 M McGavick R 39.9 3 others 3.2
2008	Obama 57.7 McCain 40.5 6 others	C Gregoire D 53.2 D Rossi R 46.8	
2010			P Murray D 52.4 D Rossi R 47.6
2012	Obama 56.2 Romney 41.3	J Inslee D 51.5 R McKenna R 48.5	M Cantwell D 60.5 M Baumgartner R 39.6
2014			
2016	Clinton 52.6 Trump 36.9 Johnson Lib 5.0 others 5.5	J Inslee D 54.5 B Bryant R 45.5	P Murray D 59.1 C Vance R 40.9

Washington Elections to the U.S. House, Districts 1–5

Washington had six House seats in 1950, added a seventh in 1952, an eighth in 1982, a ninth in 1992, and a tenth in 2012. In the 1950s, District 1 was just west of Puget Sound; District 2 was north of Seattle plus the northern half of the Olympic Peninsula; District 3, the southwest; District 4, south and east of the Cascades; District 5, north and east of the Cascades; District 6, just east of Seattle; and District 7, at large. Through the 1960s and 1970s, except for small changes, District 1 was Seattle; District 2, north of Seattle; District 3, still the southwest; District 4, immediately east of the Cascades; District 5, Spokane and nearby; District 6, Tacoma and the area west; and District 7, south Seattle and across the Sound. This configuration held through the 1980s, with the new 8th District to include suburbs along south Puget Sound and east across Lake Washington (Bellevue, Mercer Island). The new 9th District, from 1992, included suburbs from Seattle south to Tacoma, including Seatac Airport. The new 10th District, from 2012, was carved from parts of District 3 around Olympia and adjacent areas.

	DISTRICT 1	DISTRICT 2	DISTRICT 3	DISTRICT 4	DISTRICT 5
1950	Mitchell D 51.4 Powell R 47.9 2 others	Jackson D 61.1 H Wilson R 38.1	Mack R 53.0 Quarnstrom D 46.7	Holmes R 64.3 Little D 35.7	Horan R 54.8 Dellwo D 45.3
1952	Pelly R 51.3 Bullitt D 48.3	Westland R 54.3 Henson D 45.6	Mack R 53.3 Quarnstrom D 46.6	Holmes R 67.6 Bryan D 32.5	Horan R 56.0 Dellwo D 44.0
1954	Pelly R 52.6 Mitchell D 47.4	Westland R 52.2 Henson D 47.8	Mack R 64.8 Tisdale D 35.1	Holmes 61.0 Yoder D 39.0	Horan R 58.5 Garton D 41.4
1956	Pelly R 58.1 JB Wilson D 41.9	Westland R 56.0 Peterson D 44.0	Mack R 56.5 McCoy D 43.5	Holmes R 50.4 LeRoux D 49.6	Horan R 53.7 Delaney D 46.3
1958	Pelly R 70.1 Odman D 29.9	Westland R 53.7 Mitchell D 46.1	Mack R 60.8 Meyers D 38.8	May R 53.9 LeRoux D 45.7	Horan R 53.2 Delaney D 46.3 Con 0.5
1960	Pelly R 70.2 Holman D 29.8	Westland R 60.1 Peterson D 39.9	Hansen D 49.6 Nordquist R 43.8	May R 58.8 Mundy D 40.0	Horan R 59.3 Gallagher D 40.6
1962	Pelly R 73.8 Bryant D 26.3	Westland R 59.8 Moore D 40.2	Hansen D 65.3 Alexander R 34.6	May R 67.0 Gallant D 33.0	Horan R 64.4 Gallagher D 35.6
1964	Pelly R 60.0 Palmason D 40.1	Meeds D 54.9 Westland R 45.1	Hansen D 70.2 Anderson R 29.8	May R 65.3 Huza D 34.8	Foley D 53.4 Horan R 46.4
1966	Pelly R 80.3 Bryant D 19.7	Meeds D 60.7 EM Smith R 36.0 2 others	Hansen D 65.8 Kisor R 34.2	May R 62.1 Bansmer D 30.3 Paxton conserv 7.7	Foley D 56.6 Powers R 43.4
1968	Pelly R 61.4 Cole D 37.7 other	Meeds D 56.2 Turner D 43.8	Hansen D 56.8 Adams R 43.2	May R 66.8 Lukson D 33.2	Foley D 56.7 Bond R 43.2
1970	Pelly R 64.4 Hughes D 32.0 2 others	Meeds D 72.8 McBride R 27.2	Hansen D 59.1 McConkey R 40.9	McCormack D 52.5 May R 47.4	Foley D 67.0 Gamble R 33.0
1972	Pritchard R 50.3 Hempelmann D 49.1 other	Meeds D 60.4 Reams R 39.6	Hansen D 66.3 McConkey R 33.7	McCormack D 52.1 Bledsoe R 47.9	Foley D 81.3 Privette R 18.7
1974	Pritchard R 69.5 Knedlik D 28.7 2 others	Meeds D 59.8 Reed R 39.0 other	Bonker D 60.9 Kramer R 38.1 other	McCormack D 58.9 Paxton R 41.1	Foley D 64.4 Gage R 35.6
1976	Pritchard R 71.9 Wood D 25.8 2 others	Meeds D 49.2 Garner R 49.0 2 others	Bonker D 70.8 Elhart R 28.0 other	McCormack D 57.8 Granger R 41.0 2 others	Foley D 58.0 Alton R 40.6 2 others
1978	Pritchard R 64.0 Niemi D 33.7 other	Swift D 51.4 Garner R 48.6	Bonker D 58.6 Bennett R 41.4	McCormack D 61.1 Roylance R 38.9	Foley D 48.0 Alton R 42.8 Tonasket ind 9.3
1980	Pritchard R 78.3 Drake D 18.1 other 3.6	Swift D 63.9 Snider R 32.6 other	Bonker D 62.7 Culp R 37.3	Morrison R 57.4 McCormack D 42.6	Foley D 51.9 Sonneland R 48.1
1982	Pritchard R 67.6 Long D 32.4	Swift D 59.6 Houchen R 40.4	Bonker D 60.0 Quigg R 36.8 other	Morrison R 69.8 Kilbury D 28.6 other	Foley D 64.3 Sonneland R 35.7
1984	Miller R 56.3 Evans D 43.7	Swift D 58.6 Klauder R 38.6 other	Bonker D 71.0 Elder R 28.9	Morrison R 76.1 Epperson R 23.9	Foley D 69.7 Hebner R 30.3
1986	Miller R 51.4 Lindquist D 48.6	Swift D 72.2 Talman R 27.8	Bonker D 73.5 Illing R 26.5	Morrison R 72.1 Goedecke D 27.9	Foley D 74.7 Wakefield R 25.3
1988	Miller R 55.4 Lindquist D 44.6	Swift D 100	Unsoeld D 50.14 Wight R 49.86	Morrison R 74.5 Golob D 25.5	Foley R 76.4 Derby R 23.6
1990	Miller R 52.0 Sullivan D 47.9	Swift D 50.5 D Smith R 41.2 McCord Lib 8.3	Unsoeld D 53.7 Williams R 46.3	Morrison R 70.6 Hougen D 29.3	Foley D 68.8 Derby R 31.2
1992	Cantwell D 54.8 Nelson R 42.0 2 others	Swift D 52.1 Metcalf R 42.0 2 others	Unsoeld D 56.0 Fiske R 44.0	Inslee D 50.9 Hastings R 49.1	Foley D 55.2 Sonneland R 44.8
1994	White R 51.6 Cantwell D 48.3	Metcalf R 54.7 Spanel D 45.3	L Smith R 52.0 Unsoeld D 44.5 Gun Control 3.4	Hastings R 53.3 Inslee D 46.7	Nethercutt R 50.9 Foley D 49.1
1996	White R 53.7 Coopersmith D 46.3	Metcalf R 48.5 Quigley D 47.8 NLP 3.7	L Smith R 50.2 Baird D 49.8	Hastings R 52.9 Locke D 47.1	Nethercutt R 55.6 Olson D 44.4
1998	Inslee D 49.8 Rhite R 44.1 Am Her 5.1[1]	Metcalf R 55.2 Cammermeyer D 44.8	Baird D 54.7 Benton R 45.4	Hastings R 69.1 Pross D 24.4 other	Nethercutt R 56.9' Lyons D 38.0 Am Her 5.0
2000	Inslee D 54.6 McDonald R 42.6 Lib	Larsen D 50.0 Koster R 45.9 2 others	Baird D 53.4 Matson R 40.6 Lib 3.0	Hastings R 61.0 Davis D 37.3 Lib	Nethercutt R 57.3 Keefe D 38.9 Lib
2002	Inslee D 55.7 Marine R 41.3 Lib	Larsen D 50.0 N Smith R 45.7 Lib + Green	Baird D 61.7 Zarelli R 38.3	Hastings R 66.9 Mason D 33.1	Nethercutt R 62.7 Haggin D 32.2 Lib
2004	Inslee D 62.3 Eastwood R 36.0 Lib	Larsen D 63.9 Sinclair R 33.6 Lib	Baird D 61.9 Crowson R 38.1	Hastings R 62.6 Matheson D 37.4	McMorris R 59.7 Barbieri D 40.3
2006	Inslee D 67.7 Ishmael R 32.3	Larsen D 64.2 Roulstone R 35.8	Baird D 63.1 Messmore R 36.9	Hastings R 59.9 Wright D 40.1	McMorris R 56.4 Goldmark D 43.6
2008	Inslee D 67.8 Ishmael R 32.2	Larsen D 62.4 Bart R 37.6	Baird D 64.0 Delavar R 36.0	Hastings R 63.1 Fearing D 36.9	McMorris Rodgers R 65.3 Mays D 34.7
2010	Inslee D 57.6 Watkins R 42.3	Larsen D 51.1 Koster R 48.9	Herrera Beutler R 53.0 Heck D 47.0	Hastings R 67.6 Clough D 32.4	McMorris Rodgers R 63.6 Romeyn D 36.3
2012	DelBene D 53.9 Koster R 46.1	Larsen D 61.1 Matthews R 38.9	Herrera Beutler R 60.4 Haugen D 39.6	Hastings R 66.2 Baechler D 33.8	McMorris Rodgers R 61.9 Cowan D 38.1
2014	DelBene D 55.0 P Celis R 45.0	Larsen D 60.6 Guillot R 39.4	Herrera Beutler R 61.5 Dingethal D 38.5	Newhouse R 50.8 Didier R 49.2	McMorris Rodgers R 60.7 Pakootas D 39.3
2016	DelBene D 55.4 Sutherland R 44.6	Larsen D 64.0 Hennemann R 36.0	Herrera Beutler R 61.8 Moeller D 38.2	Newhouse R 57.6 Didier R 42.4	McMorris Rodgers R 59.6 Pakootas D 40.4

[1] American Heritage Party, also known as the Christian Liberty Party, a Washington State affiliate of the U.S. Taxpayers Party.

Washington Elections to the U.S. House, Districts 6–10

	DISTRICT 6	DISTRICT 7	DISTRICT 8	DISTRICT 9	DISTRICT 10
1950	Tollefson R 60.5 Coffee D 38.9				
1952	Tollefson R 59.8 O'Connell D 40.2	(at large) Magnuson D 50.5 Canwell R 49.5 other			
1954	Tollefson R 55.2 McCutcheon D 44.7	(at large) Magnuson D 57.3 Canwell R 42.2 SLP 0.5			
1956	Tollefson R 54.0 McCutcheon D 46.0	(at large) Magnuson D 58.5 P Evans R 41.5			
1958	Tollefson R 53.5 Coffee D 45.8 Con 0.7	D Magnuson D 70.6 Jones R 29.0 Con 0.4			
1960	Tollefson R 56.5 McCutcheon D 43.6	Magnuson D 95,663 Stender R 95,524			
1962	Tollefson R 71.0 Olson D 28.9	Stinson R 56.6 Magnuson D 43.4			
1964	Hicks D 52.1 Tollefson R 47.9	Adams D 55.6 Stinson R 44.4			
1966	Hicks D 60.4 Mahler R 39.6	Adams D 62.7 Munn R 36.1 Peace Fr 1.2			
1968	Hicks D 55.8 Chase R 43.2 conserv 1.0	Adams D 65.5 Eberle R 34.1 Peace Fr 0.4			
1970	Hicks D 69.4 Jarstad R 29.8 SWP 0.8	Adams D 66.6 Lewis R 31.8 SWP 1.6			
1972	Hicks D 72.0 Lowry R 27.9	Adams D 85.4 Freeman R 12.1 write-in 2.5			
1974	Hicks D 71.8 Nalley R 28.2	Adams D 71.1 Pritchard R 28.9			
1976	Dicks D 73.5 Reynolds R 25.3 other	Adams D 73.0 Pritchard R 25.3 2 others			
1978	Dicks D 60.9 Beaver R 37.4 SWP 1.7	Lowry D 50.8 Cunningham R 44.5			
1980	Dicks D 53.6 Beaver R 46.4	Lowry D 57.2 Dunlap R 42.7			
1982	Dicks D 62.5 Haley R 33.1 Anderson ind 4.3	Lowry D 70.9 Dorse R 29.1	Chandler R 57.0 Bland D 43.0		
1984	Dicks D 66.2 Lonergan R 32.3 Lib	Lowry D 70.5 Dorse R 28.9 SWP 0.7	Chandler R 62.4 Lamson D 37.6		
1986	Dicks R 71.2 Braaten R 28.8	Lowry D 72.6 McDonald R 27.4	Chandler R 65.2 Giles D 34.8		
1988	Dicks D 67.6 Cook R 32.4	McDermott D 76.3 Edwards R 23.7	Chandler R 70.8 Kean D 29.1		
1990	Dicks D 61.4 Mueller R 38.6	McDermott D 72.4 Penberthy R 24.1 SWP 3.7	Chandler R 56.2 Giles D 43.8		
1992	Dicks D 64.2 Phillips R 28.0 Donnelly ind 6.1 Lib 1.7	McDermott D 86.2 Hampson R 21.0 ind 2.8	Dunn R 60.4 Tamblyn D 33.9 Adams ind 5.7	Kreidler D 52.1 Reichbauer R 43.2 2 others	
1994	Dicks D 58.4 Gregg R 41.6	McDermott D 75.2 Harris R 24.9	Dunn R 76.1 Wyrick D 23.9	Tate R 51.8 Kreidler D 48.2	
1996	Dicks D 65.9 Tinsley R 30.2 2 others	McDermott D 81.0 Kleschen R 19.0	Dunn R 65.4 Little D 34.6	Smith D 50.1 Tate R 47.3 NLP 2.6	
1998	Dicks D 68.4 Lawrence R 31.6	McDermott D 88.2 Lippmann Reform 9.4 SWP 2.4	Dunn R 59.7 Behrens-Benedict D 40.3	Smith D 64.6 Taber R 35.3	
2000	Dicks D 64.7 Lawrence R 31.1 Lib	McDermott D 72.8 Green 19.6 Lib 7.6	Dunn R 62.2 Behrens-Benedict D 35.6	Smith D 61.7 Vance R 35.0 Lib	
2002	Dicks D 64.2 Lawrence R 31.4 Lib	McDermott D 74.1 Cassady R 21.9 Lib	Dunn R 59.8 Behrens-Benedict D 37.3 Lib	Smith D 58.5 Casada R 38.5 Lib	
2004	Dicks D 69.0 Cloud R 31.0	McDermott D 80.7 Cassady R 19.3	Reichert R 51.5 Ross D 46.7 Lib	Smith D 63.3 Lord R 34.4 Green 2.3	
2006	Dicks D 70.6 Cloud R 29.4	McDermott D 79.4 Beren R 15.7 Lib	Reichert R 51.5 Burner D 48.5	Smith D 65.7 Cofchin R 34.3	
2008	Dicks D 66.9 Cloud R 33.1	McDermott D 83.7 Beren R 16.4	Reichert R 52.8 Burner D 47.2	Smith D 65.4 Postma R 34.6	
2010	Dicks D 58.0 Cloud R 42.0	McDermott D 83.0 Jeffers-Schroder ind 17.0	Reichert R 52.0 DelBene D 48.0	Smith D 54.8 Muri R 45.2	
2012	Kilmer D 59.0 Driscoll R 41.0	McDermott D 79.7 Bemis R 20.3	Reichert R 59.7 Porterfield D 40.3	Smith D 71.6 Postma R 28.4	Heck D 58.6 Muri R 41.4
2014	Kilmer D 63.0 McClendon R 37.0	McDermott D 81.0 Keller R 19.0	Reichert R 63.3 Ritchie D 36.7	Smith D 70.8 Basler R 29.2	Heck D 54.7 McDonald R 45.3
2016	Kilmer D 61.5 Bloom R 38.5	Jayapal D 56.0 Walkinshaw D 40.04	Reichert R 60.2 Ventrella D 39.8	Smith D 72.9 Basler R 27.1	Heck D 58.7 Postma R 41.3

318   APPENDIX

Wyoming Election Results

Wyoming has had one at-large House district since statehood.

	PRESIDENT	GOVERNOR	SENATOR	HOUSE AT-LARGE
1950		F Barrett R (no data)		W Harrison R 54.6 J Clark D 45.6
1952	Eisenhower 62.6 Stevenson 37.0 3 others		F Barrett R 51.7 J O'Mahoney D 48.3	W Harrison R 60.1 R Rose D 39.9
1954		M Simpson R 50.5 W Jackson D 49.5	J O'Mahoney D 51.5 W Harrison D 48.4	K Thomson R 56.2 S Tully D 43.8
1956	Eisenhower 60.1 Stevenson 40.0			K Thomson R 58.2 J O'Callaghan 41.8
1958		JJ Hickey D 48.9 M Simpson R 46.6	G McGee D 50.8 F Barrett R 49.1	K Thomson R 53.6 R Whitaker D 46.4
1960	Nixon 4.8 Kennedy 45.2		K Thomson R 56.3 R Whitaker D 43.6	W Harrison R 52.3 H Armstrong D 47.7
1962		C Hansen R 54.5 J Gage D 45.5	M Simpson R 57.8 (unexp term) J Hickey D 42.1	W Harrison R 61.4 L Mankus D 38.6
1964	Johnson 56.6 Goldwater 43.4		G McGee D 54.0 J Wold R 46.0	T Roncalio D 50.8 W Harrison R 49.2
1966		S Hathaway R 54.3 E Wilkerson D 45.7	C Hansen R 51.8 T Roncalio D 48.2	W Harrison R 52.8 A Christian D 47.2
1968	Nixon 5.7 Humphrey 35.5 Wallace 8.7			J Wold R 62.8 V Linford D 37.3
1970		S Hathaway R 62.8 J Rooney D 37.2	G McGee D 55.8 J Wold R 44.2	T Roncalio D 50.3 H Roberts R 49.7
1972	Nixon 69.0 McGovern 30.5 Am Ind 0.5		C Hansen R 71.3 M Vinich D 28.7	T Roncalio D 51.7 W Kidd R 48.3
1974		E Herschler D 55.9 D Jones R 44.1		T Roncalio D 54.7 T Stroock R 45.3
1976	Ford 59.3 Carter 39.8		M Wallop R 54.6 G McGee D 45.4	T Roncalio D 56.4 L Hart R 43.5
1978		E Herschler D 50.9 J Ostlund R 49.1	R Whitaker D 62.1 A Simpson R 37.9	R Cheney R 58.7 W Bagley D 41.3
1980	Reagan 62.6 Carter 28.0 ind 6.8 Lib			R Cheney R 68.6 J Rogers D 31.4
1982		E Herschler D 63.1 W Morton R 36.9	M Wallop R 56.6 R McDaniel D 43.4	R Cheney R 71.1 T Hommel D 28.9
1984	Reagan 70.5 Mondale 28.3 Lib		A Simpson R 78.3 V Ryan D 21.7	R Cheney R 73.6 H McFadden D 24.4 Lib 2.0
1986		M Sullivan D 54.0 P Simpson R 46.0		R Cheney R 69.5 R Gilmore D 30.5
1988	Bush 60.5 Dukakis 38.0 2 others		M Wallop R 50.3 J Vinich D 49.6	R Cheney R 66.6 B Sharratt D 31.8 2 others 1.4
1990		M Sullivan D 65.4 M Mead R 34.6	A Simpson R 64.0 K Helling D 36.0	C Thomas R 55.1 P Maxfield D 44.9
1992	Bush 39.7 Clinton 34.1 Perot 25.7 2 others			C Thomas R 57.8 J Herschler D 39.3 Lib 2.9
1994		J Geringer R58.7 K Karpan D 40.2 Lib 1.1	C Thomas R 58.9 M Sullivan D 39.3 Lib 1.8	B Cubin R 53.2 B Schuster D 41.3 Lib 5.5
1996	Dole 49.8 Clinton 36.8 ind + Reform 12.2 2 others		M Enzi R 54.1 K Karpan D 42.2 2 others 3.7	B Cubin R 55.2 P Maxfield D 40.8 Lib 3.9
1998		J Geringer R 55.6 J Vinich D 40.5 D Dawson Lib 3.9		B Cubin R 57.8 S Farris D 38.7 Lib 3.5
2000	Bush 69.2 Gore 28.3 4 others		C Thomas 73.7 M Logan D 22.0 Lib 4.2	B Cubin R 66.8 M Green D 28.5 2 others 4.7
2002		D Freudenthal D 50.0 E Bebout R 47.9 Lib 2.1	M Enzi R 72.9 J Corcoran D 27.1	B Cubin R 60.5 R Akin D 36.2 Lib 3.3
2004	Bush 68.7 Kerry 29.0 ind 1.4 2 others			B Cubin R 55.2 T Ladd D 41.8 Lib 3.0
2006		D Freudenthal D 69.9 R Hunkins R 30.0	C Thomas R 68.9 D Groutage D 29.4	B Cubin R 47.6 G Trauner D 47.0 Lib + write-ins 5.4
2008	McCain 64.7 Obama 32.5 2 others		J Barrasso R 73.4 (unexp term) N Carter D 26.5 M Enzi R 75.6 (full term) C Rothfuss D 24.2	C Lummis R 52.6 G Trauner D 42.8 Lib 4.6
2010		M Mead R 65.7 L Petersen D 22.9 T Haynes ind 7.3		C Lummis R 69.0 D Wendt D 24.0 Lib 7.0
2012	Romney 69 Obama 28		J Barrasso R 75.9 T Chesnut D 21.6 ind 2.5	C Lummis R 70.1 C Henrichsen D 24.2 2 others 5.7
2014		M Mead R 62.5 P Gosar D 28.9	M Enzi R 72.3 C Hardy D 17.6 C Gottschall ind 8.0	C Lummis R 68.6 R Grayson D 23.0 2 others 8.4
2016	Trump 68.2 Clinton D 21.9			L Cheney R 62.2 R Greene D 30.1 others 7.7

Notes

INTRODUCTION

1. Gelman et al., *Red State, Blue State*, 236, affirms the red-blue code's beginning date of 2000, citing Tom Zeller's "Ideas and Trends" article in the *New York Times* of Feb. 8, 2004, which also mentions several earlier party-political color schemes.

2. In 2000, George W. Bush (R) won 271 electoral votes and 50,455,130 popular votes (47.9 percent); Al Gore (D) won 266 electoral votes and 50,997,291 popular votes (48.4 percent). The Green Party candidate, Ralph Nader, won no electoral votes but 2,882,863 popular votes (2.7 percent). Deskins, Walton, and Puckett, *Presidential Elections*, 521, 524. In 2016, Donald J. Trump (R) won 304 electoral votes and 62,984,825 popular votes (46.1 percent); Hillary Clinton (D) won 227 electoral votes and 65,853,516 popular votes (48.2 percent). Federal Election Commission, Official Results, Jan. 30, 2017.

3. The census's West region encompasses Alaska, Arizona, California, Colorado, Hawaii, Idaho, Montana, Nevada, New Mexico, Oregon, Utah, Washington, and Wyoming. The six Great Plains states, from north to south, are North Dakota, South Dakota, Nebraska, Kansas, Oklahoma, and Texas. Most of the three hundred respondents to a 1990 survey asking "Where is the West?" included the Plains states. Nugent, "Where Is the West?"

4. Election results for the three federal offices may be found on the website of the clerk of the U.S. House of Representatives. State governors and legislatures are usually accessible from the office of the secretary of state of each state, or in some cases from the board of election commissioners or similar office. Besides the election returns, I rely on the biennial *Almanac of American Politics*, which began in the early 1970s; Neal Peirce's books on the Great Plains, Pacific, and Rocky Mountain states, and Richard Lowitt's *Politics in the Postwar American West*. The much-maligned *Wikipedia* has proved helpful, especially for governors' contests and for its lists of governors and senators for each state. See the appendix.

5. For a critique of recent political culture history, which does not deal with elections, parties, and the like, see Deverell, "Claims and Reclaims," esp. 530–31; and Frederick Logevall and Kenneth Osgood, "Why Did We Stop Teaching Political History?" op-ed, *New York Times*, Aug. 29, 2016. For a defense of political culture history, see Julian Zelizer, "Political History Is Doing AOK," in *Process* (blog

of the Organization of American Historians), www.processhistory.org, Aug. 31, 2016. Raffaella Baritono seconds Logevall and Osgood and documents the vigor of political history in "Introduction: Political History Today."

CHAPTER 1

1. Key, *Southern Politics*; Gastil, *Cultural Regions*, 187, 201. Gastil also observed that "wherever there are Southern Baptists there is Southern culture" (53). Peirce, *Great Plains States;* Elazar's well-known *Closing of the Metropolitan Frontier* does not include Oklahoma.

2. The historiography on modern conservatism is now huge. I cite and employ here only some very recent ones: Zelizer, "Reflections," 371, 373–74. Also helpful in analyzing conservatism and its several strands is Phillips-Fein, "Conservatism," esp. 24, 731, followed by Lassiter, "Political History," esp. 761, and McGirr, "Now That Historians Know So Much," esp. 765, both from the *Journal of American History*'s "Conservatism: A Round Table" issue; the "Roundtable" addressed the Tea Party movement but appeared before it was in full bloom. Coming a bit later were Formisano, *Tea Party*, and Skocpol and Williamson, *Tea Party*.

3. Bissett, *Agrarian Socialism*; and Jim Bissett, "Socialist Party," in *Encyclopedia of Oklahoma History and Culture*.

4. Worth Robert Miller, "Populist Party," in *Encyclopedia of Oklahoma History and Culture*, www.okhistory.org/publications/encyclopediaonline.php, and more extensively, Miller's book, *Oklahoma Populism*.

5. The 2016 result was not atypical. Trump won 65.3 percent, Hillary Clinton 28.9 percent, and the Libertarian Gary Johnson 5.7 percent.

6. Following the Republican pioneers Henry Bellmon and Dewey Bartlett, the state's governors have been Democrats David Hall in 1970, Boren in 1974, and George Nigh in 1978 and 1982. Bellmon returned in 1986. Democrat David Walters followed in 1990. Then came Republican (and conservative Catholic) Frank Keating in 1994 and 1998. Democrat Brad Henry won in 2002 and 2006. Republican Mary Fallin won in 2010 and again in 2014. As the *Almanac of American Politics 2012*, 1349, records, she was the first woman and first Republican elected lieutenant governor, in 1994 and subsequently, and held the office until 2006, when she was elected to the U.S. House for two terms from the Oklahoma City district.

7. James Davis of Oklahoma State University quoted in *International Business Times*, Mar. 6, 2012, www.ibtimes.com/articles/310220/20120306/santorum-oklahoma-win-primary-votes.htm.

8. Scales and Goble, *Oklahoma Politics*, 303–6.

9. Ibid., 307–29 (quotes 324, 329). Or, as Henry Bellmon delicately put it in his autobiography, Kennedy "was philosophically unacceptable in our state." Bellmon, *Life and Times*, 220.

10. Bellmon, *Life and Times*, 220.

11. Ibid., 123–25.

12. Scales and Goble, *Oklahoma Politics*, 330.

13. Only about 61,000 people voted in the Republican primary, and Bellmon won less than 57,000 of them. But he defeated Atkinson by 392,200 to 315,400. Where did all those new Republicans come from? Probably the Gary faction of the Democrats.

14. Atkinson 231,867, Gary 230,914. Gary had outpolled Atkinson by about 85,000 votes in the first primary, indicating that Atkinson snared well over half of the other candidates' supporters. In the runoff, Gary's strongest counties were mostly traditional rural Democratic bastions; Atkinson's were more urban—Oklahoma and Tulsa, Cleveland (Norman), Comanche (Lawton), and Okmulgee.

15. At that time, governors could not run for a second consecutive term. A constitutional amendment changed this in 1966. On the primary, runoff, and Gary people voting for Bellmon, see Carolyn G. Hanneman, "Bellmon, Henry Louis (1921–)," in *Encyclopedia of Oklahoma History and Culture*, www.okhistory.org/publications/encyclopediaonline.php.

16. Sullivant column, *Daily Oklahoman*, Nov. 2, 1966.

17. Bellmon, *Life and Times*, 171.

18. Hanneman, "Bellmon, Henry Louis (1921–)." A reapportionment referendum passed in the 1962 election, and in 1964 federal judges redistricted after the largely rural (and endangered) legislators balked. "The state's Republicans benefited," according to Baird and Goble, *Oklahoma*, 242.

19. Bellmon, *Life and Times*, 287. Years later, on the Senate budget committee, Bellmon opposed Ronald Reagan's supply-side economics.

20. Bellmon won over 470,000 votes to Monroney's 419,700. Comparing Monroney's support in his first (1950) win to his 1968 loss, he continued to carry the southern counties but lost some in the northeast. Comparing the counties that Harris won in 1966 to Monroney's in 1968, Harris carried, and Monroney did not carry, Roger Mills, Dewey, Custer, and Washita in the west; Canadian, Cleveland, Lincoln, and Payne in the center; Adair, Cherokee, Rogers, Wagoner, Craig, Mayes Ottawa, and Delaware in the northeast and east. It is unclear whether this reflects Republican erosion of Democratic strength or Bellmon's own personal appeal—probably both.

21. Bellmon, *Life and Times*, 294.

22. Ronald Keith Gaddie, "Republican Party," in *Encyclopedia of Oklahoma History and Culture*, www.okhistory.org/publications/encyclopediaonline.php.

23. U.S. Bureau of the Census, "Oklahoma: Population of Counties by Decennial Census: 1900 to 1990," www.census/gov/population/cencounts/ok190090.txt; and Oklahoma Department of Commerce, "Census Counts and Annual Estimates of the Resident Population for Counties of Oklahoma, April 1, 2000 to April 1, 2010." Oklahoma City: Oklahoma Department of Commerce, April 2012.

24. Conversation with W. David Baird, Oct. 11, 2011.

25. Scales and Goble, *Oklahoma Politics*, 334, 338–39. An agribusinessman had to be familiar with complex machinery, center-pivot irrigation, management methods, and much else. A degree in agronomy and an MBA were highly desirable.

26. Peirce, *Great Plains States*, 274; Oklahoma Department of Libraries, *Oklahoma Almanac 2011–2012*, 935; Nugent, *Into the West*, 338–39, 342–43.

27. Oklahoma Department of Libraries, *Oklahoma Almanac 2011–2012*, 923.

28. Lowitt, *Fred Harris*, 2.

29. Harris, *Does People Do It?*, 74 (quote), 75, 80 (quote); Lowitt, *Fred Harris*, 3–5 (quote).

30. Harris's strengths were the usual southern and northeastern counties, but he was also strong (for a Democrat) in Canadian, just west of Oklahoma City, and Cleveland, just south of it. He lost Oklahoma County, as Democrats normally did, but by less than four thousand votes, which no Republican could make up for elsewhere.

31. Harris, *Does People Do It?*, 131, 133.

32. Bloodworth, "Fred Harris's New Populism," 211–12.

33. In 1992, independent Ross Perot did even better, taking 317,000 votes, or 23 percent of the total, but he did not carry any counties. His presence may, however, have loosened some Democratic allegiances, as Wallace's probably did in 1968.

34. Hall's vote was 338,560, Bartlett's 335,741.

35. *Daily Oklahoman*, Nov. 1, 1974. This was partly campaign rhetoric; Gary and Edmondson had been on the outs for years. Nonetheless, it reflects an underlying, and intensifying, conservatism. For letters to the editor of the *Oklahoman* expressing far-right views, see the issues of Oct. 30, 1966, and Nov. 5, 1972.

36. *Almanac of American Politics 1974*, 825–26.

37. Ibid., 833.

38. *Almanac of American Politics 1984*, 971.

39. *Almanac of American Politics 1994*, 1041. Also, *Almanac of American Politics 1984*, 965–66.

40. *Almanac of American Politics 1984*, 967–68; *Almanac of American Politics 1994*, 1044–47, 1050–51.

41. Huckaby and Gaddie, "Carson Defeats Ewing," 46.

42. Gaddie, "Congressional Seat Swings," 704.

43. Quotes in this paragraph are from an excellent article detailing the 1994 election and the efforts of the Religious Right, particularly in 1994: Bednar and Hertzke, "Christian Right."

44. Leonard, "Southern Crossroads," 32. For other excellent discussions of the connection in Oklahoma between the Religious Right and the GOP, see Gaddie and Buchanan, "Oklahoma: GOP Realignment," 224; and other of Gaddie's writings.

CHAPTER 2

1. Campbell, *Gone to Texas*, 405.

2. United States Bureau of the Census, *Historical Statistics*, ser. 203, 1:35.

3. Davidson, *Race and Class*, 51.

4. Enloe and Seager, *Real State of America*, 38. Texas and Oklahoma were in the lowest category of voter participation, 49–59 percent in the 2008 presidential election.

5. Paul Burka, "Left Out," *Texas Monthly* 30:11 (Nov. 2002).

6. Davidson, *Race and Class*, 139.

7. Ibid., 239. Also, Phillips, "Texan by Color," 10, 28.

8. Davidson, *Race and Class*, 40–60, esp. tables on 43, 48; also 29, 42.

9. Ibid., 203.

10. Cullen, "From 'Turn Texas Loose' to the Tea Party," 3.

11. Davidson, *Race and Class*, 159–60.

12. Ibid., 46.

13. Key, *Southern Politics*, 255, 257, 259.

14. Parker, *Lone Star Nation*, 58; Dobbs, *Yellow Dogs and Republicans*, 27.

15. Dallas Morning News, *Texas Almanac 1952–1953*, 492.

16. Maxwell et al., *Texas Politics Today*, 20. Also, Robert Draper, "Death of a Fixer," *Texas Monthly* 20:11 (Nov. 1992); and Davis, "Authoritarian Political Systems."

17. Dobbs, *Yellow Dogs and Republicans*, 55, 67.

18. Campbell, *Gone to Texas*, 416.

19. Bridges, *Twilight*, 7.

20. Maxwell, *Texas Politics Today*, 13 (emphasis added).

21. Dobbs, *Yellow Dogs and Republicans*, 5, 90–91, 149.

22. Nancy Beck Young, "Democratic Party," in *Handbook of Texas Online*, https://tshaonline.org/handbook, 7; Dobbs, *Yellow Dogs and Republicans*, 62–64.

23. Peirce, *Great Plains States*, 304; Green, *Establishment in Texas Politics*, 141.

24. Dobbs, *Yellow Dogs and Democrats*, chaps. 6–7.

25. Green and Botson, "Looking for Lefty," 126; Davidson, *Race and Class*, 164–66.

26. Green, *Establishment in Texas Politics*, 165.

27. "Overview of the Collection" (finding aid), Bruce Alger Collection, Dallas Public Library, www.dallaslibrary2.org/texas/archives/MA83-11.html.

28. Fairbanks, "Failure of Urban Renewal," 312–13.

29. Campbell, *Gone to Texas*, 419.

30. Champagne, *Congressman Sam Rayburn*, esp. 161–67.

31. For an excellent discussion, see Davidson, *Race and Class*, 51–58 (quotes 51, 56).

32. Green, *Establishment in Texas Politics*, 173.

33. Knaggs, *Two-Party Texas*, 13, 14.

34. *Texas Observer*, editorial, "A Vote for Tower," May 20, 1961, in Miller, *Fifty Years*, 161–62. Further detail is in Campbell, *Gone to Texas*, 434.

35. Miller, *Fifty Years*.

36. Gregory Curtis, "Pooped Parties," *Texas Monthly* 21:3 (Mar. 1993).

37. Obituary of John Tower, *New York Times*, Apr. 6, 1991.

38. See, for example, Zach Vaughn, "The Rise of Two-Party Texas," in his blog, *Wandering Reveries*, Jan. 10, 2011. http://wanderingreveries.blogspot.com/2011/01/rise-of-two-party-texas.html

39. Bridges, *Twilight*, 52.

40. Davidson, *Race and Class*, 198.

41. Cramer, *What It Takes*, 411.

42. Clayson, *Freedom Is Not Enough*, 147.

43. Young, "Democratic Party," 8.

44. The statewide vote for president in 1968 gave Humphrey 41.1 percent, Nixon 39.9 percent, and Wallace 18.97 percent. Of the six Great Plains states, Texas's Wallace percentage was second only to Oklahoma's, at 20.33.

45. Garcia, *Reagan's Comeback*, 168, 141.

46. Ibid., 5, 9 (quote), 60–61, 141.

47. Davidson, *Race and Class*, 59–60, 189.

48. Peter Adams, letter to the *New York Times Book Review*, Jan. 29, 2012.

49. Parker, *Lone Star Nation*, 61–65.

50. McCall, *Power of the Texas Governor*, 30–32.

51. The vote in the general election was Briscoe 1,633,493, Grover 1,533,986, and Ramsey Muñiz of La Raza Unida 214,118; Dallas Morning News, *Texas Almanac 1974–1975*, 529.

52. Davidson, *Race and Class*, chap. 9, details this beautifully.

53. Campbell, *Gone to Texas*, 442.

54. Burka, "Left Out."

55. McCall, *Power of the Texas Governor*, 55.

56. Bridges, *Twilight*, vii.

57. Knaggs, *Two-Party Texas*, 207.

58. Ibid., 207, 227.

59. Garcia, *Reagan's Comeback*, 181.

60. Green, *Establishment in Texas Politics*, 209.

61. Lutz and Tedin, *Perspectives on American and Texas Politics*, 227; Maxwell, *Texas Politics Today*, 124.

62. Bland, *Texas Government Today*, 90, 107.

63. Wiggins, Hamm, and Balanoff, "1982 Gubernatorial Transition."

64. McCall, *Power of the Texas Governor*, 54–55.

65. Ibid., 56.

66. Ibid., 68–69.

67. Ibid., 72.

68. Bland, *Texas Government Today*, 27.

69. McCall, *Power of the Texas Governor*, 87 and chap. 7, "Clements's Second Term."

70. Knaggs, *Two-Party Texas*, 298.

71. Tannahill and Bedichek, *Texas Government*, 154.

72. Ibid., tab. 4.2, 155.

73. Ibid., 155, 158 (quote).

74. Ibid., 160.

75. Much has been written on Ann Richards's victory in 1990. Tolleson-Rinehart and Stanley, *Claytie and the Lady*, focus on "sex and gender roles in the Texas political culture," 4. A more purely biographical account is Reid, *Let the People In*.

76. Tolleson-Rinehart and Stanley, *Claytie and the Lady,* 68–69; McCall, *Power of the Texas Governor,* 98.

77. McCall, *Power of the Texas Governor,* 100; Tolleson-Rinehart and Stanley, *Claytie and the Lady,* 77.

78. Williams statement in 2011, quoted in Wuthnow, *Rough Country,* 383.

79. David Oshinsky, "The Last Liberal," *Texas Monthly* 40:10 (Oct. 2012).

80. Richards prized her endorsement by Sarah Weddington, who had been the lead attorney in the *Roe v. Wade* case of 1973; see Procter, "Texas Gubernatorial Election," 246.

81. Paul Burka, "Bill's Bungle," *Texas Monthly* 20:12 (Dec. 1992).

82. Wuthnow, *Rough Country,* 390.

83. Wiman, *My Bright Abyss,* 33.

84. Meyer, *Son,* 54.

85. Wuthnow, *Rough Country,* 272.

86. Green et al., "Soul of the South," 268.

87. By no means were all Southern Baptists conservative on political issues. Some supported gay rights and, through the Texas Freedom Network, which attracted 60,000 members and several hundred "progressive clergy" by 2010, opposed teaching creationism and intelligent design. Wuthnow, *Rough Country,* 322, 426.

88. Ramet, "'Fighting for the Christian Nation,'" 432.

89. Wuthnow, *Rough Country,* 322.

90. Ramet, "Fighting for the Christian Nation,'" 436; Lamare, Polinard, and Wrinkle, "Texas: Religion and Politics," 61.

91. Randall Balmer, "Trump's Success with Evangelical Voters Isn't Surprising. It Was Inevitable," *Washington Post,* May 16, 2016, www.washingtonpost.com/posteverything/wp/2016/05/16.

92. Bruce, "Texas," 69–70.

93. Ellis, "Alternative Politics," 361, 364, 372–76.

94. Laura Foxworth, "Southern Baptists for Life and the Challenge of Delivering the Southern Baptist Convention to the Pro-Life Movement," paper presented at the session "Abortion and Right Politics," Organization of American Historians annual meeting, Atlanta, April 2014.

95. Lamare, Polinard, and Wrinkle, "Texas: Religion and Politics," 63, 66; Lamare, Polinard, and Wrinkle, "Texas: Lone Star(Wars) State," 252; Bruce, "Texas," 70–78.

96. Lamare, Polinard, and Wrinkle, "Texas: Religion and Politics," 63–64. On school boards and the state board of education, see Grieder, *Big, Hot,* 153.

97. Kay Bailey Hutchinson defeated Democrat Bob Krueger in a special election in May 1993 to fill Bentsen's term, and in 1994 she defeated Richard Fisher for a full term. She was reelected in 2000 and 2006 for two more full terms.

98. Paul Burka, "Filling the Shoes," *Texas Monthly* 25:8 (August 1997).

99. Gregory Curtis, "The Last Whimper," *Texas Monthly* 26:1 (Jan. 1998), 7.

100. Patricia Kilday Hart, "Party Poopers," *Texas Monthly* 29:5 (May 2001),

54–57. Protected by the Voting Rights Act of 1965 and court rulings, minority districts and their Democratic incumbents were not at risk. They were Sheila Jackson Lee, Houston, District 18; Eddie Bernice Johnson, Dallas, District 30; Ruben Hinojosa, Mercedes, District 15; Silvestre Reyes, El Paso, District 16; Charlie Gonzalez, San Antonio, District 20; Ciro Rodriguez, San Antonio, District 28; Solomon Ortiz, Corpus Christi, District 27; and Gene Green, Houston, District 29, who although an Anglo represented a district that was heavily Hispanic.

101. In this paragraph I follow the *Almanac of American Politics 2004*, 1510–11. Very helpful also is Hart, "Party Poopers."

102. Bickerstaff, *Lines in the Sand*, 9. This volume is the authoritative account of the 2003 redistricting. Bickerstaff is a former assistant state attorney general, "a private attorney [often] retained to represent governments and government officials, and . . . a professor" at the University of Texas School of Law (viii). His story ends in mid-2006. DeLay's difficulties continued for several more years.

103. *Almanac of American Politics 2004*, 1511. The ten were Max Sandlin, Marshall, District 1; Jim Turner, Crockett, District 2; Ralph Hall, Rockwall, District 4; Nick Lampson, Beaumont, District 9; Lloyd Doggett, Austin, District 10; Chet Edwards, Waco, District 11; Charlie Stenholm, Avoca, District 17; Martin Frost, Arlington, District 24; Chris Bell, Houston, District 25; and Gene Green, Houston, District 29. Hall, Doggett, Edwards, and Green survived, though not all of them for long.

104. Bickerstaff, *Lines in the Sand*, 294–96; *Almanac of American Politics 2004*, 1511.

105. *Almanac of American Politics 2012*, 1520–21.

106. Bickerstaff, *Lines in the Sand*, 327, 332–38.

107. Grieder, *Big, Hot*, 155–57; McKee, Teigen, and Turgeon, "Partisan Impact"; *Almanac of American Politics 2012*, 1405–6.

108. Bickerstaff, *Lines in the Sand*, 236, 260.

109. Ibid., 308, 313, 382.

110. *Almanac of American Politics 2014*, 1566–67.

111. Grieder, "Through the Looking Glass," *Texas Monthly* 43:2 (Feb. 2015), 18–20.

112. Brian D. Sweany, "The Next Four Years," *Texas Monthly* 42:12 (Dec. 2014), 24.

113. Paul Burka, "Our Number Is Up," *Texas Monthly* 30:10 (Oct. 2002).

114. Parker, *Lone Star Nation*, 67, 174.

115. Cal Jillson, political scientist at Southern Methodist University, in *New York Times*, Oct. 28, 2017, 3.

116. Paul Burka, "Minority Report," *Texas Monthly* 35:1 (Jan. 2007).

117. Wuthnow, *Rough Country*, 429.

118. Paul Burka, "Out to Pasture," *Texas Monthly*, 42:10 (Oct. 2014). 22–28.

119. In 2016, Hillary Clinton carried the metropolitan counties of Harris (Houston), Dallas, Bexar (San Antonio), Travis (Austin), and El Paso. Tarrant (Fort Worth) went for Trump.

120. Paul Burka, "Two-Party Animal," *Texas Monthly* 36:12 (Dec. 2008).

121. Mimi Swartz, "Red but Not Relevant," *New York Times*, May 17, 2016.

CHAPTER 3

1. Although I use the voting returns for federal elections found online under clerk of the House of Representatives, and one would consider this the gold standard of reliable sources, even it is not error-free—as when it reversed the votes for U.S. senator in the 1978 Wyoming election. Curiously, a search of the Library of Congress catalog under the subject heading "[name of state]—Politics and Government, 1951—" produced almost nothing for the Dakotas, Wyoming, and certain other states, and little on Kansas or Nebraska. Biographies of people who were nationally prominent, such as George McGovern, do appear, but little else. The historiography is thinner than it should be. Historians of these red states have a nearly open field to cultivate.

2. Wood, *Survival of Rural America*, subtitle of chap. 3.

3. Spillman, "Kansan Ethos."

4. *Almanac of American Politics 1984*, 430.

5. Peirce, *Great Plains States*, 228, 221.

6. Ibid., 228.

7. Ibid., 227.

8. Cramer, *What It Takes*, 746–47.

9. Cigler, Joslyn, and Loomis, "Kansas Christian Right," 147.

10. Flentje and Aistrup, *Kansas Politics*, 25. Roy's son was quoted in his obituary saying, "He delivered more than 8,000 babies." *Topeka Capital-Journal* online, May 28, 2014.

11. Cigler, Joslyn, and Loomis, "Kansas Christian Right," 146.

12. *Almanac of American Politics 1994*, 489; Cigler, Joslyn, and Loomis, "Kansas Christian Right," 150.

13. *Almanac of American Politics 1994*, 492.

14. Cigler, Joslyn, and Loomis, "Kansas Christian Right," 150–51.

15. Flentje and Aistrup, *Kansas Politics*, 26–27.

16. It did not prohibit teaching Darwinism; it simply excluded it from material to be tested. Cigler, Joslyn, and Loomis, 154–56.

17. Ibid., 162.

18. Bryan Lowry, Oliver Morrison, and Matt Riedi, "Berger Beats Bruce, McGinn Keeps Seat in 'Brutal' Night for Conservatives," *Wichita Eagle*, Aug. 2, 2016, www.Kansas.com/news.politics-government/election/article93377897; Tim Carpenter, "Political Tide in Kansas Runs against Republican Gov. Brownback," *Topeka Capital-Journal*, Aug. 3, 2016.

19. The best biographies are Michael Kazin, *Godly Hero: The Life of William Jennings Bryan* and Richard Lowitt's three volume series *George W. Norris*.

20. A. G. Sulzberger, "Rural Legislators' Power Ebbs as Populations Shift," *New York Times*, June 2, 2011. My thanks to Jon Lauck for bringing this to my attention.

21. "Frank B. Morrison," *Wikipedia* biography.

22. Peirce, *Great Plains States*, 205.

23. Clem, "Popular Representation," 71.

24. *Congressional Record*, 16392 (Dec. 2, 1954).

25. Colon, "Elected Woman," 258–59.

26. Kincaid, "Over His Dead Body," 97n5; March, "Official Report."

27. *Almanac of American Politics 1974*, 582, 583.

28. Ibid., 579.

29. *Almanac of American Politics 1984*, 695–96; *Almanac of American Politics 1996*, 807–8.

30. *Almanac of American Politics 2012*, 978.

31. "Deb Fischer," *Wikipedia* biography.

32. *Almanac of American Politics 2016*, 1095.

33. *Almanac of American Politics 2014*, 1013–14.

34. Sarah Posner, "In Tea Party Senate Candidate's Dissertation, a Nostalgia for a Populist Christian Nation," May 20, 2014, *Religion Dispatches*, www.religiondispatches.org.

35. *Almanac of American Politics 2016*, 1097–99.

36. Hachey, "American Profiles on Capitol Hill," 153. I am indebted to the *Wikipedia* biography of Mundt for this reference.

37. Harry McPherson, quoted in Peirce, *Great Plains States*, 181.

38. On McGovern's wartime experiences, see McGovern, *Grassroots*, 23–28; Taylor, "Violence of War," 24–30; and Knock, *Rise of a Prairie Statesman*, chap. 4.

39. On McGovern's attraction to Stevenson, see Knock, *Rise of a Prairie Statesman*, 143–44.

40. Ibid., 91–97.

41. McGovern, *Grassroots*, esp. 47–58. For McGovern's party building and successful campaign for the House in 1956, see Knock, *Rise of a Prairie Statesman*, chap. 8.

42. Peirce, *Great Plains States*, 184, 186; *Almanac of American Politics 1974*, 928–29.

43. O'Regan and Stambough, "From the Grassroots," 38.

44. *Almanac of American Politics 1984*, 1081

45. Hoover and Emery, "South Dakota Governance," 221–22.

46. *Almanac of American Politics 2010*, 1364.

47. Ibid., 1357.

48. The story is told in Lauck, *Daschle vs. Thune*.

49. Janklow obituary, *New York Times*, Jan. 13, 2012.

50. *Almanac of American Politics 2014*, 1517. In 2007, after marrying former Texas representative Max Sandlin, Stephanie Herseth became known as Stephanie Herseth Sandlin.

51. Peirce, *Great Plains States*, 168–69.

52. *Wahpeton Daily News*, Apr. 26, 2013; thanks to *Wikipedia* for this reference.

53. Danbom, "Part of the Nation," 180.

54. Ibid., 178.

55. *Almanac of American Politics 1994*, 974–75.

56. *Almanac of American Politics 2012*, 1250.

57. *Almanac of American Politics 2016*, 1395.

58. Ibid., 1391.

59. "What Are Trump's Views on Climate Change? Some Clues Emerge," *New York Times*, May 21, 2016.

60. *Almanac of American Politics 2016*, 1388.

61. U.S. Census estimate; www.census.gov/quickfacts/table/PST045215/38.

62. U.S. Census Bureau, "Annual Estimates of the Resident Population for Incorporated Places: April 1, 2010 to July 1, 2015."

63. *Almanac of American Politics 1974*, 1117. According to *Almanac of American Politics 1994*, 1405, in 1992 "the northern two-thirds of Wyoming voted 42% for George Bush, and Ross Perot's 27% here almost topped Bill Clinton's 31%. . . . the southern tier of counties, from Cheyenne through Laramie to Evanston, usually votes Democratic, and voted 40%–36% for Bill Clinton."

64. *Almanac of American Politics 2012*, 1785.

65. Roberts and Bieber-Roberts, "'Politics Is Personal,'" 295.

66. Earlier Democratic winners were Bryan in 1896; Wilson in 1912 and 1916; Franklin Roosevelt in 1932, 1936, and 1940; and Truman in 1948.

67. His dissertation was titled "The Founding Fathers and Entangling Alliances."

68. Quoted in Peirce, *Mountain States of America*, 82.

69. "Gale W. McGee," *Wikipedia* biography.

70. *Almanac of American Politics 2016*, 2031, 2034, 2035. Louisiana has two quite conservative senators, but not as purely so as Enzi and Barrasso.

71. Peirce, *Rocky Mountain States*, 82.

72. Roberts and Bieber-Roberts, "'Politics Is Personal,'" 301.

73. Peirce, *Mountain States*, 78.

74. Ibid., 81.

75. Roberts and Bieber-Roberts, "'Politics Is Personal,'" 295.

76. *Almanac of American Politics 1994*, 1405.

77. As I argued in my Tanner lecture to the Mormon History Association in 2009; see Nugent, "Mormons and America's Empires."

78. Deskins, Walton, and Puckett, *Presidential Elections*.

79. "J. Bracken Lee Is Dead at 97: Was Blunt Governor of Utah," *New York Times*, Oct. 22, 1996; "Bracken Lee, Colorful Utah Maverick, Dies," *Deseret News*, Oct. 21, 1996.

80. John S. McCormick, "Calvin L. Rampton," *Utah History Encyclopedia*, www.historytogo.utah.gov/people/calvinlrampton; "Calvin Rampton, Former Utah Governor, Dies at 93," *Deseret Morning News*, Sep. 18, 2007.

81. John McCormick, "Scott M. Matheson," *Utah History Encyclopedia*, www.historytogo.utah.gov/people/scottmmatheson.

82. "Olene Walker, Utah's First Female Governor, Dies at 85," *New York Times*, Nov. 29, 2015.

83. *Almanac of American Politics 2016*, 1835.

84. *Almanac of American Politics 1974*, 1018.

85. "Obituary: Senator Frank E. Moss," *Deseret News*, Jan. 31, 2003.

86. *Almanac of American Politics 1974*, 1019.

87. *Almanac of American Politics 2014*, 1681; *Almanac of American Politics 2016*, 1839.

88. *Almanac of American Politics 2014*, 1689.

89. Alexander, "Emergence," 260.

90. Shaw, "Harassment, Hate."

91. Kevin Sullivan, "A Fortress against Fear: In the Rural Pacific Northwest, Prepping for the Day It Hits the Fan," *Washington Post*, Aug. 27, 2016, www.washingtonpost.com/sf/national/wp2016/08/27/a-fortress; "Preparing for Chaos," *The Week*, Oct. 14, 2016, 40–41.

92. Peirce, *Mountain States*, 139–40.

93. Ibid., 140.

94. Andrus obituary, *New York Times*, Aug. 26, 2017.

95. Evans obituary, *Coeur d'Alene Press*, July 9, 2014.

96. "C. L. Otter," OnTheIssues.org, www.ontheissues.org/House/Butch_Otter.htm.

97. Peirce, *Mountain States*, 141.

98. *Almanac of American Politics 1974*, 252.

99. Dant, "Making Wilderness Work."

100. Peirce, *Mountain States*, 149.

101. "Frank Church," *Wikipedia*. According to this, NCPAC—the National Conservative Political Action Committee—funded the effort to defeat Church.

102. *Almanac of American Politics 1984*, 313, 316–17.

103. McClure obituary, *New York Times*, Mar. 3, 2011.

104. *Almanac of American Politics 1994*, 372.

105. *Almanac of American Politics 2016*, 575, 578.

106. Stallings's voting record is tabulated at "Rep. Richard Stallings," www.govtrack.us/congress/members/Richard_Stallings/410251.

107. Slotnick, "1960 Election in Alaska," 302–4. Also informative is Naske, "'Little Men' Demand Statehood." On the struggle for statehood, see Whitehead, *Alaska, Hawaii*.

108. Greg Williams, "Population Growth and Migration in Alaska," in CensusScope.org/us/s2/chart_popl.html.

109. *Almanac of American Politics 2012*, 4; *Almanac of American Politics 2016*, 73.

110. *Almanac of American Politics 1984*, 26; *Almanac of American Politics 1994*, 27; *Almanac of American Politics 2004*, 80.

111. *Almanac of American Politics 1994*, 31. Regarding the other significant third-party candidates in recent decades, George Wallace took 12.1 percent of the Alaskan vote, slightly below his national average of 13.5 percent, and John

Anderson in 1980 won 7.0 percent in Alaska, close to his national average of 6.6 percent. Libertarian and Green Party candidates have run in many Alaskan elections, but their votes have usually been in the 3–5 percent range, except for Hickel's victory for governor in 1990—after which he identified as a Republican again. Ralph Nader, the Green candidate in 2000, captured 10 percent in Alaska, far above his 2.7 percent national average.

112. *Almanac of American Politics 2010*, 65.

113. *Almanac of American Politics 2014*, 42; *Almanac of American Politics 2016*, 63; *Almanac of American Politics 2018*, 57.

114. *Almanac of American Politics 1974*, 23–24.

115. *Almanac of American Politics 1984*, 28, 30–31.

116. *Almanac of American Politics 1994*, 35–36.

117. *Almanac of American Politics 2012*, 52.

118. *Almanac of American Politics 2014*, 52.

119. The contract ultimately went to TransCanada, a Canadian company. *Almanac of American Politics 2010*, 63.

120. "New Leader for Alaska Traversed Unlikely Path," *New York Times*, Nov. 25, 2014.

121. "To Reinvigorate Production, Alaska Grants a Tax Break to Oil Companies," *New York Times*, April 16, 2013.

122. "Drop in Oil Prices Now Hits Home in Alaska," *New York Times*, July 16, 2016.

CHAPTER 4

1. "Pinto Democrat" meant, without great precision, one who was rural based, fairly conservative, and of Texas origins.

2. These and the following population figures are from the U.S. decennial censuses and intervening estimates.

3. Rex, "Migration," 1, 13–14; Peirce, *Mountain States*, 218.

4. Peirce, *Mountain States*, 215, 219.

5. Ibid., 222.

6. Ibid.; Prof. James H. Madison, personal communication, Sep. 16, 2016.

7. Needham, *Power Lines*, 99–100.

8. Needham, "Sunbelt Imperialism," 241.

9. Goldberg, *Barry Goldwater*, 84–85.

10. Ibid., 99.

11. Ibid., 247; Peirce, *Mountain States*, 221.

12. Peirce, *Mountain States*, 226.

13. Ibid., 223.

14. *Almanac of American Politics 1994*, 36; "Evan Mecham, 83; Was Removed as Arizona Governor," *Washington Post*, obituary, Feb. 23, 2008.

15. "Rose Mofford, 94, Ex-governor of Arizona," *New York Times*, obituary, Sep. 17, 2016; "List of Governors of Arizona," *Wikipedia*. Symington was convicted of fraud, but the conviction was later thrown out.

16. *Almanac of American Politics 2004*, 98.

17. *Almanac of American Politics 2016*, 82.

18. *Almanac of American Politics 2014*, 63.

19. "A Radical Senator," *Montana: The Magazine of Western History* 66:1 (Spring 2016), 57; Farley, "Rocky Mountain Radicals."

20. "Mike Mansfield, Longtime Leader of Senate Democrats, Dies at 98," *New York Times*, obituary, Oct. 6, 2001.

21. Swanson, "Lee Metcalf," parts 1 and 2.

22. *Almanac of American Politics 2010*, 902.

23. "Conrad Burns, 81, Plain-Spoken Ex-senator," *New York Times*, obituary, May 2, 2016. Burns was never charged with wrongdoing.

24. *Almanac of American Politics 2012*, 1000; *Almanac of American Politics 2016*, 1082. He has scored well with labor unions, the ACLU, and even the League of Conservation Voters, and decidedly not with the American Conservative Union. See also Andrew Romano, "The Democrats' Last, Best Hope," *Newsweek*, May 9, 2011, 48–51.

25. "Max Baucus," U.S. Department of State, https://2009-2017.state.gov/r/pa/ei/biog/221450.htm.

26. *Almanac of American Politics 1984*, 687; *Almanac of American Politics 1994*, 760; *Almanac of American Politics 2004*, 953; *Almanac of American Politics 2014*, 996–97.

27. *Almanac of American Politics 2014*, 997.

28. "Montana Ex-guardsman Now Must Fight to Keep Senate Seat Given to Him," *New York Times*, Mar. 24, 2014; "Senator's Thesis Turns Out to Be Remix of Other's Works, Uncited," *New York Times*, July 23, 2014.

29. "Former Dem Congressman Declines to Enter Montana Senate Race," *Washington Post*, Aug. 13, 2013.

30. *Almanac of American Politics 1984*, 683–84.

31. *Almanac of American Politics 2010*, 895.

32. *Almanac of American Politics 2012*, 968–70.

33. Green, *Nevada*, 247.

34. Richard N. Velotta, "Harry Reid: Pat McCarran's Name Shouldn't Be on Anything," *Las Vegas Sun*, Aug. 25, 2012; "McCarran Dies," *Las Vegas Sun*, Sep. 29, 1954; David Greenberg, review of Michael J. Ybarra, *Washington Gone Crazy: Senator Pat McCarran and the Great American Communist Hunt*, *New York Times*, Oct. 31, 2004.

35. Green, *Nevada*, 254.

36. Edwards, "Gambling and Politics," 156.

37. Census figures from www.census.gov.

38. U.S. Census figures and estimate.

39. Nevada Secretary of State, "January 2015 Voter Registration Statistics Total Voters by County and Party," www.nvsos.gov/Modules/ShowDocument.aspx?documentid=3610.

40. "Walter S. Baring, Jr.," *Wikipedia* biography.

41. Peirce, *Mountain States*, 178; *Almanac of American Politics 1974*, 591.

42. "George Malone," *Online Nevada Encyclopedia*, www.onlinenevada.org/articles/george-malone.

43. Green, *Nevada*, 272.

44. A. D. Hopkins, "Grant Sawyer," *Las Vegas Review-Journal*, Feb. 7, 1999; Green, *Nevada*, 318.

45. Green, *Nevada*, 190–91, 318–19.

46. David Stout, "Howard Cannon, 90, Senator Who Served Four Terms, Dies," *New York Times*, Mar. 7, 2002. The vote was Cannon 67,336, Laxalt 67,288.

47. In the words of the *Almanac of American Politics 1984*, 705.

48. Green, *Nevada*, 327–28.

49. The result was Laxalt 79,605, Reid 78,981, with Jack Doyle, Independent American, taking 10,887.

50. Green, *Nevada*, 349.

51. *New York Times*, obituary, June 13, 2013; *Washington Post*, obituary, June 12, 2013; *Almanac of American Politics 1994*, 786.

52. In what proved to be his final campaign, 2010, Reid defeated Tea Party Republican Sharron Angle, 50 percent to 45, winning both Clark and Washoe Counties, while Angle won all the others. *Almanac of American Politics 2012*, 1001.

53. *Almanac of American Politics 2004*, 983; *Almanac of American Politics 2010*, 923.

54. *Almanac of American Politics 2010*, 924.

55. *Almanac of American Politics 2016*, 1111.

56. McCarran's last victory was in 1950, Malone's in 1952; of course, they had won before 1950. Alan Bible (D) won in 1954 (to fill McCarran's uncompleted term), 1956, 1962, and 1968. Howard Cannon (D) won in 1958, 1964, 1970, and 1976. Paul Laxalt (R) won in 1974 and 1980. Chic Hecht won only in 1982. Harry Reid first won in 1986, then again in 1992, 1998, 2004, and 2010. Richard Bryan (D) won in 1988 and 1994. John Ensign (R) won in 2000 and 2006. Dean Heller (R) won in 2012, and Catherine Cortez Masto (D) in 2016.

57. Daum, Duffy, and Straayer, *State of Change*, 3–4.

58. *New York Times*, obituary of Allott, Jan. 13, 1989.

59. Cannon, Review of *Wayne Aspinall*, 649 (quote)–52.

60. Steven C. Schulte, "Wayne Aspinall," *Colorado Encyclopedia*, www.coloradoencyclopedia.org/article/wayne-aspinall.

61. August, Review of *Wayne Aspinall*, 389.

62. Cannon, Review of *Wayne Aspinall*, 651. "It was not so much that Aspinall lost touch with his longtime constituents as that he had thousands of new metropolitan constituents in 1972 who had never shared his views."

63. Peirce, *Mountain States*, 40, 45–48.

64. Daum, Duffy, and Straayer, *State of Change*, 11.

65. Ken Schroeppel, "Denver County Remains Population Growth News," March 31, 2013, *Denver Urbanism*, www.denverurbanism.com/2013/03.

66. *Almanac of American Politics 1994*, 213.

67. *Almanac of American Politics 2010*, 278.

68. *Almanac of American Politics 2004*, 325.

69. *Almanac of American Politics 2010*, 273. The other three were Quark Software founder Tim Gill, medical technology heiress Patricia Stryker, and geophysicist and MicroMAX software creator Rutt Bridges.

70. Daum, Duffy, and Straayer, *State of Change*, 41.

71. *Almanac of American Politics 2016*, 326: The senate had eighteen Republicans and seventeen Democrats; the house, thirty-three Democrats, thirty-one Republicans, with one vacancy.

72. Nate Silver, "How Will Republicans Take Advantage of Bingaman's Retirement?," *FiveThirtyEight*, Feb. 18, 2011.

73. Edwin Mechem of New Mexico is not to be confused with Evan Mecham of Arizona.

74. New Mexico Office of the State Historian, "US Senator Dennis Chavez," http://newmexicohistory.org/people/
us-senator-dennis-chavez-from-new-mexico-1935-1962.

75. Peirce, *Mountain States*, 266, 267. See also "Clinton Presba Anderson," *Wikipedia*.

76. *Almanac of American Politics 1996*, 882.

77. *Almanac of American Politics 2004*, 1071.

78. This is the same Ed Foreman who earlier won a single term from a not-too-distant Texas district.

79. Republicans Mechem in 1950, 1952, 1956, and 1960; David Cargo, 1966 and 1968; Garrey Carruthers in 1986; Gary Johnson in 1994 and 1998; and Susana Martinez in 2010 and 2014. Democrats John F. Simms in 1954; John Burroughs in 1958; Jack M. Campbell in 1962 and 1964; Bruce King in 1970; Jerry Apodaca in 1974; Bruce King again in 1978; Toney Anaya in 1982; Bruce King yet again in 1990; and Bill Richardson in 2002 and 2006.

CHAPTER 5

1. Goldschmidt, "1952 Elections in Oregon," 124.

2. The early twentieth-century "Oregon System" is well described in Johnson, *Radical Middle Class*.

3. Toy, "Ku Klux Klan."

4. From 1900 to 1950 the U.S. population roughly doubled from 76 million to 151 million. In that half century Oregon more than tripled, from 414,000 to 1.5 million; the census's West region quadrupled from 4.3 to 20.2 million. United States Bureau of the Census, *Historical Statistics*, chap. A.

5. The closest margin was Gore's in 2000, with 47.0 percent over George W. Bush's 46.5. But in that election Green Party candidate Ralph Nader took 5.0 percent, much of which would likely have gone to Gore if Nader had not run. Other prominent third-party candidates apparently did not affect the two-party outcome: George Wallace took 6.1 percent in 1968, John Anderson 9.5 percent in 1980, and Ross Perot 24.2 percent in 1992 and 8.8 percent in 1996. The Perot

candidacies kept Bill Clinton from capturing 50 percent of the popular vote, but Dukakis (51.3 percent), Kerry (51.4 percent), Obama (56.7 and 54.2 percent), and Hillary Clinton (50.1 percent) did so.

6. *Almanac of American Politics 2004*, 1329–30; *Almanac of American Politics 2010*, 1238.

7. For example, the historian and planning expert Carl Abbott: "As late as the 1960s, patterns of political affiliation were similar across the different regions of the state. . . . The strongest contrast, that between the less Democratic mid–Willamette Valley on the one hand and the more Democratic North Coast and Multnomah County on the other hand, was no more than 10 percentage points for 1966–70. The regional differences were enough for politicians to notice but not enough to generate talk about 'two Oregons.'" Abbott, "From Urban Frontier," 87.

8. Clucas, Henkels, and Steel, *Oregon Politics*, 114, 127–28.

9. Holland et al., "Declining Economic Interdependence," 83.

10. *Almanac of American Politics 1974*, 845.

11. *Almanac of American Politics 1994*, 1066.

12. Clucas, Henkels, and Steel, *Oregon Politics*, 120–21.

13. *Almanac of American Politics 1984*, 992–93; *Almanac of American Politics 2004*, 1345.

14. William G. Robbins tells the boom-and-bust story in *Hard Times in Paradise*.

15. "Oregon's Economy: Overview," *Oregon Blue Book*, http://bluebook.state.or.us/facts/economy; Craig Wollner, "Silicon Forest," *Oregon Encyclopedia*, https://oregonencyclopedia.org/articles/silicon_forest/#.WjKuNK2ZPkE.

16. Jeff Mapes, "The Photo Vault: Charles 'Iron Pants' Martin's Tumultuous Reign," *Oregonian*, Dec. 25, 2012. Paul Kleppner also discusses Martin in "Politics without Parties." Kleppner writes, "At one point he [Martin] commended the suggestion that the state's aged and feeble-minded wards should be chloroformed, claiming it would save the state $300,000 on the next biennial budget if 900 or so of them were 'put out of their misery'" (323).

17. Murrell, "Hunting Reds," 378–79; William G. Robbins, "Oregon Commonwealth Federation," *Oregon Encyclopedia*, https://oregonencyclopedia.org/articles/?i=oep&search_text=Oregon+Commonwealth+Federation. The CIO is the Congress of Industrial Organizations.

18. Gary Murrell, "Martin, Charles (1863–1946)," *Oregon Encyclopedia*, https://oregonencyclopedia.org/articles/martin_charles_1863_1946_/#.WiXIdq2ZOJY.

19. Goldschmidt, "1952 Elections in Oregon," 123–26.

20. Robbins, *Man for All Seasons*, 47, 49. This volume is now the best source on Sweetland.

21. Ibid., 105–6.

22. Burton, *Democrats of Oregon*, 1. Morgan (1914–2012) served one term in the Oregon house, chaired the state Democratic Party in 1955, and was Oregon Public Utility Commissioner (1957–59) and Federal Power Commissioner

(1961). Sweetland's dates are 1910–2006. See "Howard V. Morgan Obituary," *Oregonian*, Apr. 22, 2012, http://obits.oregonlive.com/obituaries/oregon/obituary.aspx?pid=157186154.

23. So described by Congressman Earl Blumenauer upon Sweetland's death on September 10, 2006, in Kari Chisholm, "Monroe Sweetland," *BlueOregon*, www.blueoregon.com/2006/09/monroe_sweetlan. Sweetland did not leave a helpful autobiography, as Henry Bellmon of Oklahoma did, but see Robbins, *Man for All Seasons*.

24. LaLande, "Oregon's Last Conservative," 243.

25. Burton, *Democrats of Oregon*, 129 (quote), 130.

26. Ibid., 126–27. Howard Morgan later stated that 1954 and the Neuberger unseating of Cordon "was the big breakthrough. It was not until 1956 that we carried every statewide office except that of secretary of state, which Mark Hatfield held." Hansen, "Making of the Modern Democratic Party," 382.

27. A thorough discussion of Hells Canyon leading up to the 1956 election is Bessey, "Political Issues" ("acrimonious dispute" quote, 676).

28. Swarthout, "1956 Election in Oregon," 142–50. Compare the 1952 legislature, where Democrats won only eleven of sixty house and three of thirty senate seats (142).

29. LaLande, "Oregon's Last Conservative," 253.

30. Burton, *Democrats of Oregon*, 139.

31. Swarthout, "1956 Election in Oregon," 146–48. See as well Ceplair, "Foreign Policy."

32. Swarthout, "1958 Election in Oregon," esp. 328–30, 343 (quote 363).

33. Peirce, *Pacific States*, 199. Hatfield was the first "new Republican," followed by Tom McCall (elected governor in 1966) and Bob Packwood (elected senator in 1968).

34. Drukman, "Oregon's Most Famous Feud."

35. Neuberger's widow, Maurine, was elected to his Senate seat in 1960 for a full term, but she declined to run for reelection in 1966.

36. Swarthout, "1956 Election in Oregon," 144. Samuel W. McCall (d. 1923) was elected to the U.S. House in 1892 and reelected nine times. He was also elected governor in 1915, 1916, and 1917. Thomas W. Lawson (d. 1925) was a cofounder of the Amalgamated Copper Company and was involved in both manipulation and reform of the stock markets.

37. For these details on McCall's career, I am indebted to Brent Walth's biography, *Fire at Eden's Gate*, 109, 116, 142–47, 150–61. The John Birch Society did not gain much traction in Oregon; see Toy, "Right Side of the 1960s."

38. Walth, *Fire at Eden's Gate*, 243.

39. Walth, "No Deposit, No Return," credits certain legislators for the original impetus for the bill, with an initially hesitant McCall coming on board in 1971.

40. An accurate assessment of McCall's achievements is Robbins, *Oregon*, 154–55.

41. Allman, "1968 Elections in Oregon," 525.

42. Walth, *Fire at Eden's Gate*, 331, 334; Clucas, "Political Legacy," 463, 466.

43. Robbins, *Landscapes of Conflict*, 267, 288.

44. *Oregonian*, Nov. 7, 1974. Dellenback "is widely regarded as a conservative Republican, and yet he has the most liberal voting record of the Oregon congressional delegation," wrote Zeigler and Smith, in "1970 Election in Oregon," 333; but the voters correctly realized that Weaver was more progressive still.

45. Clucas, "Political Legacy," 474; Johnson, *Standing at the Water's Edge*.

46. Goldschmidt successfully courted business support as well as the more usual backing from teachers and labor. Goldschmidt "swept most of the Willamette Valley and coastal counties, while Paulus won in Washington and Clackamas" (west and south of Portland) and east of the Cascades. Multnomah voted strongly for Goldschmidt. *Oregonian*, Nov. 5 and 6, 1986.

47. Nearly fifteen years later it became known that he had a sexual relationship with a fourteen-year-old girl in the 1970s when he was mayor of Portland. By then the statute of limitations precluded prosecution, but in 1990 he would have been in jeopardy. Presumably, fear of exposure kept him from running.

48. This and much of the following information on the OCA is from Lunch, "Oregon" (quote 231).

49. Ibid., 242.

50. Marc Ramirez, "Lon Mabon Sets 'Em Straight," *Seattle Times*, Oct. 3, 1993.

51. Personal communication from William G. Robbins, Feb. 24, 2013.

52. For detail on Roberts's career, see her autobiography, *Up the Capitol Steps*; and Tollestrup, "Women and Oregon Political History."

53. *Almanac of American Politics 1994*, 1062. Furse was a vineyard owner and founder of the Oregon Peace Institute. She survived the Republican "Contract with America" year in 1994 by 121,147 votes to the Republican's 120,846, a margin of 301 after a recount.

54. Katherine G. Seelye, "The Packwood Case," *New York Times*, Sept. 8, 1995.

55. "Facing conservatives in Oregon who threatened to mount a serious primary challenge, Mr. Hatfield declined to run for reelection in 1996." "Mark Hatfield Dies: Former Oregon Senator Was 89," *Washington Post*, obituary, Aug. 7, 2011.

56. *Almanac of American Politics, 2004*, 1332.

57. Abbott, *Greater Portland*, 140, 142.

58. Johnston, "Parties and Politics," 199.

59. Killen and Shibley, "Surveying the Religious Landscape," 29, 30, 41, 43.

60. Floyd McKay, "Oregon Governor's Race: Bizarre," in *Crosscut: News of the Great Nearby*, October 13, 2010, http://crosscut.com/2010/10/13/oregon/20248/Oregon-governor-s-race:-Bizarre.

61. *Almanac of American Politics, 2010*, 1231; *Almanac of American Politics, 2012*, 1336.

62. "In December 1984, four of the five counties with the highest unemployment percentages were all timber dependent" (Curry, Coos, Baker, and Douglas), while "the four major metro areas had relatively low percentages." Robbins, "Town and Country" 74. "Gone are blue-collar jobs in the mills and woods; in their place a

new service- and servant-oriented economy has emerged with low-paying, part-time service sector jobs with no benefits and increasingly unaffordable housing. Bend and Ashland are 'Aspenized' examples of new Western communities" (75–76).

63. Reid Wilson, "Best State in America: Oregon, for Its Lack of Corruption," *Washington Post* online, Aug. 22, 2014, citing a Justice Department report in 2013 stating that in the preceding decade forty-two public officials in Oregon were convicted for corruption; Texas had 775.

CHAPTER 6

1. Nugent, *Into the West*, 228.
2. Rogin and Shover, *Political Change in California*, 113.
3. Jonas, "Western Politics," 454; also Bell, *California Crucible*, 12.
4. Gregory, "Upton Sinclair's 1934 EPIC Campaign," 54–55.
5. Lee, *California Votes*, 26–29.
6. Bakersfield and Kern County, for example; see Jennifer Medina, "'We're Our Own State Here': In California, Hope for a G.O.P. Bastion," *New York Times*, Nov. 20, 2016.
7. For a brief survey of ballot initiatives, see Schrag, "Drowning Democracy."
8. Putnam, *Modern California Politics*, 41.
9. *Los Angeles Times*, Nov. 9, 1950; Bell, *California Crucible*, 59.
10. Putnam, *Modern California Politics*, 32.
11. Bell, *California Crucible*, 17. After Warren left California to become chief justice, the CRA moved rightward; it backed Barry Goldwater in the 1964 presidential race.
12. Findley, "Cross-Filing," 702 (quote)–10.
13. Jacobs, *Rage for Justice*, 40–41.
14. Titus and Nixon, "1948 Elections in California," 97.
15. Bell, *California Crucible*, 88.
16. Jacobs, *Rage for Justice*, 31; Putnam, *Modern California Politics*, 146–47.
17. Boyarsky, *Big Daddy*, 20.
18. Jacobs, *Rage for Justice*, 72.
19. Montgomery and Johnson, *One Step from the White House*, 248.
20. Putnam, *Modern California Politics*, 48.
21. Anderson, "1958 Election in California," 291.
22. Putnam, *Modern California Politics*, 48.
23. Bell, *California Crucible*, 155.
24. Cannon, *Ronnie and Jesse*, 109–10.
25. Anderson and Lee, "1962 Election in California," esp. 417.
26. "Jesse Unruh," *State Net* (Sacramento), Nov. 1, 1999.
27. Brown, *Basic Brown*, 90.
28. Bell, *California Crucible*, 169.
29. Allswang, *Initiative and Referendum*, 74–75.
30. Cannon, *Governor Reagan*, 147.
31. Bell, *California Crucible*, 216.

32. Boyarski, *Big Daddy*, 130–31.

33. Hardy and Sohner, "Constitutional Challenge," 764.

34. Provost, *Bernard L. Hyink's Politics*, 107.

35. Putnam, *Modern California Politics*, 53.

36. Anderson and Lee, "1966 Election in California," 537–38.

37. Evans, *Education of Ronald Reagan*; Joshua Zeitz, "How Did Ronald Reagan Become a Conservative?," *American Heritage.com*, Jan. 22, 2007.

38. Anderson and Lee, "1966 Election in California," 540, 543.

39. Dallek, *Right Moment*, x.

40. Anderson and Lee, "1966 Election in California," 550 (citing a Field Poll of October 1966), 554.

41. Bell, *California Crucible*, 237.

42. Schuparra, *Triumph of the Right*, 145.

43. Schrag, *Paradise Lost*, 48.

44. Putnam, *Modern California Politics*, 61.

45. Dionne, *Why the Right*, 91.

46. Anderson and Bell, "1970 Election in California," 272.

47. Schuparra, *Triumph of the Right*, 147.

48. Bell, *California Crucible*, 101.

49. Jacobs, *Rage for Justice*, 49–50. Jacobs explains that the San Francisco police had arrested Chinatown residents for setting off firecrackers during the Chinese New Year. Burton promoted the legalization of firecrackers on the grounds that the New Year had a "religious nature . . . just as Catholics used candles and Jews yarmulkes. He would make it a First Amendment issue."

50. Ibid., chap. 14.

51. Richardson, *Willie Brown*, 56; Brown, *Basic Brown*, 32.

52. Field, quoted in Peirce, *Pacific States*, 33.

53. *Almanac of American Politics 1984*, 70–71.

54. Bell, *California Crucible*, 247.

55. Jacobs, *Rage for Justice*, 280.

56. Ibid., 282–87.

57. Bell, *California Crucible*, 271.

58. Ibid.

59. Cahn, Schockman, and Shafie, *Rethinking California*, 31.

60. Rapoport, *California Dreaming*, 169.

61. Allswang, *Initiative and Referendum*, 104–11 (quote, 107); Bell, *California Crucible*, 272–75; Bollens and Williams, *Jerry Brown*, 174–75.

62. Smith, "Howard Jarvis," esp. 188.

63. Brown, *Basic Brown*, 124.

64. "Greater than Two to One Majority Continues to Back Prop. 13," Field Poll 2390, Sep. 23, 2011; Schrag, *California*, 17–18; Dan Walters, "Democrats Win Big in California, but Now What?" *Sacramento Bee*, Nov. 8, 2012.

65. Bell, *California Crucible*, 275.

66. Rapoport, *California Dreaming*, 237.

67. Putnam, *Modern California Politics*, 90 (quote); Jacobs, *Rage for Justice*, 410.

68. Since 1971, California has had more members of Congress (forty-three, then forty-five in 1981, and climbing) than state senators (forty).

69. Richardson, *Willie Brown*, 279.

70. An excellent recounting of the 1981 reapportionment process, containing far more detail than I can explain here and centering on Phillip Burton's role in it, is Jacobs, *Rage for Justice*, chap. 18.

71. John Jacobs, "Burton and Boxer," *State Net* (Sacramento), Mar. 1, 1999. Boxer and John Burton remained close political allies. See also Sandalow, *Madam Speaker*, 71.

72. Jacobs, *Rage for Justice*, 199–202, 445, 489; Povich, *Nancy Pelosi*, 17.

73. Putnam, *Modern California Politics*, 92–94.

74. *Los Angeles Times*, Nov. 3 and 4, 1982.

75. *Almanac of American Politics 1984*, 72–73.

76. Ibid., 74.

77. Richardson, *Willie Brown*, 296, 297, 303.

78. Boyarsky, *Big Daddy*, 203, 205–6.

79. Didion, *Where I Was From*, 115, 131, 133, 134. For another account of the economic "free fall," see Starr, *Coast of Dreams*, 238–46.

80. Didion, *Where I Was From*, 130.

81. Lou Cannon and A. G. Block, "Surviving the Republican Train Wreck," *State Net* (Sacramento), Jan. 1, 2001, 4.

82. *Almanac of American Politics 2010*, 130.

83. *Almanac of American Politics 2016*, 142.

84. Jacobs, *Rage for Justice*, 494.

85. Ibid., 495.

86. "Voting in the 1992 General Election," *California Opinion Index* (Field Poll), Jan. 1993.

87. "Exit polls showed that if Perot had not been on the ballot, 38 percent of his supporters would have voted for Bush, 38 percent would have voted for Clinton, and the rest would not have voted at all. Clinton would have won an outright majority if Perot had not rejoined the contest. . . . It's important to remember that Perot drew his support from the middle of the middle." Dionne, *Why the Right*, 107–8. These are national figures, but it is likely that California approximated them.

88. Baldassare, *California in the New Millennium*, 7.

89. Nelson, *Democrats under Siege* , 17.

90. Richardson, *Willie Brown*, 376–79; Brown, *Basic Brown*, 215–23.

91. Starr, *Coast of Dreams*, 197–99.

92. *California Opinion Index* (Field Poll), Jan. 1995.

93. This paragraph and quotes (emphasis added) from Cahn, Schockman, and Shafie, *Rethinking California*, 166–69, in addition to the sources cited.

94. See Schrag, *California*, 11; Cherny, "Direct Democracy," 5. My thanks to Professor Cherny for sending me his essay.

95. *California Opinion Index* (Field Poll), "Voting in the 1994 General Election," Jan. 1995, 1.

96. "Prop. 187," *State Net* (Sacramento), Nov. 14, 1994.

97. Starr, *Coast of Dreams*, 208–16 (quote, 211).

98. Allswang, *Initiative and Referendum*, 208–12. For extended discussion of Prop 209 and subsequent measures, see HoSang, *Racial Propositions*, chap. 7.

99. HoSang, *Racial Propositions*, 231–42 (quote 232); "Bilingual Education Initiative, Prop. 227, Continues to Get Overwhelming Voter Support," Field Poll 1875, Mar. 20, 1998; Starr, *Coast of Dreams*, 220.

100. Allswang, *Initiative and Referendum*, 229–33 (quote 229).

101. Manzano, "Latinos in the Sunbelt," 346–47.

102. *California Opinion Index* (Field Poll), "Voting in California's 1998 General Election," Jan. 1999.

103. *Almanac of American Politics 2004*, 154.

104. Lou Cannon and A. G. Block, "Surviving the Republican Train Wreck," *State Net* (Sacramento), Jan. 1, 2001.

105. A detailed account is in Starr, *Coast of Dreams*, 588–603.

106. Ibid., 622.

107. *State Net* (Sacramento), Aug. 23, 2002.

108. "How to Win a Campaign for Governor," *State Net* (Sacramento), Dec. 1, 2002.

109. Barreto, "Latino Immigrants," 79.

110. Carl M. Cannon, "GOP California Dreams," *State Net* (Sacramento), Feb. 1, 2003, 2.

111. For details see Provost, *Bernard L. Hyink's Politics*, 53–55.

112. "Three California Election Megatrends," Field Poll, Feb. 2006.

113. Field Poll 2285, Sep. 16, 2008.

114. Michael Lewis, "California and Bust," *Vanity Fair*, Nov. 2011, 232.

115. *Almanac of American Politics 2012*, 121.

116. Field Poll 2286, Sep. 17, 2008.

117. Cherny, "Direct Democracy," 8.

118. Field Poll 2362, Oct. 28, 2010.

119. Cherny, "Direct Democracy," 9.

120. Quoted in Dan Balz, "Texas, California Embody Red-Blue Divide," *Washington Post*, Dec. 28, 2013.

121. Cherny, "Direct Democracy, 10.

122. Field Poll 2499, Feb. 24, 2015.

123. Field Poll 2439, Feb. 22, 2013.

124. Lorentzen, "Golden State of Grace," 20–32.

125. Soper, "California," 219.

126. Ibid., 211–15 (quotes 215).

127. Field Poll 2350, July 21, 1010.

128. Formisano, *Tea Party*, refers only once to the California Tea Party Patriots,

"a scattered network of enthusiasts," 34; Skocpol and Williamson, *Tea Party*, has no index entry for California.

129. Field Poll 2325, Jan. 26, 2010. Both sets of figures are below the levels of many other states.

130. For example, Dan Balz, "Texas, California Embody Red-Blue Divide," *Washington Post*, Dec. 28, 2013.

131. Fred Barnes, in *Weekly Standard*, quoted in *Chicago Tribune*, editorial page, July 10, 2014.

132. Dionne, *Why the Right*, 457. Ted Lieu was first elected in 2014 as the congressman for the 33rd District, which includes Santa Monica and other parts of the westside.

133. E. J. Dionne Jr., "Can the GOP Learn from California?," *Washington Post*, Apr. 19, 2015. Becerra became attorney general of California in 2016, after Kamala Harris was elected U.S. senator.

134. Frey, *Diversity Explosion*, esp. chap. 12.

135. Chris Haire, "For First Time since Depression, Orange County Goes Blue in Presidential Election," *Orange County Register*, Nov. 10, 2016, http://www.ocregister.com/2016/11/10/for-first-time-since-depression-orange-county-goes-blue-in-presidential-election.

136. "California Results," *New York Times*, Jan. 4, 2017.

137. Adam Nagourney, "A New Class of Democratic Leaders Is on the Rise in California," *New York Times*, Dec. 9, 2016.

CHAPTER 7

1. Melendy, "Labor and Ethnicity," 88.

2. For a detailed discussion with many direct quotes from segregationists, see Ziker, "Segregationists Confront American Empire."

3. Peirce, *Pacific States*, 331; *World Population Review*, "Hawaii Population 2016."

4. Melendy, "Labor and Ethnicity," 83. Melendy continues: "The Big Five usually controlled the governor's office, the legislature, and a coterie of friendly judges."

5. Ibid., 84.

6. Tamura, "Ordinary People," 139; Richards, Review of *Fighting in Paradise*, 873.

7. Peirce, *Pacific States*, 332, quoting the *Honolulu Advertiser*.

8. Deskins, Walton, and Puckett, *Presidential Elections*, 442.

9. A. A. Smyser, "A Biography of Ex-gov. William Quinn," *Honolulu Star-Bulletin*, Mar. 31 and Apr. 2, 1998.

10. Ibid.; Quinn obituary, *Honolulu Advertiser*, Aug. 30, 2006, and *Honolulu Star-Bulletin*, Aug. 30, 2006.

11. *Almanac of American Politics 1974*, 304, 305; *Almanac of American Politics 1984*, 360.

12. Robert D. Johnston, "Linda Lingle," *Jewish Women's Archive*, https://jwa.org/encyclopedia/article/Lingle-Linda.

13. *Almanac of American Politics 2004*, 494. The 2010 *Almanac* put it this way:

"As big agriculture shriveled, the ILWU has become overshadowed by the 44,000-member Hawaii Government Employees Association" (454). The post-mortem on her second term, in the 2012 *Almanac,* stated that "her acrimonious fights with public employee unions resulted in spending cuts, furloughs, and delayed tax refunds when the state faced huge deficits in 2009 and 2010. . . . Union-backed Democrats made gains in legislative elections, and as Lingle left office, Hawaii had the most lopsided legislative majorities in the nation" (477–78). The spreads at that time were senate, twenty-four Democrats, one Republican; house forty-three Democrats, eight Republicans. *Almanac of American Politics 2012,* 479.

14. After leaving the governorship she did some teaching and lecturing, and then in January 2015 she became a "senior adviser" to the fiercely anti-union governor of Illinois, Bruce Rauner. Befitting his background in finance rather than politics, Rauner termed Lingle the "C.O.O." (chief operating officer)—not an official title—of Illinois for the eighteen months she served. "Linda Lingle," *Wikipedia.* Also, "Hiram Fong Dead at 97," *Honolulu Advertiser,* obituary. Aug. 18, 2004.

15. "Hawaii Governor Falls to Democratic Primary Challenger," *Washington Post,* Aug. 10, 2014.

16. "The ILWU is probably why Republican Sen. Hiram Fong is still in the Senate. . . . Fong wore the tag of a Republican liberal [those were the days of Rockefeller] during the late 1950s and 1960s. But in recent years, he has lined up with increasing regularity behind the Nixon Administration. . . . in 1970, [that] proved fairly unpopular with the voters, and Democrat Cecil Heftel . . . almost scored an upset over Fong. The ILWU undoubtedly delivered more votes to the incumbent Senator than the slim majority by which he won the 1970 election." *Almanac of American Politics 1974,* 242.

17. "Spark M. Matsunaga Dies at 73: Senator Led Fight for Reparations," *New York Times,* obituary, April 18, 1990.

18. *Almanac of American Politics 2010,* 463.

19. *Washington Post,* Aug. 16, 2014.

20. "Mark Takai, 49, a Congressman from Hawaii," *New York Times,* obituary, July 23, 2016.

21. *Washington Post,* Jan. 2, 2014.

22. *Almanac of American Politics 2014,* 507; *Almanac of American Politics 2016,* 555.

23. *Almanac of American Politics 2018,* 570.

24. *Almanac of American Politics 1974,* 1057.

25. *Seattle Times,* Aug. 23, 2017.

26. Kit Oldham, "Magnuson, Warren G. (1905–1989)," *HistoryLinkOrg,* Oct. 14, 2003, www.historylink.org/File/5569; "Warren G. Magnuson Dies at 84," *New York Times,* obituary, May 21, 1989; "Magnuson, Warren Grant," *Biographical Directory of the U.S. Congress,* http://bioguide.congress.gov/scripts/biodisplay.pl?index=M000053.

27. As recounted in *Almanac of American Politics 2016,* 1929.

28. *Almanac of American Politics 2004*, 1678, 1681; *Almanac of American Politics 2016*, 1929, 1933.

29. "Albert Rosellini, Former Washington Governor, Dies at 101," *New York Times*, obituary, Oct. 11, 2011; "Gov. Rosellini: Out of Office since 1965, Not Out of Sight," *Seattle Times*, obituary, Oct. 10, 2011; "Albert Rosellini Obituary," *Legacy.com*, legacy.com/ns/albert-rosellini-obituary/154023856; Walt Crowley, "Rosellini, Albert Dean," *HistoryLinkOrg*, Jan. 30, 2003, www.historylink.org/file/5156.

30. "FBI Didn't Think Much of Washington's Gov. Rosellini, Files Show," *Seattle Times*, June 13, 2013.

31. Peirce, *Pacific States*, 240.

32. Cassandra Tate, "Evans, Daniel J. (b. 1925) and Nancy Bell Evans (b. 1933)," *HistoryLinkOrg*, Dec. 15, 2004, www.historylink.org/file/7167.

33. "Dixy Lee Ray," *Legacy Washington*, www.sos.wa.gov/legacy/biographies/DixyLeeRay.aspx; Paula Becker, "Ray, Dixy Lee (2014–1994)," *HistoryLinkOrg*, Nov. 20, 2004, www.historylink.org/file/601.

34. "John Spellman: Politics Never Broke His Heart," www.sos.wa.gov/legacy/stories/john-spellman; *Seattle Times*, obituary, Mar. 16, 2013; *New York Times*, obituary, Mar. 19, 2013.

35. *Almanac of American Politics 1994*, 1334.

36. Goodman and Baker, *State of Washington*. In 2012, however, two Democratic senators crossed over, creating Republican control for a time. *New York Times*, Dec. 27, 2012.

37. *Almanac of American Politics 2012*, 1711; *Almanac of American Politics 2016*, 1943.

38. Deskins, Walton, and Puckett, *Presidential Elections*.

REFLECTIONS

1. The first four-year election for governor took place in Arizona in 1970, Colorado in 1962, Kansas in 1974, Nebraska in 1966, New Mexico in 1970, North Dakota in 1964, South Dakota in 1974, and Texas in 1974.

2. California, enacted in 1990 and effective 1996 (assembly) and 1998 (senate); Colorado, enacted 1990 and effective 1998; Oklahoma, 1990 and 2004; Arizona, 1992 and 2000; Montana, 1992 and 2000; South Dakota, 1992 and 2000; Nevada, 1996 and 2010; Nebraska, 2000 and 2006. See National Conference of State Legislatures, "The Term-Limited States," www.ncsl.org/research/about-state-legislatures/chart-of-term-limits-states.aspx.

3. These states were Oregon, enacted 1992 and repealed 2002; Washington, 1992 and 1998; Wyoming, 1992 and 2004; Idaho, 1994 and 2002; and Utah, 1994 and 2003. Ibid.

4. *U.S. Term Limits, Inc. v. Thornton*, 514 U.S. 779 (1995).

5. A thorough discussion of the pros and cons is League of Women Voters, New York State, "Study of Term Limits: Legislative and Statewide Offices,"

2014, www.lwvny.org/programs-studies/term-limits/2014/Final-Term-Limit-Study-Guide.pdf.

6. Greenberg, "Term Limits." DeMint resigned a few years later to become president of the Heritage Foundation, a conservative think tank.

7. The largest contributors to the elections total came, not surprisingly, from California (1,545) and Texas (980). Contributing the fewest were Alaska (81), Wyoming (92), and North Dakota (106).

8. These numbers are for defeats in general elections. They do not include cases in which incumbents were defeated in primaries or through other party selection mechanisms. The Tea Party leader Tim Huelskamp, for example, lost renomination in the Republican primary in Kansas District 1 in 2016, and Utah senator Bob Bennett was denied renomination by Tea Party insurgents at his state's Republican Party convention of 2010.

9. The act was effectively nullified by the Supreme Court in *Shelby County v. Holder*, 570 U.S. 2 (2013).

10. "Redistricting Commissions: State Legislative Plans," *National Conference of State Legislatures*, www.ncsl.or/research/redistricting/2009-redistricting-commissions-table.aspx.

11. Damore, "Reapportionment and Redistricting," 164.

12. David Remnick, "It Happened Here," *New Yorker*, Nov. 28, 2016, 57.

13. William H. Frey, "The Demographic Blowback That Elected Donald Trump," *Brookings: The Avenue*, Nov. 10, 2016, www.brookings.edu/blog/the-avenue/2016/11/10.

14. Trump's edge in Pennsylvania (20 electoral votes) was 44,292; in Michigan (16), 10,704; in Wisconsin (10), 22,748. Trump won Florida (29) by 112,911 popular votes, that is, 48.6 percent to Clinton's 47.4 percent.

15. State, national, and county election results for 2016 are from www.nytimes.com/elections/results. The national popular vote totals were Clinton, 65,853,516; Trump, 62,984,825, giving Clinton a plurality over Trump of 2,868,691. Federal Election Commission, Official Results, Jan. 30, 2017.

16. "Texas Counties: 2016 Presidential Election," www.texascounties.net/statistics/presidentialelection2016.

17. Dan Balz, "Red, Blue States Move in Opposite Directions in a New Era of Single-Party Control," *Washington Post*, Dec. 29, 2013, www.washingtonpost.com/politics/red-blue-states-move-in-opposite-directions.

18. Dan Balz, "Texas, California Embody Red-Blue Divide," *Washington Post*, Dec. 29, 2013, www.washingtonpost.com/politics/texas-california-embody-red-blued-divide/2013/12/29.

19. Alan Howard, "Hawaii Should Consider Seceding from the United States," *Honolulu Star-Advertiser*, Nov. 29, 2016. I thank Professors Charlene Avallone and Chip Hughes for sending this to me.

Sources Cited

Newspaper articles and online entities are documented in full in this volume's endnotes.

Abbott, Carl. "From Urban Frontier to Metropolitan Region: Oregon's Cities from 1870 to 2008." *Oregon Historical Quarterly* 110 (Spring 2009): 74–95.

———. *Greater Portland: Urban Life and Landscape in the Pacific Northwest*. Philadelphia: University of Pennsylvania Press, 2001.

Ahuja, Sunil, and Robert Dewhirst. *The Roads to Congress 2000*. Belmont, Calif.: Wadsworth/Thomson Learning, 2002.

Alexander, Thomas G. "The Emergence of a Republican Majority in Utah, 1970–1992." In Richard Lowitt, ed., *Politics in the Postwar American West*, 260–76. Norman: University of Oklahoma Press, 1995.

Allman, Joseph M. "The 1968 Elections in Oregon." *Western Political Quarterly* 22 (Sep. 1969): 517–25.

Allswang, John M. *The Initiative and Referendum in California, 1898–1998*. Stanford, Calif.: Stanford University Press, 2000.

Almanac of American Politics. Biennial. Editors and publishers vary.

1974. Barone, Michael, Grant Ujifusa, and Douglas Matthews, eds. Boston: Gambit, 1972.

1984. Barone, Michael, and Grant Ujifusa, eds. Washington, D.C.: National Journal, 1983.

1994. Barone, Michael, and Grant Ujifusa, eds. Washington, D.C.: National Journal, 1993.

1996. Barone, Michael, and Grant Ujifusa, eds. Washington, D.C.: National Journal, 1995.

2004. Barone, Michael, and Richard E. Cohen, eds. Washington, D.C.: National Journal, 2003.

2010. Barone, Michael, and Richard E. Cohen, eds. Washington, D.C.: National Journal, 2009.

2012. Barone, Michael, and Chuck McCutcheon, eds. Chicago: University of Chicago Press, 2011.

2014. Michael Barone, Chuck McCutcheon, Sean Trende, Josh Kraushaar, and David Wasserman, eds. Chicago: University of Chicago Press, 2013.

2016. Richard E. Cohen, James A. Barnes, with Keating Holland, eds. [n.p.] Columbia Books and Information Services, National Journal, 2015.

2018. Richard E. Cohen, with James A. Barnes. Columbia Books and Information Services, National Journal, 2017.

Anderson, Totton J. "The 1958 Election in California." *Western Political Quarterly* 12 (Mar. 1959): 276–300.

Anderson, Totton J., and Charles G. Bell. "The 1970 Election in California." *Western Political Quarterly*, 24 (June 1971): 252–73.

Anderson, Totton J., and Eugene C. Lee. "The 1962 Election in California." *Western Political Quarterly* 16 (June 1963): 396–420.

August, Jack L., Jr. Review of *Wayne Aspinall and the Shaping of the American West*, by Steven C. Schulte. *Western Historical Quarterly* 34 (Aug. 2003): 389.

Baird, W. David, and Danney Goble. *Oklahoma: A History.* Norman: University of Oklahoma Press, 2008.

Baldassare, Mark. *California in the New Millennium: The Changing Social and Political Landscape.* Berkeley: University of California Press, 2000.

Baritono, Raffaella. "Introduction: Political History Today." *Ricerche di Storia Politica*, Oct. 2017, 3–6.

Barreto, Matt A. "Latino Immigrants at the Polls: Foreign-Born Voter Turnout in the 2002 Election." *Political Research Quarterly* 58 (Mar. 2005): 79–86.

Bednar, Nancy L., and Allen D. Hertzke. "The Christian Right and Republican Realignment in Oklahoma." *PS: Political Science and Politics* 28:1 (Mar. 1995): 11–15.

Bell, Jonathan. *California Crucible: The Forging of Modern American Liberalism.* Philadelphia: University of Pennsylvania Press, 2012.

Bellmon, Henry, with Pat Bellmon. *The Life and Times of Henry Bellmon.* Tulsa, Okla.: Council Oaks Books, 1992.

Bessey, Roy F. "The Political Issues of the Hells Canyon Controversy." *Western Political Quarterly* 9 (Sep. 1956): 676–90.

Bickerstaff, Steve. *Lines in the Sand: Congressional Redistricting in Texas and the Downfall of Tom DeLay.* Austin: University of Texas Press, 2007.

Bissett, Jim. *Agrarian Socialism in America: Marx, Jefferson, and Jesus in the Oklahoma Countryside, 1904–1920.* Norman: University of Oklahoma Press, 1999.

Bland, Randall W., et al. *Texas Government Today.* 5th ed. Pacific Grove, Calif.: Brooks/Cole, 1992.

Bloodworth, Jeff. "Fred Harris's New Populism and the Demise of Heartland Liberalism." *Chronicles of Oklahoma*, 88 (Summer 2010): 196–221.

Bollens, John C., and G. Robert Williams. *Jerry Brown in a Plain Brown Wrapper.* Pacific Palisades, Calif.: Palisades, 1978.

Boyarsky, Bill. *Big Daddy: Jesse Unruh and the Art of Power Politics.* Berkeley: University of California Press, 2008.

Bridges, Kenneth. *Twilight of the Texas Democrats: The 1978 Governor's Race.* College Station: Texas A&M Press, 2008.

Brown, Willie. *Basic Brown: My Life and Our Times.* New York: Simon and Schuster, 2008.

Bruce, John M. "Texas: The Emergence of the Christian Right." In Mark J. Rozell and Clyde Wilcox, eds., *God at the Grassroots: The Christian Right in the 1994 Election,* 67–90. Lanham, Md.: Rowman and Littlefield, 1995.

Bullock, Charles S., III, and Mark J. Rozell. *The New Politics of the Old South: An Introduction to Southern Politics.* Lanham, Md.: Rowman and Littlefield, 1998.

Burton, Robert E. *Democrats of Oregon: The Pattern of Minority Politics, 1900–1956.* Eugene: University of Oregon, 1970.

Cahn, Matthew Alan, H. Eric Schockman, and David M. Shafie, *Rethinking California: Politics and Policy in the Golden State.* Upper Saddle River, N.J.: Prentice-Hall, 2001.

Campbell, Randolph B. *Gone to Texas: The Lone Star State.* 2d ed. New York: Oxford University Press, 2012.

Cannon, Brian Q. Review of *Wayne Aspinall and the Shaping of the American West,* by Steven C. Schulte, and *The Politics of Western Water: The Congressional Career of Wayne Aspinall,* by Stephen C. Sturgeon. *Pacific Historical Review* 72 (Nov. 2003): 649–52.

Cannon, Lou. *Governor Reagan: His Rise to Power.* New York: Public Affairs, 2003.

———. *Ronnie and Jesse: A Political Odyssey.* Garden City, N.Y.: Doubleday, 1969.

Ceplair, Larry. "The Foreign Policy of Senator Wayne L. Morse." *Oregon Historical Quarterly* 113 (Spring 2012): 6–35.

Champagne, Anthony. *Congressman Sam Rayburn.* New Brunswick, N.J.: Rutgers University Press, 1984.

Cherny, Robert. "Direct Democracy and Legislative Dysfunction: California Politics since 1978." *Siècles* 37 (2013): 1–13, http://siècles.revues.org/1130.

Cigler, Alan J., Mark Joslyn, and Burdett A. Loomis. "The Kansas Christian Right and the Evolution of Republican Politics." In John C. Green, Mark J. Rozell, and Clyde Wilcox, *The Christian Right in American Politics: Marching to the Millennium,* 145–66. Washington, D.C.: Georgetown University Press, 2003.

Clayson, William S. *Freedom Is Not Enough: The War on Poverty and the Civil Rights Movement in Texas.* Austin: University of Texas Press, 2010.

Clem, Alan L. "Popular Representation and Senate Vacancies." *Midwest Journal of Political Science* 10 (Feb. 1966): 52–77.

Clucas, Richard A. "The Political Legacy of Robert W. Straub." *Oregon Historical Quarterly* 104 (Winter 2003): 462–77.

Clucas, Richard A., Mark Henkels, and Brent S. Steel, eds. *Oregon Politics and Government: Progressives versus Conservative Populists.* Lincoln: University of Nebraska Press, 2005.

Colon, Frank T. "The Elected Woman." *Social Studies* 58 (Nov. 1967): 256–61.

Cramer, Richard Ben. *What It Takes: The Road to the White House.* New York: Random House, 1992.

Cullen, David O'Donald. "From 'Turn Texas Loose' to the Tea Party: Origins of the Texas Right." In David O'Donald Cullen and Kyle G. Wilkison, eds., *The Texas Right: The Radical Roots of Lone Star Conservatism*, 1–9. College Station: Texas A&M University Press, 2014.

Cullen, David O'Donald, and Kyle G. Wilkison, eds. *The Texas Left: The Radical Roots of Lone Star Liberalism*. College Station: Texas A&M Press, 2010.

———, eds. *The Texas Right: The Radical Roots of Lone Star Conservatism*. College Station: Texas A&M University Press, 2014.

Dallas Morning News. *Texas Almanac, 1952–1953*. Dallas, Tex.: A. H. Belo, 1951.

———. *Texas Almanac 1974–1975*. Dallas, Tex.: A. H. Belo, 1973.

Dallek, Matthew. *The Right Moment: Ronald Reagan's First Victory and the Decisive Turning Point in American Politics*. New York: Free Press, 2000.

Damore, David F. "Reapportionment and Redistricting in the Mountain West." In Ruy Teixeira, ed., *America's New Swing Region: Changing Politics and Demographics in the Mountain West*, 153–86. Washington, D.C.: Brookings Institution Press, 2012.

Danbom, David B. "A Part of the Nation and apart from the Nation: North Dakota Politics since 1945." In Richard Lowitt, ed., *Politics in the Postwar American West*, 174–84. Norman: University of Oklahoma Press, 1995.

Dant, Sara. "Making Wilderness Work: Frank Church and the American Wilderness Movement." *Pacific Historical Review* 77 (May 2008): 237–72.

Daum, Courtenay W., Robert J. Duffy, and John A. Straayer. *State of Change: Colorado Politics in the Twenty-First Century*. Boulder: University Press of Colorado, 2011.

Davidson, Chandler. *Race and Class in Texas Politics*. Princeton, N.J.: Princeton University Press, 1990.

Davis, Katherine A. "Authoritarian Political Systems in South Texas: Patron Politics in the Rio Grande Valley." In William Earl Maxwell et al., eds., *Texas Politics Today*, 4th ed., 89–92. St. Paul, Minn.: West, 1987.

Deskins, Donald R., Jr., Hanes Walton Jr., and Sherman C. Puckett. *Presidential Elections, 1789–2008: County, State, and National Mapping of Election Data*. Ann Arbor: University of Michigan Press, 2010.

Deverell, William. "Claims and Reclaims in the American West." *Reviews in American History* 38 (Sep. 2010): 527–32.

Didion, Joan. *Where I Was From*. New York: Alfred A. Knopf, 2003.

Dionne, E. J., Jr. *Why the Right Went Wrong: Conservatism—From Goldwater to the Tea Party and Beyond*. New York: Simon and Schuster, 2016.

Dobbs, Ricky F. *Yellow Dogs and Republicans: Allan Shivers and Texas Two-Party Politics*. College Station: Texas A&M University Press, 2005.

Drukman, Mason. "Oregon's Most Famous Feud: Wayne Morse versus Richard Neuberger." *Oregon Historical Quarterly* 95 (Fall 1994): 300–67.

Edwards, Jerome E. "Gambling and Politics in Nevada." In Richard Lowitt, ed., *Politics in the Postwar American West*, 147–61. Norman: University of Oklahoma Press, 1995.

Elazar, Daniel J. *Closing of the Metropolitan Frontier: Cities of the Prairie Revisited.* New Brunswick, N.J.: Transaction, 2002.

Ellis, Blake A. "An Alternative Politics: Texas Baptists and the Rise of the Christian Right, 1975–1985." *Southwestern Historical Quarterly* 112 (April 2009): 361–86.

Enloe, Cynthia, and Joni Seager. *The Real State of America Atlas: Mapping the Myths and Truths of the United States.* New York: Penguin, 2011.

Evans, Thomas W. *The Education of Ronald Reagan: The General Electric Years and the Untold Story of His Conversion to Conservatism.* New York: Columbia University Press, 2006.

Fairbanks, Robert B. "The Failure of Urban Renewal in the Southwest: From City Needs to Individual Rights." *Western Historical Quarterly* 37 (Autumn 2006): 303–25.

Farley, Bill. "Rocky Mountain Radicals: Copper King James A. Murray, Senator James E. Murray, and Seventy-Eight Years of Montana Politics, 1883–1961." *Montana: The Magazine of Western History* 66 (Spring 2016): 39–58.

Findley, James C. "Cross-Filing and the Progressive Movement in California Politics." *Western Political Quarterly* 12 (Sep. 1959): 699–711.

Flentje, H. Edward, and Joseph A. Aistrup. *Kansas Politics and Government: The Clash of Political Cultures.* Lincoln: University of Nebraska Press, 2010.

Formisano, Ronald P. *The Tea Party: A Brief History.* Baltimore, Md.: Johns Hopkins University Press, 2012.

Foxworth, Laura. Paper delivered at the Abortion and Right Politics session, Organization of American Historians annual meeting, Atlanta, April 2014.

Frey, William H. *Diversity Explosion: How New Racial Demographics Are Remaking America.* Washington, D.C.: Brookings Institution Press, 2015.

Gaddie, Ronald Keith. "Congressional Seat Swings: Revisiting Exposure in House Elections." *Political Research Quarterly* 50 (Sep. 1997): 699–710.

Gaddie, Ronald Keith, and Scott E. Buchanan. "Oklahoma GOP Realignment in the Buckle of the Bible Belt." In Charles S. Bullock III and Mark J. Rozell, *The New Politics of the Old South: An Introduction to Southern Politics*, 205–26. Lanham, Md.: Rowman and Littlefield, 1998.

Garcia, Gilbert. *Reagan's Comeback: Four Weeks in Texas That Changed American Politics Forever.* San Antonio, Tex.: Trinity University Press, 2012.

Gastil, Raymond D. *Cultural Regions of the United States.* Seattle: University of Washington Press, 1975.

Gelman, Andrew, David Park, Boris Shor,and Jeronimo Cortina. *Red State, Blue State, Rich State, Poor State: Why Americans Vote the Way They Do.* Princeton, N.J.: Princeton University Press, 2010.

Goldberg, Robert Alan. *Barry Goldwater.* New Haven, Conn.: Yale University Press, 1995.

Goldschmidt, Maure L. "The 1952 Elections in Oregon." *Western Political Quarterly* 6 (Mar. 1953): 123–26.

Goodman, Hunter G., and Barbara Baker, comps. *State of Washington: Members of the Legislature 1889–2014*. Olympia, Wash.: Legislative Information Center, 2014.

Green, George Norris. *The Establishment in Texas Politics: The Primitive Years, 1938–1957.* Westport, Conn.: Greenwood Press, 1979.

Green, George Norris, and Michael R. Botson Jr. "Looking for Lefty: Liberal/Left Activism and Texas Labor, 1920–1960s." In David O'Donald Cullen and Kyle G. Wilkison, eds., *The Texas Left: The Radical Roots of Lone Star Liberalism*, 112–31. College Station: Texas A&M Press, 2010.

Green, John C., Lyman A. Kellstedt, Corwin E. Smidt, and James L. Guth. "The Soul of the South: Religion and the New Electoral Order." In Charles S. Bullock III and Mark J. Rozell, *The New Politics of the Old South: An Introduction to Southern Politics*, 261–76. Lanham, Md.: Rowman and Littlefield, 1998.

Green, John C., Mark J. Rozell, and Clyde Wilcox. *The Christian Right in American Politics: Marching to the Millennium*. Washington, D.C.: Georgetown University Press, 2003.

Green, Michael S. *Nevada: A History of the Silver State*. Reno: University of Nevada Press, 2015.

Greenberg, Dan. "Term Limits: The Only Way to Clean Up Congress." *Heritage Foundation*, Aug. 10, 1944, www.heritage.org/political-process/report/term-limits-the-only-way-clean-congress.

Gregory, James N. "Upton Sinclair's 1934 EPIC Campaign: Anatomy of a Political Movement." *Labor: Studies in Working-Class History of the Americas* 12 (Dec. 2015): 51–81.

Grieder, Erica. *Big, Hot, Cheap, and Right: What America Can Learn from the Strange Genius of Texas*. New York: Public Affairs, 2013.

Hachey, Thomas. "American Profiles on Capitol Hill: A Confidential Study for the British Foreign Office in 1943." *Wisconsin Magazine of History* 57 (Winter 1973–74): 141–53.

Hansen, Clark. "The Making of the Modern Democratic Party in Oregon: An Interview with Howard Morgan." *Oregon Historical Quarterly* 95 (Fall 1994): 368–95.

Hardy, Leroy C., and Charles P. Sohner. "Constitutional Challenge and Political Response: California Reapportionment, 1965." *Western Political Quarterly* 23 (Dec. 1970): 733–51.

Harris, Fred. *Does People Do It? A Memoir*. Norman: University of Oklahoma Press, 2008.

Hibbard, Michael, Ethan Seltzer, Bruce Weber, and Beth Emshoff. *Toward One Oregon: Rural-Urban Interdependence and the Evolution of a State*. Corvallis: Oregon State University Press, 2011.

Holland, David, Paul Lewin, Bruce Sorte, and Bruce Weber. "The Declining Economic Interdependence of the Portland Metropolitan Core and Its Periphery." In Michael Hibbard et al., *Toward One Oregon: Rural-Urban Interdependence and the Evolution of a State*, 79–98. Corvallis: Oregon State University Press, 2011.

Hoover, Herbert T., and Steven C. Emery. "South Dakota Governance since 1945." In Richard Lowitt, ed., *Politics in the Postwar American West*, 221–38. Norman: University of Oklahoma Press, 1995.

HoSang, Daniel Martinez. *Racial Propositions: Ballot Initiatives and the Making of Postwar California*. Berkeley: University of California Press, 2010.

Huckaby, Melody R., and Ronald Keith Gaddie. "Carson Defeats Ewing in Oklahoma's Second District Race." In Sunil Ahuja and Robert Dewhirst, *The Roads to Congress 2000*, 45–60. Belmont, Calif.: Wadsworth/Thomson Learning, 2002.

Jacobs, John. *A Rage for Justice: The Passion and Politics of Phillip Burton*. Berkeley: University of California Press, 1995.

Johnson, Charles K. *Standing at the Water's Edge: Bob Straub's Battle for the Soul of Oregon*. Corvallis: Oregon State University Press, 2012.

Johnston, Robert D. "Parties and Politics in Oregon History." *Oregon Historical Quarterly* 110 (Summer 2009): 194–201.

———. *The Radical Middle Class: Populist Democracy and the Question of Capitalism in Progressive Era Portland*. Princeton, N.J.: Princeton University Press, 2003.

Jonas, Frank H. "Western Politics." In Frank H. Jonas, ed., *Politics in the American West*, 443–67. Salt Lake City: University of Utah Press, 1969.

Kazin, Michael. *Godly Hero: The Life of William Jennings Bryan*. New York: Knopf, 2006.

Key, V. O. *Southern Politics in State and Nation*. New York: Alfred A. Knopf, 1949.

Killen, Patricia O'Connell, and Mark A. Shibley, with assistance from Kellee Boyer and Kellie A. Riley. "Surveying the Religious Landscape: Historical Trends and Current Patterns in Oregon, Washington, and Alaska." In Patricia O'Connell Killen and Mark Silk, *Religion and Public Life in the Pacific Northwest: The None Zone*, 25–50. Walnut Creek, Calif.: AltaMira Press, 2004.

Kincaid, Diane D. "Over His Dead Body: A Positive Perspective on Widows in the U.S. Congress." *Western Historical Quarterly* 31 (Mar. 1976): 96–104.

Kleppner, Paul. "Politics without Parties: The Western States, 1900–1984." In Gerald D. Nash and Richard W. Etulain, eds., *The Twentieth-Century West: Historical Interpretations*, 295–338. Albuquerque: University of New Mexico Press, 1989.

Knaggs, John R. *Two-Party Texas: The John Tower Era, 1961–1984*. Austin, Tex.: Eakin Press, 1986.

Knock, Thomas J. *The Rise of a Prairie Statesman: The Life and Times of George McGovern*. Princeton, N.J.: Princeton University Press, 2016.

Lalande, Jeff. "Oregon's Last Conservative Senator: Some Light upon the Little-Known Career of Guy Cordon." *Oregon Historical Quarterly* 110 (Summer 2009): 228–61.

Lamare, James W., Jerry L. Polinard, and Robert W. Wrinkle. "Texas: Lone Star(Wars) State." In Charles S. Bullock III and Mark J. Rozell, *The New Politics of the Old South: An Introduction to Southern Politics*, 245–57. Lanham, Md.: Rowman and Littlefield, 1998.

———. "Texas: Religion and Politics in God's Country." In John C. Green, Mark J. Rozell, and Clyde Wilcox, *The Christian Right in American Politics: Marching to the Millennium*, 59–78. Washington, D.C.: Georgetown University Press, 2003.

Lassiter, Matthew D. "Political History beyond the Red-Blue Divide." *Journal of American History* 98 (Dec. 2011): 760–64.

Lauck, Jon. *Daschle vs. Thune: Anatomy of a High-Plains Senate Race*. Norman: University of Oklahoma Press, 2007.

Lee, Eugene C. *California Votes 1928–1960: A Review and Analysis of Registration and Voting*. Berkeley: University of California Institute of Governmental Studies, 1963.

Leonard, Bill. "The Southern Crossroads: Religion and Demography." In William Lindsey and Mark Silk, eds., *Religion and Public Life in the Southern Crossroads: Showdown States*, 27–54. Walnut Creek, Calif.: AltaMira Press, 2005.

Lindsey, William, and Mark Silk, eds. *Religion and Public Life in the Southern Crossroads: Showdown States*. Walnut Creek, Calif.: AltaMira Press, 2005.

Lorentzen, Lois Ann. "Golden State of Grace." *Boom: A Journal of California* 5 (Winter 2015): 20–32.

Lowitt, Richard. *George W. Norris: The Making of a Progressive, 1861–1912*. Syracuse, N.Y.: Syracuse University Press, 1963.

———. *George W. Norris: The Persistence of a Progressive, 1913–1933*. Champagne: University of Illinois Press, 1971.

———. *George W. Norris: The Triumph of a Progressive, 1933–1944*. Champagne: University of Illinois Press, 1978.

———. *Fred Harris: His Journey from Liberalism to Populism*. Lanham, Md.: Rowman and Littlefield, 2002.

———, ed. *Politics in the Postwar American West*. Norman: University of Oklahoma Press, 1995.

Lunch, William M. "Oregon: Identity and Politics in the Northwest." In Mark J. Rozell and Clyde Wilcox, eds., *God at the Grassroots: The Christian Right in the 1994 Election*, 227–51. Lanham, Md.: Rowman and Littlefield, 1995.

Lutz, Donald S., and Kent L. Tedin. *Perspectives on American and Texas Politics: A Collection of Essays*. 2d ed. Dubuque, Iowa: Kendall/Hunt, 1989.

Manzano, Sylvia. "Latinos in the Sunbelt: Political Implications of Demographic Change." In Michelle Nickerson and Darren Dochuk, eds., *Sunbelt Rising: The Politics of Space, Place, and Region*, 335–60. Philadelphia: University of Pennsylvania Press, 2011.

Marsh, Frank, comp. "Official Report of the Board of State Canvassers of the State of Nebraska," for Primary Election August 10, 1954; General Election November 2, 1954. Lincoln(?): 1954(?).

Maxwell, William Earl, et al., eds. *Texas Politics Today*. 4th ed. St. Paul, Minn.: West, 1987.

McCall, Brian. *The Power of the Texas Governor: Connally to Bush*. Austin: University of Texas Press, 2009.

McGirr, Lisa. "Now That Historians Know So Much about the Right, How Should We Best Approach the Study of Conservatism?" *Journal of American History* 98 (Dec. 2011): 765–70.

McGovern, George. *Grassroots: The Autobiography of George McGovern*. New York: Random House, 1977.

McKee, Seth C., Jeremy M. Teigen, and Mathiew Turgon. "The Partisan Impact of Congressional Redistricting: The Case of Texas, 2001–2003." *Social Science Quarterly* 87 (June 2006): 308–17.

Melendy, H. Brett. "Labor and Ethnicity in Hawaiian Politics." In Richard Lowitt, ed., *Politics in the Postwar American West*, 82–93. Norman: University of Oklahoma Press, 1995.

Meyer, Philipp. *The Son: A Novel*. New York: HarperCollins, 2013.

Miller, Char, ed. *Fifty Years of the Texas Observer*. San Antonio, Tex.: Trinity University Press, 2004.

Miller, Worth Robert. *Oklahoma Populism: A History of the People's Party in the Oklahoma Territory*. Norman: University of Oklahoma Press, 1987.

Montgomery, Gayle B., and James W. Johnson. *One Step from the White House: The Rise and Fall of Senator William F. Knowland*. Berkeley: University of California Press, 1978.

Murrell, Gary. "Hunting Reds in Oregon, 1935–1939." *Oregon Historical Quarterly* 100 (Winter 1999): 374–401.

Nash, Gerald D., and Richard W. Etulain, eds. *The Twentieth-Century West: Historical Interpretations*. Albuquerque: University of New Mexico Press, 1989.

Naske, Claus-M. "'Little Men' Demand Statehood for Alaska." *Journal of the West* 13 (Oct. 1974): 40–50.

Needham, Andrew. *Power Lines: Phoenix and the Making of the Modern Southwest*. Princeton, N.J.: Princeton University Press, 2014.

———. "Sunbelt Imperialism: Boosters, Navajos, and Energy Development in the Metropolitan Southwest." In Michelle Nickerson and Darren Dochuk, eds., *Sunbelt Rising: The Politics of Space, Place, and Region*, 240–64. Philadelphia: University of Pennsylvania Press, 2011.

Nelson, Albert J. *Democrats under Siege in the Sunbelt Megastates*. Westport, Conn.: Praeger, 1996.

Nickerson, Michelle, and Darren Dochuk, eds. *Sunbelt Rising: The Politics of Space, Place, and Region*. Philadelphia: University of Pennsylvania Press, 2011.

Nugent, Walter. *Into the West: The Story of Its People*. New York: Alfred A. Knopf, 1999.

———. "The Mormons and America's Empires." *Journal of Mormon History* 36 (Spring 2010): 1–27.

———. "Where Is the West? Report on a Survey." *Montana: The Magazine of Western History* 42 (Summer 1992), 2–23.

Oklahoma Department of Libraries. *Oklahoma Almanac 2011–2012.* Oklahoma City, Okla.: Oklahoma Department of Libraries, 2011.

O'Regan, Valerie R., and Stephen J. Stambough. "From the Grassroots: Building the South Dakota Democratic Party." In Robert P. Watson, ed., *George McGovern: A Political Life, A Political Legacy,* 38–49. Pierre, S.D.: South Dakota State Historical Society Press, 2004.

Parker, Richard. *Lone Star Nation: How Texas Will Transform America.* New York: Penguin Books, 2014.

Peirce, Neal R. *The Great Plains States of America: People, Politics, and Power in the Nine Great Plains States.* New York: W. W. Norton, 1972, 1973.

———. *The Mountain States of America: People, Politics, and Power in the Eight Rocky Mountain States.* New York: W. W. Norton, 1972.

———. *The Pacific States of America: People, Politics, and Power in the Five Pacific Basin States.* New York: W. W. Norton, 1972.

Phillips, Michael. "Texan by Color: The Racialization of the Lone Star State." In David O'Donald Cullen and Kyle G. Wilkison, eds., *The Texas Right: The Radical Roots of Lone Star Conservatism,* 10–33. College Station: Texas A&M University Press, 2014.

Phillips-Fein, Kim. "Conservatism: A State of the Field." *Journal of American History* 98 (Dec. 2011): 723–43.

Povich, Elaine S. *Nancy Pelosi: A Biography.* Westport, Conn.: Greenwood Press, 2008.

Procter, Ben. "The Texas Gubernatorial Election of 1990: Claytie versus the Lady." In Richard Lowitt, ed., *Politics in the Postwar American West,* 239–59. Norman: University of Oklahoma Press, 1995.

Provost, David H. *Bernard L. Hyink's Politics and Government in California.* 17th ed. New York: Pearson Longman, 2007.

Putnam, Jackson K. *Modern California Politics.* 2nd ed. San Francisco, Calif.: Boyd and Fraser, 1984.

Ramet, Sabrina P. "'Fighting for the Christian Nation': The Christian Right and American Politics." *Journal of Human Rights* 4 (2005): 431–42.

Rapoport, Roger. *California Dreaming: The Political Odyssey of Pat and Jerry Brown.* Berkeley, Calif.: Nolo Press, 1982.

Reid, Jan. *Let the People In: The Life and Times of Ann Richards.* Austin: University of Texas Press, 2012.

Rex, Tom. "Migration to and from Arizona: A Report from the Office of the University Economist." [Tempe]: Arizona State University School of Business, 2016.

Richards, Lawrence. Review of *Fighting in Paradise: Labor Unions, Racism, and Communists in the Making of Modern Hawaii,* by Gerald Horne. *American Historical Review* 118 (June 2013): 873–74.

Richardson, James. *Willie Brown: A Biography*. Berkeley: University of California Press, 1996.

Robbins, William G. *Hard Times in Paradise: Coos Bay, Oregon*. Seattle: University of Washington Press, 2006.

———. *Landscapes of Conflict: The Oregon Story, 1940–2000*. Seattle: University of Washington Press, 2004.

———. *A Man for All Seasons: Monroe Sweetland and the Liberal Paradox*. Corvallis: Oregon State University Press, 2015.

———. *Oregon: This Storied Land*. Portland: Oregon Historical Society Press, 2005.

———. "Town and Country in Oregon: A Conflicted Legacy." In Michael Hibbard et al., *Toward One Oregon: Rural-Urban Interdependence and the Evolution of a State*, 59–78. Corvallis: Oregon State University Press, 2011.

Roberts, Barbara. *Up the Capitol Steps: A Woman's March to the Governorship*. Corvallis: Oregon State University Press, 2011.

Roberts, Phil, and Peggy Bieber-Roberts. "'Politics Is Personal': Postwar Wyoming Politics and the Media." In Richard Lowitt, ed., *Politics in the Postwar American West*, 295–308. Norman: University of Oklahoma Press, 1995.

Roche, Jeff, ed. *The Political Culture of the New West*. Lawrence: University Press of Kansas, 2008.

Rogin, Michael Paul, and John L. Shover. *Political Change in California: Critical Elections and Social Movements, 1890–1966*. Westport, Conn.: Greenwood, 1970.

Rozell, Mark J., and Clyde Wilcox, eds. *God at the Grassroots: The Christian Right in the 1994 Election*. Lanham, Md.: Rowman and Littlefield, 1995.

Sandalow, Marc. *Madam Speaker: Nancy Pelosi's Life, Times, and Rise to Power*. New York: Modern Times, 2008.

Scales, James R., and Danney Goble. *Oklahoma Politics: A History*. Norman: University of Oklahoma Press, 1982.

Schrag, Peter. *California: America's High-Stakes Experiment*. Berkeley: University of California Press, 2006.

———. "Drowning Democracy: Our Century of Voter Initiatives." *Boom: A Journal of California* 1 (Fall 2011): 13–29.

———. *Paradise Lost: California's Experience, America's Future*. New York: New Press, 1998.

Schuparra, Kurt. *Triumph of the Right: The Rise of the California Conservative Movement, 1945–1966*. Armonk, N.Y.: M. E. Sharpe, 1998.

Shaw, Stephen. "Harassment, Hate, and Human Rights in Idaho." In Richard Lowitt, ed., *Politics in the Postwar American West*, 94–105. Norman: University of Oklahoma Press, 1995.

Skocpol, Theda, and Vanessa Williamson. *The Tea Party and the Remaking of Republican Conservatism*. New York: Oxford University Press, 2012.

Slotnick, Herman E. "The 1960 Election in Alaska." *Western Political Quarterly* 14 (Mar. 1961): 300–304.

Smith, Daniel A. "Howard Jarvis, Populist Entrepreneur: Reevaluating the Causes of Proposition 13." *Social Science History* 23 (Summer 1999): 173–210.

Socolofsky, Homer E. *Kansas Governors*. Lawrence: University of Kansas Press, 1990.

Soper, J. Christopher. "California: Christian Conservative Influence in a Liberal State." In Mark J. Rozell and Clyde Wilcox, eds., *God at the Grassroots: The Christian Right in the 1994 Election*, 211–26. Lanham, Md.: Rowman and Littlefield, 1995.

Spillman, Patricia R. "The Kansan Ethos in the Last Three Decades of the Nineteenth Century." Master's thesis, School of Graduate and Professional Studies of the Emporia State University, 1980.

Starr, Kevin. *Coast of Dreams: California on the Edge, 1990–2003*. New York: Alfred A. Knopf, 2004.

Swanson, Frederick H. "Lee Metcalf and the Politics of Preservation: Part 1, A Positive Program of Development." *Montana: The Magazine of Western History* 63 (Spring 2013): 3–23.

———. "Lee Metcalf and the Politics of Preservation: Part 2. Conflict, Compromise, and the Art of Leadership." *Montana: The Magazine of Western History* 63 (Summer 2013): 58–96.

Swarthout, John M. "The 1956 Election in Oregon." *Western Political Quarterly* 10 (Mar. 1957): 142–50.

———. "The 1958 Election in Oregon." *Western Political Quarterly* 12 (Mar. 1959): 328–454.

———. "The 1960 Election in Oregon." *Western Political Quarterly* 14 (Mar. 1961): 355–64.

Tamura, Eileen H. "Ordinary People." In Alan M. Kraut and David A. Gerber, eds., *Ethnic Historians and the Mainstream: Shaping the Nation's Immigration Story*, 128–44. New Brunswick, N.J.: Rutgers University Press, 2013.

Tannahill, Neal, and Wendell M. Bedichek. *Texas Government: Policy and Politics*. 3d ed. Glenview, Ill.: Scott, Foresman, 1989.

Taylor, Michael J. C. "The Violence of War and the Mark of Leadership: The Significance of McGovern's Air Force Service during World War II." In Robert P. Watson, ed., *George McGovern: A Political Life, A Political Legacy*. Pierre: South Dakota State Historical Society Press, 2004.

Teixeira, Ruy, ed. *America's New Swing Region: Changing Politics and Demographics in the Mountain West*. Washington, D.C.: Brookings Institution Press, 2012.

Titus, Charles H., and Charles R. Nixon. "The 1948 Elections in California." *Western Political Quarterly* 2 (Mar. 1949): 97–102.

Tolleson-Rinehart, Sue, and Jeanie R. Stanley. *Claytie and the Lady: Ann Richards, Gender, and Politics in Texas*. Austin: University of Texas Press, 1994.

Tollestrup, Jessica. "Women and Oregon Political History: The Research and Writing of *Up the Capitol Steps*." *Oregon Historical Quarterly* 113 (Fall 2012): 478–91.

Toy, Eckard V. "The Ku Klux Klan in Oregon." In G. Thomas Edwards and Carlos A. Schwantes, *Experiences in a Promised Land: Essays in Pacific Northwest History*. Seattle: University of Washington Press, 1986.

———. "The Right Side of the 1960s: The Origin of the John Birch Society in the Pacific Northwest." *Oregon Historical Quarterly* 105 (Summer 2004): 260–83.

United States Bureau of the Census. *Historical Statistics of the United States, Colonial Times to 1970. Bicentennial Edition*. Washington, D.C.: U.S. Government Printing Office, 1975. Vols. 1, 2.

Walth, Brent. *Fire at Eden's Gate: Tom McCall and the Oregon Story*. Portland: Oregon Historical Society Press, 1994.

———. "No Deposit, No Return: Richard Chambers, Tom McCall, and the Oregon Bottle Bill." *Oregon Historical Quarterly* 95 (Fall 1994): 278–99.

Watson, Robert P., ed. *George McGovern: A Political Life, A Political Legacy*. Pierre: South Dakota State Historical Society Press, 2004.

Whitehead, John. *Alaska, Hawaii, and the Battle for Statehood*. Albuquerque: University of New Mexico Press, 2004.

Wiggins, Charles W., Keith E. Hamm, and Howard R. Balanoff. "The 1982 Gubernatorial Transition in Texas: Appointments." In William Earl Maxwell et al., eds., *Texas Politics Today*, 4th ed., 232–34. St. Paul, Minn.: West, 1987.

Wiman, Christian. *My Bright Abyss: Meditation of a Modern Believer*. New York: Farrar, Straus and Giroux, 2013.

Wood, Richard E. *Survival of Rural America*. Lawrence: University Press of Kansas, 2008.

Wuthnow, Robert. *Rough Country: How Texas Became America's Most Powerful Bible-Belt State*. Princeton, N.J.: Princeton University Press, 2014.

Zeigler, L. Harmon, and Barbara Leigh Smith. "The 1970 Election in Oregon." *Western Political Quarterly* 24 (June 1971): 325–38.

Zelizer, Julian. "Reflections: Rethinking the History of American Conservatism." *Reviews in American History* 38 (June 2010): 367–92.

Ziker, Ann K. "Segregationists Confront American Empire: The Conservative White South and the Question of Hawaiian Statehood, 1947–1959." *Pacific Historical Review* 76 (Aug. 2007): 439–65.

Acknowledgments

Several friends and colleagues sped me along with tips and suggestions about sources and bibliography. My thanks to Virginia Scharff and Richard Etulain of the University of New Mexico, who guided me to their in-house bibliography. David Chappell of the University of Oklahoma Department of History put me onto the research and writing on Oklahoma politics by R. Keith Gaddie of the OU Department of Political Science. My thanks also to Professor Gaddie for refereeing a draft of my chapter on Oklahoma. Bob Cherny of the Department of History at San Francisco State University alerted me to the Field Polls of California public opinion, and he also sent me a copy of his article on recent California politics in *Siècles*, which proved to be very helpful. Robert Johnston, of the University of Illinois at Chicago and Jeff Ostler of the University of Oregon, experts on Oregon history, read an early draft of my Oregon chapter and made very useful comments. Brian Baird, six-term member of Congress for Washington's 3rd District (1999–2011), and the husband of my daughter Rachel, read and commented trenchantly on my Hawaii-Washington chapter and the concluding "Reflections."

I am grateful to the Western History Association's Program Committee for the 2014 meeting at Newport Beach, California, and its cochairs Cathleen Cahill and Ernesto Chavez, who included me on that program for our session on Oklahoma and Oregon. Deep thanks to W. David Baird (Pepperdine University) for chairing the session, to Bill Robbins (University of Oregon) for his paper on Oregon, to Derek Everett (Colorado State) for his paper on secessionist movements, and to Kimberly Jensen (Western Oregon University) and Charles Rankin (University of Oklahoma Press) for commenting. Thanks also to the audience and their questions.

The Northwestern University Library, the research library closest to and most convenient for me, allowed me unlimited access to its collections, even though I am not a staff member or an alumnus. As an emeritus professor at the University of Notre Dame, I continue to enjoy online access to its library, including its data bases and extensive online journals and newspapers. I also thank Notre Dame's Office of Information Technology for dependable and friendly tech support.

Chuck Rankin, an old friend and on this occasion my editor-publisher, has been enthusiastic about this book project ever since I approached him with it several years ago. His readings of chapters as I churned them out have been morale builders as well as essential correctives (though I hasten to say that I am to blame for remaining errors). I am grateful also for the prompt and kind attention of Steven Baker, managing editor at the University of Oklahoma Press. John Thomas has been an eagle-eyed, yet gentle copy editor. Bethany Mowry, editorial assistant to Chuck, has been invaluable in seeking photographs and permissions to reproduce them.

Suellen Hoy, spouse, sustainer, consultant, and editor-critic from start to finish, is my indispensable support. I thank her for thinking up the title, and for her forbearance as I worked on this book for several years. Together we do history in our own *Tír na nÓg*.

Highland Park, Illinois
Spring 2018

Index